Second Edition

GREYSON DAUGHTREY

JOHN B. WOODS

PHYSICAL EDUCATION AND INTRAMURAL PROGRAMS:

Organization and Administration

1976

W. B. SAUNDERS COMPANY   PHILADELPHIA • LONDON • TORONTO

W. B. Saunders Company: West Washington Square
Philadelphia, PA   19105

1 St. Anne's Road
Eastbourne, East Sussex BN21 3UN, England

833 Oxford Street
Toronto, Ontario M8Z 5T9, Canada

Physical Education and Intramural Programs: Organization and Administration
ISBN 0-7216-2884-2

© 1976 by W. B. Saunders Company.   Copyright 1971 by W. B. Saunders Company.   Copyright under the International Copyright Union.   All rights reserved.   This book is protected by copyright.   No part of it may be reproduced, stored in a retrieval system, or transmitted in any form or by any means, electronic, mechanical, photocopying, recording, or otherwise, without written permission from the publisher.   Made in the United States of America.   Press of W. B. Saunders Company.   Library of Congress catalog card number 75-5045.

Last digit is the print number: 9   8   7   6   5   4   3   2   1

ABOUT THE AUTHORS

GREYSON DAUGHTREY

Greyson Daughtrey has served the profession as a teacher, coach, administrator, and writer. His teaching career includes twenty years of experience, from the elementary school level through the graduate school. He successfully coached several sports at both the secondary and college levels. His degrees were earned at the College of William & Mary and the University of Michigan. He has contributed many articles to professional journals and, in addition to the present text, he authored *Effective Teaching in Physical Education for Secondary Schools*, published by W. B. Saunders Company.

Mr. Daughtrey is internationally known for his far-sighted administration of the physical education program in the Norfolk Public Schools, which has long received comparable status with the academic curriculum in such factors as requirement, class size, personnel, facilities and budget.

For over twenty-five years, under his leadership, the program has included such innovative components as lifetime sports instruction, highly organized intramural and extramural programs in both elementary and secondary levels; teaching station concept, team teaching, and selectives in the secondary schools; and equal educational opportunity for both boys and girls in all phases of physical education. First as a teacher and later as an administrator, he continuously emphasized the importance of quality instruction as the medium of survival for physical education. A staunch advocate of school-community relations, he interprets the program to the many publics through massive demonstrations and Health Education Fairs involving thousands of students from all schools in the community, supported by broad-based community assistance.

Among the many professional organizations and societies of which he is a member are the American Alliance for Health, Physical Education, and Recreation; Fellow, American School Health Association; Who's Who in American Education; Royal Society of Health; and Phi Delta Kappa. He has served as president of both the Virginia AAHPER and the Council of City and County Directors (from which he received the Channing Mann Award), and as a consultant to the President's Council on Physical Fitness and Sports. He was recently appointed Editor of *Directions*, a publication of the Council of City and County Directors.

JOHN B. WOODS

Professor Woods is a teacher and administrator in the Department of Physical Education, College of Education, University of Wyoming. Prior to joining the faculty at the University of Wyoming in 1965 as Head of the Department of Health, Physical Education and Recreation, Dr. Woods both taught and coached in the states of Minnesota and Washington. A naturalized citizen, he received his elementary and secondary education in Winnipeg, Canada, before seeking his baccalaureate at Bemidji State College. He was awarded his Master of Science degree by Washington State University and received his Doctor of Philosophy in Physical Education and Higher Education from the University of Minnesota.

Dr. Woods travels extensively, visiting schools and colleges in both the United States and Canada, studying organizational and administrative procedures that may facilitate the development of professionally sound physical education and intramural programs. In 1972 he was awarded a visiting professorship by the School of Physical Education at the University of Otago in Dunedin, New Zealand. His visit to New Zealand and the South Pacific further reinforced his interest in intradisciplinary and international approaches to the many aspects of education. During the past ten years, Professor Woods has held professional office at both state and district levels. He is a past president of the Wyoming Association for Health, Physical Education and Recreation, and a past vice-president for Physical Education of the Central District of the AAHPER. He has also served on evaluation committees for both the North Central Association of Colleges and Secondary Schools and the National College Association for Teacher Education. Dr. Woods is an active author, contributing to many professional and research journals, and is a co-author of another recent text, entitled *Student Teaching: The Entrance to Professional Physical Education.*

PREFACE TO THE SECOND EDITION

Since the publication of the first edition of this text, several significant changes have occurred in the organization and administration of physical education and intramural sports programs at both the school and university levels. After a period of turmoil and rapid change, educational institutions have become much more concerned and involved with the year-to-year problems of survival.

In the preface to the first edition, we stated that it was imperative to provide our students with the necessary tools with which to cope with the demands placed on teachers and administrators. This second edition is also dedicated to that purpose. It attempts to provide students and teachers with the modern and practical techniques and procedures that are necessary for the successful organization and administration of today's physical education and intramural sports programs. The text has been totally revised in order to provide viable materials and information for the organization and administration of programs that presently exist as well as for those programs which should be initiated.

The length of the text has been reduced and in some instances chapters have been combined in order to provide a more functional approach. Increased emphasis has been placed on the supervision and organization of physical education and intramural sports programs, reflecting the present practice of offering a combined course in order to strengthen both programs by providing close cooperation and appropriate integration.

The second edition is published with the addition of two ancillary materials. The authors have developed both a *Resource Manual* for students and an *Instructor's Manual* to accompany the basic text. The *Resource Manual*, which includes both organizational and resource aids, provides a resource supplement for the text. In some instances materials which were deemed to be "aids" were deleted from the text and included with the manual. In order to facilitate usage of these materials, tear-out pages are provided, with the publisher's permission to photocopy all materials. The new *Instructor's Manual* contains teaching aids for the instructor to use in the presentation of various text areas as well as materials for student evaluation.

Like the first edition, the second edition is organized into four main subject matter areas. *Part I* presents an overview of physical education, including historical development, philosophical foundations, critical issues, present trends, public relations, and an introduction to organization and administration. *Part II* provides many viable programs and concepts involved in the organization and administration of both elementary and secondary school physical education. These materials are both modernistic and practical in nature, and highlight organizational and administrative procedures and techniques that are necessary for present programs and appropriate for future direction. Included are discussions on curriculum patterns, developing the physical education curriculum, organization of programs, classroom management, facilities, and budgeting. *Part III* provides the physical educator with materials and programs for intramural sports, health programs, interschool athletics, physical education for the exceptional child, recreation, and outdoor education, which in many schools and colleges are included as administrative phases of physical education. *Part IV* presents a brief introduction and overview of functional administrative procedures for the organization and supervision of physical education and intramural programs in higher education. Materials are included for both men's and women's programs, and emphasis is placed on physical education as a united discipline.

The authors have attempted to present a modernistic approach to the organization and administration of physical education and intramural programs. It is hoped that students and their instructors will find this text and its supplements to be of professional value and interest.

GREYSON DAUGHTREY
JOHN B. WOODS

ACKNOWLEDGMENTS

Were it not for the professional opportunities and stimulation provided by many of our professors and colleagues, our sincere interest in scholastic and academic administration would not have been developed. Administration is certainly both a science and an art, and individuals indeed learn "by doing."

We wish to express our sincere appreciation to the many educators who assisted us in this undertaking by providing both professional counsel and beneficial materials. Without this assistance, it would have been virtually impossible to undertake this work. We are also deeply appreciative of the professional support and interest which was shown for our first edition. A sincere attempt was made by the authors to contact many of the instructors who adopted the first edition, in order to solicit recommendations for constructive change. We have tried to provide a second edition which, together with the *Resource Manual* and *Instructor's Manual,* will offer a complete supervision and administrative combination which meets the needs and interests of both students and instructors.

A special note of appreciation and gratitude is extended to the following people: Mr. Charles E. Fisher, Coordinator of Intramural Sports Programs at the University of Wyoming, for his valuable contributions in the area of intramural sports programs and the nature and use of facilities; Dr. Neil W. Hattlestad, Director of Graduate Research, South Dakota State University, for compiling and writing the *Instructor's Manual;* and the architectural firm of McGaughy, Marshall and McMillan for providing several drawings.

The authors are also deeply appreciative of the time, effort, and dedication of Mrs. Lou Ann Paterra, Mrs. Caroline Hough, Mrs. Elise Green, and Miss JoAnne Tyburczy, who typed and edited the manuscript.

G.D.
J.B.W.

CONTENTS

PHYSICAL EDUCATION AND INTRAMURAL PROGRAMS:

Organization and Administration

I

TOWARD THE 21st CENTURY—FROM THE PAST TO THE FUTURE

Reprinted from H. A. Harris: *Sport in Greece and Rome.*
Copyright © 1972 by Thames and Hudson. Used by
permission of Cornell University Press.

CHAPTER ONE

Historical Development and Philosophical Foundations

Where have we come from and where are we going? These two questions are frequently asked and are most difficult to answer. Both pupil and teacher will continue to probe the history of educational thought in an attempt to provide new insight and understanding for the future of our profession.

A student of administration will quickly ask, "Of what interest in an administrative text is the historical development of physical education and sport?" This question can best be answered by the following quotation:

Each recurrent crisis in society gives fresh impetus to the study of educational history and philosophy. The swift sequence of great events quickens an interest in the past. As men try to plan for a better future, historical chapters suddenly assume a new proportion and stand in need of reconsideration.[1]

We realize, of course, that this administrative text need not repeat the depth and detail of manuscripts written with

5

the sole purpose of presenting a history of physical education. Yet a brief overview of our past is essential in a modern administrative work, because never in the history of education have past and present administrative decision making been considered so essential to the professional course we will follow as we approach the 21st century. The future direction of the supervision and administration of physical education and intramural sports will rely heavily upon experiences from the past. Students, teachers, and administrators are all seeking guidance and leadership pertaining to instructional and behavioral objectives, differentiated staffing, variable scheduling, educational systems analysis, educational accountability, open access curricula, inner-city programs, independent study, and systematic instruction.

The innovative educational programs of the sixties and early seventies will continue as long as they are "responsible" programs for the future. No longer will the majority of educational taxpayers be satisfied merely with modern equipment, innovative methods, futuristic school facilities, and "well qualified" teachers. The public is demanding that students know how to read and write when they graduate from high school and that reasonable standards of academic attainment have been achieved. Accountability studies are demanding that schools show that expenditures of public monies are educationally justified in relationship to expected outcomes. National assessment programs in physical education must indeed attempt to answer the questions, where have we come from, where are we now, and where are we going?

EARLY HISTORICAL DEVELOPMENT

The historical development of what we now call physical education, or the new concept of human performance, may, for clarification, be segmented into three broad areas of study: the development of formal and informal education; sport; and physical education.

Formal and Informal Education

Physical education can trace its historical beginnings to ancient oriental nations, and to Greece and Rome. This period of history is usually referred to as the period of ancient cultures. Historians then proceed from the Teutonic invasions to our modern day society.[2]

In general terms we can define informal education as learning that is acquired through everyday experiences, and formal education is usually thought of as learning which takes place in a formal setting with a parent, teacher, or instructor presenting organized and planned materials.

Some form of informal education has existed in the world since the beginning of human life. Factual material dealing with the education of prehistoric man is naturally very limited; however, it is generally agreed that in order for civilization to have progressed, some education was certainly necessary.

Most of the highly professionalized formal education dealing with sport and physical education did not begin until the turn of the 20th century. This is not to say that the Greeks and Romans did not take their games' and contests seriously. Formal and informal learning certainly took place in the development of physical fitness for war and the attainment of skill for competitive games.

Ancient Oriental Influences

Early man was primarily concerned with survival. His life was hard and most of his waking hours were devoted to hunting for food. Formal and informal education consisted of learning the physical skills necessary for self-preservation.

It is believed that the first civilizations to directly affect the nature of man's history were those which developed on the eastern aspect of the Mediterranean Sea. The Chinese, on the other hand, were one of the first peoples to pass from the primitive state of early man to a more civilized one. The history of China begins approximately 2500 years before Christianity.

Egypt. The oldest records found in Egypt date back to 5000 B.C. Because of a remarkable history and the recording and preservation of historical records, Egypt is generally considered to be the birthplace of modern civilization.

Historical study reveals that formalized instruction in sport skills was not practiced in the schools of ancient Egypt. As the country progressed to a civilized culture there is evidence that the people participated in activities such as swimming, dance, wrestling, and gymnastics. Most formal instruction was, however, limited to the children of the nobility and the royal family. Folk dancing was popular and common among the lower classes. The Egyptians were apparently very fond of sports and included various activities in their religious rituals. Warriors received instruction in combat skills and physical fitness for war.

Mesopotamia, Babylonia, and Assyria. Although these countries shared an important place in the history of mankind, they placed little emphasis on sports and games. Hunting and military skills were, however, in evidence. Archery was practiced for war, and swimming and horsemanship were activities found in Mesopotamia. Babylonian and Assyrian history notes some boxing and wrestling, and dancing and singing were popular among the common people.

China. Early Chinese history, as interpreted by present-day historians, emphasized many different physical activities. Because of China's vast historical span, these activities had different aims at different periods.

Early education was concerned with physical activities and some forms of body conditioning, whereas later periods stressed the intellectual approach of Confucianism and Buddhism. It is said that the Chou Dynasty (1122–255 B.C.) provided some sport education in an organized national school system. Sports and games that developed in China were, as in other early civilizations, developed for military purposes. Boxing can be traced to approximately 700 B.C., and primitive football, jiujitsu, and wrestling were recorded between 300 and 250 B.C.

"The term for Chinese boxing is *chung-kuo ch'uan*. Chung-kuo means Chinese and ch'uan may mean simply "fist", or it may refer to a system that makes little use of the fist."[3] "Kung-Fu" is not a system of boxing. This term may mean task, work performed, special skills, strength, or ability, and is a generic term for exercise. The term used for martial arts is *wu-shu*. *T'ai-chi* is a type of Chinese boxing in which meditation in activity is practiced. Currently, *T'ai-chi* is spreading throughout the world and is becoming a standardized type of medical therapy on the Chinese mainland because of its health value. As in most ancient societies, dancing was popular, and music and dance played an important part in life for both pleasure and prestige.

India and Iran. In India, which has a recorded history of civilization perhaps as ancient as that of China, physical activity was not promoted, because of religious teachings that promoted instead self-denial and the abstinence of activity, including physical enjoyments. The teachings of Buddha prohibited most of the sports and games practiced by other early civilizations.

The culture of Persia (Iran, as it is known today) presents to the historian a bridge between the ideals of the Orient and those of the Occident. From early times the people of the Persian and Mede tribes hunted, rode, and fought. Persian education was primarily moral and physical. In direct contrast to the education in India and China, intellectual training was not thought to be useful and was not encouraged. Physical programs were organized to prepare young men for war. Activities included running, throwing the javelin, and the use of the sling to hurl stones. Social dance activities were suppressed because of religious teachings, but professional dance apparently flourished.

Greek and Roman Influences

Greek and Roman history reveals the most interesting and significant aspects of our historical past. Primarily because of their geographical proximity to early Oriental civilization, Greece and Rome were the first European lands to become civilized and to bridge the Eastern and Western worlds.

Greece. Greece has often been called the "birthplace of Western culture." These peoples were the first in Europe to attain an advanced type of civilization. Their history is commonly presented as an early period of the Aegean and Homeric ages and the history of the Spartan and Athenian peoples. This structural presentation is necessary because Greece was not a single nation, but rather a collection of small political or governmental units.

Greek society was based on a strict class structure. It is estimated that 400 years before the birth of Christ, the city of Athens was populated mostly by slaves. Greek "citizens" were not bothered by the normal burdens of life and were free to serve the state. Greek education as such was therefore reserved for the citizens of the state and not for the slaves.

Early historical records indicate that the ancient Aegeans practiced hunting activities (with the bow and arrow), swimming, boxing, and wrestling. Some of these activities date back as far as 2000 to 1000 B.C. The early part of the Homeric period, which extended over decades, was very primitive. Warfare was the basic pattern of life and physical activity was devoted to total development, with a sincere love of physical effort. Early Greek gymnastics were practiced, with funeral games and chariot races, as described in *The Iliad* and *The Odyssey*.

By the fifth and fourth centuries B.C., the early periods of the Aegeans and the Homeric Greeks had passed and the golden age of the Spartan Greeks had arrived. Wealth, democratic forms of government, and public education were in evidence by the fifth century B.C. Spartans devoted themselves almost exclusively to military endeavors and thus these peoples excelled in physical fitness activities. Young women and girls were also conditioned physically in order to bear healthy children.

Physical programs included running, fighting, leaping, swimming, hunting, wrestling, boxing, ball-playing, riding bareback, throwing the discus and the javelin, and hiking. The Olympian games were first recorded in 720 B.C., when a Spartan victory was recorded in a long distance race.

In later centuries, the development of education and learning in Athens became quite different from that of the Spartans. In Athens the family made many of the important decisions. In general the Athenians were more liberal, progressive, and democratic than were the Spartans.

Sports and physical activities were important aspects of Athenian life. It is from this culture that we obtained our basic belief in education *through or by way of* the physical, rather than striving just to attain physical attributes alone.

Physical training for war was as much in evidence in Athens as it was in Sparta. Gymnastic schools were called *palestrae*, and activities consisted of running, throwing the discus and javelin, wrestling, and boxing. Bathing and swimming facilities for cleanliness were maintained near every palestra.

The life of the Greeks also offered many informal learning experiences. Community festivals and the famed Panhellenic competitions (which were held to honor the gods) became very well organized. The Olympic Games were a national festival and were held every four years at Olympia. These famous games first began 776 years before the birth of Christ.

Rome. Physical fitness and the promotion of athletic activities continued into the Roman era of history toward the same basic goal as was found among the Greeks. The duty of a Roman family was to serve the state, and the Roman state developed with the belief that it would someday rule the world.

In the early Roman period children were raised as citizen-soldiers. It is said that the power of Rome was found in the moral and physical strength of her youth. By 265 B.C. Italy (and by 31 B.C. all of the Mediterranean world) was under the dictatorship of Rome.

In the later stages of Roman civilization great emphasis was placed on the education of youth in order that they might take their places as statesmen in the world. Gymnastics were promoted for military purposes and it was considered very important to know how to swim. Horse and chariot races were popular on Roman holidays, and gladiatorial contests were held at funeral games beginning about 264 B.C.

The Roman Empire was soon plagued with moral decay. The circus and amphitheater became slaughterhouses during gladiatorial exhibitions, and the *thermae*, or public baths, became a place of luxurious and idle living. Greek athletes presented gymnastic exhibitions in Rome in 186 B.C., but they were too ascetic to become popular. As Roman children and adults became more sedentary because of their affluence, the empire continued to decay until it ultimately fell in A.D. 476.

The Middle Ages and the Renaissance

As Roman influence weakened in the civilized world, Teutonic barbarians from the north quickly overran Europe. In A.D. 376 the Visigoths began their invasion and controlled Spain for over 100 years. These barbarian invasions into a highly civilized part of the world produced the "Dark Ages," and most education and learning ceased to advance.

These rugged peoples, however, provided strenuous physical training for their youth. Boys learned to hunt, run foot races, wrestle, throw spears, and participate in ball games.

The Christian Era. During the Dark Ages most educational enlightenment was fostered by the Christian church. Christianity taught that an individual should be concerned with his soul and that the development of physical powers was a waste of time. Thus most churchmen of this age were strongly opposed to sports activities. Some of the early church leaders who were trained in the eastern part of the Holy Roman Empire did, however, allow limited physical activity.

In approximately A.D. 525, monasteries were organized in Europe. Monasticism promoted the nourishment of the spirit rather than of the physical body, thus creating a setback in the development of sports and physical activities.

The Medieval Era. The Medieval

Figure 1–1. "Running Girl." (From Stobart, J. B.: The Glory That Was Greece. London: Sidgwick and Jackson, Ltd., 1911.)

period of history came into being after the establishment of Christianity. Society of that time needed some type of social and political structure, so feudalism, manorialism, and chivalry evolved.

Like the cultures which preceded them, the peoples of the Medieval era trained their youth for war. A difference existed, however, in that children of this age were also required to observe social and moral customs, practice religious beliefs, and promote gallantry. Physical activity played an important part in chivalric education. Boys were taught vigorous physical exercises to strengthen themselves for war.

The Renaissance. The period of the Renaissance marked the awakening of thought and learning that took place between the 14th and 17th centuries. Study during this period of history centered around classic philosophy, literature, and art. "Humanists" were men who were concerned with the affairs of man rather than with the divinities.

Italy fostered the so-called Humanistic movement and education and schools thrived. In the late 14th and 15th centuries daily exercises were compulsory and children played games, rode horseback, fenced, and were instructed in archery. Competition was also encouraged in wrestling and swimming.

In the 16th century, English Humanists wrote of the value of recreation for the body, and play and exercise were promoted. Such activities as tennis, fencing, dancing, archery, wrestling, running, riding, swimming, and lifting dumbbells were in evidence.

The Enlightenment

The 18th century was a period of transition to modern political, social, religious, and educational ideals. This century saw the creation of Basedow's Philanthropinum school in 1774. This school was the first of its kind to admit all people and provide gymnastics in the daily program. Basedow's ideals were like those of Rousseau in that he believed that natural growth required play and exercise. Johann F. Guts Muths (1759-1839) became the grandfather of German gymnastics and the modern founder of what was soon to be known as modern physical education.

The late 18th and early 19th centuries saw the creation of the German Turnverein or gymnastic societies. Historians give credit to Friedrich L. Jahn for initiating this movement. In 1811 and 1812 Jahn promoted his movement by conducting gymnastic games using balance-beams, vertical ropes, ladders, horizontal bars, and high-jumping and pole-vaulting equipment. By the 1920's camping and hiking became popular in Germany, and youth hostels could be found all over the country.

Modern Europe provided much of the sport and educational background for what we now refer to as physical education. Continental European countries provided a more formalized system of gymnastics and movement activities, while England provided a less regimented approach by means of games and contests. World Wars I and II had a great influence on physical education and sport. Physical activity produced healthy youth for war, a practice that has been in effect for thousands of years. Games and contests were also of value in creating diversions from pain and suffering.

THE HISTORY OF AMERICAN PHYSICAL EDUCATION

"There have been few definitive works tracing the rise of sport in America. Those that exist have recognized the colonial or puritan influence on much of American sporting history."[4] Physical education historians who have traced the rise of contests and physical activities in the United States generally organize their materials into four distinct periods. These are the Colonial Period, 1600's to the 1780's; the Provincial Period, 1780's to the 1880's; the Decline of European Influence, 1880's to the 1920's; and the true American Emphasis from the 1920's to the present.

English Colonial Period

There is no doubt that a great many of the people who were involved with the English emigration to the colonies objected to organized sport. In fact, this was one of the objections the Puritans had in thir quarrel with the Anglican church of England.

During the early part of this period very little if any organized sport activities were permitted. Toward the latter part of the period a heavy influx of new colonists, who were not Puritans, began to participate in recreational activities.

Provincial Period

By the 19th century organized sport was beginning to materialize, and the introduction of gymnastics in 1823 at the Round Hill School in Northampton, Massachusetts, marked the beginning of formalized instruction on a large scale. The state of Massachusetts continued to dominate the field with the establishment of the first American college gymnasium at Harvard College in 1826. In 1833 Oberlin College was founded and admitted both women and blacks.

The first attempt to prepare teachers of physical education in the United States occurred at Dio Lewis's Normal Institute in 1861. Instruction was given in Swedish medical gymnastics.

Although it was later abolished, the first state-wide mandatory physical education program was established in California in 1866. As early as 1868, Mankato State Teachers' College of Minnesota offered a type of teacher-training course in physical education. The first important decade of American physical education began in 1880 when many sound teacher-training programs were established across the country. In 1893 Harvard College became the first college to confer an academic degree in physical education.

Decline of European Influence

Toward the latter part of the 1800's the influence of foreign systems of physical training began to wane. Up to this time most activity programs had consisted primarily of regimented cadence-type drills and gymnastics. The Old World emphasis, as fostered and promoted by the Turners and the immigrants who were followers of Jahn, began to give way to less formalized physical activities.

In the 1890's entrance requirements, selective admission, and guidance and placement programs were initiated in many American colleges. By 1911 the entrance requirements of the professional physical education program at the University of Wisconsin were organic vigor, aptitude for a high degree of motor efficiency, evidence of the ability for strong leadership, and sound health.

"History demonstrates that educational purposes change from time to time, as social circumstances change, and as outlooks on life change accordingly. What it means to be educated is contingent on a specific place and time."[5] We should not educate for yesterday's world.

THE EMERGENCE OF PROFESSIONAL PHYSICAL EDUCATION

The years from 1920 to 1930 marked a dramatic change in the American way of life. The philosophical thought of John Dewey promoted deep thought and educational change. Physical education made quite rapid advances toward individual, dual, and team sports. In the early 1900's educators began to replace physicians as directors of professional programs. Sports participation was stressed and remedial physical education, aquatics, water safety, and health education were presented.

Figure 1–2. Cricket was a popular team sport in early America as it was in many English speaking countries. (Courtesy of The Dunedin New Zealand Evening Star.)

Elementary Physical Education

In the early 1900's physical education in the elementary schools was still strongly dominated by the formal system. By 1925 city supervisors of physical education were employed to organize programs and assist classroom teachers. In cities whose elementary schools had physical education the subject was required for 150 minutes per week for grades one through six.

By 1930 laws requiring physical education in the public schools had been enacted in 36 states. "Twenty states had appointed state directors of physical education, and a few others. . . were working in this direction."[6]

During the Second World War physical education at the elementary level was usually scheduled daily and consisted of 30-minute periods. Activities included games, folk dance, story plays, stunts and tumbling, and health instruction. At this time a grading system of "satisfactory" or "unsatisfactory" was in effect at the elementary level.

Secondary Physical Education

In 1924 a great number of American secondary schools did not require physical education because they did not have gymnasiums. If any activity was offered other than interscholastic athletics it was of the formal type.

A study conducted in 1932, however, revealed that the trend in high school programs was away from formal-type activities and toward informal games and sports. At this time in the history of secondary physical education approximately 75 per cent of the secondary schools required physical education.

During the war years of the 1940's many secondary school physical education programs were involved with the physical development of youth for war.

Physical Education in Colleges and Universities

Physical education at the college and university levels continued to develop programs for general student activity and professional programs for students desiring major preparation. As was noted earlier, the first attempt to prepare teachers in our profession occurred in 1861. Sixty-four years later it was estimated that approximately 75 institutions began to offer degree courses in physical education between 1920 and 1925.

The financial depression of the 1930's brought about a greater emphasis on student selection and admission. A study conducted as early as 1934 illustrated that physical education majors stood at the bottom of all teaching fields in the range and depth of their academic training. Prior to this study the most prevalent specialized curriculum in physical education was for athletic coaching.

During the Second World War a great emphasis was naturally placed on physical fitness training programs. Following the war a conference of directors of graduate study in physical education was held in 1946 at Père Marquette State Park, Illinois, and a National Conference on Undergraduate Professional Preparation was held at Jackson's Mill, West Virginia, in 1948. These conferences emphasized the need for a cultural background for successful teaching.

Physical Education Since 1950— "The Battle of the Systems"

Professional physical education at all levels in the educational spectrum has undergone modification and revision during this last half of the 20th century. The communistic influence in various parts of the world and the struggle for peace, combined with modern advances in scientific technology, have all had their effect.

Sociological trends have indicated that our populations are continuing to shift from metropolitan to suburban areas. To add to the many worries of the educational community, the increasing "knowledge boom" which faces us as we approach the 21st century is placing a severe strain on administrators, who must decide what material is to be taught and how it all can be accommodated.

In 1952 the Kraus-Weber minimum muscular fitness test brought to the attention of the American public the fact that 56.6 per cent of children who were tested in the eastern states failed one or more of the items on this test. In a later study, European children selected to participate averaged only 8.2 per cent failures. Because of the implications of these test results, the President's Council on Youth Fitness was established at Annapolis in 1956. The establishment of this council was quickly followed by the creation of a Youth Fitness Test Battery designed by the American Association for Health, Physical Education and Recreation. This association is now known as the American Alliance for Health, Physical Education and Recreation, and the Council on Youth Fitness is now called the President's Council on Physical Fitness and Sports.

This emphasis on youth fitness was continued by the late Presidents John F. Kennedy and Dwight D. Eisenhower and is still being actively promoted by the federal government and professional associations.

As we approach the turn of the century, many problems face our profession. Among those considered to be the most severe and which will be presented in later chapters are the jeopardy of required programs at all levels; the strengthening of undergraduate and graduate professional programs; the relationship of both men's and women's interscholastic and intercollegiate athletics to physical education; the direction of and relationships between national organizations for health, physical education, and recreation; and the future emphasis of our programs for a rapidly changing urban society.

THE INTRODUCTION OF INTERSCHOLASTIC AND INTERCOLLEGIATE ATHLETICS

With the vast flow of immigrants prior to the Civil War, many different sports were introduced in America. Most of these, however, were of a recreational nature and were not highly organized.

Baseball became popular after the Civil War, and in 1875 the National League was formed, followed by the American League in 1900.

Intercollegiate sports had their beginning with the formation of the Rowing Association of American Colleges in 1871. After this date, the eastern colleges and universities began competing against each other in such sports as rugby, cricket, lacrosse, fencing, and ice hockey. The first golf championship was held in 1897, the NCAA championships beginning in 1939.

The first recorded athletic organization was the National Amateur Gymnastic and Athletic Tournament Association, which was formed in New York in 1873. This was followed in 1888 by the American Athletic Union, which became the first national organization to represent amateur sports.

The Intercollegiate Athletic Association (which later became the National Collegiate Athletic Association) was founded in 1906. The organization of the nation's so-called "small colleges" did not take place until 1940 when the National Association of Intercollegiate Basketball was formed in Kansas City. In 1952 this organization became the National Association of Intercollegiate Athletics.

Interscholastic athletics for boys was quite prominent as early as 1907, with participation in football, track and field, rowing, baseball, basketball, ice hockey, tennis, and golf. Some attempt was made to regulate high school competition with the formation of the Athletic Leagues in New York and New Jersey as early as 1895. By 1916 high school athletic leagues had begun in Illinois, Indiana, Iowa, Michigan, and Wisconsin. These organizations then formed the North Central Interscholastic Athletic Conference.

In an attempt to further control interscholastic athletics, the National Federation of High School Athletic Associations was formed in 1923. In 1925 the National Association of Secondary School Principals endorsed the National Federation of State High School Associations (NFSHSA), as it is now called, as the agency to represent high school athletics in their interstate and national aspects. The division of girls' and women's sports of the American Association for Health, Physical Education and Recreation has provided the guidelines for women's interscholastic and intercollegiate athletic competition. For the past several years, the question of women's rights and equal opportunities has focused on the changing philosophy of high schools towards girls' interscholastic athletic competition. The DGWS, NFSHSA, and the National Association of Girls and Women in Sport of the AAHPER are working toward common guidelines and policies for both college and high school levels. The Association for Intercollegiate Athletics for Women (AIAW) is rapidly expanding, encompassing many colleges and universities throughout the United States and Canada. This association is attempting to provide the same type of organizational and administrative service for women's intercollegiate athletics as the NCAA provides for men.

THE HISTORY AND DEVELOPMENT OF PROFESSIONAL ORGANIZATIONS

The following brief historical review of selected professional organizations is presented in order to further illustrate the historical development of physical education and related professional organizations.

American Alliance for Health, Physical Education and Recreation (AAHPER)

In 1885 William G. Anderson became the founder and first president of the American Association for the Advancement of Physical Education. This organization provided the basic structure and framework for what is now called the American Alliance for Health, Physical Education and Recreation.

In 1903 the name of this, our first professonal organization, was changed to the American Physical Education Asso-

ciation; in 1937 it was renamed the American Association for Health and Physical Education and became a member organization of the National Education Association. In 1938 the name was changed again to the American Association for Health, Physical Education and Recreation.

In 1969, because of changing form and function, the association became an *affiliate* member of the National Education Association and recorded some 50,000 active members.

The new American Alliance, ratified in 1974, is composed of seven associations. The new *American Association for Leisure and Recreational Services*, formerly the Recreation Division, is made up of some 12 committees, which deal with various functions from community school recreation to professional preparation. The *American School and Community Safety Association*, previously the Safety Division, is made up of seven special interest areas. The *Association for the Advancement of Health Education*, formerly the School Health Division, deals with interest areas from elementary education to professional preparation, research, and administration. The *Association for Research, Administration and Professional Councils*, previously the General Division, deals with aquatics, college and university administration, city and county directors, outdoor education and camping, international relations, measurement and evaluation, and physical fitness. The former division of girls' and women's sports is now the *National Association for Girls and Women in Sport*. The six interest areas for this association are athletic administration, club sports (intramurals, coaching, intercollegiates) association for intercollegiate athletics for women, interscholastics, and officiating. The former divisions of physical education and men's athletics are now combined into the *National Association for Sport and Physical Education*. There are 23 interest areas in this association, including PEPI,* kinesiology, sports psycholo-

---

*Physical Education Public Information Project.

gy, curriculum, adapted physical education, college and university administration, and elementary and secondary school physical education. The new *National Dance Association*, formerly the Dance Division, is made up of six interest areas, including commissions on theatre, dance, and related arts.

Members of this new alliance will be permitted to indicate their area of professional interest and concern. The operating funds for the seven associations will be determined according to the one or two choices made by each individual member. Opportunities for participation by voting, holding office, or receiving services will also be determined by interest choice.

Publications of the Alliance are many and varied, but all deal with the professional advancement of physical education, athletics and sport. Publications include the *Journal of Health, Physical Education and Recreation*, the *Research Quarterly* and *Up Date*.

For further information contact: AAHPER, 1201 16th Street, N.W., Washington, D.C. 20036.

American Academy of Physical Education (AAPE)

The American Academy of Physical Education was founded in 1930. The Academy is committed to the following goals: advancing knowledge and understanding, stimulating research and scientific concerns, and interpreting positions and disseminating relevant points of view on physical education in this and other nations.

The Academy limits the number of active Fellows at any one time to 100. Such membership is limited to those actively employed in one or more of the fields of health education, physical education, and recreation. The Academy charges its Fellows to continue the development of professional excellence. From time to time the Academy publishes papers presented by Fellows, position statements and studies developed and approved by the Academy, as well

as the R. Tait McKenzie Memorial Lectures.

For further information contact: AAHPER, 1201 16th Street, N.W., Washington, D.C. 20036.

American College of Sports Medicine (ACSM)

Among the objectives of this organization are the following: to promote and advance medical and other scientific studies dealing with the effects of sport and other physical activities on the health of human beings; to initiate, promote and correlate research in these fields; to establish and maintain a sports medicine library. There are presently five chartered regional chapters of the American College of Sports Medicine. Additional regional chapters are being developed throughout the United States as the interest of members dictates. Membership is open to any individual interested in sports medicine. Basic requirements for membership are a doctorate or graduate degree in a field related to health, physical education, or biology. Publications include the quarterly issue of the *Journal of Medicine and Science in Sports* and *The Encyclopedia of Sports Sciences and Medicine*.

For further information contact: American College of Sports Medicine, 1440 Monroe Street, Madison, Wisconsin 53706.

American Federation of Teachers (AFT)

"The American Federation of Teachers is an autonomous national union of preschool, elementary, secondary, and college classroom teachers, affiliated with the American Federation of Labor — Congress of Industrial Organizations." The AFT was organized on April 16, 1916, when eight local unions of teachers met in Chicago to form a national organization and secure a charter from the American Federation of Labor. The AFT received its national charter on May 9, 1916.

The American Federation of Teachers reports that during 1960 to 1962 there was a 34 per cent increase in AFT membership. In 1974 the Federation reported some 400,000 members and was considered to be one of the fastest growing unions in the world. The AFT states that a labor affiliation gives the Federation and its members the support of more than 14 million members of unions in the AFL-CIO. In its literature, the AFT maintains that local unions and state federations affiliated with the American Federation of Teachers are autonomous. The Federation has a constitution which outlines the rights and duties of affiliated organizations. The AFT's governing body is its annual convention. Delegates to this convention are elected by local union members. The main governing and administrative body is the executive council of 20 vice-presidents and the president, who is a full-time officer. The president and vice-presidents are subject to election every two years. Vice-presidents, who are assigned to specific geographical areas, serve without remuneration.

The 1974 action programs of state and local federations as recorded by the organization were as follows: to promote a single salary schedule for teachers based on training and experience, starting at $10,000 and reaching $25,000 in five annual increments; to recognize the rights of teachers everywhere to organize, negotiate, and bargain collectively; to promote more effective school programs; to provide reduced class sizes, specialized teachers, and the necessary teaching aids; to upgrade education in urban areas; to promote state tenure laws to protect teachers from being discharged without proven cause; to eliminate overcrowding in classrooms; and to acquire better retirement pensions as well as improved programs for sick leave and hospitalization. The motto of the American Federation of Teachers is "democracy in education . . . education for democracy."

For further information contact: American Federation of Teachers, AFL-CIO, 1012 14th Street, N.W., Washington, D.C. 20005.

Canadian Association for Health, Physical Education and Recreation* (CAHPER)

The Canadian Association for Health, Physical Education and Recreation was founded in 1933. Biannual conventions were held until 1944, when the first annual convention was held in Winnipeg, Manitoba.

The organization of professional physical education associations in Canada is of relatively recent origin. In 1922, in the city of Toronto, Ontario, a district physical education club was formed, and a year later the province of Quebec Physical Education Association was established. Through the combined efforts of these two provincial associations, the Canadian Physical Education Association was organized in 1933. In 1950 the CPEA (today known as the CAHPER) incorporated and obtained a charter from the federal government. Since its early beginnings, the Canadian Association has experienced a steady professional growth and has had a strong influence on the promotion of professional physical education in Canada.

The National Physical Fitness Act, which was passed in October, 1943, also played a significant role in the development of physical education in Canada. The appointment of a National Council on Physical Fitness consisting of representatives from each of the Canadian provinces did much to encourage programs and to promote the training of physical education teachers and recreation leaders. In 1954 the National Physical Fitness Act was repealed and in its place a National Council of Health and Safety assumed the responsibilities for physical fitness and physical education. Since 1961 financial federal assistance has provided the necessary resources for the promotion of physical education, leisure time activities, and amateur sports in Canada.

Among the publications of CAHPER is the *Canadian Journal for Health, Physical Education and Recreation,* which is

_____

*(L'Association Canadienne Pour La Santé, L'Education Physique et la Recreation.)

published bimonthly beginning in September.

For further information contact: The Canadian Association for Health, Physical Education and Recreation, Administrative Centre for Sport and Recreation, 333 River Road, Venier City, Ontario, Canada.

National Association for Physical Education of College Women (NAPECW)

The National Association for Physical Education of College Women is a nonprofit organization founded in 1924 for the purpose of studying problems relating to college and university departments of physical education for women. This association was originally founded in 1910 as the Association of Directors of Physical Education for Women. In 1914 the title of the organization was changed to the Society of Directors of Physical Education in Colleges for Women.

In addition to the national association, there are five affiliate district associations (Eastern, Southern, Midwest, Central, and Western) which offer further opportunity for professional fellowship among teachers of college physical education.

The original purposes of the association have been expanded to include the promotion of professional growth and competency among its members and the stimulation of professional understanding in the development of new ideas. Membership in the association is open to women members of departments of physical education in both two- and four-year colleges and universities. Active members of the association must first hold membership in their district association. The national association publishes a biennial record of the business of the association; a report of the biennial workshop; *Spectrum*, the association newsletter; and *Quest*, a joint publication with the National College Physical Education Association for Men.

For further information contact: The Department of Physical Education for Women, University of Wisconsin, Madison, Wisconsin 53705.

National College Physical Education Association for Men (NCPEAM)

The National College Physical Education Association for Men was founded in 1897 and was then named the Society of College Gymnasium Directors. In 1908 the organization became the Society of Directors of Physical Education in Colleges, and in 1933 the name of the organization was changed to the College Physical Education Association. The basic aim of the NCPEAM is "the advancement of physical education in institutions of higher learning." The objectives of the organization are as follows:
— To awaken and promote an intelligent interest in and improvement of teaching and administrative standards
— To acquire and disseminate accurate professional information
— To establish techniques of promotion that insure an adequate and comprehensive program
— To pursue research that advances the physical education profession
— To assist all members of the association in accomplishing the above objectives

Publications of the association include the annual *Proceedings* and *Quest*, which is published jointly by the Association and the National Association for Physical Education of College Women.

For further information contact: The Secretary-Treasurer, 108 Cooke Hall, University of Minnesota, Minneapolis, Minnesota 55455.

National Collegiate Athletic Association (NCAA)

The National Collegiate Athletic Association was first formed in 1905 and was originally named the Intercollegiate Athletic Association of the United States. This association is the organization through which the colleges and universities of the United States act on athletic matters at the national level. It is a voluntary association of more than 770 institutions, conferences, and organizations "devoted to the sound administration of intercollegiate athletics."

The association lists 10 basic purposes, among which are the following: to uphold the principle of institutional control of and responsibility for all intercollegiate athletics, in conformity with the association's constitution and by-laws; to study all phases of competitive athletics and establish basic rules and procedures in order that colleges and universities of the United States may maintain their athletic activities on a high level. At its first special convention in 1973, NCAA delegates voted to divide the membership of their organization into three legislative and competitive divisions. Each member college was given the opportunity to elect its division through self-determination. An 18-member Board of Control is responsible for establishing and directing the general policy of the association.

For further information contact: The National Collegiate Athletic Association, P.O. Box 1906, Shawnee Mission, Kansas 66222.

National Education Association (NEA)

The National Education Association of the United States was first organized in 1857 as the National Teachers' Association. The basic purpose of this early organization was to elevate the character and advance the interest of the profession of teaching and to promote the cause of popular education in the United States. The name of the association was later changed in 1870 to the National Educational Association. In 1907 the National Education Association of the United States was incorporated under a special act of Congress approved in 1906.

Any person who is actively engaged in the profession of teaching or other educational work, or any other person interested in advancing the cause of education, is eligible for membership in the association.

The NEA's expressed goals are to promote an independent united teaching profession, professional excellence, and economic security for all educators, and to provide leadership in solving social problems. The organization hopes to meet a membership goal of some 1.9 million educators by the fiscal year 1976–77. For the 1973–74 fiscal year, the association reported a total budget of some 31.6 million dollars, which was expended for programs, basic support, goal areas, administrative services, and governance.

For further information contact: The National Education Association, 1201 16th Street, N.W., Washington, D.C. 20036.

National Federation of State High School Associations (NFSHSA)

The National Federation of State High School (Athletic) Associations was first organized and formed in 1920 in Chicago. The secretary of the Illinois High School Athletic Association invited representatives from several neighboring states and state associations to come to Chicago to discuss problems that had resulted from high school contests organized by colleges and universities or by other clubs or promoters. At this first meeting it was decided that the welfare of the high schools required that a more active part in the control of such athletic activities be exercised by the high school administrators themselves through their individual state organizations. This control necessitated the formation of a national organization. In 1922 the Chicago meeting was attended by representatives from 11 states and the name of the National Federation of State High School Athletic Associations was adopted.

The basic legislative body for this association is a National Council made up of one representative from each member state association. The executive body is the executive committee of eight state Board of Control members from the eight territorial sections of the United States, as outlined in the Association's constitution. The Federation now consists of 50 individual state high school athletic and/or activities associations and the association of the District of Columbia. Also affiliated are seven interscholastic organizations from the Canadian provinces of Alberta, British Columbia, Manitoba, New Brunswick, Nova Scotia, Ontario, and Saskatchewan.

The Federation was organized primarily to secure proper adherence to the eligibility rules of the various state associations in interstate contests and meets. At the present time, no national athletic meet or tournament is sanctioned. Meets or tournaments which involve the schools of more than one state are sanctioned in accordance with definite limitations in connection with the distance to be traveled, the type of sponsor, the amount of school time involved, and the extent to which such events interfere with other participation. The National Federation is a service organization and assists schools and state associations in a variety of ways.

For further information contact: The National Federation of State High School Associations, 400 Leslie Street, Elgin, Illinois 60120.

National Foundation for Health, Physical Education and Recreation (NFHPER)

The first annual meeting of the National Foundation for Health, Physical Education and Recreation was held in 1967 in Las Vegas, Nevada. The board of directors of the foundation expressed the purposes of their organization as follows: "The association serves its members' immediate goals; serves their welfare in those personal and professional ways delineated in the Constitution." The foundation also serves the long range purposes and goals of the professions of health, physical education, and recreation, enabling the profession to make its contribution to people and to education. The foundation supports various professional projects, including PEPI, student scholarships, and the maintenance of archives.

For further information contact: The National Foundation for Health, Physical Education and Recreation, 1201 16th Street, N.W., Washington, D.C. 20036.

National Intramural Association (NIA)
National Intramural Sports Council (NISC)

The National Intramural Association was founded in 1950 at Dillard University in New Orleans. The basic purpose of this organization is to encourage the exchange of ideas and to stimulate professional growth among its members.

The early growth of intramurals in America was quite disorganized, and until the 1920's, programs were very difficult to determine. However, as early as 1857 at Princeton University, attempts were being made to organize the first intramural sports contests. "As the intramural movement expanded, there was an increasing effort to set standards for improvement through the formation of various professional intramural organizations. The individual intramural directors realized their problems could be solved by meeting as a group to share their experiences."[7] In 1950 Dr. William Wasson, at Dillard University, formed the first national association. This was the first national group devoted entirely to intramural sports; the basic concept came into being largely as a result of a Carnegie Grant to study the intramural programs in black colleges. Charter members of the NIA were the following: Albany State College, Arkansas State College, Bethuen-Cookman College, Dillard University, North Carolina College, Southern University, Texas State University, Tillotson College, Tuskegee Institute, Wiley College, and Xavier University of New Orleans.

In addition to its basic purpose of organizing and encouraging the exchange of ideas, the association states additional objectives as follows: to promote and encourage intramural and recreational programs; to serve as a medium for the publication of research papers on intramurals; to act as a placement service agency; and to provide consultant services. The National Intramural Association is primarily a college and university service organization, so in 1966 the National Intramural Sports Council was formed as a joint project of the division of men's athletics and the division of girls' and women's sports of the American Association for Health, Physical Education and Recreation. The Intramural Sports Council provides a service organization to meet the needs of schools throughout the country. Both the NIA and the NISC promote "a sport for everyone, and everyone in a sport." Publications of the NIA include the annual conference proceedings.

For further information contact: The National Intramural Association, Texas Tech University, Lubbock, Texas 79409.

National Recreation and Park Association (NRPA)

The National Recreation and Park Association is an independent non-profit service organization. It draws its membership from both the United States and Canada. This organization is dedicated to the improvement of park and recreation leadership, programs, and facilities. The NRPA traces its history to 1898 when the New England Association of Parks Superintendents was founded in Boston, Massachusetts. The association took its present form in 1965 through the merger of six major professional and citizen organizations.

Policy for this organization is set by a board of trustees representing both the professional and the public interest. All members are provided opportunities to participate in the formulation of policy and program. The association provides services through publications, institutes, and workshops, as well as through direct consultation and technical assistance. Publications include the *Journal of Leisure Research, Therapeutic Recreation Journal*, and *Parks and Recreation*, a monthly magazine.

For further information contact: The National Recreation and Park Association, 1601 North Kent Street, Arlington, Virginia 22209.

Phi Epsilon Kappa (PEK)

Phi Epsilon Kappa was founded in 1913 by the students and faculty at the Normal College of the American Gymnastics Union in Indianapolis, Indiana. This professional fraternity for physical educators was initiated to bind members together and to promote a friendly atmosphere among members of the profession.

More than 23,000 members have been initiated into this fraternity since its conception in 1913. Among the objectives of this professional fraternity are "to further the individual welfare of its members and to foster scientific research in the fields of health education, physical education, recreation education and safety education." Publications include the *Physical Educator*, and membership is available through the various collegiate chapters located in colleges and universities throughout the United States.

For further information contact: Business Manager, 4000 Meadows Drive, Suite L-24, Indianapolis, Indiana 46205.

Society of State Directors of Health, Physical Education and Recreation (SSDHPER)

The Society of State Directors of Health, Physical Education and Recreation was first organized and formed in 1926 in New York City. Some 16 state directors of physical education and health education, who had met informally in the early 1920's, were the individuals who made up the early association. The Society lists five basic purposes, among which are the following: "the promotion of sound programs of physical education including appropriate athletics at preschool, elementary, secondary, and post-secondary school levels; and to study problems affecting the quality of programs and to implement procedures for their solution." The Society is composed of state directors of health, physical education, and recreation, and their associates. Membership is open to state directors or consultants of health, physical education, and recreation or to the persons certified by the chief state school officer as being primarily responsible for state programs in these fields. Associate memberships are available for those who have duties in one of these disciplines.

Over the years, the Society has issued numerous proclamations, resolutions, and proceedings which have had an impact on school, college, and community programs. The major publication of the association is *A Statement of Basic Beliefs—The School Programs in Health, Physical Education and Recreation*. A newsletter is also issued periodically to society members.

For further information contact: Secretary-Treasurer, The Society of State Directors of Health, Physical Education and Recreation, 9805 Hillridge Drive, Kensington, Maryland 20795.

PHILOSOPHICAL FOUNDATIONS FOR PHYSICAL EDUCATION

As we have just observed, physical education and sport are not an innovation of the 20th century. They existed in all the early civilizations in some form, depending upon the emphasis and ideals of each society.

The old exercise period known as "physical training" has now become the complex and extensive subject area of professional physical education. "Its new content is a sequence of experiences in which children learn to move as they move to learn more about themselves and their world."[8]

It is important now to discuss the philosophical background and present nature of the modernization of our profession.

Philosophy is defined in several different ways. A standard definition is: "a study of the processes governing thought and conduct; theory or investigation of the principles or laws that regulate the universe and underlie all knowledge and reality."[9] Another definition is: "that branch of learning (or that science) which investigates, evaluates, and integrates knowledge of reality as best as possible into one or more systems embodying all available wisdom about the universe."[10]

Philosophy in Education

Philosophy, like any other branch of learning, is composed of several subdivisions or categories. These are generally viewed as:

1. Metaphysics—questions about reality;
2. Epistemology—acquisition of knowledge;
3. Logic—exact relating of ideas;
4. Axiology—system of values.

Most educators believe that education is of a practical nature, therefore placing educational philosophy in category 4. As physical education is a vital part of our educational system, a philosophy of physical education is a philosophy based on or for a system of values.

Philosophical differences among groups and individuals play a great part in determining the direction that formalized education will follow. These differences are often referred to as "philosophical tendencies" and may be categorized as naturalism, realism, idealism, and pragmatism. *Naturalism* is a philosophical theory which emphasizes that the physical nature of the universe is self-explanatory and that scientific laws can explain all phenomena. *Realism* is the facing of facts and practicality, or the belief that universals have objective reality and exist in themselves. *Idealism* promotes a rational order in the universe based on a conception of things the way they ought to be according to the mind of the individual. *Pragmatism* deals with the belief that we learn truth by doing, and that validity is only achieved when the practical results are tested.

It is of course vital that an educator develop a personal philosophy in order to be most effective in his work. It is even more important that an individual holding an administrative position develop a philosophy for his life and for his profession. A well-thought-out personal and professional philosophy will be of immense value in assisting with the decision-making which any administrator faces. The achievement of a unified philosophy within a school district, school, or department will create a maximum drive toward the desired goals.

Philosophy in Physical Education

"Specifically, there appear to be three major philosophies of physical, health, and recreation education in regard to educational values. They are experimentalism, or perhaps pragmatic naturalism, which emphasizes the concept of total fitness rather than physical fitness alone; realism, which typically accepts education of the physical as the primary emphasis in the field; and idealism, which is basically an essentialistic position that stresses education of the physical and yet believes in education through the physical as well. The delineation of these three positions does represent progress, but it doesn't tell us anything about the possibility of consensus and where we go from here."[11]

Some teachers are *"concerned existentialists"* and hold that each person exists as an individual in a purposeless universe. Free will to survive is emphasized, and a concern for life and living is dominant through games of self-expression. The existentialist is a provocator of thought and attempts to enlighten the child to the moral dimensions of life. A *pragmatist* attempts to guide students so they can find successful solutions to the many problems of life as they arise. The pragmatic teacher emphasizes *how* to think rather than *what* to think. This type of socialized approach to learning stresses group decision making in games and contests. A great deal of opportunity is provided for the free interchange of ideas and the continuous evaluation of progress. A physical education teacher who follows the *idealist* philosophy believes that the teacher is the most important entity in the child's life and that facilities, equipment, and supplies are not nearly as important as setting an example of wholesome, vigorous living and stimulating students to develop their full creative powers. Creative effort, discussion, and self-initiated activities are the focal point of an idealist's physical education program. The *realist*, on the other

hand, rejects many of the idealist's approaches to education. The realist believes that students should be brought into contact with the real world through such things as activity experiments, demonstrations, and the exposure to the application of scientific principles.

It may well be that if a national or even international unanimity of purpose is desired by us in the profession, we should seek out those who profess the philosophical tendencies which best exemplify the desired outcomes. One would suspect that a combination of one or more "tendencies" of thought might well produce a satisfactory philosophy upon which to base the profession.

Philosophy and Principles

"Principles are general concepts based either upon pertinent scientific facts or upon philosophic judgment that arises out of insight and/or experience."[12]

Once a philosophy has been established through insight, experience, and understanding, and scientific facts have been discovered, principles may be formed. If principles are based on well-established facts, they are not apt to change. Principles based on philosophical thought, however, may be subject to frequent change.

An individual's personal and professional philosophy is the basic underlying factor in the determination of principles for any of the many aspects of our profession.

MODERN CONCEPTS OF PHYSICAL EDUCATION

Once one has developed a professional *philosophy* and then formulated basic guiding *principles*, the next step is to outline *objectives* or *aims*, in order to advance toward a desired goal. These three criteria have provided the basis for many statements of general educational principles and/or objectives, during the past 50 years.

These principles for attainment, or

statements for being, as they are sometimes referred to, have been emphasized and analyzed for years in many professional texts. Some of the more noteworthy analyses are: the Seven Cardinal Principles of Education, as presented in 1918; the objectives of educational purposes presented by the American Youth Commission in 1937; and the four purposes of education as prepared by the Educational Policies Commission of the National Education Association of Secondary School Principals in 1947.

Although these statements of objectives and principles have been adapted to meet the needs of almost every discipline in the academic spectrum, it is true that *in every statement the health, fitness, and recreational needs of children and youth have been stressed.* The historical influence of these statements upon physical education has naturally been great. "There appears to be no question that the role of physical, health, and recreation education in the educational pattern will vary depending on the final or ultimate aims of education to which the individual subscribes. Specific educational objectives must be chosen in the light of these ultimate goals."[13]

Eighteen "goals of education" as presently listed by Phi Delta Kappa are:

1. Develop skills in reading, writing, speaking, and listening
2. Develop pride in work and a feeling of self-worth
3. Develop good character and self-respect
4. Develop a desire for learning now and in the future
5. Learn to respect and get along with people with whom we work and live
6. Learn how to examine and use information
7. Gain a general education
8. Learn how to be a good citizen
9. Learn about and try to understand the changes that take place in the world
10. Understand and practice democratic ideas and ideals
11. Learn how to respect and get along with people who think, dress, and act differently
12. Understand and practice the skills of family living
13. Gain information needed to make job selections
14. Learn how to be a good manager of money, property, and resources
15. Practice and understand the ideas of health and safety
16. Develop skills to enter a specific field of work
17. Learn how to use leisure time
18. Appreciate culture and beauty in the world

Of these goals, number 15 applies directly to physical education, stressing (a) establishment of an effective individual physical fitness program; (b) development of an understanding of good physical health and well-being; (c) establishment of sound personal health habits and information; (d) development of a concern for public health and safety.

Physical Education in a Constantly Changing Society

Since World War II there have been many statements of physical education objectives, aims, and purposes for children, youth, and adults. It is unfortunate that many institutions required that such "statements of truth" be committed to memory, so that students would never forget the importance of the development of "organic power and vigor." In offering purposes or objectives for any goal attainment we must be sure that we understand realistically what we are trying to accomplish. Zeigler states that much of the field of physical education and sport is "out of step" with the large majority of the younger generation, because the present *rate* of change is increasing so sharply. We must attempt to eliminate this credibility gap immediately, or the profession cannot display *accountability, relevance,* and *involvement.*[14] Many schools and colleges are attempting to provide programs that will develop human values through sports. In 1973, Springfield College sponsored a national conference on this important contemporary issue.

In 1965 the American Association for

Health, Physical Education and Recreation presented the following as *the major educational purposes of physical education:*[15]

1. To help children learn to move skillfully and effectively not only in exercise, games, sports, and dances but also in all active life situations.

2. To develop understandings of voluntary movement and the ways in which individuals may organize their own movements to accomplish the significant purposes of their lives.

3. To enrich understanding of space, time, mass-energy relationships, and related concepts.

4. To extend understanding of socially approved patterns of personal behavior, with particular reference to the interpersonal interactions of games and sports.

5. To condition the heart, lungs, muscles, and other organic systems to respond to increased demands by imposing progressively greater demands upon them.

Although over 10 years old, these purposes were developed upon a basic underlying philosophy that is believed to be professionally sound. The "now" physical education still follows these basic objectives but strives to make activities more valuable and enjoyable for *all* students. Lifetime sports, freedom of choice, and student-centered coeducational activities are all a part of the new physical education image. Our modern concept is that a physically educated person is one who has acquired knowledge, skills, and an appreciation of his or her body and how it works. Then, because of the development of a positive attitude toward movement, we are motivated to use these skills for a happy, productive life.

Modern Technology and Sedentary Living

Modern advances in industrial and business technology continue to proceed at an ever-increasing rate, in spite of the depletion of energy reserves. These advances make possible more leisure time and more modern conveniences. Modern conveniences are naturally not considered "conveniences" or "modern" unless they eliminate all or part of our human energy expenditure, either at work or at play. Because of a continued worldwide shortage of fossil fuels, the 21st century may well be characterized by even shorter work weeks, increased leisure time, and other advances that may eliminate more and more opportunities for children and adults to be physically active. The physically educated person will be one who is concerned with his physical self and who will recognize that a healthy, vigorous individual is much better able to sustain environmental forces and meet life's challenges. If he has learned to move effectively and efficiently, an individual will realize that his skills have fitted him for a lifetime of enjoyable movement experiences. He will also appreciate physical activity and express joy and satisfaction in movement experiences such as games, sports, dance, and play.

In the coming years, will there be a place for a profession that promotes individual and group activities which are physical in nature? This question is one of many that will have to be answered if physical education, as we know it today in our schools and colleges, is to survive. It is of interest to refer back in history to the decadent life and physical decay of Rome and to compare this with the direction of present-day life in the United States and in many other countries throughout the world.

Domains of Learning

In attempting to provide instructional programs to educate children and youth, classifications have been formulated for the teaching-learning process in order to provide meaningful direction. Physical education objectives have been classified in "learning domains" just as they have for other aspects of the school curriculum. The three domains of learning in physical education are:

Psychomotor Domain—includes the technical aspects of movement in the form of sports, exercise, and dance.

Cognitive Domain—includes the knowledge and interpretive abilities associated with participation in a physical activity. Some of the more common learning areas in physical education are the strategies used in playing various sports and games; the rules governing such activities; the inherent values of physical activities; the historical background of sport and physical education; and game courtesies and sport etiquette.

Affective Domain—includes the emotional and social behavioral patterns that are involved in formulating an individual's interests, appreciations, attitudes, ideals, habits, and, perhaps most important, values and judgments.

Most authors writing about the "dimensions" of domains of learning agree that these domains are further subdivided into different levels. Such levels represent the degree of involvement of particular behavioral patterns. Levels of *psychomotor* behavior include perception, mental, physical, or emotional readiness, guided response, and overt response. Levels of *cognitive* behavior include knowledge, comprehension, synthesis, evaluation, and application. Levels of *affective* behavior include responding, organization, valuing, and receiving or attending.

When teachers attempt to specify and measure instructional objectives, they should first determine the classes of behaviors reflected in those objectives. Thus, objectives are classified into cognitive, affective, and psychomotor domains. The major reasons for classifying objectives are to avoid concentrating on one or two categories to the exclusion of others; to make sure that instruction is provided for prerequisite objectives before attempting to teach more complex ones; and to assure that the appropriate instruments are employed to evaluate the desired objectives.[16] A teacher must be careful, however, to recognize that one of the major drawbacks of classifying behaviors is the tendency to place a specific objective in one behavioral domain when it more properly should be placed in two or more. It is often difficult to isolate the behavioral domains present in any given objective.

Elementary and Secondary School Concepts

In most educational settings, statements of concepts, principles, objectives, and aims are first related to curriculum development. Physical education, like other academic areas in the school setting, has been actively involved in attempting to formulate behavioral objectives and to institute such objectives in the instructional process. Behavioral objectives are generally considered to be statements which describe what students will be able to do after completing a prescribed unit of instruction. A basic behavioral objective, which should be sought at the elementary school level, is the understanding of voluntary movement as a significant function of man. Individual development and self-identification are two extremely important concepts to be taught at the secondary school level. At either the elementary or secondary level, modern functional secondary school programs should promote a wide range of individual and dual activities. The ultimate behavioral objective is to produce a physically educated person, as mentioned previously. Our programs should attempt to develop men and women capable of fully utilizing their opportunities for education, recreation, and creative work. Cardiovascular and respiratory endurance characterizes a movement-oriented individual—one who realizes that physical activity is beneficial because vigorous physical activity improves human body functions.

The NOW physical education, which is being promoted in the middle and late 1970's, places maximum emphasis upon finding ways to make physical education more valuable and more palatable for all students. Youth are being introduced to activities that are considered to be lifetime sports—that is, activities in which they can participate for the rest of their lives. Students at all grade levels are being provided with more freedom to select physical education activities in cooperation with their teachers. Teachers and schools are supplementing programs with resources in the local community as well as providing coeducational student-centered curricula.

Inner-City Programs. Inner-city physical education programs are receiving a great deal of emphasis as we approach the 21st century. Physical educators in urban centers are faced with the difficult challenge of making physical education relevant to the youth who live and go to school in large urban areas.

Perhaps the most critical area of need involves the continued struggle to provide more and better indoor and outdoor facilities and equipment. In many instances, older facilities may be renovated and used creatively to provide a realistic teacher-student ratio. It is certainly recognized that students living in large cities deserve to have the same quality programs as those who live in the suburbs. Individualizing programs to meet student needs and involving students in the organization and planning of dynamic and interesting programs are approaches that are producing desirable results. Humanization, involvement, broadened basis of competition, mini courses, and weekend physical education experiences are very worthwhile approaches which will be discussed in detail in Part II of this text.

Multi-Unit Organization. The open school concept at the elementary level continues to promote new, imaginative, and creative play experiences for children. Continuum I, which encompasses nursery, kindergarten, and grades 1 and 2 (i.e., ages 4 through 8), usually stresses the social development of the young child under the tutelage of master teachers as the main facilitators of learning. Scheduling changes are sometimes made daily in order to meet the needs of each child as they are diagnosed. Children in play experiences as well as in other parts of the curriculum are provided with both structured and unstructured time. Each teacher in the continuum usually works with children of various ages, and an attempt is made to provide individually guided education for each child. Continuum II (ages 8 through 12) is usually composed of grade levels 3 through 6. Programs in this continuum may be implemented in standard self-contained classrooms or in an open school concept. "Learning Centers" may be established in science, math, social studies, language arts, and physical education. Many such programs are patterned after an instructional model known as I.G.E.—Individualized Guided Education. Learning involvement permits each child to receive individual teacher guidance and self-choice of material. Mode of learning and self-pacing receives the greatest emphasis in this continuum. Continuum III (ages 12 through 15) is usually regarded as the "middle school." The middle school or "the school in the middle" is recognized as an idea whose time has come. For many years, educators have recognized that youth in the early stages of adolescence have special problems in bridging the gap between elementary and high school. The junior high school was, and is, an attempt to provide an appropriate transition between the elementary and high school grades. Modern day middle schools may encompass grade levels 7, 8, and 9 or may begin as low as the fifth grade. In some instances middle schools encompass grades 6, 7, and 8, the ninth grade being placed in the traditional high school. In the third continuum, or middle school, the student is the focal point of the program. Student input is encouraged, and the building of student responsibility is a primary aim of the entire middle school curriculum. At this point, student schedules may be arranged on the basis of student needs and interests. Many, if not all, classes consist of children of various ages, and a wide variety of electives are usually available to students throughout their academic day. Many units in physical education, varying in length from two to four weeks, are often provided in both the second and third continuum in order to provide a wide variety of physical activities to meet the needs of students.

Performance, Competency, and Accountability. Although many programs of instruction are still conducted on a traditional basis, a variety of approaches toward the "now" physical education are being attempted throughout the country, from primary grades through high school. Team teaching, coordinated program planning, and the use of supplemental activity areas are deemed to be three of the most important criteria in the establishment of programs designed to meet the needs of all students. Whether or not accountability in American public education will prove to be one of the most important educational movements in the decade of the 1970's remains to be seen. Nevertheless, the federal government, taxpayers, and unhappy parents have transformed the term accountability from a theoretical notion to a formidable force in American education. To the layman, accountability means that public schools must prove that students at various levels have met some reasonable standard of achievement. The concept also implies or infers that schools must show that they use federal and state funds wisely and that expenditures of money justify educational outcomes. Several public opinion polls in the early seventies consistently recorded substantial majorities favoring teacher accountability. Because of the demand for accountability and competency-based instruction (C.B.I.), physical education teachers are being challenged to demonstrate that they are providing specific functional skills as well as a definite field of knowledge and behaviors which can be identified. Accountability, C.B.I., and performance discrepancy will be discussed in greater depth in Chapter 2 as some of the critical issues facing physical education.

Concepts in Intramural Sports

During the 1970's concepts in intramural sports, which evolved as schools attempted to improve physical education programs, were concerned with coeducational activities, recreational competition, and the modification of activities and programs which were already in existence.

Most school intramural sports programs became involved in attempting to meet the needs and interests of students. The addition of a wider variety of coeducational activities resulted because of student demands. The California Sports Day, a totally recreationally oriented program, is an excellent example of new offerings and interests; intramurals will be discussed in detail in Chapter 12. In some schools, highly competitive intramural coeducational activities have been initiated.

Modifications of present programs and activities have been evolving over the past several years. Regular baseball or softball has developed into "slow pitch," and tackle football has been modified and well received as "touch" or "flag" football. Such changes in activities and activity rules have developed in order to include more students of lesser skill in intramural programs and also to eliminate strenuous conditioning programs. Sports which have had their rules modified are also more readily adaptable to coeducational programs. Some excellent examples are innertube water polo, broomball hockey, and mini soccer. The Charlottesville (Virginia) School System adopted the middle school concept several years ago, including grades 6, 7, and 8. When this restructuring occurred, Charlottesville eliminated interscholastic athletics from the middle school and in their place stressed the inclusion of an outstanding program of intramural sports for both boys and girls. This exemplary program includes a wide diversification of sports offerings and is well supported by trained staff and excellent facilities.

Recreational competition has also been widely accepted by students in intramural sports. Many activities which are recreational in nature yet have some competitive aspects are being added to intramural sports programs throughout the country. Many such activities are one-day events and include a wide diversification of activities, ranging from wrist wrestling to bicycle races, relays, tugs of war, kite flying, and frisbee contests. Organized activities which are noncompetitive also meet the needs and interests of many students. The most popular of these are sports clubs for such activities as scuba diving, rock climbing, cycling, and self-defense or the martial arts.

College and University Concepts

During the mid-1970's, institutions of higher learning experienced a gradual withdrawal from student and faculty activism. The student unrest of the sixties and early seventies was followed by a period characterized as "the return to academics."

Students and faculty alike tended to refer to this seeming disinterest as a period of student apathy. As college enrollments declined, both administrators and faculty devoted much more time to student-centered interests. Active student recruitment and the re-emphasis of endowed giving are in evidence in both private and public institutions. As enrollments have continued to stabilize or decline, many state and private universities have been forced to curtail high-cost programs and to release nontenured and tenured faculty. The release of tenured faculty has brought about a great deal of campus unrest and facilitated conflict between university administrators, faculty, and professional and union organizations. It is believed that this confrontation over the necessary termination of faculty contracts may well bring about the unionization of college and university faculties 10 to 15 years before collective bargaining would have otherwise occurred.

The limitations of academic funding brought about by dwindling enrollments have seriously affected physical education programs in some institutions. In several states, schools and colleges have been required to release faculty in physical education departments and to curtail selected programs.

Accountability and competency-based instruction have also been demanded in institutions of higher learning. Administrators and their faculties are involved in thorough "in house" evaluations in an attempt to determine whether or not basic instruction programs as well as professional curricula indeed meet the needs of students and society. An in-depth study of these and other significant concepts will be discussed in Part IV.

THE PURPOSE AND IMPORTANCE OF PHYSICAL EDUCATION

Of what importance are sport and physical education to our culture? Who needs physical education or physical activities? Such questions and many more pertaining to the usefulness of physical education are asked repeatedly and are often difficult to answer. The physical educator and the physical education administrator must be able to respond in simple, logical, meaningful terms, or else their programs will be in jeopardy. The era of the uninformed public who could be satisfactorily answered in glittering generalities has long ago ceased to exist.

Any statement of the importance of or need for physical education programs, at any educational level, will of course be based upon an individual's personal and professional philosophies. The determination of these philosophies is the basic step in deciding what is important in life and what needs exist.

Value judgments are, in many instances, very difficult to make, yet few individuals would take issue with the importance of leading a *healthful life.* Indeed, health has been man's greatest concern since the earliest civilizations. Physical educators and physical education programs are primarily interested in the development and maintenance of a high level of health—not just average health, but superior health; not just physiological health, but mental and emotional health as well.

As we approach the 21st century, medical research continues to document and support the fact that the physical self thrives on vigorous activity and that all healthy body systems function more efficiently when they are subjected to some cardiovascular and circulatory overload. Physicians and physical education practitioners can document that physical activity assists in the control of obesity; improves organic function; assists in the reduction of mental stress and tension; and contributes greatly to an individual's overall mental health. The importance of physical activity and the need for teaching physical education is well known and generally well accepted. As many nations continue to emphasize physical fitness, the recognition of the importance of teaching physical education in many instances is not the major problem. One of the profession's greatest obstacles lies in the development of a positive attitude toward regular physical activity on the part of physical educators themselves. We must lead the way and set the example; we must indeed practice what we preach.

Human Movement and the Acquisition of Physical Skills

Two of the more important purposes for teaching physical education to children and adults are to develop a specific level of physical fitness and to develop neuromuscular skills. The acquisition of both fitness and skill is essential for the proper functioning of the individual as a moving motor mechanism. There is little doubt that the physical education and activity needs of youth differ greatly today from those of the past, owing to the rapid social and economic changes that have taken place in recent years. Consequently, the objectives of our contemporary physical education programs must be adjusted to meet the needs and demands of new cultural patterns as they develop. In many ways students must be considered the consumers of our products, as they are the direct recipients of the activities we use to illustrate concepts of human movement. *We must use our many and varied programs to develop a positive attitude toward continued physical activity for life and living.* If we fail in the development of a healthful attitude toward active physical participation, we are literally wasting our time with subsequent curricula, facilities, and innovation.

Scott[17] believes that physical educators can assist in seeing that physical activity has an even greater meaning for the "consumer," if we attempt to eliminate some of the elaborate paraphernalia with which we surround our teaching. Although change is agonizing, Scott states that we must ask ourselves, "Should we force everyone to engage in our instructional programs?" "Should we force people into movement experiences they dislike?" If sport is to be enjoyed and used by individuals as a pleasurable experience, then rules, regulations, and requirements, which *force* structured play, may well be incongruous. Physical education programs should assist each participant to *learn* and *understand* as well as *enjoy* what physical fitness and physical education is and what it can do. Basic concepts regarding the purposes of our programs should include knowledge and skill concerning the human body and how it functions, physical activity for a healthy organism, the acquisition of skills for leisure-time activities, and the development of a healthful mental and social well-being. As a result of movement education and the acquisition of useful physical skills, our students should then be capable of successfully meeting the needs of their daily lives, including leisure-time activity needs and needs that may develop in emergency situations.

Personal and Educational Values

Many authors have devoted pages, chapters, and entire texts to attempts to answer the many questions and ramifications surrounding the purpose and importance of physical education. Why teach physical education? Of what value is physical education in our nation's schools? Of what value are physical education and interscholastic activities in relation to educational problems? Are there any psychological and physiological bases for teaching physical education? These and many similar questions have been asked for decades by superintendents, principals, physical education teachers, and teachers in colleges and universities. In an attempt to provide an answer to some of these questions and, indeed, define what physical education actually is, Thompson[18] states that "physical education is a way of education through physical activities that are selected to provide an environment conducive to human growth, development, and behavior, which in turn contribute to the development of a better citizen."

The authors would amend this definition of physical education to state "physical education *should be* a way of education. . . ."[11] All too often physical activities in our schools and colleges are not selected to provide an environment conducive to mental, emotional, and physical growth. Nor are they selected to provide maximum development and acceptable behavioral patterns. Realistically, many programs throughout the country are selected primarily on the type and nature of available indoor and outdoor facilities as well as on the specific interest and expertise of physical education teachers. Almost all school districts and school systems believe that schools should meet "needs and interests," and challenge the abilities of each individual child within their schools. Personal and educational values can certainly be obtained from physical education classes if this philosophy is adhered to for all disciplines within the school, physical education included. Antiquated facilities, overloaded classes of 60 to 90 pupils, disinterested or ill-prepared teachers, and haphazard scheduling of classes have all contributed to student dislike, absenteeism, and the development of undesirable attitudes.

For activities to be of value, curriculum planning in physical education must provide for much more than just sports activities that are thought to be interesting and fun. Physical educators have known for many years that each child needs to develop a positive and satisfying self image, through acceptance, success, and sufficient attention from peers and teachers. We must ask ourselves whether our programs are promoting activity situations that will reinforce each child's individual and personal needs in the development of image, acceptability, success, and attention. Ironically, too many physical education programs, because of teacher thoughtlessness or lack of correct methodology, encourage game and activity situations in which a child's self image can easily be destroyed through rejection by peers and lack of success.

As stated previously, excellent documentation exists to support the need for daily physical education programs for grades kindergarten through college. Activities and athletic programs *may* assist in lowering the number of school dropouts and reducing delinquency and crime. There is also considerable research data available to show that selected motor aptitude tests correlate positively and significantly with intellectual performance. Several experimental programs have also demonstrated a significant improvement in the academic performance of children exposed to selected physical education programs. Our single most important contribution, however, still remains in the area of the development of physical fitness. A physiological basis for physical education and the development of cardiovascular fitness is actively supported by many medical associations. It is in this area that the most scientific research has been undertaken. It must be emphasized, however, that entire physical education programs should not be changed to provide sole concentration on the development of cardiovascular respiratory fitness. Physical education periods of 40 to 60 minutes duration, two or three times a week, can only *assist* in fitness development. It is recognized that the development of a positive attitude, so that the student will carry on physical activities which contribute to total fitness outside of formalized class instruction, is of far greater importance.

What students gain in personal and educational values is directly related to the interest, instructional capabilities, and teaching methodology of the physical education teacher. Teaching methods that promote negative learning should have been discarded years ago, yet we still see instances where a student is required to do push-ups, sit-ups or run laps for punishment. After completing such punishment (*in the form of physical activity*), students and adults are then encouraged to undertake the same activities because they are beneficial for their physical well-being. Understandably, adults violently refuse to become involved in jogging or calisthenic programs because of unpleasant experiences with such activities in the past. Psychologists and others interested in the growing needs of boys and girls ask physical educators why children enter formalized activity programs with a positive and healthful attitude toward play only to leave them several years later with a very negative attitude toward physical education. Self-evaluation may well reveal that practices and procedures which we employ when children first come into contact with changing and showering for physical activity may have little educational value and may, indeed, foster fear and humiliation for many students. As physical educators, we are well accustomed to locker room and shower areas; but the very act of changing clothes and showering with other students may prove to be a very traumatic experience for some children. For this reason, physical education programs should have one of the finest student orientation periods when "formalized" programs begin, in the second or third continuum.

There are many personal and educational values in a well-conceived and well-taught physical education activity program. If curricula are developed which stimulate the activity and psychological needs of individuals as well as of groups of children, and if interested and professionally competent teachers provide viable instruction, much can be derived from physical education. In a well-conceived and well-conducted program, physical activity is a pleasurable experience. Students *do* learn to understand themselves and others and they *do* develop neuromuscular skills which lead to physical fitness for living. The concept of "I'm okay, you're okay," indeed becomes a reality.

REFERENCES

1. D. B. Van Dalen, E. D. Mitchell, and B. L. Bennett: *A World History of Physical Education.* Englewood Cliffs, N.J.: Prentice-Hall, Inc., 1953, p. 5.
2. E. A. Rice, J. L. Hutchinson, and M. Lee: *A Brief History of Physical Education.* New York: The Ronald Press Co., 1958, pp. 3–47.
3. Donn F. Draeger and Robert W. Smith: *Asian Fighting Arts.* Tokyo: Kodansha International Let., 1969, p. 12.
4. John A. Lucas: "A Prelude to the Rise of Sport: Antebellum America, 1850–1860." *Quest,* XI, December, 1968, p: 50.
5. G. Wesley Sowards and Mary Margaret Scobey: *The Changing Curriculum and the Elementary Teacher.* San Francisco: Wadsworth Publishing Co., 1961, p. 131.
6. C. W. Hackensmith: *History of Physical Education.* New York: Harper & Row, 1966, p. 449.
7. Pat Mueller: *Intramurals: Programming and Administration.* New York: The Ronald Press Co., 1971, p. 19.
8. *This is Physical Education.* Washington, D.C.: AAHPER, 1965, p. 1.
9. *Webster's New World Dictionary.* Cleveland: The World Publishing Co., 1962, p. 1099.
10. Earle F. Zeigler: *Philosophical Foundations for Physical, Health and Recreation Education.* Englewood Cliffs, N.J.: Prentice-Hall, Inc., 1964, p. 11.
11. *Ibid.,* p. 254.
12. Jesse F. Williams: *The Principles of Physical Education.* Philadelphia: W. B. Saunders Co., 1964, p. 16.
13. Zeigler, *op. cit.,* p. 254.
14. Earle F. Zeigler: "Five Stances That Have Got To Go." *JOHPER,* Washington, D.C.: AAHPER, September, 1973, p. 48.
15. *This is Physical Education, op. cit.,* p. 1.
16. Robert J. Kibler, Larry L. Barker, and David T. Miles: *Behavioral Objectives and Instruction.* Boston: Allen & Bacon, Inc., 1970, p. 44.
17. Phebe M. Scott: *The Agony of Change.* Proceedings of the Central Association for Physical Education of College Women, Fall Conference, Overland Park, Kansas, 1971.
18. John C. Thompson: *Physical Education for the Nineteen Seventies.* Englewood Cliffs, N.J.: Prentice-Hall, Inc., 1971, p. 1.

SUGGESTED READINGS

Kleinman, Seymour: "New Uses for an Old System" *JOHPER*, September, 1974, p. 21.

Lucas, John A.: "A Prelude to the Rise of Sport: Antebellum America, 1850–1860." *Quest*, XI, December, 1968, p. 50.

Scott, Phebe M.: *The Agony of Change.* Proceedings of the Central Association for Physical Education of College Women, Fall Conference, Overland Park, Kansas, 1971.

Thompson, John C.: *Physical Education for the Nineteen Seventies.* Englewood Cliffs, N.J.; Prentice-Hall, Inc., 1971, Chapter 1.

Zeigler, Earle F.: *Philosophical Foundations for Physical, Health and Recreation Education.* Englewood Cliffs, N.J.: Prentice-Hall, Inc., 1964, Chapters 3 and 4.

Zeigler, Earle F.: "Five Stances That Have Got To Go." *JOHPER.* Washington, D.C.: AAHPER, Sept., 1973, p. 48.

CHAPTER TWO

Critical Issues and Present Trends

Several trends and current issues were presented briefly in the preceding chapter because they were considered to be issues pertaining to basic philosophical foundations. An additional overview of these and other areas of interest is now provided; this will be especially useful in later chapters when we deal with the supervision and administration of elementary and secondary schools, colleges, and universities. Specific objectives and programs for these specialized areas will be presented in those chapters which deal with each area individually.

PRESENT STATUS AND THE CHALLENGES OF THE FUTURE

The present status of professional physical education is open to question. In order to determine this status, one must first define the type of program and the academic or service level at which it is being offered.

33

There is no doubt that many of our public school and college programs are considered excellent both in scope and quality. Other programs, however, are quite mediocre or inadequate as judged by students, teachers, and the general public. Many educators have supported the belief that the basic foundation upon which American public education rests at the elementary and secondary levels is *quality education for all*. If this is true, what are physical educators doing to meet this objective?

As was mentioned in Chapter 1, schools are concerned with learning domains, performance objectives, accountability, individually guided education, and student participation in the determination and selection of curricula. All of these concepts are direct attempts to improve the quality of education in our schools and to provide greater *responsibility* in education, and they all have a direct effect on physical education programs. To a large extent, the status of physical education curricula within any given school or school district depends upon the goals and objectives of the schools in which programs are found. The following excerpt is from a statement by a physical education teacher in a large metropolitan high school.

There was a time, up to the late sixties, when we used to innovate with demonstrations, combining boys' and girls' classes in all areas of activity. The trend toward individual expression has taken away the controls we once used and, in a way, we are now outmoded. I feel I am now more of a custodian of a gymnasium and less a teacher. We try to individualize and often have multi-activities at the same time ... however, there are beehives of activity. The kids are doing their thing, as they say! Some youngsters would play "21" all year round, and some groups would play floor hockey without let-up, and gymnastic oriented youngsters utilize apparatus, the trampoline being ever popular.

Of course, this is but a single illustration, provided by a single teacher from a specific school setting. However, it does tend to illustrate an individual teacher's expression of what has happened to physical education because of changes which have occurred since the late 1960's. The nature and scope of present physical education programs, at all education levels, depends primarily upon the physical education teacher's professional preparation, experience, and willingness and ability to cope with the constantly changing educational spectrum, without sacrificing the established curricula proved necessary for the development of children.

Future Challenges

Burton C. Brunner[1] asks the question, "How will today's physical education classes be remembered?" Will they be remembered for quality instruction, breadth as well as depth, and carry-over values for later life? Or will they be remembered as dull, unimaginative, dogmatic, compulsory programs, which contributed little, if anything, to a student's present or future well-being? Fortunately, physical educators are in a position to make present programs worthwhile, *if they will only take the time and make the effort that is required*. The "now" physical education demands devotion and creativity from its teachers.

As one can well realize, there are many challenges for the future for any academic profession in our modern world. Perhaps the challenge is even greater in physical education than in other disciplines. Five of our most pressing tasks, as we approach the 21st century, are:

1. The formation of clear, concise statements of philosophical objectives for the national nature and scope of professional physical education.
2. The improvement of facilities, programs, and instruction at all educational levels to meet the ever-changing needs and interests of students and adults.
3. The establishment of a strong and prestigious profession for physical education, which will work in close cooperation with agencies and organizations primarily concerned with health education, recreation, and athletics.
4. The ability to continue to educate the general public concerning the nature of and

need for physical activity, and the ability to promote and maintain a physically active populace.

5. Improvement of the quality of instruction through the development of stronger teacher education programs, with emphasis on in-depth knowledge of what to teach and how to teach it.

Present and future challenges in physical education will be directly related to changing influences in American education in general. Surveys conducted in the early 1970's revealed that approximately half of the teachers in the United States thought that teaching as a profession was improving, while 4 out of 10 thought the profession was on the decline. Studies conducted during the same period showed that almost 30 per cent of all parents were unhappy or dissatisfied with their children's education. A paramount challenge to American education has been to improve this image as well as to develop alternate methods for financing public schools. Changes in financing, early childhood education, collective bargaining, teacher shortages and surpluses, parent involvement, student participation, and the use of para-professionals will no doubt continue to provide educational challenges for the future. Proposals by both parents and teachers will have their effect on physical education programs.

CRITICAL ISSUES

In 1956 a study was undertaken in the "Big Ten" universities to determine basic issues facing the profession. At that time these issues or problems were presented as:

1. The need for better public relations directed toward a better understanding of physical education by the public.
2. The improvement of impoverished curricula in physical education.
3. The recruitment, selection, preparation, and retention of professional personnel.
4. Athletic problems at all levels.
5. The need for basic professional philosophy.
6. The need for professional status.

7. The emphasis for general, liberal, and cultural aspects within the profession.
8. The need to strengthen elementary physical education programs.
9. The impending crisis in student enrollments.
10. The need for practical research.
11. Professional problems and differences among teachers of health education, physical education, and recreation.
12. Evaluation and grading.
13. Specialized *vs* generalized professional preparation.
14. Accreditation and certification.
15. Academic credit for physical education.
16. Quality instruction.
17. Higher salaries for attracting quality teachers.[2]

Although these basic issues were formulated, presented, and discussed some 20 years ago, most are still significant issues. A great deal of progress has, of course, been made since 1956. PEPI has provided vastly improved public relations, and positive contributions have been made in physical education curricula by the concentration on meeting the interests and needs of children in rapidly changing metropolitan and urban centers. The profession will always be concerned with the recruitment and preparation of students to become master teachers. In 20 years some of the problems facing physical education and interscholastic or intercollegiate athletics have been alleviated, but many problems still exist. Elementary physical education programs have, in many instances, been significantly strengthened. The crises in student enrollments in 1956 involved dealing with massive increases, while present problems facing the profession are concerned with decreasing enrollments. Most teachers agree that there is a need for practical research. Some of the problems involving the relationships between health education, physical education, and recreation have been alleviated by the formation of new associations for each of these professional areas within the new American Alliance for Health, Physical Education and Recreation. Evaluation and grading, as well as the dilemma of whether to prepare teachers to be specialists or generalists, is as evident today as it was 20 years ago. Problems concerning accreditation and certification have stabilized, as has academic credit for physical education. Quality instruction and higher salaries for teachers are still a very vital part of the professional objectives of both the NEA and the AFT.

Accountability, competency-based teacher education, educational funding, learning freedoms, and countless other changing influences in American education are additional crucial professional problems for every educational level.

Basic Aims, Objectives, and Principles

National aims to be reached by the elementary, secondary, and university levels are not easily formulated. Many scholars and professional organizations have presented specific aims, objectives, and statements of worthy purposes, but these suggestions vary as much as individual thought and belief vary. The aims and objectives of physical education should have a basic underlying philosophy: the mental, emotional, and physiological health of the individual.

Aims. The term "aim" is usually defined in relationship to objectives. A deferred aim may be an objective whose attainment is not expected until after one or more goals or objectives have been reached. An aim is usually considered to be a type of "guiding" objective that gives direction and leads to the attainment of a specific goal.

Objectives. Objectives are considered to be more narrow and perhaps more practical than aims, and are usually a specific standard or goal to be achieved. Objectives serve as a guide directed toward achievement and are usually stated in exact terms. "Behavioral" objectives are statements describing what students will be able to do after completing a prescribed task. "There are objectives and there are objectives—some are commonly associated with goals; some are developed as principles leading to some desired results; and some are less exact and are more of a feeling or are in the realm of the philo-

sophical. Objectives can serve as stimulus or as guidelines. They can even be used as an excuse for inaction or postponement of action. In fact, *objective* is a word that can cover a great many human activities."[3] Performance objectives should have the following qualities: the learner and the instructor have a common understanding as to what is to be accomplished, and the learner and the instructor have a common and firm set of criteria by which the learner's progress and level of competency may be assessed at any specific point in time.

Principles. "A principle is a guiding rule for general action toward some goal and is based on scientific fact or authoritative opinion."[4] According to the authors of this quotation, specific procedures in physical education will vary for each established goal. If our efforts are to be effective, we should act according to *principle,* and not through whim or opportunism. Principles are related to policy in that they provide the professional guides upon which policies are based.

In attempting to clarify the domain of physical education as a discipline, Lawrence G. Rarick presents the following points:

1. Physical education as a discipline is concerned with the mechanics of human movement, with the mode of acquisition and control of movement patterns, and with the psychological factors affecting movement responses.
2. Physical education is concerned with the physiology of man under the stresses of exercise, sports, and dance, and with the immediate and lasting effects of physical activity.
3. The historical and cultural aspects of physical education and dance occupy a prominent place in our discipline. The roles of sports and dance in the cultures which have preceded ours and in our own culture need to be fully explored.
4. Lastly, in physical education we are aware that man does not function alone. Individual and group interactions in games, sports, and dance are an important area, one which needs our attention. As yet, we have no rationale for explaining the diversified behavior patterns of individuals and groups as either participants or spectators.[5]

Rarick agrees that professional physical education has not yet come of age, and at present there is still no agreement among many of our scholars as to its primary focus.

Bookwalter and VanderZwaag believe that a basic *aim* of physical education is "the optimum development, integration, and adjustment physically, mentally, and socially of the individual through guided instruction and participation in selected total body sports, rhythmic, and gymnastic activities conducted according to social and hygienic standards."[6] The physical education teachers at Marshalltown Community School District in Marshalltown, Iowa, believe that their basic philosophy is to provide all students with learning experiences so that they will have the opportunity for organic fitness, neuromuscular development, social adjustment, emotional expression, and interpretive understanding. The goal of the physical education staff in this school district is to provide a complete sequence of physical education activities for both boys and girls that will provide each student with skills for post-school recreational activities, skills for leisure time, and a life-long interest in physical fitness.

In every aspect of public education there is a trend to place more and more of the responsibilities of child development upon the teacher. For this reason we must be careful that in our statements of purpose we do not attempt to "aim" at more than we can possibly hope to accomplish. Whether or not a teacher can do equal justice to physical, mental, emotional, and social objectives remains a moot question.

Objectives appropriate for specific grade levels and child growth and development levels must also be formulated. Victor P. Dauer suggests the following as definable purposes for the elementary school:

1. The development and maintenance of suitable levels of physical fitness.
2. Competency in useful physical skills and management of the body.
3. The development of desirable social standards and ethical concepts.
4. The acquisition of safety skills and habits.

5. The enjoyment of wholesome recreation.
6. Desirable personal adjustments.[7]

"Movement competency and basic skills are the emphasis on the primary level. Acquiring more precise skills is a learning experience centered in the intermediate grades. Management of the body is stressed throughout, with experiences which give opportunity for the child to use his body in a variety of situations."[8]

Charles Silberman, author of *Crisis in the Classroom*, believes that no matter what aims or objectives we have for education, school does not need to be the grim, joyless place that most schools are depicted to be. Silberman believes that schools can:

—be human and still educate well
—be genuinely concerned with gaiety and joy and individual growth and fulfillment with sacrificing concern for intellectual discipline and development
—be simultaneously child-centered and subject- or knowledge-centered
—stress esthetic and moral education without weakening the three R's

The revision of basic objectives carried over from elementary levels to college and university programs does not appear to be sizably altered. Senior high school programs should be designed to foster and promote individual and dual sports. Specific objectives for secondary school physical education are found in detail in Part II of this text. College and university curricula depend to a large extent upon the needs and interests of college-age youth. It is evident that if a college student had a sound and adequate physical education background in public school, his young-adult program should be geared to a higher level of attainment and to a more diversified acquisition of skill than that of a student with an inadequate background.

General Education and Physical Education

The term general education means a broad type of education, one which attempts to develop abilities and attitudes but does not *specifically* prepare the student to seek a special vocation or avocation. "This kind of education has been defined as that part of the total education of the student which deals primarily with common persistent problems of the individual and of society (as they interact) and which gives meaning and commonness of purpose to life."[9]

In courses considered to be of an introductory nature, there will be students who may become interested in the subject matter and wish to concentrate in a specific area, as well as those who wish a general education. Jones et al. state that "general education is that part of the total educational program which the student needs just because he is a human being and a member of society."[10]

Physical education activity programs, which are offered from kindergarten through college, are considered to be basic instructional programs that contribute to each individual's general education. Such programs are not to be confused with activity-methodology courses, which are offered in colleges for those who have expressed the desire to concentrate or specialize in professional physical education.

The specific contributions of basic instructional programs *may* be very worthwhile if they follow well-founded aims and objectives. Once again we must be very careful that we do not flatly state that *all* physical education activities do, in fact, make such contributions. As teachers who are dedicated to educational objectives we must make sure that our aims and objectives for general programs in physical education adhere to those aims and objectives presented for the grade level we teach.

Utilizing motor activities as a means of reaching the general goals of education is a phenomenon of the 20th century. Education of and through the physical was presented, accepted, and implemented during the early 1900's. Early physical educators such as Hetherington, Williams, and Nash did much to promote the acceptance of physical education as a vital aspect of general education during a time of changing educa-

tional philosophy. Education "of" the physical was joined during the later part of the century by education "through" the physical, and the "new" physical education attempted to achieve general education goals through the medium of motor activity. Siedentop does not believe that the idea of education through the physical is a sufficient base for contemporary programs of physical education. He states:

We appear to be in a period of theoretical transition within physical education, and it is still difficult to determine the exact direction in which we will move. It does appear that education through the physical, as traditionally formulated, has reached its peak as the primary theoretical concept undergirding programs of physical education and is presently being challenged on several fronts. It might be that the concept has sufficient strength and merit to prevail as the major theory of American physical education, but it will probably have to undergo some modification if it is to retain its position.[11]

If education through the physical still refers to the old seven cardinal principles developed in 1918, then physical educators should indeed be re-evaluating and re-examining their goals as they pertain to general education. Several critical issues revolve around whether or not physical education programs are in harmony with the goals of general education as currently expressed by the Educational Policies Commission. Why students develop avoidance behavior patterns in many physical education classes remains to be explained, as does the validity of the widespread idea that physical education programs can develop moral character, desirable attitudes, and positive value judgments. Future curricula might well provide education neither of the physical nor through the physical, but education for the future well-being of mankind.

Professional Preparation

A periodic review of professional literature reveals that the professional preparation of teachers has long been a critical issue. In almost every statement of problems facing the profession, the improvement of our product—teachers—has been mentioned. Educators at the college level have been quick to place the "blame" for poor student achievement on elementary and secondary school teachers, while these teachers, in turn, believe that the quality of teachers is directly dependent upon colleges and universities.

There is no doubt that any profession, if it seeks to attain quality, must have a high-caliber membership. This is perhaps more true for teachers than for many other disciplines. Yet, in untold instances, we continue to graduate individuals who have little if any interest in teaching physical education and who, in some cases, are certainly not "quality products." These unfortunate occurrences have been brought about, in part, by the association between "high-powered" intercollegiate athletics and professional programs in physical education.

The pursuit of excellence in professional preparation for both the recruitment of able and interested students and the employment of viable, confident faculty is certainly a stated objective that receives little argument among those in the profession. The problem arising in this worthwhile pursuit, however, deals largely with defining the term "excellence."

Most faculty members in educational institutions today have idealistic standards and are meticulous in their class preparation and instruction. They are concerned about their image and their success and want to be respected for their teaching, their scholarship, and their coaching . . . . In the pursuit of excellence it is especially important that the administration set worthy goals; for there can also be excellence in the pursuit of objectives that are inimical to education and to society. Every staff member must accept the underlying assumption that the goals for which the organization exists, and its members strive, are worthwhile and sound.[12]

National associations, state agencies, college and university associations, and private interest groups have all shown an active interest in the improvement of undergraduate standards in physical ed-

ucation. The AAHPER has developed several guidelines for the professional preparation of physical education teachers, as have many colleges and universities. It is safe to state that most institutions offering a major area of specialization in physical education adhere to these nationally accepted and recognized criteria, but the problem is that these criteria are adhered to only in part. A professional department may well have one of the finest curricula in the country—on paper—and yet employ professors who are not competent while at the same time promoting a very liberal policy with respect to the elimination of academically unqualified students. This type of undergraduate preparation the profession can well do without.

We, the authors, firmly believe that quality attracts quality, and that the quickest and most desirable way to improve the status and prestige of our profession is to attract and maintain quality students.

The many ramifications of professional preparation will be discussed in Part IV of the text. Specific critical issues and present trends will be presented dealing with student selection and retention, general vs specialized curricula, program evaluation, and interdisciplinary relationships.

Programs and Curricula

Curriculum in its broadest sense is defined as that which is to be taught or learned. It refers to what is to be taught for the sake of the individual, the society, and the subject. "The factors which are allowed to determine the curriculum within a school system should come from the nature of the learner and the needs and demands of society."[13]

Every interested student, parent, and teacher continually questions the course of study that is recommended for the attainment of specified goals. The establishment of worthwhile and practical programs of study has been a critical issue for many years and should remain so. It is by continually questioning and

Figure 2–1. "Home-made" LaCrosse sticks make recreational physical education activities more enjoyable and provide a constructive learning experience. (Courtesy of the University of Wyoming.)

evaluating our curricula that we attempt to provide education for today and tomorrow, rather than for yesterday. Any curriculum should be developed in accordance with a philosophy of education so that all materials present a harmonious interrelationship.[14] The determination of school and college physical education curricula for the needs of our changing society is one of our most critical issues.

As we approach the 21st century, the future of learning is faced with a massive task of change. In attempting to achieve educational goals, educators are faced with the question of what and how children learn. Until recently we believed that the school was the most powerful part of the learning environment; we now know that it is not. A great deal of the subject matter of today's learning is unrealistically narrow. Much of what has been proposed and accepted for programs and curricula has been based on a Western culture looking more to the past than to the future. Declining public confidence in the schools, as well as the realization that serious problems exist not only in the schools of our large cities but also in the suburban and rural areas, brought about the "accountability" em-

phasis of the late sixties and early seventies. As discussed in Chapter 1, schools are now held accountable for the relevance of their programs, and "accountability" and "performance-based education" have become common pedagogical terms. The national drive for accountability in education became so strong in the early seventies that in 1972 the National Education Association passed a resolution on accountability. The NEA recognized that the term "accountability," as applied to public education, is subject to varied interpretations. The Association maintained that educational excellence for each child is the objective of the education system and that educators can be accountable only to the degree that they share responsibility in educational decision making and to the degree that other parties who share this responsibility—legislators, other government officials, school boards, parents, students, and taxpayers—are also held accountable. The NEA seeks the proper base professionally, legally, and legislatively for educators to achieve optimum and appropriate accountability programs.

Most people agree that everyone, including teachers and school administrators, should be held accountable for their work. But what many individuals object to and fear is the oversimplified concept that defines accountability as the sole responsibility of the teacher or principal. Even though the Educational Testing Service of Princeton, New Jersey, does not include physical education activities in their *Interest Index* because both boys and girls say they like 90 per cent or more of their physical education activities, physical education as part of the total educational spectrum is still faced with accountability and assessment in education. A major task brought about by the accountability emphasis is that of determining pupil performance. In order to determine pupil performance, the objectives for pupil learning must be translated into appropriate teaching competencies. Learning objectives for programs and curricula are called *performance objectives* and are directly concerned with learning domains.

A statement released in 1974 by Dr. Helen D. Wise, President of the National Education Association, on "an assessment of the Michigan accountability system" revealed that an evaluation of the Michigan Assessment Program showed the implementation of accountability systems to be counterproductive.[15] This assessment of the Michigan school system reported that evaluation of teachers on the basis of their students' test scores is possibly one of the most unfortunate potentialities of the Michigan program. Although test scores are good indicators of socio-economic status, they are not good measures of what is actually taught in school.

Interscholastic and Intercollegiate Athletics

Professional and administrative problems appear to multiply when interscholastic and intercollegiate athletic programs are initiated. The focal point of most problems pertaining to athletics on any level is the double objective of providing sound basic instructional programs in physical education while at the same time conducting successful athletic programs.

The old adage that there are just so many hours in a working day is certainly true as far as the teacher-coach is concerned. The difficulties in attempting to achieve a satisfactory winning record while at the same time keeping abreast of the many ramifications and changes in teaching methodology and curricular innovation are certainly more than a teacher-coach can cope with, unless provided with a realistic reduction in teaching load.

The main reason given for this cleavage was to attempt to improve the quality of instruction in basic activity programs. This same trend has also been witnessed in large colleges and universities where each year more and more individual departments and schools of physical education are being created as administrative units distinct from divisions of intercollegiate athletics.

It is a fact that in schools or colleges in which there exists administrative pressure (or permissiveness) regarding "big time" athletics, physical education programs may suffer when coaches must both teach and coach. As athletic pressures mount, professional programs of scope and quality vanish. In this circumstance the only alternative is to make a distinction of programs.

Four of the most critical issues facing interscholastic-intercollegiate athletics are as follows: the participation of girls in competitive sports, spectator control and crime in large metropolitan centers, the use of drugs and ergogenic aids, and the financial support of athletics.

Girls in Competitive Sports. In 1973 the National Commission on the Reform of Secondary Education proposed a set of new national goals. One of these was to eliminate sexism in schools:

> School boards and administrators at the local level must provide opportunities for female students to participate in programs of competitive team sports that are comparable to the opportunities for males. The programs must be adequately funded through regular school budgets.
>
> Outstanding female athletes must not be excluded from competition as members of male teams in non-contact sports. The fact that a school offers the same team sport for girls should not foreclose this option.
>
> State activities associations should be required by statute to eliminate from their constitutions and by-laws all constraints to full participation in competitive team sports by females.
>
> If state activities associations are to continue to have jurisdiction over female sports, they should be required by state statute to have equal sex representation on all boards supervising boys' and girls' athletics.[16]

Although the recommendations made by this commission are considered to be controversial and perhaps extreme, there is little doubt that interscholastic and intercollegiate athletic programs for girls and women have finally arrived at their rightful place in competitive sports. Public school athletic associations and conferences throughout the country are becoming rapidly involved in competitive sports programs for girls, and federal Health, Education and Welfare funds under Title IX are providing new dimensions for women's intercollegiate athletics. Specific recommendations for interscholastic and intercollegiate athletic programs for girls and women will be found in Parts III and IV of this text.

Spectator Control. As our large cities in the United States have grown, their school systems have witnessed an alarming deterioration in both the quality and scope of their programs. Some educators believe that our large city school systems are on the verge of complete collapse. Some 20 or 25 years ago, many large city school systems were considered to be among the best in the country. Today, these same schools are considered to be near the bottom in total academic quality. In many of our larger cities, crime has become a part of the normal experience in many high schools and reform is desperately needed.

The sharp rise in crime in large city schools has created many problems regarding spectator control at interscholastic athletic events. In some instances, in Detroit, Chicago, and Los Angeles, for example, high school athletic events have been conducted without spectators because school officials were unable to control gang wars and indiscriminate fighting. Riots within schools and on school property have caused countless thousands of dollars in property damage, and have forced school administrators to move contests to "neutral" school facilities and to ban spectators. There appears to be very little that can be done to curb this type of student conduct without the full support of school administrators, teachers, and students. Rules for student conduct at the John F. Kennedy Junior/Senior High School in Denver, Colorado, present the following preamble:

A. The right to attend a public school and receive instruction being a political privilege rather than a private right, the State may impose such disciplinary measures as it sees fit on those who attend. *Corpus Juris Secundum.*
B. Objectives of the policies pertaining to pupil behavior:
(1) to facilitate teaching and learning in the classroom.
(2) to help develop proper attitudes to-

ward law and order in the schools and community.
(3) to educate our youth to observe accepted rules of conduct.
(4) to aid in the fulfillment of the responsibility invested in the schools by the state of Colorado.
C. Since the chief purpose of the schools is to educate those pupils in its charge, acts of behavior which tend to conflict with the educational program of the district, or which are harmful to the welfare of other pupils, will not be tolerated.
D. Respect for constituted authority and obedience to this authority are essential lessons to qualify one for the duties of citizenship, and the classroom is an appropriate place to teach these lessons.

Student misconduct should not be tolerated, as it can severely jeopardize the entire present and future of interscholastics. Student participants should follow the fundamentals of good sportsmanship. They should show respect for their opponents and for the officials. They should know, understand, and appreciate the rules of the game which they are playing and maintain their self-control. There is no doubt that the coach bears the greatest responsibility for sportsmanship. A coach's influence is a very significant factor in the development of attitudes and behavior patterns of his players. If a coach does not demonstrate good sportsmanship, then it is extremely difficult to expect his players, the student body, or the community to do so. If it is expected that militant demonstrations will be staged at an athletic contest, school administrators and coaches should be prepared in advance with specific control measures. Games should begin on time and advance planning should be undertaken for the possible use of police and limitations for admission. The AAHPER has stated that "A public agency may refuse to admit a person to an activity for a good cause only, and may not make arbitrary or invidious discriminations. Evidence of past misconduct on the premises or evidence that admission would jeopardize safe conduct of the event may suffice."[17] And: "I am convinced that most behavior problems at athletic contests are caused by a small band of delinquents and drop-out students. We must not forget the many fine youngsters who do benefit from school programs nor lose sight of the educational value of inter-scholastic athletics. Further, effective spectator conduct can be realized by team effort within every community and with the attitude that something worth-while is worth keeping and fighting for."[18]

Drugs, Ergogenic Aids, and Pornography. Drug abuse in schools is a remarkably complex problem. Many teachers and coaches know little about the drug culture, despite the fact that they deal daily with students who are members of it. It is generally agreed in medical circles that more misinformation exists about drugs than about practically any other subject. A vast majority of teachers in our high schools have had little or no training to prepare them for dealing with students who appear in class under the influence of drugs. Decisions about drug use are made by isolated individuals with little or no coordination of purpose or design. Many more facts are needed about the effects of drugs on both the individual and the society of which he is a part.

High school drug cultures still remain in some schools in many cities. Although the middle seventies saw an apparent decline in the use of hard drugs by both high school and college students, there is some evidence that federally funded programs for "crash" drug education classes may have done more harm than good. Some of these emergency programs, rather than discouraging the use of drugs, resulted in aroused curiosity on the part of many children to participate in their local "drug gang." Teachers and coaches must obtain scientific facts about drugs in order that children and adolescents may assess the wisdom of becoming involved with drugs of any kind. "In the last analysis, no one can make a binding decision for another. No one can escape the fact that the individual must decide for himself what his attitude and practice will be in regard to the use of drugs. One of the major functions of our society is to educate the young person so that he does his own thinking,

exercises his own judgment, and makes his own decisions about drugs as well as about any other subject."[19]

The use of ergogenic aids by athletic teams is also a critical consideration. An ergogenic is any work-producing aid that can be used to increase body performance. Ergogenics may be in the form of pills to be ingested or they may be massage machines or stretching devices. A detailed presentation concerning health education is found in Chapter 11.

In some schools pornography has found its way into the classroom, and there is little legal precedent for protecting the teacher who attempts to deal with the various problems that pornography presents. There are few court cases dealing with the teacher's role in handling this problem, and educators certainly recognize that this is not the preferred way to learn about human reproduction. Whether or not pornography in the classroom can be considered criminal remains to be decided by the courts.

Financing Athletics. One of the most critical issues facing interscholastic and intercollegiate athletic programs lies in the area of finance. Since 1972 numerous reports have claimed that some educational school systems in the United States are on the threshold of financial disaster. Taxpayers continue to reject school bond issues and tax levies in unprecedented numbers. Major school systems, such as those of Chicago and Philadelphia, are facing bankruptcy. Moreover, in the past several years, some 40 of the nation's largest school districts have been operating under crisis conditions because of severe financial problems.

Many educators believe that the major pathway to school finance reform is legislative and not judicial. The changes needed to improve educational equality will be legislated by school boards, state legislatures, and the United States Congress. The heaviest responsibility will continue to lie with the states, because it is still felt that education is a state responsibility. It is hoped that there will be an increase of federal school support (above the 7 per cent level) and that court decisions in opposition to an educational system based mainly on the wealth of a community (as it is a denial of equal educational opportunity) will do much to alleviate the financial crisis. Regardless of the type of state plan for funding and distribution, a major portion of the burden of financing public school education should not lie with property owners but should indeed encompass other taxes that reflect the wealth of a particular state.

When school districts have financial difficulties, there is an inevitable effect upon school athletic programs. In several of our large cities, athletic teams and contests have been canceled because of lack of financial support. In some cities, gifts from private corporations and public donations have provided the necessary funding to enable high school athletic conferences to continue. In other cases, however, entire athletic programs have been eliminated and selected sports have not been reinstated. The critical issue of funding for interscholastic athletics will remain until states and school districts can determine a more equitable way to finance education. A further discussion concerning athletic finance is presented in Chapter 13.

It must be reiterated that individual athletic programs may be quite unique in scope and content, necessitating the formation of principles to meet the needs of a particular situation. Specifics regarding extra pay for coaching, athletics for junior high schools, financial problems, public pressure, and relationships to other school programs are presented in Chapter 13.

The Relationship of Physical Education to Recreation and Health Education

Action and reaction have been prevalent during the past over the national organization of the three professional areas that have been housed under the same administrative roof since 1938. It has long been apparent that health education and recreation have become "adult" members of the national organiza-

tion. In April 1969 the American Association for Health, Physical Education and Recreation voted to become a national affiliate of the National Education Association, and in 1974 a new alliance of "associations" was formed which included an Association for Leisure and Recreational Services and an Association for the Advancement of Health Education.

In 1966 the National Recreation and Park Association was formed as an independent nonprofit service organization dedicated to the advancement and enhancement of the park and recreation movement and to the conservation of natural and human resources. This organization was formed through the merger of several well-established associations in the park and recreation field. One of these is the Society of Park and Recreation Educators, whose members either hold joint memberships in the AAHPER and the NRPA or belong only to the NRPA. The Society of Park and Recreation Educators is the "administrative voice" for professional recreation throughout the United States.

Critical problems have existed and still exist among physical educators, health educators, and recreation educators in the professional preparation and employment of students. The general public, for the most part, has not recognized differences among these professionals, and physical educators are often employed to teach health education and to conduct community and state recreation programs. Health educators object to unqualified individuals teaching health, and recreation specialists have strenuously objected to community programs being directed by physical educators who have little or no professional preparation in community recreation programs.

Many colleges and universities have separate departments or administrative divisions for recreation, park administration, and health education. These separations are necessitated by the tremendous expansion of knowledge and subject matter in each of the fields. It is impossible today for one individual to acquire expertise in all three areas. In fact, some undergraduate physical education programs now permit students to concentrate on a specific field within the larger program of studies. In health education emphases are being shifted from costly "crisis care" to promotion of positive health and prevention of disability. The Department of Health, Education and Welfare is doing its utmost to develop and implement proposals of the President's Committee on Health Education.

Resolutions endorsed by the National Education Association, American Association for School Administrators, National Congress for Parents and Teachers, American Medical Association, American Pediatrics Association, Council of Chief State School Officers, National School Boards Association, and National Association of State Boards of Education have urged the development of comprehensive health education programs as an essential part of every school program.[20] As comprehensive school health education programs continue to be initiated and state legislation continues to demand and support health programs, there will be a continuing need for certified health education teachers. The AAHPER endorses the development of certification programs in health education and urges that states develop health education certification standards requiring separate subject area preparation for health education teachers and that state departments establish health education as an academic subject area.

This recognition that recreation and health education are separate professional entities is also being experienced in Canada. Recent articles in Canadian journals relate that CAHPER is changing its structure in order to more clearly meet the needs and demands for recreation and park administration, health education, and physical education and sport.

Interdisciplinary Commonality — Coeducational and Cooperative Programs

The benefits derived from the sharing of knowledge and new ideas are invaluable. Unfortunately, considerable concern for sharing ideas in physical education has led to little constructive action.

Witness: the many junior and senior high school programs where there has been a complete separation between men's and women's departments; athletic programs separated from physical education in our public schools; the professional departments and colleges at the university level that have built an "academic wall" around their administrative unit and duplicate many offerings that should be common to all disciplines; and the continuing battle between many college and university physical education departments regarding duplication of course offerings, faculty, and facilities. These are but a few of the areas in which little if any attempt is made toward a type of interdisciplinary commonality. It is indeed encouraging, however, to witness the improvement in physical education programs at the college and university level that took place during the early and middle seventies when many separate departments of men's and women's physical education were combined. This administrative and organizational change occurred at such institutions as Oregon State University, Iowa State University, and the University of Minnesota.

The lack of cooperation within the various administrative branches of our profession has been a problem for many years. If professional physical education is to move forward and become a strong discipline, it must be a *united* discipline. Interdisciplinary cooperative effort is an absolute necessity for the survival and advancement of our profession. In many instances, the separation of men's and women's programs cannot be justified, and the increased financial expenditure cannot be supported.

Law and Teacher Liability

The physical education administrator should be more knowledgeable than any other administrator or teacher about the many ramifications of legal liability for pupil injury. This is especially true at public school levels, where more injuries occur in intramural and varsity athletics and in physical education classes than anywhere else. The majority of legal court cases involving accidents to pupils result from physical education and athletic activities. The National Safety Council reports that physical education and related activities account for almost two-thirds of all school jurisdiction.

Leibee states, "It is perhaps safe to say that a desire of every person who makes education his career is to help in the development and maintenance of the finest possible educational system. In his efforts to realize that desire, the professional educator may devote his ability and preparation to their fullest extent, only to see the entire scheme collapse because of the sudden occurrence of an accident."[21]

The Law and Public Education. Because education is recognized as a state interest, the law in the United States provides protection to specified groups within our school systems. The interpretation of legal and judicial references must then be made, taking into consideration the state constitution, the legislature, and the local school authorities.[22] There are many laws that deal specifically with education, but there are infinitely more that generally relate to the operation of government and affect education only because education and the educational system happen to be a part of the government. Legal operations at all levels are, of course, limited by the federal constitution, the state constitutions, and the judicial theories as to the scope of public powers.

There are many legal aspects to public education. These include the separation of church and state; the powers and duties of local school districts and officers; the use of school money and property; the employment of teachers; the discharge of teachers; teacher tenure and retirement legislation; the creation, consolidation, and alteration of school districts; school elections; and the liability of school districts, officers, and employees. This last area, *tort* liability for injuries to pupils, is perhaps the single most important aspect for immediate study and consideration by a future teacher or administrator of physical education.

The law in the United States provides special protection to various structures in our school systems. This protection also provides immunity from liability for many damages arising from injury caused by negligence. Individuals within the same organizational structure, however, may be required to provide damage payments because of a court decision that found them guilty of negligence.

Selected Legal Terms. The following definitions of selected legal terms are presented in order to familiarize the student with important concepts.[23]

ASSUMPTION OF RISK. "Involves the situation where the person subsequently injured may be said to have ventured into the relationship or situation out of which the injury arises, voluntarily and with full knowledge of the danger. He thus relieves the defendant of the duty to protect him against injury."

COMMON LAW. "The common law is that body of principles and rules relating to persons and property which arose out of custom and usage and judgments of courts offering such usages and customs. Common law is often considered as unwritten law in the sense it was not established by a legislature. The common law is distinguished from laws created by legislature."

CONTRIBUTORY NEGLIGENCE. "Is the failure by the person injured by the negligence of another to use due care for his own protection. Such contributory fault generally bars his recovery if his misconduct exposes him to the injury resulting from the defendant's negligence, and combines and concurs with that negligence in causing the injury."

DAMAGES. "Compensation awarded the plaintiff for the damage, injury, or loss suffered by him as a result of the defendant's wrongful conduct."

LIABILITY. "The condition of being subject to an obligation, performance of which is enforceable by a court; legal responsibility."

MALFEASANCE. "Evil doing, ill conduct, the commission of some act which is positively unlawful and which ought not be done at all."

MISFEASANCE. "The improper performance of some act which a man may lawfully do."

NEGLIGENCE. "Consists in the failure to act as a reasonably prudent and careful person would act under the circumstances to avoid exposing others to unreasonable danger or risk of injury or harm. It may consist of the omission to act as well as in acting affirmatively."

NONFEASANCE. "The nonperformance of some act which ought to be performed, omission to perform a required duty, or total neglect of duty."

TORT. "A term applied to a group of situations or relationships which the law recognizes as civil wrongs, and for which the courts will afford a remedy, usually in the form of an action for damages; a breach of a duty, other than one arising out of contract, giving rise to a damage action."

Negligence in the Law. Negligence is said to deal essentially with conduct. This "conduct" may be either action or inaction but *must not* be of a high quality or standard required of all persons in our society. For the successful maintenance of a suit based on negligence the following elements must be in evidence:

1. Duty to conform to a standard of behavior which will not subject others to an unreasonable risk of injury.
2. Breach of that duty—failure to exercise due care.
3. A sufficiently close causal connection between the conduct or behavior and the resulting injury.
4. Damage or injury resulting to the rights or interest of another.[24]

Negligence, then, is not necessarily based on mere carelessness. It is usually based on actions recognizable as involving unreasonable risk or danger to others. "The so-called reasonable, prudent person against whom the jury measures the defendant is, of course, a creature of the mind. He is an ideal; the good citizen who always looks where he is going; doesn't day-dream while approaching a dangerous spot in the road...."[25]

Acts that *may* be considered as negligence on the part of a physical educator or school employee are:

1. The diagnosis and treatment of an injury.
2. Failure to act (properly) in case of injury.
3. Failure to exercise a reasonable degree of care.
4. Allowing pupils who are not competent in a particular skill to use complex or potentially dangerous equipment.
5. Failure to warn pupils of danger in a danger area or activity.
6. Failure to repair or inspect instruments or equipment.
7. Failure to make preparation to prevent harm to pupils *prior* to their taking part in activities that require such preparation.

The principal *defenses* against a negligence action in cases where the defendant's negligence has been established are (a) contributory negligence, (b) assumption of risk, or (c) immunity. *Contributory negligence* is the failure by the person injured through the negligence of another to use due care for his own protection. Immunity may be claimed unless there is a statute or judicial decision to the contrary, since school districts and their officers are not liable for injuries caused by negligent performance within their legal duties.

Liability of School Districts and School Personnel. The majority of states still hold to the doctrine that the state or corporate subdivision "can do no wrong." This approach has been modified, however, by the courts and legislatures in that some have (a) abolished the immunity of school districts; (b) enacted legislation that permits districts to purchase liability insurance protecting the districts; (c) enacted legislation that permits districts to purchase liability insurance protecting employees of the districts during their employment; (d) enacted "save harmless" statutes; and (e) legislated methods of recovery other than common "tort" law.

In the United States our legal system holds that all people have a right to expect freedom from bodily injury caused by another individual. As discussed previously, negligence can be considered an issue only when a bodily injury has occurred and only if it can be proven that some act of negligence has been the cause of the injury. Teachers and school employees are responsible for the safety, health, and welfare of the students in their classes. This relationship between students and teachers is one of *in loco parentis*, which means that teachers and other school employees are serving in the place of the child's parents. In 1959 the Illinois State Supreme Court over-ruled the common-law doctrine of governmental immunity; this was the first time that a court in the United States ever ruled against this law. Since then several states have ruled against laws of governmental immunity, but a great deal of variation exists, and students and administrators should be familiar with the specific laws for their state and school district.

Physical education teachers and administrators should be especially aware of problems that may arise over emergency care, the legal aspects of teacher discipline, and the general moral behavior that is expected of school personnel. Only emergency care — not medical treatment — is to be rendered by school personnel. Laws have also been enacted specifically to protect pupils from unethical and brutal teachers. In disciplining teachers for wrongdoing, significant changes have taken place within the past several years, some of them representing decreases in restrictions on teacher conduct. The main factors that have contributed to these changes are (a) legislation and the widespread adoption of collective bargaining in education; (b) court decisions on teacher rights, especially constitutional rights; and (c) developments in the total social context.[26]

Koehler presents the following guidelines that physical educators should consider:

1. Teachers of physical education should be properly qualified or certified.
2. Instruction in physical education should occur within the rules and regulations of the state and its agencies, the profession and curriculum guidelines.

3. Personnel in physical education should be aware of the dangers and hazards in various activities and be able to anticipate and foresee inherent dangers.
4. Physical education instructional methodology should include the following techniques: supervision, ability grouping, equipment selection, first aid, equipment and facility inspection, and environmental safety for physical activities.[27]

The determination of most cases of liability in regard to negligence is a question for jury decision. It is important to realize that laymen determine the question of negligence and that their decisions may affect physical education programs. Every effort should be made to insure that activities, equipment, facilities, and programs are sound in nature and implementation. All physical education teachers should be encouraged to purchase liability insurance if state statutes are such that the teacher may be held liable for student injuries.

PRESENT TRENDS

It is questionable whether or not many of our present educational innovations should indeed be considered modern trends. Many, if not all, of our "space-age"programs are just old ideas with new wrinkles. However, there have been a number of creative changes in such areas as curriculum design and content, teaching methodology, and the nature and use of indoor and outdoor facilities. The specifics of such innovations will be presented in later chapters, dealing with areas of specialization at the elementary, secondary, or college and university levels. It is appropriate to present at this time a general overview of recent changes that were primarily brought about by new demands on the educational profession as a whole.

Visibility and Status

The continuing search for professional status is certainly not a modern trend, yet for years physical educators have been talking about the emergence and development of a "profession." This search for a strong, unified discipline is just as true today as it was 20 years ago.

Concepts in Transition

Educational programs in schools and colleges must continue to change in order to meet the demands of an advanced, modern civilization. Requests for change have ranged from statements demanding more individualized programs of study to the demands of students and faculty for a voice in the formation of institutional policies.

New trends and concepts are developed in part through research, which provides educators with the materials to trigger behavior changes. Studies have indicated that *educational innovation* involves (a) the development of new curricula; (b) the development of new teacher education programs (internships and the like); (c) investigation in educational technology (educational television); (d) school reorganization, such as nongrading and team-teaching; and (e) school integration and compensatory education.

Modernizing Curricula. During the 1960's physical education programs had three apparent emphases: perceptual-motor development, a multi-disciplinary approach to learning, and movement education. These approaches continue to characterize many physical education curricula today. We are also witnessing an increased emphasis on the contribution of motor activity to the affective domain. Movement education still maintains as its major goal the efficient movement of children for all of life's activities. Other goals of movement education are to gain a knowledge, understanding, and development of creative skills as well as a knowledge of how we learn. Educators concerned with perceptual-motor development work primarily with children who have some type of learning disability. Considerable research has supported the success of motor activities in clinical situations. Perceptual-motor programs may be focused on such areas as visual perception, kinesthetic aware-

Figure 2–2. Fourth- and 5th-grade children are introduced to variations of tennis-paddle ball, by using gymnasium "multi-courts" which swing out from the walls. This type of equipment gives variety to physical education activities.

ness, space orientation, and general motor skill development.

The multi-disciplinary approach developed during the middle seventies tended to focus on the affective domain, with educators emphasizing the arts, the quality and quantity of life style, and creativity. "Throughout the country increased interest also can be found in integrating various subject matter areas around a general concept. There are programs, for example, in which art, music, science, and physical education have united to focus on such concepts as balance, force, and direction to help the child gain cognitive understandings through a variety of subject matter experiences."[28] Whether this approach is beneficial to physical education remains to be seen.

Annarino[29] believes that a modern high school physical education program should include student selection of a multi-media individualized approach. He believes that students should be permitted to progress at their own rate and that an opportunity should be provided for students to participate in in-depth learning. This approach is implemented much the same as other mini courses, with the use of individualized

instructional packets, diagnostic pre-
tests, audiovisual aids, and the achievement of predetermined competencies.
After a student passes the minimal skill
and cognitive competencies for an individualized instructional packet, he takes
a final written examination. Depending
upon the formative evaluations and final
written grades, the student may elect to
work toward a higher competency level
for a specific mini-activity or select another activity and follow the same learning package.

Among the innovative physical education goals and objectives presented by
Klappholtz for implementation by the
year 1980 are the following:

1. Physical education supervisors, department chairmen, and teachers at all levels—
primary school through senior high—should
meet and determine what they consider to be
the terminal objectives that students should
achieve by graduation.
2. Administrators and teachers should work
together to establish performance or behavioral objectives for each student at each grade
level.
3. Physical educators and administrators
should make every effort to individualize and
personalize the physical education program at
every level to meet the individual needs of
every student.[30]

Some experienced physical educators,
however, are extremely concerned about
some of the practices that are occurring as
a result of modernizing curricula. They
fear that in our haste to create relevant
and innovative physical education programs, we may well be creating curricula
and instructional problems that may severely damage physical education programs in the future.

In spite of attempts to modernize curricula, the available evidence indicates
that most schools and school systems
have remained typically conservative.
The concept of nongrading, for example,
has taken hold in only a very few physical education programs. Flexible modular scheduling has replaced the traditional three- or five-day schedule in
some schools. Modular scheduling is designed to provide individualized instruction and to develop student responsibility, discipline, and self-direction.

In attempting to install programs to
foster student self-direction, physical
educators in some schools have implemented what is called contract learning.
This type of learning may provide an opportunity for the successful use of individualized instruction at the secondary
school level. Learning competencies are
established so that students are made
aware of specific learning tasks or skills
which are required for successful completion of a "contract." Some contract
learning programs are also organized on
a coeducational basis and are designed
to meet individual needs through the
development of contracts for individual
and dual sport activities. Students participating in this type of learning experience can progress at their own rate,
since the contract approach tends to reduce peer pressures which force students to progress at a pace beyond their
capabilities.

Contract learning also recommends
that physical educators consider boys
and girls as total, integrated beings. We
must remember that each child brings
much more than just his physical self
into our gymnasiums and onto our playing fields. Children also bring their
minds, their emotions, and their unique
personal and social traits.

During the past 10 years, lifetime
sports have done much to further the
concept of individual differences. Physical education teachers at the secondary
level have formulated independent
study projects, contract learning, required
electives, and other innovative approaches revolving around student involvement and student expresson of specific interests.

Recreation and physical education
programs for the physically handicapped
and mentally retarded have increased
substantially in the past 10 years.
Suggested criteria for evaluating curricular changes include the following:

1. Do they develop in students the basic
"learning to learn" skills?
2. Do they work to develop the inherent
talents of each individual?
3. Do they provide opportunities for students to enhance their employment options
and career interests?
4. Do they teach students how to live in a

changing environment and teach them about strategies for social change?

"A changing, growing society cannot afford to allow its educational system to stand still, nor can it afford to underutilize its most valuable community resources. Every school district should begin assessing all possible options open to it in order to maximize the social, emotional, and intellectual growth of all students."[31]

Perhaps the most significant philosophical statement regarding the function of physical education in changing school programs is presented by Brownell when he states that *the true function of physical education and athletics deals with realistic contributions made by these programs to the overall and avowed purposes sought by the school in its total curriculum.*[32] Our programs should therefore attempt to provide a realistic contribution to the expressed purposes of an institution. As future demands and new research indicate the need for change, physical education programs must be able to adapt. Our academic institutions must be aware of new demands and current research in order to prepare prospective teachers for a "modern market place."

Educational Resource Management Systems. Some educational concepts that have received considerable attention during the 1970's deal with Instructional Systems, Educational Resource Management Systems, or Educational Systems Analysis. It is necessary to provide a brief review of these concepts, as they are important to future supervisors or administrators of physical education programs.

The term *systems*, as we use it today, relates to a systems concept that was designed and implemented during and after the Second World War. Problem-solving systems and machine systems (weapons systems) are excellent examples of systems approaches used during a time of war. Banathy[33] states that the purpose of a system is realized through processes in which interacting components of the system engage in order to produce a predetermined output. In order to sustain itself, a system must produce an output which satisfies a "suprasystem." "The key criterion by which the effectiveness or adequacy of the performance of a system can be evaluated is how closely the output of the system satisfies the purpose for which it exists."[34]

In education, systems analysis, systems approach, and systems development are terms which have been widely used as educators attempt to develop a conceptual design for a system of planning, programming, budgeting, and evaluating (PPBES). The following are the most important criteria for the development of a systems approach in education or physical education: a clear definition of the purpose of the system, the determination of the characteristics of input, the consideration of alternatives and the identification of what has to be accomplished, the implementation of the system and testing of output, and the identification and implementation of required adjustments in order to insure the attainment of specific goals and objectives.

Transforming these major systems strategies into the "domain" of education requires planning in the following areas:

1. Formulating specific learning objectives
2. Developing tests to measure the degree to which the learner has attained the objectives
3. Examining the input characteristics and capabilities of the learners
4. Identifying whatever has to be learned so that the learner will be able to perform as expected
5. Considering alternatives from which to select learning content, learning experiences, and components
6. Installing the system and collecting information from the findings of performance testing and systems evaluation
7. Regulating the system[35]

These aspects of systems strategies provide the basic quantitative-scientific techniques that assist the educational administrator in the decision-making process. The vast size and overall complexity of educational organizations have created a need for efficient and rapid methods of analysis planning and communications control in educational administrative functions.[36] The most difficult and important part of the entire systems analysis approach involves the *establishment of very specific objectives.* It is readily apparent that objectives cannot be stated in general terms, because of the quantitative nature of systems and the fact that the system is attempting to define the most feasible, suitable, and acceptable means for accomplishing a given purpose.

Educational concepts are directly related to and indeed dependent upon the determination of *specific objectives*, their placement in some type of sequence, and analysis of them. This determination and analysis may be the most difficult job of all when one considers the many aspects of teaching.

Career Education. The early seventies witnessed a renewed emphasis and concentration on career education in American schools. With the assistance of state and federal funding, career education programs were implemented and supported in the first, second, and third continuums. Children in grades 1 and 2 were introduced to career education in the form of developing dexterity and manual skill in every conceivable area of interest from lapidary to rather elaborate craft and jewelry design.

Emphases in career education have been based on providing opportunities within the educational setting for children to experience beginning skills which may develop interests for later life. It is relatively easy to identify and arouse student interest in careers from the cognitive school subjects, but quite difficult to arouse talents and interests of a physical nature.

A much more enriching career life can be offered students if a combination of physical, cognitive, and affective interests are met. Students who demonstrate an interest in a high level of physical activity may very well find the greatest career enjoyment by pursuing careers that permit them to be physically active. An example is the student who may demonstrate a high cognitive talent for mathematics as well as for physical activity, and thus may wish to pursue a career in a type of engineering which keeps him physically active. Naturally

the most common career orientation for those who enjoy sports and physical activity is physical education, recreation, dance, and coaching.

Career education can be initiated as early as the 7th grade by permitting students to assist teachers in many educational and sport skills settings. An excellent example of this is the PELT (Physical Education Leadership Training) program which is in operation in the Norfolk, Virginia, public schools. This exemplary program provides a very specific organization, administration, and supervision so that specific objectives and goals are reached (see Chapter 8 for greater detail). In addition to providing opportunities in career education by assisting in the teaching of classes, some schools provide courses for credit, with students receiving basic instruction on how to teach sports skills to younger students. Other avenues of interest highlighting career education for physical education deal with diversified occupation programs where students work part-time in the city recreation department, park department, YMCA, YWCA, or private sports clubs and health spas. Interested students may also find part-time employment that will develop interests for a future career in the areas of recreational therapy or physical therapy, scouting, teaching sport and recreational skills to senior citizens, and working in various housing and apartment complexes which have incorporated recreational facilities and are in need of part-time instructors.

At present, health-related careers are receiving financial assistance and a great deal of attention from both state and federal health agencies. Recent state legislative actions recommending that health teachers have a major program of study in health education will do much to promote school health programs.

The total concept of motor development can relate to career education in that motor movement is that phase of the total educational process that contributes to the total fitness, growth, development, and skill acquisition of the child, primarily through movement-oriented experiences. Recent research has documented that underlying the development of fundamental motor skills and abilities are factors such as motivation, readiness to learn, and sensory and perceptual-motor difficulties. There is increasing evidence to support the statement that perceptual-motor competency is closely associated with academic learning, particularly reading and writing readiness and achievement. Perceptual-motor training may aid in the development of both reading and motor skills.

It is unfortunate that some physical education teachers at the secondary school level have avoided the introduction of career education programs because of the possibility of creating auxiliary personnel or "future teacher's aids" who could later be used in the schools in some instances to replace physical education teachers. Since the late 1960's, when federal funds were available from the Elementary and Secondary Education Act, the Manpower Development and Training Act, the Education Professions Development Act, and the Economic Opportunity Act, the use of teacher's aids and auxiliary personnel has become widespread. Such auxiliary personnel programs vary greatly from one school or school district to another, and depend a great deal upon the particular situation, school needs, and the sources and degree of funding. Physical education teachers must be involved with the planning and implementation of such programs in order to insure that the quality of present programs does not deteriorate, and that early problems in the development of auxiliary personnel programs are met effectively.

Teachers and Teaching. In any discussion of teachers and teaching dealing with the promotion and maintenance of professionalism, questions always arise. All educators recognize that there is a need for a clear definition of professionalism and of the responsibilities of teachers and administrators in school development and improvement. Problems of concern involve educational preparation, certification, teacher supply and demand, professional status, teachers' rights, evaluation of teaching competency, in-service training, and negotiations involving collective bargaining.

To further illustrate the key issues facing education in the early seventies, Phi Delta Kappa, the professional fraternity for men in education, conducted a study to consider the development of means by which the fraternity might (1) define attributes of the professional educator; (2) produce guidelines for selection of persons for admission to professional preparation; (3) identify the ideal college and university training prior to certification; (4) improve certification standards; (5) improve rural definitions of education positions and specialties; (6) establish in-service evaluation in training procedures for continuous professional improvement.

As early as 1971, predictions were being made that collective bargaining by teachers would move from the local to the state level. Collective bargaining on a state-wide level will certainly influence educational policies and practices. The combining of the NEA and the AFT into a semi-united organization will do much to secure uniformity of pay scales and benefits for employees in many educational organizations. This united organization for negotiating with employers will certainly have some effect upon the methods by which school districts raise money, as will the year-round school concept. General provisions which are usually included in any negotiations or master agreements between teacher associations and school boards include a specific statement as to the intent of the parties concerned. Such statements include a neutral agreement that both parties wish to provide the best possible education for students and to expand the post-graduation options for all youth. It is usually recognized by both parties that cooperation is necessary to formulate an agreement if it is to be an asset to the civic and educational communities and a substantial benefit to the school district. Statements of agreement also usually contain provisions dealing with discrimination, association rights, teacher rights, negotiating procedures, grievance procedures, teacher leave provisions, teaching conditions, student discipline, and various other provisions ranging from class size to salary and teachers' stipends. Examples of areas usually included under teachers' rights are dismissal and nonrenewal of contract, teaching of controversial issues, deprivation of additional compensation, and general policies and procedures.

Teacher grievances are usually an indication that there has been a violation, misinterpretation, or inequitable application of any of the provisions included in the master agreement between the teacher association and the board of education. An "aggrieved person" is a member of the teachers' association or negotiating unit who is presently employed in the school or school district and who asserts a grievance. A grievance is usually initiated when a written complaint is delivered to the aggrieved person's principal or other administrator by the association, faculty representative, or any other association representative. Grievance procedures then follow a specific organizational plan working through several levels of the organization of the school district.

Other areas of interest to teachers which are usually included in master agreements are teaching conditions, teacher aids, student's rights, teacher assessment, and complaints against teachers. The specific statements of policy and criteria for these and many other aspects of the constitutional rights for teachers should be determined by the present or prospective teacher for his respective school and school district. An excellent handbook on the rights of teachers has been prepared by David Rubin.[37] This guide sets forth the constitutional rights for teachers under present law and offers suggestions on how teachers can protect their individual rights. The Constitution, of course, is not the only source of a teacher's rights, as has just been discussed. Rights are further defined by individual teaching contracts, any relevant collective agreement, policies of the state and local boards of education, state and federal statutes, and state constitutional provisions.

During the early and middle seventies, the teaching profession experienced an increasing dissatisfaction with course-credit credentials for certifying teachers, which resulted in various proposals for performance or competency-based teacher's certification. Efforts have been and are being made to develop objective criteria for evaluating the quality of teacher performance. Many colleges of education have increased the number of hours of clinical experience that their students must obtain and have provided a great diversification of experiences. Early experiences in freshman and sophomore years coupled with increased supervision by faculty and master teachers have been witnessed in many professional preparation programs. Such approaches may not, however, provide the necessary qualities for competent teaching in our rapidly changing world, and schools of education may have to re-examine their curricula and clinical experience programs in order to insure that those who are certified have completed performance or competency-based certification programs. A greater emphasis on teacher performance and a recognition of merit by merit salary increases and promotion, and less emphasis on teaching credentials, may do much to assist our educational system to respond more rapidly to the changing demands of society and students. Continuing teacher contracts and tenure for teachers, if not established under professional criteria, tend to promote incompetency and provide less concern for excellence in education and more tolerance for mediocrity.

The 1970's have witnessed a teacher surplus in many academic disciplines, and the immediate impact of this change from shortage to surplus upon schools of education has been a reduction of student admissions. Educators are quick to point out that the supply of graduates prepared to teach is inadequate for the number of teaching-related positions that *should* be created in our nation's schools. Limited financial resources, however, often preclude the addition of needed specialists in such areas as health education. More teachers must be recruited for minority groups and the disadvantaged, and special in-service education programs should be provided in order to facilitate the acquisition of new skills and the renewal of knowledge by teachers who are already teaching.

There is little doubt that there will be a great deal of difference between teachers who were prepared in the 1950's and those who will be prepared in the 1980's. As we approach the 21st century, more and more teachers will be members of organizations which engage in collective bargaining. Teachers who were prepared in the fifties traditionally were respectful of authority, the establishment, and the bureaucracy in the educational system. This professionalism and elitism is being replaced by the types of action demonstrated by other unionized groups, such as teamsters, brewery workers, and auto workers.[38]

"We need courageous leaders in curriculum reform, the revision of educational finance and the re-ordering of priorities. We need to place the future of our children and grandchildren before the narrow interest of individuals who would save their pocketbooks and sacrifice the minds, motivation, and intelligence of our future adults of the year 2000."[39]

State and Federal Funding

Although some educators are reluctant to agree, there is little doubt that all levels of education will have to depend heavily upon both state and federal support in the immediate future. The fantastic expenditure of funds for public education is already placing a severe burden on local school districts and colleges and universities. The impact of increased costs is causing budgetary difficulties for many colleges and universities at the present time, and the major impact may yet be felt at the public school level.

Most of the present school organization patterns in the metropolitan areas came into being because of a lack of planning for rapid population expansion. After World War II, there was a steady decline of city systems, and "lighthouse" school systems developed rapidly in suburbs. The shift in quality edu-

cational systems from the cities to the suburbs was brought about by the migration of more affluent families to suburbia and the influx of less fortunate families into the cities. Our society has failed in meeting the fiscal requirements of our cities and in providing equality of educational opportunity.

"Increasingly, the cities have become the receptacles for the poor and the black, while their surrounding suburbs have become the growing enclaves of the white middle class."[40] Two distinct factors appear to work against equality of educational opportunity in metropolitan areas. First, the distribution of fiscal resources is unequal, providing insufficient funding for the city schools while giving vast amounts to the suburbs to educate a relatively small number of students. Second, the ratio and socioeconomic distribution of the population between city and suburbs prevents a meaningful level of school integration.

Present patterns of state financial aid do not permit the equalizing of educational support for city and suburban schools. It is a fact that many cities receive less financial support from the states per student than do their wealthy suburbs. Many more financial demands are made upon tax funds in metropolitan areas than in non-metropolitan areas. Usually local financial ability is based on the overburdened property tax, which is not sufficient to meet the demands of metropolitan areas. As a result, cities look to the greater resources available from state and federal funding. State responsibility in education has been clearly established, with state constitutions normally requiring legislatures to establish and maintain systems of free public education that provide for uniform and efficient education practices throughout the state. Although operating locally, school districts nevertheless remain the responsibility of state government. There is a great deal of diversity, however, in the interpretation of this responsibility among states: Hawaii and Delaware, for example, maintain a very strong state control, while Nebraska and South Dakota maintain a low level of control, with average state contributions to public education in the early seventies ranging from 40 to 46 per cent of all local public elementary and secondary education expenditures.

The somewhat controversial idea that the federal government will have to play an increasing role in funding public education is today approaching wide acceptance.[41] The United States Constitution does not refer specifically to education; however, Article I, Section VIII, which is referred to as the general "welfare clause," has opened the way for federal support of public education.

Many educators believe that today's educational problems have been created by past actions and inaction of local and state governments. State aid for education has always favored suburbs over cities and thus has tended to accelerate the outflow of middle and upper class citizens, who are usually the city's largest tax resource, to the suburbs. State-aid-to-education formulas have not kept pace with educational needs. In some states, per-student expenditures differ by ratios of two and sometimes three to one within single states. Recent state legislation in California may set the precedent in forcing states to present more realistic state-aid formulas that would place new priorities on present state resources. Also, as reapportionment of legislative districts continues, urban areas will be provided with more equal representation in state legislatures, and Congress will achieve a larger voice in the allocation of resources. The great fear expressed by educators is that with "outside" financial assistance will come "outside" control.

Legislation. Since the early 1960's federal programs have been enacted and funded in an attempt to improve education for all and to extend compensatory advantages to those who have suffered educational deprivation. Innovative programs have been sought which will enhance readiness for learning.

The federal government is a major source of financial support and technical assistance to the country's schools and universities. This support is provided primarily through the United States Office of Education (OE). The OE is a major component of the Education Division of the United States Department of Health, Education and Welfare. OE administers programs covering virtually every level and aspect of education. In 1974 OE's funding level approximated some 6 billion dollars; this was in addition to the appropriation of 75 million dollars for the National Institute of Education, the other major component of the HEW Education Division.

The OE is still distributing funds for Title I of the Elementary and Secondary Education Act, which came into being in 1965 and is designed to meet the total education of boys and girls and to point to a new multi-discipline approach to educational problems. Title I provides financial assistance to local educational agencies for special educational programs in areas having high concentrations of children from low-income families.

In 1974 OE funds were available to institutions, agencies, and organizations for elementary and secondary education programs, as well as for post-secondary education programs, education of the handicapped, occupational, adult, and vocational education, teacher and other professional training, student assistance, and research. Of particular interest to physical educators are funds which may be available under the Economic Opportunity Act to extend into primary grades the educational gains made by deprived children in Head Start or similar pre-school programs. Such funds may be used in the area of motor development. Programs for disadvantaged children under Title I of the Elementary and Secondary Education Act are designed to meet the educational needs of deprived children, including, in certain instances, motor skill development.

The Drug Abuse Education Act administered by OE provides funding for drug abuse education and related activities. Established in 1970, its main purpose is the organization and training of drug education leaders at state and local levels.

The OE also provides assistance for

physical education and recreation for the handicapped under Title VI—legislation dealing with education of the handicapped. This assistance goes toward research in physical education and recreation for handicapped children.

On June 23, 1972, the Education Amendments Act was enacted. This legislation was enacted by both houses of Congress and signed by the President in order to end all discrimination in education based on sex. It is designed to eliminate sexist discrimination in curriculum, activities, admissions policies, and financial aid.[42] Title IX states that no person shall on the basis of sex be excluded from participation in, be denied the benefit of, or be subjected to discrimination under any educational program receiving financial assistance.

The regulations pertaining to the Education Amendments Act were published in 1974 in the Federal Register. They state that schools cannot discriminate on the basis of sex in awarding scholarships. The Department of Health, Education and Welfare is the governmental agency responsible for the interpretation of these regulations. The regulations are lengthy and detailed, and cover many facets of discrimination, including job discrimination, fringe benefits, lodging, and counseling.

Title IX should do much to promote interdisciplinary togetherness and to assist schools and colleges in the development of coeducational activities. The greatest single change will no doubt come about in competitive athletic programs, where some discrimination existed in the awarding of athletic scholarships and the participation of women in competitive sports.

In 1973 and 1974, three Senate-House sports bills to determine an amateur sports board for the United States received a great deal of political and professional attention. These bills were an attempt to provide an amateur sports board, which would be empowered to issue charters to organizations granting authority with regard to U.S. participation in international competition. This governing board would be authorized to mediate disputes between chartered sports associations or between a sports association and an athlete. The necessity for such an amateurs' sports board in the United States was brought about by the increasing and insurmountable conflicts between the NCAA, the AAU, and now between the NEAA and the AAHPER/AIAW (Association for Intercollegiate Athletics for Women). Various components of the bill apply to the authority to charter U.S. sports associations for Olympic Games programs and such other programs as are found by the board to be appropriate for a charter under the Act. Divisions within the sports board were provided for athletic facilities, health and safety, and Olympic study. A National Sports Development Foundation was also established and authorized to accept private gifts and donations and matching contributions from federal government sources in order to promote and encourage athletic activity and physical fitness programs.

Federal support programs are, of course, directly dependent upon the appropriation of funds, and such appropriations will vary considerably because of changing attitudes in Congress. For current and detailed information regarding programs, the appropriate federal governing agencies should be contacted. The following publications will also provide information about such funding:

Education U.S.A.—A newsletter published by the National School Public Relations Association, 1201 16th St. N.W., Washington, D.C.

The Chronicle of Higher Education—A higher education newspaper which may be ordered from Editorial Projects for Education, 3301 North Charles St., Baltimore, Maryland.

Research in Education—A monthly catalog which provides up-to-date information about educational research sponsored by the Bureau of Research, U.S. Office of Education. Write to the Superintendent of Documents, U.S. Government Printing Office, Washington, D.C.

Washington Newsletter—A publication covering news on federal support programs and projects of particular interest to related areas of AAHPER. Specific items may be ordered through AAHPER, 1201 16th St. N.W., Washington, D.C.

REFERENCES

1. Burton C. Brunner: "How Will Today's Physical Education Classes Be Remembered in 1989?" *JOPHER*, February, 1969, p. 42.
2. Robert J. Francis: "1956 Study of Basic Issues Facing the Profession." Washington, D.C.: AAHPER, December, 1960.
3. Tom Kepner and Lanny Sparks: *Objectives Marketplace Game*, National Special Media Institutes, 1972.
4. Carl W. Bookwalter and Harold J. VanderZwaag: *Foundations and Principles of Physical Education.* Philadelphia: W. B. Saunders Co., 1969, p. 1.
5. Lawrence G. Rarick: "The Domain of Physical Education as a Discipline." *Quest*, IX, December, 1967, p. 49.
6. Bookwalter and VanderZwaag, *op.cit.*, p. 4.
7. Victor P. Dauer: *Dynamic Physical Education for Elementary School Children.* Minneapolis: Burgess Publishing Co. 1968, p. 4.
8. *Ibid.*, p. 5.
9. Francis C. Rosencrance: *The American College and Its Teachers.* New York: The Macmillan Co. 1962, p. 97.
10. J. James Jones, C. Jackson Salisbury, and Ralph L. Spencer: *Secondary School Administration.* New York: McGraw-Hill Book Co., 1969, p. 194.
11. Daryl Siedentop: *Physical Education, Introductory Analysis.* Dubuque, Iowa: Wm. C. Brown Co., 1972, p. 91.
12. J. Tillman Hall *et al.*: *Administration: Principles, Theory and Practice— With Applications to Physical Education.* Pacific Palisades, Calif.: Goodyear Publishing Co., 1973, pp. 52–53.
13. Jones, Salisbury, and Spencer, *op. cit.*, p. 202.
14. Jesse F. Williams, Clifford L. Brownell, and Elmon L. Vernier: *The Administration of Health Education and Physical Education.* Philadelphia: W. B. Saunders Co., 1964, p. 67.
15. Helen D. Wise: *An Assessment of the Michigan Accountability System.* Washington, D.C.: Public Information Unit, Communications Services, National Education Association, p. 1.
16. "The Reform of Secondary Education." *News Exchange*, Vol. 15, No. 4, December, 1973.
17. "Crowd Control for High School Athletics." *The National Council of Secondary School Athletic Directors.* Washington, D. C.: AAHPER, 1970, p. 34.
18. *Ibid.*, p. 32.
19. Oliver E. Byrd: *Medical Readings on Drug Abuse.* Reading, Mass.: Addison-Wesley Publishing Co., 1970, p. v.
20. "Separate Certification for Health Education Teachers." *School Health Review*, March–April, 1974, p. 3.
21. Howard C. Leibee: *Tort Liability for Injuries to Pupils.* Ann Arbor, Mich: Campus Publishers, 1965, p. 1.
22. Robert R. Hamilton and Paul R. Mort: *The Law and Public Education.* Brooklyn, N.Y.: The Foundation Press, 1959, p. 1.
23. Leibee, *op. cit.*, pp. 2–7.
24. *Ibid.*, pp. 8–9.
25. *Ibid.*, p. 10.
26. Floyd G. Delon: *Substantive Legal Aspects of Teacher Discipline.* Topeka, Kansas: National Organization on Legal Problems of Education, 1972, p. 52.
27. Robert W. Koehler: *Prudence Brother, Prudence.* Normal, Ill.: Illinois State University, 1973, p. 5.
28. Margie Hanson: "Directions and Thrusts." *Physical Education.* Washington, D. C.: AAHPER, 1973, p. 1.
29. Anthony A. Annarino: *High School Mini-Activity Physical Education Programs Based on a Multi-Media Individualized Approach.* West Lafayette, Indiana: Department of Physical Education, Purdue University.
30. Lowell A. Klappholtz: "Innovation Physical Education Goals and Objectives for 1980." *Physical Education Perspective*, May, 1974, p. 1.
31. Robert Green and Barbara Parness: "Seeking the Best-Alternative Schools from Traditional Surroundings." *Teacher's Voice*, Michigan Education Association, June, 1973, p. 11.
32. Clifford Brownell: "The Role of Health, Physical Education and Recreation in the Space Age." *National Association of Secondary School Principals*, Vol. 44, No. 256, May, 1960, p. 5.
33. Bela H. Banathy: *Instructional Systems.* Palo Alto, Calif.: Fearon Publishers, 1968, p. 12.
34. *Ibid.*, p. 1.
35. *Ibid.*, p. 32.
36. Frank W. Banghart: *Educational Systems Analysis.* London: The Macmillan Co., 1969, p. 4.

37. David Rubin: *The Rights of Teachers—The Basic ACLU Guide to a Teacher's Constitutional Rights.* New York: Discus Books, 1972.
38. Wilber J. Cohen: *Changing Influences in American Education.* Ann Arbor, Mich.: University of Michigan, 1972, p. 17.
39. *Ibid.,* p. 5.
40. Henry M. Levin: "Financing Schools in a Metropolitan Context." *Metropolitan School Organization: Basic Problems and Patterns.* Berkeley, Calif.: McCutchan Publishing Corp., 1972, p. 37.
41. Mike M. Milstein: "Roles of State and Federal Government." *Metropolitan School Organization: Basic Problems and Patterns.* Berkeley, Calif.: McCutchan Publishing Corp., 1972, p. 50.
42. Marjorie Blaufarb: "Opportunity Knocks Through Title Nine." *Up Date.* Washington, D.C.: AAHPER, January, 1974, p. 1.

SUGGESTED READINGS

Blaufarb, Marjorie: "Opportunity Knocks Through Title Nine." *Up Date.* Washington, D.C.: AAHPER, January, 1974.
Brunner, Burton C.: "How Will Today's Physical Education Classes Be Remembered in 1989?" *JOHPER,* February, 1969.
Delon, Floyd G.: *Substantive Legal Aspects of Teacher Discipline.* Topeka, Kan.: National Organization on Legal Problems of Education, 1972.
"Grantsmanship: How to Develop and Write Proposals." Wyoming State Department of Education, Cheyenne, 1971.
Rarick, Lawrence G.: "The Domain of Physical Education As a Discipline." *QUEST, IX,* December, 1967.
"The Reform of Secondary Education." *News Exchange,* Vol. 15, No. 4, December, 1973.

CHAPTER THREE

Public Relations: School-Community Communication

Administrators, teachers, and students often tend to forget that public education is a form of social institution, which is financed and maintained by everyone – not just those who have children in our public schools. Thus, educational objectives and curricula must be established for the benefit of *all* people.

Effective communication and public relations play an indispensable role in the operation of public institutions. They also play an indispensable role in the operation of each discipline within such institutions. The local community and the general public at large must continually be kept informed of educational programs if they are expected to continue providing financial and moral support. It is common nature for people to criticize the use of tax funds and question mandatory programs if they have never been provided with clear, concise statements of purpose and progress.

"Differences in background, education, and expectation result in different social and political values. These are probably the greatest handicaps to effective communication and the most difficult to overcome."[1]

COMMUNICATION: THE INDISPENSABLE VEHICLE

It has often been stated that one of the true "arts" of modern man is the "art of communication." Communication has been called the foundation of cooperative group activity, or the vehicle which provides the thread that binds an organization together by ensuring common understanding. Another interesting definition of communication is "the process of transmitting cues in order to modify human behavior."[2] In any event, the art or act of communicating is one of our most important learned behaviors and is of the *utmost* importance in administration. Communication implies action, and when used effectively in public relations it may be combined with persuasion in an effort to sway or influence public opinion. Communication is the most vital aspect of public relations. There are a myriad of public relation materials, resources, and approaches available to educators. Examples of "ideas in action" provided by the National School Public Relations Association (NSPRA) include the following: the use of communication to generate public support for increased educational funding; creative endeavors with newspapers, closed circuit TV programs, in-service training, building and area meetings; information programs designed to answer questions and to solicit support for exemplary programs; techniques in communication for feeling the pulse of the community; and programs designed to personalize large city school systems.

Communication problems usually grow out of the size and complexity of the modern urban school system, the diverse interests of various staff groups, the specialization of responsibilities, the proliferation of new programs, the uncertainty of finances, and the crisis atmosphere itself.[3] Physical educators are just beginning to realize that providing viable curricula and meeting the needs and interest of students is not enough; exemplary programs worthy of publicity must be "sold" to the general public. Public support is not automatic but is usually the result of sound communication programs which have been conscientiously planned, developed, and implemented. The single most important person in any public relations program is the teacher, administrator, or individual providing the communication.

A teacher's image is a composite reflection of teachers as they meet pupils, administrators, and the general public. In many instances, if physical educators can "sell" themselves, they will be able to generate the necessary support to improve curricula and programs.

Public sentiment is everything. With public sentiment nothing can fail; without it, nothing can succeed. He who molds public sentiment goes deeper than he who enacts statutes or pronounces decisions. He makes statutes or decisions possible or impossible to execute.

Abraham Lincoln

Basic Principles and Mechanics of Communication

The conveyance of ideas is one of the most complex aspects of human relations. Educators are very much involved in human relations and in the conveyance of ideas, because they are usually attempting to promote new programs or concepts. The educational administrator must "communicate" if he desires to be successful. In fact, a clear statement of purpose, universally understood, is an outstanding guarantee of effective administration. "Sound administration starts with the communication of a statement, or at least a clear recognition of goals to be achieved."[4]

In most organizations communication is seen to have two basic functions: (1) to give and receive *direction;* and (2) to give and receive *information.* Hardwick and Landuyt state that knowledge is power, and there are times when certain knowledge may give a colleague or other associate the capacity to do harm to the communicating administrator or the entity he represents.[5] Also, an administrator who tends to be somewhat "loquacious" should be sensitive to the danger of overstepping the bounds of ethical behavior.

In considering basic principles of communication, Hardwick and Landuyt state that an administrator should ask himself five basic questions before he communicates:

1. What is the main purpose of my communication?
2. Do I have collateral aims? If so, what are they, and should they be sought in this effort at communication?
3. Is there anything extraneous in the planned message?
4. Does it include ideas which will unnecessarily place me or my organization in jeopardy?
5. Am I including anything which violates ethical principles and honor?[6]

In working with individuals and groups in a given community, an administrator must use effective methods of communication and interaction. Many different approaches have been outlined to characterize this relationship:

1. *Indifference*—the school and community are separate and unrelated, and there should be little, if any, interaction.
2. *Publicity*—selling the school or organization to the public.
3. *Interpretation*—educational interpretation as a one-way means of communicating to inform the community.
4. *Cooperative endeavor*—a two-way means of communication or a process of interaction.[7]

One can quickly see that the first three approaches are not usually effective. The cooperative endeavor of the institution and the community, or the general public working together, is the most effective approach.

Additional mechanics of communication that are of importance to the administrator are (a) quantity, (b) accuracy, (c) frequency, and (d) emotional appeal. Before entering into com-

munication the initiator must measure the quantity of his "vehicle" to gauge whether or not it is appropriate to the task for which it is designed; the conveyance must then be accurate, be of a frequency to obtain results, and in some cases possess emotional appeal.

Formal Communication. Formal communication is the planned system made up of procedures and channels of formal authority in an organization. Objectives of this type of communication are to transmit policy decisions, obtain a return "flow" of information from employees, and inform employees of the aims and objectives of the institution.

Informal Communication. Informal communication deals with informal, interpersonal contacts. Communication in this system is based upon such things as friendship, mutual confidence, and informal sources of information. It is often considered the most important part of a "communication system."

The traditional "seven C's" of communication have been in evidence for many years but, nevertheless, are still pertinent.

1. *Credibility*—Communication must have truth, and the receivers of communication must have a high regard for the source of the communication and respect its credibility.
2. *Context*—Communication programs must be in harmony with the basic realities of the environment in which communication exists. The multi-media of communication are supplementary to the past and present acts of the communicator.
3. *Content*—Communication must have meaning for the individual or group that is receiving the message. Relevance and reward are important aspects of content.
4. *Clarity*—Any communication must be placed in a context that can be readily understood by the receiver. The communicated information must mean the same to the receiver as it does to the communicator. Generally speaking, the greater the distance the communication has to travel, the more simplified it should be.
5. *Continuity and Consistency*—Communication is a continual process and it requires frequent repetition to achieve maximal penetration.
6. *Channels*—Channels of communication should be established and used. Such chan-

nels should be ones which are easily determined and used by the group or individual who is to receive the communication.

7. *Capability*—Communication must take into consideration the capability of the individuals who are going to receive the message. Communications are usually most effective when they require the least effort on the part of the receiver to understand what is being communicated. Capability includes factors such as habit, reading ability, availability of knowledge, and intellectual capacity.

EDUCATIONAL COMMUNICATION AND PUBLIC RELATIONS

Communication within an educational setting is usually organized into two distinct communication "systems." These are the interaction between the organization and the so-called "plural publics," and communication to give and receive direction and information within the organization itself. Many of the basic mechanics of communication in general are common to both of these systems. *It must be remembered, however, that communication is considered to be only an intermediate goal, since the ultimate goal is the successful execution of programs to meet established objectives.*

Many individuals and groups have defined public relations and, surprisingly enough, with some degree of agreement. A definition by the American Association of School Administrators in 1950 stated that "Public relations seeks to bring about a harmony of understanding between any group and the public it serves and upon whose good will it depends."[8] In 1968 the executive committee of the National School Public Relations Association adopted the following definition for educational public relations:

Educational public relations is a planned and systematic two-way process of communication between an educational organization and its internal and external publics. Its program serves to stimulate a better understanding of the role, objectives, accomplishments, and needs of the organization. Educational public relations is a management function which interprets public attitudes, identifies the policies and procedures of an individual organization with the public interests, and executes a program of action to encourage public involvement and to earn public understanding and acceptance.

In this definition, the term educational organization includes school districts, community colleges, and national, regional, state, or local associations and agencies. The NSPRA developed standards for educational public relations programs as well as standards for educational public relations professionals in the late 1960's. The specifics of these standards may be obtained from the NSPRA, 1201 16th Street, N.W., Washington, D.C. 20036.

In 1972 the NSPRA also developed an evaluation instrument for educational public relations programs. This instrument was designed to serve as a basis for evaluating the extent to which schools or organizations have made provisions for organizing and conducting a formal public relations program as advocated by NSPRA. It was *not* designed to provide an indication of how good or bad public relations programs are, nor was it designed to assess the product of a public relations program. This instrument and others like it were developed in an attempt to improve educational communication and public relations in educational communities across the country.

One cannot underestimate the value of excellent community relationships, especially in our public elementary and secondary schools. This is also true of today's funding of colleges and universities, although in this case the "vehicle" is of a somewhat different nature. The fact remains, however, that public education at any level is directly dependent upon the support of the public and on public taxation, and failure to recognize this fundamental principle is a cardinal error in public administration.

An assumption sometimes made regarding public relations programs is that popular support for any cause, regardless of its merit, can be built up merely by repeated statements of advice or warning, with little factual data to back up such statements. This has not proved to be true, and effective public relations is based upon actual needs and worthwhile service.

For years physical educators have been giving lip service to clichés, memorized during their undergraduate preparation. In many cases such blanket statements cannot be substantiated in practical programs. The public of today is a well-informed and by and large a well-educated public that cannot be deceived by glittering generalities. "Clearly public relations programs can stimulate interest and awareness, but they cannot create a point of view which is at odds with individual experience."[9]

Personalizing "The System"

School public relations, then, is an attempt to convey information and to stimulate interest and awareness in academic programs of value. The American Association of School Administrators states that the specific purposes of school public relations are:

1. To inform the public as to the work of the school.
2. To establish confidence in schools.
3. To rally support for proper maintenance of the educational program.
4. To develop awareness of the importance of education in a democracy.
5. To improve the partnership concept by uniting parents and teachers in meeting the educational needs of the children.
6. To integrate the home, school, and community in improving the educational opportunities for all children.
7. To evaluate the offering of the school in meeting the needs of the children of the community.
8. To correct misunderstandings as to the aims and activities of the school.[10]

The overall theme that permeates many statements of community relations is that good public relations depends largely upon good public service to the community. Constructive criticism is needed in order to maintain the quality and integrity in our public institutions, yet critical attacks by individuals or groups that are based on fact are easily dispelled by an excellent public information service.

People genuinely interested in education seek information from their local schools or from state institutions in which they have a specific interest. The nature of their requests for such information, of course, varies according to the time period in history and local and national events. Typical requests include:

— Descriptions of the instructional program, and recent innovations.
— The nature and education of teachers and faculty.
— Student enrollments.
— The construction and use of new facilities.
— What the public can do to assist school programs.
— What the future may present in terms of needs and enrollments.
— The appropriation of funds for the institution, salaries, and general operational budgets.

An administrator of physical education may well be called upon to develop and perform the following tasks, if he wishes to promote a successful community relations program:

1. Develop faculty appreciation of the importance of good community relations.
2. Interpret system-wide policies and develop supplementary physical education policies with his faculty.
3. Secure, present, and interpret school or college information for faculty use.
4. Develop a coordinated and positive program for community relations.
5. Effect two-way interpretation of educational problems between school personnel and patrons.
6. Coordinate activities with every educational level, from the primary grades through college.[11]

Between 1960 and 1970, the number of school districts in the United States decreased from some 40,000 to approximately 19,000. This national move to consolidate school districts provided a better financial base for a larger consolidated district while creating many administrative and personnel problems. It is argued that although larger school districts can provide better quality and a broader range of education for students, such consolidation may prove to be quite traumatic for the teaching staff. "Personalizing the system" is an approach that has been used with considerable success as a communication technique which can eliminate a "communication crisis." In large suburban areas, teachers often complain of a lack of communication, and administrators perceive the problem as being more a lack of the personal face-to-face contact that was a virtue of smaller school districts. One specific technique that can help bridge the communication gap is the designation of an information staff to provide a staff newsletter, professional level materials, recruitment brochures, orientation materials, teacher handbooks, and explanations of curriculum development. In addition, "communication committees" of teachers and administrators can be formulated to study school problems.

Public relations in education, as in other social agencies, must convey information to and stimulate interest in many *publics*. The general public is composed of many smaller publics and each of these publics, or "plural publics" as they are often referred to, has special social, economic, and political interests. As was previously stated, public education is supported by *all* the people, not just by the parents of the children in school; therefore *all* people must be kept informed of the nature and scope of every public educational institution.

Support and Opposition

In many public schools a typical public relations program is one which provides press releases for the local media and conducts information programs to inform parents about school programs. Public relations is frequently perceived as a one-way process of "giving the word."

Fessler[12] believes that there is a need for a much more sophisticated approach to school public relations. This educator believes that school public relations programs should consider the following: (1) the varied and often conflicting referent groups with which the public schools

must contend; (2) emphasizing the need for two-way interaction; and (3) identifying specific communication needs that enable schools to aim appropriate messages at appropriate sources. In order to plan a meaningful public relations program, a school needs to gather relevant data regarding the position the school wishes to take; the "referent" group perception of the school position; and the referent group expectation of the school position. The referent group, or group to which the communication is directed, will express differing levels of satisfaction or dissatisfaction, depending upon the group's philosophical agreement or disagreement with a school's position. Four specific patterns of *support and opposition* then tend to emerge.

One pattern which may emerge is *support* of the school's position or objectives. In this instance the group to which the communication is aimed perceives itself to have the same expectations as those being expressed by the school. The pattern of support is one in which communication, satisfaction, and philosophical agreement are high. A pattern of *opposition* occurs when the group or general public accurately perceives the actual position of the school but has expectations that are different from its perception of the school's position. "This pattern describes a situation where the referent group knows the school's position but believes the position ought to be something different."[13] A pattern of *"tenuous support"* will exist when the public misperceives the position of the school, that is, has expectations that are in agreement with its *perceptions* of the school position, resulting in high satisfaction, but that are in disagreement with the *actual* school position. In this instance, it can be assumed that if communications were improved, the pattern would turn into one of opposition. *"Tenuous opposition"* results when the group misperceives the position of the school, has expectations that are in disagreement with its perceptions, and has expectations that are in agreement with the position held by the school. In this instance, if communications were improved, the public would realize its high measure of philosophical consolidation with the school's position, and the pattern would become one of support.

These support and opposition constructs presented by Fessler provide suggestions for prescribing a tailor-made public relations program. In this way, teachers and administrators would be able to diagnose needs and prescribe specific communication actions to meet those needs, and both community relations and community understandings would be improved.

PUBLIC RELATIONS AND PHYSICAL EDUCATION—EFFECTIVE IDEAS IN ACTION

Public relations, or community relations, have been sadly overlooked in many physical education programs across the country. It is true that considerable national emphasis and "advertising" have been undertaken by federal and national professional organizations, yet a great deal more needs to be done at the local community level.

The term "community" means many things to many people. Schools usually view their "community" in terms of formal and informal groupings of people. There are subgroups within the over-all community, and each one of these subgroups has different perceptions of the educational institution. "The school's community is, in reality, composed of a number of overlapping groups of people in which individuals may hold membership."[14] It is important that physical educators realize that this structure exists and that they do everything they can to inform each subgroup of the nature and purpose of the profession. This is sometimes very difficult in a large city where the populace is very diversified. It is possible, however, to inform adequately the "subcommunity group" directly connected with local students and the area of the community or state served by the institution. Teachers and administrators of physical education themselves must truly comprehend and believe in the

value of physical education before they can effectively promote their programs. The time is past when "overfed" and "underactive" physical educators can promote the "do as I say, not as I do" philosophy. Once the administrator himself truly believes in his program he can use his knowledge to establish and promote sound community relations.

Basic principles or established "truths" that we as a profession urgently need to inform the public about are the following:

1. Professional undergraduate and graduate preparation in physical education is different from participation in an intercollegiate athletic program.
2. Interscholastic athletic programs are not desirable substitutes for basic instruction programs in physical education.
3. Because an individual was an outstanding athlete does not necessarily mean he is an outstanding coach or physical educator.
4. Physical education, professional recreation, and health education are different academic disciplines and should be treated as such.
5. Professional physical education does not *have to be* a "dumping ground" for academically unqualified students.
6. Physical activity is absolutely essential for the health of the human organism.

To repeat, *"quality attracts quality"* and the finest way to promote *any* discipline is to staff the discipline with outstanding individuals who are admired and respected in their local and national community. In this way the plural publics will be much more likely to believe the "truths" that these professionals are attempting to promote.

Physical Education Public Information

No single physical education agency or organization has done as much or been as successful as PEPI—Physical Education Public Information. PEPI was developed by the Physical Education Division of the American Association for Health, Physical Education and Recreation in 1971–72. PEPI was created and designed to educate the public regarding the vital contribution of physical education to children and youth. The project emphasizes the use of local media—press, radio, and television—as a means of gaining greater public understanding.

The basic PR problem which PEPI faced was an attempted clarification of the distorted views that many of the "plural publics" held regarding physical education. PR programs sponsored by PEPI stressed the need for physical education for all children and its indispensability in the structure that supports the student's ability to absorb knowledge and to learn from experiences. Basic concepts that are stressed by PEPI's programs are: (1) physical education is health insurance; (2) physical education contributes to academic achievements; (3) physical education provides experiences and skills which last a lifetime; (4) physical education helps in developing a positive self image in the ability to compete and to cooperate with others. PEPI coordinators and others interested in planning better community relations meet for general workshops at different locations around the country. These sessions are devoted to the following:

1. Public information
2. Techniques for communicating with the public
3. Media operations
4. Techniques for interviews and talk shows
5. Major concepts in physical education
6. Analysis of spot announcements, talk shows, documentaries
7. Distribution of spots, newspaper articles
8. Local issues and problems

PEPI materials are available which provide specific recommendations on how to improve public relations in physical education. These materials deal with obtaining radio and television interviews, means of acquiring service time in radio, public service broadcasting, news releases, and other materials designed to improve PR for the "now" physical education. For further information regarding PEPI programs and assistance in public relations, write to AAHPER in Washington, D. C.

Community Relations—Plural Publics

Identifying the many publics to which public relations programs should be aimed is not an easy task, and is one that is difficult for the average physical education teacher to work into an already crowded schedule of activities. The many individual agencies and organizations within a community which must be reached by a good public relations program are often referred to as "plural publics." In attempting to identify such publics, teachers, supervisors, and administrators should remember that physical education public relations programs should attempt to reach everyone. The children under our tutelage are usually considered to be the best vehicle by which to transport a positive image about our programs. Parents, employees, and other teachers in the school are all people who count. Those individuals who make laws, school policy, and funding decisions should be contacted through a positive, constructive communications program. Physical educators should be aware of every existing opportunity to open or create communication channels. Many educators have not fully recognized the value of parental understanding of and support for education. One of our basic needs in communicating with representatives of local radio and television stations is the need to build a rapport and to create positive attitudes towards physical education. We must make the media aware of the difference between physical education and interscholastic athletics. The following is a list of ways to communicate with important "publics." Keep in mind that not all will apply to every group in every instance.

— Personal conversations
— Demonstrations
— PTA programs
— Local and national public media
— Face-to-face contact
— Posters and other visual materials
— Report cards
— Open houses for media personnel
— Letters to the editor
— Public meetings
— Recreation and social activities

—Participation in local education associations
—Brochures and booklets on health, physical education, and recreation
—Programs that physically involve parents

In putting our message across to the many publics, we must study the types of information that parents and the local community should have and the types of data that would be most impressive. Experts in the PR field state that we should sell our programs the same way anything else in our society is sold. Educational "verbiage" will probably continue within our profession, but it must be eliminated to a large degree for public consumption. Our communication programs must be within the easy understanding of the publics to which they are geared, and they must be factual and concise so that the individuals for which they are intended will take the time to listen.

One of the most promising developments within the past 10 years has been the creation of community relations departments within public school systems. An excellent example of such a program is that conducted by the Toledo public schools. This school system supports a very active and well-designed community relations department. A division of this department is provided for physical education. The physical education division and the community relations department in Toledo have as their motto "service for all."

The major tasks in developing sound relations between an institution and its "communities" are (a) organizing and planning a program, (b) securing information about the community, and (c) providing for two-way communication between the instructional staff and laymen. The effectiveness of agencies, avenues, and media will depend largely on the characteristics of a community, the abilities and experience of the faculty, and the nature of the problems that are encountered.

As has often been stated, "the best public relations is a worthwhile product." This is certainly true in education. Physical educators should not overlook the students in their classes as vehicles for the promotion of excellent community relations. Nevertheless, administrators must be familiar with the media and procedures for "internal" and "external" communication of philosophies and programs.

Avenues for Communication. The first place an administrator should look in attempting to promote effective community relations is to his faculty. Individual faculty members more than likely play the most important role in the development of effective public relations. Public relations programs deal with fundamental attitudes, and a faculty composed of able people who truly believe in what they are doing, combined with an efficient community relations program, will prove to be very successful. Moreover, an outstanding faculty is invaluable in the promotion of the profession both within the administrative structure of the institution and in the public at large.

If conducted correctly, a most effective medium for supplying parents with information is the scheduling of parental visits. Such visitations should provide time for parents and interested persons to visit classes in health education and physical education. Teachers should be proud of worthwhile programs and wish to present such programs for parents to witness. If possible the teacher should try to contact parents personally to invite them to visit when their child is participating. If personal contact is not possible, general announcements of physical education visitation periods can be sent home with the students. Other media should be prepared for visitation periods, such as attractive bulletin boards pertaining to physical education programs, exhibits placed at strategic locations, and educational materials provided for parents to take home.

Voltmer and Esslinger state that parents are primarily interested in:

1. The progress and achievement of their children.
2. Methods of instruction.
3. Health and physical fitness of their children.
4. The program of activities.

Figure 3–1. Children enrolled in a second continuum use the natural resources of their community to construct a "rope bridge" as part of an innovative physical education class. Such activities create community interest in school programs. (Courtesy of the University School, University of Wyoming.)

5. Need for physical education.
6. The objectives of physical education.
7. Intramural athletics.
8. Teachers of physical education.
9. Physical education facilities.
10. Attendance and behavior of pupils in physical education.[15]

Student activities that may do much to promote school-community relations for physical education cover a wide range of possibilities. Teachers wishing to make use of such activities, however, must make certain that they have competent students promoting worthwhile programs before such action is undertaken.

Many types of demonstrations are extensively used in order to promote understanding and to generate support. The presentation of special programs for PTA groups, a physical education or school "open house," and play days are some of the more widely used techniques. The main purpose of such activities should be to attempt to *inform* the general public of what we are doing and not just to provide entertainment.

City-wide intramural programs bring together pupils from several schools and provide a medium for demonstrating to the public a phase of the overall school program. The public should be invited to attend intramural tournaments or play days. Coeducational gymnastic demonstrations have proved to be a most successful means of public relations. Such demonstrations have a very worthwhile appeal to a large majority of the community and are thoroughly enjoyed by the participants.

Advisory committees may be school board committees or local school committees, and are made up of both school personnel and lay consultants. The committee meets periodically to discuss problems and to make resolutions and recommendations to the physical education department or to the local school board. If correctly conducted, these groups can do much for the advancement and promotion of physical education programs in the school and community.

New concepts in *mass media* also hold great promise for bringing physical education programs to the public. The use of video tapes will have a tremendous impact. Tapes of physical education activities can be made during actual instruction periods and then shown by local television stations. Newspapers are not a new media for our use, but new dimen-

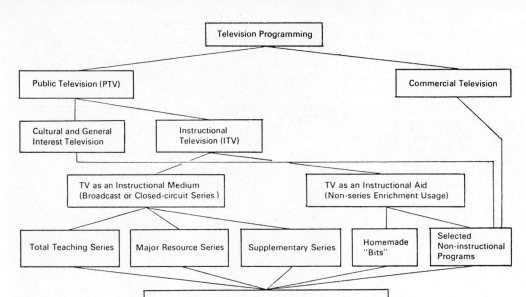

Figure 3–2. Television: production and utilization in physical education. (Courtesy of AAHPER.)

sions in this media should certainly be investigated.

The general public has come to recognize that television is perhaps one of the most important communication mechanisms ever designed and may well even be our major source of public information. Instructional television during the past 10 years has produced a considerable impact on children and youth and has still not reached its expected potential. The realities and potentialities of TV are apparent when it is reported that there are thousands of elementary school boys and girls who receive televised physical education lessons followed by activity sessions in gymnasiums.[16]

Closed circuit television or video tape recordings are used throughout the world to analyze athletic performance. Video tapes have been used for years by prospective student teachers to analyze experimental teaching lessons. These widely differing examples of television usage clearly indicate that the use of this medium has been discovered by physical educators, and that we have found many effective ways to use this valuable resource.

School visitations, student activities, and the use of mass media are perhaps three of the most commonly used techniques for informing the public of physical education objectives and programs.

REFERENCES

1. John M. Pfiffner and Robert V. Presthus: *Public Adminstration.* New York: The Ronald Press Co., 1960, p. 133.
2. *Ibid.,* p. 134.
3. *Communication Ideas in Action.* Washington, D.C.: National School Public Relations Association, 1970, p. 51.
4. William H. Newman: *Administrative Action—The Techniques of Organization and Management.* Englewood Cliffs, N.J.: Prentice-Hall, Inc., 1963, p. 18.
5. C. T. Hardwick and B. F. Landuyt: *Administrative Strategy and Decision Making.* Cincinnati: South-Western Publishing Co., 1966, p. 388.
6. *Ibid.,* p. 389.

7. James J. Jones and Irving W. Stout: *School Public Relations: Issues and Cases*. New York: G. P. Putnam's Sons, 1960, pp. 7–10.
8. *Public Relations for America's Schools, Twenty-Eighth Yearbook*. Washington, D.C.: American Association of School Administrators, 1950, p. 12.
9. Pfiffner and Presthus, *op. cit.*, p. 174.
10. *Public Relations for America's Schools, op. cit.*, p. 14.
11. Lester W. Anderson and Lauren A. VanDyke: *Secondary School Administration*. Boston: Houghton Mifflin Co., 1963, p. 476.
12. Ralph Fessler: "Support and Opposition in School-Community Relations." In *Planning and Changing, A Journal for School Administrators*. Normal, Ill.: Illinois State University, Spring, 1973, p. 29.
13. *Ibid.*, p. 32.
14. Henry J. Otto and David C. Sanders: *Elementary School Organization and Administration*. New York: Appleton-Century-Crofts, Inc., 1964, pp. 56, 278.
15. Edward F. Voltmer and Arthur A. Esslinger: *The Organization and Administration of Physical Education*. New York: Appleton-Century-Crofts, Inc., 1967, p. 460.
16. *TV Production and Utilization in Physical Education*. Washington, D.C.: AAHPER, 1971.

SUGGESTED READINGS

Bucher, Charles A.: "What's Happening in Education Today?" *JOHPER*, September, 1974, p. 30.
Communication Ideas in Action. Washington, D.C.: National School Public Relations Association, 1970.
Fessler, Ralph: "Support and Opposition in School-Community Relations." In *Planning and Changing, A Journal for School Administrators*. Normal, Ill.: Illinois State University, Spring, 1973.
"PEPI-Grams." *JOHPER* (Physical Education Public Information Reports).
Stanley, Philip L.: "Implementing Off-Campus Activities." *JOHPER*, June, 1974.
TV Production and Utilization in Physical Education. Washington, D.C.: AAHPER, 1971.

CHAPTER FOUR

An Introduction to Organization and Administration

Now that we have reviewed the historical development of sport and physical education as well as our philosophical foundations, modern trends, public relations, and communication, let us turn to the focal point of this text, *organization and administration*. This introductory chapter to administration will present the fundamental and common concepts that are appropriate for any level of educational administration. These concepts and theories have been drawn from many educational organizations as well as from business and industry, since we can learn much by leaving our own discipline.

BASIC TERMS AND CONCEPTS

School and public libraries have many books and periodicals dealing with the "skill" of administration. Without administration, any type of organization would be almost impossible to form, and if it were formed, it could not function.

There are three basic types of organization and administration:

1. The leader-centered organization in which positions, power, and authority are delegated by the leader.
2. The organization in which positions are assigned on the basis of tradition.
3. The bureaucratic type of organization in which members of the organization and management are recruited to fill established positions. This type of organization breaks the absolute power of the leader.

Administration and supervision encompass many different aspects of a total organizational structure. Administration deals with the management of personnel, human relations, production, and organizational planning. All of these diverse responsibilities are encompassed in the definition of the term administration, which states that administration is "the broad coordination of the activities of people inside some organized group."

Most of the productive work of our society is carried out or conducted by structuring groups into some type of organization. These organizations usually have certain typical features. These features or characteristics involve a purpose for the organization; physical properties or some type of financial base; systematic ways of accomplishing a goal, aim, or purpose; and some type of organizational structure or internal division. "Knowing the boundaries of an organization is important for several reasons. First, it tells us the domain over which affairs are administered for and on behalf of the organization. Second, we are able to determine the personnel component which holds membership in the organization. Third, we can follow out the consequences of decisions made in the organization because the organization can be viewed as a closed system in which decisions about change have limited and discernible internal consequences."[1]

Administration

"Administration is the guidance, leadership, and control of the efforts of a group of individuals toward some common goal."[2] Because almost every definition of the term administration presents the "goal-oriented" approach, you can see why it is imperative to establish a direction. Without something to work toward there would be no reason to direct progress; thus, an administrator's task would be impossible. *Autocratic administration* is the use of the administrator's power or authority to operate and control all others in the organization. This type of administration places unlimited power and authority in the hands of one person, to be used as he or she sees fit. *Democratic administration* is a type of administration which makes use of constructive group thinking and promotes sharing ideas in a united endeavor toward decision making. The nature and use of both of these approaches to administration will be presented later in this chapter.

Organization

Organization has been defined in many different ways by many different people. Two definitions that we may wish to consider are "a systematic preparation for action" and "the structuring of individuals and functions into productive relationships."[3] "Organization seeks a pattern of skills and responsibilities that will ensure coordination and unity of purpose through supervision."[4] *The objective of both administration and organization is to control the environment, with administration providing the direction for the organization.*

In attempting to provide a definition and a description of the term organization we must again realize that it is extremely difficult to provide a single definition which fulfills every need. In many instances, "organization" is referred to as a process or a result of arranging or grouping together interdependent elements into a logical functioning unit. Descriptions of organization include structure or order as a systematic preparation for some type of action. The term structure or structuring is often used in relationship to the grouping of individuals or units so that they can function in some productive manner. Organization seeks a pattern of skills and responsibilities that will insure coordination and unity of purpose through supervision.

"Line-and-staff" organization is a type of organization that establishes a specific line of authority and responsibility from the chief administrator through subordinates and to the employees or to the individuals who make up the organization.

Supervision

The terms *supervision* and *supervisor* have been in evidence for many years and are said to date back in usage to the 1870's. Efforts to define these terms have been just as numerous as the attempts to provide definite parameters for administration and organization. A realistic definition of supervision is one which provides some aspect of individual or group leadership. *A supervisor is an individual, usually an official, who oversees or directs, and one who is in charge of a specific segment of an organization.* The term supervision infers or implies that individuals or groups are being supervised, directed, or managed. Supervision may be either autocratic or democratic and it may be either specific or general. *General supervision* occurs when a supervisor is responsible for the actions of a group of individuals within general physical or organizational premises, while *specific supervision* occurs when the supervisor is working directly with individuals or groups. An educational

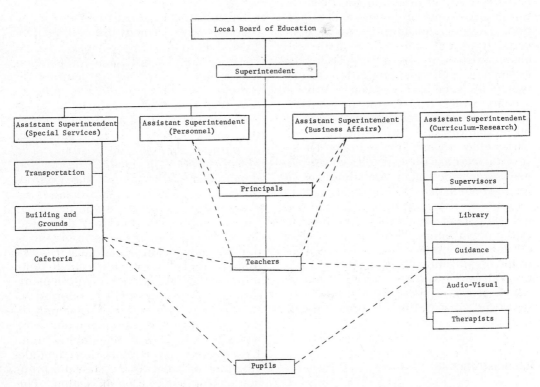

Figure 4–1. An example of the administrative organization of public education.

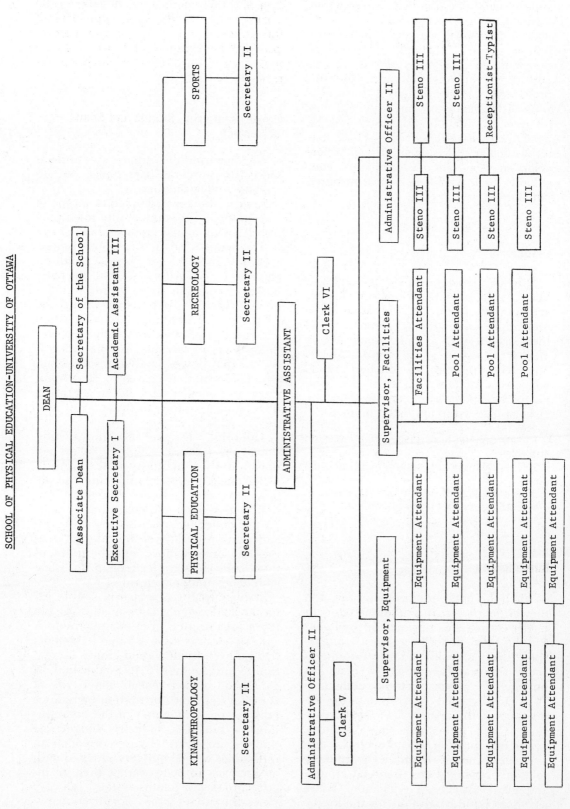

Figure 4–2. An example of an organizational chart depicting both academic and service responsibilities.

supervisor is an individual who provides leadership and direction for teachers and other educational workers. Such direction is usually involved with meeting the aims and objectives of the specific educational organization and with improvement of instruction. Educational supervision involves some aspect of professional stimulation and growth and the design and construction of teaching materials and methods. Educational supervisors may be called coordinators, consultants, or in some instances, resource personnel.

Leadership

A leader is one who is the guiding head of an organization. In many instances the leader is the administrator—the department head, dean, or president. *Leadership is considered as the ability to lead.* A nonstrategic leader is one who follows established rules, whereas a strategic leader is one who meets the situation as it arises. Four key tasks of leadership are listed below:

1. The definition of institutional mission and role.
2. The institutional embodiment of purpose.
3. The defense of institutional integrity.
4. The ordering of internal conflict.

Bureaucracy

When the number of people subject to the direction of the administrator or leader exceeds his personal span of control, he must delegate authority and responsibility to a subleader or intermediary and thus a *bureaucracy* is created. A bureaucracy is constructively defined as "a form of social organization for administering the affairs of a formal organization."[5] If it becomes large enough, every organization will develop a bureaucracy. They are found in government, religious organizations, fraternal groups, and many aspects of education. There are three basic conditions for the forma-

tion of a bureaucracy: (a) the size of the organization; (b) the limited purpose of the organization; and (c) the heterogeneous background of those who are members or participants in the organization.

Power, Authority, Status, and Span of Control

We have used the terms power and authority in previous paragraphs, but do we know what they mean?

Power. Power is defined as a type of "latent force." It is the ability to employ force, not its actual employment. Power is a concept used in describing human relations. It is neither force nor authority, but is intimately related to both. Power is coercive, as compared to influence, which is persuasive in nature. Power stands behind every association and sustains its structure; without power there is no organization and no order. It is said that power is always successful; when it is not, it ceases to be power. Power is necessary in order to get things done, and it resides in those with prestige.

Authority. Defined as "the institutionalized right to employ power, not power itself,"[6] authority is the right to make decisions that will guide the actions of individuals or of groups. "Authority based on rational grounds rests on the belief by subordinates in the legality and propriety of the rules governing the organization, and the right of those elevated to leadership to issue commands under such rules."[7]

Status. Status is a clearly visible external mark which distinguishes people in an organization from one another. "A status system is a set of value judgments that ranks individuals and groups in relation to one another."[8] An established organization always reveals some type of status system and the system includes a rank for every member of the organization. In business, industry, and education we are aware of cases in which an individual was completely satisfied with an increase in status rather than an increase in pay. A "status system" is a very powerful system in any organization.

Span of Control. The "span of control" concept is an important aspect of organization and administration. It was previously stated that a bureaucracy is formed when an administrator's personal span of control becomes so large that he cannot provide individual direction. The degree of individual direction that an administrator can offer depends upon the number of individuals for whom he is responsible and the amount of time he can devote to each. Since the leader's span of control is often limited, sub-leaders must be appointed.

Decision Making

"The fine art of executive decision consists in not deciding questions that are not now pertinent, in not deciding prematurely, in not making decisions that cannot be made effective, and in not making decisions that others should make."[9]

The occasions for having to make decisions arise from:
1. Authoritative communication from superiors.
2. Cases referred by subordinates for decision.
3. Cases initiated by the administrator himself.[10]

Many leaders or administrators do not like to make decisions. Personal decisions have to be made by the administrator, whereas the responsibility of making organizational decisions can often be delegated. Barnard[11] states that the capacity to make decisions may be developed by training and especially by experience. An administrator can pursue the following courses in making a decision:

1. Decide to act (positive decisions).
2. Decide and not act (negative decisions).
3. Decide and reserve action.
4. Decide not to decide.

Administrative decision making is the most difficult task a leader faces because most men wish to avoid criticism and the responsibility for failure. The administrator may be obliged to make "top-level" decisions, but he should distribute responsibility so that others can make less important decisions.

THE NATURE OF ADMINISTRATIVE PROCESSES

During the past several years there has been a marked change in emphasis within the fundamental principles and practices of human relations. This change has emphasized a redirection from the practice of strict authoritarian systems to a much more democratic approach. Coupled with this change toward cooperative thinking and decision making is the modernization of American public education, with its present emphasis on "adaptability" and "conceptual design." Schools of today must reflect the needs of society and attempt to prepare the citizens of the future. With these changes have come opportunities for democratic participation in administration.

Several years ago, educational administrators placed a great deal of emphasis on processes and procedures which were not considered to be "unique" in school administration. Concentration was placed on educational finance, school plant design, school business management, legal aspects of education, and curriculum and instruction. These issues still remain important today but the nature and scope of educational administration has changed. Present day school management is also concerned with the various aspects and components of decision making, leadership, politics, social systems, management science, and the processes involved in planning, organizing, stimulating, coordinating, and appraising.[12] Supervisors and administrators usually make things happen through other people, and educational administration today is placing much more emphasis on issues other than the traditional problems centered around school finance and school plant design.

In management and administration, the administrator can be expected to be actively involved in planning, delegating authority and responsibility, initiating programs and concepts, making decisions, communicating with other individuals within the organization, selecting and retaining staff, and promoting good public relations. A competent and knowledgeable administrator will understand clearly what the job entails and what his or her responsibilities are as well as the delegation of power and authority which the position controls. In providing effective leadership, an administrator will encourage a climate where innovation is accepted and he will effectively delegate authority and responsibility to those working in sub-administrative positions within the organization. Cooperation with others is a necessity and administrative support should be provided for employees so they are able to conduct the affairs of the organization.

Administrators must exercise a degree of consistency in administrative decision making and their decisions must be consistent with the established policies, procedures, and objectives of the organization. Decisions should be made promptly but not hastily, and they should be realistic and based on the principles of sound decision making. As discussed in the chapter on communication, the leader or administrator must be kept informed and he in turn must keep the individuals within his organization informed by means of good public relations procedures. A good administrator will listen with understanding and purpose and will react favorably to constructive criticism of his own work. A leader must be able to express himself clearly and effectively in writing, speaking, and overall manner. One of an administrator's greatest responsibilities is the selection and employment of competent and well qualified individuals for positions in the organization. A systematic evaluation of employees is usually one of the responsibilities of an administrator, as well as the responsibility to maintain a positive atmosphere for the development of members of his organization. The success and advancement of the organization is an administrator's most important goal.

Basic Principles of Democratic Administration

The fundamental principles of democratic administration may be summarized as follows:[13]

1. Democratic administration accords to a group and the individuals composing it the responsibilities for participation in the making of decisions that affect undertakings of the group and the activities and the interests of the individuals composing the group.
2. This does not necessarily mean that each person exercises administrative responsibilities, but that the administration provides the situation and procedure by which the individuals of various sorts of groups in the schools may cooperate in planning.
3. Democratic administration attempts to locate the leadership and encourage its exercise by each person in accordance with his abilities, capacities, background, experience, interests, and needs.
4. Democratic administration provides for such flexibility of organization that adjustments may be made from time to time in the matter of human relationships, as the occasion and developments may seem to indicate.
5. Democratic administration recognizes the unusual instinctive urge to creative activity among human beings, and allows for its expression in planning and carrying out education programs and procedures.

Many educators have pointed out that democracy is the most misunderstood term in educational administration. Griffith states that there are six erroneous meanings of educational democracy that are very prevalent.[14]

Error 1.   Democratic administration is a laissez-faire procedure.
Error 2.   Democratic administration means guiding persons to accept an administrator's viewpoint.
Error 3.   Democratic administration avoids the firm exercise of authority and insistence on obedience.
Error 4.   Democratic administration means majority rule.
Error 5.   Democratic administration is a means of avoiding unpleasant decisions.
Error 6.   Democratic administration means the absence of formality.

The beginning administrator must realize that democratic administration does not mean abdicating authority or evading responsibility. An administrator's proposed solution to a problem may be the correct course, even though his faculty considers it in error and unworkable. The majority is not always correct, and a majority opinion may be based upon ignorance or fear of change.

As we have stated before, a basic quality of a good educational administrator is the ability to enable the teachers to achieve their objectives with a minimum expenditure of time and effort and the least interference with other institutional activities.

Most of the work which falls within the duties of any administrator can be divided into the following basic processes:

Plan — Determining what shall be undertaken — the formation of objectives, policies, programs, methodology, and schedules.

Organize — Grouping of materials and activities into the administrative units necessary to carry out the plans made in step one.

Direct — Directing and guiding those operations necessary to meet objectives. Issuing instructions and providing motivation for those who are to carry out the instructions.

Coordinate — Coordinating the total effort of the leader's administrative unit and seeing that operational results conform to the plans.

Evaluate — Evaluating the total plan to attempt to determine if the established objectives have been met. (This step may include the comparison of actual results against an internal or external standard.)

The purpose of most organizational plans is the maximum utilization of the available resources in order to accomplish assigned tasks or to meet planned objectives. "School administration has only one purpose: That purpose is to facilitate the total educational program of the community."[15]

Performance-Based Administration

Performance-based administration is a widely discussed innovation which has arisen in public education during the past several years. Attempting to put administration on a "performance base" has come about as a dimension of educational accountability. Naturally, there are many ramifications to any determination of performance. Many discrepancies may exist, such as the difference between *actual* performance and *desired* performance. This difference is called a *performance discrepancy* and examples of performance discrepancies can be found throughout education. Whenever problems exist, a difference has been detected between what is desired and what is actually happening.

In discussing performance-based administration, the first thing that must be established or determined is the definition and listing of *performance objectives* for the specific supervisory or administrative position. Statements concerning goals and objectives of the programs under the authority and responsibility of the administrator are essential information in order to attempt to determine a performance base. Administrative performance objectives must be established and clearly defined, with a division of objectives into sub-objectives which becomes more definitive and designed to relate specific responsibility areas. A realistic planning of performance objectives requires that many individuals be consulted and that objectives be considered and carefully analyzed before the determination is made as to which are to be used in the evaluation of performance. Once this is established and an evaluation is made of what is and what should be, results can furnish the administrator or his superiors with information which would not have been available otherwise. Such information could prompt new insight and decisions which lead to the continuous improvement of programs.

Educational Management Systems (EMS) came about because of the demand that educators and educational systems be held accountable for their product. This "system's approach" to educational management is also concerned with *performance-based administration*. This analysis or assessment is made to determine *where* administrators perform essential tasks and also to define exactly what an administrator *does.* The identification of specific results of administrative action can then be recorded. In determining performance indicators, questions are asked relating to when results are accomplished; what has been accomplished; and what types of things are observable positive results. An attempt is also made to identify the categories of activities for which a supervisor or administrator is responsible. Questions asked are: where does the administrator perform; where *should* he or she be performing as an administrator of a specific program; and what are the intended accomplishments? Appropriate performance indicators are determined for each position focusing on pre-established results.

"Traditionally, educational institutions have reflected the moral principles and values of the adult society. Parents employed educators to operate the schools but retained the power to determine the nature of the schools. Administrators must be accountable to the public for the discharge of their responsibilities. Accountability requires combined efforts of community and educators in determining the educational purpose, defining functions, judging results, and taking corrective actions."[16]

ADMINISTRATIVE PERSONNEL

Administration is said to be both a "social technique" and a "distinct skill." As previously stated, the good administrator is one who enables a group to achieve their objectives. The administrator or leader must recognize the dynamics of each different situation if he is to perform his function of bringing the group to their goal. What then makes a good administrator or leader?

From Traits to Functions

Before World War II most of the emphasis in studies of leadership attempted to isolate unique physical, intellectual, class, or personality traits that could differentiate leaders from others. The trend today is to investigate the whole complex of intentions, actions, and consequences as a social involvement. "Democratic leadership implies a profound understanding of the natural roots of competence and consensus and an unqualified commitment to the derived ethics, justice and open communications."[17]

Many educational administrators believe that administration is very much learned and that effective performance in the administrator's job calls for extraordinary development of ego and superego capacities. It also may be true that administration is never fully learned, and that no one is ever able to transmit to another more than a part of administrative skill.

Basic Qualities

Administration is considered so much of a skill that in business and industry capable executives can move from one post to another and do an outstanding job in each position. In educational administration as it pertains to physical education, the administrator who has had professional experience and an in-depth educational preparation is usually the leader who knows what desirable goals are and how to advance toward them.

An administrator must have a useful formal education. An educated man possesses a set of values and knowledge about an area of reality. It is said that the educated man is likely to value truth; the ignorant man is likely to accept convenience and expediency. "The educated man avoids glittering generalities; the ignorant man is most likely to traffic in them."[18] Ignorance breeds dogmatism.

Selected basic qualities for an administrator of physical education are:

1. A strong academic training in the subject matter of physical education.
2. A clear recognition of the professional goals to be achieved.
3. The possession of requisite mental ability.
4. A willingness to exert individual effort to accomplish professional objectives.
5. A willingness to adapt to social change and to be flexible, so that he or she may function well in many different situations.

6. The possession of a personal quality that contributes to leadership and is acceptable to faculty, students, and the general public.

7. A sound personality and personal health habits that follow the healthful ideals of the profession.

8. An ability to express himself accurately and forcefully in speaking and writing.

Several studies have been undertaken in recent years which indicate that there is very little difference in technical skill ability among successful and unsuccessful school administrators. The difference between these two groups in "human skills" and "conceptual skills," however, was considered great. These three skills are defined as:[19]

Conceptual Skill — The ability to see the enterprise as a whole; it includes recognizing how the various functions of the organization depend on one another, and how changes in any one part may affect all the others.
Human Skill — The executive's ability to work effectively as a group member and to build cooperative effort within the team he leads. A leader must understand himself and other people and be outstanding in human relations.
Technical Skill — A proficiency in and understanding of a specific type of activity, particularly one involving methods, processes, procedures, or techniques. Technical skill involves a specialized knowledge in the use of specific tools and techniques of a discipline.

An administrator's "creative potential" is also an important aspect of the basic qualities that lead to successful leadership. Such potential may be evaluated in terms of:

Interest in problem solving
Creative expectancy (confidence)
Feeling of security
Intellectual curiosity (questioning attitude)
Broad interest in increasing knowledge
Good memory
Ability to observe
Depth
Ability to concentrate
Open-mindedness
Flexibility (mental)
Imagination
Originality
Large and varied vocabulary
Sense of humor

Independence
Discernment, perception
Good judgment (in the field of the problem)
Patience
Articulateness
Energy
Idea fluency (quick thinking)
Nerve
Intuitiveness
Self-starter quality, self-discipline
Serendipity (luck)
Contrary nature
Drive

If professional physical education is to continue to strive for excellence in its many programs, individuals who are not academically prepared in physical education should not be employed to administer such programs. Once again, "quality seeks quality," and a well-qualified, competent administrator should be able to attract an excellent faculty.

The Director

The director of physical education has many responsibilities ranging from the supervision and evaluation of teachers to the administration of the budget. However, there is no delineation of these responsibilities based on sound research.

Probably the most comprehensive inquiry into the major roles and duties of the director was made by the New York State Council of Administrators of Health, Physical Education, and Recreation. Thirty-six members of this body were interviewed using a measurement instrument involving 93 duties. The administrators selected for interviews met the following criteria: (1) certification as an administrator, (2) a minimum of three years experience in the position, and (3) an allotment of at least half of their professional time to administering programs in grades one through twelve.

The survey revealed that 21 of the 93 duties were essential for adequate performance of the administrative function. Among the 21 duties were major roles such as (1) stimulating and developing professional staff leadership, (2) scheduling athletic contests and making arrangements for procedures involved in the interschool contests, (3) organizing and

Figure 4–3. In-service activities. (Courtesy of Norfolk Public Schools.)

supervising the management of instructional materials, (4) arranging conferences with staff members in preparation for visits and observation, (5) supervising athletic contests, (6) recommending policies for control of athletic contests, (7) initiating and approving requisitions and purchase orders, (8) evaluating teachers' instructional planning and assisting in developing instructional materials, (9) developing efficient office management procedures, (10) overseeing all records of athletes to determine eligibility, etc., (11) working with professional organizations to improve professional service, (12) scheduling and regulating the equitable use of all facilities for school and community use, and (13) providing for the administration and supervision of all intramural and extramural activities.[20] These duties are discussed more thoroughly in the resource manual.

One major task that directors face is the planning of in-service programs. These programs are designed to improve instruction and are prevalent in many areas of the country. There is a trend for school districts to sponsor their own in-service programs without university dominance. Many staff development departments have been formed as a part of the administrative function.

Staff development is becoming such an important phase of instruction that funds from state and federal agencies are available to finance such programs. Some districts reimburse teachers for participating in these programs. Others provide substitutes for teachers in order to free them for in-service training.

In-service planning may include students demonstrating skills and techniques or it may be restricted to teachers participating in the various procedures involved in effective instruction. A combination of both plans is probably the best arrangement.

As the planning progresses, it may be advisable to procure local sports performers and college specialists to provide the expertise necessary for skill demonstrations.

In addition to securing local specialists for in-service education, teachers from the various schools should be selected to provide leadership roles in conducting the programs. These teachers may be given written instruction in how to conduct overall assignments. These assignments should include information on the importance of teaching skills, correct demonstration of skills, encouraging teacher participation, providing time for evaluation of the program, utilization of available time, apprising teachers of available supportive materials, demonstrating the most effective teaching methods, and explaining effective group organization.

Although actual knowledge of teaching skills is basic to in-service participation, information in related areas such as the use of multi-media equipment, developing lesson plans, and effective teaching methods and procedures should be provided. Apprising teachers of local, state, and national trends is important and time should be allowed in the in-service planning for discussion of developments and trends.

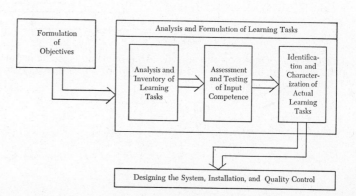

Figure 4–4. The formation of objectives should systematically lead to learning tasks and the overall design of the system. (From Banathy, B. H.: *Instructional Systems.* Palo Alto, Calif.: Fearon Publishers.)

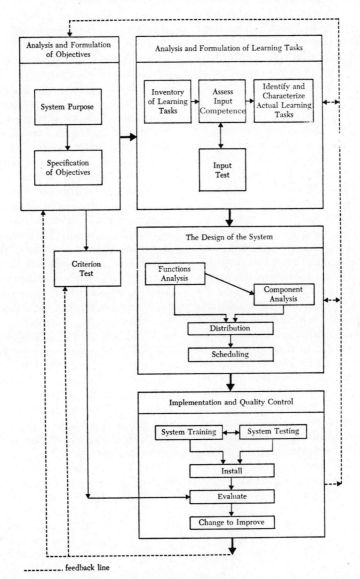

Figure 4-5. Once objectives have been formulated, specific learning tasks are undertaken which lead to the design of the system and implementation. (From Banathy, B. H.: *Instructional Systems.* Palo Alto, Calif.: Fearon Publishers.)

The Supervisor

A "supervisor" is defined as a teacher, administrator or resource person who is charged with responsibility for overseeing and improving instructional methods.

An *education supervisor* is one who has the responsibility of assisting teachers to improve their instruction and helping them with the development of an interesting and viable curriculum which will meet the needs and interests of the students as well as the objectives of the program. Whatever definition or meaning is adopted, a supervisor's duties are directly dependent upon an official position description. A supervisory position should only entail those duties and responsibilities which are delegated to it by a higher administrative authority or administrative board of control.

Supervision of physical education was first begun by employing school specialists to provide in-service training for regular teachers so that they could teach physical education in their classes. In discussing the differences and similarities between administration and supervision, some authors believe that "basically, as far as physical education is concerned, the ultimate goal is the same for both administration and supervision."[21] These two terms have so many common functions that it is extremely difficult to separate them entirely. It is generally believed that administration encompasses a much larger area of responsibility than does supervision and that there is a greater delegation of authority to an administrator than to a supervisor. Because of this delegation of authority and greater degree of responsibility, an administrator may be more authoritative than a supervisor, but he also carries greater responsibility for dealing with budgets, supplies, facilities, and the employment of personnel. A supervisor is more directly related to the teacher-pupil learning situation and must work well in a cooperative arrangement with teachers in order to obtain desired results. A supervisor must relate well to the person or persons he or she is supervising and desires to assist.

Many of the duties and functions of an educational supervisor are much the same as those of a director of physical education and athletics, or of a chairperson of health and physical education. Once again the specific responsibilities of the position should be determined and presented in a well organized manner by a principal, superintendent, or school board. A responsibility which is probably the most important and should be given the greatest emphasis is the responsibility for *leadership*. A physical education supervisor must be able to lead and provide an example for teachers in knowledge, skill, and teaching methods. This leadership is of great importance in providing in-service training and for providing the organizational leadership necessary to conduct teaching workshops and clinics. As is true in most administrative or supervisory positions, supervision may be provided through either horizontal or vertical approaches. *Horizontal supervision* provides for a physical education specialist to be responsible for supervision and assistance within a specified grade level or levels for all the schools in an area, city or district. An example would be a supervisor (specialist or coordinator) at the elementary schools. *Vertical supervision* finds the supervisor responsible for the supervision of physical education in all grades, elementary through high school. This type of supervision has the advantage that it should provide a continuity of program for all grade levels in a given school or school district.

The Department Chairperson or Head

The department head or chairperson is the leader of a specialized administrative unit. A "chairperson" is usually the spokesman for a group of individuals, such as the departmental faculty. He or she represents the group at school or college administrative meetings and relates the wishes of the group in a democratic manner. A literal definition of a department head, however, signifies or implies that this leader is the "head" of the faculty, and has the power and authority to make administrative decisions personally, if desired. The degree or amount of authority delegated to either a department head or to a department chairperson is directly dependent upon the wishes of the administration to which he is subordinate.

The term "chairperson" or "chairone" has gained wide acceptance because the term "chairman" is not deemed appropriate for female administrators. During the past six or seven years, especially at the college level, but also in many school systems, women have played a much more prominent role in organization, supervision, and administration. Federal and state legislation forbidding discrimination against minorities and women has done much to promote the recognition of the leadership capabilities of women in physical education. Many college or university departments of physical education across the country are now headed by female administrators, and the administrative title of general usage is that of a *chairperson*.

The duties and responsibilities of a chairperson of a department of physical education and athletics in a public school are quite complex and diversified. Duties usually involve responsibilities pertaining to administration, facilities, equipment, supplies, curriculum, budget and finance, supervision of faculty, health and safety, extracurricular activities, and interscholastic athletics for both men and women. The most important and significant delegated responsibility is that of providing professional leadership for the department in order to insure that the efforts of the department are devoted to the attainment of the goals and objectives of the school.

The Dean

The dean is that member of a college or university administration in charge of all the faculties in a school or college. A dean of a school or college of physical education is usually administratively responsible for several different departments, such as Physical Education (co-educational curricula), Health Education, Intramurals, and Recreation and Park Administration.

Junior and senior high schools in some cities have become so large that the delegation of responsibility requires administrators, other than assistant principals, who are in charge of several departments or a division. In this instance, schools have created Deanships. It is not at all uncommon (in large city school systems) to find a dean of student affairs, auxiliary services, and academic curricula.

Supervisor or Director of Intramural Sports

Intramural sports programs for both boys and girls, and men and women, are rapidly increasing in both scope and quality in schools and colleges. School administrators are finally realizing the benefits which children derive from a well conceived and well conducted intramural sports program. The administration of intramural sports depends to a large extent upon the academic level at which the programs are found. Traditionally, in junior and senior high schools, IM activities are supervised and directed within the department of physical education and athletics. The department head or chairperson is therefore responsible for the nature and scope of the program. At the college or university level, programs may be housed in the department of physical education, the division of intercollegiate athletics, or as a separate administrative unit under the jurisdiction of a Dean of Student Activities or a Dean of Student Life. "A strong director, either man or woman, will eliminate most weaknesses of either plan, and will work with all human and natural resources to produce a functional program that will meet the needs, interests, and hopes of all youth."[22]

In many schools the director or supervisor of IM sports is not designated as a specific individual. Many programs still remain under the supervision of physical education teachers and coaches, with responsibility shared by several teachers rather than the sole responsibility for the program resting with one individual.

This organizational approach does not provide continuity for intramural programs, and it is considered a much better administrative approach to delegate the authority and responsibility for conducting an exemplary program to both male and female physical education teachers or other interested faculty members. In this way, intramural programs do not get slighted and they do not act as a specific recruiting agency for interscholastic athletics. When physical education teachers are given this they should be released from other school assignments.

The general duties and responsibilities of an intramural director are:

to determine the guiding principles and general policies for intramural sports.

to serve the total recreational needs of the student body by means of a carefully devised program of activities.

to emphasize events and activities that will have both in-school value and will carry over into adulthood.

to provide the most efficient methods for arrangement of competition, encouraging competition for the fun of playing and not for possible rewards.

to constantly work with the school administration through individuals and committees, councils, faculty groups, etc.

to do research and professional studies to determine the best practices for conducting intramural programs.

to provide personal conferences and consultations with students on any matters pertaining to sports information, program mechanics and health and safety.

to provide the supervision of actual competition as well as the meetings and conferences with school managers and organizers.

to provide the planning and organization for the total intramural sports program including the construction of schedules and the determination of events.

to provide budget recommendations for the ordering of all equipment and supplies.

to provide intramural publications such as intramural handbooks for student information and to provide program reports to the administration as well as to the news media.

The Director of Interscholastic Athletics

The responsibility for interscholastic athletics for both boys and girls varies considerably from state to state and from school district to school district. The most common organizational plan finds the administrator who is the director of physical education also responsible for the supervision and control of interscholastic athletics. At present, these administrators are usually male and are in charge of both boys' and girls' physical education programs as well as interscholastic athletics and intramurals. The present emphasis and interest being experienced in interscholastic activities for girls has necessitated the initiation of female administrators for the girls' programs. Whatever the delegation of responsibility for interscholastic athletic programs, the final authority rests with the school board or the board of education. The district superintendent of schools is the administrator who is employed to represent the school board and to implement its policies. The high school or junior high school principal is usually directly responsible for the interscholastic athletic programs within his or her school. Athletics are a vital part of a school's curriculum, and school principals are charged by the superintendent with the authority and responsibility for the organization and administration of these programs. This delegation of responsibility is then passed down to the director of physical education and athletics, and he must support the wishes and policy recommendations of the school board and other educational administrators. Principals are usually directly responsible for the eligibility of students who participate.

The position of athletic director in most large schools is one that entails a great deal of responsibility and importance in the development and maintenance of programs. As schools and school districts experience financial problems, athletic directors are increasingly pressed to provide the necessary program funding. The many duties and responsibilities of this position are presented in detail in a later chapter; however, they usually include: scheduling of activities; hiring of officials; purchase and maintenance of equipment and supplies; selection of faculty to coach; and the construction, design and maintenance of indoor and outdoor facilities. The athletic director is also expected to recommend athletic policies to the principal which are then submitted to the superintendent.[23] This responsibility of policy recommendation makes it mandatory that athletic directors fully understand and abide by the governing philosophy, objectives, and principles of state high school athletic associations as well as adhere to those overall policies established by their school and school district.

The most important responsibility for a high school athletic director is the successful management of athletic contests. The athletic director and the coaches under his supervision are directly responsible for the many phases of contest management. These responsibilities include: contracts, eligibility, athletic officials, permission to participate, physical examinations, equipment, supplies, facilities, publicity, tickets, and concessions, as well as everything from ushers and programs to entertainment and decorations. As discussed in a previous chapter, effective crowd control is one of the most serious problems facing directors of interscholastic athletics in large city school systems.

HUMAN RELATIONS IN ADMINISTRATION

Human relationships are interactions among people, and administrative relationships deal with such aspects as power, authority, motivation, morale, and status. We have previously discussed or defined these terms in a general manner; now let us probe a bit deeper to see their importance to an administrator.

Human Relations and Power and Authority

To be a successful administrator the leader must have the power and author-

ity to act. "Good administration is seen as proper action taken in the light of realism—the realism imposed through the course taken, anticipated as possible by the administrator's colleagues in the organization, by his friendly associates outside, or particularly by his opposition anywhere."[24]

In order to fulfill his administrative role in an organization, the leader should:

1. Maintain interest in the welfare of the group.
2. Understand the group, its purpose, and members that have the most influence on group opinion.
3. Understand resources, personal and material, which the group controls.
4. Set standards for the group, define a goal, develop a plan of action, and provide direction.
5. Win support of the influential group members.
6. Assign performance responsibilities.
7. Project a plan beyond its performance.
8. Use influence to discipline minority members.
9. Move ahead and expect to be followed.

All effective administration demands the possession and use of power to some degree. This we must not forget, since it is as true today as it was in the days of true autocracy. Power has been identified with prestige, influence, eminence, competence, ability, and knowledge. The administrator interacts with members of his organization through power relations and authority relations. In this interaction the administrator has power in the form of authority in the "institutionalized" form, and power itself in the "informal" organization. "Power stands behind every association and sustains its structure. Without power there is no organization and without power there is no order."[25]

Motivation, Morale, and Status

A subordinate must have confidence in his leader if the organization is to be effective in meeting its purpose. The leader must have power and authority to act, and such authority should be based upon rational grounds. If such is the case, subordinates will believe in the legality and propriety of the rules governing the organization and the right of those elevated to leadership to issue directives under such rules.

These conditions must be met if the administrator is to be effective in motivating his subordinates and in creating positive morale. At any subordinate or administrative level, individuals want to be involved in decision making in some manner. Morale can be greatly improved and self-motivation increased if employees are permitted and even encouraged to assist with the establishment of standards, goals, and programs. Such involvement will tend to increase the morale of the organization, although the measurement of a morale level at any given time is considered to be very difficult because it is comparative and its elements are largely subjective in nature. In business and industry a low level of morale is considered part of the typical picture of a bureaucracy. "The bureaucrat is viewed as weighed down with rules, procedures, and red tape, mired in his own particular rut, uninterested in getting out of it and unable to do so if he would. Likewise he is loath to exert any great effort to advance the work of the enterprise."[26] Among large corporations the company with a high level of morale is quite rare.

Status consists of the external markings which distinguish and rank individuals in relation to one another. It entails a set of value judgments of "better" or "more important." Any established organization always has a type of status system, and status always exists in a system since there is no such thing as a solitary status.

A successful administrator will attempt to improve morale by involving individuals in decisions about their own work. He will also find that this technique may help to motivate people and provide them with some measure of status. *Morale and status are vital considerations in the attempt to motivate individuals to strive toward achieving the purposes of the organization.*

ORGANIZATION AND SUPERVISORY FUNCTIONS IN SCHOOLS

It is now appropriate to present a brief overview of the organization and administration of physical education in schools, since this material will serve as an introduction to Parts II and III, which deal specifically with this area.

State and Local Authority

In the United States public education is a function of the state; therefore, the state is the supreme authority for all public schools in its jurisdiction. In most states there is a state board of education, which functions to discharge such authority. What the state can and cannot control is limited in some states by the powers of local school districts. Generally, however, state boards of education control the appropriation of state funds, the curriculum, and teacher certification.

Local authority is vested in a board of education for a school district, and such boards have the power and authority to levy taxes in order to support schools in their district. In the state of Wyoming, local school districts are provided with a great deal of "educational autonomy" and have far more power and authority than the state board of education in determining curriculum. The state only sets forth general guidelines for the districts to follow.

At the local level, school boards delegate authority and responsibility to a superintendent of schools, who exercises the authority of the board. Elementary and secondary school principals are then responsible to the superintendent.

The Organization of Elementary and Secondary Schools

The introduction of "accountability" and "performance" to American public school education has made innovation and the implementation of new or redesigned curricula much more possible than was true of public education fifteen or twenty years ago. The general public, as well as teachers and administrators, appears to be embarked on a national commitment to explore and initiate new and exciting ways of changing and improving American education. Individuals in all walks of life are now much more receptive toward educational innovation than at any other time in the history of education in the United States. This concentration on the continual search for new and more effective ways to stimulate learning has naturally caused some changes and concern in the organization, supervision, and administration of schools.

Innovations or new concepts which have been evidenced in the past several years and which have caused change in the structure of administration and organization are:[27] (1) nongraded schools, dual progress plans, continuous learning plans, and flexible scheduling practices; (2) self-contained classrooms giving way to departmentalization at the high school level and core programs and team teaching at the elementary level; (3) composition and size of class groups with the initiation of homogeneous grouping and then the promotion of heterogeneous grouping coupled with the concept of varying class size; (4) educational technology, with new technological aids providing changes in organization through individualizing instruction and making use of language laboratories and teaching machines; (5) content changes in various subject matter fields, particularly in mathematics, foreign languages, and science, with the individualized approach to education bringing about change in organization and administration; and (7) changes associated with method evidenced in the fact that teachers are now more apt to change their teaching methods and techniques as different goals and objectives undergo critical analysis and adjustment.

The old "traditional" or "standard" school design provided a general organizational pattern of a self-contained classroom whereby one teacher had the responsibility for instructing the same group of students for the same amount of time each day. This form of school organ-

izational pattern was prevalent in the 18th and 19th centuries when very few ways existed for transmitting knowledge to students except via a teacher. More group oriented instruction occurred with the development of communication technologies which came into wide usage in the 20th century. The adoption of the Carnegie unit in the early 1900's gave further support to individual learning. The Carnegie unit was the first attempt in American education to insure some national standard of quality, since all students were required to spend a definite period of time on a subject for each unit of credit earned. In some educational circles the Carnegie unit is no longer acceptable and is considered as a crude indicator of learning.

The need to recognize individual differences in learning is of great importance today, yet many obstacles impede the progress of educational change, particularly change related to organizational patterns. Criticism of today's organizational patterns in schools centers around the control of students. High school teachers and administrators are accused of becoming specialists in the control of large groups of students at catastrophic expense to their opportunity to learn. Organizational patterns which have evolved in an attempt to "free" curricula are flexible scheduling, modular scheduling, and variable course structuring (variable modular scheduling). Proponents of VCS and VMS state that variable course structuring permits organizational structures to support desirable educational goals with the emphasis on individual learning. Flexible modular scheduling usually consists of three phases: a phase for large group instruction; one for small group instruction; and a phase for individualized instruction in a laboratory type situation. Many schools have adapted physical education curricula to correspond to the scheduling practices of other courses. In physical education, at the beginning of each activity unit, a large group session may be held in which introductory material is discussed and assignments provided. Subsequent instructional periods are provided, followed by a laboratory or practical experience session. These laboratory periods usually allow a child to reinforce his physical skills and practice activities in which he needs additional reinforcement. The progression of activities and courses usually moves from very simple to the more complex motor skills.

Another organizational concept, which has been attempting to gain headway in the past ten years, is the proposal for "year-round community schools." Proposals for year-round schools are usually based on a more efficient use of facilities and teachers. With rising school costs, some citizens, especially those who are familiar with business management and efficiency concepts, feel that school facilities should be utilized twelve months of the year. Opponents of this concept are usually teachers who desire to have their summers "free", or parents and educators who believe that children deserve and require time in the summer for creative play and relaxation. Some parents who vacation in the months of June, July or August do not wish to plan their family's recreational activities at various other times during the school year, dependent upon their children's educational schedule. The entire concept, however, of year-round community schools is not geared solely to children and youth attending grades K through 12. Many of the benefits claimed by the supporters of the year-round concept involve benefits to the total community with wide participation by both children and adults.

OFFICE MANAGEMENT

A well-organized and efficient office is a very important administrative responsibility and one which is all too often overlooked by physical education and athletic administrators. If an office is well-organized and efficiently staffed, an excellent impression is conveyed to all those in the school or college.

Just as office management is an important aspect of business administration, it is also very important in any educational organization. In a departmental or cen-

tral office setting, information about personnel, equipment, and the objectives of the school are coordinated and disseminated. *Office work is said to be synonymous with information processing* and the good "management" of information is one of the foundations of most successful organizations. As with every other aspect of the school, *office management deals with people* and an effective office must be people oriented. An administrator's chief function in dealing with the delegated responsibilities of office management is to make the best possible use of resources and personnel as the department strives to reach its objectives.

Organizational Patterns

Modern day "office management" may be organized into five basic areas:[28] (1) general office management; (2) data processing; (3) systems analysis; (4) managerial functions; and (5) office personnel. A general discussion of *office management* usually deals with the overall management function of administrators, as well as office organization and an office manager's role in that organization.

Data processing is a very important aspect of most business offices and deals with computing, duplicating, office media, correspondence, and records. Many business offices are also concerned with *systems analysis,* and various "systems tools" deal with everything from time-motion study to form and layout analysis. Office working conditions (environment analysis) are a vital part of the overall systems analysis approach.

Managerial functions usually deal with the planning and organization for overall office management. *Quality* and *cost* control are perhaps the two most crucial areas which are usually presented in a discussion of the many managerial functions of office management. *Office personnel* is also one of the more critical aspects of office management as this area deals with job analysis, fringe benefits, salary, position evaluation, employee selection, and motivation of employees.

General Office Procedures

Time is a very important and valuable commodity for administrators, teachers, and clerical staff. It is important that a great deal of careful thought be devoted to the organization and supervision of office procedures. Teachers and staff should fully understand all office functions relating to "how", "where", and "when". Teachers and secretaries must adopt systematic procedures in order to operate at maximum efficiency with minimum expenditures of time and motion. *Advanced planning is a critical consideration for any school or college office.*

The Office. The physical education, intramural, and athletic office is by nature a very complex and busy organizational area. Few departments have the necessary space and secretarial staff to meet the many needs and demands for conducting physical education, athletic, recreational, and intramural programs. It is safe to say that most departmental offices are understaffed, underequipped, and crowded into very small space allocations.

If we consider that a physical education office must process information dealing with students, personnel, schedules, and facilities, as much support as possible should be provided for secretarial and clerical assistance. Secretaries usually devote the greatest percentage of their workday to the primary function of "office paper moving activities". These activities relate to preparing and duplicating tests and records, distributing these materials, and filing or storing student grades, activity schedules, and various athletic and instructional records. Data dealing with "paper moving activities" come to the department from many sources both internal and external. To be useful to the administrator and to teachers the input data received in the central office must be processed in a series of operations that eventually combine the material received into a useful coordinated output.

Any office, whether it be an administrative office or a secretarial workroom, should be airy, bright, and cheerful. Administrators should do their utmost to acquire the necessary physical space to accommodate required office furniture, equipment, and staff for the department. Whenever possible, secretaries should be permitted to choose the specific type of equipment which they would like to use. It has been demonstrated many times that if this administrative procedure is followed, the work output and morale of any clerical staff is significantly improved. Recognizing that most office personnel are overworked and underpaid, a departmental office must still present a pleasant atmosphere as it is usually the first contact between the department and the educational community.

Management Functions. Office management for the majority of physical education and athletic offices is a direct responsibility of the director or chairperson of the department. The scope and magnitude of "office operations" is naturally directly related to the size of the school in which the department is located. Unfortunately, most physical education administrators do not have enough hours in the day to keep abreast of new developments in office organization and management. As a result, office efficiency levels in many departments are very poor. Administrators must therefore do their utmost to keep up to date themselves and to see that their office staff does as well. Whenever possible, office procedures should be analyzed and, where necessary, innovations made and changes instituted. Every experienced administrator recognizes that office work is not just a necessary but minor area within his or her organization. Office management in today's schools and colleges is quickly becoming much more than a clerical-oriented approach. "Office work has suffered too long from inexact measurement, subjective standards, and loose control. Control is a primary function of management. There can be no control without standards and there can be no standards without measurement."[29]

Most physical educators are concerned with management as it pertains to a small office situation. In this type of office almost all of the paperwork and record keeping is handled by one individual. Such a secretary or clerical assist-

Figure 4–6. A bright, cheerful secretary creates an enjoyable office atmosphere.

ant must be the proverbial "jack of all trades", and must perform an entire range of clerical activities as well as being the administrator's "good right arm". Even though the office may be small and staffed by a single individual, basic principles of good office management should be followed. It is perhaps even more important for responsibilities to be clearly defined and planning to be well organized in a small office than it is in a large one. Efficient procedures are just as important for the physical education office as they are for the principal's office, and an up-to-date approach to problem solving can eliminate wasted time and inefficiency regardless of the size of the office.

Data Processing. The words "data processing" have grown to be synonymous with the use of computers. This is somewhat of a misconception because a great deal of data processing was, is, and will continue to be, conducted with paper and pencil.[30] In the educational environment data processing usually infers or implies the use of many different techniques and procedures. Among these are computing, duplicating, communicating, filing, record keeping, reporting, budgeting, and ordering equipment and supplies. Computing processes will not be discussed here because very few physical education departments at either the school or college level are fortunate enough to have data processing "hardware" available at the departmental level.

Duplicating processes include such things as: multi-copying (carbon copies, automatic typewriters, spirit and stencil processes, and off-set duplication); copying (photography, contact reproduction, xerography); and various forms of imprinting (signature machines, impression stamps and addressing methods). *Communicating processes* are usually thought to be one of the most difficult responsibilities of the secretary or clerical assistant. Communication, as discussed previously, usually involves the accurate transmission of knowledge, ideas, or opinions to the administrator, teachers, or students. Office communications may be external or internal in nature. External communication involves such things as mail service, telephone, and centrex; while internal communication involves messenger service, mechanical methods of carrying, and intercommunication systems. Secretarial correspondence is a most important aspect of data processing and the communicating process. Filing systems and their administration may also be included.

Many different types of filing media are available in today's modern offices and the various methods of organization and control of correspondence and filing should be systematically reviewed by the administrator and the secretarial staff in order to insure that modern methods are providing a high level of office efficiency. It is unfortunate that many educational offices operate at very poor efficiency levels because of inadequate funding to provide modern equipment and/or the lack of knowledge on the part of the administrator and the secretarial staff regarding the nature and use of new office techniques.

Office Personnel

Conscientious, efficient, and pleasant office personnel are vital members of any organization. Effective performance by office staff is nearly as important to the achievement of departmental goals as the performance of administrators and teachers. Many administrators consider an efficient and well-qualified secretary indispensable. Senior office personnel not only contribute significantly to the total office operation but they are also instrumental in training junior secretaries, clerical assistants, and part-time student employees.

Position Analysis. In many educational offices at both school and college levels there are well-defined differences among positions. Position analysis (job description) involves specific descriptions for various secretarial positions as well as for clerical assistants. The basic objectives in any position analysis are to determine what positions are required, the nature of these positions, and what skills, knowledge, and experience are necessary. *Job descriptions* should describe as simply, uniformly, and clearly as possible what constitutes each position. In other words, what are the daily, weekly, or monthly responsibilities and duties? *Job specifications* theoretically differ from job descriptions in that they enumerate tasks which make up the position described and often tell how frequently the tasks are performed. It is common for job specifications to include the amount and type of education or formal training required and the types of special machines or equipment which are to be used. The following section gives a sample of job descriptions.

SECRETARIAL JOB DESCRIPTIONS

JUNIOR SECRETARY, GRADE I. Takes and transcribes dictation involving limited and simple vocabulary with ordinary skill and speed. Works under supervision. May perform minor and related clerical duties. Includes beginners.

JUNIOR SECRETARY, GRADE II. Takes and transcribes dictation of difficult nature involving varied vocabulary and frequent use of unusual words and expressions. Requires considerable skill, accuracy, and speed. May take dictation by shorthand notes or machine. May also keep files, keep records, and perform other related clerical duties. Requires experience.

SECRETARY, GRADE III. A junior secretary, Grade II, who is assigned to an administrative office and, in addition to taking and transcribing dictation, sets up and maintains the files and records, and takes care of routine office functions without supervision. Little or no responsibility for meeting people, arranging appointments, handling correspondence; seldom handles confidential information.

SENIOR SECRETARY, GRADE IV. Serves as secretary to an official of the organization. (This grade is not intended to include secretaries to major administrative or executive officials of large organizations.) In addition to the functions performed by the Secretary, Grade III, meets and interviews people, schedules appointments, handles correspondence not requiring a dictated reply, and allocates mail to subordinates. In general, by the use of considerable judgment and experience relieves official of minor administrative duties.*

Employee Selection. It is often stated that an office can be no more effective than the individuals who work in it. If they are provided with the opportunity, departmental administrators should attempt to employ the best possible individual for each office position. Every attempt should be made to employ individuals who like to work in an office and who enjoy relating to both students and faculty. Such people should have the necessary training for the work they are to undertake as well as any special qualifications and attitudes necessary to work in the many diversified areas found in departments of health, physical education, recreation, athletics, and intramurals. Obviously, this is no simple task.

Prospective employees should be required to submit a letter of application

---

*Courtesy of Southwestern Publishing Company.

and appear for a personal interview. Letters of recommendation from former employers as well as the results of specific achievement and aptitude tests should also be included in the formal application. It is common for most organizations to require a trial employment prior to a continuing employment agreement. Every administrator is desirous of selecting a secretary who is both conscientious and loyal. The administrator and the senior departmental secretary should work as a team, with concentrated effort and an in-depth understanding of each other. It is common practice, where freedom of choice is permitted, for new administrators to choose their own senior secretary. Where this choice is not permitted or when a new administrator does not desire to employ a new secretary, conflicts often develop because of "shared loyalty", and/or the unwillingness of a long-tenured secretary to initiate change.

Orientation or induction periods should be provided for all new office employees. These orientation periods provide "training time" for secretaries to become acquainted with required work procedures and to adjust to pre-established work patterns. Tact, business ethics, loyalty, and discretion as they pertain to specific office tasks must be acquired during this orientation period.

Office Procedures and Secretarial Responsibilities. In a typical physical education office, office procedures and secretarial responsibilities usually include almost every type of assignment. Schedules must be prepared, tests typed, student records maintained, competition results distributed, letters written, and travel arrangements confirmed. General and specific office procedures must therefore be clearly defined and recorded so they are readily available to all office personnel and teachers. If there are two or more office personnel working together, authority or leadership roles must be established either officially or unofficially. "Office leadership" is usually delegated or assigned to the senior secretary. This individual is then responsible for the overall coordination of the total office. This type of supervisor should plan, organize, and control the work of other employees, both those who are full-time and those who are part-time assistants. The senior secretary who assumes, or is delegated this supervisory role should clearly understand the nature and degree of delegated authority and responsibility.

The departmental chairperson should also make it very clear to all other office personnel what their delegated responsibilities are and the specific degree of delegated authority (to make decisions) which their position holds.

REFERENCES

1. Robert Dubin: *Human Relations in Administration*. Englewood Cliffs, N.J.: Prentice-Hall, Inc., 1961, p. 26.
2. William H. Newman: *Administrative Action—The Techniques of Organization and Management*. Englewood Cliffs, N.J.: Prentice-Hall, Inc., 1963, p. 1.
3. John M. Pfiffner and Robert V. Presthus: *Public Administration*. New York: The Ronald Press Company, 1960, p. 5.
4. *Ibid.*, p. 5.
5. Robert Dubin, *op. cit.*, p. 140.
6. *Ibid.*, p. 262.
7. *Ibid.*, p. 277.
8. *Ibid.*, p. 283.
9. Chester I. Barnard: *The Functions of the Executive*. Cambridge, Mass.: Harvard University Press, 1938, p. 188.
10. *Ibid.*, p. 190.
11. *Ibid.*, p. 189.
12. American Association of School Administrators: *Management by Objectives and Results—A Guidebook for Today's School Executives*. Arlington, Virginia, 1973, p. 2.
13. Harl R. Douglass: *Modern Administration of Secondary Schools*. Boston: Ginn and Company, 1954, p. 9.
14. Francis Griffith: "Six Mistaken Meanings of Democratic Administration." *Phi Delta Kappan*, October, 1966, p. 59.
15. James J. Jones, C. Jackson Salisbury, and Ralph L. Spencer: *Secondary School Administration*. New York: McGraw-Hill Book Co., 1969, p. 93.
16. Conrad Driner: *Administrators and Accountability, Accountability in American Education*. Boston: Allyn and Bacon, Inc., 1972, p. 135.
17. R. K. Ready: *The Administrator's Job: Issues and Dilemmas*. New York: McGraw-Hill Book Co., 1967, p. 32.
18. Dubin, *op. cit.*, p. 3.
19. Newman, *op. cit.*, p. 1.
20. John F. Foley: "Critical Duties of Administrators of Health, Physical Education, and Recreation," *Directions*, Council of City and County Directors, September, 1965.
21. James H. Humphrey, Alice M. Love, and Leslie W. Irwin: *Principles and Techniques of Supervision in Physical Education*. Dubuque, Iowa: Wm. C. Brown Co., 1972, p. 4.
22. Louis E. Means: *Intramurals—Their Organization and Administration*. Englewood Cliffs, N.J.: Prentice-Hall, Inc., 1973, p. 27.
23. Charles E. Forsythe and Irvin A. Keller: *Administration of High School Athletics*. Englewood Cliffs, N.J.: Prentice-Hall, Inc., 1972, p. 147.
24. C. T. Hardwick and B. F. Landuyt: *Administrative Strategy and Decision Making*. Cincinnati: South-Western Publishing Co., 1966, p. 3.
25. Robert Bierstedt: "Power and Social Organization." *American Sociological Review*, No. 15, December, 1950, pp. 730–736.
26. Marshall E. Dimock and Howard K. Hyde: TNEC Monograph No. 11, "Bureaucracy and Trusteeship in Large Corporation." Washington, D.C.: U.S. Government Printing Office, 1940, p. 33.
27. David W. Beggs and Edward G. Buffie: *Independent Study, Bold New Venture*. Bloomington, Ind.: Indiana University Press, 1971, p. 206.
28. Irene Place, Charles B. Hicks, and Robin L. Wilkinson: *Office Management*. San Francisco: Canfield Press, 1971, p. xii.
29. *Ibid.*, p. 57.
30. *Ibid.*, p. 48.

SUGGESTED READINGS

American Association of School Administrators: *Management by Objectives and Results—A Guidebook for Today's School Executives:* Arlington, Virginia, 1973, p. 2

Dubin, Robert: *Human Relations in Administration.* Englewood Cliffs, N.J.: Prentice-Hall, Inc., 1961, p. 26.

Humphrey, James H., Alice M. Love, and Leslie W. Irwin: *Principles and Techniques of Supervision in Physical Education.* Dubuque, Iowa: Wm. C. Brown Co. 1972, p. 4.

Place, Irene, Charles B. Hicks, and Robin L. Wilkinson: *Office Management.* San Francisco: Canfield Press, 1971, p. xii.

Woodward, Theodore, John A. Pendery, and Howard L. Newhouse: *Secretarial Office Procedures for Colleges.* Chicago: South-Western Publishing Co., 1972.

II
STRUCTURING PHYSICAL EDUCATION IN SCHOOLS

CHAPTER FIVE

Organizational Procedures and Designs

BASIC ADMINISTRATIVE FOUNDATIONS

Before instructional procedures can be initiated, classes formed, and activities begun, certain administrative foundations must be determined. Instructional programs in physical education must have foundations to build on just as academic programs must, since without such foundations there can be no effective plans for developing instruction.

Daily Participation

There is sufficient evidence that physical education should be a required program from kindergarten through grade 12. However, since physical education is a comparatively recent addition to the school curriculum, it has never enjoyed the respected place in the curriculum that academic subjects have held. Although physical education makes a tremendous contribution to health, a defi-

101

nite policy requiring physical education has been noticeably lacking.

Although in some school systems physical education is mandatory from kindergarten through the 12th grade, for the most part the inclusion of physical education in the curriculum is erratic and uncertain. Figure 5–1 verifies this statement. The requirement is the program, and as the requirement is gradually chipped away, the program likewise disappears. In places where the state requirement is dropped in certain grades, participation in physical education gradually decreases until there is none at all. All subject areas that maintain a constant place in the curriculum, such as English, do so because they are required.

Many national groups whose membership consists of a cross section of educators, physicians, lay people, and others strongly recommend a daily program in physical education. The President's

Council on Physical Fitness and Sports at its quarterly meeting on May 26, 1971, unanimously recommended that "All school children in grades K–12 should be required to participate in daily programs of physical education emphasizing the development of physical fitness and sports skills."[1]

Over the years, other groups of national importance, such as the National Conference for the Mobilization of Health Education and Physical Education[2] and the National Conference on Fitness of Secondary Youth,[3] have strongly recommended a daily requirement in physical education on the secondary level.

More recently, the Society of State Directors of Health, Physical Education and Recreation issued the following statement, which covered all aspects of required physical education from prekindergarten through grade 12:

(Text continued on page 105)

TIME AND GRADE REQUIREMENTS FOR PHYSICAL EDUCATION IN ELEMENTARY AND SECONDARY SCHOOLS—STATES AND POSSESSIONS

State	Required by Law or Regulation	Time Requirement	Grade Requirement
Alabama	Yes	1-6—30 m/day; 7-8—daily; 9-12—1 credit	1 through 12
Alaska	Yes	1-8 required but no time specified; 9-12—1 credit	1 through 12; secondary 1 credit required
Arizona	No	Recommended only; 1-3—10% of day; 4-8—14% of day; 9-12 not specified	None
Arkansas	Yes	1-8 required but no time specified; 9-12—1 credit	1 through 12; secondary 1 credit required
California	Yes	1-6—200 m/2 wks; 7-12—400 m/2 wks	1 through 12
Colorado	No	None (Physical education in grades 1 through 12 is required for state accreditation)	Non-regulatory state
Connecticut	Yes	Not specified	Required by law in elementary and secondary schools; grade level optional
Delaware	Yes	1-6—suggested 200-250 m/wk; 7-8—2 periods/wk; 9-10—2 periods/wk one semester, 3 periods/wk adjacent semester; 11-12 elective	1 through 10; 11-12 elective (effective April 1970)
District of Columbia	Yes	Grade 1—150 m/wk; 2-6—125 m/wk (combined with health); 7-9—90 m/wk; 10-11—3 periods/wk; 12 elective	1 through 12
Florida	Yes	1-6—daily period; 7-8—90 periods/yr (2 55-m periods/wk); 9-12—2 credits	1 through 8; 9-12—2 credits

Figure 5–1. Time and grade requirements for physical education. (From Greene, Andrew: "State Legal Requirements for Physical Education." Washington, D.C.: *JOHPER*, April, 1971, p. 19.)

Illustration continued on the opposite page

State	Required by Law or Regulation	Time Requirement	Grade Requirement
Georgia	Yes	1-8—30 m/day (combined HE & PE)	1 through 8
Hawaii	Yes	K-6—90 m/wk; 7-10—½ credit/yr	K through 10
Idaho	Yes	1-8 not required; 9-12—1 credit	9-12—1 credit
Illinois	Yes	1-12 daily period equal in length to other subject periods	1 through 12
Indiana	Yes	1-6—10% of day recommended; 7-8—15% of day recommended; 9-12—1 credit	9 through 12—1 credit required
Iowa	Yes	50 m/wk minimum	1 through 12
Kansas	Yes	9-12—55 m/day	1 through 8 recommended only; 9-12 required
Kentucky	Yes	1-8—120 m/wk; 9-12—1 semester (suggested in 9 or 10)	1 through 8; 9 through 12—1 semester or ½ credit for graduation
Louisiana	Yes	1-8—120 m/wk; 9-12—150 m/wk minimum, 300 m/wk maximum	1 through 12
Maine	Yes	1-11—2 periods/wk for all pupils in public schools	1 through 11
Maryland	Yes	1-6 required but no time specified; 7-8 daily period; 9 daily where possible, 9-12—1 credit	1 through 12; 9-12—1 credit
Massachusetts	Yes	1-6—90 m/wk; 7-12—120 m/wk	1 through 12
Michigan	Yes	Not specified	Not specified
Minnesota	Yes	1-6—30 m/day; 7-10—2 55-min periods/wk	1 through 10
Mississippi	Yes	1-6—20 to 30 m/day	1 through 6
Missouri	Yes (use voluntary classification plan)	1-6—2 30-min periods/wk; 7-12 required but no time specified	1 through 12
Montana	Yes	1-3—15 m/day; 4-6—20 m/day; 7-8—30 m/day; 9-10—3 periods/wk	1 through 10
Nebraska	No	None by law; for accreditation—elementary 150 m/wk; secondary 2 55-m periods/wk	Can get accreditation for meeting indicated requirements
Nevada	Yes	1-8 not specified; 9-12—3 years 5 daily periods/wk	9 through 12—3 years required
New Hampshire	No	None	New law in 1972 will require PE at all levels
New Jersey	Yes	1-12—150 m/wk	1 through 12 (includes some health education)
New Mexico	Yes	1-3—125 m/wk; 4-6—150 m/wk; 7-8 equivalent of 1 period/day for 1 year; 9-12 equivalent of 1 period/day for 1 year	1 through 6; 7-8 equivalent of 1 period/day for 1 year; 9-12 equivalent of 1 period/day for 1 year
New York	Yes	1-6—120 m/wk.; 7-12—300 m/wk	1 through 12
North Carolina	Yes	1-8—150 m/wk; 9 daily period (combined with health)	1 through 9

Figure 5-1 continued

Illustration continued on the following page.

State	Required by Law or Regulation	Time Requirement	Grade Requirement
North Dakota	Yes	Daily instruction for all	1 through 12
Ohio	Yes	1-8—100 m/wk; 9-12—2 periods/wk for 2 years	1 through 12 (dependent upon fulfillment of 2 yr requirement)
Oklahoma	No	None	None
Oregon	Yes	K-3—10% of school day; 4-6—15% of school day; 7-8—35-45 m/day; 9-10—45-60 m/day; 11-12 optional	K through 10; 11-12 optional but strongly recommended
Pennsylvania	Yes	1-6 daily but no time specified; 7-12—2 periods/wk but no time specified	1 through 12
Rhode Island	Yes	1-12 average of 20 m/day (combined with health)	1 through 12
South Carolina	Yes	1-6 daily period; 7-8—2 or 3 periods/wk; 9-12—1 credit	1 through 8; 9 through 12—1 credit required for graduation (may apply 2 credits toward graduation)
South Dakota	Yes	1-9—90 m/wk	1 through 9
Tennessee	Yes	1-6—30 m/day; 7-8—1 hr twice weekly or 45 m alternate days or 30 m/day; 9-12—1 credit	1 through 12; 9 through 12—1 credit required
Texas	Yes	1-6 required but no time specified; 7-8—130 clock hrs/yr (minimum); 9-12—1½ credits (240 clock hrs)	1 through 12; 9 through 12—1½ credits required
Utah	Yes	1-6—30 m/day recommended; 7-9—1 semester; 10-12—1 semester in 2 of 3 grades	7 through 12 (time requirements indicated)
Vermont	Yes	1-8 no time specified; 9-12—1 credit	1 through 12
Virginia	Yes	1-8 no time specified; 9-12—3 credits required of combined health & physical education	1 through 12
Washington	Yes	1-8—20 m/day; 9-12—90 m/wk	1 through 12
West Virginia	Yes	1-6—30 m/day; 7-8—1 period/day; 9-12—minimum of 2 periods/wk	1 through 12
Wisconsin	Yes	1-6 daily period; 7-12—3 periods/wk	1 through 12
Wyoming	Yes	1-8 required but no time specified	1 through 8

POSSESSIONS

State	Required by Law or Regulation	Time Requirement	Grade Requirement
Canal Zone	Yes	1-6—30 m/day; 7-12—55 m/day	1 through 12
Guam	Yes	1-6 no time specified; 7 and 9—1 period/day; 10 and 11—1 period/day	1 through 6; 7 and 9; 10 and 11
Puerto Rico	Yes	1-6—80 m/wk; 7-9—50 m/wk; 10-12—250 m/wk elective	1 through 9; 10 through 12 elective
Virgin Islands	Yes	1-6—45 m/wk; 7-10—180 m/wk	1 through 10

Figure 5-1 continued

Physical education is essential for all students from pre-kindergarten through grade 12. The daily instructional period for elementary school students (pre-K, K–6) should be at least 30 minutes in length, exclusive of time allotted for dressing, showering, recess, free and/or supervised play periods, and noon-hour activities.

The minimum instructional class period for middle schools and junior and senior high schools should be a standard class period daily, except where the length and frequency of the class periods are altered to offer students a more comprehensive program. Where modular or flexible scheduling is used, care should be taken to involve students in some combination of at least 300 minutes of physical education per week spread over three or more days.[4]

Two position papers on physical education appeared in 1971. One listed the essentials of a quality elementary program, and the other stated guidelines for secondary physical education. Both of these publications recommended daily physical education. On the elementary level, they agreed that "to best serve the activity needs of children, a daily program is recommended."[5] The paper dealing with secondary education firmly stated that "a daily instructional period of directed physical education should be provided for all secondary school students equivalent in length to that found in the regular school pattern."[6]

Outstanding educators have for many years pointed out the need for requiring physical education. James B. Conant, a leading educator, has said "I am convinced that ideally a period of physical education should be required of all students in grades 1 through 12 every day...."[7]

Further emphasizing the importance of requiring physical education, Paul Briggs, Superintendent of Schools, Cleveland, Ohio, stated, "...revitalized, expanded programs are needed in urban America."[8]

Physicians also have endorsed the need for requirements in physical education. Fred Allman, Jr., M.D., of Atlanta, Georgia, states, "I feel very strongly that physical education should be required for all children, grades 1 through 12." He justifies his stand by the following reasons:

Socioeconomic changes which have taken place in the past 20 years have placed a new responsibility on physical education programs and instructors. Recent medical research has indicated that degenerative disease and increased mortality are associated with a sedentary life and that physical fitness improves physiological efficiency and results in an increase in endurance, strength, and agility. People who exercise regularly live longer and are less likely to suffer from degenerative diseases. Good health habits must be learned and practiced during the adolescent years and carried out all through life.[9]

Other physicians support a required daily program for all students in all grades. Their opinions may be summarized by Thomas Quigley of Boston, who says:

Generations of experience have established that the growing young body needs and should have daily, supervised exercise. It seems tragic to see a state or school district take or consider the backward step of deleting the requirement of daily health and physical instruction in the schools.[10]

In addition to the tremendous support given physical education for physiological and fitness reasons, there is much research to show that the level of physical fitness has a direct relationship to academic achievement. Gruber noted this in an address to the American Association for the Advancement of Science, saying, "All children should have daily physical education."[11]

The American Medical Association for many years has supported physical education in schools and colleges. At Miami Beach in 1960, the House of Delegates of the Association passed the following resolution:

Whereas, the medical profession has helped to pioneer physical education in our schools and colleges and thereafter has encouraged and supported sound programs in this field; and

Whereas, there is increasing evidence that proper exercise is a significant factor in the maintenance of health and the prevention of degenerative disease; and

Whereas, advancing automation has reduced the amount of physical activity in daily living, although the need for exercise to foster proper development of our young people remains constant; and

Whereas, there is a growing need for the development of physical skills that can be applied throughout life in the constructive and wholesome use of leisure time; and

Whereas, in an age of mounting tensions, enjoyable physical activity can be helpful in the relief of stress and strain, and consequently in preserving mental health; therefore be it

Resolved, that the American Medical Association through its various divisions and departments and its constituent and component medical societies do everything feasible to encourage effective instruction in physical education in our schools and colleges.[12]

A convincing argument for daily physical education participation is the research by Johnson. His study attempted to show the relationship of daily physical education classes as opposed to merely two or three classes per week on *physical fitness,* skill performance, adipose tissue, and growth. The results indicated that students who were involved in the daily program were superior in *fitness* and skill performance, and had less adipose tissue than those who were scheduled for physical education only two or three days per week. It is generally agreed that physical fitness is a basic objective of physical education. This study should reinforce the efforts of administrators to provide daily programs for all students.[13]

Research discloses that boys and girls during the formative years need between three and five hours of vigorous activity daily for normal growth and development. This daily requirement is necessary to provide motivation, instruction, and guidance for all students in activities that may be carried over to after-school participation.

A recent survey of adult participation indicated the need for more physical education in the elementary schools. The report showed that only 47 per cent of the individuals surveyed had had any physical education in elementary school.[14] Physical education should receive high priority in elementary school, since it is during the early years that lifetime attitudes toward exercise are formed.

It should be noted that not all physical education teachers and administrators feel that a physical education program should be required. Some argue that because many students dislike the program, to force them to participate is foolish, since the outcome would be of doubtful value. However, many students dislike not only physical education but also English, mathematics, and many other subjects. The answer is to change the content and the teaching procedure to make the program more interesting—not to drop the requirement. In physical education, offering a choice of activities within the requirement is one trend that offers considerable promise in developing interest in the subject. (See Chapter 7.) A second argument against required physical education is that physical education is natural and that a majority of students would elect it if they had an option. This argument is not consistent with the facts. In those schools where the requirement has been dropped, the program has gradually disappeared. To offset this trend, supervised play or recreational programs may be offered, but this is not true physical education.

Since health and fitness are basic objectives of physical education, it seems logical to require all students to participate in a daily program as recommended by medical and educational groups and leaders. A promising trend is the increase in the physical education requirement on the state level during the six-year period from 1964 to 1970. The most noticeable increase has been on the elementary level. Figure 5–1 provides an overview of state regulations regarding time and grade requirements for physical education.

However, it is dangerous for teachers to assume that the requirement itself can serve as protection against poor and uninteresting programs. Teachers should, within the requirement, develop plans for making instruction as interesting and effective as possible.

The authors of this text strongly support a daily requirement in physical education. The supporting evidence for this requirement in the preceding paragraphs has been developed to enable teachers and physical education leaders to impress superintendents, curriculum planners, board members, and others with the importance of providing adequate time for physical education in the school program.

Credit

Administrators, while laying the groundwork for the school curriculum, should be aware of the need for and the importance of physical education, and assign to it the same credit toward graduation that is traditionally assigned to academic subjects. Experience reveals that for subjects in the curriculum to maintain a position of respectability, they must carry credit toward graduation. Although the need for credit in physical education is apparent, only token recognition has been given. In school systems where physical education is placed on the same credit basis as other subjects in the curriculum, not only is the program respected by teachers and students but also greater interest is shown by students, and a more effective program is the result.

Under no circumstances, however, should the credit for physical education be used to justify poor administrative techniques. When a student has *valid reasons* for failing to achieve the required credits in physical education, his promotion or graduation should not be denied because of such credit deficiency. One valid reason would be physical disability. Court rulings in such matters have nearly always been in favor of the student. A case in point involved a disabled 17-year-old girl who lacked a quarter of a credit and was not granted a diploma. She had undergone a serious spinal injury which precluded her participation in physical education. The court ruled in favor of the student and she was granted a diploma.[15] For individuals who are physically unable to participate in physical education, some type of alternative program should be provided. Attending classes, observing procedures, and writing papers on the program constitute an alternative that is fair to both the student and the teacher. When teachers and administrators refuse to be flexible in extreme cases such as the one just described, the resulting actions by the parents and courts will undoubtedly produce unfavorable attitudes toward the program.

Teachers and Class Size

Administrators should give considerable attention to the number of teachers needed for the program and the size of the classes they are to teach. Just as the student-teacher ratio is carefully determined for academic subjects, a definite policy should be made and adhered to for physical education. Not only is it extremely difficult to effectively teach classes that range from 50 to 100 students, but the supervision required to insure adequate safety is almost impossible.

Various suggestions have been offered regarding the number of teachers and the size of classes in physical education. *Guidelines for Secondary Physical Education* recommends that class size be comparable to other subjects but with variations where necessary.[16] On the elementary level, the prevailing opinion seems to be that the number of different classes assigned per day is a better criterion for determining teaching load than the actual number of hours spent teaching.[17] Realistically, 30 to 40 students per teacher would seem to be a practical class size. With this student-teacher ratio, the number of teachers needed is easily determined.

The Number of Stations and Teachers Needed. The number of stations and teachers needed in physical education should be determined the same way as for other subjects. The elements involved are the number of students assigned, the average class size, the number of periods in the day, and the types of activities involved. These elements, placed in the following formula, provide a sound guideline for determining the number of stations needed.

$$\frac{\text{Number of students}}{\text{assigned to physical}} \times \frac{\text{Number of periods}}{\text{Total number of class}}$$
$$\frac{\text{education}}{\text{Class load}} \times \frac{\text{class meets weekly}}{\text{periods in school week}}$$

= Number of stations needed

In a junior high school with 1200 students enrolled daily in physical education, a class size of 40 students per teacher, and a six-bell day, the number of stations would be calculated as follows:

$$\frac{1200}{40} \times \frac{5}{30} = \frac{6000}{1200} \text{ or 5 stations needed}$$

The number of stations needed in the elementary school may be determined by the following formula:

$$\frac{\text{Number}}{\text{of classrooms}} \times \frac{\begin{array}{c}\text{Number of physical} \\ \text{education periods per} \\ \text{week per class}\end{array}}{\begin{array}{c}\text{Total periods in} \\ \text{school week}\end{array}}$$

= Number of stations needed

In an elementary school with 24 classrooms and ten 30-minute periods daily, the number of stations needed may be determined as follows:

$$24 \times \frac{5}{50} = \frac{120}{50} = 2.4 \text{ or 2 stations needed}$$

The same formula determines the number of teachers needed to provide instruction. In the first situation shown above, six teachers would be needed, since each usually has a free period for planning in a six-bell day. The same procedure is followed in the elementary school with a minimum of two or three teachers. Teaching stations will be discussed further in Chapter 10.

INTERNAL ORGANIZATIONAL DESIGNS

Through the years many plans have evolved as educators experimented with the internal organization of schools in their efforts to provide better ways of conducting instructional programs. It is extremely difficult to determine which is the best plan, since so many variables—number of students, type of school, number of teachers, community attitudes, financial resources, equipment, and so on—are involved. However, regardless of the type of existing organization they find themselves in, physical educators should have an in-depth knowledge of all of the various plans. *An understanding of these plans may be the determining factor in establishing the status of physical education in the administrative structure.*

The generally accepted patterns of organization are (1) *horizontal* and (2) *vertical*. Each of these will be briefly discussed as it applies at both the elementary and secondary levels.

Elementary Level

Horizontal Pattern. Horizontal organization consists of the assignment of teachers to the various groups of students at the same grade level. The horizontal pattern in the elementary school is based on (1) the self-contained classroom, (2) departmentalization, (3) ability grouping, and (4) team teaching.

1. SELF-CONTAINED CLASSROOM. The self-contained classroom organization places the entire responsibility for instruction in all areas on one classroom teacher. Students remain with the same teacher the entire day throughout the year. Proponents of the self-contained classroom claim that the plan is more conducive to meeting the individual needs of young children, since the teacher spends more time with them. Opponents of the plan feel that overall instruction is weak, since one person cannot be sufficiently qualified to teach all subjects adequately. This premise is

probably the reason various innovative plans are replacing the self-contained organization in many school systems.

2. DEPARTMENTALIZATION. Various forms of departmentalization appear in many of the nation's elementary schools. As contrasted with the self-contained classroom plan, more than one teacher is involved in instruction. In some places there is a different teacher for each subject. Departmentalization requires a specialist in one or several subjects, with each subject receiving an appropriate daily time allotment. Many educators feel that children receive better instruction when specialists in the fields of physical education, music, art, English, mathematics, and so on, are responsible for the instruction.

3. ABILITY GROUPING. Ability grouping is a system that places students in relatively homogeneous groups based on intellectual capacity, academic achievement, or physical performance. Theoretically, students in such groups should proceed at their own individual speed and complete a span of work faster than they would in the traditional class. However, academic education research has not shown ability grouping to be superior to heterogeneous classification. The need for ability grouping in physical education will be discussed in Chapter 8.

4. TEAM TEACHING. Educators are continually seeking new ways of improving teaching techniques and staff utilization. A trend that is finding increasing acceptance in many schools is the team-teaching concept. Team teaching is a departure from the self-contained classroom plan in that two or more teachers, usually under a leader, work together to form an instructional team. The team plan utilizes the special talents of each teacher and provides a greater opportunity to utilize teacher time and talents more effectively. Teachers are free to plan programs, organize classes, secure materials and teach the area in which they are best qualified. One teacher may lecture or use multimedia to a large group of students while the other teachers deal with small groups for remedial work, evaluation, or individualized instruction.

Although team teaching is rapidly replacing the traditional pattern in the elementary schools, educators do not agree on its effectiveness. Views both for and against this technique have been presented by leading educators.

Colman and Budahl, for example, list several recognized limitations to team teaching:

1. Many teachers are not suited by training or disposition to engage in the cooperative planning and varied use of procedures, resources, and personnel that are essential to team teaching. In fact, it is often maintained that if a teacher is thoroughly competent in teaching his particular subject, team teaching is not necessary.

2. Team teaching calls for the use of special physical facilities that must be provided at considerable expense if not already available. Many older schools simply do not have the necessary large rooms for some phases of teaming.

3. Special planning periods must be scheduled at a time when all team members can meet. In order to make such meetings possible, the administrator sometimes must ask for concessions for team members or impose restrictions on non-team members.

4. The per-student cost of team teaching is sometimes higher than the per-student cost of conventional teaching, because many teams are comprised of nonprofessional aides, paraprofessionals, and clerical assistants in addition to full-time certified teachers.

5. The necessary impersonality of large group instruction hampers the emotional, social, and academic progress of certain students who need consistent, individual contact with their teachers. Team teachers seldom become well enough acquainted with individual students in a large group to be able to meet their needs effectively.

6. Planning essential to productive team teaching often becomes unduly complicated, and the end result may not justify the expenditure of professional time and energy. If individualized instruction in both the small and large groups is not planned with great care, team teaching may be less effective than traditional classroom instruction.[18]

Meyer, on the other hand, offers the following arguments in favor of team teaching:

HEALTH, PHYSICAL EDUCATION AND SAFETY DEPARTMENT
NORFOLK CITY PUBLIC SCHOOLS

Master Schedule For The Elementary School

Grade 1

8:30 / 8:40	Opening Exercises
9:00 / 11:00	Language Arts
11:00 / 11:20	Lunch
11:20 / 12:00	Change Classes Rest - Storytime - Sharing
12:00 / 12:45	Math
12:45 / 1:20	Social Studies Science
1:20 / 1:50	Physical Education Monday and Wednesday or Tuesday and Thursday 2 Classes on Friday
1:50 / 2:00	Evaluation Dismissal

Grade 2

8:30 / 8:40	Opening Exercises
9:00 / 11:15	Language Arts
11:20 / 11:40	Lunch
11:40 / 12:15	Storytime Art
12:20 / 12:50	Physical Education Monday and Wednesday or Tuesday and Thursday 2 Classes on Friday
12:50 / 1:00	Rest Period
1:00 / 1:30	Math
1:30 / 2:00	Social Studies Science

Grade 3

8:30 / 8:40	Opening Exercises
9:00 / 11:00	Language Arts
11:10 / 11:40	Lunch
11:50 / 12:20	Physical Education
12:30 / 1:30	Social Studies Science Handwriting
1:30 / 2:15	Math
2:15 / 2:30	Evaluation Dismissal

Grade 4

8:30 / 8:40	Opening Exercises
8:40 / 10:50	Language Arts
10:50 / 11:30	Math TV Science
11:30 / 12:10	Science
12:15 / 12:45	Lunch
12:50 / 1:20	Physical Education
1:25 / 2:20	Social Studies
2:20 / 2:30	Evaluation Dismissal

Grade 5

8:30 / 8:40	Opening Exercises
8:45 / 9:40	Math
9:40 / 10:10	Physical Education
10:10 / 11:10	Social Studies and Science
11:10 / 11:40	Strings and Activities
11:40 / 12:05	Lunch
12:05 / 12:20	Current Events
12:20 / 2:20	Language Arts
2:20 / 2:30	Evaluation Dismissal

Grade 6

8:30 / 8:40	Opening Exercises
8:40 / 9:35	Math
9:35 / 10:40	Social Studies and Science
10:50 / 11:20	Physical Education Monday 2 classes Tues.-Fri. Physical Education 1 Class
10:50 / 11:20	Physical Education 1 Class
11:10 / 11:50	Activities Strings Science TV
11:50 / 12:15	Lunch
12:15 / 2:20	Language Arts
2:20 / 2:30	Evaluation Dismissal

Grade 7

8:30 / 8:40	Opening Exercises
8:40 / 9:10	Physical Education (Boys) Girls Reading
9:10 / 9:40	Physical Education (Girls) Boys Reading
9:45 / 10:45	English or Math
10:45 / 11:40	Math or English
11:45 / 12:40	Social Studies or Science
12:45 / 1:15	Lunch
1:15 / 2:00	Science or Social Studies
2:00 / 2:30	Band, Chorus, Study

Figure 5–2. Daily master schedule for elementary school, showing physical education in the team-teaching pattern. (Courtesy of Taylor Elementary School, Norfolk, Virginia.)

1. Team teaching has tremendous potential as the vehicle essential for interdisciplinary teaching from the state of theory to one of fact.

2. The major thrust of teaming for instruction of youth is to improve the quality of instruction and individualize it; to extend specialized teaching competencies of staff; and to provide a more flexible basis or organization in terms of student, staff, time, and curriculum.[19]

A problem arising from the team-teaching procedure is the question of the place of physical education in this type of curriculum. In some instances efforts have been made to schedule large numbers of students in physical education in order to release classroom teachers for small-group instruction. This plan is unsatisfactory for two reasons: first, one teacher cannot satisfactorily teach a large number of students the skills of physical education activities; second, the element of safety should prohibit scheduling of large groups of students to a single teacher. The best that could be expected from a situation of this nature would be a supervised play period, which is not physical education.

In elementary schools the team-teaching plan that offers the best arrangement for physical education is the procedure in which full-time physical education teachers are used to teach all of the physical education program, releasing the classroom teacher for other assignments. Figure 5–2 shows a schedule of this type. Team teaching in the actual physical education class will be discussed in Chapter 8.

Vertical Pattern

Vertical organization is synonymous with the graded school. Students move upward from one grade to another after having completed the standard instructional material designed for each grade. Dissatisfaction with the graded plan led to various experiments in an attempt to allow students to progress at their own speed. The following plans illustrate attempts to break away from the graded curriculum:

1. *Multi-Graded School.* Multi-graded schools are illustrations of a departure from the graded plan in which students in two or more grades are placed in the same room. Students study in several grades at the same time.

2. *Nongraded School.* The most popular plan is the nongraded school in which all grade barriers are eliminated. This plan allows students to progress at their own rate of speed, since they are grouped by academic achievement instead of by age.

3. *Multi-Unit School.* A rather new concept in the elementary schools is the multi-unit school. This plan provides an alternative to the self-contained classroom by replacing the classroom with a nongraded instructional and research unit. Each unit consists of 100 to 150 students within the four age groups (4–6, 6–9, 8–11, 10–12) and a leader, several staff members, an intern, and aides. The second level of organization consists of the leaders and principal, who plan, implement, and evaluate.

Research shows that the multi-unit plan positively influences the achievement of students who are enrolled. Other findings indicate more individualized instruction, greater teacher morale, more teacher preparation and a decrease in delinquency.[20]

Secondary Level

The secondary level has not experimented with innovative plans to the extent that elementary level has, largely because of the pressure for college preparation, which is controlled by the Carnegie unit. However, in recent years, many high schools have provided alternatives to traditional organization plans and are experimenting with more viable programs that relate to the changing needs of society today.

Horizontal Pattern

The horizontal pattern in the secondary school usually involves either comprehensive or specialized schools. The comprehensive high school encompasses the various background interests and abilities of students in one educational center. It attempts to provide educational opportunity for all youth in the community. In the comprehensive school, students will find an array of college preparatory, vocational, general, and elective courses. The comprehensive school, truly an American invention, endeavors to offset the shortcomings of maintaining separate academic or vocational schools.

In contrast to the comprehensive high school is the specialized school which provides specialized curricula in vocational education, college preparatory, fine arts, or scientific areas. Of the specialized schools, the vocational school is the most prevalent in many large cities. Strengthened by federal funding, these schools are growing rapidly in number as more emphasis is placed on technical education. With the de-emphasizing of college preparatory education and the trend toward skill development, the vocational school can be expected to become increasingly popular, especially in metropolitan areas.

Although there is considerable debate as to which type of school provides the better education, achievement tests show that comprehensive high school students have usually made a higher average score than private college-preparatory school students in 8 out of 10 subject areas.[21]

In the horizontal pattern, physical ed-

ucation is usually on a daily requirement basis. If students are transported away from the comprehensive school to a vocational center, physical education should be scheduled in the morning, thus insuring its inclusion in the student's daily schedule.

Vertical Pattern

The vertical pattern involves the grouping of grades into administrative units for instruction. Many different plans are in current use, and there is no one "best" plan. Local conditions and philosophy must determine which grouping is most satisfactory.

There are two types of vertical patterns: the traditional and the nontraditional. The traditional organizational pattern places the first eight grades in the elementary level and the remaining four in the secondary level. It is usually known as the 8–4 plan, with the kindergarten added to the elementary level.

If we envision the nontraditional pattern as an upward arrangement of grades (K–12), it would include the several grouping plans shown in Figure 5–3. The more prevalent groupings in the vertical pattern are the junior high (6-3-3), the middle school (4-4-4), and the junior-senior high school (6-6).

In the vertical pattern, so long as the

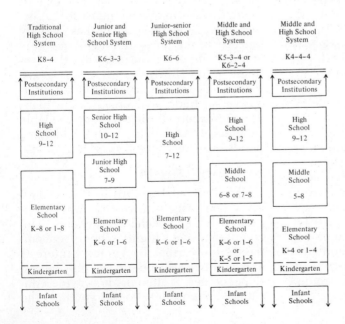

Figure 5–3. Patterns of school organization. (From Alexander, William M., et al.: *The High School: Today and Tomorrow.* New York: Holt, Rinehart & Winston, 1971, p. 8.)

daily requirement in physical education is followed, physical education enjoys respectable status in the curriculum.

TYPES OF SCHOOLS AND HOW THEY AFFECT PHYSICAL EDUCATION

The Community School

The community school plan provides a reciprocal opportunity between schools and the community for the use of facilities, instructional ideas, learning experiences, and leadership. The community school concept is best illustrated by the program in Flint, Michigan, which is sponsored by the Mott Foundation. The entire educational community is involved in the many facets of the program. Schools are never closed, and the facilities are always available. A visit to the schools discloses a variety of programs, from swimming to Bishop sewing. In some sections of the city the school may be the center for major community activities, bringing together people of all ages, ethnic groups, and economic status.

The Flint program, which involves many cooperating organizations, is an example of what may be accomplished when public and private enterprise mutually accept a challenge. The board of trustees of the Mott Foundation selected the Flint Board of Education to administer its grants for the development of health, recreation, and educational programs.

Community schools are in operation today in many sections of the country. In 1971 it was reported that there were 1920 community schools scattered throughout the nation.[22] Some of the more outstanding programs exist in Los Angeles, California; Monterey, California; Dade County, Florida; New Haven, Connecticut; and Springfield, Ohio.

The major reason for the strong support for community education is that it makes economic sense. In many areas, costly school plants remain idle for long periods of time. Coordinating the use of these buildings 24 hours a day for all people seems logical and practical. New buildings that are planned for school-community use can provide more facilities for both school and community, since duplication of construction is eliminated.

Physical education occupies an important place in the community school concept. However, balance in the use of facilities must be carefully maintained. The joint use of facilities, gymnasiums, playgrounds, classrooms, and other areas is practical, and if carefully planned and carried out under strong supervision, the entire community will benefit. The advantages of the community school system far outweigh the minor problems that arise from mutual use, particularly from an economic consideration.

The Year-Round School

The year-round school grew out of the movement to provide better quality education through the fuller use of existing facilities. It seems logical, because of increased enrollment, rising building costs, high interest rates and other factors, that educators should embrace the year-round school concept. Objections, such as inconvenience to parents because of the change in schedule and other scheduling problems, have been mentioned. However, these objections are being overcome because of the economic advantages and quality education provided by year-round education.

Changing Times describes the most popular extended year plans: (1) the 45-15 plan, (2) the four-quarter plan, and (3) the quinmester plan. (See Figure 5–4.)

45-15 plan. School is open for 240 class days instead of 180. The students are divided into four groups of equal size. Every group attends classes for four nine-week sessions (45 school days) with each session separated by a three-week vacation (15 school days). Groups start three weeks apart, so only three of the four groups are using the school at any one time. Result: The building serves 33⅓% more students than it could hold all at once.

Four-quarter plan. This plan calls for 240 class days divided into 60-day quarters. There are four groups of students, each of which attends classes for three quarters and takes one

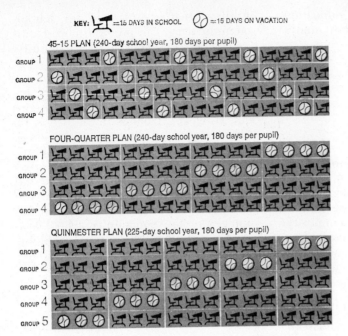

KEY: ⊢⊥ =15 DAYS IN SCHOOL ◯ =15 DAYS ON VACATION

45-15 PLAN (240-day school year, 180 days per pupil)

GROUP 1
GROUP 2
GROUP 3
GROUP 4

FOUR-QUARTER PLAN (240-day school year, 180 days per pupil)

GROUP 1
GROUP 2
GROUP 3
GROUP 4

QUINMESTER PLAN (225-day school year, 180 days per pupil)

GROUP 1
GROUP 2
GROUP 3
GROUP 4
GROUP 5

Figure 5–4. Plans for the year-round school. (From "Are You Ready For Year-Round Schools?" Changing Times, The Kiplinger Magazine, May, 1974.)

quarter off. Only three of the groups use the school at the same time.

Since this system can result in some students always taking their vacations in the winter months, educators have devised a *rotating* four-quarter plan. Under rotating quarters the vacation periods of the groups are changed each year so that, over the course of four years, each group gets one during the nice-weather months.

Quinmester plan. The school year consists of 225 class days, divided into five 45-day sections. There are five groups of students, each of which attends classes for four of the sections and takes one section off. Vacations are staggered so that one of the groups is on vacation during each section.[23]

In planning for the year-round school, administrators are confronted with the problem of how to schedule the physical education program. The program conducted in Dade County Public Schools of Miami, Florida, is an excellent example of how physical education operates in the year-round school plan.

In the Dade County district, two senior high schools and one junior high school experimented with the quinmester plan for operating year-round schools. The plan consists of five 9-week sessions which include 180 teaching

days and cover 12 months. The 9-week sessions are called "quins" and students may elect any four of the five quins or they may decide to elect all five of them. Most of the courses are elective and are arranged by the health and physical education advisory council. Seventy units of instruction were identified, including activities from both team and individual sports, of which a large number are coeducational. Health education is also included in the plan; 10 courses are offered, of which two are required by the state.

Four quins in physical education and two in health education are required for graduation. Students earn a quin credit upon satisfactory completion of each 9-week course.[24]

Alternative School

The alternative school is the most far-reaching of the trends discussed in providing options and in freeing students from the confines of the traditional curriculum. According to *Education U.S.A.*, the number of alternative schools increased from 464 in 1972 to 1000 in 1973.[25] Alternative public schools may be found in hundreds of communities in 30 states.

The alternative school attempts to provide options for all students in all aspects of the school and community. Mario Fantini, Dean of Education at New Paltz College in New York, states that "Traditional schooling is not right for everybody, but neither is nongraded, continuous progress education. . . . The main idea behind alternatives is matching teaching and learning styles. Just switching some kids from one classroom to another to match them with the teacher that is best for them doesn't cost a cent."[26]

The alternative movement grew out of the efforts of students, parents, and teachers in the grass roots of the community to provide more alternatives to the traditional curriculum without affecting the rights of those students and parents who still desired the benefits obtained from the traditional curriculum.

Some of the more prevalent types of alternative public schools that are currently operating are: open schools, schools without walls, various types of centers, schools-within-a-school, ethnic schools, educational parks, and nonpublic alternatives.[27]

Since the alternative school concept is based on the needs of the community, it will succeed only if the community assists the teachers and administrators in the planning and evaluation. Cooperative effort between school and community results in improvement in teacher morale; lower incidence of drugs, vandalism, and delinquency; and less truancy.

Although there are many advantages to the alternative school, certain guidelines are necessary if the concept is to succeed. Fantini lists several:

1. The alternative must be made available to students, teachers, and parents by choice. It cannot be superimposed.
2. It cannot claim the capacity to replace existing alternatives like the standard school. Premature claims of superiority, belittling the worth of other alternatives, tend to create a negative political climate.
3. It must give evidence of being geared to the attainment of a comprehensive set of educational objectives: those for which the

school is accountable and not merely selected ones.
4. It is not designed to promote exclusiveness—racial, religious, or socio-economic. Equal access must be guaranteed.
5. It is not dependent on significant amounts of extra money to implement and does not increase the per-student expenditures beyond those of established options. The idea is to utilize existing resources differently—perhaps more effectively.[28]

Physical education is in a position to benefit more in alternative education than other subjects in the curriculum. For those schools that have inadequate facilities, community bowling alleys, golf courses, swimming pools, skating rinks, and other facilities are available. Privately operated facilities may be used for a small fee or at no cost, since these facilities remain idle during the day.

Alternative physical education is provided in many schools throughout the country. North High School, Downers Grove, Illinois, offers alternatives in such activities as bowling, golf, hiking, horseback riding, skating, skiing, swimming, and tennis. The community, school, and home are all used for conducting these activities.[29]

INNOVATIVE TRENDS AFFECTING PHYSICAL EDUCATION

Flexible Scheduling

An innovation that has revolutionized curriculum planning in some places is a procedure known as flexible scheduling. Flexible scheduling broadly defined would be any arrangement in which the traditional scheduling procedure is altered to permit more individualization of instruction and a different system of scheduling the time of both students and teachers.

There are two types of flexible scheduling. The first retains the traditional required schedule, but provides greater choice of courses and more flexibility in content. Retaining the traditional daily period but initiating innovation within the period, changing teachers in some classes, and using the team approach would be other illustrations of this type. *Modular scheduling* is the second approach to flexible scheduling. This plan provides for periods that vary in length and frequency. The school day is divided into several 15- or 20-minute modules as contrasted to the traditional six or seven periods. The number of modules assigned to a subject is determined by the needs of the students and the nature of the particular subject. Modular scheduling disregards the usual concept that each subject in the curriculum needs the same allotment of time, which in the secondary school is usually one period of 50 to 60 minutes.

Modular scheduling usually provides for three types of instruction: large group, small group, and independent study.

Large Group Instruction. Some aspects of instruction in physical education, such as tests, multi-media orienta-tion in an activity, and demonstrations and lectures by outstanding authorities or experts, may be presented effectively in large groups by one teacher. This arrangement releases teachers for other assignments, and provides facilities for different programs, and allows more time for other subjects. However, without careful and imaginative planning, large group instruction may become boring and ineffective. There is very little individual instruction, and teacher-student interaction is impossible.

Small Group Instruction. Small group instruction is the ideal teaching arrangement for physical education. In small group situations, individual instruction becomes a reality, teacher-student interaction is possible, and progression in performance is more easily detected.

Independent Study. Theoretically, independent study allows the student to

TIME	MOD	M	T	W	Th	F
8:30- 8:50	1	7th L.G. Sec. A-B	7th Sec. A-B	7th Sec. A-B	7th Sec. A-B	7th Sec. A-B
8:50- 9:10	2	7th L.G. Sec. C-D	Small Groups	Small Groups	Small Groups	Small Groups
9:10- 9:30	3	Open	7th Sec. C-D	7th Sec. C-D	7th Sec. C	7th Sec. D
9:30- 9:50	4	Lab.	Small Groups		Indep. Study	Indep. Study
9:50-10:10	5				Open Lab	Open Lab
10:10-10:30	6	6th L.G. Sec. A-B	6th Sec. A-B	6th Sec. A-B	6th Sec. A-B	6th Sec. A-B
10:30-10:50	7	6th L.G. Sec. C-D	Small Groups	Small Groups	Small Groups	Sm. Grs.
10:50-11:10	8	Open Sec. C-D	6th Sec. C-D	6th Sec. C-D	6th Sec. C-D	6th
11:10-11:30	9	Lab.	Small Groups	Small Groups	Small Groups	Small Groups
11:30-11:50	10	Adapted P.E.L.G.	Adapted P.E.	Adapted Ind. St.	Adapted P.E.	Adapted P.E.
11:50-12:10	11		Small Groups		Small Groups	Small Groups
12:10-12:30	12	OPEN LABORATORY				
12:30-12:50	13	8th Sec. A-B	8th Sec. A-B	8th Sec. A-B	8th Sec. A-B	8th Sec. A-B
12:50- 1:10	14	Large Group	Indep. Study	Small Groups	Small Groups	Small Groups
1:10- 1:30	15	8th Sec. C-D	8th Sec. C-D			
1:30- 1:50	16	Large Group	Indep. Study	8th Sec. C-D	8th Sec. C-D	8th Sec. C-D
1:50- 2:10	17			Small Group	Small Group	Indep. Study
2:10- 2:30	18					
2:30- 2:50	19	OPEN LABORATORY				
2:50- 3:10	20	(Conferences, remedial help, practice)				

6th grade Sections A,B,C,D   *Grouped according to needs*

7th grade Sections A,B   *Average ability*
    Sections C,D   *High interest and ability; self-motivated; beginning independent study.*

8th grade Sections A,B   *Average ability; beginning independent study*
    Sections C,D   *More highly skilled and motivated*

Figure 5–5. A modular schedule for junior high school physical education. (From Heitman, Helen M.: "Rationale for Change." In *Organizational Patterns for Instruction in Physical Education.* Washington, D.C.: AAHPER, 1971, p. 14.)

pursue a topic in depth, provides the opportunity for self-motivation, and self-evaluation, and develops the resourcefulness for research. However, the success of this phase of flexible scheduling depends on the type of student, the facilities available, the location of the school, the environment, and a careful consideration of the offerings available.

The average student has his time divided into about 12 to 18 hours per week on large group instruction, about six hours in small group instruction, and 12 hours in independent study. See Figure 5–5 for an example of modular scheduling in the junior high school.

The modular scheduling plan provides more time for certain subjects and allows all students adequate time to study in depth those areas which they may need to spend more time on. The modular plan transforms the traditional schedule from a rigid arrangement to one that may be altered at will.

Some places have experimented with modular scheduling in physical education. Ridgewood High School, Norridge, Illinois, has used the modular scheduling plan for several years. The school day consists of twenty 20-minute modules. The number of modules and class scheduling depend on the needs, objectives, facilities, and type of program involved.

At Ridgewood, the schedule is planned around six-day cycles rather than a five-day week. The freshman and sophomore students meet three times each cycle for 80 minutes (4 modules). Junior and senior students meet four times each cycle for 60 minutes (3 modules). In planning, ample time is provided for large group instruction, small group instruction, and independent study.

Independent study in physical education at Ridgewood offers tremendous advantages, and the results seem to have been very satisfying, largely because the student gets to spend additional time doing what he wishes. He may elect to spend this time on physical education skill improvement, individual sports, remedial exercises, rhythms, or other areas of physical education. The goals of phys-

ical education independent study (PEIS) at Ridgewood are clearly outlined as follows:

1. Give freshmen and sophomores a chance for recreative, social, and physical study.
2. Give juniors and seniors a chance to shoulder the responsibility of individualized work.
3. Create carry-over interest and skill in a variety of recreational sports and games to be participated in in later life.
4. Give each student a chance to work on any individualized sport in which he wishes to further his knowledge and skill, progress at his own rate.

In addition to independent study, the program at Ridgewood provides two modules of large group study during each cycle. These periods are used for tests and group discussion and lectures by experts.

By overlapping scheduled classes, the gymnasium is never void of students. For example, Class A meets from 10:00 A.M. to 11:00 A.M., Class B from 10:40 A.M. to 11:40 A.M. Class A reports to the gymnasium at 10:00 A.M. and is dismissed at 10:50 A.M. The first and last 10 minutes are spent changing classes. Class B is in the locker room from 10:40 A.M. to 10:50 A.M. and takes the place of Class A in the gymnasium at 10:50 A.M. The time saved in the locker room during the course of the day increases the available time from 7 classes to 10 classes in both boys' and girls' physical education. Aides are employed to supervise the locker room, freeing teachers to teach.

An innovation that has proved effective at Ridgewood is assigning three teachers to two classes. This is made possible by increasing the class size of two classes. The released teacher is available for individual help and individualized instruction.[30]

There are some educational leaders who feel that flexible scheduling is the answer to many problems which confront them in the quest for effective instruction. They offer the following reasons for their stand:

1. Because scheduling is no longer restricted to the standard six- or seven-period day, many areas of instruction may be included in the curriculum, allowing the student to have a wider choice of subjects in his program.

2. The very nature of flexible scheduling provides for the inclusion of many procedures conducive to effective teaching, such as block scheduling, multiple periods, homogeneous grouping, and programed instruction.

3. Instructional groups of various sizes may be scheduled, which would more nearly meet the needs of students and subject emphasis than the traditional plan of the fixed teacher load of 30 or 40 students.

4. Flexible scheduling provides time for individualized study, remedial and enrichment programs, and teacher planning that would otherwise be unavailable.

5. A better utilization of teacher potential and experience is possible through flexible scheduling practices.

Notwithstanding these examples of successful experiences, not all educators agree that flexible scheduling is a solution to the problems of physical education. Administrators opposed to flexible scheduling offer the following criticisms:

1. Administrators should consistently remember that physical education is a skill subject for which continuity of instruction time is vitally important.

2. Adequate facilities are basic to modular scheduling. If facilities are not sufficient, the effort for flexible scheduling in physical education would be unsatisfactory and impractical.

3. Teachers may be unprepared for this approach, and the resulting program built around unprepared teachers would be ineffective.

4. In large schools with many curriculum offerings, modular scheduling is very complex. Computers are frequently used to process the scheduling of the many areas of instruction. The resulting program in physical education may be unsatisfactory as a result of the complexity.

5. Unless carefully organized, flexible scheduling allows too much free time and permissiveness.

Some parents also have voiced strong opposition to modular scheduling. Richard Gorton discusses a number of objections that parents have made against this form of curriculum procedure:

1. What's wrong with the present schedule?

2. I don't see how my child can learn when he is under no teacher direction.

3. Don't the children have too much freedom under this new plan?

4. Isn't this program just for the college-bound?

5. Won't this program hurt my child's chances of getting into college or obtaining a scholarship?[31]

For many years the basic scheduling problem in including physical education in the school curriculum has been the justification of reserving one period in a six- or seven-period day for physical education. The traditional subjects take up several periods daily, with one period usually devoted to physical education. However, recent innovations in curriculum design have presented even greater difficulties in scheduling physical education on a daily basis.

Those schools that have experimented with modular scheduling find the same defective element—unscheduled time. Until some alternative is found to solve the many problems that occur when students are given large amounts of free time, modular scheduling cannot be considered a successful innovation.

The adverse effects of modular scheduling on physical education are revealed in a study by the California Department of Health Education, Physical Education, Athletics and Recreation. Twelve schools and 2400 students were involved. Six of the schools were on modular scheduling and six operated on daily scheduling.

Stan LeProtti, director of the study, made the following observation:

The advantage alluded to by exponents of flexible scheduling . . . is not attainable under the conditions which presently exist. Students do not respond according to theory; staff does not function effectively to the extent claimed; and existing facilities do not accommodate the scheduling practice.

In those flexible schedules which provide elongated time periods i.e., 90 or 120 minutes for physical education on an irregular basis, the process of program administration and instruction is simply slowed down. That is, students take longer to dress, teachers take longer to take the roll, and students spend more time standing or sitting during the instructional phase of the program.[32]

In the modular scheduling curriculum, physical education is usually allotted three periods weekly (or in a six-day block of time).

The modular scheduling curriculum relegates physical education to such a low level that several crucial questions are raised. What is the status of physical education in the curriculum? Will the daily needs of children be met under the modular plan? Will the time allotment for physical education be decreased? It should be re-emphasized here that the bulk of opinion indicates the need for daily physical education in grades K through 12.

An alternative to modular scheduling in physical education is the elective plan, which allows for flexibility and innovative teaching *within the daily requirement.* This approach is discussed in Chapter 7.

Educational Television

Teaching by closed-circuit television has made such an impact on education that all subjects in the curriculum have been affected. Many advantages accrue from this innovation. Through the medium of television, many programs utilizing maps, exhibits, paintings, and the like, that would otherwise be beyond the realm of traditional instruction are brought to the classroom. Television permits outstanding teachers to bring their experience and ability to many more students than they could ever reach in the traditional classroom. Concise, effective lessons may be taped and stored for future use. As shown in the following paragraphs, however, there are arguments both for and against educational television.

Douglass presents several arguments in favor of the use of educational television:

1. It provides an opportunity of using superior teachers to teach a large number of students economically.

2. It is most effective with large groups and instructional methods, such as demonstrations and lectures.

3. Better than any other tool, it allows students to see or hear events as they occur.[33]

John Scanlon also lists some advantages of educational television that merit consideration:

1. It can vastly extend the reach of the nation's best teachers—particularly those in the subject matter areas in which good teachers are scarce.
2. It can bring to students educational experiences far beyond the potential of conventional teaching in the classroom.
3. It has been found that televised instruction requires the student to accept more responsibility for his own learning than is the case with conventional methods of instruction.
4. One other important result of the experimentation to date has been a more effective use of teaching time and classroom space.
5. The use of superior teachers on television has proved an important means of upgrading the quality of other teachers, particularly beginning teachers.[34]

The major disadvantage of educational television is the tremendous cost of the initial installation and the rising costs of maintenance of the station, television sets, and personnel, which have prevented many cities from experimenting with this innovation. DeYoung and Wynn advance other arguments against educational television:

1. Conventional television instruction lacks the capacity to accommodate the individual differences of learners.
2. It forces the television teacher to depend largely upon the lecture method of teaching, with its well-known limitations.[35]

A recent report of the National Commission on the Reform of Secondary Education states that "One of the monumental failures of modern education is the medium of educational television." The Commission further points out that the "Twin lock steps of high school scheduling and television programming made the result a disaster for the secondary schools that seriously tried to follow through." The Commission concludes that "In instructional television, what has not been film has been lecture, most of it no better than a good, average live lecture by a local teacher, lacking all interaction between teachers and the taught."[36]

Educational television as a supplementary teaching device may be desirable. However, experimentation shows that the claims made by its founders have not been realized. The school systems of both the District of Columbia and the state of New Jersey found that as a basic teaching device it was inadequate, and therefore eliminated it from their budgets. DeYoung and Wynn record a review of 400 research studies showing that students learn about as well with instructional television as they do in the typical classroom. They show that television is most successful in the elementary school, whereas in the secondary schools and colleges the traditional classroom appears to produce better results.[37]

Differentiated Staffing

In an effort to improve instruction by finding better ways of utilizing the talents of teachers who are already em-

ployed, individual staffing procedures have been initiated in many school districts. These procedures have prompted administrators to re-examine the traditional concepts that all teachers have equal ability and should have the same class load.

In differentiated staffing teachers are recognized for their competency in certain tasks and receive remuneration for these competencies. Some teachers have leadership ability and should be considered for department heads, while others have great in-depth knowledge and could serve effectively as instructional leaders in their particular field, assisting other teachers in their teaching.

The effectiveness of differentiated staffing is emphasized by Rand and English. They describe a model in which teachers are selected for their experience and qualifications in particular areas and receive additional remuneration for increased professional responsibility (see Figure 5–6).

The advantages of differentiated staffing are obvious. With teachers actively involved in the improvement of the instructional process, all aspects of the administration and supervisory functions are strengthened. However, differential staffing challenges one of the most zealously guarded assumptions of teachers.

				Non-tenure	REGULAR SALARY SCHEDULE PLUS FACTORS
			Non-tenure	TEACHING RESEARCH ASSOCIATE Doctorate or equivalent	Twelve Months ($16,000-20,000)
		Non-tenure	TEACHING CURRICULUM ASSOCIATE M.S., M.A., or equivalent		Eleven Months ($14,000-16,000)
	Tenure	SENIOR TEACHER M.S., M.A., or equivalent			Ten to Eleven Months ($11,000-14,000)
Non-tenure	STAFF TEACHER B.A. Degree plus 1 year				Ten Months ($6,000-11,000)
ACADEMIC ASSISTANT A.A. or B.A. Degree					Ten Months ($4,000-5,000)
Some teaching responsibilities	100 percent teaching responsibilities	4/5's staff teaching responsibilities	3/5's-4/5's staff teaching responsibilities	3/5's staff teaching responsibilities	
EDUCATIONAL TECHNICIANS					

Figure 5–6. A model of differentiated staffing. (From Rand, M. John, and Fenwick English: "Towards a Differentiated Teaching Staff." *Phi Delta Kappan*, January, 1968, p. 267.)

Since public education began, the myth that all teachers are equal has frustrated efforts to award merit pay for exceptional teaching service. For the present, differentiated staffing is just a dream, but perhaps in a few years some of the traditional barriers will be overcome and teachers will be allowed to assist with the improvement of instruction and receive commensurate pay for this leadership.

Behavioral or Performance Objectives

In the quest for accountability and the renewed efforts to improve the quality of instruction, educators have revived the behavioral or performance objectives that were prevalent in the late fifties.

The outline of performance objectives lists three domains: (1) cognitive, (2) affective, and (3) psychomotor. The *cognitive domain,* explored by Bloom,[38] consists of intellectual objectives such as knowledge and understanding. Bloom includes six categories, arranged in hierarchical order as follows: (1) knowledge, (2) comprehension, (3) application, (4) analysis, (5) synthesis, and (6) evaluation. Krathwohl[39] developed the *affective domain,* outlining the objectives that pertain to interests, attitudes, appreciation, and adjustment. He also lists categories in hierarchical order: (1) receiving, (2) responding, (3) valuing, (4) organization, and (5) characterization by a value or value complex. The *psychomotor domain,* pertaining to ob-

Taxonomy Categories	Illustrative General Instructional Objectives	Illustrative Behavioral Terms for Stating Specific Learning Outcomes
(Development of categories in this domain is still underway)	Writes smoothly and legibly Draws accurate reproduction of a picture (or map, biology specimen, etc.) Sets up laboratory equipment quickly and correctly Types with speed and accuracy Operates a sewing maching skillfully Operates a power saw safely and skillfully Performs skillfully on the violin Performs a dance step correctly Demonstrates correct form in swimming Demonstrates skill in driving an automobile Repairs an electric motor quickly and effectively Creates new ways of performing (creative dance, etc.)	Assembles, builds, calibrates, changes, cleans, composes, connects, constructs, corrects, creates, designs, dismantles, drills, fastens, fixes, follows, grinds, grips, hammers, heats, hooks, identifies, locates, makes, manipulates, mends, mixes, nails, paints, sands, saws, sharpens, sets, sews, sketches, starts, stirs, uses, weighs, wraps

Figure 5–7. "The Psychomotor Domain." (From Gronland, Norman, E.: *Stating Behavioral Objectives for Classroom Instruction.* London: The MacMillan Co., 1970, p. 24.)

jectives in teaching motor skills, is given a comprehensive treatment in a recent publication by Singer.[40]

The psychomotor domain is the most important of the three domains in physical education. Figure 5–7 lists the objectives and terms in the psychomotor domain which should be helpful to physical education teachers and administrators.

The purpose of stating objectives in behavioral terms, as opposed to general objectives, is to offer a practical approach for teaching and learning. Setting behavioral or performance objectives gives the teacher a more concise and specific outline of what the learner should accomplish in his step-by-step approach to a goal. Those who advocate the use of performance objectives point out that it is one definite procedure whereby teachers can detect improvement and see the effectiveness of their teaching. The stating of objectives charts the course of instruction for a definite period of time, whether it be a day, a week, or a year, and enables both teacher and student to clearly identify the goals which they are striving to attain. Finally, the use of performance objectives is extremely effective in the evaluation of the program of instruction. In these days of accountability, the performance-based curriculum may be used to apprise the public of the status of education.

A major reason for the writing and use of performance objectives is the need for determining the terminal behavior in the affective domain. For years education has been deeply concerned with the dissemination of instructional material and factual information in the cognitive domain. The question may justifiably be raised that if the use of this material fails to alter behavior or attitudes, have not the time and effort been wasted? In drug education, for example, if the facts presented to a class do not alter the attitude of the students toward drug usage, why continue the program? Outstanding leaders in education and psychology advocate measurement of performance in the affective domain. Mager strongly favors the use of such objectives to determine the pattern of behavior.[41]

However, not all educational leaders subscribe to the performance objective approach in curriculum planning and teaching. They agree that objectives are necessary, but do not believe that they should be written in behavioral terms. Some of their criticisms are:

1. The list of objectives for an area will become so voluminous that they will never be used.
2. The time consumed in writing objectives could be better spent in other activities.
3. Teachers should be concerned with cognitive instruction and leave the affective domain to others.
4. Stating specific objectives places a brake on creativity.
5. The statement of specific objectives may develop a rigid, inflexible curriculum.
6. Mass development of objectives which are used to change behavior may be a dangerous procedure from a societal point of view.

Before embarking on a performance-based curriculum in physical education, teachers and administrators should weigh the pros and cons and arrive at a decision that will be effective and practical. Some physical educators have used written performance objectives effectively as goals for performance in the instructional program. Although some attention has been given to the cognitive domain (knowledge) and the affective domain (behavior), the basic thrust in physical education has been in the psychomotor domain.

TEACHING RESPONSIBILITY IN THE ELEMENTARY SCHOOL

Probably one of the major causes of the confusion and lack of continuity in the elementary program is the way in which teaching responsibility has been assigned. At present, several plans are used in the elementary school program.

Classroom Teacher

In the majority of elementary schools in America, the classroom teacher is responsible, with or without assistance, for the instruction in physical education, in addition to teaching other subjects such as history, mathematics, science, language arts, music, and art and performing a multiplicity of other duties.

The educators who advocate that the classroom teacher should assume the entire responsibility for physical education instruction offer the following reasons for supporting this view:

1. The classroom teacher has more comprehensive knowledge of the needs of children and is more familiar with their growth and development patterns.

2. He or she is better qualified to coordinate the various areas and place physical education in proper perspective.

3. Since the students are with the classroom teacher during the entire day, it is easier to determine when the children should have physical education.

4. It is less expensive to include physical education in the curriculum when the classroom teacher is responsible for the instruction.

Leaders who oppose this plan are extremely strong in their convictions because they feel that:

1. The classroom teacher is not qualified to teach many of the intricate skills involved in physical education. Certain movements and skills, if not taught correctly, may seriously injure the student. Because of this lack of qualification the resulting program too often is impotent and meaningless.

2. The majority of classroom teachers are not interested in teaching physical education. If they had been, they would have studied physical education as a major in college.

3. Many classroom teachers are physically unable to teach the skills of physical education.

Classroom Teacher Assisted by a Specialist

A second plan calls for placing a specialist in the schools who assists the regular classroom teacher by demonstrating the correct skills and procedures; he also shares the responsibility for supplemen-

ting and strengthening the physical education program. The physical education specialist should inspire, stimulate, and be a source of skilled help to the classroom teacher. To carry out these responsibilities effectively, the specialist must:

1. Pre-plan with the classroom teacher.

2. Organize activities in a general way for the entire year and plan the program in detail for periods of not less than six weeks.

3. Act as a leader or consultant to the classroom teacher in supervising physical education activities. The physical education teacher also teaches specific skills, games, and rhythmics. The classroom teacher must be present at all times so that he can carry on these activities without the physical education teacher.

4. Be responsible for obtaining and issuing needed supplies and equipment in the schools, keeping them in repair, and checking them periodically.

5. Give assistance in the planning, organizing, and carrying out of any school program or project pertaining to his field. Since the specialist is usually not in the same school every day, this responsibility assumes, of course, that he will be notified in advance of any project in which he is called upon to participate.

All Instruction by a Qualified Physical Education Teacher

The most desirable plan is to have a qualified physical education teacher who is responsible for all instruction in physical education. Individuals who relegate the teaching of physical education to the classroom teacher and expect anything remotely approaching quality education should acquaint themselves with the facts. At a national conference in 1961, the American Association of Health and Physical Education and Recreation has this to say about the problem:

Every effort should be made to provide elementary school children with specialists in physical education who can teach the broad and diversified program in skills, attitudes, and outcomes for which physical education is designed.[42]

In 1959 St. Louis experimented with having physical education teachers assume the instruction in the elementary school. The result was eminently satisfactory in that the physical education specialist is better qualified to teach his specialty than is the classroom teacher.[43]

Many cities and counties throughout the country are now employing full-time physical education teachers in the elementary schools. This trend is emphasized when teachers' associations bargain with the administration for released time. When full-time physical education teachers are employed, classroom teachers are relieved of their physical education responsibility.

Some localities that have employed full-time teachers for all elementary schools are Prince George County, Maryland; Dade County, Florida; Pittsburgh, Pennsylvania; Rochester, New York; Cedar Rapids, Iowa; and Towson, Maryland.

Hallstrom, in a study of 15 fourth-grade classrooms in Omaha, Nebraska, found that the effectiveness of the specialist in teaching physical education exceeded that of other methods of assigned responsibility.[44]

During the summer of 1968, the Elementary School Physical Education Commission surveyed 229 school systems in an effort to determine current operational practices in the administration of elementary physical education. One of the components of the survey involved the personnel teaching physical education. The results indicated that the specialist spends less time teaching in the primary grades than in the upper elementary level.[45] Figure 5–8 shows the various personnel assignments for teaching discussed earlier in the chapter.

Irrespective of the criticisms of such a program, the classroom teacher is responsible for the instruction in physical education in the majority of classrooms across the country. This is true primarily because of the cost of employing specialists in physical education. Until administrators and the public become fully convinced of the need for physical education teachers in the elementary school, ways must be devised to continue teaching physical education in the elementary school in the most effective manner possible.

There are some places where classroom teachers seem to be teaching physical education satisfactorily. The program in San Francisco, involving 104 elementary schools and 1700 teachers, is an example of such a program. "The vast corps of dedicated teachers...can be enlisted readily if the professional physical education teachers are prepared to give supplementary training and assistance," says Viola Beck, the supervisor of the program. She suggests three principles to support her belief:

1. The influence of whatever professional leadership is available must be spread as far as possible. If there are too few physical educators to teach the children daily, concentrate on teaching the teachers.
2. Involve classroom teachers in the process of deciding what their program is to include.
3. Work together as a team to involve good

	K	1	2	3	4	5	6
Classroom teacher with no assistance from specialist	46	31	31	30	22	20	19
Classroom teacher with only consultative assistance from specialist	74	91	85	79	63	62	85
Specialist and classroom teacher sharing the responsibility	47	101	100	98	96	94	93
Specialist with no supportive help from the classroom teacher	20	63	66	78	108	114	115

Figure 5–8. Chart of personnel involved in teaching physical education. (From Elementary Schools Physical Education Survey. Washington, D.C.: AAHPER, 1968.)

teaching aids, instructional guides, workshops, demonstrations and in-service training.[46]

TEACHING RESPONSIBILITY IN THE SECONDARY SCHOOL

In the secondary school, instruction is usually the responsibility of the specialist in physical education. The departmentalized organization is most prevalent. Under this plan the various subject matter areas are divided into departments, usually with a chairperson to provide leadership and assistance to teachers.

Department Chairperson

In many places the department chairperson is given supervisory responsibility in addition to the usual duties. This expanded role has grown out of the need for a qualified person who can work with teachers and assist them in improving the instructional program.

The Department Head and Supervision. The role of the department head as a supervisor is fraught with many problems. It would seem that to assign an experienced teacher as the head of a group of teachers to provide supervision and help would be a practical approach to improving instruction. However, this is not always true, for the following reasons:

1. Persons who are selected as department heads are too often not qualified for this responsibility. They may be good teachers, but are not able to master the delicate balance that must exist between helping teachers with routine administrative procedures and assisting with the improvement of teaching methods and techniques. The latter involves supervision, which immediately places the chairperson in a different role.
2. Too little time is provided for chairpersons to appraise fairly the competence of teachers in the department. Usually one or two periods are allotted for the performance of these duties, which obviously is insufficient.
3. It is difficult for a fellow teacher, who teaches as a member of the department, suddenly to become a supervisor and be accepted by the other teachers. It is awkward for the chairperson to have coffee breaks with teachers, to participate in the daily school routine, and then to have to evaluate colleagues objectively.
4. The additional responsibilities that are assumed by the department head outweigh the salary differential that is usually granted.

Those in favor of the department chairperson plan point out the following:

1. Although the principal is the recognized supervisory officer, rarely is a principal qualified to perform this function in several areas of instruction.
2. When there are several teachers in a department, it is necessary to have one person to serve as a liaison between the department and the administration of the school and the central office.
3. A competent chairperson may assist teachers with their daily instructional problems. This is particularly true with new teachers.
4. A qualified chairperson may serve as a leader in improving instruction within the department.

Administrative Duties of the Department Chairperson. In addition to supervisory responsibilities, the chairperson must perform the following administrative duties:*

1. Arrange meetings of the department.
2. Serve as a leader in developing guidebooks and other instructional material.
3. Assist in the selection of textbooks.
4. Assist the principal with requisitioning supplies and equipment.
5. Assist in the preparation of the budget.
6. Take inventory of supplies and equipment.
7. Help teachers with instructional problems (extremely important for new teachers).
8. Attend school and city-wide meetings on curriculum instruction and other meetings concerned with the operation of the schools.
9. Attend faculty meetings and other meetings arranged by the principal.
10. Interview prospective teachers.
11. Assist with scheduling and assignment of teachers in the various grade levels.
12. Keep informed about current teaching methods and materials.

---

*The resource manual includes other duties.

13. Report departmental problems to the principal.

14. Serve as a liaison between the department and the administration of the school and system.

15. Serve on committees to coordinate city-wide programs.

16. Participate in local, state, and national programs for the improvement of education.

17. Assist in the assignment of teachers to the areas of instruction they are best qualified to teach.

Departmental Organization

The John Dewey High School in Brooklyn, New York, uses a comprehensive handbook which outlines uniform policies and procedures for the department. The handbook includes such areas as student responsibilities, students' programs, responsibilities of the teacher, locker room supervision, student evaluation, special programs, teacher programming, and health guidance.[47] These items illustrate the general components which are usually involved in organizing a department. Local conditions, however, determine these components, and they will vary from school to school.

PLACEMENT OF STUDENTS

Another foundation of effective administrative planning is the proper scheduling of students to physical education classes. A definite policy should be established for this administrative function.

Students should be scheduled for physical education as they are for other required subjects, but unfortunately this is rarely the case. Too often students are scheduled without regard for grade, size of class, or balance of the teacher-student ratio. From an effective teaching standpoint, adequate scheduling is one of the most important procedures in administrative responsibility. Often physical education is the last subject scheduled, with the result that students are grouped in a haphazard, unbalanced manner. Not only do teachers find it difficult to teach in such situations, but the attitudes and achievement potential of students are adversely affected.

Characteristics of an Effective Schedule

There are several characteristics that are noticeable in an effective schedule. A good schedule should:

1. Be sufficiently flexible so as to include traditional or innovative plans, various school programs, and alternative programs.
2. Provide for equal distribution of students in classes.
3. Include state and local time allotments.
4. Be efficiently developed so as to provide smooth operation of the instructional program.
5. Provide sufficient planning time for all teachers.
6. Take into consideration the varying abilities of all students.
7. Anticipate fluctuating enrollments and utilize teaching stations accordingly.
8. Assign teachers to subjects or areas of their choice and those they are best qualified to teach.
9. Utilize computerization but not to the detriment of the individual student.

Steps in Scheduling

Several steps are recommended in scheduling students to physical education classes. The procedures differ somewhat for the various grade levels, as the following paragraphs illustrate.

Elementary School Scheduling. Scheduling in the elementary school involves the scheduling of classes rather than of students. In schools where there is a physical education specialist to assist the classroom teacher, guidelines must be established to determine the number of teachers needed for the program, the number of days a specialist is needed in a particular school, and the number of periods the specialist meets with classroom teachers daily. Assuming that all students and teachers need the services of the physical education specialist, the following plan is suggested:

1. The physical education specialist should meet the classroom teacher for a 30-minute period at least one period each week. This period should be used to review the material taught during the week and to introduce new material to be taught the other four days of the week.

2. Physical education teachers should teach a minimum of eight or nine 30-minute class periods daily. The number of periods is determined by the number of teachers in the school. The school day usually consists of a maximum of ten 30-minute periods. A teaching load of eight periods daily is a fair load for the physical education teacher.

3. The number of classes the physical education teacher meets with daily divided by the number of classroom teachers determines the number of days the physical education teacher is scheduled for a particular school. *Example*: There are 24 classroom teachers in the school; 24 divided by 8 equals 3. Thus the physical education teacher is assigned to the school three days each week. The other two days are spent in a smaller school.

These guidelines should be used as the starting point for preparing the schedule. It is the principal's responsibility to prepare the schedule; however, in many places this responsibility is delegated to the physical education teacher. The following steps, essential in schedule construction, facilitate the task, regardless of whose responsibility it becomes.

1. Obtain from the principal a list of teachers, with grade and classroom assignments, lunchroom, television, band, or orchestra, and recess schedules for teachers in each grade level. No effective schedule can be made unless all of these factors are considered.

2. Block off scheduled times (television classes, lunch, and recess periods, etc.) by grade levels, eliminating time that cannot be used.

3. Block off time that remains each day for all the days to show when classes can be scheduled for all grade levels. It is necessary to consider all grade levels at once, since of the several times during the day that a particular grade level can be scheduled, only one may be the best time, considering all the factors involved.

4. According to the number of days assigned to the school and the number of teachers in each grade level, set up the schedule, assigning teachers in a particular grade level the same time each day so that they will have physical education at the same time each day of the week. *Example*: Suppose a school has six 5th-grade classes and the specialist is assigned to the school three days. After determining the above factors, it is found that from 10 to 11 o'clock each day is the best available time to assign classes for the 5th grade. The schedule should then read as shown in Figure 5–9. This schedule means that three 5th-grade classroom teachers will be on the playground from 10:00 to 10:30 each day, and three more from 10:30 to 11:00.

5. Once the schedule has been organized, changes should be made only by the classroom teacher within the block of time allotted, unless they are absolutely necessary in order to adjust to some other phase of the curriculum.

In addition to the five steps just listed, the following suggestions will be helpful in preparing the schedule and in maintaining a cooperative working relationship:

1. Work with art and music teachers in making out schedule, to avoid conflict.

2. Use teacher suggestions in making out the schedule.

3. Explain to teachers that the time designated for physical education should be the same each day. If conflicts exist between departments, make out alternate schedules for days when the specialist is not in the school. Make sure that the alternate schedule time for each teacher is shown on the schedule.

4. In constructing schedules, allow a minimum of eight classes each day. Additional time should be used for teacher workshops and conferences with principal and teachers.

5. Avoid scheduling classes during the first 15 minutes of the school day. This time is used by classroom teachers to take attendance, conduct opening exercises, and so on. The physical education teacher should use this time to check and repair equipment, set up equipment for classes, meet with squad leaders, notify teachers about where he will meet them that day, and hold conferences for discussing problems of organization and instruction.

Health and physical education teachers should submit the schedule to the principal in the format shown in Figure 5–9. After the schedule is approved by the principal, a mimeographed copy

TIME	DAILY	GRADE	ROOM	IN CLASSROOM
10:00–10:30	Teacher A	5	102	Monday
	Teacher B	5	103	Tuesday
	Teacher C	5	104	Wednesday
10:30–11:00	Teacher D	5	107	Monday
	Teacher E	5	108	Tuesday
	Teacher F	5	109	Wednesday

Figure 5-9. A suggested schedule for three teachers.

should be posted in each classroom and on the office bulletin board. Multiple copies (three or more, as requested) should be presented to the central office of the physical education department.

Scheduling in the Junior and Senior High School. Scheduling students in physical education differs greatly between junior high school and elementary school. Factors such as departmentalization and curriculum design affect the scheduling process at the upper levels.

Senior high school scheduling differs from that of the junior high school in that more variables are involved. An overview of the senior high school reveals a large number of elective and required subjects, and sometimes terminal subjects in which part of the day is scheduled away from school on an expanded vocational program, all of which must be considered when developing the schedule.

Planning the Schedule for the Junior and Senior High School. Planning the schedule for the junior and senior high school is a most difficult task when appropriate time allotments and student-teacher ratios must be calculated for so many different subjects. Too often physical education is scheduled last, resulting in a student-teacher ratio that is unreasonable. The procedures presented below are usually followed by experienced schedule makers, and administrative heads in physical education should urge that physical education be scheduled for the same amount of time as

other required subjects. The following steps in schedule making are outlined as guide for the physical education department head of a senior high school, but may be applied to junior high school as well.

1. *Planning letter to parents.* Letters are sent to all parents for their approval, as shown in Figure 5-10. The proposed program that has been cooperatively planned by the counselor and student is sent home on a *subject selection registration blank* for the parents' approval and signature.

2. The subject selection registration blanks are returned to counselors, who use them to prepare planning cards.

3. *Planning cards* are sent to the department chairman, who codes each subject in his respective subject area.

4. *Information to junior high schools.* All information pertaining to the program of studies, offerings, census cards, course selections, planning cards, and coding is sent to all the junior high schools that feed into the high school.

5. *IBM cards.* All course code numbers are punched into the planning cards.

6. *Validation.* The codes are validated through the IBM machine.

7. *Course summary.* A summary of all course offerings by subjects is made by homeroom teachers.

8. *Tallies.* Tallies noting the number of sections needed are sent to department heads.

9. *Master schedule.* Assignments, along with homeroom numbers, are placed in the skeletal master schedule.

10. *Checking master schedules.* The master schedule is checked to insure that sufficient sections are available to meet the anticipated load, to avoid duplications of

SUBJECT SELECTION REGISTRATION BLANK

Please complete subjects passed in years previous to present selection.

Student's Name _____ Last _____ First _____ Middle _____ Student Number _____ Grade Level _____

School _____ (Currently Attending) _____ Birth Date _____ Parents' Name _____

Address _____ Phone: Home _____ Business _____

7th Grade		8th Grade		9th Grade	
Course Title	Grade	Course Title	Unit	Course Title	Unit
English 7		English 8	1	English 1	1
P.E. and Health		P. E. and Health	1	World History/Geog.	1
Social Studies 7				P. E. and Health	1
Mathematics 7					
Life Science					
Exploratory					
		Alternate		Alternate	
		Alternate		Alternate	
Total Subjects Passed for Year		Total Units for Year		Total Units for Year	

10th Grade		11th Grade		12th Grade	
Course Title	Unit	Course Title	Unit	Course Title	Unit
English 2	1	English 3	1	English 4	1
P. E. and Health	1	U. S. & Va. History	1	U. S. & Va. Government	1/2
				___(Soc. St.)	1/2
Alternate		Alternate		Alternate	
Alternate		Alternate		Alternate	
Total Units for Year		Total Units for Year		Total Units for Year	

Date _____, 197__ _____ Signature of Student _____ Signature of Parent

Instructions for Completing Registration Form

The student should:
1. Choose the subjects best suited to meet his or her needs, interests, abilities, attitudes, and goals.
2. Confer with parents, counselors, and teachers for help in making wise selections.
3. List the subjects completed successfully and passed in previous years.
4. List subjects selected, making certain all previous requirements have been met.
5. Fill out the remainder of the current grade column so that the minimum of units, but not more than six units, are indicated (exclusive of alternates).
6. List at least two alternative electives in case of scheduling conflicts.
7. Choose subjects very carefully. Changes which are necessary because of summer school courses or for other valid reasons should be requested no later than the last weekday in August.

NOTE: The courses to be scheduled are dependent on student choice and teacher availability.

Figure 5–10. A planning letter to parents allows parents and students to cooperatively plan their educational experiences. (Courtesy of Booker T. Washington High School, Norfolk, Virginia.)

assignments, to check invalid cards, and to verify teacher names and course offerings.

11. *Computer.* Cards for master schedule offerings are punched for use in the computer.

12. *Summer school students.* All planning cards for summer school students are pulled for updating and course adjustments.

13. *Final computer procedure.* Planning cards, properly punched, are sent to the computer along with the master schedule offerings and information about teachers, subjects, room numbers, periods, and available seats.

Innovative Scheduling

The preceding discussion has covered the procedures involved in traditional scheduling. In recent years, however, many schools have experimented with more innovative ways of scheduling in an attempt to provide more time and choices in curriculum for the variety of programs that are essential for a comprehensive secondary school curriculum. The procedure that has received the greatest attention—modular or flexible scheduling—was described earlier in this chapter. Another plan that would allow more choices is the elective program. This plan works harmoniously with the physical education schedule since the *program is required and innovations occur within the requirement.* The elective plan is discussed in Chapter 7.

PHYSICAL EDUCATION AND EDUCATIONAL EXPERIMENTATION

The question arises, what effects do various types of schools, designs, and organization plans have on the status of physical education? One simple answer to this question is impossible, since local conditions, philosophy, and decisions usually determine what areas of instruction should be included in the program and how much time should be allocated to each of them. However, it may be safely stated that if the daily requirement is maintained, irrespective of the type of organization, physical education will maintain a proper position in the curriculum.

It is extremely important for administrators to insist on the daily requirement, since too often, when decisions about time allotments are made, physical education suffers. A case in point is flexible or modular scheduling, which is based on the theory that some subjects require more modules and fewer classes weekly than others. On what basis is this decision made? Surely there is no scientific evidence to show that English should have more modules or weekly time than history or physical education. The decision is usually an empirical one, with physical education leaders exercising little effect on the decision making. The decision usually results in physical education being scheduled three days per week, which ignores the recommendations of physicians and physical education leaders that all students should have physical education daily for normal growth and development.

It is the opinion of the authors of this text that physical education is basically different from academic areas in that it is a *movement* program. Movement is essential for health and fitness, and is certainly as important as English or history to the total education of children.

Although physical education subscribes to trends and endeavors to implant the procedures and findings of academic research in its teaching, it does not necessarily follow that these findings are applicable to physical education. Although the affective and cognitive domains are involved to a certain extent, physical education operates basically in the psychomotor domain, since it is skill and movement oriented.

Physical education leaders and administrators should study the academic research and experimentation that have been done in their field, but they should not blindly subscribe to these findings and recommendations, since they are not always effective. A study by the Ford Foundation substantiates this premise. The study found that, during the 1960's, many innovative programs were initiated which influenced staffing, scheduling, technology, and training in physical education. Although the Ford Foundation invested 30 million dollars in these programs, it concluded there were no lasting or significant results, and most of the innovations were eventually abandoned.[48]

In 1973 the Charles F. Kettering Foundation established the National Commission on the Reform of Secondary Education. The publication of the Commission, *The Reform of Secondary Education*, lists the innovations that received the most funding from foundations and the U. S. Office of Education. They are:

Team Teaching
Modular Scheduling
Nongraded Schools
Programmed Learning
Individualized Instruction

Computer Assisted Instruction
Independent Study
Learning Centers
Open Plan Schools
Language Laboratory
Behavioral Objectives
Differentiated Staffing

The findings of the Commission paralleled the Ford Foundation's conclusions in that "the decade of change and innovation in the schools had little or no lasting effect on the content of school programs or the quality of teaching and learning."[49]

REFERENCES

1. *Newsletter.* Washington, D. C.: President's Council on Physical Fitness and Sports, June, 1971, p. 14.
2. "A Physical Education Program for Today's Youth." Washington, D. C.: National Conference for Mobilization of Health Education, Physical Education, and Recreation, March, 1951.
3. "Youth and Fitness—A Program for Secondary Schools." Report of the National Conference on Fitness of Secondary Youth. Washington, D. C.: AAHPER, 1959, p. 24.
4. The Society of State Directors of Health, Physical Education, and Recreation: *School Programs in Health, Physical Education, and Recreation, a Statement of Beliefs.* Washington, D. C.: AAHPER, 1973, p. 7.
5. "Essentials of a Quality Elementary Physical Education Program: A Position Paper." *JOHPER*, April, 1971, p.42.
6. "Guidelines for Secondary School Physical Education: A Position Paper." *JOHPER*, April, 1971, p. 47.
7. James B. Conant: "Required Physical Education Must be Retained in California's Schools." California Association for Health, Physical Education and Recreation, 1961, p. 7.
8. "An Inner City Superintendent Supports Physical Education." *Physical Education Newsletter*, June 1, 1971.
9. *What Physicians Say about Physical Education.* Washington, D. C.: President's Council on Physical Fitness and Sports, undated.
10. *Ibid.*
11. Joseph Gruber: "Exercise and Mental Performance." Address before the American Association for the Advancement of Science, Dallas, December, 1968.
12. American Medical Association, Report of the House of Delegates, Miami Beach, 1960.
13. LaVon C. Johnson: "Effects of 5-Day-a-Week vs. 2- and 3-Day-a-Week Physical Education Class on Fitness, Skill, Adipose Tissue, and Growth." *Research Quarterly*, AAHPER, March, 1969, p. 93.
14. Charles A. Bucher: "National Adult Physical Fitness Survey, Some Implications." *JOHPER*, January, 1974, p. 27.
15. Virginian-Pilot, Norfolk, Virginia, June 20, 1974.
16. "Guidelines for Secondary School Physical Education: A Position Paper." *JOHPER*, April, 1971, p. 47.
17. "Essentials of a Quality Elementary School Physical Education Program: A Position Paper." *JOHPER*, April, 1971, p. 42.
18. Clyde Colman and Leon Budahl: "Necessary Ingredients for Good Team Teaching." *Bulletin, National Association of Secondary School Principals*, January, 1973, p. 41.
19. James Meyer: "Teaming—A First Step in Interdisciplinary Teaching." *The Clearing House*, March, 1969, p. 407.
20. "436 Schools Join Multi-Unit Bandwagon." *Education 1972.* Washington, D. C.: National School Public Relations Association, 1972, p. 20.
21. Herbert L. Brown, Jr.: "Are the Public Schools Doing Their Job?" *The Saturday Evening Post,* September 21, 1957.
22. John Minzey: "Community Education: An Amalgam of Many Views." *Phi Delta Kappan*, November, 1972, p. 150.
23. "Are you Ready for Year-Round Schools?" *Changing Times*, May, 1973, p. 46.

24. Hy Rothstein and Robert F. Adams: "Quinmester Extended Year Plan." *JOHPER*, September, 1971, p. 30.
25. "Alternative Schools Seek Broader Acceptance." *Education U.S.A.* Washington, D.C.: National School Public Relations Association, October 15, 1973, p. 39.
26. *Ibid.*, p. 39.
27. Vernan H. Smith: "Options in Public Education: The Quiet Revolution." *Phi Delta Kappan*, March, 1973, p. 434.
28. Mario Fantini: "Alternatives Within Public Schools." *Phi Delta Kappan*, March, 1973, p. 445.
29. Mimeographed materials from Downers Grove Public Schools, Downers Grove, Ill., 1974.
30. "Modular Scheduling Leads to Use of Facilities Every Minute of the Day." *Physical Education Newsletter*, December 15, 1973.
31. Richard A. Gorton: "Parental Resistance to Modular Scheduling." *The Clearing House*, March, 1969, pp. 392–396.
32. "California Supports Value of Daily Programs." *Newsletter*. Washington, D. C.: Council on Physical Fitness and Sports, December, 1971.
33. Harl Douglass: *The High School Curriculum*, 3rd ed. New York: The Ronald Press Co., 1964, p. 586.
34. John Scanlon: "Classroom T.V. Enters a New Era." In Woodring and Scanlon: *American Education Today*. New York: McGraw-Hill Book Co., 1963, pp. 219–227.
35. Chris DeYoung and Richard Wynn: *American Education*, 7th ed. New York: McGraw-Hill Book Co., 1972, p. 48.
36. B. Frank Brown: *The Reform of Secondary Education*. New York: McGraw-Hill Book Co., 1973, p. 88.
37. DeYoung and Wynn, *op. cit.*, p. 400.
38. Benjamin S. Bloom and D. R. Krathwohl: *Taxonomy of Educational Objectives; Handbook I: Cognitive Domain*. New York: David McKay Co. 1956.
39. D. R. Krathwohl *et al.*: *Taxonomy of Educational Objectives: Handbook II: Affective Domain*. New York: David McKay Co. 1964.
40. Robert N. Singer: *The Psychomotor Domain: Movement Behavior*. Philadelphia: Lea & Febiger, 1972.
41. Robert F. Mager: *Preparing Instructional Objectives*. Palo Alto, Calif.: Fearon Publishers, 1962, p. 3.
42. Doris Hutchinson: "Obtaining Quality Instruction for Elementary School Children." *Administering City and County School Programs*, Report of a National Conference. Washington, D. C.: AAHPER, 1961, p. 24.
43. Louis Kittlaus: "The Physical Education Specialist vs. the Classroom Teacher." *Administering City and County School Programs*, Report of a National Conference. Washington, D. C.: AAHPER, 1961, pp. 79–80.
44. Thomas Lynn Hallstrom: "An Exploratory Study of the Effect of Special Teacher, Combination Special-Classroom Teacher, and Classroom Teacher Instruction Upon Certain Aspects of Physical Fitness and Motor Skill Development." Research Study No.1, reprinted from Dissertation Abstracts, Colorado State College, 1966.
45. Don Brault, Chairman: *Elementary Schools' Physical Education Teacher Status Survey*. Elementary School Physical Education Commission. Washington, D. C.: AAHPER, 1968.
46. Viola Beck: "The Classroom Teacher is the Key." *JOHPER*, November–December, 1963, p. 23.
47. Joel Kass, Assistant Principal, John Dewey High School, Brooklyn, New York. Mimeographed materials sent on request.
48. B. Frank Brown: *The Reform of Secondary Education*. New York: McGraw-Hill Book Co., 1973, p. 7.
49. *Ibid.*, p. 7.

SUGGESTED READINGS

Alexander, William M., Galen J. Saylor, and Emmett L. Williams: *The High School, Today and Tommorrow*. New York: Holt, Rinehart & Winston, 1971.
Anderson, Lester W., and Lauren A. Van Dyke: *Secondary School Administration*. Boston: Houghton Mifflin Co., 1972.
De Young, Chris A., and Richard Wynn: *American Education*, 7th ed. New York: McGraw-Hill Book Co., 1972.
Jones, James A., C. Jackson Salisbury, and Ralph L. Spencer: *Secondary School Administration*. New York: McGraw-Hill Book Co., 1969.
McLain, John D.: *Year-Round Education, Economic, Educational and Sociological Factors*. Berkeley, Calif.: McCutchan Publishing Corp. 1973.
Strom, Robert D., and E. Paul Torrence: *Education For Affective Achievement*. Chicago: Rand McNally & Co., 1973.

Courtesy of Silverton Public Schools, Silverton, Colorado.

CHAPTER SIX

Developing the Physical Education Curriculum

NEED FOR CURRICULUM CHANGE

The need for changes in curriculum is revealed in the increasing dissatisfaction of parents and students with present educational offerings. Of the 10 problems confronting the public schools, the 1974 Gallup Poll listed poor curriculum as ninth.[1] The National Commission on the Reform of Secondary Education states: "Our large city school systems are on the verge of complete collapse. Two decades ago the cities operated the best school systems in the United States. Today these schools are at the bottom in academic accomplishment."[2] Nationwide problems of school attendance, crime, assaults on teachers and students, noticeable decline in achievement, and lack of interest in education are symptoms of conditions which are forcing educators to initiate steps in curriculum change.

For many years the basic purpose of secondary education was preparation for college. In recent years the emphasis has changed from college preparatory to

133

include planning for careers that involve instruction in skills. The curriculum must accommodate this change in order to meet the new demands of society. Problems at the elementary level that have high priority for study are in the areas of reading, individualized instruction, career education, and physical education.

In all levels of education, innovations in scheduling, school organization, alternative education, and teaching methods are rapidly gaining ground. In addition, the advances of technology with the socio-economic changes that follow point to the need for constant curriculum revision. Cohen outlines 11 changes in our society that will affect curriculum revision far into the 21st century:

1. Changes in financing school expenditures
2. Early childhood education
3. Desegregation, busing, and quality education
4. Collective bargaining
5. Substitutions for teacher certification
6. Innovation and experimentation
7. Teacher shortages and teacher surplus
8. Parental involvement and student preparation
9. Expectations from education
10. Education and social problems
11. National legislative developments[3]

DEFINITION OF CURRICULUM

Although there are many definitions of curriculum, one both adequate and comprehensive would include all the experiences, situations, and activities under school authority which involve positive learning in both in-school and out-of-school programs.

This broad concept of curriculum presents a multiplicity of problems for individuals and groups who are concerned with planning and teaching. Whereas curriculum planning in the early years of American education was relatively simple, the future will challenge the best efforts of everyone. The findings of research in child growth and development, the psychology of learning, and educational sociology have influenced curriculum development. Increasing industrialization has created new economic problems. Two world wars, the era of depression, the present global confrontation, international uneasiness, socio-economic problems accompanied by spiraling costs and inflation are placing such demands on the curriculum that educators are alarmed. They feel that the curriculum must be adapted to the aim of assisting students in meeting the many new problems that will confront them when they leave school and go out into the world.

In order to educate students to meet actual life situations, many innovative programs have been tried and others are on the horizon. The subject fields are no longer inviolate educational entities. Moreover, there seems to be an all-out effort to devise relevant educational experiences for students to keep them from prematurely leaving school.

Physical education leaders are asking the question, What will be the status of physical education in the curriculum of the future? Since 1918 when the Seven Cardinal Principles of Education were formulated, health has been foremost among the objectives of education. Since physical education makes a direct contribution to health, leaders in the field have felt secure in the status that physical education has retained in the school curriculum.

In 1973, an educational goal-searching program was launched by Phi Delta Kappa, the prestigious educational fraternity. Not since the establishment of the Seven Cardinal Principles in 1918 has such an extensive effort been made to determine the goals of American education. Eighteen goals of education were sent to 1020 members of Phi Delta Kappa, who were asked to rate them according to their own convictions. The 60 per cent return was tabulated and the goals ranked as shown in Chapter 1.[4]

In *The Reform of Secondary Education*, 32 recommendations were made to improve the educational scene in the secondary schools of the country. These

APPENDIX B NATIONAL GOALS IN HISTORICAL PERSPECTIVE	
CARDINAL PRINCIPLES OF 1918	NATIONAL GOALS OF 1973
Health (Physical Fitness)	Adjustment to Change (Mental Health)
Command of Fundamental Processes	Communication Skills Computation Skills
Vocation	Occupational Competence
Civic Education	Responsibility for Citizenship Respect for Law and Authority Appreciation of Others
Worthy Home Membership Worthy Use of Leisure Ethical Character	Knowledge of Self, Critical Thinking, Clarification of Values, Economic Understanding, the Achievements of Man, Nature and Environment

--- (Broken Line) - Separates interrelated goals

—— (Solid Line) - Separates unrelated goals

Figure 6-1. National goals of education. (From Brown, B. F.: *The Reform of Secondary Education.* New York: McGraw-Hill Book Co., 1973, p. 188.)

recommendations will no doubt have far-reaching effects on the secondary school curriculum.[5] Figure 6-1 shows the relationship of the proposed reforms to the Seven Cardinal Principles.

After reviewing the two studies on goals of education, some leaders may become concerned with the status of physical education. In 1918, the Seven Cardinal Principles listed health first, but approximately 60 years later Phi Delta Kappa has suggested 18 goals and ranked health fifteenth. *The Reform of Secondary Education* does not even include physical education among its 32 recommendations. It does suggest that mental health replace physical fitness.

These reports raise many questions. Why is physical education not listed in either study? Health is vaguely mentioned in both studies. Physical education makes contributions to health, but the question remains, Why was the area of physical education overlooked?

The Phi Delta Kappa study includes physical fitness as a part of its fifteenth goal, but physical fitness is *not* physical education. Physical fitness is an objective of physical education.

The Reform of Secondary Education will have a strong impact on the secondary curriculum, and many educators will follow the recommendations which it makes. Physical education will have to be reassessed and a strong program of interpretation launched if it is to remain within the curriculum outlined in this report.

The remainder of this chapter will be devoted to suggested procedures in developing a physical education curriculum consistent with the changing curriculum emphases that are influencing education in America's schools.

CONSIDERATIONS IN CURRICULUM CHANGE

Curriculum Patterns

Curriculum pattern refers to the plan to be used for designing the total curriculum. It is the style or format that serves as a guide in developing the various components to be included in the curriculum. The major patterns that affect curriculum development are (1) traditional curriculum and (2) innovative curriculum.

Traditional Curriculum. The traditional curriculum is characterized by its adherence to the conventional patterns of organization, methods of teaching, and placement of learning experiences in the various subject areas which have dominated school curricula over the years. The traditional curriculum is inflexible and textbook-oriented, with little provision made for the interests and needs of students.

Other characteristics of the traditional curriculum are (1) undue emphasis on competition for grades, (2) the promotion and failure concept, (3) the measurement of progress by norms, (4) an emphasis on order and decorum, (5) the use of teaching methods that prevent student response, (6) subject areas without relevance, and (7) formal classroom organization.

Students usually enter the 1st grade and proceed grade by grade through to the 12th, meeting teacher-made obstacles at each grade level. These obstacles consist of pre-planned bits of knowledge that must be absorbed by the student in order for him to be placed in the next grade level.

On the elementary level teachers and administrators have largely broken away from the traditional curriculum, but unfortunately the secondary schools for the most part are still adhering to it.

Innovative Curriculum. The innovative curriculum is characterized by change and diversity. Such procedures as flexible and elective scheduling, team teaching, individualized instruction, open schools, and differentiated staffing are observed in many school programs today. In curriculum development the values of these innovations should be carefully examined before including them in the physical education planning.

Factors Affecting Curriculum Development

There are many factors that must be considered in the development of any curriculum in education. These factors either directly or indirectly influence the effectiveness of curriculum implementation.

Accountability. One of the most important of the current movements involving the educational process is the trend to hold teachers accountable to the public for the effectiveness of instruction. The rising costs of education and the failure of many students to attain minimal reading and mathematical skills have caused taxpayers to question the value of education as it presently exists.

Recent lawsuits by concerned parents who are not satisfied with instruction, particularly in reading skills, are a grave indication of what the future may hold for education if it does not improve. As the issue of accountability gains momentum, certain dubious practices by teachers are unveiled. Parents are questioning such procedures as failure to recognize nonlearners and to provide special instruction for them. Too often students are promoted each year without acquiring sufficient reading skills to cope with the instructional content demanded in the succeeding level.

Teachers in California are required by law to be accountable for their teaching effectiveness. Thirty-three states have accountability by legislation pending and nine others are studying such requirements.

Plans for determining accountability include the assessment of student progress, observations for evaluation, and achievement standards. The use of behavioral or performance objectives for observation and evaluation is already routine practice in many places. The advantages and disadvantages of these objectives have been discussed in Chapter 5.

How does the accountability movement affect physical education? This question is not easily answered. Before any satisfactory reply can be made, the objectives of physical education must be developed. How many teachers and physical education leaders know what the purposes are in physical education? Is the program designed to prepare for leisure time participation? If so, to what extent are we attaining these goals?

The accountability movement has far-reaching implications for every subject area in the curriculum. No longer can instruction based upon outmoded objectives be tolerated. Each area of instruction must justify its existence in the curriculum. Can physical education leaders convince the taxpaying public that physical education is a necessary educational component? The need for physical education, which involves millions of dollars annually for salaries, equipment, and facilities, must be justified.

Computers in Physical Education. Another innovation that involves physical education on a limited scale is the computer. Computers are used not only for complex scheduling procedures (modular scheduling) but also for recording grades and the results of extensive testing programs.

Systems Approach. Budgetary problems arising from the continual spiraling of educational costs have prompted educators to look at the systems approach in curriculum construction. This approach brings teachers, administrators, the school board, and the community together to study the priorities, needs, and costs of education. Priorities are established and objectives are developed to evaluate the effectiveness of the program.

When the curriculum is developed and the content selected, each item should be weighed against possible alternatives. Teaching procedures are organized to relate to each phase of the curriculum content. The objectives are usually written in performance terms, which provide a more accurate measure of progress.

Conceptual Approach to Teaching. Good describes conceptual teaching as a "method of teaching which emphasizes the usefulness of learning through the formation of consistent, generalized symbolic ideas."[6] Teachers who prescribe the instructional content are seldom, if ever, aware that very little discovery and intellectual stimulation are involved. Through the conceptual approach the teacher, by generalizing, can make the instructional content more relevant and stimulating. Through the use of many teaching aids and media, students will make discoveries on their own and strive toward attaining their potential. As the teacher draws on the general interests of students, he is able to lead them step by step to a better grasp of the area of instruction.

Thoughtful physical education teachers have been applying the principles of conceptual instruction for many years. Reduced to its simplest proportions, conceptual teaching in physical education involves, in addition to the teaching of skills, the inclusion of all knowledge related to the skill. In teaching the skills of tennis, for example, the student should know about the leisure-time aspects of the sport. He should understand the social opportunities open to him through playing tennis in coeducational situations. The student, as he is led through the various progressions in learning the game, will gradually gain insight into his tennis potential and discover new social, mental, physical, and emotional relationships in his involvement with friends and community.

Humanizing the Physical Education Curriculum. In these days of transition, all education administrators are deeply concerned with personnel practices. Too frequently teachers are left to their own devices to succeed or fail. It is generally recognized by experienced administrators that most teachers need expert assistance from principals, supervisors, department heads, and fellow teachers. Many of the problems growing out of teacher-student relationships would be avoided if new teachers were actively included in departmental meetings and if better communication between teachers and administrators was initiated and maintained.

Teachers must be made to feel that they are a part of the school and the department in which they work. In recent years, because of integration, many students and faculty members have been reassigned to schools which are unfamiliar to them, and sometimes adjustment to the new schools is extremely difficult. An alert administrator should schedule orientation programs for both old and new teachers and provide time and opportunity for all teachers to communicate with one another. In-service programs should be planned, and all new and reassigned teachers should be given important assignments in these programs.

Some school systems have developed programs to help teachers in overcoming prejudice and misunderstanding. One such program was planned by the public school system of Montgomery County, Maryland. An important part of the program was the publication of a booklet entitled *Primer of Understanding,* prepared in an attempt to overcome prejudice and translate the expressions of black students into standard English.[7] Distributed to teachers, it served as an aid to communication and greater understanding.

Through staff development services involving in-service programs, teachers become familiar with the many facets of instruction which play important roles in shaping attitudes of students toward each other and toward their teachers. Teachers, as they work together in the development of the curriculum, learn to communicate and understand one another.

In Palo Alto, California, a multicultural advisory committee of the Unified School District states that "A multiculturally integrated curriculum and instructional program is one which enables students to develop and function more perceptively, honestly, and creatively in all areas of intellectual and social interaction." The committee further states that this type of curriculum may be developed by acquiring a knowledge and understanding of :

1. the root cultures of mankind
2. the American subcultures
3. the characteristics of racism, prejudice, and destructive ethnocentrism
4. the techniques of rational analysis
5. practical human relations
6. the practical methods of solving problems[8]

A number of school systems have incorporated in the curriculum materials such as guides and supplementary aids. These materials make the classes more interesting, lessen disruptive behavior, and assist students in developing a positive self-image.

Physical education administrators and teachers assigned to develop curriculum guides should attempt to make the content more relevant to the needs, interests, and desires of all students. Some suggestions are:

1. Provide individualized instruction in leisure-time activities for all students, irrespective of sex, race, color, creed, size, and ability.
2. Plan and provide intramural programs for all students rather than for a select few.
3. Develop co-recreational programs for all students at all levels.
4. Teach the dances and rhythmical activities of various ethnic groups.

PHYSICAL EDUCATION AND TYPES OF CURRICULUM

The program in physical education is highly sensitive to the various curriculum patterns in the American school system. There are five major curriculum patterns, which vary in different sections of the country from the traditional to the experimental types. These are discussed in the following paragraphs.

The Subject Curriculum

The subject curriculum is the traditional pattern of curriculum organization that relies on the teaching of a number of separate subjects, such as civics, history, and geography. In the strictest interpretation of this type of curriculum, the teacher plans the content of the subject and relies upon the textbook as the basic guide.

The areas that constitute the subject curriculum are usually required and are placed at the various grade levels. Some subjects receive more time than others, according to the opinion of curriculum committees and individuals who have the authority to make these decisions. English, for instance, is usually required daily each year in the secondary school. In many places physical education from grades 1 through 12 is also required by state law.

Physical Education in the Subject Curriculum. Physical education is usually treated as a separate subject and is scheduled daily. Leaders in the field have, for many years, pressed for this daily requirement in order that physical education maintain a respectable position in the curriculum. Although the daily requirement has been the goal, many schools still do not grant this amount of time to the program. Although many weaknesses have developed in the subject curriculum, it does provide a vehicle for separate emphasis on physical education in a grade K through 12 arrangement.

The Correlated Curriculum

The correlated curriculum attempts to recognize and utilize the relationships among subjects without destroying the identity of any subject. As an example, English, history, art, and music are often taught as an interrelated whole under such designations as American Studies or Western Civilization, without destroying the identity of any of the individual courses.

Physical Education in the Correlated Curriculum. There are many ways in which other subjects in the curriculum may be correlated with physical education. Health education, for example, may be correlated with physical education without destroying the identity of either

subject. Such areas as personal responsibility and cleanliness, athletic health problems and knowledge, sanitation, health and social problems, and, finally, a survey of the physical education plant and services may be taught adequately in the combined arrangement. The art department may assist in the construction of posters and other materials for exhibitions. The vocational department may construct equipment for use in the instructional program in physical education.

A clear distinction should be made between correlation and integration. As explained above, in a correlated curriculum certain relationships between two subjects may be recognized without losing the identity of either subject. On the other hand, integration may fuse relationships between subjects to the extent that a subject disappears completely. A certain amount of correlation may exist between physical education and other subjects to the advantage of all subjects, whereas integration, when carried to the extreme, may eventually destroy a program in physical education. The premise that physical education is basically movement and that daily movement is necessary for normal growth and development precludes successful attempts to integrate physical education with other subjects.

The Broad-Fields Curriculum

The broad-fields approach is an attempt to modify the traditional subject-centered curriculum. This approach seeks to eliminate the sharp lines of demarcation in the subject curriculum, to bring together the knowledge common to the subjects involved, and to study them in a broader context. An illustration is the way biology is currently taught. Biology, as taught in the secondary schools, covers the fields of botany, physiology, zoology, anatomy, and bacteriology, combining pertinent elements of these areas into one instructional unit.

Physical Education in the Broad-Fields Curriculum. The broad-fields approach to curriculum design has probably affected physical education more than any other type of curriculum construction. In their efforts to include everything in the curriculum, administrators frequently attempt to combine related areas into one broad subject. Health education and physical education, for example, are taught as a unit in public schools throughout the country, with safety education also being included in many schools. Such combinations may serve to augment physical education, and the curriculum of the future may combine health education and physical education into a broad administrative unit in order to find a place for these two areas.

The Core Curriculum

In the core curriculum, subjects are required but time allotments and content are varied to meet the needs of the individual student. The content for the class is usually predetermined by teachers and students and eliminates the traditional subject barriers. Current block-scheduling designs indicate a revival of this concept under new terminology.

Physical Education in the Core Curriculum. Physical education in the core curriculum school is usually organized as a subject-centered area of instruction. Although some authors have suggested plans and opportunities for using the core philosophy in physical education, administrators still schedule physical education as a separate subject.

The Experience Curriculum

The experience curriculum represents an effort to relate teaching to the situations and problems that confront children in everyday living. Teachers help students to understand problems in the world at large and to make decisions relating to life.

The most important characteristic of the experience curriculum is its relevance to the problems of youth. Although the knowledge and experience of several subject areas may be mobilized

to concentrate on a particular problem, the results may be questioned. The results are doubtful because of the enormous time factor involved, the lack of continuity in general education, and the inability of students to successfully assume much of the planning procedure.

Physical Education and the Experience Curriculum. Physical education programs have for many years felt the influence of the experience curriculum. Planning the physical education program based on the experience curriculum concept involves the inclusion of the play pattern, which practically eliminates teaching. Although play is an important element in physical education, one can easily see how the "play" concept could rule out such major objectives of physical education as the development of fitness, instruction and orientation in sports, and dance and rhythmic programs, all of which are so necessary for normal growth and development.

The brief overview of the curriculum patterns just presented and the relationship of physical education to these patterns point to a definite conclusion. Except in the broad-fields curriculum, physical education remains a separate subject in the curriculum planning process throughout the nation. This is as it should be, since the major goal of physical education is to provide an opportunity for boys and girls to participate daily in activities that will promote their physical growth. To accomplish this aim, there must first be a separate place for physical education in the school program. Innovations that have proved successful may then be incorporated within the daily instructional classes.

PRINCIPLES OF CURRICULUM DEVELOPMENT

For the curriculum to be functional and responsive to socio-economic changes, guidelines to curriculum development are necessary. DeYoung and Wynn divide the principles for curriculum development into two groups: (1) the nature of the curriculum and (2) the process of curriculum development.

The Nature of the Curriculum

1. The curriculum should be rooted in a philosophy of education.

2. The curriculum should accommodate a wide range of individual abilities and needs of students.

3. The curriculum should be life-centered, shaped by both the present and future needs of the individual and society.

4. The curriculum should be well balanced.

The Process of Curriculum Development

1. Curriculum building should be a cooperative enterprise.

2. Evaluation is essential for curriculum improvement.

3. Curriculum support systems should be adequate.

4. Curriculum development should be a systematic process.[9]

SCOPE AND SEQUENCE

The extent of offerings that are found in the curriculum is referred to as *scope*. The curriculum may consist of a narrow range of activities, or there may be a diversified program consisting of many areas of instruction. In curriculum development, all of the research that is involved, the time spent in planning, and the final selection of activities result in the scope of offerings which is referred to as the curriculum.

Sequence is concerned with the placement of the scope of activities, or where they fall in the instructional pattern. It refers to the grade placement and continuity in which learning experiences occur. Figure 6–2A shows the scope and sequence of one activity and includes the grade placement of the skills of the activity for junior and senior high schools. Other plans outline the curriculum areas of instruction (scope), the time allotment, and the placement of all activities by grades (sequence). (See Figure 6-2B.)

ELEMENTS AND STEPS IN CURRICULUM CONSTRUCTION

The curriculum should be developed step by step, with input from the school personnel, from community groups, and from the vast array of knowledge and materials available from many sources. The steps should include (1) general agreement that a need exists for curriculum development, (2) pre-planning, (3) investigating the field, (4) implementing, and (5) appraisal of results. Each step involves a number of elements that are essential in developing the total physical education curriculum. Committees should be formed for each of the steps and the elements assigned. Figure 6–3 outlines such an arrangement.

Of the many elements involved in the construction of the physical education curriculum, probably the most important is the *selection of activities*. There are literally hundreds of activities that may be included in the program; Bancroft lists more than 500.[10] At this point many questions are raised. Which of the numerous activities should be excluded? On what basis are activities selected for the curriculum? Should the selection of activities be left to the discretion of the teacher? If the teacher selects them, on what basis is the selection made? The gravity of the problem of curriculum content in our nation's schools is pointed out in a study by the Battle Creek Physical Education Curriculum Project, which stated that "It appears that a primary need in physical education is one of establishing a systematic method of selecting, organizing, and evaluating curriculum content so that the relevant knowledges, skills, and values may be incorporated into the teacher-learning situation."[11]

CURRENT METHODS OF SELECTING ACTIVITIES

While there are several approaches to the selection of activities for the physical education curriculum, three of the most commonly used—individual judgment, empirical method, and the questionnaire method—merit separate discussion.

Text continued on page 144

SCOPE AND SEQUENCE (Grade Placement of Skills)

CHART I: NORMAL PROGRAM

Time Allotment for Activities Based on 5 periods per week; every semester.

This chart offers suggested time allotment for the entire course of study. Adjustment may be made in accordance with local facilities, equipment, and personnel. On a basis of 180 periods per year, 15 have been allotted for organization and orientation, 10 periods in the Fall and 5 in the Spring.

ACTIVITY	Jr. H.S. (Per. per year)			Sr. H.S. (Per. per year)		
	7th	8th	9th	10th	11th	12th
CONDITIONING AND PHYSICAL FITNESS TESTING	30	15	30	15	15	15
DANCE						
Folk and Square	15			15		
Social			15			15
GYMNASTICS	30	30	15	30	30*	15
Apparatus, Tumbling, Ropes, Rebound Tumbling						
INDIVIDUAL AND DUAL SPORTS						
Bowling			15		15	
Handball		15		15		
Golf		15				15
Tennis	15					15
Others: (Ping-Pong, Badminton Paddle Tennis, Tetherball, etc.)					15*	
TEAM SPORTS						
Basketball	15		30	30		30
Soccer		30		15	15*	15
Softball (Baseball)	15	15	15	15	30*	
Touch Football	15		15	15	30*	
Volleyball		15	15	15	15*	15
TRACK AND FIELD	15	15	15	15		30
AQUATICS	(If facilities are available)					
GAMES	(If time permits)			(If time permits)		
Low Organization, Contests, Relays, Self-Testing, Mass Games						
TOTALS	165	165	165	165	165	165

A

*Schools offering Hygiene (Health Teaching) in the 11th Year should omit these 15-period units and give 30-period units for only 15 periods.

Figure 6-2. *A*, Scope and sequence of activities for the secondary schools. *B*, Scope and sequence in golf. (From *Physical Education for Boys, Grades 7–12; A*, p. 11; *B*, p. 269. Courtesy of the Board of Education, New York City.)

GOLF

SCOPE AND SEQUENCE: (Grade Placement of Skills in Golf)

GUIDE
B — Basic skills
R — Review skills

	JUNIOR HIGH SCHOOL			SENIOR HIGH SCHOOL		
GRADE:	7	8	9	10	11	12
KNOWLEDGE						
Basic rules of the game		B				B
Golf etiquette, sportsmanship		B				B
Glossary of terms used		B				B
Safety precautions		B				B
Equipment, and care of equipment		B				B
SKILLS						
Warmup exercises		B				B
Grip		B				R
Stance		B				R
Backswing		B				R
Downswing		B				R
Putting		B				R
Short Irons (5-9 iron)		B				R
Half swing (punch)		B				R
Full swing (shoulder level)		B				R
Long Irons (2-4)						B
Half swing (punch)						B
Full swing (shoulder level)						B
Woods						
#3 Wood (Brassie)		B				R
#1 Wood (Driver)						B
#2, 4 Wood						B
Chipping						
Pitch and run						B
Pitch						B
Sand shots						B
Correction of errors						
Slice		B				B
Hook		B				B
Smother		B				B
Topping		B				B
Shank		B				B
KNOWLEDGE AND SKILL TESTS		B				B
LEADUP DRILLS AND EXERCISES		B				B
CULMINATING ACTIVITY (Trip to golf course; Intramural Tournament)		B				B

B

Figure 6–2. *continued*

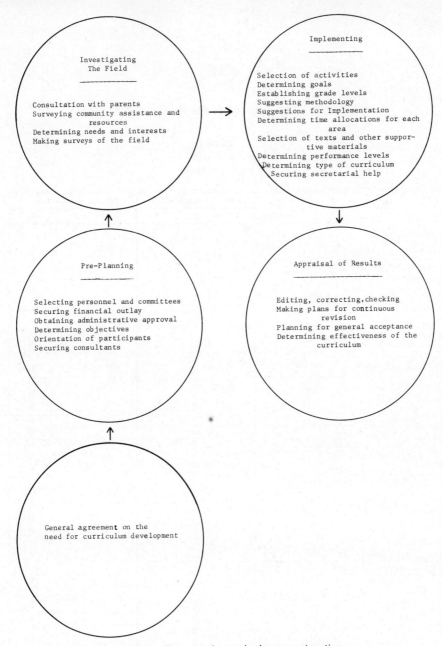

Figure 6-3. Elements in curriculum construction.

Individual Judgment

This method is the most prevalent one for selecting the activities to be taught in the physical education program. Unfortunately, many activities that are dangerous and unsound and that make no contribution to the health of boys and girls are included in programs because teachers or coaches like them and not because research or scientific considerations have indicated their desirability.

Teachers almost universally are allowed to determine curriculum content without the assistance of qualified supervision or a scientifically developed guidebook. When placed in this dilemma, they usually resort to an arbitrary selection of activities, often determined by what they happened to participate in at college. Since they may lack the scientific judgment in the selection of physical education activities, the curriculum is allowed to deteriorate. Such a careless approach to curriculum construction would not be accepted in the academic program.

Generally, the teachers of physical education also coach athletic teams, and too often they restrict the physical education class to the development of those skills involved in the athletic program. Programs developed around this philosophy have hurt physical education throughout the country because they are unscientific, inadequate, and inconsiderate of the educational needs and interests of all students.

The Empirical Method

In many places the curriculum is based on the writings of a few leaders who, through observation and practical experience, determine what should be included in the curriculum. This approach has some merit, but too often the selection of content may result in unsound activities that may adversely affect the health and safety of children. An illustration of how this approach may result in negative outcomes is the universal acceptance of the sit-up with extended knees as an abdominal exercise. For half a century physical educators faithfully included this exercise in the curriculum, and it is still done in some schools today even though recent research has shown that the sit-up is not an abdominal exercise unless the knees are flexed. Furthermore, sit-ups when done with the knees extended may accentuate the postural condition of lordosis in some children.

The Questionnaire

A popular procedure in determining which activities should be taught is the questionnaire survey. The two most commonly used types of surveys are the survey of *participants* and the survey of *leaders* in physical education. Surveys of participants show by the actual experience which activities meet their needs.

A study conducted by the Opinion Research Corporation of Princeton for the President's Council on Physical Fitness and Sports revealed startling findings concerning the extent of exercise by Americans 22 years of age or older. The survey was made in 360 communities throughout the country and presents an accurate picture of what adult participants do to promote their personal fitness. The survey indicated that most of the respondents during their school years participated in team sports such as basketball, football, and baseball rather than lifetime sports such as golf, tennis, and handball.[12]

From time to time, surveys have been made of the opinions of leaders to assist in the selection of activities for the physical education curriculum. The most extensive attempt to construct a curriculum in physical education based on the opinions of leaders was made by La Porte.[13] The revised edition of this book took note of the need for determining participant interests and found a high correlation between the interest appeal of the prevailing activities and the ones in the revised edition.

The importance of selecting activities scientifically for the physical education curriculum cannot be overemphasized. It has been shown in the preceding paragraphs why many current approaches to the selection of activities are unsound. Programs that were sufficient to meet the needs of individuals during the past 40 years are not appropriate for the future. Recent research showing the importance of lifetime activities, total fitness, and emotional stability necessitates taking a new look at curriculum content and the criteria for its evaluation. Evidence points to the need for a more scientific approach to the selection of activities that compose the program in physical education.

Curriculum construction and the selection of activities for the program are tedious and time-consuming procedures, but when educators and parents realize that the health and fitness of children depend upon their efforts, the task becomes both challenging and satisfying.

The first step in the scientific selection of curriculum content is the establishment of criteria to measure or evaluate each activity. These criteria should take into consideration the fundamental needs of children. A review of the literature reveals such a large number of criteria that to list them all here would be both impractical and unnecessary.

In order that the selection of content be sound, the criteria should be few in number and stated as realistically as possible. With this premise in mind, several criteria are discussed at length on the following pages.

GENERAL CRITERIA

A careful study of the field reveals several general criteria that should be used in determining the activities for the physical education curriculum. These criteria should include all of the essentials necessary for a sound and scientific selection of activities. The activities, once selected, may be safely used anywhere in the country. The following general criteria merit consideration for curriculum planners who desire a curriculum that is designed to meet the needs of all children.

The Activities Should be Consistent with Basic Objectives of Physical Education

Too often objectives are carefully laid down at the beginning but are soon forgotten in the course of the program. Only those activities that meet the established objectives of the program should be included in the program.

Many objectives have been developed by professional leaders and groups. Those developed by Rosentswieg from a study of 100 college physical educators seem appropriate for present use: (1) organic vigor, (2) neuromuscular skills,

(3) leisure-time activities, (4) self-realization, and (5) emotional stability.[14]

The Activities Should Be Safe and Should Contribute to Health and Fitness

Teachers are responsible by law for the safety of all students in their classes. They must assure parents that the activities taught are safe. Those which are unsafe should be excluded from the program.

Many court decisions have been handed down in which teachers have been declared negligent. Such court actions come under the phase of law known as *tort law*, described further in Chapter 2. The physical education administrator should be familiar with the applicable sections of tort law.

In organizing the instructional program, several precautions should be taken to assist teachers in the prevention of accidents:

Teachers should stay with their classes. Teachers should never leave their classes. If they should leave and an accident occurs while they are away, it is a simple matter to prove negligence. *The Wall Street Journal* reports a verdict of $300,000 against a teacher in New Jersey. The teacher had left the class, and while he was gone a student was seriously injured on a springboard.[15]

Exclude unsafe activities. Recent research shows that some activities are extremely dangerous. A case in point is the trampoline. Zimmerman shows that "Based on the number of hours of participation, injuries occurred twice as frequently in colleges as they did in the high schools. Therefore, the teaching of the sport is not only dangerous but it loses all carry-over value for the student."[16]

Tumbling would meet the objectives of trampolining just as well, with fewer accident possibilities. Boxing is another illustration of a sport that can be replaced with a less dangerous one: wrestling meets all of the objectives of boxing and is much safer.

Use correct teaching procedures. There is a correct way of teaching all activities in the physical education curriculum. The teacher should know these since he is a specialist in the field; a teacher who violates these procedures may be judged negligent in an accident case. *Physical Education Newsletter* describes a case in which the New York City School Board was held liable for injuries sustained by a boy who was "overmatched" in a kickball game. The students were matched by numbers instead of by height or weight. The teacher and Board of Education were held guilty of negligence.[17]

Organize classes correctly. Proper class organization plays an important role in reducing accidents. Many court cases have found teachers negligent because of poor class organization. *Physical Education Newsletter* reports a case in which a girl was injured playing indoor line soccer. The court claimed the teacher was more interested in securing active participation by as many students as possible than in the safety of her students.[18]

Articles in professional periodicals and other publications offer sufficient evidence to conclude that many of the traditional exercises used by teachers are contraindicated and should be excluded from the curriculum. Not only do the exercises fall short of what they are supposed to do, but too often they also have serious anatomical implications that may adversely affect the health and fitness of boys and girls. Some of these movements are deep-knee bends,[19, 20] sit-ups,[21–24] leg-lifts,[22, 23] toe-touching,[25] push-ups,[26] and the back-arch.[27] Students of physical education should study in depth the opinions and comments of the authors listed in these references.

The traditional exercises just mentioned have been studied and found to be unsatisfactory for inclusion in the physical education curriculum. There are other contraindicated movements that have not received as much attention as those listed but which need to be carefully evaluated before they are included. One of these is the "split." There are instances where serious damage has been done by forcing all girls to perform the split. Many girls are anatomically unable to accomplish the movement, and to force it may seriously damage the sacrum.

The entire field of conditioning exercises or *calisthenics* has been under scrutiny for many years. This group of activities was originally a part of the gymnastics program and, according to Williams, survived because the exercises were inexpensive, required very little time, did not demand specially trained teachers, could be conducted in the classroom, and required no equipment.[28]

Calisthenics do not produce fitness, but when used as warm-up exercises related to teaching a sport, they may be acceptable. However, some teachers use them indiscriminately, allowing them to dominate the curriculum. This is clearly contraindicated, and many leaders in physical education vigorously oppose calisthenics altogether. Hetherington, at the turn of the century, when gymnastics dominated physical education, stated:

The emphasis in selection for a curriculum of activities in the school to meet the needs of children and present-day social demands must be on the natural or big-muscle play activities—the natural activities are educationally more valuable than gymnastic drills. They give a certain development of intellectual, emotional, nervous, and organic powers not given in the same degree by any kind of activity in child life, and it is impossible to gain the broad and more significant phases of these values through drills.[29]

Cowell, a more recent leader in physical education, stated that "When natural activities were substituted for formal gymnastics, it brought physical education into greater harmony with biological laws, which resulted in a better approach to meet the needs of all children."[30] Calisthenics, contrived and unnatural, have no scientific basis for appearing in the curriculum. They have been retained year after year, probably because many of them were used for corrective purposes, and teachers have continued to accept them without question. Flint states that "Although most exercises are planned to accomplish certain purposes, sometimes the types of movement involved make it impossible to meet the objectives and the results would be unsatisfactory."[31]

Many calisthenic movements, such as those mentioned above, unless performed properly, may cause serious damage to the body. On the other hand, natural, "big-muscle" movements are beneficial for normal growth and development, and contribute to the health and fitness of children.

"Warm-up" exercises are acceptable, provided they incorporate the actual movement involved in the major activity that follows. For example, a batter can improve his game by swinging two bats before batting, and a pitcher by throwing moderately before he enters the game. It would be absurd for the batter or the pitcher to perform push-ups or sit-ups prior to playing. Flint explains that there should be a scientific basis to the use of calisthenics, and states that "... if activities are selected without meeting individual needs and unless their execution is supervised carefully, a dangerous practice may be the result."[32]

A recent study of the values of the warm-up was reported in the *Journal of Health, Physical Education and Recreation.* If the best possible results are desired, then the warm-up is necessary, according to 95 per cent of the studies reported. The following conclusions summarized the findings in the report:

1. Fourteen of 22 studies showed significant improvement in performance following warm-up.
2. Seven of the 22 studies showed improvement in performance following warm-up, but the improvement was not statistically significant.
3. One of the studies showed a decrease in muscular strength following passive warm-up, but muscular endurance was not affected.
4. A vigorous, long warm-up appears to contribute more to better performance than does a moderate, shorter warm-up.
5. A related type warm-up seems to improve performance more than an unrelated warm-up.
6. Attitude appears to have an influence upon the degree of improvement of performance following warm-up.[33]

Physical education teachers in each grade and throughout their daily instruction should continually try to develop in each child a positive attitude toward physical education. Movement is one of the basic urges of man and it is natural for normal children to be active. Physi-

cal education teachers should take advantage of this natural desire for movement and teach those skills which are important for normal growth and development and which will motivate students to continue physical activity throughout their lives.

It is disheartening to observe children playing joyously for years in their daily routine who suddenly undergo a complete change of attitude toward physical education. This change sometimes is so pronounced that it approaches rebellion when students are assigned to a physical education class.

Probably one of the causes of this change is the attitude of the teacher. The domineering, militaristic, whistle-blowing type of teacher who relies on a strictly formal and uninteresting method of teaching a class is sure to encounter hostility toward both himself and the program. Another cause of disinterest among students is the type of activities included in the program. The contraindicated movements mentioned earlier and other meaningless calisthenics are almost guaranteed to turn students against the program. On the other hand, activities that involve fundamental movements such as running, jumping, throwing, and catching are always interesting to students. When sports are taught that include these movements, the interest in physical education is high. Students are thirsty for effective instruction in tennis, bowling, golf, handball, basketball, swimming, modern dance, and other activities that include the movements mentioned above.

Finally, the dedicated teacher should familiarize himself with the yearly growth needs of children and the activities that are suitable for these needs. Lack of knowledge will lead to the use of the wrong activity and eventually cause the student to lose interest in physical education.

The Activities Should Involve Instruction

In surveying the list of possible activities that might be included in the physical education program, one can readily see that many require no instruction. When "frill" activities involving machines, gadgets, and many types of calisthenics are used, the need for a teacher rapidly diminishes. Unfortunately, programs completely dominated by calisthenics are not uncommon. Many types of fitness activities involving obstacle races, bars, and climbing apparatus likewise require little, if any, instruction, and in fact dominate the elementary program in many places precisely because no instruction is necessary and students may exercise on their own. The authors do not wish to imply that all of these activities should be excluded from the total program, but if the curriculum is to be an instruction-oriented one, then many of them should receive careful scrutiny before they are included.

For example, some schools include such activities as roller skating in the curriculum, even though almost all students learn to skate before entering school. Why should valuable instructional time be spent by the teacher watching a group of students skate? An alternative to this arrangement would be to teach the skills of figure skating, which involves a sophisticated level of instruction and thus could be justified for being included in the curriculum.

Activities Should Include Movement Education

A trend that seems to be gaining popularity, particularly in the elementary level, is *movement education*. Godfrey and Kephart define movement education as "that aspect either of physical education or classroom education which deals with the development and training in basic movement patterns as differentiated from movement skills."[34] Movement patterns are sometimes classified into three groups: (1) *locomotion movements,* which include walking, running, skipping, jumping, leaping, hopping, galloping, and sliding; (2) *nonlocomotion movements,* such as swinging, twisting, bending, pushing, pulling, stretching, and lifting; and (3) *manipulative movements* — throwing, catching, striking, and kicking. Williams, in his *Principles of Physical Education*, as early as 1925 referred to the natural, fundamental movements of man and the importance of including these movements in the program of physical education. He maintained this concept of physical education throughout his life and it was still included in the final edition of his text.[35]

Experimentation with curriculum revision in an effort to improve the quality of instructional content and teaching procedures led to research in psychology and kinesiology that has provided a greater insight into what physical education really is. Although physical education is primarily movement, more seems to be involved than just the teaching of skills, particularly in the kindergarten and primary grades. The advocates of movement education maintain that early basic experiences in the fundamental movements are prerequisites to more effective skill instruction in later years. They feel that experiences in jumping, running, hanging, walking, pushing, throwing, and catching serve as the foundation for all physical education. As the child moves through space, employing these movements, he becomes more aware of them and therefore will be better prepared to master the complex skills of sports and other activities. As the child experiences sensations of space, force, and handling objects in his exploration of the world of movement, he becomes exhilarated by the kinesthetic adjustments of his body. He develops confidence as he learns, through the use of objects, to make the perceptual judgments necessary to perform various tasks. For example, when the child catches a ball, he makes more perceptual judgments than he does when throwing it. To catch an object involves visual tracing of the object's flight and adjusting the various parts of the body to receive it. Running a dash does not require as many perceptual judgments as running over a bench or a hurdle. Dribbling a basketball requires more adjustments when an opponent is guarding the dribbler. Walking on a railroad tie requires more insight and balance than

Figure 6-4. *A* and *B,* A test for perceptual motor activities. (Courtesy of Hutchinson Public Schools, Hutchinson, Kansas.)

Administering the Developmental Perceptual-Motor Rating Survey

Educators in Hutchinson, Kans., follow these instructions when giving the district's perceptual-motor rating survey to kindergarten children.

Items 1-4 survey the child's achievement level in balance, posture, and laterality.

Material: Walking Board

Room approximately 8 x 12 ft., free of obstacles, sufficient space to clear wall or objects in all four activities. Possible credit on each item: 4, 3, 2, or 1.

1. *Walking Board: Forward*
   Position child on floor at one end of board. Tell child, "Get upon the board and walk to the other end."
2. *Jumping*
   Position child in center of free area. Tell child "Place both feet together. Jump one step forward." Follow this with "Place both feet together as before. Make one long jump."
3. *Hop*
   Position child as in jumping task. *Task A*—Right foot: Say to child, "Stand on your right foot with your left foot off the floor. Jump one foot forward without putting your left foot down." Ask child to do the same task standing on the left foot. *Task B*—As above, two hops on right, two on left.
4. *Skip*
   Position child at one end of free area. Say to him "Skip to the wall over there and back to where you started."
5. *Identification of Body Parts* (Vital to Space Localization)
   Position child in free area as in previous items. Tell the child to stand facing you. Say to him: Touch your shoulders, hips, head, ankles, ears, feet, eyes, elbows, and mouth.
6. *Imitation of Movement*
   Neuromuscular control and translation of visual clues into motor movement. Examiner will position arms as shown, and child will be asked to imitate. Examiner's reference: Make stick figure as on summary sheet.
   Position as follows: (a) bilateral, (b) unilateral, (c) bilateral, (d) contralateral, (e) unilateral, (f) contralateral, (g) bilateral. Instruct child to stand facing you at distance of two feet. (free area) Say to child "I am going to move my arms freely (demonstrate several positions) and want you to move your arms just as I do each time." (Parallel if child moves right arm when examiner moves right arm.)
7. *Chalkboard Drawings—Problems of Directionality*
   Task A—Circle: Instruct child to step to chalkboard and draw a circle. Note on summary sheet: preferred hand, size of drawing, position with respect to child's midline, accuracy and direction of production. Structure task for him if necessary. Illustrate size, place dot on board for center of circle.
   Task B—Lines (lateral) Place 2 x's, 20 to 24 inches apart. Ask child to stand midway between 2 x's. Ask him to draw a line from one x to the other. Note on summary sheet: preferred hand, movement of body and direction of movement. Child may change hands when crossing midline. May move whole body, hips, etc.
8. *Ocular Control*
   Eye movement control—following a target.
   Materials: penlight or pencil with thumbtack in eraser.
   Procedure: Seat child in chair opposite examiner. Move penlight in arc, telling him you want his eyes to follow wherever it moves. Hold light 20 inches before child's face and at his eye level. *Task A:* Both eyes. Move light along arc of a circle with radius of about 20 inches, having its center at a point between child's eyes. Same for vertical arc. Assign rating.
9. *Visual Achievement Forms*
   Perceptual-Motor Match
   Materials: Four visual achievement forms, one 8 1/2 x 11 sheet of plain white paper, two pencils reasonably sharp, desk or table suitable for size of child.
   Procedure: Seat child comfortably at desk. Lay each form, one at a time, flat on desk above top of sheet of paper on which child is instructed to copy the form. Allow child to manipulate paper as he chooses. Each form must be presented as the first. Say to child "Make one like this." (circle) If child asks where to begin on paper, tell him he may draw it wherever he likes, but there are four forms.
   Do not structure the task for him, as to size, direction, and placement on paper.

For details on scoring the test, write the Editor, Physical Education Newsletter, *100 Garfield Avenue, New London, Conn. 06320 and we'll send them to you.*

B

Figure 6–4. *continued*

walking on the ground. When performing basic movements, the body is continually adjusting and refining the movements as the task becomes more involved. This exploration and refinement of fundamental movements is movement education. Successful performance in these movements provides a foundation for efficiency in the acquisition of skills and a more successful performance in movement experiences throughout life.

The values that accrue from a basic program in movement education may be summarized in the following statements:

1. Success is within the reach of every child because the goals are personal. Quality performance (at different levels) is stressed, expected, and usually obtained from the children.

2. Self-discipline and self-direction are expected results. The child must make decisions constantly, and he is held responsible for them.

3. The situation provides a laboratory for freedom to create, to express, and to try out one's own solutions without fear of being a loser or a "dub."

4. When game elements are added—an "it" or a "goal"—the child is ready for the challenge because he has attained a comfortable degree of skill.

5. Although children are quite serious and totally involved in the teaching-learning situation, satisfaction and fun result. This is movement with a purpose and is so recognized by the child; it is exciting to him, as skills develop and success is experienced.[36]

The Activities Should Involve Perceptual-Motor Skills

The teaching of skills has always been a basic objective of physical education. Morehouse and Miller discuss the relation of skills to the nervous system, stating, "The development of motor skills of various types, one of the major objectives of physical education, consists primarily of improvement in the speed and accuracy with which the nervous system coordinates activity."[37]

No one questions the importance of teaching motor skills, yet some leaders feel that better long-range results can be achieved if the learner analyzes the mental processes employed in performing the movement, thus developing an awareness of the learning process. Programs that use this approach in teaching skills are called perceptual-motor programs. Fleming defines perceptual-motor programs as "A means of teaching the child use of the body mechanisms which serve to monitor and control body positions and movement and enable him to derive meaning from sensory experiences."[38]

Psychologists and leaders in child development have advocated the need for experiences in early motor development in order that the child perceive interrelationships in the world around him. Recent studies have led optometrists to believe that lack of motor coordination contributes to visual problems. Many psychologists feel that skills and movements which enable children to coordinate eye-body movements (hands and feet), to achieve an awareness of directionality and laterality, to adjust to postural and balance changes, and to understand body-image are basic to all learning. Nature provides the opportunity for children to develop these skills under normal conditions. However, many children today do not grow and develop in a normal setting, and as a result enter school without sufficient ability to participate in the usual learning process.

The study of perceptual-motor development reveals certain basic concepts. For example, it has been known for years that as the body grows, the motor system develops first. It is also known that not only do motor learnings develop first but they also play a great role in intellectual development during the early years. Since all learning takes place and is manifested through the senses (sight, hearing, kinesthetic sense), it is important that all of these avenues of learning be developed early in life. Unfortunately, too many children enter school without having had the play and movement experience necessary for the development of basic motor skills. Inadequate performance in these skills, in turn, prevents these children from satisfactorily learning how to read, write, and spell; they thus become frustrated, lose interest in school, and become susceptible to the adverse social behavior that is so frequently seen in our schools today.

Considerable attention is presently focused on training in perceptual-motor skills and on the proper performance of these skills in relation to academic learning. This focus has grown out of the studies that have been made in an effort to find the reasons why such a high percentage of children cannot read, write, or spell. However, despite these studies, which clearly show that sound programs in physical education may improve reading ability and other learning skills, a climate of confusion prevails which prevents teachers and administrators from utilizing the fundamental concepts that are necessary in all learning situations.

Too often the assumption is made that all students in a 1st-grade class are ready to learn and that learning will take place if the traditional teaching procedures are used. This assumption may apply to the majority of students, but a fact that has been ignored is that many children enter school without the perceptual-motor skills that are necessary for learning.

A balanced program in physical educaiton not only provides gross motor learning (large-muscle activity) but also emphasizes perceptual-motor experiences in grades K–3. Unfortunately, although there is evidence to show that daily participation in a well-planned physical education program is extremely important as a means for improving academic learning, many students do not have the opportunity for this participation.[39] Tight schedules, an insufficient number of physical education teachers in the elementary schools, and lack of adequate teaching space are the chief reasons for the inadequate physical education programs that exist in the nation's elementary schools. Until these conditions are corrected, many children will not reach a simple level of performance in basic education (reading, writing, and spelling) and millions may never reach their full potential.

Students, before entering school, should be screened to determine deficiencies in perceptual-motor skills. The screening should involve simple tests that reveal the areas in which the deficiency occurs. An intensive developmental program should follow the screening tests for those students who are deficient in certain skills. The program, which should be a natural one involving movements that assist in the improvement of perceptual-motor skills, should be an integral part of the physical education program for grades K–3. The students requiring further development, although they are scheduled with other students, should receive considerable individualized instruction. Teachers of physical education should emphasize instruction in perceptual-motor skills in grades K–3 regardless of whether students are screened prior to entering school. The process is important, since deficiencies in motor learning may underlie the lack of successful performance in academic education.

Some school systems have developed diagnostic tests to identify deficiencies in perceptual-motor development. One such test, developed in Hutchinson, Kansas, is shown in Figure 6–4 *A* and *B*.

The Activities Should be Based on the Growth and Development Needs of the Students

Boys and girls do not grow and mature in the same way. Not only do they differ anatomically at any particular age, but there are marked physiological and psychological differences.

Among the most important criteria to be used in developing the physical education curriculum scientifically are the growth and development statistics of children. Studies show that students are maturing earlier today both physically and sexually,[40] and these studies should be considered when students are evaluated and assigned to instructional groups.

Activities Should Consider Sex Variations

An important factor which should be taken into consideration when planning the curriculum is the ruling of the Department of Health, Education and Welfare under the guidelines of Title IX. Although there is considerable confusion about exactly how Title IX is to be implemented, there is no doubt that the ruling will have far-reaching effects on the physical education curriculum.

Title IX affects every aspect of instruction, as the following statement illustrates. Title IX provides that "No person in the United States shall on the basis of sex, be excluded from participation in, be denied the benefits of, or be subjected to discrimination under any education program or activity receiving Federal financial assistance."[40a]

In the specific application to physical education, the ruling states:

86.34 Access to course offerings.

A recipient shall not provide any course or otherwise carry out any of its education program or activity separately on the basis of sex, or require or refuse participation therein by any of its students on such basis, including health, physical education, industrial, business, vocational technical, home economics, music, and adult education courses.

(a) With respect to classes and activities in physical education at the elementary school level, the recipient shall comply fully with this section as expeditiously as possible but in no event later than one year from the effective date of this regulation. With respect to physical education classes and activities at the secondary and post-secondary levels, the recipient shall comply fully with this section as expeditiously as possible but in no event later than three years from the effective date of this regulation.

(b) This section does not prohibit grouping of students in physical education classes and activities by ability as assessed by objective standards of individual performance developed and applied without regard to sex.

(c) This section does not prohibit separation of students by sex within physical education classes or activities during participation in wrestling, boxing, rugby, ice hockey, football, basketball, and other sports, the purpose or major activity of which involves bodily contact.

(d) Where use of a single standard of measuring skill or progress in a physical education class has an adverse effect on members of one sex, the recipient shall use appropriate standards which do not have such effect.

(e) Portions of classes in elementary and secondary schools which deal exclusively with human sexuality may be conducted in separate sessions for boys and girls.[40a]

Although Title IX emphasizes the need for a reevaluation of programs for girls, the fact remains that anatomically girls are different from boys. All of the arguments for providing equal opportunity for girls in such matters as participation in interscholastic sports, equal time in the curriculum, adequate facilities, comparable supplies and equipment, coeducational activities, and competition are valid. In addition, it may be acceptable for *some* girls to participate with boys in *some* contact sports. *However, for the majority of girls taking physical education, careful attention should be given to the inclusion of certain activities especially suited to girls.*

For instance, as girls approach puberty, they find it difficult to perform activities that involve hanging by the arms. Williams cites medical opinion regarding these activities and states that "Many of the activities on the parallel bars, long horse, flying rings, traveling rings, and horizontal ladder, that girls can do equally well as boys before puberty, become wholly undesirable for them afterward."[41] He further elaborates on activities of this nature by showing that girls and women should:

... not be asked to engage in weight-lifting, to perform muscular feats on apparatus... The strength developed in modern dance is not only more suitable for girls and women than the strength acquired from stunts on heavy apparatus, but also it will arrive sooner and stay longer. The strength developed in swimming, hockey, skating, and tennis is not only far preferable in type for girls and women than the strength acquired in weight-lifting, but also more efficient and enduring.[41]

The issue of participation of girls in certain sports will be controversial for years to come. Physical education leaders must be aware of the emotional overtones and carefully apprise administrators, teachers, and the public of (1) the difference between participating in interschool athletics and physical education, and (2) the anatomical and physiological structure of girls, which definitely points to the exclusion of some activities from the girls' physical education curriculum.

The physiological differences that exist between boys and girls are clearly described by McNight and Hult. They explain that the chief cause of the difference is the development in females of the hormone estrogen, which inhibits the growth of muscle tissue and enhances the growth of adipose tissue. The male hormone androgen, in contrast, promotes the growth of muscle tissue. McNight and Holt conclude that:

It should be clear, however, that physiological differences dictate that the male athlete will not only remain superior in sports requiring muscular strength and speed, but will also reach a higher level of training because of these factors.[42]

Rather than succumb to the propaganda that accompanies the performance of women in the Olympic games and professional exhibitions shown on television, it would be more logical to study in depth the anatomical differences between men and women. There is no question about the value of providing women full opportunity to participate in all activities of their choosing. However, all persons who are responsible for developing physical education curricula should remember that the instructional program is usually required and must be treated differently from programs which are voluntary. To require a girl in an instructional class to participate in an activity for which she is physiologically or anatomically unsuited is to invite legal procedures in case of injury. The basic reason that girls' classes have been conducted separately from boys' is that with the approach of puberty, there are definite anatomical and physiological differences between boys and girls. A further discussion of this subject will be found in Chapter 13.

LOCAL CRITERIA

Because of varying local conditions, there is a need for specific criteria to determine which activities are best suited for use in a particular area. In adapting the curriculum to local needs, the following criteria should be met.

Activities Should be Relatively Inexpensive

There are many activities which meet all of the objectives but are more expensive than others that could be used. Some types of apparatus, for example, such as parallel bars, meet the objectives of physical education but are expensive and can only be used by small groups of students at any one time. Wrestling, on the other hand, also meets the desired objectives of physical education and a large number of students may be taught at the same time. A teacher with one standard wrestling mat can teach as many as 40 students simultaneously, whereas many parallel bars would be necessary to teach a comparable number, thus making the latter activity prohibitively expensive in many places.

The Activities Should be Acceptable to the Community

In some instances, the community is the final judge of whether or not an activity shall be taught. Dancing is an activity that may meet community opposition in some parts of the country. The teacher may have to eliminate dancing at first and substitute some other activity. With proper interpretation through a public relations program, dancing may eventually be accepted. In the meantime, the citizens pay taxes and support education, and they have the right to say what is to be taught in the program.

The Activities Should be Interesting

Rarely does one observe students running out of the school building to perform calisthenics. Rather, they begin to throw, run, jump, kick, and catch, and this is as it should be. The instructional program must motivate movement beyond the class period if students are to meet exercise requirements for normal growth and development.

Since motivation is the keystone of all learning, it is essential that the interest factor receive adequate consideration in the development of the curriculum. If students are not interested in an activity or have developed over the years a hearty dislike for it, motivation will be lacking and even the best instruction will be unsatisfactory.

Several surveys have been made to determine the interests and attitudes of students toward physical education. One such survey was developed at Prairie High School in Cedar Rapids, Iowa. It consisted of 49 statements in which students expressed their feelings about physical education. Each statement was rated on a scale as follows: Strongly agree, 5 points; moderately agree, 4 points; undecided, 3 points; moderately disagree, 2 points; strongly disagree, 1 point. The results of the survey assisted the teachers in evaluating and modifying the program and in keeping abreast of changing student interests.

Many of the comments of the students have been most interesting and revealing. For example, in the 1973 survey, 60.86 per cent of the students stated that they disagreed with the statement "I take physical education because it is required." The 1973 survey showed that:

1. Students are aware of many of the benefits that physical activities provide.
2. Students feel that physical education and physical activity contribute to improved physical fitness.
3. Students feel that the instructor has a great deal of effect on whether they like the physical education class or not.
4. Students have definite opinions about specific activities taught in the program.
5. Students strongly support the school's "open gyms" program.
6. Students believe that physical education classes are enjoyable.[43]

Frank P. Bolden, director of secondary physical education, District of Columbia Public Schools, uses student interests in curriculum construction. In a recent curriculum revision program, in addition to studying curriculum guides of other districts and having discussions with outstanding leaders, the interests of students were taken into account. An interest survey form was developed in which students were requested to respond to five statements: (1) list interests in team sports; (2) list interests in individual sports; (3) list interests in coeducational activities; (4) list activities that should be included in the program; (5) list number of classes desired per week. Bolden feels that the interest survey is helpful in planning relevant activities for students.[44]

Although surveys may assist in determining student interest, they should not be the sole determinant in the selection of activities for the program. Student interest may be erratic, and frequently students are swayed by their emotions rather than by logic. Local popularity of a specific activity may lead the masses to participate in that activity alone rather than develop ability in several sports. For example, in some sections of the country, because of the strong public relations program for professional basketball, many students are oblivious of the need for developing skills in lifetime sports activities.

Interest surveys should be made only after students have had an intensive orientation in a wide variety of activities. In order for a student to select an activity wisely, he must have experienced the values and thrills that accrue from performance in many activities.

Teachers who develop programs involving pre-survey—exploration—post-survey—will find that the second survey reveals entirely different likes and dislikes of activities than were shown in the first survey.

The Activities Should Not be Time-Consuming

Time plays an important role in determining the value of an activity in the curriculum. Softball offers a vivid example. Usually, when teachers include softball in the program, they resort to the traditional arrangement of 10 on each side, with 10 in the field and 10 at bat. However, many classes are too large to accommodate this situation and there are often many more than 10 at bat and in the field. Thus the chances are remote that every batter will get a turn during a period, and the same applies to players in the field. Many students never touch the ball the entire period, which results in rapid loss of interest in the program. If the softball program cannot be organized into small groups so that everyone is hitting and fielding many times during the period, then it should be dropped from the curriculum.

Criterion of Relative Value

Sometimes a decision must be made as to which of several desirable activities should be selected for the curriculum. A number of activities may meet all of the criteria, yet, because of the time element, some must be dropped. For example, touch football, soccer, and speedball all meet the established objectives, but because of the time factor only one may be selected. It is at this point that the relative value of each activity must be determined, and community choice comes into play. If football is highly popular in a particular locality, it may be selected instead of the other two; in other sections of the country, soccer may be more popular. The teacher should remember that activities taught in the curriculum should be a part of after-school and community planning, to encourage participation beyond school hours. Thus, community choice rather than the personal choice of the teacher should be the criterion.

For a summary of the general and local criteria for selecting activities, see Figure 6–5.

THE PROGRAM OF PHYSICAL FITNESS

Physical fitness is an objective of physical education and an integral phase of total fitness. However, a grave problem of interpretation confronts administrators and teachers of physical education. Many individuals and groups without scientific evidence are defining physical fitness and prescribing activities that should be used to achieve it. In many places these interpretations have

resulted in programs and activities that are questionable and that require further study by administrators in order to determine the nature of physical fitness and its relation to the physical education offering.

Physical fitness varies in kind and degree from individual to individual and from program to program. There are different types of fitness to suit different purposes; for instance, programs designed for war require a type of fitness that is entirely different from programs designed for peace. The fitness level necessary for the interschool athletic program is neither necessary nor desirable for the majority of students in the physical education program. Individuals training for tennis are involved in an entirely different fitness plan from those individuals who are practicing wrestling. The overriding problem is to find the level of fitness that is desirable or necessary for each individual.

Many programs today are based on the findings of certain fitness tests that are often scientifically unsound and do not provide a true indication of fitness. As an outgrowth of these tests, programs in calisthenics and gymnastics have been promoted, although they should have been replaced many years ago by sports and games involving the fundamental movements of man. Some of these programs in calisthenics and gymnastics, many involving machines and gadgets, are undemocratic, militaristic, and contrary to the concepts of the American way of life, since they are taught in a regimented manner that simulates procedures used in the preparation for war.

The development of fitness should not depend on calisthenics and apparatus. That this approach is unsatisfactory was shown as early as 1943 in a study by Wilbur, which found that games are better than formal gymnastics in building strength, in establishing body coordination, agility, and control, and in reaching a high level of physical fitness.[45]

To achieve the desired level of fitness and maintain it requires motivation. Sports involving the basic movements discussed earlier not only provide the necessary ingredients for producing fitness but also have their own built-in incentive for continuous exercise. The formal conditioning programs advocated by so many have only temporary value. An example of this is the training program of the Air Force Cadets in World War II. Their conditioning program consisted of running, grass drills, guerilla exercises, and obstacle courses. These cadets, at the time of their graduation, showed a very high level of fitness, but soon afterward this peak of fitness was lost, since as pilots they no longer were required to participate in the formal programs.[46]

The reason for the failure of conditioning programs is boredom. How many physical education teachers and administrators who advocate calisthenics, conditioning, and the like actually participate in them themselves? How many individuals who lead relatively sedentary lives resort to these conditioning programs for exercise? The answer to both of these questions is very few. However, you will find many of these people on the golf courses, tennis courts, and bowling alleys, and even more would frequent these places if they had been taught the skills of lifetime sports in the secondary schools.

Weiss substantiates this premise by stating that sports are fun, challenging, and carry their own built-in incentive for continuous exercise. He further states that:

They are competitive in a way that cannot be matched by non-sport physical conditioning activities. In fact, participants are often so motivated by sports that they gladly submit to supplementary physical conditioning exercises to gain a bit of strength, power, or endurance that it takes to beat the opponent. We need to revise our strategy. We don't seem to be succeeding very well in making our youth take their fitness medicine. We should turn more and more to sports through intramurals, play days, and community recreational programs.[46]

Cureton offers more recent and convincing evidence concerning the fallacy of using calisthenics, weight-training, and isometric programs in developing physical fitness. He did a study of activities that would produce changes in the cardiovascular system. The results of the study showed that the best activities for

developing fitness are swimming, walking, jogging, skating, and skiing. The study revealed that the weight-training and isometric programs are least effective.[47]

Siedentop observes that the traditional five or 10 minutes of calisthenics is largely worthless. It does not seem to contribute either to health fitness or to any specific motor-performance fitness. In addition, he states there is no evidence to show that such activities as the push-up and sit-up cause any meaningful increase in health, fitness, or performance in specific sports activities.[48]

Karpovich and Sinning, in their discussion of physical fitness, make a most challenging statement. They point out that:

It seems more logical to conclude that beyond a certain indispensable minimum of fitness, an additional improvement in physical fitness has no effect upon health, no matter how one defines the word. Excessive physical activities, on the other hand, may be definitely detrimental to persons with some diseases.[49]

The conclusion that may be drawn from the preceding discussion of physical fitness is that a well-balanced program of vigorous activities and sports that include continuous running and other fundamental movements will suffice in developing the level of physiological fitness necessary for health and happiness.

SUGGESTED PROCEDURES IN THE SELECTION OF ACTIVITIES

Designing a curriculum in physical education is a task of such importance that the help of many people is necessary. Individuals who are selected to assist in this task should have a background of scientific preparation, dedication to the improvement of education, and successful teaching experience. A survey of any school system or school usually reveals a number of teachers who meet these qualifications. These teachers should represent a cross section of the city or school and should serve on the central committee for curriculum

SELECTING ACTIVITIES FOR PHYSICAL EDUCATION

GENERAL CRITERIA: Activities should	5	4	3	2	1	TOTAL
1. Be consistent with the objectives of physical education						
a. organic vigor						
b. neuromuscular skills						
c. leisure time						
d. self realization						
e. emotional stability						
2. Be safe and contribute to health and fitness						
3. Involve instruction						
4. Include movement education						
5. Involve perceptual-motor skills						
6. Be based on the growth needs of students						
7. Consider sex variations						
LOCAL CRITERIA: Activities Should						
8. Be relatively inexpensive						
9. Be acceptable by the community						
10. Not be time consuming						
11. Be interesting						
12. Have relative value						

Figure 6–5. Selecting activities for the physical education curriculum.

construction. Once the committee has been formed, the following steps should be taken: (1) encourage each member to suggest activities that he feels should be in the curriculum; (2) develop criteria; (3) weigh value for each criterion; (4) evaluate each activity by the criteria; (5) after having evaluated the activities, list them according to rank; (6) eliminate certain activities by using the criterion of relative value. Figure 6–5 may be helpful in selecting activities. Each activity suggested for inclusion in the curriculum should be evaluated by the criteria shown in the figure.

THE CURRICULUM GUIDE

The development of the total school curriculum involves many facets of in-struction, all necessary for the operation of a school program. Philosophy must be determined, scheduling procedures established, the number of teachers and classrooms determined, the types of curricula chosen, and the innovations decided upon. These are only a few of the many areas that constitute modern curriculum development.

The curriculum guide usually consists of a number of instructional units relating to a central theme. For example, a guide in health education would contain units on such topics as communicable disease, personal hygiene, safety, emotional health, and the physiology of exercise. In addition to outlining material, the guide may contain suggestions for the teacher on methods of teaching, student activities, supplementary material, and other aids necessary for effective instruction.

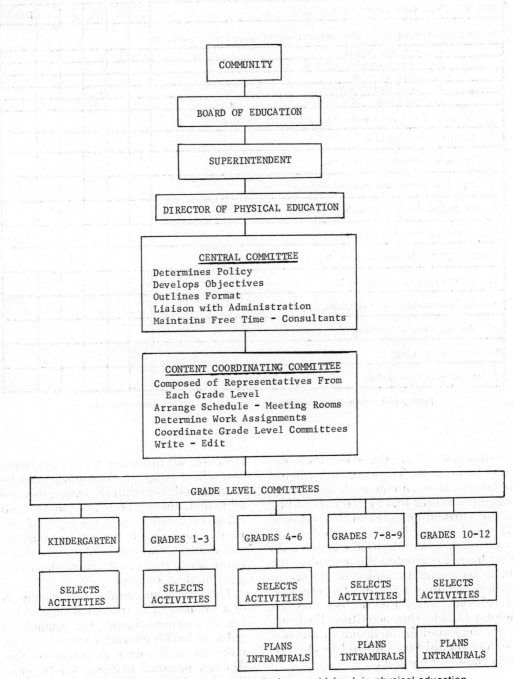

Figure 6-6. Committee pattern for developing a guidebook in physical education.

Construction of the Guide

Organization of a Committee. The interest in developing a guide usually arises from the impetus given by teachers and administrators to provide an outline of basic content in a particular discipline. As plans materialize, the importance of selecting a number of qualified people to formulate plans becomes apparent.

In order that a guide be functional and effective, it should be developed by as many interested individuals as possible. Participation by teachers and specialists develops rapport among the various individuals responsible for implementing the program and also provides in-service training for teachers.

Individuals who have been selected to help construct the guide should be placed on appropriate committees. These individuals should be teachers and others, such as principals and lay people, who have had a background in physical education. Arbitrary selection of committee members before studying their backgrounds frequently creates problems and may delay the production of the book.

Although many individuals are necessary for the development of the guide, the final writing should be delegated to a select few or perhaps to one person who is especially well qualified for the task. This will provide for continuity and consistency of style.

Many systems and schools have developed guides for physical education. Although programs vary, a clearly defined pattern of assigning committees and functions exists. Figure 6–6 illustrates a committee pattern that should be of assistance in the development of an effective guide.

When work begins on the construction of a guidebook and materials have been collected from various sources, the general criteria presented in the following paragraphs should be helpful to committee members.

Guidebook Characteristics. It is extremely important to develop clear-cut procedures to assist planners in construction of the guide. This is necessary in order to provide direction and prevent wasteful effort. Douglass lists 12 characteristics that all guides have in common which should be helpful to committee members.

1. Statement of a social and education philosophy
2. Statement of the accepted basic principles of learning
3. Clearly defined conception of the curriculum
4. Statement of the aims of education
5. Scope and area of curriculum and course guides
6. Sequence and time allotment
7. Determination of content materials and activities
8. Suggested organization of materials and activities
9. Suggested teaching procedures
10. Suggested evaluation procedures
11. Student-teacher reference materials
12. Mechanical makeup of course guides[50]

Yearly Calendar. There are many plans for arranging curriculum activities for daily, weekly, monthly, and yearly instruction. Some schools and cities have the activities outlined and described in a guidebook, with the activities grouped on cards that may be filed and used as needed. One city has arranged the entire curriculum on a 9" × 12" card which outlines the elementary program from grades K to 7. The activities are arranged by weeks and grades, with page references which refer to the guidebook for descriptions of the activities. This arrangement of content serves several purposes:

1. Teachers do not have to carry a bulky guide with them at all times.
2. The cards serve as a weekly check on what has been taught by the classroom teacher and the specialist teacher.
3. Teachers have an outline of what should be taught for the entire year.
4. Students know what is taught day by day and what to expect in future lessons.
5. The plan provides daily lesson guides for the classroom teacher and specialist.

The curriculum described above is shown in Figure 6–7.

Norfolk City Schools

HEALTH, PHYSICAL AND SAFETY EDUCATION DEPARTMENT
BASIC ELEMENTARY SCHOOL CURRICULUM
FIRST SEMESTER

TEACHER ______________________ SQUAD LEADER ______________________

GRADE ______________________ SCHOOL ______________________ ASSISTANT SQUAD LEADER ______________________

Weeks	Kindergarten - Grade 1	Grade 2	Grade 3	M	T	W	T	F	Grade 4	Grade 5	Grade 6	Grade 7	Weeks
									1st SIX WEEKS				
1	Organization pp. 16 - 39	Organization pp. 16 - 39	Organization pp. 16 - 39						Organization pp. 16 - 39	Organization pp. 16 - 39	Organization pp. 16 - 39	Organization pp. 16 - 39	1
	Apparatus (Daily) p. 115	Apparatus (Daily) p. 115	Apparatus (Daily) p. 115						Apparatus (Da.) pp. 115-119	Exercises (Daily) p. 114	Exercises (Daily) p. 114	Exercises (Daily) p. 114	
	Relays (Daily) p. 44	Relays (Daily) p. 44	Relays (Daily) p. 47						Relays (Daily) p. 50	Relays (Daily) p. 53	Relays (Daily) p. 57	Relays (Daily) p. 57	
2	Circle Activities p. 88	Circle Activities p. 88	Circle Activities p. 88						Newcomb p. 258	Serve Ball p. 259	Volleyball Skills pp. 242-260	Volleyball Skills pp. 242-260	2
	Relay Race Relays p. 97	Relay Race Relays p. 97	Relay Race Relays p. 97						Circle Activities p. 88	Circle Activities p. 88	Bombardment p. 107	Bombardment p. 107	
3	Back to Back p. 85	Magic Carpet p. 94	Boundary Ball p. 103						Serve Ball p. 259	Shower Ball p. 259	Volleyball Skills pp. 242-260	Volleyball Skills pp. 242-260	3
	Automobile Relay p. 85	All Fours Relay p. 84	All Up Relay p. 84						Circle Chase p. 89	Circle Chase p. 89	Capture the Bacon p. 112	Capture the Bacon p. 112	
4	Busy Bee p. 87	Squirrels in Trees p. 98	Keep Away p. 105						Shower Ball p. 259	Cage Volleyball p. 259	Volleyball pp. 242-260	Volleyball pp. 242-260	4
	Heel and Toe Relay p. 92	Relay Race Relay p. 97	Circle Race p. 103						Circle Race p. 103	Circle Race p. 103	Circle Chase p. 89	Circle Chase p. 89	
5	Circle Chase p. 89	Back to Back p. 85	Boundary Ball p. 103						Cage Volleyball p. 259	Cage Volleyball p. 259	Volleyball pp. 242-260	Volleyball pp. 242-260	5
	All Four Relay p. 84	Automobile Relay p. 85	Leap Frog Relay p. 105						All Run Relay p. 101	Arch Ball Relay p. 85	Cage Volleyball p. 259	Cage Volleyball p. 259	
6	Fire on Mountain p. 99	Busy Bee p. 87	Boundary Ball Tournament						Hook On p. 113	Hook On p. 113	Hook On p. 113	Hook On p. 113	6
	Hop Scotch p. 93	Hop Scotch p. 93	Hop Scotch p. 93						Newcomb-Serve Ball Tourn.	Cage Volleyball Tournament	School Volleyball Tournament p. 61		
									2nd SIX WEEKS				
1	Apparatus (Daily) p. 115	Apparatus (Daily) p. 115	Apparatus (Daily) p. 115						Circle Chase p. 89	Exercises (Daily) p. 114	Exercises (Daily) p. 114	Exercises (Daily) p. 114	1
	Relays (Daily) p. 44	Relays (Daily) p. 44	Relays (Daily) p. 47						Relays (Daily) p. 50	Relays (Daily) p. 53	Relays (Daily) p. 57	Relays (Daily) p. 57	
	Rope Rhythmics p. 194	Rope Rhythmics p. 194	Rope Rhythmics p. 194						Rope Rhythmics p. 194	Rope Rhythmics p. 194	Rope Rhythmics p. 194	Rope Rhythmics p. 194	
2	Brownies & Fairies p. 86	Follow the Leader p. 92	Soccer Skills p. 209						Bowling p. 111	Bowling p. 111	Bowling p. 111	Bowling p. 111	2
	All Up Relay p. 84	Kangaroo Relay p. 99	Arch Ball Relay p. 85						Cage Volleyball p. 259	Cage Volleyball p. 259	City-wide Volleyball Tournament p. 69		
3	Cowboys and Indians p. 90	Flowers and Wind p. 91	Drive Ball p. 214						Soccer Skills p. 209	Soccer Skills p. 209	Soccer Skills p. 209	Soccer Skills p. 209	3
	Arch Ball Relay p. 85	All Up Relay p. 84	Carry & Fetch Relay p. 87						Four Square p. 109	Four Square p. 109	Four Square p. 109	Four Square p. 109	
4	Ball Handling Skills p. 122	Ball Handling Skills p. 122	Ball Handling Skills p. 122						Drive Ball p. 214	Drive Ball p. 214	Soccer pp. 208 - 215	Soccer pp. 208 - 215	4
	Overhead Pass Relay p. 96	Overhead Pass Relay p. 96	Five Trips p. 91						Hand Polo p. 110	Hand Polo p. 110	Punt Ball p. 230	Punt Back p. 230	
5	Flowers and the Wind p. 91	Five Trips p. 91	Soccer Skills p. 209						Soccer pp. 208 - 215	Soccer pp. 208 - 215	Soccer pp. 208 - 215	Soccer pp. 208 - 215	5
	Goat Butting Relay p. 92	Carry & Fetch Relay p. 87	Figure 8 Relay p. 104						All Run Relay p. 101	Leap Frog Relay p. 113	Football Keep Away p. 229	Football Keep Away p. 229	
6	Follow the Leader p. 92	Cowboys and Indians p. 90	Drive Ball Tournament						Soccer pp. 208 - 215	Capture the Bacon p. 112	Touch Football pp. 226 - 237	Touch Football p. 226	6
	Kangaroo Relay p. 99	Arch Ball Relay p. 85	Kangaroo Relay p. 99						Drive Ball Tournament	Soccer Tournament	Soccer Tournament	Soccer Tournament	
									3rd SIX WEEKS				
1	Rope Rhythmics pp. 194 - 207	Rope Rhythmics pp. 194 - 207	Rope Rhythmics pp. 194 - 207						Rope Rhythmics p. 194	Basketball Unit of Instruction pp. 120 - 135			1
	Individual Movements &	Individual Movements &	Individual Movements &						Individual Movements &	Basketball Skills p. 122	Basketball Skills p. 122	Basketball Skills p. 122	
	Ball Rhythmics pp. 142 - 148	Ball Rhythmics pp. 142 - 148	Ball Rhythmics pp. 149 - 154						Ball Rhythmics pp. 155 - 165	Circle Touch Ball p. 125	Circle Touch Ball p. 125	One Goal Basketball p. 133	
2	Magic Carpet p. 94	Brownies & Fairies p. 86	Modified Soccer pp. 208 - 215						Bowling p. 111	Corner Goal Ball p. 131	Sideline Basketball p. 134	Around the World p. 129	2
	Carry and Fetch Relay p. 87	Goat Butting Relay p. 92	Shuttle Relay p. 240						Hand Polo p. 110	Four Passes & Shoot p. 133	Basketball "21" p. 128	Arch Goal Ball Relay p. 127	
3	Squirrels in Trees p. 98	Magic Carpet p. 94	Modified Soccer pp. 208 - 215						Four Square p. 109	End Ball p. 132	Six Hole Basketball p. 130	Basketball p. 135	3
	Kangaroo Relay p. 99	Carry and Fetch Relay p. 87	Clasp Tag p. 103						Relay Race p. 97	One Goal Basketball p. 133	One Goal Basketball p. 133	Figure "8" p. 127	
4	Sing & Do Album I	Review Rhythmics p. 143	Review Rhythmics pp. 145 - 148						Review Rhy. pp. 149-154	Review Rhy. pp. 155-165	Review Rhy. pp. 166-178	Review Rhy. pp. 179-184	4
	Push the Business On p. 142	Sing & Do Album I	Three Pin Bowling p. 106						Rag Hockey p. 106	Rag Hockey p. 106	Rag Hockey p. 106	Rag Hockey p. 106	
5	Sing & Do Album II	Sing & Do Album II	Yankee Doodle p. 149						Camptown Races p. 155	Red River Valley p. 166	Dribble, Pivot & Pass p. 63	Dribble, Pivot & Pass p. 63	5
	Mexican Social Dance p. 143	Saturday Afternoon p. 145	Rag Hockey p. 106						Circle Chase p. 89	Sicilian Circle p. 168	Figure 8 Dribble & Pass p. 64	Figure 8 Dribble & Pass p. 64	
6	Jolly is the Miller p. 143	Walking My Partner p. 145	Pop Goes the Weasel p. 150						Green Sleeves p. 156	Trallen p. 170	Basketball-Fitness Run p. 64	Basketball-Fitness Run p. 64	6
	Fire Engine p. 99	Follow the Leader p. 92	Follow the Leader p. 92						Circle Race p. 103		Annual Basketball Relays p. 70		

SEE BACK OF CARD FOR IMPORTANT INSTRUCTION AND TESTING PROGRAM

PE-3—72

A

Figure 6–7. Basic elementary school curriculum. *A*, Outdoor program. *B*, Indoor program.

PHYSICAL PROFICIENCY TEST

NAMES Check √ Passed—Failed ★	Age	Pull-Up (Boys) Flexed Arm Hang (Girls)		Sit-Up (Knees Flexed)		Standing Broad Jump		Shuttle Run		50-Yard Dash		600-Yard Run-Walk	
		P	F	P	F	P	F	P	F	P	F	P	F
1													
2													
3													
4													
5													
6													
7													
8													
9													
10													
11													
12													

Number Pupils Scoring Satisfactory or Better on All Tests _____

Number Pupils Below Satisfactory on One or More Tests _____

Total Number Pupils Tested _____

★ Passed—Average or Above

INCLEMENT WEATHER ACTIVITIES

Kindergarten and 1st Grade

Lesson No.	GAMES	RELAYS	Lessons Taught
1	Cat and Mice p. 87	Automobile p. 85	
2	Changing Seats p. 88	All Up p. 84	
3	Circle Activities p. 88	Arch Ball p. 85	
4	Classroom Tag p. 89	Carry and Fetch p. 87	
5	Follow the Leader p. 92	Relays p. 97	

2nd GRADE

1	Circle Activities p. 88	Carry and Fetch p. 87	
2	Magic Carpet p. 94	Heel and Toe p. 92	
3	Musical Arches p. 95	Kangaroo p. 99	
4	Ring Master p. 97	Overhead Pass p. 96	
5	Simon Says p. 98	Relays p. 97	

3rd GRADE

1	Three Pin Bowling p. 106	Arch Ball p. 85	
2	Rag Hockey p. 106	Blackboard p. 102	
3	Musical Arches p. 95	Around the Row p. 102	
4	Circle Activities p. 88	Figure 8 p. 104	
5	Classroom Tag p. 89	Relays p. 97	

4th GRADE

1	Changing Seats p. 88	Arch Ball p. 85	
2	Circle Activities p. 88	Around the Row p. 102	
3	Coffee, Tea or Milk p. 108	Blackboard p. 102	
4	Rag Hockey p. 106	Carry and Fetch p. 87	
5	Three Pin Bowling p. 106	Overhead Pass p. 96	

5th GRADE

1	A Dozen Ways p. 112	All Up p. 84	
2	Circle Activities p. 88	Around The Row p. 102	
3	Coffee, Tea or Milk p. 108	Blackboard p. 102	
4	Rag Hockey p. 106	Geography p. 113	
5	Bowling p. 111	Circle Pass p. 108	

6th and 7th GRADES

1	Circle Activities p. 88	All Up p. 84	
2	Rag Hockey p. 106	Geography p. 113	
3	3 Pin Bowling p. 106	Overhead p. 96	
4	Bowling p. 111	Circle Pass p. 108	
5	A Dozen Ways p. 112	Blackboard p. 102	

INSTRUCTIONS

1. Developmental exercises should be daily procedure beginning with the fifth grade.
2. Objective tests should be given as indicated and recorded. Test results must be turned in to the physical education office prior to June 1st.
3. During winter program (December through mid-March), outside activities should be given when possible.
4. Inclement weather activities should be given by lessons and checked as indicated.
5. Softball is scheduled for grades six and seven only during the last four weeks of the school year.
6. "P" denotes page in 1971 Revision of Elementary Guidebook for description of activity.
7. All activities should be set up separately for boys and girls due to variance in growth patterns.

DAILY OUTLINE OF THIRTY-MINUTE PHYSICAL EDUCATION PROGRAM

5 mins.: Developmental Movements to music—walking, hopping, skipping, running, etc.; rope skipping to music; conditioning exercises (5th - 7th Grades only).

5 mins.: Review previous activities.

15 mins.: Instruction in skills; rules pertaining to activities; practice of skills; participation.

5 mins.: Skills laboratory—Relays and formations placing skills taught in a complete situation.

B

Figure 6-7. *continued*

REFERENCES

1. George H. Gallup: "Sixth Annual Gallup Poll of Public Attitudes Toward Education." *Phi Delta Kappan*, September, 1974, p. 21.
2. B. Frank Brown: *The Reform of Secondary Education*. New York: McGraw-Hill Book Co., 1973, p. 8.
3. Wilbur J. Cohen: "Changing Influences in American Education." *Innovator*. Ann Arbor: The University of Michigan, School of Education, December, 1972.
4. Harold Spears: "Kappans Ponder the Goals of Education." *Phi Delta Kappan*, September, 1973, pp. 31–32.
5. B. Frank Brown: *op. cit.*, p. 13.
6. Carter V. Good: *Dictionary of Education*, 3rd ed. New York: McGraw-Hill Book Co., 1973, p. 588.
7. *Human Relations—Current Trends in School Policies and Programs*. Washington, D. C.: National School Public Relations Association, 1972, p. 12.
8. *Ibid.*, p. 21.
9. Chris A. DeYoung and Richard Wynn: *American Education*, 7th ed. New York: McGraw-Hill Book Co., 1972, p. 361. (For additional reading in this area, the following sources are recommended: Lester W. Anderson and Lauren A. Van Dyke: *Secondary School Administration*, 2nd ed. New York: Houghton Mifflin Co., 1973, p. 107; Jack J. Wickert: "Criteria for Curriculum Development." Washington, D. C.: *Educational Leadership Journal*, Association for Supervision and Curriculum Development, January, 1973, p. 361.)
10. Jesse H. Bancroft: *Games*. New York: The Macmillan Co., 1942.
11. Paul Vogel (Program Director): *The Battle Creek Physical Education Curriculum Project*. Battle Creek, Mich., 1969. (From printed materials sent on request.)
12. Charles Bucher: "National Adult Physical Fitness Survey: Some Implications." *JOHPER*, January 1974, p. 25.
13. John M. Cooper and Clinton Strong: *The Physical Education Curriculum*. Los. Angeles: Lucus Brothers, 1973.
14. Joel Rosentswieg: "A Ranking of the Objectives of Physical Education." *Research Quarterly*, Vol. 40, 1969, p. 783.
15. Wall Street Journal, November 2, 1964.
16. Helen M. Zimmerman: "Accident Experience with Trampolines." *Research Quarterly*, December, 1956, pp. 452–455.
17. "In the Courts—Negligence on the Playground and in the Gym." *Physical Education Newsletter*, October 15, 1963.
18. "Too Many in Mass Games Can Lead to Physical Injuries." *Physical Education Newsletter*, August, 1963.
19. Charles L. Lowman: "A Message to School Health Services." *Journal of School Health*, January 1962, p. 18.
20. American Medical Association: *Health Education Services*, September, 1961, p. 26.
21. Marilyn Flint: "Selecting Exercises." *JOHPER*, February, 1964, p. 19.
22. Lowman, *op. cit.*, p. 18.
23. Flint, *op. cit.*, p. 20.
24. Dale O. Nelson, "Focus on Two Fitness Exercises," *JOHPER*, May, 1964, p. 23.
25. Marilyn Flint, *op. cit.*, p. 20.
26. Charles Lowman, *op. cit.*, p. 18.
27. Marilyn Flint, *op. cit.*, p. 21.
28. Jesse F. Williams: *Principles of Physical Education*, 8th ed. Philadelphia: W. B. Saunders Co., 1964, p. 306.
29. Clark Hetherington: *School Program in Physical Education*. New York: World Book Co., 1922, p. 54.
30. Charles C. Cowell: *Scientific Foundations of Physical Education*. New York: Harper & Brothers, 1953, p. 44.
31. Flint, *op. cit.*, p. 19.
32. Flint, *op. cit.*, p. 19.
33. Tom Neuberger: "What the Research Quarterly Says about Warm-Up." *JOHPER*, October, 1969, p. 77.
34. Barbara B. Godfrey and Newell C. Kephart: *Movement Patterns and Motor Education.* New York: Appleton-Century Crofts, Inc. 1969, p. 19.
35. Williams, *op. cit.*, p. 341.
36. Elizabeth A. Ludwig: "Toward an Understanding of Basic Movement Education in the Elementary Schools." *JOHPER*, March, 1968, p. 77.
37. Laurence E. Morehouse and Augustus T. Miller: *Physiology of Exercise*, 6th ed. St. Louis: C. V. Mosby Co., 1971, p. 21.

38. James W. Fleming: "Perceptual Motor Programs." In Robert N. Singer: *Psychomotor Domain: Movement Behavior.* Philadelphia: Lea & Febiger, 1972, p. 251.
39. Joseph J. Gruber: "Exercise and Mental Performance." Address before the American Association for the Advancement of Science, Dallas, December, 1968.
40. Brown, *op. cit.,* p. 41.
40a. Federal Register, Part II. Washington, D.C.: Department of Health, Education and Welfare. June 4, 1975, pp. 24128 and 24141.
41. Williams, *op. cit.,* p. 119.
42. Dorothy McNight and Joan Hult: "Competitive Athletics for Girls — We Must Act." *JOHPER,* June, 1974, p. 45.
43. "Finding Out What Students Think about Physical Education," *Physical Education Newsletter,* January 1, 1973.
44. Seeking Student Opinion, the First Step in Curriculum Revision." *Physical Education Newsletter,* September 15, 1973.
45. E. A. Wilbur: "A Comparative Study of Physical Fitness Indices as Measured by Two Programs of Physical Education: The Sports Method and the Apparatus Method." *Research Quarterly,* October, 1943, p. 20.
46. Raymond Weiss: "Do Sports Produce Fitness?" *JOHPER,* March, 1961, pp. 21–56.
47. T. K. Cureton: "The Relative Value of Various Exercise Conditioning Programs to Improve Cardiovascular Status and Prevent Heart Disease." *Journal of Sports, Medicine, and Physical Fitness,* March, 1965, p. 54.
48. Daryl Siedentop: *Physical Education: Introductory Analysis.* Dubuque, Iowa: Wm. C. Brown Co., 1972, p. 81.
49. Peter V. Karpovich and Wayne E. Sinning: *Physiology of Muscular Activity,* 4th ed. Phhiladelphia: W. B. Saunders Co., 1971, p. 270.
50. Harl R. Douglass: *The High School Curriculum.* New York: The Ronald Press Co., 1964, pp. 280–289.

SUGGESTED READINGS

Cratty, Bryant J.: *Psychomotor Behavior in Education and Sport.* Springfield, Ill.: Charles C Thomas, 1974.
Doll, Ronald C., and Ruth C. Cook: *The Elementary School Curriculum.* Boston: Allyn & Bacon, Inc., 1973.
Mackenzie, Moslin M.: *Toward a New Curriculum in Physical Education.* New York: McGraw-Hill Book Co., 1969.
Siedentop, Daryl: *Physical Education, An Introductory Analysis.* Dubuque, Iowa: Wm. C. Brown Co., 1972.
Vannier, Maryhelen, Mildred Foster, and David Gallahue: *Teaching Physical Education in Elementary Schools,* 5th ed. Philadelphia: W. B. Saunders Co., 1973.
Willgoose, Carl E.: *The Curriculum in Physical Education,* 2nd ed.: Englewood Cliffs, N.J. Prentice-Hall, Inc., 1974.

CHAPTER SEVEN

Organization and Administration of School Programs

The purpose of this chapter is to aid the administrator in fitting the program which he and his staff or colleagues have designed into the total school milieu. He must know how to organize the program in relation to the physical plant, the curriculum pattern, and the teaching staff. He must determine the logical segmentation of the content in order to fit the activity to the developmental characteristics and growth needs of the children and youth within the age span of the school level and grade. Moreover, he must see that the overall program is administered so that the students will not only be oriented to a variety of activities but will also be motivated to participate and become skillful enough in a few chosen activities to participate after school as well.

The division of most American schools into age levels—kindergarten, the primary and intermediate schools, and the junior and senior high schools—provides natural categories for considering the organization and administration of physical education programs in each division. A more recent division—the middle school—will also be discussed.

KINDERGARTEN

The most important age for learning is the span of years from birth until the child enters the first grade. Many educational leaders have long suspected that the first five years of life have a profound bearing on intelligence. Bloom found that by the time a child reaches the age of 4 he has developed 40 per cent of his mature intelligence and from ages 4 to 8 realizes another 30 per cent.[1]

These findings have had tremendous impact on educational thinking and at the same time have increased the public's awareness of the importance of the kindergarten.

Aims of Kindergarten

It was pointed out earlier in the text that all children are endowed by nature with the urge for movement. For normal growth and development, children must have several hours of vigorous activity daily. In addition to the urge for movement, there are other needs of the 5-year-old.

Children at this age need to participate in all types of activities involving perceptual motor skills, which include spatial relationships. They should experience the joy of movement through self-experience and play with other children in situations that are simple and nonstructured. In their daily programs, attention should be given to providing for the development of a positive self-image through successful performance in skills. Programs for kindergarten children should encourage positive health habits and allow ample time for alternating rest with play, since both are essential for normal growth and development.

Physical Education in the Kindergarten

Activities designed for the first grade are usually suitable for kindergarten children. The teacher and the administration should not fail to provide ample time for movement in the schedule. The importance of providing time for vigorous exercise for these students cannot be overemphasized. Activities developed around the fundamental movements of running, jumping, throwing, climbing, dancing, swinging, creeping, and catching should constitute the bulk of the program for kindergarten children. There is no place in the program for unnatural "calisthenics" and other contrived artificial movements that violate the natural urge for movement manifested in the fundamental movements mentioned above. Note the manner in which these fundamental movements are incorporated in the sample curriculum for the primary grades in Figure 7–1.

THE ELEMENTARY PROGRAM

For a number of years the emphasis on physical education has been greatest in the secondary schools. The secondary school program is usually a required part of the curriculum, with qualified teachers employed to provide the instruction. Such is not the case in most elementary schools, even though study and research indicate that the most important years of the child's life are the elementary years. Few elementary schools in the country, in fact, have full-time qualified physical education teachers responsible for the instruction.

In 1968 a nationwide study by the Elementary School Physical Education Commission on Physical Education Teacher Status revealed that in 229 school systems, there were only 564 full-time specialists. Chapter 5 (Figure 5–8) shows the results of the survey. However, there are indications that the elementary program is improving. A later survey by the Commission reveals that because of classroom teachers' negotiations for released time, there is a steady increase of elementary physical education teachers. For the 1974–75 school year, the Commission in another survey reported that Salem, Oregon, had an increase from 93 to 103; Decatur, Georgia, 9 to

SAMPLE PROGRAM FOR THE PRIMARY LEVEL (GRADES K-3)

1. Fundamental Locomotor and Non-Locomotor Movements 20%
    Opportunities to explore basic skills such as
    the walk, run, hop, gallop, skip, bend, reach,
    stretch, bounce, push, pull, swing, and sustain.

2. Rhythmic Activities (could be combined with number 1) 20%
    Performing locomotor activities in even and uneven rhythm;
    Tom-tom rhythms; Creative rhythms (animals, toys);
    Dramatic rhythms; Singing Games and Folk Dances
    (How Do You Do My Partner, Shoemaker's Dance,
    Looby Loo, Mulberry Bush, Chimes of Dunkirk,
    Skip to My Lou, Hokey Pokey, Broom Dance).

3. Games 30%
    Chasing, running, tagging, jumping, leaping games
    such as Fire Engine, Hill Dill, Squirrel in Tree,
    Midnight Chinese Wall, Policeman, Old Witch, Fox
    and Geese, Boiler Burst, Touch the Corner, and various relays.

4. Self-testing Activities 30%

    Swimming should be offered if a pool is available.

                                                        Total 100%

    NOTE: Descriptions of above typical activities will be found in most
          game books and elementary school manuals. The activities
          listed are merely samplings.

Figure 7–1. A sample program for the primary level. (From Cooper, John M., and Clinton Strong: *The Physical Education Curriculum.* Columbia, Mo.: Lucas Brothers, 1973, p. 39.)

13; Marietta, Georgia, 14 to 20; Kansas City, Missouri, 11 to 24; Shreveport, Louisiana, 12 to 18; Pensacola, Florida, 33 to 41; Lubbock, Texas, 16 to 24; Fairfax County, Virginia, 140 to 145; Montgomery County, Maryland, 87 to 90.

Philosophy of the Elementary Program

For over 200 years the importance of elementary instruction has been extolled by men of high esteem, including such leaders as Horace Mann, Harry Barnard, John Dewey, William H. Kilpatrick, and James Russell Lowell. The views of these great Americans and the efforts of many educators have been summarized by the Educational Policies Commission in its stand for free, compulsory elementary education. The Commission has stated, "Of all the educational institutions, the elementary school teaches the greatest number of Americans for the longest time. It is, therefore, a cornerstone of the American promise of equal opportunity."[2]

Perhaps the time has arrived when the public has become sufficiently enlightened that attention can be focused on the crucial need for revitalizing the physical education program in the elementary schools of America. A recent optimistic overview by Hanson indicates that the future of elementary physical education can be exciting. She cites four trends that indicate this:

1. There is a nationwide surge of interest in elementary school physical education.
2. Curriculum planners are seeking to provide programs aimed at total development of all children, and they are recognizing the vital role physical education plays in the

physical and overall development of young people.

3. The stress on problem-solving and creative approaches in all teaching, as a result of implementing modern learning theories, serves to challenge physical educators to employ compatible methods in their classes.

4. Perceptual motor programs are receiving a good deal of attention from people both within and outside physical education.[3]

Hanson cautions, however, that we still have problems that must be dealt with if we are to make a significant contribution to education.

A philosophy of elementary education is needed to define and clarify the future needs of children. Such a philosophy of elementary education may be developed from the six concerns of elementary education outlined in *The Elementary School We Need,* published by the Association for Supervision and Curriculum Development. There are six commitments: (1) a concern for creative activity; (2) a concern for the development of values consistent with democratic living; (3) a concern for the development of skills for effective participation in a democratic society; (4) a concern for the development of understandings of the social and scientific world; (5) a concern for the mental health and personality development of children; and (6) a concern for the health and physical development of children. Because the last concern cited has particular significance for physical education, a summary of the Association's presentation of it is given here:

In many ways, elementary schools seek not only to maintain but also to improve the health status of children. Through planned programs of physical education, health education, and safety education, as well as through physical examinations, elementary schools demonstrate a major concern for health and physical development. Many cooperative efforts are undertaken with community agencies in these areas. In addition, the willingness of elementary schools to adapt their programs to provide for the physical needs of children has made it possible for many students who have serious physical handicaps to enter regular school programs.[4]

Classification and Time Allotment of Activities

Each of the various classifications of activities selected for the instructional program should be given a certain percentage of time in the curriculum. This is important in order to prevent a single activity from dominating the instructional program. These percentages are flexible and may vary with the locality, but they offer a guide toward developing a varied curriculum. Figure 7-2 shows the time allotment and classification of the content of activities as suggested by Vannier.

Improving the Elementary Program

As has been said, there is much evidence that instruction in physical education in the elementary schools of America needs to be improved. A study of 222,415 New York State students in 1964 confirmed that physical education is least adequate in the elementary school. As an outgrowth of the study, George H. Grover, director of the Division of Health, Physical Education and Recreation, recommended 10 steps to improve the quality of physical education in the elementary school:

1. Require appropriate medical examinations and take all possible steps to secure correction of any remediable defects.

2. Schedule a daily physical education period of at least 30 minutes — exclusive of time needed for dressing and showering.

3. Devote at least half of each period to vigorous physical activity.

4. Keep classes to a maximum size of 35.

5. Employ certified teachers of physical education.

6. Provide sufficient indoor teaching stations and locker and shower facilities for all physical education classes.

7. Identify the physically underdeveloped child early in the school year and provide special developmental activities and periodic testing.

8. Organize intramural and extramural activities for both boys and girls beginning in the third or fourth grade.

9. Require boys and girls to change into

	K	1	2	3	4	5	6
GAMES AND SPORTS	10%	15%	25%	30%	40%	50%	50%
Low organized games	10	15	20	10	10	0	0
Relays	0	0	5	10	5	5	5
Lead-up games	0	0	0	10	25	45	45
Official sports	0	0	0	0	0	0	0
RHYTHMICS	30%	25%	25%	25%	20%	20%	20%
Fundamentals	15	10	10	5	5	5	5
Creative Rhythm	15	10	10	10	5	5	5
Folk & Square Dance	0	5	5	10	10	10	10
SELF-TESTING	60%	60%	50%	45%	40%	30%	30%
Conditioning	0	5	5	10	10	10	10
Movement exploration	40	30	30	15	10	0	0
Stunts	10	10	5	5	0	0	0
Tumbling	0	5	5	5	10	10	10
Hand apparatus	10	10	5	5	0	0	0
Large apparatus	0	0	5	5	10	10	10

Figure 7–2. Classification and time allotment of activities. (From Vannier, Maryhelen, *et al.*: *Teaching Physical Education in Elementary Schools*, 5th ed. Philadelphia: W. B. Saunders Co., 1973, p. 159.)

physical education uniforms beginning in the third or fourth grade.

10. Offer health education in each grade with sufficient time to teach the necessary content.[5]

The Opinion Research Corporation of Princeton conducted the National Adult Fitness Survey for the President's Council on Physical Fitness and Sports. The survey revealed that 53 per cent of the individuals involved in the survey had no elementary physical education.[6]

John Puckett in an article published in the *Physical Educator* expresses concern

Figure 7–3. Elementary education is the cornerstone of democracy.

that in many school systems the secondary schools receive preference over the elementary schools in the areas of leadership, equipment, and supplies. He feels that in order to achieve recognized objectives, existing elementary programs must be improved. He offers several suggestions for improving the program, such as making it the responsibility of administrators to promote better programs, planning a variety of activities in the program, developing testing programs, placing physical education teachers in all schools, providing sufficient funds for equipment and supplies, and providing opportunity for classroom teachers to improve themselves in physical education.[7]

If the activities in the elementary school are studied closely, the teaching of skills in games and sports reflects an increasing emphasis as students progress through the various grade levels. Many activities such as mimetics, tag games, singing games, and others that were emphasized in the earlier years are no longer allotted large proportions of time in the curriculum. It is interesting to note the emphasis on various activities in the middle school, which is the next level to be studied.

THE MIDDLE SCHOOL

The middle school, a relatively new movement in school organization, is designed to provide pre-adolescents with offerings planned to really meet their basic needs and interests. Children are maturing earlier, and sixth graders are frequently misplaced in the existing elementary school. In the middle school, students are no longer required to participate in the junior high school programs, which often reflect the senior high programs in curriculum, organization, and extracurricular activities. As with most pioneer programs, the middle school has been subjected to educational scrutiny. However, in spite of criticism, the middle school has shown phenomenal growth in the emergence of new grade combinations. Surveys show that middle school grade classifications have increased from only 20 of 443 schools reporting in 1964 to 2298 in 1970.[8] The most popular combination seems to be grades 6−8, found in 58.2 per cent of the schools.

As the middle school has developed around the rationale of meeting the needs of early adolescents, different procedures have been explored. Team teaching, the individualization of instruction, student guidance, flexible scheduling, exploration, the interest approach, and improving the self-image of students have all been successfully employed. Daily programs of physical education are common in most middle school curriculums.

Purposes of the Middle School

As the middle school movement gains momentum, the need for establishing definite purposes becomes evident. Based on the needs and characteristics of pre-adolescents, the middle school should:

1. Provide activities that are interesting and relevant for pre-adolescent students.
2. Provide classroom situations and extra-class programs that are based on individual abilities of students and that allow each student to achieve varying degrees of success.
3. Provide exploration in a wide variety of activities.
4. Provide an organizational pattern that allows students a smooth adjustment to the demands of the senior high school.
5. Emphasize guidance in all areas of instruction.
6. Provide for counseling in cases of deviant behavior problems and unusual intellectual manifestations.
7. Provide programs that recognize the physical, mental, emotional, and social characteristics of children.
8. Provide for individualized instruction through the use of innovative staff development programs.
9. Provide activities, organizations, and teaching procedures that allow students to develop latent creative potentiality.
10. Provide activities that meet the physiological needs of early adolescence.

Physical Education in the Middle School

The theme which is explained in purpose number three has far-ranging implications for the physical education program. Exploration and orientation have always been basic purposes of the junior high school, and it seems logical to examine the middle school curriculum with exploration and orientation as guidelines.

The middle school curriculum in physical education should be organized and developed just as the curriculum was constructed for the junior high school. Although exploration and orientation should always be the prevailing criteria, *the activities should be different from those in the junior high.* Recent research indicates that most middle school instructional content consists of traditional activities heavily influenced by the senior high school curriculum.[9] It seems logical to study the total curriculum, elementary and senior high school, in order that the middle school offerings become a natural part of the total program. If the exploration plan is followed, then students should spend some time in a wide variety of activities that will enable them to make an intelligent choice of activities in the senior

SCHOOLS	ACTIVITIES	PROCEDURES
Middletown Middle School Middletown, Rhode Island	Instruction ——— Teach skills in stunts, tumbling, basketball, apparatus, volleyball, tennis, badminton, track and field.	•Sexes integrated for instruction •Segregation of sexes for team play •Team teaching
C. L. Scarborough Middle School Mobile, Alabama	Teach skills in archery, golf, folk dancing, gymnastics, rhythms, track, creative dance, shuffle board, table tennis and horseshoes	•Coeducation for 50% of the activities •Emphasis on life-time activities
Orchard Middle School Solon, Ohio	Extra-Class ——— Mini-Courses	•Selectives •Interest Survey
Walker-Grant Middle School Fredericksburg, Virginia	Mini-Courses Individual and lifetime activities	•Electives •Clubs
Owen J. Roberts Middle School Pottstown, Pennsylvania	Teach spelunking, juggling, bowling, swimming, diving, skiing, square dance, golf, and gymnastics	•Hobby and interest
Sennet Middle School Madison, Wisconsin	Recreational games, individual activities, and sports and team sports	•Open laboratory •Selectives •Small groups •Large groups
Beachwood Middle School Beachwood, Ohio	Skills of tag football, softball, kickball, soccer, hockey, wrestling, basketball, gymnastics, volleyball, track, tumbling, archery, golf	•Open laboratory •Independent study

Figure 7–4. Innovative programs in the middle school. (Adapted from Munson, Corlee, and Elba Stafford: "Middle Schools: A Variety of Approaches to Physical Education." *JOHPER*, February, 1974, p. 29.)

high school. Figure 7–4 shows several schools that are experimenting with innovative programs and includes the activities and procedures involved in implementing the program.

The next level of organization is the junior high school. Although a striking similarity exists between the junior high school and the middle school, there are some differences, which become apparent when one compares the purposes of the two types of schools.

THE JUNIOR HIGH SCHOOL PROGRAM

Purposes of the Junior High School

For a number of years educators have debated the purpose and organization of the junior high school and even the need for such an entity. Conant states:

Because of wide diversity in school organization, professional disagreement, and my own observations, I conclude that the place of grades 7, 8, and 9 in the organization of a school system is of less importance than the program provided for adolescent youth.[10]

The junior high school was founded on the double premise that a smoother transition period between childhood and adolescence is necessary in the schools and that the sudden change from the child-centered program of the elementary school to the subject-dominated curriculum of the high school might be alleviated by the junior high school. Proponents of the junior high school feel that, when properly planned around this premise, the junior high school program more nearly meets the needs of adolescents than does any other organizational pattern.

Bossing and Cramer feel that in a maturing democracy, such as exists in the United States, educational programs exist for the youth. They feel that the junior high school can best prepare students to live in a democracy by allowing them to develop attitudes and beliefs that will prepare them for adjusting to democratic living. Among the many educational needs for the adolescent's educational well-being is some provision for the development of mental and physical fitness.[11]

Since students are motivated to acquire knowledge in many activities, they are prepared to make a wise program selection in the senior high school. A number of years ago, Nash et al. advocated more exploration in the junior high school.[12]

Exploration in the Junior High School

In addition to the usual objectives of secondary education, the junior high school places emphasis on guidance, integration, and socialization in the development of a curriculum designed to meet the needs of boys and girls.

One objective that has priority over all other efforts in the junior high school is the exploration by students of many activities. Students should be encouraged to explore, discover, and develop innate potentialities. This objective has valuable implications for the organization

and administration of physical education in the junior high school.

Exploration in physical education requires a careful survey of activities and considerable study of time allotment. One city has used the exploration approach in teaching for 25 years. All of the schools are designed around six teaching stations, with a teacher assigned to each station. The curriculum is planned to allow an equal amount of time for exploration and discovery in each activity. Students are grouped by ability and are encouraged to improve their skill techniques, acquire knowledge of rules, and learn the purposes of each activity. The entire program attempts to prepare each student for the elective program in the senior high schools.[13]

Classification and Time Allotment of Activities

Because of the heavy emphasis on spectator sports and the impact of the inter-school program upon the content of the instructional program, classifications for the various physical education activities must be developed to insure that no single activity or group of activities dominates the curriculum. Although time allotments in terms of percentages are necessary and may in fact assist in providing direction for the program, they should be adaptable to the varying needs of individual schools and systems.

There are several plans for allocating time for the various groups of activities. The school system in Arkansas uses a sound classification and allotment of time of activities for teaching physical education throughout the state. The plan is developed around six groups of activities, with time allocations for each grade: (1) rhythmic activities; (2) team activities; (3) individual activities; (4) self-testing activities; (5) games and relays; and (6) body mechanics and conditioning exercises. The entire program is shown in Figure 7–5A.

In cities and districts that have supervisors and curriculum planning committees, local programs prevail. Programs planned on the local level are usually ef-

TYPE OF ACTIVITY	SEVENTH GRADE Boys	Girls	EIGHTH GRADE Boys	Girls	NINTH GRADE Boys	Girls	TENTH GRADE Boys	Girls	ELEVENTH GRADE Boys	Girls	TWELFTH GRADE Boys	Girls	SAMPLE ACTIVITIES
Rhythmic Activities	15%	30%	15%	30%	15%	30%	10%	30%	10%	30%	10%	30%	Fundamentals of rhythms, folk games, mixers, square dancing, modern dance, singing games.
Team Activities (Highly organized team sports)	30	25	30	25	30	30	35	30	35	30	35	30	Basketball, baseball, touch football, volleyball, soccer, speedball, field hockey, field ball, speed-a-way.
Individual activities (Individual sports and recreational activities)	20	20	20	20	20	20	30	30	30	30	30	30	Tennis, golf, badminton, bowling, archery, table tennis, handball, shuffle board, track and field, horseshoes, deck tennis, aerial darts, paddle tennis, fly and bait casting, swimming, skating, quiet games, camping, canoeing and boating.
Self Testing Activities	15	10	15	10	15	10	20	5	20	5	20	5	Tumbling, pyramid building, apparatus activities, wrestling, individual and dual stunts, rope climbing, rope jumping, and trampoline activities.
Games and Relays	15	10	15	10	15	5							Wheelbarrow relay, two-legged relay, crab walk race, obstacle race, leap frog relay, overhead relay goalthrowing relay, dodge ball, keep-away.
Body Mechanics and Conditioning Activities	5	5	5	5	5	5	5	5	5	5	5	5	Fundamentals and practice of walking, running, sitting, lifting, pushing, carrying, standing. Exercises for strength and endurance. Example:

A

Figure 7–5. *See opposite page for legend.*

TYPE OF ACTIVITY	SEVENTH GRADE	EIGHTH GRADE	NINTH GRADE
Team Sports	40–50%	30–40%	30–40%
Gymnastics and Tumbling	20%	20–30%	20–30%
Individual Sports	11–20%	15–20%	15–20%
Rhythms and Dance	10–15%	15–20%	20–25%
Physical Fitness	5%	5%	5%
Other	5%	5%	5%

B

Figure 7–5. Time allotments for activities for boys and girls according to grade. (A courtesy of State Department of Education, Little Rock, Arkansas; B from Seattle Public Schools, Publication Guide for Junior High School Girls, Seattle, Washington, 1968.)

fective, since local individuals assist with the planning and take pride in using materials they have developed, resulting in a successful program.

The classification and time allotment of activities developed for girls in the Seattle Public School (Figure 7–5B) will serve as an example of local planning.

It is interesting to note the varying percentages of time allotted to activities taught in the junior high school. A study of physical education programs reveals the heavy emphasis on team sports and the exclusion of individual activities. Figure 7–6 illustrates how some schools are devising instruction to more nearly approach the objectives of the junior high school. The senior high school program, which is described next, will further emphasize the importance of instruction in activities that may be practiced beyond school years.

SCHOOLS	ACTIVITIES	PROCEDURES
	Instruction	
Edgewood Junior High School, New Brighton, Minnesota	Instruction in individual sports, team sports, lifetime sports, folk and modern dance, field hockey, and conditioning	• Coeducational • Team teaching • Differentiated staffing
Roosevelt Junior High School, Eugene, Oregon	Instruction in track and field, outdoor education, team and lifetime sports, dance, weight lifting, cycling, jogging, yoga and swimming	• Elective program • Team teaching for track and field and outdoor education • Coeducational
Vermillion Junior High School, Vermillion, South Dakota	Extra-Class Roller skating, golf, tumbling, baton twirling, backpacking, judo, fishing, fencing, bowling, table tennis, archery, weight lifting	• Mini courses • Selectives
Old Orchard Junior High School, Skokie, Illinois	Individual and team sports	• Intramurals • Supplements instructional program

Figure 7–6. Innovative programs in the junior high school. (From Munson, Corlee, and Elba Stafford: "Middle Schools: A Variety of Approaches to Physical Education." JOHPER, February, 1964, p. 29.)

THE SENIOR HIGH SCHOOL PROGRAM

Purposes of the Senior High School Program

The objectives of secondary education have already been described in Chapter 2. However, it seems desirable to mention briefly the basic purposes of the senior high school commonly agreed upon. Grieder and Romine suggest the following widely accepted functions of the senior high school: the integrative function, the differentiative function, the propaedeutic function, the socializing function, the exploratory function, and the guidance and counseling function. The differentiative function has particular significance for physical education and therefore deserves mention.

Differentiative function. It is very desirable that the program for secondary education identify the interests and special abilities of students and provide preparation for the development of specialized abilities as a means of providing leaders and workers in all of the various important aspects of American industry, culture, and work.[14]

Although physical education in the secondary school shares all of the general objectives of education as well as the specific objectives outlined above, the differentiative function is of special concern for physical education teachers in the senior high school. It is on this premise that the elective program, discussed in the following paragraphs, is based.

The elective program does not imply that the student elects physical education. It suggests that the student *elects activities within the requirement.*

Election of Activities

By the time he reaches senior high school, a student will have formed intense likes and dislikes for various activities, based on his own anatomical structure, physiological limitations, and psychological attitude. The senior high school student should no longer be required to follow the program of prescribed activities for the elementary, middle, or junior high schools. Having progressed through a required program of activities in the elementary school and an exploration program in the junior high school, he should be allowed a choice of activities in the senior high school. This choice of activities allows students to follow their interests in certain activities and with the assistance of teachers to attain that degree of skill performance which their potential will permit.

Although, until recently, election of activities on a planned basis was rare in the schools, it has been recognized as a necessary goal. As early as 1951, Nash et al. anticipated the importance of students' election of activities.[15] More recently, attention has been given to the advantages of student electives over the traditional curriculum.

All elective programs should be preceded by a period of exploration to allow the student to make a wise selection of activities. Without having participated in a particular activity, students are incapable of determining whether they like it or not. The exploration period should be scheduled in the junior high school; however, if this is not possible, the first year of the senior high school should provide for a well-planned exploration program.

The student-choice plan for electives, when planned properly, has many advantages. It improves the quality of instruction, motivates students to learn, and minimizes many of the problems frequently found in the senior high school. Some of the advantages of the plan are immediately apparent.

Develops Better Performance. When students are able to specialize in the activity of their choice, they derive more enjoyment from the instruction and are able to develop a degree of excellence in performance that will motivate them to participate in the activity throughout their lives.

Recognizes Varying Abilities. Boys and girls differ anatomically, physiologically, and psychologically. These differences predispose students to excel in certain activities and to perform poorly in others. Continual failure causes students to develop antagonism toward an activity, while successful performance provides them with a feeling of accomplishment. The choice of activities takes into account natural differences and enhances the quality of instruction.

Provides for Innovative Teaching Procedures. It has been established that the purpose of the senior high school program is to provide students with the opportunity for specialization in order for them to develop a high level of skill performance. To accomplish this, the best instruction possible by those teachers best qualified is necessary. Although teachers are expected to teach several activities, they rarely excel in more than one or two. Team teaching in conjunction with student choice allows for the reassignment of a teacher to the proper activity. For example, in one plan, 120 students are assigned to each period during the day, with three teachers responsible for the instruction. Students are allowed to choose one of three activities (hockey, volleyball, basketball) in which they wish to receive instruction. After the students have made their choices, the three teachers assign themselves to the activities they are best qualified to teach. In this plan, teachers not only teach the activity which they like and for which they are best qualified but they also work cooperatively in planning and organizing teaching procedures and assisting students in the selection of activities and with other details.

An example of the manner in which this plan provides for better staff utilization is the placement of coaches in the proper activity. Most coaches are specialists excelling in one or two activities. Student choice, when combined with team teaching, places students and coaches in the activity they like, the result being a more effective instructional program.

Develops Class Decorum. In an electives program, students are more eager to cooperate by reporting to class promptly and dressing quickly; they refrain from bringing notes to be excused, and they enter the learning situation with more interest. Too often students who dislike a program do not participate

and create problems for the teacher. In contrast, when all students are participating in activities they themselves have selected, disciplinary problems are rare.

Provides for Better Class Management. The electives program is so interesting to students that they become more cooperative in matters of dress, attendance, and participation. Thus teachers are able to spend more time teaching rather than doing organizational minutia.

For many students, the senior high school is the terminal period in physical education. If the program is to have meaning and attain the desired objectives, it should offer an instructional program that not only provides for immediate health needs for every student but also motivates all students to participate in physical activity beyond their years in school.

Examples of Elective Programs

Some cities have already instituted elective programs which have produced effective teaching situations, offering concrete evidence of the value of this approach in curriculum organization.

The required elective program designed for the girls of Niles North High School, Skokie, Illinois, deserves mention. The program was planned after careful analysis of the needs of the school and consideration of several factors which were weighed before initiating the program. These factors were (1) philosophy; (2) grouping by grade levels; (3) available teachers, stations, and equipment; (4) length of marking periods; (5) skill background of students; and (6) dedication of the department chairman.

The plan at Niles North High School operates from a modular scheduling team-teaching arrangement with classes scheduled on a five-day cycle. The entire school schedule is programed and computerized.

Students make their selections each six weeks, with the first day of each cycle set aside for reorganization, which includes the assignment of teachers and students.

CYCLES	ACTIVITIES OFFERED		
First Six Weeks	Hockey Driver Safety Archery	Tennis Badminton Driver Training	Health Bowling Ice Skating
Second Six Weeks	Driver Safety Field Hockey Speedaway	Adv. Basketball Folk Dance Driver Training	Health Bowling Ice Skating
Third Six Weeks	Basketball Modern Dance Personal Development	Health Driver Training Driver Safety	Prog. Gymnastics Bowling Ice Skating
Fourth Six Weeks	Adv. Volleyball Modern Dance Apparatus	Driver Safety Driver Training Rhy. Gymnastics	Ice Skating Bowling
Fifth Six Weeks	Volleyball Apparatus Folk Dance	Health Driver Safety Driver Training	Ice Skating Bowling Flag Football
Final Six Weeks	May Day Fun for the Family Bowling	Track & Field Driver Training Health	Softball Driver Safety Ice Skating

Figure 7–7. A sample elective program. (From "Required Electives for High School Girls." *Physical Education Newsletter.* December 1, 1972.)

The activities that compose the program are grouped under eight categories: aquatics, individual sports, team sports, gymnastics, dance, self-testing, miscellaneous, and class instruction.[16]

Another example of a program developed around electives is illustrated by the curriculum offerings for girls in the high school program of Granite City, Illinois. The program, which is required in grades 10 through 12, is divided into six cycles, each six weeks in length. Figure 7–7 outlines the offerings by grades. An outstanding feature of the plan is the summer school program, which may be substituted for one cycle of regular physical education.

Although the girls have a diversified program, they must meet the following requirements for graduation:

1. Earn eight semesters' credit in health and physical education (two in the 9th grade).
2. Take one unit each of beginning hockey, beginning modern dance, beginning apparatus, driver safety, and health.
3. Pass three units of team sports (all may be in the same activity).
4. Complete two units of individual sports activities selected from archery, tennis, badminton, track and field, bowling, skating, golf, or fun for the family.[17]

John Dewey High School in Brooklyn, New York, offers a comprehensive program in electives for boys and girls. Figure 7–8 provides the scope and sequence of the entire program.[18]

Other schools which have successfully initiated required electives programs are Cheltenham High School, Wyncote, Pennsylvania,[19] and Gloucester High School, Gloucester, Massachusetts.[20] Both of these schools have achieved the major purposes of an electives program: (1) more relevancy is developed, and (2) more in-depth instruction is possible. East Syracuse—Minoa Central Schools, East Syracuse, New York, initiated a pilot electives program in 1973. The program emphasizes a varied curriculum which includes lifetime activities and the use of community facilities.[21]

Classification and Time Allotment

Just as the classification of activities and the allotment of time for them are desirable for the junior high school program, so is the arrangement of activities necessary for the senior high school. It was pointed out that in the junior high school undue emphasis is usually placed on team sports, as revealed in a study of current senior high school guidebooks

JOHN DEWEY HIGH SCHOOL
Brooklyn, New York

Boys Course Offerings: 1973-74

TYPE OF COURSE		1	2	3	4	5
Exploratory Physical Education NEW STUDENTS 9th & 10th Grades		9111 Football Track	9112 Gymnastics "A" Basketball	9113 Wrestling Gymnastics "B"	9114 Soccer Volleyball	9115 Softball Tennis/Paddle Ball
Beginner's Electives *Courses for beginners only: all others to be combined with Intermediate	Life Sports	Paddle Ball/ Hand Ball	*Bowling	*Badminton & Table Tennis	*Fencing	*Tennis
	Team Sports	Football	Soccer	Hockey	Volleyball	Softball
	Miscellaneous	Track	Basketball	Gymnastics A/B		Track
			*Golf	Wrestling		
Intermediate Electives	Life Sports	Paddle Ball/ Hand Ball	Bowling	Badminton & Table Tennis	Fencing	Tennis
	Team Sports	Football	Soccer	Hockey	Volleyball	Softball
	Miscellaneous	Track	Basketball	Gymnastics A/B		Track
			Golf	Wrestling		
Advanced Electives **Separate from Intermediate class. All others combined with Intermediate Classes.	Life Sports	Paddle Ball & Hand Ball	Bowling	Badminton & Table Tennis	Fencing	Tennis
	Team Sports	Football	Soccer	Hockey	Volleyball	Softball
	Miscellaneous	Track	**Basketball	**Basketball		Track
			Golf	**Gymnastics A/B		
				**Wrestling		

Figure 7–8. A comprehensive electives program. (Courtesy of John Dewey High School, Brooklyn, New York.)

Illustration continued on the following page

on both the state and local levels. This proposed allotment of time for individual sports is encouraging, but considerable effort is required if individual sports are to gain a respectable place in the physical education curriculum. In the revised edition of *The Physical Education Curriculum* (Figure 7-9), a more favorable emphasis is placed on individual sports for the senior high level.

ADAPTING THE EXPLORATION AND ELECTIVE PLANS

The materials and programs just presented describe ways in which the exploration and electives procedures may be incorporated into the school curriculum. Each school, of course, must operate its physical education program according to its own philosophy; most administrators will find, however, that the patterns recommended here can usually be adjusted to fit their needs.

Junior-Senior High School

The junior high school provides the opportunity for students to acquaint themselves with a variety of activities, whereas the senior high school gives them the chance to participate in the activities of their choice and to develop a high level of skill in their chosen activity. This arrangement is a practical one, and the results are satisfactory when the city or district operates uniformly under a city-wide curriculum with a uniform guidebook. However, if there is no uniform plan and each school arranges its own curriculum, this arrangement is less adaptable, since students who transfer from one school to another may not be properly oriented to make a wise choice of activities. In such situations each school might initiate its own plan of exploration and electives. For instance, in the junior high school, students in the 7th grade might be involved in the exploration phase while those in the 8th and 9th grades would have a choice of activities. In the senior high school,

		Boys Course Offerings: 1973-74				
TYPE OF COURSE		1	2	3	4	5
Miscellaneous	Leaders in Training	Track Football	Basketball Gymnastics "A"	Gymnastics "B" Wrestling	Volleyball Soccer	Tennis/Paddle Ball Softball
	Power Training	Track Football	Basketball Gymnastics "A"	Gymnastics "B" Badminton & Table Tennis	Volleyball Soccer	Softball Paddle Ball
Electives	Weight Training	Weight Training	Weight Training	Weight Training	Weight Training	Weight Training
	Leaders	Leaders	Leaders	Leaders	Leaders	Leaders
Co-Ed		4891 Self-Defense	4892 Self-Defense	4893 Self-Defense	4894 Self-Defense	4895 Self-Defense
		Co-Ed: 9811 Paddle/Hand Ball	Co-Ed: 9812 Volleyball	Co-Ed: 9813 Bowling	Co-Ed: 9814 Badminton/ Table Tennis	Co-Ed: 9815 Tennis
Electives		9741 Intermediate Folk Dance	9742 Intermediate Folk Dance	9743 Intermediate Folk Dance	9744 Intermediate Folk Dance	9745 Intermediate Folk Dance
		9791 Advanced Folk Dance	9792 Advanced Folk Dance	9793 Advanced Folk Dance	9794 Advanced Folk Dance	9795 Advanced Folk Dance
		Yoga	Yoga	Yoga	Yoga	Yoga

Figure 7-8. *continued*

Illustration continued on the opposite page

JOHN DEWEY HIGH SCHOOL
Brooklyn, New York

Girls Course Offerings: 1973-74

TYPE OF COURSE		1	2	3	4	5
Exploration Physical Education NEW STUDENTS		9161 Movement Exploration	9162 Volleyball Gymnastics "A"	9163 Basketball Gymnastics "B"	9164 Folk Dance Badminton	9165 Softball Track
Beginner's Electives	Life Sports	*Tennis	Paddle Ball/ Hand Ball	*Fencing	*Bowling/ Badminton	*Golf/Archery
*For Beginners Only.	Team Sports	*Field Hockey Speed-A-Way	Volleyball	Basketball	Track	Softball
	Gymnastics	Conditioning for Gymnastics	Gymnastics "A"	Gymnastics "B"		
Intermediate Electives	Life Sports	Tennis	Paddle Ball/ Hand Ball	Fencing	Bowling/ Badminton	Golf/Archery
	Team Sports	Field Hockey Speed-A-Way	Volleyball	Basketball	Track	Softball
	Gymnastics	Conditioning for Gymnastics	Gymnastics "A"	Gymnastics "B"		
Advanced Electives	Life Sports	Tennis	Paddle Ball/ Hand Ball	Fencing	Bowling/ Badminton	Golf/Archery
**Separate course: all others to be combined with intermediate course.	Team Sports	Field Hockey Speed-A-Way	**Volleyball	**Basketball	Track	**Softball
	Gymnastics	Conditioning for Gymnastics	Gymnastics "A"	Gymnastics "B"		
Miscellaneous Electives	Leaders Training	4351 Tennis Field Hockey	4352 Gymnastics "A"	4353 Gymnastics "B"	4354 Volleyball Basketball	4355 Track Softball
	Slimnastics	Slimnastics	Slimnastics	Slimnastics	Slimnastics	Slimnastics
Co-Ed Activities		9891 Self-Defense Co-Ed: 9811 Yoga	9892 Self-Defense Co-Ed: 9812 Yoga	9893 Self-Defense Co-Ed: 9813 Yoga	9894 Self-Defense Co-Ed: 9814 Yoga	9895 Self-Defense Co-Ed: 9815 Yoga

Figure 7–8. *continued*

10th-grade students would be oriented to the various activities in that grade while 11th- and 12th-grade students would choose the activities they wished to pursue.

Other School Plans

There are many patterns of secondary school organization other than the junior-senior high arrangement. (See Chapter 5 for other patterns.) In all of these plans, the rule to follow would be to place the exploration program in one or two lower grades and follow this with an electives program in the upper grades.

An exploration-elective organizational plan is followed in the John Dewey High School, Brooklyn, New York. All new students must explore 5 phases in

SAMPLE PROGRAM FOR THE JUNIOR HIGH SCHOOL (Grades 7-9)
AND SENIOR HIGH SCHOOL (Grades 10-12)

	Junior High		Senior High	
	Boys Weeks	Girls Weeks	Boys Weeks	Girls Weeks
1. Survival and water safety Swimming - Diving - Life Saving ...	18	18	12	12
2. Dancing and Rhythms Folk - Square - Social - Modern (Girls)	12	18	12	18
3. Team Sports a. Court and Diamond Games Volleyball - Softball - Basketball-Modified Basketball (Junior High Girls)	18	18	12	12
b. Field Sports Soccer - Speedball - Touch or Flag Football - Flickerball (Boys) — Fieldball - Field Hockey	18	12	18	12
4. Tumbling Gymnastics Tumbling - Pyramids - Apparatus - Trampoline - Relays - Stunts - Body Mechanics and Body Building	12	12	12	12
5. Individual and Dual Sports a. Tennis - Badminton - Handball Bowling, Track and Field - Wrestling - Golf and Archery ..	15	15	30*	30*
b. Additional Sports and Activities selected from the following list: Boating and Canoeing - Hiking and Camping - Horseshoes - Fencing - Fly and Bait Casting - Paddle Tennis - Riding - Skating - Snowshoeing - Squash - Table Tennis - Weight Training - Outdoor Education - Other Recreational Activities; or, devote more time to dual activities listed under "a" but many should be in co-educational activities	15	15	12	12
	Total of 108 Weeks		Total of 108 Weeks	

*Some choice permitted where feasible.

The time allotments are approximate in terms of relative values, and are subject to minor adjustment. They are listed in terms of weeks. A given activity can be concentrated in one year with a specific number of weeks or it may be split between two of the three years or distributed equally between the three years according to preference of a given school. For suggestions on schedule see Table VIII. If possible it is often desirable to schedule the activities to fit seasonal sports.

Figure 7-9. A modern curriculum, showing increased emphasis on individual sports instruction. (From Cooper, John M., and Clinton Strong: *The Physical Education Curriculum.* Columbia, Mo.: Lucas Brothers, 1973, p. 42.)

Exploratory Physical Education. After completing the required exploratory program, students may select any physical education activity offered in the curriculum.[22] See Figure 7–8 for the entire program.

Many schools and school divisions require only one year of physical education on the secondary level. In such situations, it is difficult to provide electives programs. Perhaps the best way to institute the program would be to arrange for exploration in the last year of elementary school. The person administering physical education in the secondary schools should explain the need for this type of program to the elementary school principals involved, and arrangements for the program should be set up in meetings with the elementary school classroom teachers or physical education teacher.

Some difficulties may arise in providing elementary schools with the required equipment, since there is usually a pronounced difference between elementary and secondary school activities. However, by using audio-visual aids and by arranging for high school teachers to visit the elementary school, a modified exploration program may be effectively implemented.

LIFETIME SPORTS

In the discussion of junior high school plans, we noted that instruction is inadequate in activities that can be continued after students finish school. Although the need is great for more instruction in lifetime activities, research has shown that four out of five high school graduates receive no instruction in these activities and that 80 per cent of the nation's public schools do not offer instruction in golf, tennis, bowling, or badminton.[23]

Many leaders in physical education through the years have advocated more emphasis on individual sports that have carry-over value beyond the school years. Williams,[24] Karl and Carolyn Bookwalter,[25] Brownell and Hagman,[26] and Oberteuffer and Ulrich[27] are a few of these leaders. In many school programs, team sports dominate the curriculum at the expense of individual or dual sports

such as golf, tennis, swimming, and bowling. Because of this, the student is deprived of learning skills that he can use throughout life. One should remember that only one out of every thousand students plays football after leaving school.[28]

PROGRAM IMPROVEMENT

Irrespective of the types of curriculum a school system has devised, effective instruction requires that both administrator and teaching personnel recognize the necessity for continuous effort to improve the performance of the classroom teacher. There are many examples of both formal and informal programs of in-service education throughout the country. One example is the program sponsored by the California State Department of Education and the California Committee on Fitness. Under a cooperative plan, these two agencies designated 22 schools to serve as physical education demonstration centers. The purpose is to spotlight outstanding programs that teachers and administrators may visit, observe, and, it is hoped, translate into improvements in their own schools (see Figure 7–10).

Criteria were established by physical educators for determining the schools to be chosen. In examining these criteria, the reader will agree that they may very well serve as standards for outstanding programs throughout the country.

EVALUATION OF THE SCHOOL PROGRAM

A continuing responsibility of the administrator of physical education, whether he be a director of a large system, a department head, or a teaching specialist, is to evaluate the program to determine to what extent objectives are being met. An obvious first step is to determine the standards by which to measure effectiveness.

There have been many attempts by individuals and groups to evaluate the overall school program in physical education. The committee for the National Study of Secondary School Evaluation developed the criteria that are used to evaluate pro-

CRITERIA FOR SELECTING OUTSTANDING PROGRAMS

1. All physical education teachers in the school must have a college major or minor in physical education.

2. A school's facilities must be appropriate for the total instructional program, including general physical education, gymnastics, and aquatics.

3. Physical examinations are required for all students.

4. The curriculum is designated to permit the maximum development of each student.

5. The physical education course of study is well-balanced, up-to-date, and outlines specifically what is expected at each grade level in each unit.

6. For a boys' program to qualify for demonstration purposes, it must meet state standards in seven of the following eight activities: aquatics, body mechanics, combatives, gymnastics and tumbling, individual and dual sports, recreational games, rhythm and dance, and team sports. For a girls' program to qualify for demonstration purposes, it must meet state standards in six of the following seven activities: aquatics, body mechanics, gymnastics and tumbling, individual and dual sports, recreational games, rhythm and dance, and team sports.

7. The school must offer, in grades 7–12, opportunities for students to participate in organized intramural and extramural activities. Senior and four year high schools must also offer a well-balanced interscholastic program.

8. The program must offer instruction aimed at improving skills, developing total body coordination and physical fitness, teaching course content, and inculcating knowledge of how physical fitness is developed and maintained.

9. There must be a progressive sequence for the teaching of each course and unit in the physical education program.

10. There must be an established time allotment for the teaching of each activity in a physical education period.

11. During each period, vigorous activities must be adapted to individual capacities.

12. Classes must be organized to allow for the assignment of students to physical education on the basis of such individual factors as health, skill development, and grade level.

13. The school must offer special instruction for students with physical limitations and inadequate skills.

14. Other activities or subjects may not be substituted for regular physical education.

15. Successful completion of the physical education course of study is required for graduation.

16. An evaluation of each student's progress is based on objective measurement of the goals specified in each unit or course.

17. Physical or motor fitness tests are given to all students twice a year and are used as one basis for identifying underdeveloped students, adapting instruction to individual needs, and appraising students' progress.

18. The school gives skill and knowledge tests in physical education to help determine student achievement.

19. The school has a well-defined grading procedure for physical education—consistent with grading procedures used in other subjects and well understood by students and parents.

20. The program is evaluated constantly using the evaluative criteria established by the California Association of Secondary School Administrators.

21. The school takes steps and establishes priorities to implement the findings of periodic evaluation.

22. The physical education staff holds regular meetings to discuss the instructional program with an eye toward improving instructional methods and revising the course of study.[42]

Figure 7–10. Criteria for selecting outstanding programs. (From "Elements of an Outstanding Physical Education Program—Would Your School Have Been Chosen?" *Physical Education Newsletter*, May 1, 1967.

I. ORGANIZATION

Checklist

1. The program, including interschool athletics, is under the direction of a specialist in physical education. . . . . na 1 2 3 4
2. Courses are required in all grade levels of the secondary school. . . . . na 1 2 3 4
3. Consideration is given to abilities and needs of students in assigning them to physical education classes. . . . . na 1 2 3 4
4. Supplementary instruction is provided for students with deficiencies in ability or physical education background. . . na 1 2 3 4
5. Provision is made for regular department staff meetings for curriculum planning. . . . . na 1 2 3 4
6. The organizational pattern permits flexibility in the assignment of staff for effective use of their special abilities. . . na 1 2 3 4
7. Class size is such that it permits effective teaching. . . . . . . na 1 2 3 4
8. The community is kept informed of the purposes and goals of physical education, intramural activities, and interschool athletics.* . . . . na 1 2 3 4
9. The total program, including interschool athletics, is adequately financed through the regular school budget. . . . . na 1 2 3 4
10. The interschool athletic program is under the control and administration of school authorities. . . . . na 1 2 3 4
11. Adequate time is provided in each class period for showers and dressing. . . na 1 2 3 4
12. Minimum state eligibility standards for interschool athletics are subscribed to and enforced. . . . . . . na 1 2 3 4

* *Interschool athletics* is interpreted as including playdays, sports days, informal interschool games, and organized interscholastic athletics.

13. In addition to recommended periodic medical examinations, such examinations are required before participation in athletics. . . . . na 1 2 3 4
14. Medical assistance is readily available in case of student injuries. . . . . na 1 2 3 4
15. Consideration is given in teachers' schedules for planning, organizing, and supervising intramural and interschool athletics. . . . . na 1 2 3 4
16. Opportunity is made available to parents and students for insurance coverage of all boys and girls engaging in sports and competitive activities. . . . . na 1 2 3 4
17. Protective equipment is provided according to the demands of the program. . . na 1 2 3 4
18. Parental permission is required for students to participate in competitive sports or other activities that require travel. . na 1 2 3 4
19. Interschool and intramural schedules are reasonable in terms of the demand upon students' time and the distances traveled. na 1 2 3 4
20. Men and women physical education teachers cooperatively plan and conduct co-educational instruction and activities. . na 1 2 3 4
21. Teachers from the various grade levels plan together to develop a sequential program in physical education. . . . . na 1 2 3 4
22. Teachers of the same grade level plan together to develop the physical education program at that level. . . . . . na 1 2 3 4

23. na 1 2 3 4

Supplementary Data

1. Describe the allotment of time for physical education, including adapted physical education classes.

2. Describe policies and practices for excusing students from classes.

3. Describe class assignment procedures.

Evaluations

a) *To what degree are physical education activities provided for all students?* . . . . na 1 2 3 4
b) *How satisfactorily do time allotments meet instructional needs?* . . . . na 1 2 3 4
c) *How satisfactory are the controls and safeguards for all athletic activities?* . . . . . . na 1 2 3 4

Comments

Figure 7–11. Evaluation checklist. (From *Evaluation Criteria*, 4th ed. Washington, D.C.: National Study of Secondary School Evaluation, 1969, p. 187.)

grams of physical education for secondary schools throughout the nation. These criteria are listed in Figure 7–1.

With the assistance of already existing evaluative criteria and self-evaluation plans, local districts sometimes find it advisable to develop their own plans for evaluation. Regardless of the approach used, it is advisable to evaluate programs periodically. A highly recommended procedure is to invite outside specialists to visit schools and, through the use of reliable instruments such as the one illustrated here, to evaluate the program and make recommendations for improvement.

REFERENCES

1. Benjamin Bloom: *Stability and Change in Human Characteristics.* New York: John Wiley & Sons, 1964, p. 69.
2. Educational Policies Commission: *Contemporary Issues in Elementary Education.* Washington: National Education Association, 1960, p. 3.
3. Marjorie Hanson: "Elementary School Physical Education Today." *JOHPER*, January, 1969, p. 36.
4. George Manolakes: "The Elementary School We Need." Association for Supervision and Curriculum Development. Washington, D.C.: National Education Association, 1965, pp. 20–21.
5. "Ten Steps to a Stronger Elementary Fitness Program." *Physical Education Newsletter*, October 15, 1964.
6. Charles A. Bucher: "National Adult Fitness Survey: Some Implications." *JOHPER*, January, 1974, p. 27.
7. John Puckett: "An Emphasis on Elementary School Physical Education—Goal: A Superior Program for All." *Physical Educator*, May, 1965, pp. 83–84.
8. Thomas Gatewood: "What Research Says about the Middle School." *Educational Leadership* (Journal of the Association for Supervision and Curriculum Development), December, 1973, p. 221.
9. Elba Stafford: "Middle Schools: Status of Physical Education Programs." *JOHPER*, February, 1974, p. 26.
10. James Conant: *Education in the Junior High School Years.* Princeton: Educational Testing Service, 1960, p. 12.
11. Nelson Bossing and Roscoe V. Cramer: *The Junior High School.* Boston: Houghton Mifflin Co., 1965, pp. 62–63.
12. Jay B. Nash, *et al.: Physical Education: Organization and Administration*, New York: A. S. Barnes & Co., 1951, p. 303.
13. *Building Healthier Youth.* Norfolk Public Schools, Norfolk, Virginia, 1976.
14. Clavin Grieder and Stephen Romine: *American Education.* New York: The Ronald Press Co., 1965, pp. 312–313.
15. Nash *et al., op. cit.*, p. 304.
16. "Things to Consider in Planning a Selectives Program." *Physical Education Newsletter*, March 1, 1974.
17. "Required Electives for High School Girls." *Physical Education Newsletter*, December 1, 1972.
18. John Dewey High School, Brooklyn, New York. Materials sent on request.
19. "Suggestions for Scheduling Required Electives in Physical Education." *Physical Education Newsletter*, December 1, 1973.
20. "Required Electives for Juniors and Seniors." *Physical Education Newsletter*, September 1, 1972.
21. "Varied Offerings Feature Required Electives for High School Seniors." *Physical Education Newsletter*, May 1, 1973.
22. John Dewey High School, *op. cit.*
23. Editorial. *Physical Education Newsletter*, January 1, 1967.
24. Jesse F. Williams: *Principles of Physical Education*, 8th ed. Philadelphia: W. B. Saunders Co., 1964, p. 354.
25. Karl Bookwalter and Carolyn Bookwalter: "Fitness for Secondary School Youth." *Bulletin, National Association of Secondary School Principals*, March, 1956, p. 52.
26. Clifford Brownell and Patricia Hagman: *Physical Education: Foundations and Principles.* New York: McGraw-Hill Book Co., 1951, p. 138.
27. Delbert Oberteuffer and Celeste Ulrich: *Physical Education*, 3rd ed. New York: Harper & Row, 1962, p. 298.
28. Charles Bucher: *Foundations of Physical Education*, 7th ed. St. Louis: C. V. Mosby Co., 1975, p. 57.

SUGGESTED READINGS

Brown, B. Frank: *The Reform of Secondary Education.* New York: McGraw-Hill Book Co., 1973.
Bucher, Charles A.: *Foundations of Physical Education*, 7th ed. St. Louis: C. V. Mosby Co., 1975.
DeYoung, Chris A., and Richard Wynn: *American Education*, 7th ed. New York: McGraw-Hill Book Co., 1972.

CHAPTER EIGHT

Organization for Classroom Management

TEACHER-STUDENT RELATIONSHIPS

Probably the greatest challenge in a teacher's career is meeting his class for the first time. In a brief period of 50 or 60 minutes, all of the information gained from methods, organization, principles, psychology, physiology of exercise, and other college courses must be condensed into one capsule of knowledgeable procedure. The mass of information needed for effective teaching at this point may be summarized in one word—organization.

The importance of organization of effort, mechanics of control, teacher-student relationships, teacher-principal rapport, teaching materials, methods of motivation, and other factors involved in conducting the class cannot be overemphasized. Experience has shown that in order to meld these factors into an effective class period, proper teacher-student relationships must be established the first time the teacher meets his class, since it is during the first meeting that

187

students form their lasting impressions of the teacher. The teacher who seeks popularity or who places himself on a level with his students invariably loses control and respect and jeopardizes his potential for success. The teacher should maintain his position as a leader and project an image of confidence and maturity that students can respect. He must be friendly yet firm, informal yet forceful. The new teacher often finds a balance between these attitudes difficult to achieve. Nevertheless, in order to teach effectively, the teacher must establish rapport early between himself and his students.

In addition, he must consider problems of discipline. Although much has been written about disciplinary measures, most of it is not applicable to physical education. Since deep-seated character traits and primitive urges are frequently brought to the surface in a class in which physical activity is involved, an entirely different approach should be taken in handling sensitive disciplinary problems. The physical education teacher must be a keen, practical psychologist. He must be able to understand and analyze the causes of adverse behavior and guide students toward purposeful activity.

Many students who create behavior problems for the teacher have inherent leadership potential, but the quality takes the form of bullying, exhibitionism, or boisterousness. The teacher must win the confidence of such students and place them in a position of leadership; this will help to develop an atmosphere of orderly conduct in the class and provide a more acceptable outlet for leadership abilities.

Some of the factors involved in deviant behavior and acceptable procedures to counteract it are suggested on the following pages.

DEVIANT BEHAVIOR

Although we have always had deviant behavior, in recent years the situation has worsened. Not only are the delinquent acts more vicious, but they are more widespread. No longer is adverse behavior a problem of a few large cities; it now exists in all areas of the country. In 1973, Lee Dolson, former president of the San Francisco Classroom Teachers Association, stated that "Teachers are in a state of fear. . . . It's time society is held accountable for the destruction of the teaching profession."[1]

In New York City, where there were 541 recorded attacks on teachers in 1972, Albert Shanker, President of the United Federation of Teachers, said that "Many teachers must work in a state of fear and be subjected to continuing assaults, harassment, intimidation, and insults. . . . Teachers have been doused with lighter fluid and set afire; others were raped and robbed, and there have been students so badly assaulted that they required plastic surgery."[2]

The conditions described by Shanker have become so serious and so prevalent that student behavior is now the number one problem of the nation's schools. The Sixth Annual Gallup Poll of the major problems confronting the schools listed for the sixth consecutive year the problem of discipline in the schools as the first concern.[3] The controversy arising between administrators and board members regarding corporal punishment, for example, has forced many superintendents to resign. The focal point of the corporal punishment battle rests on the public demand for restraint of the disruptive actions of students in the schools as opposed to court rulings upholding the rights of students under the constitution.

The behavior crisis in the schools brings the teacher to the front of the firing line, charged with the responsibility of teaching in an atmosphere of disruption and chaos.

Causes of Deviant Behavior

There is no single cause or group that is totally responsible for the deviant behavior in the schools of America: the schools, the teachers, the parents, and society itself must all share the blame.

Schools. Investigations of the conditions in education today reveal that the schools themselves are major producers of delinquency. For a large number of students, the curriculum is uninteresting and the school experience frustrating. Students are forced to remain in classes which they feel provide no experiences to assist them in earning a living. The curriculum in many places is antiquated and far removed from the needs of today's youth.

Because of the traditional requirements, administrators must regulate the school so that conformity in attendance, attitudes, and the behavior of students is rigidly enforced. When students, owing to these regulatory procedures, attend classes only to find them uninteresting and the instruction inadequate, rebellion is their natural course of action.

Teachers. Teachers are accused of contributing to the problem of deviant behavior. Some teachers use coercion, punishment, sarcasm, and intimidation to insure that their students perform in the manner that they prescribe. It is not surprising that students become aggressive and hostile toward teachers who use the authoritarian approach rather than logic, understanding, affection, and innovative teaching procedures.

Parents. Some groups feel that parents should be blamed for the deviant behavior that disrupts the classroom. These critics say that parents will not cooperate or support teachers in their efforts to maintain discipline in the classroom. They claim that not only do parents fail to cooperate but many of them even encourage their children to defy existing authority. It is not uncommon, for example, for parents to cover up for their children when they are truant, fail to report to class, or intimidate the teacher and other students.

Society. Not all critics place the blame for deviant behavior on the schools, teachers, and parents. Some feel that the present upsurge of behavior problems in the schools is a worldwide trend that reveals a general decline of respect for law, order, and the "establishment" in general. Many educational leaders feel that more attention should be given to financing education rather than to rehabilitation.

That education is in serious financial trouble was pointed out by James A. Harris, president of the National Education Association for the year 1974, who revealed the startling fact that in many states more money is spent to incarcerate children than to educate them. As an example, he cites the state of Iowa, where $9000 is spent yearly to maintain a student in a juvenile home and only $1050 to educate a student who causes no trouble. Other typical state expenditures on correctional procedures are as follows: Maryland, $18,000; Illinois and Michigan, $10,000; Virginia, $3877; and District of Columbia, $7469.[4]

Other Causes. In addition to the causes of behavior problems just described there are other contributing factors. Poor race relations, overcrowded schools and classrooms, school gangs, and lack of religious influence are just some of the negative influences on the behavior of students. In a survey of discipline problems in 682 urban schools, sponsored by the National Association of Secondary School Principals, the following conclusions were made:

1. The size of the student body is a more important variable than the size of the city in which the school is located.
2. Integrated schools with higher percentages of black students are less likely to be disrupted if such schools also have high percentages of black staff.
3. Disruption and average daily attendance are directly related. Where average daily attendance is lower, disruption is higher and vice versa.[5]

Corporal Punishment

Because of the universal increase in deviant behavior in the schools, the question of corporal punishment has become controversial to the extent that it may be banned from the schools entirely. While many school administrators and teachers still advocate corporal punishment, the opposition by parents and various groups has become so strong that many states have eliminated it.

The American Civil Liberties Union and the Task Force on Corporal Punishment of the National Education Association vigorously oppose the use of corporal punishment. The Task Force, following a national survey, stated that "Teachers and other school personnel abhor physical violence of persons toward each other, no matter what the form—alley fights, gang warfare, repression by law enforcement agencies, or war between nations."[6] The Task Force lists the following conclusions drawn from the survey:

1. Physical punishment usually has to be used over and over again to be even minimally effective.

2. Teaching that might is right increases rather than decreases a student's disruptive behavior.

3. Corporal punishment is used much more often against students who are smaller and weaker than the teacher; it is used more frequently against poor children and members of minority groups than against children of white, middle-class families.

4. In many cases, corporal punishment causes lasting psychological damage to children.

5. Corporal punishment increases aggressive hostility rather than increasing self-discipline.

6. The availability of corporal punishment discourages teachers from pursuing other, and better, avenues of discipline.

7. Any set limitations on the use of corporal punishment are usually ignored.[7]

The Task Force, among its many recommendations, asks for a statute allowing that physical restraint be used only to protect teachers and students, to prevent injury, to protect property, or to gain possession of a weapon. It calls for outlawing all forms of corporal punishment except under the conditions outlined. The Task Force also recommends short- and long-range measures to be used in coping with disruptive behavior.[8]

The American Civil Liberties Union takes the stand that in addition to being ineffective, physical punishment is illegal. The Union states that the Constitution provides "That no one shall be deprived of life, liberty, or property without due process of law. . . ." Implicit in these provisions, the Union claimed "is the right to bodily integrity, the violation of which must be interpreted as a deprivation of liberty."[9] Recent court rulings have substantiated this stand. A suit involving the spanking of a fourth grader who was not given due process was decided in favor of the boy and his mother. Although the damages were small ($200), the suit may have set a precedent because it required due process for a summary punishment (punishment which is administered without a hearing or due process).[10]

The news media have also taken a stand against corporal punishment. They paint a vivid picture of the extremes to which adults may go in administering punishment. The Los Angeles *Times* reports cases in which children were beaten with split baseball bats, rubber hose, and slotted paddles. The *Times* calls corporal punishment "That most ineffective and archaic practice, a holdover from the darker ages of education when students cowered in terror of a blow to the head or a birch to the posterior."[11]

Guides for Alleviating Deviant Behavior

Curbing deviant behavior is a most difficult undertaking. Teachers are untrained in the procedures necessary for coping with the problems arising from the conflicts common in today's classroom. Education in the past was taught in an authoritarian setting. Students did what the teacher demanded or they were punished. Each teacher had his own code of behavior, and students had to adjust to these varying standards or risk failure, sarcasm, or social disapproval.

With the furor now centered around the use of corporal punishment and the increasing court recognition of civil rights for students, teachers no longer have strong control of the behavior of their students. Since the teacher is the key to providing effective instruction in the present climate of the classroom, he should be given the aids necessary to perform his job. Some of the procedures that may assist him are discussed in the following paragraphs.

Student Codes. Throughout the country, administrators and boards of education are developing student codes of behavior. These codes have grown out of the court rulings which guarantee new freedom for students.

In some places, such as Oregon and Michigan, the state boards have ordered districts to develop student codes. Included in the codes are not only student rights in freedom of the press, assembly, and expression but also student responsibilities. Codes should clearly outline what students may rightly do in such matters as dress, special assembly, and student government. The student should also be apprised of what he cannot do regarding alcohol, tobacco, the use of automobiles, theft, disruption, assault, and damage to property. In addition, the code should outline grievance procedures relating to suspension and expulsion.

The student code should be written by a committee appointed by the superintendent. In addition to teachers, principals, administrators, and parents, the code committee should include students. Since the purpose of the code is to point out the regulations and rights of students, it is imperative that students have a voice in formulating policy.

Rewarding Positive Behavior. There is evidence that students respond favorably when teachers reward them for positive behavior and ignore their disruptive acts. One study has reported a drop from 62 to 29 per cent in disruptive behavior following application of this principle of behavior modification.[12]

The use of behavior modification in working with deviant students is nothing new. It is an application of the reinforcement theory originally advocated by B. F. Skinner, and has produced favorable results when used in such teaching systems as programmed instruction and in mental hospitals.

The teacher is the key to developing positive behavior. Studies show that even with identical class sizes and teaching situations, some teachers have more success than others. When teachers structure complex learning situations so that students have rewarding experiences, positive results follow. In order to attain these results, teachers should plan assignments that are appropriate to the student's performance level, and present them in a sequential manner. The students should be rewarded for success in their efforts to attain established goals.

Although many educators point to the advantages that are gained from behavior modification, not all agree that this procedure is a wise one. Carrison, for one, is deeply concerned with some of the results of behavior modification. He raises three questions about the use of these procedures in dealing with discipline: (1) What other conditions may occur besides the simple one desired? (2) What type of personality modification is taking place along with behavior modification? (3) What type of society will result when it consists of individuals trained in this manner?

The first question suggests the possibility that if a student is rewarded with something pleasant for performing a particular task, he may never realize the actual value of the task itself. Carrison feels that to bribe a child by promising him the dessert if he eats his vegetables may build up a long-range dislike for vegetables, which are necessary for health. If the child is continually subjected to rewards and bribes for performing tasks in school, he will not become aware of the intrinsic values of intellectual achievement.

In answer to the second question, Carrison says that behavior modification may develop the "con artist" type of personality, causing the child to expect some reward or bribe for everything he does. The child may be unable to function without rewards, or he may become a master of "conning" the teacher in attaining the goals which are established. Since behavior modification involves manipulation, the process necessarily suppresses the truth, because the child is not aware that he is being manipulated. The question is raised, Is a procedure which does not provide the child a truthful setting educationally sound? Students trained in this manner, it is argued, would not become an asset to society.

In summary, Carrison urges that before embarking on a behavior modification course, teachers be provided with in-service programs to study the origin of behavior modification. He points out that these procedures were originally designed for use in the mental institutions, for hopeless mental patients. This being the case, behavior modification techniques should only be used by licensed psychologists and psychiatrists who are qualified to work with disturbed people.

Carrison makes the final observation that schools advocating and practicing behavior modification may become involved in legal entanglements. The legal issue is that of placing a child in therapy without parental consent under a teacher who is unlicensed and unqualified to render this treatment.[13]

Teacher-Student Conferences. In a survey of teacher opinion conducted by the Scholastic Institute of Teacher Opinion, 52 per cent of the teachers felt that having individual conferences with a student is the most effective disciplinary procedure.[14] The conference provides an effective medium of communication between the teacher and the student, one in which they will learn to understand and appreciate each other's views and attitudes toward education and life. The conference is obviously the most effective technique in dealing with the troublesome student.

Figure 8-1. Many students have great leadership potential. Placing them in leadership roles may alter their behavior and produce better adjusted students. (Courtesy of Norfolk Public Schools, Norfolk, Virginia.)

Student Leadership. Involving students in leadership roles has been proved very effective in providing challenges for many students. Leadership potential is not limited to the academically talented or socially adjusted—some of the most notorious delinquents have shown tremendous leadership ability. Placing unmotivated students or potential dropouts in leadership roles involving purposeful activity often helps them to find themselves. One program that has produced satisfying results for students of a broad range of abilities is the Physical Education Leadership Training (PELT) Program in Norfolk, Virginia. This program will be described later in the chapter. (See Figure 8-1.)

It has been clearly shown that students feel that discipline and work are essential to an effective teaching situation. The results of two surveys, one by the American College Testing Program and one by the National Association of Secondary Principals, show that students support teachers who are demanding, are strong disciplinarians, and who make them work.[15]

Good Teaching and Organization. Successful teachers point out that good teaching and the careful organization of their classes are essential to effective instruction. Students report to the physical education class with the anticipation of actively participating in activities in order to acquire and improve certain skills. When they continually do the same thing from day to day without instructional leadership, they become uninterested and disruptive. Movement is a natural urge of all individuals, and the successful teacher organizes his class so that this natural urge can be channeled along acceptable instructional lines. Students must be challenged to reach a higher level of skill performance if they are to remain interested in physical education. Failure to challenge students to improve their skill techniques leads to an atmosphere of disruption that may eventually destroy all rapport between student and teacher.

Acceptable and Unacceptable Teacher Behavior. In their associations with students, teachers have an important role in preventing disruptive behavior. Matters of discipline can be resolved only by the teachers. Administrators and supervisors can assist teachers in the improvement of instruction, but they can be of very little assistance in the improvement of teacher-student relationships. The personality of the teacher, his speech, the way he expresses himself, his confidence, and the inner attitudes he has toward students are several of the many traits that determine the success or failure of a teacher.

Experience has shown that there are several approaches and procedures that teachers should or should not employ if they are to be successful and prevent disruptive behavior. The teacher should:

1. Be aware that planning is a basic essential to effective instruction. Effective instruction is a prerequisite to order in the classroom. When teachers challenge the interest of students and the instruction leads them to a higher level of performance, very little time is available for negative behavior.

2. Be knowledgeable in the areas of instruction for which he is responsible. It does not take a long time for students to find out if the teacher is ill-prepared.

3. Be friendly, fair, firm, tolerant, and sincere with students. Many inner-city children resent the dictatorial manner in which some teachers approach their assignments.

4. Try to assist each student to find success and develop a positive self-image.

5. Always maintain the dignity of his status as a teacher. To be a "swell guy" at all costs will destroy a teacher's effectiveness, whereas the development of a climate of admiration and respect will allow him to communicate with students.

6. Always be positive in his approach and maintain a sense of humor.

7. Learn as much about each student as possible. A teacher should know about each student's life habits, family relationships, peer group, likes and dislikes, and above all his personal problems.

8. Make each class interesting and challenging. This can be done by frequent changes of routine, such as taking a field trip or bringing a guest speaker who relates to young people.

9. Be careful about mistaken judgment in decisions, and readily admit an error.

10. Be unafraid to mete out punishment when necessary and award the student when the deed merits it.

11. Be careful not to establish too many rules and regulations. However, when infractions are made, the teacher should be strong in enforcing these rules.

The teacher should *not:*

1. Inflict corporal punishment. Evidence points to the ineffectiveness of this approach, particularly in the secondary school.

2. Be maneuvered into a "point of no return" situation in which he states, "Either you do this or you will be punished."

3. Discipline all students in the class for the misbehavior of some. Procedures such as this will cause the innocent to resent and distrust the teacher.

4. Use participation in an acceptable activity as punishment. For example, to punish a student by forcing him to perform push-ups or running in place will cause the student to dislike these activities, since he will associate them with punishment.

5. Be maneuvered into an argument with students. This may be the type of battle where winning the battle means losing the war.

6. Ridicule or humiliate a student. This approach will turn the student against the teacher.

7. Attempt to force confessions from students.

8. Attempt to improve a student's behavior by comparing his actions with those of a well-behaved student. This approach will cause the student to resent the student who is less troublesome.

9. Threaten the student. To threaten him if he violates a rule usually prompts the student to deliberately break a rule.

10. Concentrate on minor offenses. This tends to weaken action for a more serious offense.

Although positive teacher-student relationships have a high priority in effective administration of the instructional program, the other factors discussed in the following paragraphs are also extremely important.

ADMINISTRATIVE DETAIL

It is good organization strategy to set aside a block of time at the beginning of each term or season for establishing procedures for taking care of attendance, records, excuses, uniforms, regulations of the department, locker assignments, towels, and student leadership.

Attendance

There are several methods of checking attendance. These include squad leaders calling the roll, roll call by the teacher, and the placing of numbers on the wall or floor, with each student standing in front of his number during the attendance check. Students assigned to exposed numbers are marked absent. These numbers may be recorded on a slip of paper and, between class periods, the absence recorded on the students' individual record cards or in the teacher's roll book (see chapter figure). Other plans involve use of a tag board and signing in and out each period.

Records

Well-planned programs require a simple but effective system of bookkeeping. Provisions should be made for recording absences, grades, daily observations, and so on. Some tools that may be used are personal record cards, squad cards, and permanent record cards.

Personal Record Card. The teacher should have a simple personal record for each student enrolled in his class. This record provides valuable assistance in guidance and in conferences with parents and administrators. An example of this type of card is shown in Figure 8–2.

Squad Card. Squad cards are widely used, and in many situations they are quite effective. Some teachers prefer the squad card to the individual or personal record card, but both may be used to advantage. Squad cards usually are designed to include the names of the squad members, attendance, test results, and other practical information about one squad, team, or group of students within the class. Such a card is shown in the resource manual that accompanies this text.

Permanent Record Card. Teachers and administrators with vision know the wisdom of keeping records of vital components of the program, such as yearly grades, yearly intramural points, comments of teachers, and other items that may be referred to during the year. These components should be recorded in a systematic manner and made available for teachers, parents, and administrators to review when necessary.

Excuses

It is inadvisable to excuse students from physical education permanently. A well-planned program consisting of a variety of activities, ability grouping within each class, and a special program of adaptives should provide for the needs of almost all students. In some instances a physician may recommend either adapting the program to the individual's needs or assigning the student to a special class. Figure 8–3 illustrates a

LEXINGTON HIGH SCHOOL PHYSICAL EDUCATION - JR.-SR. CLASS CARD

LAST NAME	FIRST	INITIAL	UNIT-H.R.	CLASS

UNIT	INSTRUCTOR	LESSONS 1	2	3	4	5	6	7	GRADE
1									
2									
3									
4									
5									
6									
7									
8									
9									
10									

Figure 8–2. Personal record card. (Courtesy of Lexington High School, Lexington, Massachusetts.)

OCEAN TOWNSHIP HIGH SCHOOL

OAKHURST, NEW JERSEY

<u>MEDICAL EXCUSE FORM</u>

<u>To the Attending Physician</u>:

The student whose name appears below is requesting, through his parents, to be
excused from the regular physical education classes at school. Such request will
only be honored by the instructor when the information has been completed and
signed by you, the attending physician, and returned to the school.

<u>To Be Completed by Student and Parent</u>:

Name of Student _____ Sex _____ Grade _____

School _____ Physical Education Teacher _____

Have you been excused from Physical Education classes for any extended period prior
to this year? (If so, state reason and for how long.) _____

_____

_____
Parent's Signature

PHYSICAL
<u>To Be Completed by Physician</u>:

It is desirable to keep all students in contact with regular physical education,
where possible. Please indicate which of the following group of activities would
be the best suited for your patient. If any group other than Group I is indicated
<u>please be sure to give your estimate of the length of time this student should</u>
<u>remain in this modified program</u> and the activities you recommend.

GROUP I   _____ No Restrictions

GROUP II   _____ No Restrictions. Excused from Shower –
                                    Length of time _____

GROUP III _____ Restricted from strenuous activity
                                    a. Omit contact sports _____
                                    b. Omit prolonged exercise _____
                                        Length of time _____

GROUP IV   _____ Omit all participation in physical acti-
                                    vities
                                    Length of time   _____
                                                       _____

Please indicate briefly the nature of the student's disability if classified other
than in Group I.

DATE: _____ DOCTOR'S SIGNATURE _____

NOTE: This form has the approval of the Monmouth Company Medical Society.

Figure 8–3. Medical excuse form for physical education. (Courtesy of Ocean Township High School,
Oakhurst, New Jersey.)

type of card used for a physician's recommendation regarding a student's participation in physical education.

Sometimes there is pressure to excuse students from physical education and substitute extracurricular activities, such as cheerleading, band practice, and drill team participation. This trend should be vigorously opposed; it usually undermines the instructional program, and it is difficult to curtail once the precedent has been established. Opposition to the substitution of extracurricular activities for physical education has been expressed by the Representative Assembly of the American Association of Health, Physical Education and Recreation. The Assembly states that "Whenever or wherever this practice prevails, children and youth are being denied their full educational rights."[16] This is a logical stand. If these activities are substituted for physical education, why not also substitute art, dramatics, vocational education, and other activities included in the curriculum? The claim that these involve physical activity is not a sound criterion for excusing the student from physical education; indeed, students building a set for a dramatic club may get even more vigorous exercise than the baton twirler, but this is insufficient reason for exempting the student from physical education.

Sometimes students are excused from physical education because they participate in interschool athletics. Although there are some arguments favoring this practice, they are not sound for the following reasons:

1. Conditioning is a basic factor in the development of athletes. The athlete reaches a plateau of development during the competitive season; after the season is over, there is a tremendous letdown and the athlete just "takes it easy" from December until August. Then, after two or three weeks of practice, he plays the first game. If he were enrolled in the physical education program, he would stay in training for the remainder of the year.

2. Athletes excused from physical education to participate in athletics miss instruction in many of the individual sports and other desirable activities offered in the physical education class. By taking physical educa-

tion, in addition to conditioning themselves, they would be learning skills that could be carried over into later life, long after interschool competition is over.

3. Many schools offer full credit toward graduation in physical education. Grades cannot be given to students if they do not attend class. Students would never be excused from mathematics or other academic subjects and expect a grade. If this policy does not apply to academic subjects, it should not apply to physical education.

Medical opinion is opposed to excusing students from physical education, as revealed in the following statement:

Excuses from physical education which deprive a young person of desirable developmental experiences in this area should not be granted unless there is a clear and overriding health reason wherein the student cannot participate except in a prescribed program of restricted physical activity. Currently, there is general agreement among both physicians and educators that when *good* programs exist, "blanket" or overall excuses from physical education are unnecessary.[17]

Uniforms and Shoes

It is desirable that students dress appropriately for physical education classes. Class morale, safety conditions, performance, and sanitary conditions are improved when students dress uniformly. A one-piece suit for girls and trunks and a shirt for boys are recommended. Rubber-soled shoes, such as tennis or basketball shoes, should be required to insure safety and improve performance of the various movements involved in the program.

There are several reasons why students should dress appropriately when participating in physical education:

Class Morale. When students dress in well-fitted uniforms, they develop self-confidence, since the suits enhance both figure and self-image.

Safety. Regulation uniforms are designed for safety. These uniforms are free of buckles, belts, and other metal adornments that may interfere with movement and cause injury. Rubber-soled shoes prevent slipping and falling, which constitute a large number of the injuries in the physical education class.

Performance. Correct attire provides freedom of movement, which in turn will allow the student to attain his peak performance. The properly fitted uniform is designed to prevent the restraint that results when students wear jeans, short-shorts or cut-offs.

Cleanliness. A clean, well-laundered suit promotes personal hygiene, prevents skin irritations, and reduces body odor. The aesthetic factor is extremely important when large groups exercise and participate in vigorous activities.

Economy. A uniform that is properly constructed provides years of functional participation, since it is rugged and designed for all situations. Wearing street clothes is unsanitary, expensive, and unsatisfactory for participation in physical education.

Students should be encouraged to purchase inexpensive uniforms and shoes. These items can usually be purchased from local stores, although some schools prefer to purchase them from the manufacturer and sell them through the school bookstore or physical education class. Selling uniforms and shoes in the physical education class itself is not satisfactory, since teachers waste valuable instruction time collecting money, keeping accounts of sales and the money on hand, and taking inventories of uniforms and shoes. In some instances, selling uniforms in class has resulted in enormous loss of money and of uniforms, which may present a real problem for the teacher and the administrator.

Regulations of the Department

Students should be apprised of the regulations of the department during the first few class meetings, A written statement outlining these regulations is far better than verbal announcements. Written material may be carried home to serve as a valuable instrument for eliminating misunderstandings and establishing rapport between the teacher and parent. Figure 8–4 shows the title page and table of contents of a handbook for students and parents which has been used successfully for many years.

Locker Assignments

Considerable time and planning should be devoted to assigning lockers. All of the details involved in this procedure should be completed the first week of school. The numbers and combinations may be recorded on a permanent record card (see resource manual) or master sheet and filed in the central office.

Towel Program

There are two widely used plans for handling of towels: (1) students are assessed fees to cover the costs of purchasing and laundering towels, or (2) the school assumes the cost of the program. The first is the more common. In this plan, students pay a fee of two or three dollars for the year; this fee is usually sufficient to defray expenses. Local laundries bid for the service, and deliver and collect towels daily. This arrangement is more practical than laundering the towels in the school. However, some schools do launder the towels; in such cases, machines must be purchased and someone should be employed to supervise the program. It is neither a practical nor a sound policy to delegate this responsibility to a teacher.

The second plan is the more desirable one. The school, using tax money, assumes payment of all costs for the purchase and laundering of towels. This plan eliminates fees and teacher involvement in handling money.

Student Leadership

There are many details and procedures in teaching for which students may provide valuable assistance. Each class should have a group of students organized to assist the teacher with both administrative and instructional procedures, such as issuing towels and equipment, recording results of tests, checking attendance, and attending to other details essential to the smooth and effective operation of the program. These leaders should meet periodically with

BOYS'

PHYSICAL EDUCATION HANDBOOK

ROBERT LOUIS STEVENSON INTERMEDIATE SCHOOL
ST. HELENA UNIFIED SCHOOL DISTRICT
1316 HILLVIEW PLACE – ST. HELENA, CALIFORNIA

Figure 8–4. A comprehensive physical education handbook.

the teacher to study areas involving the conduct of the class.

Leaders should be selected democratically through class elections. Those selected then choose students to become members of their squads. Many physical educators throughout the country have found the student leader organization an invaluable aid in conducting their programs. Lucille M. Burkett, chairperson of the girl's physical education department, Shaker Heights (Ohio) High School, emphasizes the importance of student leaders. Her leaders assist with taking the roll, supervising the showers and locker room, teaching skills, and performing other routine functions that are helpful in producing an efficient program.[18]

An excellent plan, which was developed for the girls' program of the New York Public Schools, describes in detail the various functions of student leader groups. The plan expands the student leader concept and involves a highly organized program for leaders in training, leaders corps, and honor leaders.[19]

A student leadership program that originates in the senior high school and extends downward into the elementary school is practiced in the Norfolk (Virginia) Public Schools. The program is called PELT (Physical Education Leadership Training) and involves juniors and seniors in all high schools.

The PELT program is designed to make unique contributions to each individual's mental, physical, emotional, and social health. It encompasses learning experiences of the physiology of exer-

TABLE OF CONTENTS

Figure 8–4. *continued*

cise course, which in turn will be integrated into the total elementary and junior high physical education programs. Upon completion of requirements established for the programs, students assist with instruction in the elementary, junior, and senior high schools (known as *laboratory schools*). Each student participating in the program receives a mark as outlined for the regular marking period. His mark, as with other disciplines, is dependent upon his work. Full credit for graduation is allowed for this course.

Objectives of PELT. The Physical Education Leadership Program is committed to the following objectives:

1. Assist with instruction in the laboratory school, particularly when the physical education teacher is not there.
2. Provide in-depth study in health and physical education for those students who want to make teaching a career.
3. Provide leadership opportunity for those students who have leadership ability; give potential dropouts an incentive to remain in school; and provide a positive approach to making school more interesting to students.
4. Provide individualized instruction for laboratory school students.

Phases of the Program. The phases and other aspects of the PELT program are described in the resource manual. Also see Figure 8–5.

A variation of the student leadership program may be observed in the Wadesboro (North Carolina) Junior High School. Rather than teaching juniors and seniors the rudiments of leadership, 8th-grade students are trained to work with 6th-grade students. Each leader is provided with a fact sheet which explains the procedures for checking attendance, caring for equipment, and assisting with instruction.[20]

A cooperative student leadership program involving the staff at Burris Laboratory School at Ball State University, Muncie, Indiana, which involves 12th-grade girls enrolled at Delta High School and teachers of Royerton Elementary Schools, should be mentioned. The curriculum for elementary students, which is a joint effort of the three groups, states several goals, among them the development of perceptual-motor skills. Authorities feel that the program creates a favorable attitude towards physical education, a change in behavioral patterns of students, and improvement in skill performance of the students.[21]

Having devoted considerable time to the mechanics of organizing classes, preparing students for instruction, and laying the groundwork for the year's program, the teacher should now be ready to teach. The organizational procedures involved in teaching are just as important as preparing students for in-

Figure 8–5. *A*, Physical education leadership training. (Courtesy of Norfolk Public Schools, Norfolk, Virginia.)

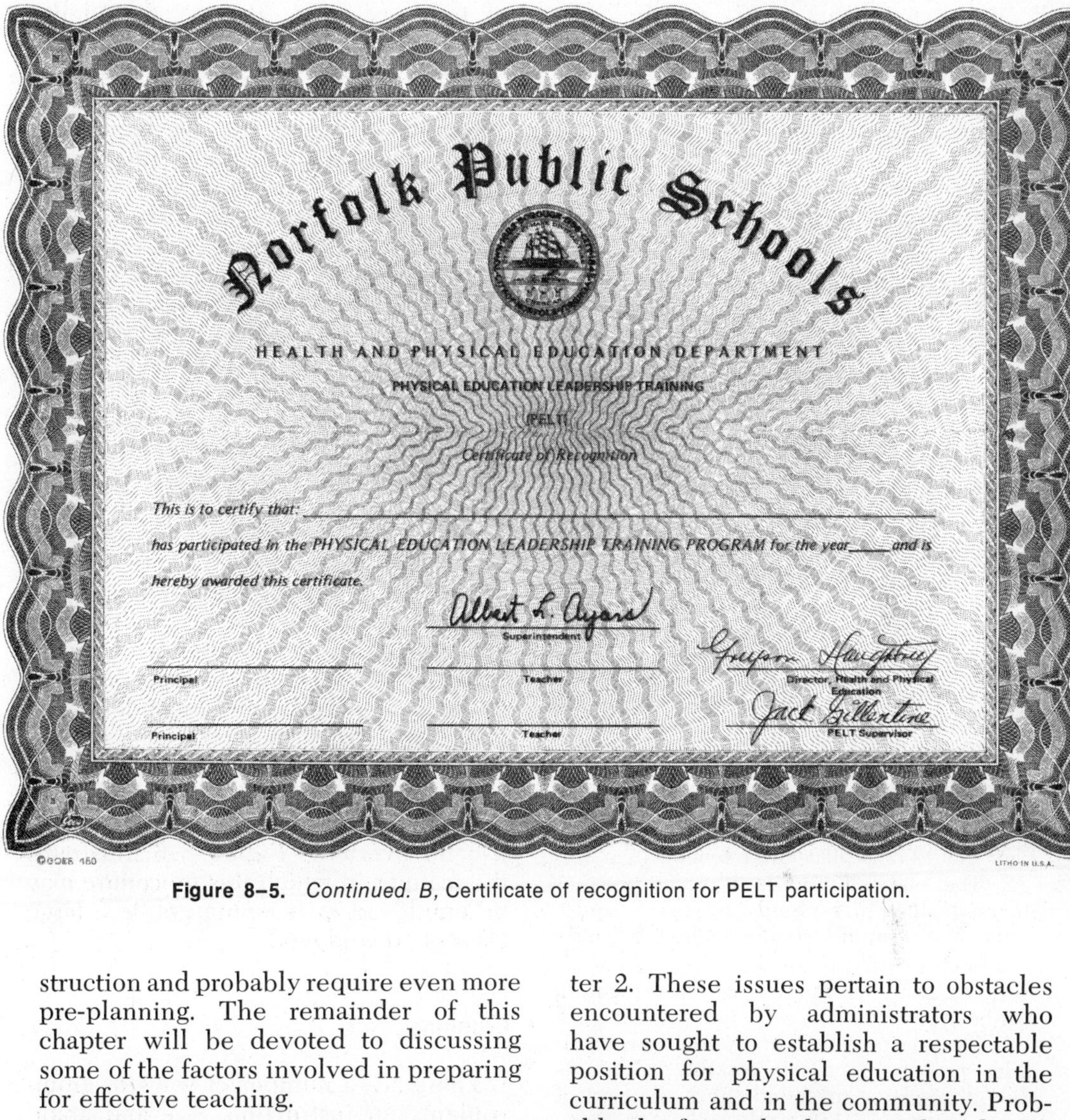

Figure 8–5. *Continued. B,* Certificate of recognition for PELT participation.

struction and probably require even more pre-planning. The remainder of this chapter will be devoted to discussing some of the factors involved in preparing for effective teaching.

ORGANIZATION FOR EFFECTIVE TEACHING

The more important guidelines for effective organization of class routine have been discussed. In addition to these guidelines and planning responsibilities, there are other basic factors to effective classroom management which are centered around the teaching process itself.

A Teaching Program

Some of the crucial issues in physical education have been discussed in Chap-

ter 2. These issues pertain to obstacles encountered by administrators who have sought to establish a respectable position for physical education in the curriculum and in the community. Probably the factor that has contributed most to the unfavorable position which the program occupies in many places is poor instruction. It is extremely difficult to sell a poor program to the board of education and to the community.

Administrators and teachers have a responsibility for evaluating the program and distinguishing between a supervised play program and a sound program of instruction based on acceptable objectives and goals. In places where physical education is planned and teaching is the rule, the program has progressed. However, there are many instances in which physical education has been either excluded from the curriculum or relegated to an obscure status. This situation exists when there is little organization and the play concept dominates the program. Authoritative opinion regarding the importance of instruction during the class periods is presented in Chapter 5. To achieve this goal, definite principles of organization must be established.

Principles of Organization

Planning for effective physical education instruction requires a tremendous background of knowledge in the psychology of learning, physiology, and teaching techniques. Moreover, the physical educator who aspires to excellence must have a high degree of organizational ability. The organizational principles presented here should be helpful for the teacher who desires to provide for individual needs and to assist students in acquiring competence in skill performance. These principles apply to all activities included in the physical education curriculum.

1. The program should be a teaching program based largely on instruction in skills. Play should take place after school.
2. The class should be divided into as many small ability groups as space, equipment, and supplies permit. When properly classified into ability groups, the needs of all students, from the handicapped to the gifted, can be met.
3. Use all equipment and other tools available; procure more if possible. Students should not have to spend the major part of the class period "waiting their turn" because of limited equipment.
4. Emphasize the need for and the value of each activity taught.
5. Discuss the importance of developing skills for better performance and carry-over.
6. Develop procedures for teaching large groups effectively through such techniques as the overflow principle. This will help to maintain a higher level of instruction. The overflow principle is described in the following paragraphs.

Teaching Large Classes

Unfortunately, most physical education teachers are faced with the problem of teaching large groups of students. Probably this is why teachers frequently resort to an informal, free-play program rather than attempt to teach skills. Developing techniques for teaching skills to large classes is a challenge that teachers must accept. Teaching the skills involved in individual sports such as bowling, tennis, and golf is extremely difficult because of the need for individualized instruction and the lack of space. While working with a few students, some teachers find it difficult to supervise and be responsible for the majority of the class, who are not involved. Thus the group that remains idle presents a disciplinary problem. One practical and effective organization procedure for teaching large groups is to provide an overflow to accommodate a large portion of the class while the teacher spends his time teaching the basic activity. The principle of this plan is to provide for instruction in the skills of a basic activity to one group while the remainder of the class participates in a team activity that accommodates large numbers safely and without the need for intensive supervision. Volleyball is the best activity to use for overflow. Figure 8–6 illustrates the manner in which this procedure may be employed in teaching golf to a large class of 40 students.

Grouping

There are a number of ways to group students for instruction. Age and grade are the most common, but are the least effective because of varying physiological, psychological, and anatomical growth and development factors. Height and weight are used frequently for activities such as basketball, in which height is important, and wrestling, in which weight is important. The grouping of students by ability, however, is the most effective method. (See resource manual for other methods of grouping.)

Ability Grouping. Irrespective of the way students are scheduled to the physical education class, they should be grouped by ability. Provision for individual differences and valid results can be

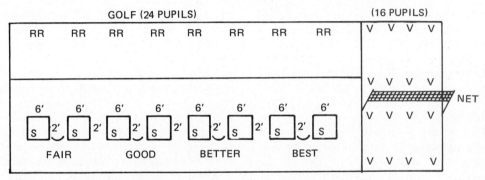

Figure 8–6. Teaching golf skills to 40 students, using the overflow plan.

attained only by devising some plan for placing students in instruction groups of similar performance levels. Physical education is a movement program, and it is not difficult to see the differences in performance within a class of students of the same age and grade. In addition to the instructional necessity of grouping by ability, the element of safety further substantiates the need for grouping. Moreover, ability grouping provides motivation for student effort. When students are grouped heterogeneously, the skilled students become bored and the unskilled develop a defeatist complex because of continual failure. Finally, grouping classes by ability enables handicapped students to find a place for satisfactory skill practice and purposeful social adjustments. Figure 8–7 shows a simple ability grouping procedure that may be applied in all programs of teaching skills.

Maximizing Benefits from Class Time Allotment

Ask any physical education teacher whether or not he has sufficient time to accomplish program objectives and his answer will most likely be that he does not. A realistic appraisal of the expanding curriculum shows, however, that there must be limitations on the amount of time allotted to any subject. Thus, the physical educator must organize the class time to derive the greatest benefit from every minute. There is an eco-

nomic principle which is quite applicable to this situation. The principle states that in order to maximize profits, the industry must use each of its scarce resources in the most effective manner; one of the scarce resources, of course, is the time available to produce the goods or services. In physical education, this means that the greatest benefits from the time allotted can be realized only if each minute is utilized to the greatest advantage.

The administrator should be familiar with effective procedures for organizing and utilizing class time. At the beginning of the semester, he should assist

Figure 8–7. Grouping students by ability for teaching the skills of hockey. The class has been divided into several ability groups. The teacher is seen just behind the center girl in the group located in the foreground. (Courtesy of Norfolk Public Schools, Norfolk, Virginia.)

the teachers in developing a standard time plan that can be followed in each daily period; for the inexperienced teacher especially, this cooperative planning is essential. Note that the emphasis here is not on how to teach but on how to best organize class time for effective teaching.

The authors feel that if one element of teaching could be singled out as contributing most significantly to the breakdown and disintegration of physical education, it would be the careless utilization of class time. When students become aware that there is either no planned activity or activity without meaning and continuity; when they are allowed to dress at leisure, linger in the shower, or dawdle at assembly or roll call; when they learn that half the class time is used in getting organized, they soon lose interest, and disciplinary problems arise.

Phases of Class Time. The allotment of time for physical education in the daily schedule usually does not exceed 30 minutes in the elementary and 60 minutes in the secondary school. The time element and the need for continuity of topics demand a careful utilization of each moment in the period if maximal benefits are to be achieved. This is particularly true in the secondary schools, where at least one-fifth of the period is devoted to dressing and showering.

A well-organized plan consists of several phases, each of which should be planned carefully. Each phase is given a time module, which remains constant, while activities within time modules may vary. The administrator must be aware of the fact that time modules are not simply assigned arbitrarily; rather, time is assigned on the basis of the intensity of activity during the class period.

EVALUATION OF STUDENTS

There should be a period evaluation of students to determine the progress they have made. Evaluation is a continuous process involving the entire spectrum of student growth and development, and is essential to guidance, motivation, group-ing, testing, and marking. Evaluation determines to what extent the student has benefited by participating in the program.

Many processes are involved in evaluation. Decisions on curriculum content may be made by individuals or groups evaluating areas of instruction empirically. Judgments may be made through the use of questionnaires for securing data. Students may evaluate a teacher according to their emotional reactions to him. Administrators may evaluate a school or several schools in light of their administrative goals. Teachers may evaluate students to determine progress and improvement. Finally, parents may evaluate the schools in terms of student accomplishment.

Several factors may be involved in the evaluation process, contributing to the confusion of its definition. Matthews states that "evaluation implies the judgment, appraisal, rating, and interpretation so fundamental to the total educational process."[22]

The words test and measurement are sometimes used synonymously with evaluation. Although the terms are related, there is an important difference. *Test* refers to an instrument which measures performance, and *measurement* is only a part of the total evaluative process. Measurement may include not only tests but also such tools as rating scales and checklists.

An example of the evaluative process would be the teacher who wishes to determine the progress his class makes toward a stated goal. He would use many tools, including performance tests, written tests, question and answer procedures, and observations. The evaluation procedures would involve stating the goal, determining the tests to be used and the tools necessary for measuring, and finally interpreting the results.

Evaluation in physical education is too broad a field to be completely covered in this text. Only the simple rudiments of evaluation will be discussed here, and the reader is urged to pursue this most important phase of physical education administration by studying the references listed at the end of the chapter.

Testing in Physical Education

There is a need for reformation of the traditional testing programs used in schools today. The pressure on students to make high grades on the various tests arbitrarily designed by teachers has developed an artificial learning situation that is primarily responsible for the problems of cheating, school dropouts, and, in some instances, poor teaching.

The dropout problem in our nation's schools is increased by unrealistic testing methods. The whole system of grading and testing must be changed. A report on the study of dropouts by the National Education Association showed that the school is usually geared to the average student. Those students who cannot meet the standards arbitrarily established by teachers are disheartened, finally lose interest, and usually drop out of school.[23]

Programs heavy in testing perpetuate the "assign, lecture, test" type of teaching that is regarded by many as the poorest procedure for helping students learn to think and reason. It is a paradox that at this time in the 20th century, with more teaching innovations made available than at any time in history, many teachers still use the threat of testing as the only motivating factor for learning.

It is not the intent of this discussion to recommend that testing be discontinued. Many leading educators believe in it, and many parents demand it. However, there is general concern about the overemphasis on the traditional programs in education that rely entirely on testing as the basis for teaching or measuring what a student has learned in a given area.

Before initiating testing programs in a school or system, administrators should review the purposes of testing. Unless there are definite reasons for developing a testing program, it would be better to abandon the idea.

Testing in physical education is an intricate and time-consuming procedure. Physical education classes are usually large, and unless the test is given for a purpose, the time involved is not justifiable. Too often tests are inefficiently administered to large groups and scored; the results are recorded, filed, and never seen again. This practice is educationally unsound, impractical, and deplorable.

There are several reasons for testing in physical education, the major ones being (1) to motivate students to continue exercise programs beyond the school day; (2) to serve as a basis for determining student progress, which may in turn be used to evaluate the level of teaching; (3) to assist the teacher in assigning marks; (4) to compare test scores with other students; (5) to provide teachers with information regarding the student, with a view toward improving instruction; (6) to assist teachers in placing students in similar ability groups; (7) to assist in determining the achievement level of students; (8) to diagnose the weaknesses and strengths of students, with emphasis on assessing future performance levels; and (9) to assist in interpreting the program to administrators and the community.

Test Evaluation. A good testing program is based on sound instruments of measurement. It is generally agreed among specialists in testing that all tests should be carefully evaluated before they are used. The teacher should have some guides to assist him in the selection of tests. A good test has certain qualities that distinguish it from a poor one, and there are several criteria for measuring these qualities. The criteria of primary importance are reliability, validity, objectivity, availability of norms, and simplicity. A *reliable* test is one that produces consistent results. For example, if a test is given to a group of students twice, the reliability of the test is determined by the degree to which the students hold the same relative positions in both tests. A test is *valid* when it measures what it is supposed to measure. A test for measuring basketball skills would not be valid for measuring the shot-put. An *objective* test is one that rules out the opinion, judgment, and influence of the scorer. Noll and Scannell list three ways of attaining objectivity: (1) questions should be stated specifically; (2) questions should require short, precise answers; (3) the test should be scored by using a previously determined scoring key.[24] *Norms* represent an accumulation of scores from large population samples and serve as standards for making comparisons. Good standardized tests usually provide norms. Although they are used as criteria for standardized tests, norms are not usually applicable to local teacher-constructed tests. Tests in physical education should be *simple*, since classes are large; unless they are simple, it is extremely difficult to administer an effective testing program. Other questions that should be asked when choosing a test are: Is it easily administered? Is it expensive? Is it easily scored? Are the results easily interpreted?

Types of Tests

There are several types of tests in physical education, the most important being knowledge tests, local achievement tests, behavioral tests, and standardized tests. A good testing program should include a variety of these tests.

Knowledge Tests. Written tests to determine the student's knowledge of an activity play an important role in all physical education programs. These tests should be given periodically to determine progress, to bring out topics that need clarification, and to provide the teacher with information that may be used for guidance, planning, and evaluation. Knowledge tests are classified into two groups:

1. *Subjective tests.* These require students to elaborate on a topic or problem; they may ask the students to discuss, compare, analyze, relate, or express opinions on topics studied in class. Subjective tests require considerable time to conduct and grade and are not practical for use in large classes. The major advantages of these tests are that they examine the depth of knowledge that the student has acquired about the topic and his ability to express himself in writing. Subjective instruments have an important place in a testing program.

2. *Objective tests.* Objective tests are written tests that call for specific answers. The four most popular types are true-false, completion, multiple-choice, and matching. These tests are practical, easily corrected, and may be satisfactorily used for large groups.

Local Achievement Tests. In addition to written tests designed to determine knowledge, tests for measuring achievement in sports skills, general motor ability, strength, and fitness are an integral part of physical education testing programs. Since activity is the predominant feature of physical education, a testing program would be incomplete unless it included a measurement of the students' progress in performing the activities. An example of a locally planned achievement test for motor fitness is shown in Figure 8–8. Another type is included in the resource manual.

Behavioral Tests. Programs designed to measure instructional results have been an integral part of education since teaching began. It is essential that the instructional process include adequate tools of measuring which will enable the teacher to determine student achievement and progress.

The major processes of developing programs include (1) establishing objectives, (2) selecting the content, (3) determining methods and procedures of instruction, (4) the actual instruction, and (5) devising ways of measuring the effectiveness of the instruction and the results.

There are a number of ways to develop instructional objectives. One plan that is gaining popularity is the behavioral approach, which was discussed in Chapter 5. If the instructional program is constructed around the development of behavioral objectives, then it has to be measured by them. The three domains—cognitive, affective, and psychomotor—have already been discussed. Although primarily concerned with the psychomotor domain, physical education also includes elements of the other two. Keeping this in mind, let us examine how the types of tests discussed earlier may be written in behavioral terms. For example, tests on a tennis skill would be:

Tennis
Skill—Forehand Return

Township of Ocean School District
Oakhurst, New Jersey

Department of Health, Safety, and Physical Education   June, 1969

BASIC MOTOR FITNESS TEST,* AGES 5-7

Name _____
          (Last)   (First)   (Age) (Grade) (School)   (Sex)

Parent's Name _____
                  (Last)   (First)   (Address)   (Phone No.)

			TEST PERIODS				
Date								
Weight								
Height								
TEST ITEM	ATTEMPTS	FACTOR MEASURED	RAW SCORE	STANDARD SCORE	RAW SCORE	STANDARD SCORE	RAW SCORE	STANDARD SCORE
1. Standing Broad Jump	2	Explosive Strength						
2. Medicine Ball Throw (5 lb)	2	Explosive Strength						
3. Tapered Balance Beam	2	Gross Body Balance						
4. Sit-Ups (Max 100)	1	Abdominal Strength						
5. Right Grip	2	Grip Strength						
6. Left Grip	2	Grip Strength						
7. Push (Manuometer)	2	Arm Strength						
8. Pull (Manuometer)	2	Arm Strength						
9. 35 Yard Dash	1	Speed						
10. 300 Yard Run	1	Endurance						
11. Endurance Index								
12. Total Standard Score								
13. Average Standard Score								

ANECDOTAL REMARKS (indicate student minimal effort by "-" and would not try by "--")

AREAS OF WEAKNESS   INDIVIDUALLY PRESCRIBED ACTIVITIES

      * Modified version of the Buttonwood Farms Motor Fitness Test: Level II, designed
by the Temple University HPER Department, Philadelphia, Pennsylvania.

Figure 8-8. Locally developed performance test. (Courtesy of Township of Ocean School District, Oakhurst, New Jersey.)

Written test
    Cognitive. The student will describe the footwork in the forehand return in one paragraph on a written test.

Performance tests
    Affective. The student displays patience and understanding while learning the forehand return.
    Psychomotor. The student will demonstrate the correct position of the feet and arms in executing the forehand return, three out of five times.

The basic difference between behavioral testing and the achievement types of tests discussed earlier is preplanning. In the behavioral approach teachers must plan and determine goals that students should attain in a given period of time. A behavioral testing program is a highly structured innovation in education.

Before embarking on a program of writing behavioral objectives, the writer must be able to define and identify the three domains. Determine to which domain each of the following activities belongs by marking *P* for psychomotor, *C* for cognitive, and *A* for affective.

The student:

1. Jumps the rope _____
2. Uses the text _____
3. Throws the ball _____
4. Concentrates on rules _____
5. Praises the official _____
6. Resists foul play _____
7. Runs a dash _____
8. Refuses a bribe _____
9. Evaluates the teacher _____
10. Dresses for physical education _____
11. Defends the coach _____
12. Serves the ball _____
13. Plans strategy _____

Although there are many critics of behavioral objectives, the fact remains that the entire process of writing and interpreting them brings about a reexamination of the instructional procedures. This, in itself, may improve instruction and assist teachers in determining the purposes of physical education.

Standardized Tests. Standardized tests may be used to compare local performances with scientifically devised norms. However, there are so many variables in physical education activities that the effectiveness of standardized tests is questionable. Because these tests are given by different people in different sections of the country under varying conditions, it is extremely difficult to provide the control necessary to achieve validity and reliability. Standardized tests may be valuable for motivating students, but it is undesirable to use them for grading or classifying students into categories of "fit" and "unfit." Rather, it is recommended that standardized tests be used for motivation in conjunction with locally prepared tests. Administrators and teachers who wish to use standardized tests may refer to those devised by the American Alliance for Health, Physical Education and Recreation.

Administrating a testing program involves considerable study and preparation. Because of the many factors that must be considered, a discussion of some of the procedures in testing is important.

Administrative Procedures in Testing

Confronted with the many facets of a testing program and the intricacies involved in administering the tests, the teacher may become discouraged and may be tempted to abandon testing altogether. The simple answer to teachers who feel that testing is important, yet are uncertain about how to proceed, is *planning.* A few hours devoted studying the situation and outlining the steps involved would shed new light on the value of testing. The following guidelines should assist the teacher in organizing plans for conducting a testing program.

Pre-Planning. Before the day arrives for giving the test, a careful survey should be made of the details involved and an orderly arrangement of them should be made. The following items should be taken care of well in advance:

1. Selection of the test or tests should be made early.
2. Announcements should be made that (a) explain the nature and purpose of the test, (b)

state what is to be tested, and (c) give a description of the test.

3. A survey of availiable equipment and supplies should be made. The equipment should be placed at the site of the test before the testing begins.

4. Test areas and sites should be selected and marked. Safety factors, identification of areas, and traffic flow should be considered.

5. Instructions should be provided to assist students in approaching each testing station in a uniform manner.

6. Student leaders should be assigned to assist with such details as recording scores, arranging students at the stations, and collecting score sheets. The leaders should be provided with written instructions well in advance. Provision should be made for essential items such as score cards, marking pencils, and score scales.

Class Organization. After the type of test and the details involved in pre-planning have been determined, the next step is the organization of the class for conducting the test. There are several possible arrangements. In giving certain tests, such as the sit-up, the teacher may have an entire class take the test at the same time. For the sit-up test, the class may be divided into two groups, with students in each group paired; on a signal from the teacher, one group takes the test while the second group counts. At the conclusion of this cycle, the two groups reverse and the test is given again. An alternative is to have each student keep his own score and report it at the end of the test (see Figure 8–9). Some teachers prefer to give tests by squad formation, recording the results on a squad card. Stations

for the various test items are arranged, and students rotate by squads from one station to another. A floor plan that may be used for testing the skills of basketball is shown in the resource manual. Sometimes teachers prefer that the student rotate from one teaching station to another, using an individual card for recording test results. Score cards are filed in a central file. Figure 8–10 illustrates the type of card that many be used for recording test results. After having taken their tests, students are permitted to go to a nontest area and participate in an overflow activity, as described on page 202. This procedure allows the teacher to concentrate on the testing program and reduces disciplinary problems that may develop if students are left without planned activity.

Giving the Test. Since students should be encouraged to perform their best, various motivational procedures are suggested. One that may be helpful is posting norms of the test items near the testing station. This allows the student to see the level he should attain or excel. Other factors that should be considered during the test period are discussion of the test, a demonstration of the test for proper form, a survey of equipment and areas to determine hazards that may present safety problems, and a brief overview of the importance of the test.

Follow-Up. After tests have been given, the teacher should collect the cards from the students or stations and file them for study. Shortly after testing, the material and scores should be an-

Figure 8–9. Testing an entire class simultaneously. (Courtesy of Norfolk Public Schools, Norfolk, Virginia.)

NEW RIVER JUNIOR HIGH SCHOOL
Physical Education Dept.
Individual Accomplishments

Student's Name_____

	Date	Age	Ht.	Wt.		Date	Age	Ht.	Wt.		Date	Age	Ht.	Wt.
1._____					4._____					7._____				
2._____					5._____					8._____				
3._____					6._____					9._____				

	Amt.	Pct.	Amt.	Pct.	Amt.	Pct.	Amt.	Pct.	Amt.	Pct.	Amt.	Pct.	Amt.	Pct.	Amt.	Pct.	Amt.	Pct.
Pull-Ups																		
Sit-Ups																		
Shuttle Run																		
Std. Brd. Jmp.																		
50 Yd. Dash																		
Softball Throw																		
600 Yd. Run-Walk																		
Dips																		
Push-Ups																		
100 Yd. Dash																		
220																		
440																		
880																		
Mile																		
High Jump																		
Pole Vault																		
Brd. Jump																		
120 L.H.																		
Shot Put																		
Discus																		

Figure 8–10. Individual card for recording test results. (From Klappholtz, Lowell: "Cumulative Physical Education Record Cards Help Chart Students Fitness Progress." In *Successful Practices in Teaching Physical Fitness.* New London, Conn.: Croft Educational Services, 1968, p. 20.)

alyzed and statistical procedures initiated. It is extremely important to interpret the results in light of the purposes developed during the pre-planning stage. Unless tests are used to improve student performance or to assist in analyzing curriculum content, they are of little value. Teachers and administrators should initiate curriculum revision and development programs based on the statistical findings of the test results.

MARKING

There is considerable controversy among educators over the value of marking or grading. Such variables as the student's attitudes, his physical, emotional, and mental health, his behavior in class, the effort he puts out, and his attendance can all affect his final grade. Because of the difficulty in determining an accurate mark for the student, multiple marking plans have been developed.

Terwilliger[25] reviewed the marking programs of 129 secondary schools. From his study, several startling conditions were revealed. It was found that 22 per cent of the schools had no standard policy for determining the basis for marks. The remaining respondents stated that absolute standard achievement (27 per cent), ability (29 per cent), and achievement matched with class notes (16 per cent) were used as a basis for assigning marks.

In addition to this lack of a firm policy, there was a wide variance in whether such factors as behavior, absence, tardiness, and effort were used in grading. Forty per cent of the administrators lowered grades for disciplinary or other reasons. Fifty per cent gave either major or minor consideration to student effort.

The results of the study revealed not only this wide variance in the policy for assigning marks but also such a lack of fairness in grading that grave doubts arise as to the justification of assigning marks unless the entire system of marking is revolutionized.

Some current trends in marking which may serve as guidelines for administrators or teachers who wish to upgrade their marking plans are:

1. Increasing recognition that marking and grading practices ought to reflect educational objectives.
2. Increase in the use of grading systems that attempt to recognize a broader range of student performance.
3. Increasing recognition that a single "mark" cannot accurately express the desired information.
4. Attempts to get away from the use of percentage points as the basis for grades, and to use instead the five-point grading system.
5. Attempts to involve parents as well as teachers in the development of new marking and grading systems.
6. Increasing recognition that the major unresolved issue is the determination of the basis of marking and grading.[26]

Marking in Physical Education

There is a lack of agreement concerning marking in physical education activities. Many teachers feel that physical education should be marked as other subjects are. They believe that student progress should be determined on the basis of tests on the material outlined for the various grades—the students either pass or fail, and individual differences, such as anatomical variations over which the student has no control, are not taken into account. Other teachers disagree; they feel that the individual differences *are* important and that effort and performance should count as well.

Several marking plans are discussed in the following paragraphs.

Marking on Improvement. There are many people who feel that marking a student on improvement is the only fair and valid way of evaluating his progress in physical education. Since the advent of behavioral objectives, entire programs in all areas of instruction have been developed around pre-test—teach—post-test procedures. One of the main objectives of education is to improve and expand learning potential. The only way to determine the degree to which a student is achieving this objective is to measure his improvement in various skills. When students are marked on improvement, individual differences are taken into consideration.

Some teachers rely entirely on improvement as a basis for testing and marking. They believe that students should be tested, taught for an interval of time, and tested again. The grade is determined by the progress made between the initial and final tests. Those who disagree with this procedure feel that it is time-consuming, and that students have a different performance level when tests are given, with improvement varying accordingly. They also feel that students may deliberately score low on the initial test in order to score high on the terminal test.

This last objection may be overcome by having the teacher tell students who deliberately score low on the initial test in order to get a higher grade that the tests are only part of the total testing program and that they should always do their best.

Finally, critics of the improvement marking plan point out that because of natural ability, some students may show a lower improvement rate on the terminal test than others; that is, the more skillful a student is, the more difficult it will be for him to show a large degree of improvement. This problem may be eliminated by grouping students on the basis of ability before the initial test.

During the summer of 1959, the Department of Physical Education at the University of Michigan, in cooperation with the University Summer School, developed a scientific marking plan that has vast implications for improving marking programs throughout the country.

Students in the Michigan plan are classified into three groups (A, B, and C) and are given initial tests and terminal tests. Improvement is noted, and a report of the student's standing is sent home to the parents (see Figure 8–11). The report card is explained as follows: Assume that the student performs four pull-ups on his initial test and that this is an average performance. The report card shows a red dot in the pull-up "0-0" cell, which is the initial test position. If he does six pull-ups in the terminal test, his per cent change would equal

$$\frac{6-4}{4} \times 100 \text{ or } 50\% \text{ change}$$

He would thus fall into the above-average group, with a blue dot placed on the 50 mark, provided the improvement is sufficient. The weekly program operates on a schedule that is planned for the three groups.

The Michigan program was acceptable to parents largely because of the meaningful factors involved in the report, an excellent teacher, good planning and use of student time, wise use of facilities, ample equipment, and the pre-planning that provided a program that was challenging for each student.[27]

Marking on Effort. There is divided

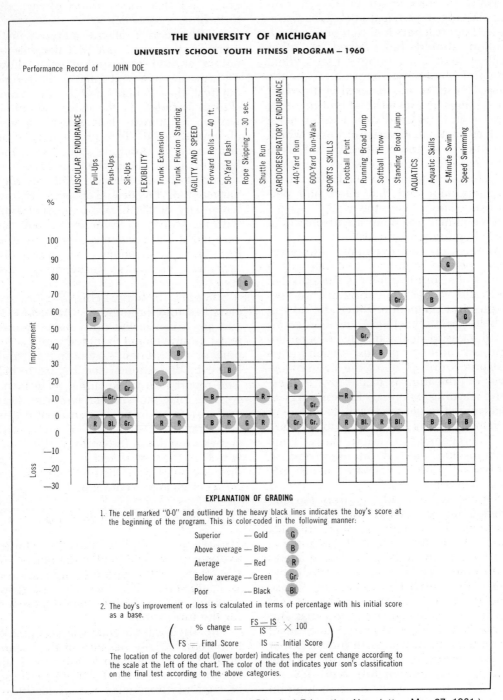

Figure 8–11. A scientific marking plan. (From *Physical Education Newsletter,* May 27, 1961.)

opinion about taking effort into account as part of the final mark. Some teachers feel that, since many students are handicapped because of body type and are unable to score well on certain tests, effort should be considered. They argue that merely because a student with a certain body type cannot attain a predetermined standard in the kip-up or the mile run does not mean that he is physiologically unfit and should fail. Those opposed to including effort as part of the final grade feel that marking in physical education should assume the same characteristics as marking in academic subjects, with achievement as the major factor involved. They argue that it is difficult to measure effort and that it penalizes those students who attain high levels of performance without exhibiting any degree of effort.

Related Factors. There is no general agreement as to what factors should be involved in the marking systems in the nation's schools. The literature reveals that such items as attendance, showering, dress, effort, skill, posture, fitness, teamwork, sportsmanship, fair play, responsibility, initiative, emotional stability, body mechanics, attitude, progress, ability, and motor performance are all widely used. There is considerable opinion that items such as attendance, showering, and dress should *not* be used in determining marks in physical education, yet the results of a study conducted among 50 practice teachers revealed that in 80 per cent of the schools they visited, the child's mark was based solely on his being present and in uniform.[28]

Marks based on these items are meaningless as measurements and have nothing to do with the learning process, performance, or achievement. Attendance, dress, and the like involve administrative policy and should be handled as such. Marking should be based on how well the student attains the objectives of the program, which concern the mental, physical, social, and emotional development of the students enrolled in the class.

The Probability Curve. This plan is often called "relative marking," because the student's progress is compared with the performances of the other class members. In some educational circles, the term norm-referenced is used. The letter system is usually used, and the final mark is determined by the relationship of the student's performance to that of the average student. This method of marking students is acceptable to many teachers because it is highly objective and reliable.

Although marking on the probability curve has its advantages, it is criticized by some because a student's mark is determined by the performance of the other students in his class rather than by his mastery of instructional skill or content.

The Absolute Method. In the absolute method, the assignment of marks is made from a predetermined level of achievement. If the level of achievement for the letter grade A is 90 per cent, then 90–100 would be the A interval.

Teachers favor this plan for marking because (1) they are familiar with it, (2) it is relatively easy to compute, and (3) it provides a definite standard for measuring achievement. The fundamental disadvantages of this method are (1) the levels of achievement lack consistency, since they are established by teachers and each teacher has his individual standards; and (2) the difficulty in recognizing the measurement errors involved in each score is formidable.

Pass-Fail Theory of Marking. The pass-fail option has become popular in some sections of the country. This plan allows students to choose the pass or fail designation rather than the traditional letter grade for the final mark. Opponents of traditional methods of marking feel that the pass-fail plan would liberalize the marking system and eliminate the pressure for marks that has become such an acute problem in education. Those favoring the pass-fail plan feel that if the pressure for marks is reduced, students will be encouraged to enroll in more elective courses.

However, experience shows that the pass-fail plan has not proved as successful as the proponents of it had predicted.

Students seem to become less motivated and lose interest when competition is decreased. The better students do not perform their best and the poorer students are not challenged to improve.

Test Factors. Obviously some test factors are more important than others. There is no absolute agreement on ranking these factors, but there can be no question about the importance of skill in the program. Physical fitness factors (including skill, strength, speed, and endurance) knowledge, emotional-social factors, and effort or attitude might be weighted as follows: physical fitness, 40 per cent; knowledge, 20 per cent; emotional-social factors, 20 per cent; and attitude-effort factors, 20 per cent. In this arrangement, physical fitness carries twice as much weight as the other factors and should be scored twice.

Unfortunately, there is no one marking system that can be used in all situations. However, there are certain criteria that may assist administrators and teachers in developing a marking program. These are discussed in the following paragraphs.

Criteria for Marking

Many leaders in education are opposed to the systems of testing and marking that exist in our schools at present. The pressure created by placing an emphasis on testing has been discussed earlier in this chapter. However, marking seems to be a part of the educational system and there are no indications that it will be discontinued. Parents and students have become accustomed to marks and expect them; teachers need them to determine progress and achievement; and school authorities demand them because of tradition.

With the varying current opinions on marking, the distance between theory and practice, and the many problems teachers face, such as large classes, it is easy to see why marking is one of the poorest procedures in physical education today. However, many educators feel that with proper planning, the establishment of definite criteria for marking, and the formulation of plans based on these criteria, sound marking programs are possible. Neilson and Jensen offer several criteria that may serve as guidelines in developing such programs:

1. *Marks should be valid.* They must truly represent the quality and quantity of student achievement for which they purportedly stand.
2. *Marks should be reliable.* They must accurately and consistently represent the same results for each student.
3. *Marks should be highly objective.* Different teachers, given the same data on a student, should arrive at the same mark. This quality is dependent upon a clearly defined marking system.
4. *Marks should be assigned on the basis of definite standards.* The standards should not differ for each student nor should they fluctuate widely from one year to the next.
5. *Marks should be capable of clear interpretation with regard to what they signify.* If the significance of an A is not evident in terms of quality and quantity of achievement, then the grade lacks meaning.
6. *Marks should be based on a system that allows for the most economical use of the teacher's time and effort.* Since marking is only one of the teacher's many tasks, only a reasonable amount of time can be justified for it.
7. *Marks should be timely.* Final marks are recorded only at the end of semesters, but for purposes of incentive, students should frequently be informed of their progress and present standing.[29]

Although no particular plan is best for all schools, the final decision should be based on weighted factors, criteria, and other information discussed earlier. The following plan may be helpful to teachers who are marking on the absolute standard.

When this plan is used, letter marks must be converted to numbers for computing the final marks.

MARKS	% SCORE	NUMBERS
A	90–100	5
B	80–89	4
C	70–79	3
D	60–69	2
E	Below 60	1

After converting marks into numbers, the following steps must be carried out: (1) determine the factors or items to be tested; (2) give each item a weight; (3) list score the student made on the item; (4) multiply the weight's number by the score; (5) divide the total points by the total weight factors; and (6) assign the mark. The following figure illustrates this procedure.

Factor	Weight	Score	Points
Physical Fitness	2	4 (B)	8
Skills	6	3 (C)	18
Knowledge	2	5 (A)	10

36/10 = 3.6 or a B

The size of classes in physical education too often precludes any sound method of marking. Planning and conducting a testing program for 200 to 300 students is a difficult task. It is essential that simple tests be devised, encompassing a few items that can be measured adequately rather than attempting to measure large numbers on a superficial basis. Administrators and others concerned with marking students must be realistic; as they plan, they must consider the number of students involved, the time consumed in testing each individual and in converting scores to marks, the difficulties encountered in scoring some events, and, finally, the hazards always present in physical education activities.

Importance of Testing and Marking

Despite all of the criticisms of testing and marking and the difficulties involved in implementing these programs, they *are* necessary. A survey submitted to 48 state superintendents revealed that the greatest weakness to be found in physical education was in the area of marking. The study also showed that the vast majority of marks are determined subjectively, without definite standards. The superintendents concluded that physical education marks were not acceptable as presently arrived at and that administrators had a right to be suspi-cious of a discipline in which teachers cannot explain how they arrived at each student's mark.[30]

COMMUNICATION WITH PARENTS

One of the purposes of marking is to apprise parents of the standing of their children in the school. The letter mark is used extensively throughout the country. Other methods of reporting to parents are the pass-fail method and the descriptive method. Some schools send parents a more comprehensive appraisal of the child's accomplishment than the mark alone.

A report to parents that illustrates good teacher-parent communication was designed by Highland Indiana School District. The Kirchner physical fitness test is administered to all boys and girls in grades 4 to 6. Teachers and administrators maintain that the test is effective, since it is short, simple, and easily administered. Figure 8–12 shows the test items, results, and the performance chart.

Sometimes it becomes necessary to apprise parents of unsatisfactory student performance in such areas as attendance, attitude, cooperation, tardiness, and personality difficulties. Poor behavior patterns in these areas, if left unresolved, may develop into adverse student-teacher relationships that may eventually affect the student's marks and even his promotion or graduation. Usually, if these problems are challenged early, they become relatively unimportant. An effective approach to alleviating most of these situations is through parental communication. A telephone call or a letter (Figure 8–13) usually suffices.

ASSIGNMENT OF HOMEWORK

Homework in physical education can be important not only for interpreting the program but also for improving skill performance. As early as 1964, homework was shown to be a useful tool in

Text continued on page 219

Highland's Physical Fitness Report Card

Student

Dear Parents:

Twice a year your child will participate in the Kirchner Physical Fitness Testing Program of the School Town of Highland. The test is given in regular physical education classes by physical education specialists to fourth, fifth, and sixth grade students. The test is given once in the fall and once again in the spring. After the spring test, you can easily compare your child's performance in each event. A circled event highlights your child's weakest test event, and practice might be in order. Please *return this form* to school after the fall test.

TEST PERFORMANCE

FALL TEST	SPRING TEST	EVENT	DESCRIPTION
		30	30 yd. dash measures leg speed
		BPU	bench push-ups measure strength & endurance
		CU	curl-ups measure strength & endurance
		SJ	squat jumps measure strength & endurance
		SBJ	standing broad jump measures power
		TOTAL	total of all points earned in all events
		AVERAGE	average score of students in your child's class
		RATING	your child's rating on national standards of age and sex (S=superior, G=good, A=average, BA= below average, P=poor)

PHYSICAL

	FALL TEST	SPRING TEST
HEIGHT		
WEIGHT		

AVERAGE PERFORMANCE CHART

		8 yrs		9 yrs		10 yrs		11 yrs		12 yrs	
		B	G	B	G	B	G	B	G	B	G
1.	30	5.8	5.9	5.4	5.5	5.4	5.5	5.0	5.2	4.9	5.3
2.	BPU	17	13	17	11	18	11	19	10	18	9
3.	CU	16	15	19	17	22	20	26	22	27	20
4.	SJ	22	22	24	24	29	25	31	28	28	23
5.	SBJ	47	44	50	47	54	50	57	53	59	53

Sex and Age

Figure 8–12. Report card for parents. (From *Physical Education Newsletter*, April 15, 1970.)

```
┌─────────────────────────────────────────────────────────────────┐
│                     JOHN DEWEY HIGH SCHOOL                        │
│                   BROOKLYN, NEW YORK 11223                        │
│                                                                   │
│  Department of Health and Physical Education                      │
│                                         Date _____      │
│                                                                   │
│  Dear _____                             │
│                                                                   │
│        As an interested parent of a student of John Dewey High    │
│  School, I know you are concerned with his or her program.        │
│  Please note the comments which have been checked. With your      │
│  help and concern, Dewey can help each student in overcoming      │
│  his or her obstacles.                                            │
│                                                                   │
│        Missing homework _____                  │
│        Inattention in class _____                  │
│        Excessive absence/lateness _____                  │
│        Lack of preparedness _____                  │
│            (books, pen, etc.)                                      │
│        Attitude in class _____                  │
│        Other _____                  │
│              _____                  │
│              _____                  │
│                                                                   │
│        I would appreciate a response to this letter in the        │
│  space below and a prompt return to my attention. Working         │
│  together we can help your son or daughter overcome obstacles     │
│  to success.                                                      │
│                                                                   │
│                             Sincerely,                            │
│                                                                   │
│                                                                   │
│                             _____         │
│                             Teacher's Name                        │
│                                                                   │
│                                                                   │
│                             _____         │
│                             Assistant Principal                   │
│                             Health and Physical Education Dept.   │
│  - - - - - - - - - - - - - - - - - - - - - - - - - - - - - - - -  │
│                         Parent's Reply                            │
│                                                                   │
│  _____        _____      │
│  Name of Student               Teacher                            │
│                                                                   │
│  _____                                           │
│  Official Class                                                   │
│                                                                   │
│  _____        │
│  _____        │
│                             _____         │
│                             Signature of Parent                   │
└─────────────────────────────────────────────────────────────────┘
```

Figure 8–13. Communication with parents. (Courtesy of John Dewey High School, Brooklyn, New York.)

ELEMENTARY HEALTH AND PHYSICAL EDUCATION CONSULTANT PROGRAM

HOME PHYSICAL FITNESS AND SKILL ABILITIES ACHIEVEMENT FORM
(Primary Grades)

ACTIVITY	PHYSICAL FITNESS	Sept.	Oct.	Nov.	Dec.	Jan.	Feb.	Mar.	Apr.
Muscular Endurance	1. Sit-ups (arms extended)								
	2. Push-ups								
	3. Step-ups (about 14")								
	4. Running in place								
Flexibility	1. Trunk flexion standing								
	2. Right leg kick								
	3. Left leg kick								
	4. Forward roll								
	5. Trunk extension standing								
Agility and Speed	1. Jump rope								
	2. Standing broad jump								
	3. Vertical jump								
	4. Run 25 yds.								
Cardio-respiratory Endurance	1. Run-walk around block								
	2. 25 yd. dash								
Balance and Coordination	1. Astride jump								
	2. Jumping jack								
	3. Jumping jack in motion								
	4. Skip								
	5. Head stand								
	6. Heel-toe walk								
ACTIVITY	SKILL ABILITY								
1. Throw a ball (accuracy 10-20 ft.)									
2. Catch a ball (No. times without missing)									
3. Bounce a ball (No. times without missing)									
4. Bounce a ball off wall (catch on 1st bounce)									
5. Catch a beanbag (No. times without missing)									
6. Bat a ball (No. times without missing)									
7. Kick a ball (accuracy and distance)									
8. Running broad jump									

We are all aware of the rapid rate of growth of first grade boys and girls. Patience and encouragement must be ever present when they are trying to do their very best. The rate of progression differs with all children; therefore, we must be extremely considerate and helpful in whatever and whenever they undertake to do any of the activities.

The activities briefly outlined above should be practiced whenever possible by the children. This will then serve as a general conditioning program whereby they will have the opportunity to be tested by their parents when the opportunity arises.

Parents should place their initials in the proper rectangle each time after observing the child perform the activities. Attempt to check the child's progress approximately the last few days in each month. Be fair with the child by giving him or her credit for only what he has done correctly. Indicate the number accomplished, etc., along with your initials.

Student's Name _____ Grade _____ Teacher's Name _____

Parent's Signature _____

Figure 8–14. Homework in physical education may be indicated for many students. (Courtesy of Livonia Public Schools, Livonia, Michigan.)

physical education, particularly for handicapped children.[31] Students should be screened in the physical education class, and those who do not achieve suggested levels of perfomrance should be encouraged to practice the activities at home.

A practical plan for assigning home-work in physical education is used by the Livonia public schools. Figure 8–14 illustrates how results of physical fitness and skill tests are recorded monthly for the period from September through April. The results are sent to the parents, who are requested to cooperate with the teacher by watching the child's progress each month.

IMPROVING INSTRUCTION THROUGH SUPERVISION

Improving instruction is one of the most difficult phases of administration. Teachers frequently do not have guide-lines to assist them in distinguishing between a good and a bad program. Since organizational procedures, methods of teaching, and curriculum content in physical education are so different from those of other subjects, administrators are sometimes uncertain about the char-acteristics of good instruction in physical education.

In order to improve instruction and provide for a more desirable climate of communication between the teacher and the administrator, a self-evaluation or self-rating plan may prove helpful. The plan should include the factors that make up good teaching. The teacher is given guidelines that indicate what is expected of him. After studying the plan, administrators would know the compo-nents of a good program and would feel more confident in discussing them with the teacher. The self-appraisal charts discussed in the next section incorporate the factors involved in effective instruc-tion for the secondary school physical education teacher, the elementary class-room teacher, and the elementary spe-cialist in physical education who visits the schools on a part-time basis. Full-time physical education teachers in the elementary school may use the chart shown for the secondary school.

Self-Appraisal Charts

Self-Appraisal Chart for the Secondary School Teacher. The purpose of the self-appraisal chart for secondary school teachers is (1) to serve as an aid in teacher self-evaluation; (2) to provide a compilation of the factors involved in ef-fective teaching that will assist teachers and administrators in a joint effort to improve instruction; and (3) to serve as an administrative tool for determining the progress made toward established objectives. (See Figure 8–15.)

Self-Appraisal Chart for the Elemen-tary Classroom Teacher. A self-appraisal chart for the elementary classroom teacher is necessary because in the ma-jority of elementary schools the class-room teacher is usually responsible for instruction in physical education. The organization as well as the administration of physical education in the elementary schools is different in many respects from that in the secondary schools. Classroom teachers are usually not qualified to teach physical education; thus, a self-appraisal chart incorporating the factors necessary for effective instruction may be of tremendous assistance to them (see Figure 8–16).

Classroom teachers should score be-tween 75 and 90 per cent on the items listed in the "yes" column. This score is based on the assumption that the teacher will receive some help from a specialist.

A self-appraisal chart for the part-time physical education specialist is a valu-able tool for improving communication between the specialist and the classroom teacher. Figure 8–17 shows the factors involved in the specialist's teaching as-signment and should serve as a guide in improving the organization and adminis-tration of the program, both prerequi-sites to quality instruction.

The specialist should score between 95 to 100 per cent on all items listed in the "yes" column. The items shown comprise his responsibilities; he should be evaluated on his performance in these categories.

	Check Yes No

I. *Class Organization*
    A. Do my pupils assemble quickly rather than waste valuable time in the locker room or loitering on the way to class? ___ ___
    B. Are my pupils dressed properly and neatly? ___ ___
    C. Are all of my pupils participating? ___ ___
    D. Do I have a sound program for pupil excuses? ___ ___
    E. Are student leaders a part of my program? ___ ___
    F. Do I always organize my class into small groups for instruction? ___ ___
    G. Do I provide enough equipment so that each pupil may perform the instructional skill many times each period? ___ ___
    H. Do I use an effective plan for checking attendance that is not unduly time consuming? ___ ___

II. *Teaching Techniques*
    A. Do I know my subject well enough to teach rather than allowing pupils to play? ___ ___
    B. Do I demonstrate skills instead of using pupils? ___ ___
    C. Do I teach developmental exercises rather than allowing pupils to lead them? ___ ___
    D. Do I use recognized teaching procedures in my skill instruction? ___ ___
    E. Do I teach skills rather than just "throwing out the ball?" ___ ___

III. *Empathy*
    A. Empathy between pupil and teacher
        1. Are my pupils inspired rather than bored? ___ ___
        2. Is morale high in my class? ___ ___
        3. Do my pupils like and respect me? ___ ___
        4. Do I enjoy teaching and working with pupils? ___ ___
        5. Are my pupils cooperative? ___ ___
        6. Do I provide guidance and assist pupils with their problems? ___ ___
    B. Empathy between the teacher and the pupil
        1. Do I attempt to interpret the program to the public through talks, television programs, or demonstrations? ___ ___
        2. Does the public appreciate what I am trying to accomplish? ___ ___
        3. Is there approval of my program from the public? ___ ___
        4. Do parents show interest in my program? ___ ___
    C. Empathy between the teacher and other school personnel
        1. Do I interpret the program to teachers and administrators? ___ ___
        2. Is there cooperation between the faculty and my department? ___ ___
        3. Do I cooperate with other teachers in the department and the faculty? ___ ___
        4. Do teachers and administrators seem to appreciate what I am trying to do in the program? ___ ___

IV. *Curriculum Content*
    A. Are the activities based on the needs of pupils? ___ ___
    B. Do I plan for individual differences by ability grouping? ___ ___
    C. Is the program planned daily? ___ ___
    D. Does the program have direction? ___ ___
    E. Is the instruction of high quality? ___ ___
    F. Are the activities in the program selected scientifically? ___ ___
    G. Do I emphasize the teaching of skills? ___ ___

Figure 8–15. A self-appraisal chart is an effective instrument for improving instruction and also for assisting administrators in evaluating teachers.

	Yes	No
H. Is the program planned to motivate pupils to further their participation?	___	___
I. Are carry-over activities taught?	___	___
J. Is each pupil involved in the instruction?	___	___
K. Does the program meet desirable objectives?	___	___
L. Are pupils allowed a choice of activities in the senior high school?	___	___
M. Are pupils allowed to master the activity of their choice?	___	___
N. Are pupil's sufficiently oriented in the junior high school to make a wise choice in the senior high school?	___	___

V. *Safety of pupils*
A. Do I always provide a safe environment for my pupils? ___ ___
B. Do I teach and discuss safety factors with my pupils? ___ ___
C. Do I know the legal aspects of teacher negligence? ___ ___
D. Do I have pupil assistance in "spotting" in activities where there is the element of danger? ___ ___

VI. *Supervision*
A. Do I always stay with my pupils in the dressing room, in the gymnasium, and on the play field? ___ ___
B. Do I spend a minimum of time in the physical education office? ___ ___
C. If I must leave my class, do I have someone replace me? ___ ___

VII. *Care of Equipment*
A. Am I careful with the use and storage of equipment? ___ ___
B. Do I teach my pupils the importance of the proper care of equipment? ___ ___
C. Do I keep an inventory of equipment and supplies? ___ ___

VIII. *Discipline*
A. Do I handle my own discipline problems? ___ ___
B. Is there a minimum of discipline problems in my class? ___ ___
C. Do I maintain reasonable decorum in my classes? ___ ___
D. Do I maintain a calm appearance in dealing with problems rather than losing control? ___ ___
E. Do I have a normal approach in working with pupils instead of a sadistic manner? ___ ___

IX. *Professional Attitude*
A. Do I hold membership in a professional organization? ___ ___
B. Do I seek self-improvement in my field through workshops, summer school, extension courses, committee work, or reading? ___ ___
C. Do I conduct myself in a manner that demands respect of pupils and teachers? ___ ___
D. Do I dress properly in class and away from class? ___ ___
E. Do I participate in efforts to identify and solve over-all school problems as a member of the faculty? ___ ___

TOTAL ___ ___

Superior teachers would score 75 per cent or more on items in the "yes" column.

Figure 8–15. *continued*

	Yes	No
Do I make preparations for my classes in physical education by studying and familiarizing myself with the objectives?	____	____
Am I familiar with the needs and necessary content of each grade level?	____	____
Do I use and can I locate reference material in physical education?	____	____
Is my program a teaching one rather than a "throwing-out-the-ball" type?	____	____
Do I provide for physical education each day rather than using the period for free time or a "coffee break?"		
Do I feel that physical education is an important phase of the total curriculum?	____	____
Do I provide for individual differences?	____	____
Do I use pupil assistants?	____	____
Do I demonstrate the proper skills involved in activities?	____	____
Do I organize the class into small groups for instruction based on ability?	____	____
Do I provide enough equipment to enable each pupil to perform skills many times during the period?	____	____
Do I stay with my classes at all times to insure safety procedures and a safe environment?	____	____
If I have the assistance of a specialist, do I take full advantage of his services?	____	____
TOTAL	____	____

Figure 8–16. Self-appraisal chart for the classroom teacher.

	Yes	No
I. *Organization*		
A. Do I explain the program to all persons concerned: parents, teachers, principals, and pupils?		
B. Do I emphasize the use of bulletin boards, assembly programs, and parent-teacher groups to interpret the program?		
C. Do I discuss fully the use of curricular materials and other instructional aids?		
D. Do I plan carefully before the class meets by marking instructional areas, locating balls, and other equipment, specifying various areas for instruction, and familiarizing the classroom teachers with the procedures for the day?		
E. During the class period do I organize the class into as many groups as possible for instruction?		
F. Do I involve the classroom teacher in the program at all times?		
G. Do I show teachers and pupils organizational procedures?		
H. Do I secure the attention of pupils before explaining the activity?		
II. *Teaching procedures*		
A. Do I use recognized teaching procedures, teaching from the easy to the more difficult?		
B. Do I teach skills carefully so that both classroom teacher and pupils understand?		
C. Do I select activities in relation to space and equipment?		
D. Do I plan for inclement weather?		
E. Do I conduct classes out-of-doors as much as possible?		
F. Do I plan for individual differences?		
G. Do I offer guidance and assistance to pupils when necessary?		
H. Do I plan programs based on interest of pupils?		
I. Do I explain activities in such a manner that time is not wasted?		
J. Are pupils taught how to move from one formation to another in an expedient manner?		
K. Is all available equipment used at all times?		
L. Do I involve the classroom teacher in planning and conducting the program?		
M. Do I explain the importance of physical education in general and the immediate activity in particular to all pupils?		
N. Do I emphasize the importance of sound organization?		
O. Do I discuss the value of leadership?		
P. Do I discuss frequently the value of health and fitness and the contribution physical education makes?		
III. *Safety of pupils*		
A. Are pupils briefed in the various aspects of safety?		
B. Is instruction in safety an integral and continuous part of the program?		
C. Do I inspect all teaching areas daily for hazards and remove hazardous items?		
D. Do I insist that pupils dress properly for safety?		
E. Do I keep reports on accidents and use the reports to eliminate the causes?		
F. Are classes organized and areas planned to reduce accidents to a minimum?		

The specialist should score 100 per cent on all items listed in the "yes" column. The items shown comprise his responsibilities; he should be evaluated on his performance in these categories.

Figure 8–17. Self-appraisal chart for the elementary physical education teacher.

REFERENCES

1. *Discipline Crisis in Schools.* Arlington, Va.: National School Public Relations Association, 1973, p. 1.
2. *Ibid.,* p. 1.
3. George H. Gallup: "Sixth Annual Gallup Poll of Public Attitudes Toward Education." *Phi Delta Kappan,* September, 1974, p. 21.
4. "Education Too Little Too Late." *Parade,* June 16, 1974, p. 5.
5 Stephen K. Bailey: *Disruption in Urban Public Secondary Schools.* Bulletin, National Association of Secondary School Principals, 1970, pp. 10–12.
6. *Discipline Crisis in Schools, op. cit.,* p. 42.
7. *Ibid,* p. 42.
8. *Ibid,* p. 43.
9. *Ibid,* p. 45.
10. "Don't Discipline without Due Process, Courts Warn." *Education U. S. A.,* May 27, 1974, p. 217.
11. *Discipline Crisis in Schools, op. cit.,* p. 46.
12. *Discipline Crisis in Schools, op. cit.,* p. 28.
13. Muriel Paskin Carrison: "The Perils of Behavior Modification." *Phi Delta Kappan,* May, 1973, p. 593.
14. "Scholastic Institute of Teacher Opinion." *Today's Education,* March-April, 1974, p. 90.
15. *Discipline Crisis in Schools, op. cit.,* p. 54.
16. Report of the Representative Assembly. *JOHPER,* May-June, 1962, p. 42.
17. Committee on Exercise and Physical Fitness: "Classification of Students for Physical Education." *JAMA,* January, 1967, p. 113.
18. "Training Leaders for Girls' Physical Education and Intramurals." *Physical Education Newsletter,* October 1, 1964.
19. New York Public Schools: *Physical Education For Girls.*
20. "Eighth Graders are Leaders." *Physical Education Newsletter,* February 1, 1971.
21. "Training High School Juniors and Seniors to Help Teach Elementary Physical Education." *Physical Education Newsletter,* November 15, 1970.
22. Donald K. Mathews: *Measurement in Physical Education,* 4th ed. Philadelphia: W. B. Saunders Co., 1973, p. 1.
23. Benjamin Fine: "School Revisions Needed." *Virginian-Pilot,* Norfolk, Virginia, January 26, 1964.
24. Victor H. Noll and Dale P. Scannell: *Introduction to Educational Measurement,* 3rd ed. New York: Houghton Mifflin Co., 1972, p. 153.
25. James S. Terwilliger: "Self-Reported Marking Practices and Policies in Public Secondary Schools." *Bulletin, National Association of Secondary School Principals,* March, 1966, pp. 5–37.
26. Chester W. Harris (ed.): *Encyclopedia of Educational Research,* 3rd ed. New York: The MacMillan Co., 1960, pp. 783–789.
27. "An Elementary Youth Fitness School at the University of Michigan." *Physical Education Newsletter,* May 27, 1961.
28. Mathews, *op. cit.,* p. 374.
29. H. P. Neilson and Clayne R. Jensen: *Measurements and Statistics in Physical Education.* Belmont, Calif.: Wadsworth Publishing Co., 1972, p. 328.
30. Editorial. *Physical Education Newsletter,* October 15, 1965.
31. Greyson Daughtrey: "Homework in Physical Education." *JOHPER,* October, 1964, p. 23.

SUGGESTED READINGS

Humphrey, James H., Alice M. Love and Leslie W. Irwin: *Principles and Techniques of Supervision in Physical Education.* Dubuque, Iowa: Wm. C. Brown Co., 1972.
Mathews, Donald K.: *Measurement in Physical Education,* 4th ed. Philadelphia: W. B. Saunders Co., 1973.
Phillips, E. Lakin, and Daniel N. Wiener: *Discipline, Achievement and Mental Health,* 2nd ed. Englewood Cliffs, N. J.: Prentice-Hall, Inc., 1972.
Safrit, Margaret J.: *Evaluation in Physical Education: Assessing Motor Behavior.* Englewood Cliffs, N.J.: Prentice-Hall, Inc., 1973.
Singer, Robert: *The Psychomotor Domain.* Philadelphia: Lea & Febiger, 1972.

Swimming pool of George Washington School No. 1 in Elizabeth, New Jersey. (Courtesy of Glazed Tile and Ceramic Mosaics; American Olean Pool, Paddock Pool Builders, Inc.)

CHAPTER NINE

Planning Physical Education Facilities

INNOVATIVE DESIGNS IN FACILITIES

Recent study and experimentation have yielded new trends in design for the construction of school facilities. Although basic concepts, such as that of having teaching stations, remain the same, innovations in design are producing teaching stations that are more functional and less expensive. This section presents some of the more important of these new designs.

A popular structure designed for large crowds and multiple use is the field house. This area may be used for physical education, intramurals, and interschool athletics. However, it has the disadvantage of all multiple-use areas — conflict of usage. Physical education is not concerned with spectators, whereas the interschool athletic program is. Thus, greater use will be made of the field house for the interschool program than for physical education.

Areas such as swimming pools and tennis courts that were previously used only for a few months of the year are now being enclosed with synthetic ma-

225

terial to provide year-round use. These synthetic covers are considerably cheaper than the traditional covers and should be considered in the planning of new construction and in modernizing older structures. An excellent example of effective use of synthetic covers is the new Charles Wright Academy Multi-Activity Center. Figure 9–1 shows the proposed project, including the floor plan and an outside view of the center.

Playground apparatus is likewise undergoing a transition, from the traditional swings, ladders, and climbing bars to more imaginative designs. Sculptured equipment is revolutionizing playground activities and attendance. Revolutionary designs are especially needed for large cities that have limited play spaces for their soaring populations.

Playground equipment designed to challenge the imagination and the play urge of children appears to be the answer to limited play areas. This equipment is stationary, may be erected on any small area, is attractive, and does not detract from the symmetry of a building or the beauty of a neighborhood. A major advantage of the playground equipped with modern apparatus is the large number of children that can play in a small area. Figure 9–2 illustrates several types of innovative playground apparatus that are both challenging and practical, particularly for elementary children.

Some sections of the country have successfully experimented with covered areas for outdoor play; thus areas formerly not used in inclement weather may now be used almost year-round.

Climate control is an extremely important factor in the construction of facilities, for the following reasons:

1. There are reasons to believe that some climatic variety stimulates our physiological processes.

2. Human efficiency does not reach a high degree in extremely cold or extremely hot climates.

3. Prolonged periods of temperature and relative humidity extremes seem to have a definite influence on increased mortality rates.

4. Day-to-day living habits are frequently the sources for dissemination of disease. For example, people being crowded together in confined spaces during the winter leads to atmospheric dissemination of many of the common diseases, such as chicken pox and measles.

5. Excessively warm or cold climate conditions influence the ability of human beings to resist infection and disease.[1]

Three major factors are involved in the design of limited shelters: (1) climate; (2) degree of utilization required; and (3) the size and scope of the program.[2]

Physical education administrators and teachers throughout the country are currently experimenting with the construction of areas to improve instruction. The innovative designs for facilities discussed on the following pages are illustrations of many local efforts to improve facilities.

Hastings, Nebraska. In Hastings, golf is such an important activity in the instructional program that a one-hole course has been developed to give students actual experience in the sport. Steve Bindas, coordinator of physical education, developed the course, which is used by both elementary and secondary school students. Instruction includes use of all clubs, etiquette, strategy, terminology, and rules. The cost of construction was small, and, according to reports on the use of the course, the money was well spent.[3]

Clayton, Missouri. Over half of the new high schools in Clayton are composed of an unheated, roofed-over area. The structures are being used to accommodate increased class sizes and extracurricular activities, to facilitate modular

Figure 9–1. Air-supported structure at Charles Wright Academy, Tacoma, Washington. (Courtesy of Donald F. Burr Association, Architects.)

VIEW FROM SOUTHEAST

MULT-ACTIVITY CENTER   Charles Wright Academy
Donald F. Burr, F.A.I.A. & Associates Architects
Tacoma, Washington

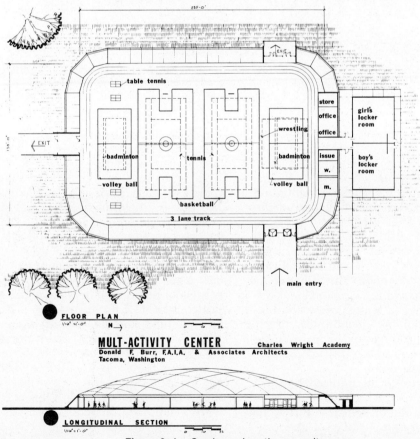

FLOOR PLAN
1/16" = 1'-0"
N →

MULT-ACTIVITY CENTER   Charles Wright Academy
Donald F. Burr, F.A.I.A. & Associates Architects
Tacoma, Washington

LONGITUDINAL SECTION
1/16" = 1'-0"

Figure 9-1. *See legend on the opposite page.*

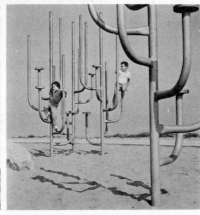

Figure 9–2. Elementary school playground apparatus should be challenging and practical. (Courtesy of Steelways' *More Fun Than Ever.* New York: American Iron and Steel Institute, March, 1969.)

scheduling, to develop the interscholastic program, and to expand the intramural program. (See Figure 9–3.)

Norfolk, Virginia. Norfolk has initiated a program for teaching swimming inexpensively through utilization of the "mini-pool." The instructional program is developed around a portable pool which may be assembled in one location and then disassembled and transported from school to school. The program is geared to teaching elementary children the basics of water safety and elementary swimming techniques. Each child is given one week of instruction. At the conclusion of the instruction, certificates are awarded.

The pools are located adjacent to the junior high school, which gives the children access to the dressing facilities and showers. A unique feature of the program is the use of the auxiliary gymna-sium, which enables the children to participate in recreational activities during inclement weather.

The program is planned for eight weeks during the summer; the maximum class size is 20 children and each period consists of one hour of instruction. Each pool has an administrator, an assistant, and two aides.

An evaluation of the program reveals that parents, children, administrators, and school board members are all enthusiastic about it. If the instruction is carefully planned and conducted properly, children lose their fear of the water and may learn to swim. Parents are grateful for having their small children taught how to swim. Since the cost of teaching such a large number of children is relatively small, administrators and school board members are extremely cooperative. The cost is small since the pools

Figure 9–3. Physical education programs may be conducted throughout the year by using outdoor covered areas. Courtesy of Clayton Public Schools, Clayton, Missouri.)

were donated to the health and physical education department by the Mayor's Youth Commission and the Norfolk Housing and Redevelopment Commision. Figure 9–4 illustrates the type of pool used in the program.

Mt. Stuart Elementary School, Ellsburg, Washington. The new elementary school at Ellsburg, Washington, incorporates innovations designed to meet the needs of the students today and in the future. The facility is planned to provide year-round physical education irrespective of weather.

The building includes four interior activity areas, each serving one group of four classrooms. The largest area (2200 square feet) serves the 4th- and 5th-grade classes located in the east wing. The second largest area (1800 square feet) is located in the north wing and serves the 3rd-grade classes and one 2nd-grade class. The smallest areas are in the south (1500 square feet) and west (1406 square feet) wings and serve grades 1 and 2 and the kindergarten. Adjacent to each of the interior areas is an outside covered play

area. The advantage of the plan is obvious: each activity area serves four classroom teachers, allowing physical education to be scheduled daily in a facility in which skills may be taught properly. Figure 9–5 shows the floor plan of the facility.

Figure 9–4. Instruction in swimming with the use of the portable mini-pool. (Courtesy of Norfolk Public Schools, Norfolk, Virginia.)

Piney Branch Middle School, Takoma Park, Maryland. An example of thoughtful planning is shown in the Piney Branch Middle School, Takoma Park, Maryland. The school was designed for school-community use and includes a swimming pool, gymnasium, and dressing rooms. Figure 9–6 illustrates how the physical education unit is arranged in conjunction with the other sections of the school.

New designs are necessary if we are to keep abreast of the rapid progress that is being made in this field. Basic to all progress in education is the interpretation of the aims and objectives to the community. Even more important is the need for informing the public about the purposes of physical education. Other examples of innovative designs in the construction of physical education facilities are shown in Figure 9–7.

PLANNING INDOOR AREAS

Administrators today are faced with many problems in regard to school construction. Changing emphases in educational philosophy, developments in modern technology, and the growing trend toward providing facilities for both large-group and independent study are just some of the problems confronting educational leaders. An acute problem currently facing administrators is the re-

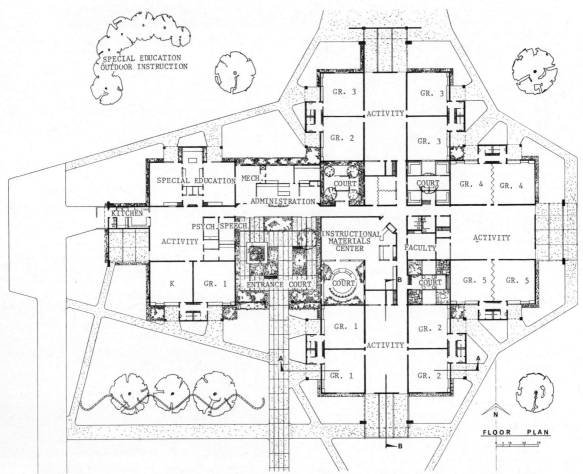

Figure 9–5. An innovative elementary school that provides four teaching stations for physical education. (From Baily, S., and L. Rawley: "A School for Today and Tomorrow." *JOHPER*, September, 1969, p. 31.)

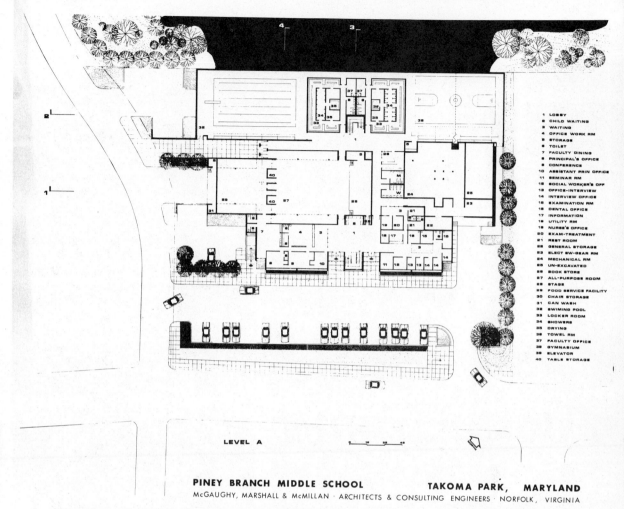

LEVEL A

PINEY BRANCH MIDDLE SCHOOL   **TAKOMA PARK, MARYLAND**
McGAUGHY, MARSHALL & McMILLAN · ARCHITECTS & CONSULTING ENGINEERS · NORFOLK, VIRGINIA

Figure 9–6. A middle school designed for physical education and recreation. (Courtesy of Takoma Park Schools, Takoma Park, Maryland.)

cent federal legislation regarding school facilities. The Department of Health, Education and Welfare stipulates that all districts that receive federal aid shall provide facilities for girls and women comparable to those provided for boys and men. Although this ruling is primarily concerned with interschool athletics, it also affects planning and construction for physical education. The section of Title IX regarding facilities clearly states that

A recipient may provide separate toilet, locker room, and shower facilities on the basis of sex, but such facilities provided for students of one sex shall be comparable to such facilities provided for students of the other sex.[3a]

In the past, superintendents usually recommended that the school districts provide the necessary standard classrooms needed to house the enrollment with little consideration of the many changes made in teaching techniques, procedures, and expanding curriculum areas. The result was that the school program had to be made to fit the school plant. Fortunately, this concept of

Figure 9–7. *See legend on the opposite page.*

school construction is now recognized as impractical. Today the superintendent is expected to keep abreast of the dynamics of our space age culture and, together with his staff and the architect, to plan school plants that meet currently changing educational demands.

Innovations in Teaching

The technological revolution and its by-products have created innovations in teaching that have surpassed anything developed on the educational horizon in 50 years. In order to meet the resultant challenge, instruction must take place in an environment that differs in many ways from the traditional school building of yesteryear. Innovations in teaching procedures have shown that merely constructing a sufficient number of traditional classrooms to house the student body will no longer meet the needs of today's youth. Examples of teaching trends that require changes in the traditional school are team teaching, educational television, teaching machines, independent study areas, instructional materials centers, and plural teaching areas in physical education.

Administrators of physical education, working as members of the joint-planning team, are generally concerned with all of these innovations and trends. Therefore, they should read professional journals in general education, and observe schools in which innovative techniques have been implemented in order to gain insight into the advantages and disadvantages of these educational changes. The trend of primary concern to physical education teachers is that of having plural teaching areas; because the administrator needs an in-depth understanding of this trend, the remainder of this chapter will be devoted to it.

Functional Construction

Functional construction of the physical plant is necessary if teachers are to perform their duties successfully. In the past, too many school buildings have been constructed without adequate planning. Architects have designed buildings without seeking advice from those within the profession who are qualified to provide the information needed for planning functional facilities in physical education.

Fortunately, there seems to be a trend toward bringing architects, administrators, and curriculum specialists together at the planning stage to provide a more functional school plant. The physical education administrator should be among the specialists whose expertise is sought to contribute to the design of a functional building. He should be familiar with the innovative trends discussed earlier in this chapter, and should have available diagrams and photographs of these trends. Finally, the administrator should have a checklist of reasons for constructing the facility and guides on how to proceed with the planning.

Guides for Functional Instruction

Some essential guidelines that should be used by administrators and architects in developing plans for construction of the physical education plant are as follows:

1. The need for the plant should be justifiable. All concerned members of the school

---

Figure 9–7. Innovative trends in the construction of physical education facilities.
A, Outdoor covered area, Riverside Elementary School, Princeton, New Jersey. (Courtesy of Kelly and Gruzen, Architects.) *B, Swimming pool with a hydraulic submersible bulkhead,* Chartiers Valley High School, Pittsburgh, Pennsylvania. (Courtesy of American Olean Ceramic Mosaics, Adolph Kiefer and Associates. Architects.) *C, Deflatable roof concept, which provides open air for the summer.* Hammocks Middle School, Mamaroneck, New York. (Courtesy of the Perkins and Will Partnership, Architects.) *D, Synthetic floor covering,* University of Wyoming, *E, Rooftop play area,* Friends Select School, Philadelphia, Pennsylvania. (Courtesy of Mirick, Pearson, Ilvonen and Batcheler Architects.) *F, Synthetic air structure cover.* (Courtesy of Thermo-flex Incorporated.)

system and the community should be apprised of this need.

2. Representatives of the community and school should be involved with the development of the initial plans.

3. The initial plan should consider such factors as cost, location and number of teaching stations, size of classes, types of activities that will be conducted, location of service areas, and accessibility for both school and community groups.

4. Innovations such as the use of folding partitions to provide teaching stations should be given careful consideration.

5. Future use of the building should be considered, with plans for additions if necessary.

6. The facility should not be designed in conjunction with the auditorium, lunchroom, or music rooms. Authorities in physical education administration recommend separate facilities for physical education, to prevent scheduling difficulties.

7. Expensive duplication of facilities for school and community use should be avoided. The facility should be planned to effectively provide for both school and community, with a gate in the corridor to prevent access to other areas of the building.

8. State and local regulations should be considered at the outset, so that expensive alterations may be avoided at a later date.

9. All sources of federal, state, and local funds and sites should be carefully explored.

10. Gymnasiums in both the elementary and secondary schools should be located in a wing of the building away from classrooms and separated by a corridor.

11. Practical planning should begin with the large gymnasium, which should include a folding partition and bleachers. This area will serve as station for basketball and other activities where spectators are involved. The folding partition provides two stations for physical education.

12. Use of synthetic floor coverings and ground coverings should be considered.

13. Various innovative trends in the construction of gymnasiums, field houses, and swimming pools should be considered.

14. Special attention should be given to providing facilities for the handicapped.

These guidelines provide a framework within which administrators, architects, and teachers can plan functional physical education facilities. Figure 9–7 shows some of the newer trends in physical education facilities.

Steps in Planning

Since physical education is an integral part of the total educational program, planning of the physical education facility should be developed in this context. Although the specifications and requirements for physical education are quite different from those of academic subjects, planning for physical education and other school facilities must be a joint venture.

Definite steps should be established and then followed in the planning of the school facility. Figure 9–8 illustrates a process that is functional and effective. It allows all individuals concerned with school programs to play an important role. Physical education personnel should be prepared to provide input at levels 2, 3, and 4 of this plan.

Once the framework for planning has been established, administrators can focus their attention on the actual procedures involved. The national trend to include qualified school personnel in the initial planning of the school plant is a welcome one, especially in physical education. The experiences and knowledge of these professionals can prove invaluable in the overall effort to bring the planning more in line with the functional aspects of design for physical education construction. Planning a school building that will provide for all the needs of modern education is a painstaking and difficult task. Each department is competing for adequate space in the plant, and many compromises must be made. Such compromises may result in structural changes in the plant, which further emphasizes the need for administrators to have a good background in planning procedures. Some of the most important planning procedures in physical education are discussed in the following paragraphs.

Development of Policy. The development of a firm policy regarding the purposes and use of the facility is important, since in many places the community uses school buildings. Too often buildings have been constructed without anticipation of community use; a facility

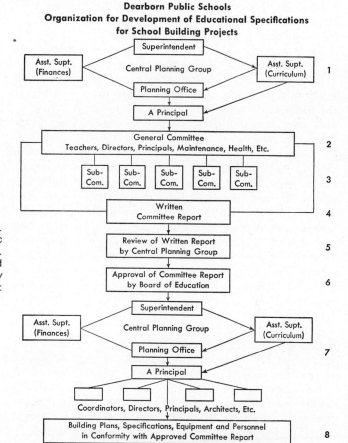

**Dearborn Public Schools
Organization for Development of Educational Specifications
for School Building Projects**

Figure 9–8. Steps in planning. (From Dearborn (Michigan) Public Schools, Staff Newsletter, Vol. 3., No. 5, 1951. In Anderson, Lester W., and Lauren A. Van Dyke: *Secondary School Administration.* Boston: Houghton Mifflin Co., 1972, p. 502.)

that is unsatisfactory for multiple programs is the obvious result. Boards of education should have a written policy concerning the function of school buildings and the extent to which the community may share the facilities. If the policy provides for community use, the building must be designed to meet these demands. In order to effectively accomplish this interaction between the school and the community, a subcommittee should be formed, consisting of school officials, lay people, architects, and others interested in the plant's use and the needs of the community. This com-

mittee should be assigned a dual responsibility:

1. To develop a broad plan defining the purpose and use of the physical education facility.

2. To make recommendations concerning sources of funds for construction of the facility, type and location of the structure, use of the facility for meeting local needs and interests, factors involved in the functional use of the plant, and, if health instruction is a part of the program, the number and location of health rooms.

General Plan. Once the purpose and use of the facility has been determined, a general plan should be given to the architect by the director of physical education or someone with the knowledge of the needs of physical education. The purpose of the general plan is to provide the architect with an overview of the physical education program, in order to guide his thinking in the initial planning. The general plan should outline the needs of the program and list the administrator's recommendation; a rough sketch of the facility should accompany the recommendations. The basic needs include enrollment, class size, areas for community use, types of instructional activities, service areas, special uses, and number and size of teaching stations. The plan should also include sketches and photographs of innovative ideas that might be included in the structure. In addition to furnishing the general plan and innovative material, the administrator should suggest that the architect visit a modern, functional building to see some of the ideas that would be desirable for inclusion in the facility.

Enrollment. An estimate should be made regarding the total enrollment of the school and the number of students scheduled for physical education. One gymnasium is adequate for 240 students scheduled daily in physical education (40 students per period, 6 periods daily), but beyond this the architect and the administration must begin to think in terms of more teaching stations. Determining the number and size of teaching stations needed is probably the most important phase of the entire planning, since the teaching station is the basic cost determinant. Chapter 6 describes a formula for determining the number of stations needed.

Class size. The ideal class size for physical education is debatable. However, it is generally agreed that 30 students per period is desirable; for most large schools, however, 40 students would be practical. Class size is also discussed in Chapter 5.

Areas for community use. Modern planning includes consideration of areas for community use; the number, types, size, and location of these areas should be

carefully determined. Usually separate office and storage rooms are adequate, since by using folding gates and partitions, the dressing rooms, showers, and stations may be readily accessible.

Types of instructional activities. It is extremely important to determine the types of instructional activities that will be included in the curriculum. For example, the ceiling height is a critical factor for some activities but not for others. A modern program includes instruction not only in team sports, such as basketball, that require a high ceiling, but also in individual sports, such as wrestling, tumbling, table tennis, rhythms, tennis, golf, and bowling, for which a high ceiling is unnecessary. Basketball is the only sport in which a high ceiling is considered desirable, and there is even some doubt as to whether the traditional 24-foot ceiling is really necessary, since modern basketball is played around the goal area and the shooting and passing involved rarely exceed a height of 16 feet. If it were not for the space needed for bleachers to accommodate spectators, basketball courts with a 16- to 18-foot ceiling would be adequate. A thorough study is needed to justify the questionable expenditure of money for expensive gymnasiums designed for basketball, which involves only a few students, to the exclusion of more practical, inexpensive areas which may be used for a variety of activities.

Service areas. Service areas — dressing rooms, showers, toilet facilities, athletic areas, offices, storage rooms, drying rooms, and laundry facilities — are essential to the comfort, health, and safety of students and are necessary for the implementation of the instructional program in physical education. Specifications for most of these areas are covered by state building codes, and it is the duty of the architect to provide adequately for them in the initial design of the building. Further discussion regarding these areas is presented later in this chapter.

Special uses. Although the facility is designed primarily for physical education instruction, special uses will be made of the stations. For example, in most schools, facilities are used jointly for interschool athletics and physical education. This necessitates the planning of standardized playing areas, provisions for spectators, and separate dressing, storage, visiting-team, and showering facilities for the interschool program. In many places the community uses the school facilities at the end of the school day, in the evenings, and during the summer. Specific arrangements are necessary if these groups are to be accommodated without interfering with normal school functions.

Provision should be made to include facilities for the handicapped. This may be done through the use of auxiliary rooms shown in Figure 9–10 and discussed on page 246. Although the trend is to admit handicapped children to regular classes, there are instances where special activities involving special facilities are necessary. Specifications for developing facilities for the handicapped are included in the resource manual.

Review of the General Plan. After the general plan, which includes the basic design for the physical education facility, has been incorporated in the total building plans, a review of the tentative plans is in order. If the general design of the facility is satisfactory to the school authorities, final specific recommendations can be made.

Specific Recommendations. The physical education administrator has provided in his general plan a set of parameters within which the architect can create an initial design to fit instructional needs. So far, however, the details—types of lockers, shower heights, floor markings, floor coverings, and so on—have not been taken care of. These are the specifics, and their inclusion or omission may mean the difference between a functional and a non-functional building.

It costs no more to design a functional plant than it does to design a non-functional one. A highly authoritative checklist shown in Figure 9–9 includes the items considered necessary in planning the physical education section of the building. This checklist should assist administrators in making sure that none of the specifics necessary for a functional facility are overlooked.

Floor Coverings. An item of extreme importance which should be determined early in the planning stage is the type of floor covering to be used. In addition to the traditional wooden floor, usually made of maple or birch, synthetic materials may be used. All-weather coverings made of rubber, asphalt, and synthetics are used for field houses. Sometimes portable wood floors are available for basketball.

Synthetic gymnasium coverings are provided by several nationally known manufacturers. Although used extensively for outdoor areas, synthetics have had only limited acceptance for indoor use, although this is likely to change in the forseeable future.

Some secondary schools have already used synthetic coverings successfully indoors. Brainerd High School, Brainerd, Minnesota; Sikeston High School, Sikeston, Missouri; and Alma High School, Alma, Michigan, have substituted such products for the traditional wood covering.

Plural Teaching Stations

All schools are composed of areas where students and teachers meet to participate in the various educational procedures that are conducive to learning. These areas vary in size and structure to meet the needs of the student and the objectives of the subject. For academic subjects these areas are known as classrooms; for physical education, they are known as gymnasiums. In planning instructional programs, formulas have been used to determine the number of classrooms necessary for academic subjects. These formulas are usually based on a recommended teacher load, such as 25, 30, or 35 students. Although recommendations have been made for classrooms or gymnasiums needed in physical education, few places use a formula in providing adequate areas for instruction. The usual procedure is to construct a gymnasium designed for basketball and allow it to be used for physical education classes. This station must suffice regardless of the number of students that are assigned to it.

Text continued on page 242

CHECK LIST FOR FACILITY PLANNERS

As an aid to those responsible for planning facilities for physical education, health education, and recreation, a check list has been prepared. The application of this check list may prevent unfortunate and costly errors.

Place the appropriate letter in the space indicated in the right-hand margin after each statement:

A — The plans meet the requirements **completely.**
B — The plans meet the requirements **only partially.**
C — The plans **fail** to meet the requirements.

Soundly-conceived plans for areas and facilities are not achieved by chance or accident, but by initiative and action of knowledgeable people acting individually, in groups, and as agencies.

GENERAL

1. A clear-cut statement has been prepared on the nature and scope of the program, and the special requirements for space, equipment, fixtures, and facilities dictated by the activities to be conducted.

2. The facility has been planned to meet the total requirements of the program as well as the special needs of those who are to be served.

3. The plans and specifications have been checked by all governmental agencies (city, county, and state) whose approval is required by law.

4. Plans for areas and facilities conform to state and local regulations and to accepted standards and practices.

5. The areas and facilities planned make possible the programs which serve the interests and needs of all the people.

6. Every available source of property or funds has been explored, evaluated, and utilized whenever appropriate.

7. All interested persons and organizations concerned with the facility have had an opportunity to share in its planning (professional educators, users, consultants, administrators, engineers, architects, program specialists, building managers, and builder—a team approach).

8. The facility and its appurtenances will fulfill the maximum demands of the program. The program has not been curtailed to fit the facility.

9. The facility has been functionally planned to meet the present and anticipated needs of specific programs, situations, and publics.

10. Future additions are included in present plans to permit economy of construction.

11. Lecture classrooms are isolated from distracting noises.

12. Storage areas for indoor and outdoor equipment are adequately sized. They are located adjacent to the gymnasiums.

13. Shelves in storage rooms are slanted toward the wall.

14. All passageways are free of obstructions; fixtures are recessed.

15. Facilities for health services, health testing, health instruction, and the first-aid and emergency-isolation rooms are suitably interrelated.

16. Buildings, specific areas, and facilities are clearly identified.

17. Locker rooms are arranged for ease of supervision.

18. Offices, teaching stations, and service facilities are properly interrelated.

19. Special needs of the physically handicapped are met, including a ramp into the building at a major entrance.

20. All "dead space" is used.

21. The building is compatible in design and comparable in quality and accommodation to other campus structures.

22. Storage rooms are accessible to the play area.

23. Workrooms, conference rooms, and staff and administrative offices are interrelated.

24. Shower and dressing facilities are provided for professional staff members and are conveniently located.

25. Thought and attention have been given to making facilities and equipment as durable and vandalproof as possible.

26. Low-cost maintenance features have been adequately considered.

27. This facility is a part of a well-integrated master plan.

28. All areas, courts, facilities, equipment, climate control, security, etc., conform rigidly to detailed standards and specifications.

29. Shelves are recessed and mirrors are supplied in appropriate places in rest rooms and dressing rooms. Mirrors are not placed above lavatories.

30. Dressing space between locker rows is adjusted to the size and age level of students.

31. Drinking fountains are conveniently placed in locker-room areas or immediately adjacent thereto.

32. Special attention is given to provision for the locking of service windows and counters, supply bins, carts, shelves, and racks.

33. Provision is made for the repair, maintenance, replacement, and off-season storage of equipment and uniforms.

34. A well-defined program for laundering and cleaning of towels, uniforms, and equipment is included in the plan.

35. Noncorrosive metal is used in dressing, drying, and shower areas except for enameled lockers.

36. Antipanic hardware is used where required by fire regulations.

37. Properly-placed hose bibbs and drains are sufficient in size and quantity to permit flushing the entire area with a water hose.

38. A water-resistant, coved base is used under the locker base and floor mat, and where floor and wall join.

39. Chalkboards and/or tackboards with map tracks are located in appropriate places in dressing rooms, hallways, and classrooms.

40. Book shelves are provided in toilet areas.

41. Space and equipment are planned in accordance with the types and number of enrollees.

42. Basement rooms, being undesirable for dressing, drying, and showering, are not planned for those purposes.

43. Spectator seating (permanent) in areas which are basically instructional is kept at a minimum. Roll-away bleachers are used primarily. Balcony seating is considered as a possibility.

44. Well-lighted and effectively-displayed trophy cases enhance the interest and beauty of the lobby.

Figure 9–9. Check list for facility planners. (From "Planning Facilities for Athletics, Physical Education, and Recreation," 1974, pp. 7 and 193. Reprinted courtesy of AAHPER and The Athletic Institute.)

45. The space under the stairs is used for storage.

46. Department heads' offices are located near the central administrative office, which includes a well-planned conference room.

47. Workrooms are located near the central office and serve as a repository for departmental materials and records.

48. The conference area includes a cloak room, lavatory, and toilet.

49. In addition to regular secretarial offices established in the central and department-chairmen's offices, a special room to house a secretarial pool for staff members is provided.

50. Staff dressing facilities are provided. These facilities may also serve game officials.

51. The community and/or neighborhood has a "round table" —planning round table.

52. All those (persons and agencies) who should be a party to planning and development are invited and actively engaged in the planning process.

53. Space and area relationships are important. They have been carefully considered.

54. Both long-range plans and immediate plans have been made.

55. The body comfort of the child, a major factor in securing maximum learning, has been considered in the plans.

56. Plans for quiet areas have been made.

57. In the planning, consideration has been given to the need for adequate recreation areas and facilities, both near and distant from the homes of people.

58. Plans recognize the primary function of recreation as being enrichment of learning through creative self-expression, self-enhancement, and the achievement of self-potential.

59. Every effort has been exercised to eliminate hazards.

60. The installation of low-hanging door closers, light fixtures, signs, and other objects in traffic areas has been avoided.

61. Warning signals—both visible and audible—are included in the plans.

62. Ramps have a slope equal to or greater than a one-foot rise in 12'.

63. Minimum landings for ramps are 5' x 5', they extend at least one foot beyond the swinging arc of a door, have at least a 6-foot clearance at the bottom, and have level platforms at 30-foot intervals on every turn.

64. Adequate locker and dressing spaces are provided.

65. The design of dressing, drying, and shower areas reduces foot traffic to a minimum and establishes clean, dry aisles for bare feet.

66. Teaching stations are properly related to service facilities.

67. Toilet facilities are adequate in number. They are located to serve all groups for which provisions are made.

68. Mail services, outgoing and incoming, are included in the plans.

69. Hallways, ramps, doorways, and elevators are designed to permit equipment to be moved easily and quickly.

70. A keying design suited to administrative and instructional needs is planned.

71. Toilets used by large groups have circulating (in and out) entrances and exits.

CLIMATE CONTROL

1. Provision is made throughout the building for climate control—heating, ventilating, and refrigerated cooling.

2. Special ventilation is provided for locker, dressing, shower, drying, and toilet rooms.

3. Heating plans permit both area and individual-room control.

4. Research areas where small animals are kept and where chemicals are used have been provided with special ventilating equipment.

5. The heating and ventilating of the wrestling gymnasium have been given special attention.

ELECTRICAL

1. Shielded, vaporproof lights are used in moisture-prevalent areas.

2. Lights in strategic areas are key-controlled.

3. Lighting intensity conforms to approved standards.

4. An adequate number of electrical outlets are strategically placed.

5. Gymnasium and auditorium lights are controlled by dimmer units.

6. Locker-room lights are mounted above the space between lockers.

7. Natural light is controlled properly for purposes of visual aids and other avoidance of glare.

8. Electrical outlet plates are installed 3' above the floor unless special use dictates other locations.

9. Controls for light switches and projection equipment are suitably located and interrelated.

10. All lights are shielded. Special protection is provided in gymnasiums, court areas, and shower rooms.

11. Lights are placed to shine between rows of lockers.

WALLS

1. Movable and folding partitions are power-operated and controlled by keyed switches.

2. Wall plates are located where needed and are firmly attached.

3. Hooks and rings for nets are placed (and recessed in walls) according to court locations and net heights.

4. Materials that clean easily and are impervious to moisture are used where moisture is prevalent.

5. Shower heads are placed at different heights—4' (elementary) to 7' (university)—for each school level.

6. Protective matting is placed permanently on the walls in the wrestling room, at the ends of basketball courts, and in other areas where such protection is needed.

7. An adequate number of drinking fountains are provided. They are properly placed (recessed in wall).

8. One wall (at least) of the dance studio has full-length mirrors.

9. All corners in locker rooms are rounded.

CEILINGS

1. Overhead-supported apparatus is secured to beams engineered to withstand stress.

2. The ceiling height is adequate for the activities to be housed.

3. Acoustical materials impervious to moisture are used in moisture-prevalent areas.

4. Skylights, being impractical, are seldom used because of problems in waterproofing roofs and the controlling of sun rays (gyms).

Figure 9–9. *Continued on the following page*

5. All ceilings except those in storage areas are acoustically treated with sound-absorbent materials. _____

FLOORS

1. Floor plates are placed where needed and are flush-mounted. _____

2. Floor design and materials conform to recommended standards and specifications. _____

3. Lines and markings are painted on floors before sealing is completed (when synthetic tape is not used). _____

4. A coved base (around lockers and where wall and floor meet) of the same water-resistant material used on floors is found in all dressing and shower rooms. _____

5. Abrasive, nonskid, slip-resistant flooring that is impervious to moisture is provided on all areas where water is used —laundry, swimming pool, shower, dressing, and drying rooms. _____

6. Floor drains are properly located and the slope of the floor is adequate for rapid drainage. _____

GYMNASIUMS AND SPECIAL ROOMS

1. Gymnasiums are planned so as to provide for safety zones (between courts, end lines, and walls) and for best utilization of space. _____

2. One gymnasium wall is free of obstructions and is finished with a smooth, hard surface for ball-rebounding activities. _____

3. The elementary-school gymnasium has: one wall free of obstructions; a minimum ceiling height of 18'; a minimum of 4,000 square feet of teaching area; and a recessed area for housing a piano. _____

4. Secondary-school gymnasiums have: a minimum ceiling height of 22'; a scoreboard; electrical outlets placed to fit with bleacher installation; wall attachments for apparatus and nets; and a power-operated, sound-insulated, and movable partition with a small pass-through door at one end. _____

5. A small spectator alcove adjoins the wrestling room and contains a drinking fountain (recessed in the wall). _____

6. Cabinets, storage closets, supply windows, and service areas have locks. _____

7. Provisions have been made for the cleaning, storing, and issuing of physical education and athletic uniforms. _____

8. Shower heads are placed at varying heights in the shower rooms on each school level. _____

9. Equipment is provided for the use of the physically handicapped. _____

10. Special provision has been made for audio and visual aids, including intercommunication systems, radio, and television. _____

11. Team dressing rooms have provisions for:

   a. hosing down room _____
   b. floors pitched to drain easily _____
   c. hot- and cold-water hose bibbs _____
   d. windows located above locker heights _____
   e. chalk, tack, and bulletin boards, and movie projection _____
   f. lockers for each team member _____
   g. drying facility for uniforms _____

12. The indoor rifle range includes:

   a. targets located 54" apart and 50' from the firing line _____
   b. 3' to 8' of space behind targets _____
   c. 12' of space behind firing line _____
   d. ceilings 8' high _____
   e. width adjusted to number of firing lines needed (1 line for each 3 students) _____
   f. a pulley device for target placement and return _____
   g. storage and repair space _____

13. Dance facilities include:

   a. 100 square feet per student _____
   b. a minimum length of 60 linear feet for modern dance _____
   c. full-height viewing mirrors on one wall (at least) of 30'; also a 20' mirror on an additional wall if possible _____
   d. acoustical drapery to cover mirrors when not used and for protection if other activities are permitted _____
   e. dispersed microphone jacks and speaker installation for music and instruction _____
   f. built-in cabinets for record players, microphones, and amplifiers, with space for equipment carts _____
   g. electrical outlets and microphone connections around perimeter of room _____
   h. an exercise bar (34" to 42" above floor) on one wall _____
   i. drapes, surface colors, floors (maple preferred), and other room appointments to enhance the room's attractiveness _____
   j. location near dressing rooms and outside entrances _____

14. Training rooms include:

   a. rooms large enough to administer adequately proper health services _____
   b. sanitary storage cabinets for medical supplies _____
   c. installation of drains for whirlpool, tubs, etc. _____
   d. installation of electrical outlets with proper capacities and voltage _____
   e. high stools for use of equipment such as whirlpool, ice tubs, etc. _____
   f. water closet, hand lavatory, and shower _____
   g. extra hand lavatory in the trainers' room proper _____
   h. adjoining dressing rooms _____
   i. installation and use of hydrotherapy and diathermy equipment in separate areas _____
   j. space for the trainer, the physician, and for the various services of this function _____
   k. corrective-exercise laboratories located conveniently and adapted to the needs of the handicapped _____

15. Coaches' rooms should provide:

   a. a sufficient number of dressing lockers for coaching staff and officials _____
   b. a security closet or cabinet for athletic equipment such as timing devices _____
   c. a sufficient number of showers and toilet facilities _____
   d. drains and faucets for hosing down the rooms where this method of cleaning is desirable and possible _____
   e. a small chalkboard and tackboard _____
   f. a small movie screen and projection table for use of coaches to review films _____

Figure 9–9. *Continued*

HANDICAPPED, DISABLED, AND AGING

Have you included those considerations that would make the facility accessible to, and usable by, the disabled and the aging? These considerations include:

1. The knowledge that the disabled and the aging will be participants in almost all activities, not merely spectators, if the facility is properly planned. _____

2. Ground-level entrance(s) or stair-free entrance(s) using inclined walk(s) or inclined ramp(s). _____

3. Uninterrupted walk surface; no abrupt changes in levels leading to the facility. _____

4. Approach walks and connecting walks no less than 4' in width. _____

5. Walks with a gradient no greater than five percent. _____

6. A ramp, when used, with rise no greater than one foot in 12'. _____

7. Flat or level surface inside and outside of all exterior doors, extending 5' from the door in the direction that the door swings, and extending one foot to each side of the door. _____

8. Flush thresholds at all doors. _____

9. Appropriate door widths, heights, and mechanical features. _____

10. At least 6' between vestibule doors in series, i.e., inside and outside doors. _____

11. Access and proximity to parking areas. _____

12. No obstructions by curbs at crosswalks, parking areas, etc. _____

13. Proper precautions (handrails, etc.) at basement-window areaways, open stairways, porches, ledges, and platforms. _____

14. Handrails on all steps and ramps. _____

15. Precautions against the placement of manholes in principal or major sidewalks. _____

16. Corridors that are at least 60" wide and without abrupt pillars or protrusions. _____

17. Floors which are nonskid and have no abrupt changes or interruptions in level. _____

18. Proper design of steps. _____

19. Access to rest rooms, water coolers, telephones, food-service areas, lounges, dressing rooms, play areas, and all auxiliary services and areas. _____

20. Elevators in multiple-story buildings. _____

21. Appropriate placement of controls to permit and to prohibit use as desired. _____

22. Sound signals for the blind, and visual signals for the deaf as counterparts to regular sound and sight signals. _____

23. Proper placement, concealment, or insulation of radiators, heat pipes, hot-water pipes, drain pipes, etc. _____

24. Referral to Appendix H, ASA-A117.1-1961, "Making Buildings and Facilities Accessible to, and Usable by, the Physically Handicapped." _____

SWIMMING POOLS

1. Has a clear-cut statement been prepared on the nature and scope of the design program and the special requirements for space, equipment, and facilities dictated by the activities to be conducted? _____

2. Has the swimming pool been planned to meet the total requirements of the program to be conducted as well as any special needs of the clientele to be served? _____

3. Have all plans and specifications been checked and approved by the local Board of Health? _____

4. Is the pool the proper depth to accommodate the various age groups and types of activities it is intended to serve? _____

5. Does the design of the pool incorporate the most current knowledge and best experience available regarding swimming pools? _____

6. If a local architect or engineer who is inexperienced in pool construction is employed, has an experienced pool consultant, architect, or engineer been called in to advise on design and equipment? _____

7. Is there adequate deep water for diving (minimum of 9' for one-meter boards, 12' for 3-meter boards, and 15' for 10-meter towers)? _____

8. Have the requirements for competitive swimming been met (7-foot lanes; 12-inch black or brown lines on the bottom; pool 1 inch longer than official measurement; depth and distance markings)? _____

9. Is there adequate deck space around the pool? Has more space been provided than that indicated by the minimum recommended deck/pool ratio? _____

10. Does the swimming instructor's office face the pool? And is there a window through which the instructor may view all the pool area? Is there a toilet-shower-dressing area next to the office for instructors? _____

11. Are recessed steps or removable ladders located on the walls so as not to interfere with competitive swimming turns? _____

12. Does a properly-constructed overflow gutter extend around the pool perimeter? _____

13. Where skimmers are used, have they been properly located so that they are not on walls where competitive swimming is to be conducted? _____

14. Have separate storage spaces been allocated for maintenance and instructional equipment? _____

15. Has the area for spectators been properly separated from the pool area? _____

16. Have all diving standards and lifeguard chairs been properly anchored? _____

17. Does the pool layout provide the most efficient control of swimmers from showers and locker rooms to the pool? Are toilet facilities provided for wet swimmers separate from the dry area? _____

18. Is the recirculation pump located below the water level? _____

19. Is there easy vertical access to the filter room for both people and material (stairway if required)? _____

20. Has the proper pitch to drains been allowed in the pool, on the pool deck, in the overflow gutter, and on the floor of shower and dressing rooms? _____

21. Has adequate space been allowed between diving boards and between the diving boards and sidewalls? _____

22. Is there adequate provision for lifesaving equipment? Pool-cleaning equipment? _____

23. Are inlets and outlets adequate in number and located so as to insure effective circulation of water in the pool? _____

24. Has consideration been given to underwater lights, underwater observation windows, and underwater speakers? _____

25. Is there a coping around the edge of the pool? _____

26. Has a pool heater been considered in northern climates in order to raise the temperature of the water? _____

27. Have underwater lights in end racing walls been located deep enough and directly below surface lane anchors, and are they on a separate circuit? _____

28. Has the plan been considered from the standpoint of handicapped persons (e.g., is there a gate adjacent to the turnstiles)? _____

Figure 9-9. *Continued on the following page*

29. Is seating for swimmers provided on the deck? _____

30. Has the recirculation-filtration system been designed to meet the anticipated future bathing load? _____

31. Has the gas chlorinator (if used) been placed in a separate room accessible from and vented to the outside? _____

32. Has the gutter waste water been valved to return to the filters, and also for direct waste? _____

INDOOR POOLS

1. Is there proper mechanical ventilation? _____

2. Is there adequate acoustical treatment of walls and ceilings? _____

3. Is there adequate overhead clearance for diving (15' above low springboards, 15' for 3-meter boards, and 10' for 10-meter platforms)? _____

4. Is there adequate lighting (50 footcandles minimum)? _____

5. Has reflection of light from the outside been kept to the minimum by proper location of windows or skylights (windows on sidewalls are not desirable)? _____

6. Are all wall bases coved to facilitate cleaning? _____

7. Is there provision for proper temperature control in the pool room for both water and air? _____

8. Can the humidity of the pool room be controlled? _____

9. Is the wall and ceiling insulation adequate to prevent "sweating"? _____

10. Are all metal fittings of noncorrosive material? _____

11. Is there a tunnel around the outside of the pool, or a trench on the deck which permits ready access to pipes? _____

OUTDOOR POOLS

1. Is the site for the pool in the best possible location (away from railroad tracks, heavy industry, trees, and open fields which are dusty)? _____

2. Have sand and grass been kept the proper distance away from the pool to prevent them from being transmitted to the pool? _____

3. Has a fence been placed around the pool to assure safety when not in use? _____

4. Has proper subsurface drainage been provided? _____

5. Is there adequate deck space for sunbathing? _____

6. Are the outdoor lights placed far enough from the pool to prevent insects from dropping into the pool? _____

7. Is the deck of nonslip material? _____

8. Is there an area set aside for eating, separated from the pool deck? _____

9. Is the bathhouse properly located, with the entrance to the pool leading to the shallow end? _____

10. If the pool shell contains a concrete finish, has the length of the pool been increased by 3 inches over the "official" size in order to permit eventual tiling of the basin without making the pool "too short"? _____

11. Are there other recreational facilities nearby for the convenience and enjoyment of swimmers? _____

12. Do diving boards or platforms face north or east? _____

13. Are lifeguard stands provided and properly located? _____

14. Has adequate parking space been provided and properly located? _____

15. Is the pool oriented correctly in relation to the sun? _____

16. Have windshields been provided in situations where heavy winds prevail? _____

Figure 9–9. *continued*

A concept that is highly recommended is to establish a formula for providing teaching stations in physical education based on the number of students enrolled in the school and a suggested teaching load per teacher. Such a formula was shown in Chapter 5 (p. 108). Some educational leaders, such as Lloyd Trump and Dorsey Baynham, envision that the school of tomorrow will include plural teaching stations in physical education rather than a gymnasium designed for basketball only.

Gymnasium Stations. Gymnasium stations constitute the largest and most expensive part of the physical education facility.

The lack of adequate teaching stations is one of the reasons that poor programs in physical education exist throughout the country. In order for physical education to provide quality instruction, there must be adequate facilities. Construction can no longer be planned for the basketball team to the exclusion of other areas needed for physical education; the standard high-ceilinged gymnasium is too expensive. Activities such as wrestling, bowling, volleyball, tumbling, rhythms, table tennis, and indoor golf may be taught in a smaller area with a 12- to 14-foot ceiling (see Figure 9–10).

Cost of construction and lack of understanding have prevented administrators from planning physical education around the teaching-station concept. Planning in physical education based on a standard gymnasium designed for basketball is costly. However, when areas such as auxiliary rooms, health rooms, swimming pools, and available spaces resulting from folding unused bleachers are considered, the teaching-station concept has a different meaning.

The physical education program of tomorrow will be designed around a sufficient number of teaching stations, a situation comparable to other areas in the curriculum. Several cities have designed new physical education plants incorporating several teaching stations. The Seattle School District initiated a unit-plan building program for secondary schools which included teaching stations formed by folding partitions. The plan was developed through a school-community study which incorporated projected enrollment needs. The building program also included gymnasiums in all elementary schools.[4]

In Denver, Colorado, new construction was planned around the needs of physical education, again by the use of folding partitions to provide necessary teaching stations. Community use was anticipated. The criteria for construction were safety, instructional adequacies, flexibility, expansibility, and economy.[5]

A building program designed around the teaching-station concept was begun in Norfolk, Virginia, in 1956. The first new junior high school in the program included six teaching stations: a gymnasium with a folding partition, one auxiliary gymnasium, and three health rooms. Since the program was initiated, all six new schools and nine older schools have been made to conform to this plan. Figure 9–11 shows the floor plan of a new eight-station school. Figure 9–12 illustrates how folding partitions may be used to form a two- or three-station teaching complex in a standard gymnasium.

A new school in Everett, Washington, utilizes balcony space for additional teaching stations.[6] In Oshkosh, Wisconsin, a new campus-type high school has been constructed which also uses balcony space for stations. These stations are used not only for physical education instruction but also for after-school programs.[7]

The new physical education plant in Rincon High School, Tucson, Arizona, was designed to provide several stations. In addition to a two-station basketball gymnasium, the plant includes three stations for wrestling and other individual sports, and a swimming pool; in addition, there is a girls' plant consisting of several stations.[8]

The Brookline High School, Brookline, Massachusetts, is an innovative plant designed for school-community use. The school has a gymnasium divided by a folding partition, a second gymnasium for gymnastics, two exercise rooms, a separate wrestling room, four full-size tennis courts, and a running track on the top floor.[9]

When planning the number of teaching stations, the administrator must also be careful to allot appropriate space for the various activities within each station. The architect needs this information to incorporate it into the design and to provide for floor markings for the activities. Figure 9–13 shows the space requirements for selected activities. Note, for example, that in the gymnasium design there must be space allotments for safety zones as well as for playing-court dimensions.

Planning for an adequate number of teaching stations is a good start for the administrator as a member of the plant-design team. But it is only a start. Equally

Figure 9–10. The auxiliary gymnasium provides a third station and is adequate for instruction in many activities, such as bowling, rhythms, wrestling, table tennis, and tumbling. The one shown above contains a folding partition, which provides two stations. (Courtesy of Booker T. Washington High School, Norfolk, Virginia.)

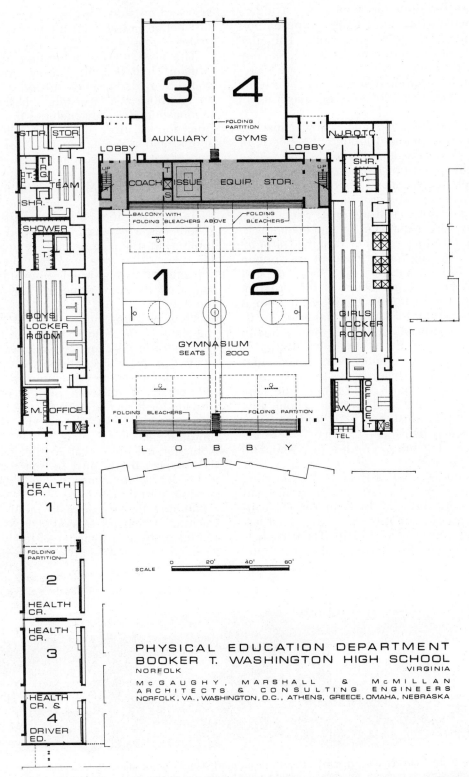

Figure 9–11. Having plural teaching stations in physical education provides incentive for quality instruction. An eight-station facility consisting of four physical education stations and four health education rooms. (Courtesy of Booker T. Washington High School, Norfolk, Virginia.)

Figure 9-12. The addition of folding partitions forms a two- or three-station complex. In the photograph the partitions are partially open. The left partition when fully open provides a large station, and the partition on the right divides the large section into two smaller ones. (Courtesy of Lake Taylor Senior High School, Norfolk, Virginia.)

Activity	Play Area in Feet	Safety Space in Feet*	Total Area in Feet
Badminton	20 x 44	6s, 8e	32 x 60
Basketball			
Jr. High instructional	42 x 74	6s, 8e	
Jr. High interscholastic	50 x 84	6s, 8e	
Sr. High interscholastic	50 x 84	6s, 8e	62 x 100
Sr. High instructional	45 x 74	6s, 8e	57 x 90
Neighborhood El. Sch.	42 x 74	6s, 8e	54 x 90
Community Junior H. S.	50 x 84	6s, 8e	62 x 100
Community Senior H. S.	50 x 84	6s, 8e	62 x 100
Competitive—DGWS	50 x 94	6s, 8e	62 x 110
Boccie	18 x 62	3s, 9e	24 x 80
Fencing, competitive	6 x 40	3s, 6e	12 x 52
instructional	3 x 30	2s, 6e	·9 x 42
Rifle (one pt.)	5 x 50	6 to 20e	5 x 70 min.
Shuffleboard	6 x 52	6s, 2e	18 x 56
Tennis			
Deck (doubles)	18 x 40	4s, 5e	26 x 50
Hand	16 x 40	4½s, 10e	25 x 60
Lawn (singles)	27 x 78	12s, 21e	51 x 120
(doubles)	36 x 78	12s, 21e	60 x 120
Paddle (singles)	16 x 44	6s, 8e	28 x 60
(doubles)	20 x 44	6s, 8e	32 x 60
Table (playing area)			9 x 31
Volleyball			
Competitive and adult	30 x 60	6s, 6e	42 x 72
Junior High	30 x 50	6s, 6e	42 x 62
Wrestling (competitive)	24 x 24	5s, 5e	36 x 36

*Safety space at the side of an area is indicated by a number followed by "e" for end and "s" for side.

Figure 9-13. Space requirements for selected indoor activities in the junior and senior high schools. (Courtesy of The Athletic Institute. From *Planning Facilities for Athletics, Physical Education, and Recreation.* Chicago: The Athletic Institute, 1974, p. 12.)

important is the ability to adjust the gymnasium stations to the various teaching loads. The next consideration, then, is to illustrate ways to make these adjustments.

When a group of 40 or 50 pupils with adequate outdoor space comes inside for instruction, problems arise. The allotted indoor space is often labeled "inadequate" for the activity. But is it really? Too often a teacher says facilities are inadequate when in reality they are adequate. It usually is a matter of changing the activity. As an illustration, let us take a class of 40 pupils that has been outdoors for touch football instruction. The outdoor space is usually adequate, since all schools have a football area; by dividing the class into several groups, the football area is large enough for all students to learn the skill of touch football. Now the same group that had ample room for sufficient movement outdoors finds itself indoors in a one-gymnasium situation. At this point many teachers will say that the space is inadequate because all 40 students cannot "play" basketball at the same time. It would take four gymnasiums for 40 students to "play" basketball. *In a situation like this, the alert teacher teaches the skills of basketball.* Instantly, the situation changes. The class is divided into many groups; four with 10 students, five with eight students, eight with five, or any other type of division of students, depending on the number of balls available. The single gymnasium is now entirely adequate and, in addition, the objectives of physical education are more readily achieved, because the teaching of skills is the teacher's main function.

Another situation involving large groups should be examined. Let us assume that a large group of students, either boys or girls, is assigned to physical education. Teachers might say that it is impossible to teach 80 to 100 students in one gymnasium. Again, this is not a fair statement. A folding partition can be used to divide the gymnasium into two teaching stations with a group on either side, as shown in Figure 9–12. The answer to the problem is the teaching of

skills and not "play" during the instructional period.

With the plan just described, many activities may be included in the program. For example, adequate instruction may be accomplished in volleyball, rhythms, basketball, tumbling, wrestling, table tennis, or bowling in either station.

A third situation arises in which the administration of the school attempts to schedule a third group of 40 or 50 students in the same standard-size gymnasium at the same period. At this point the facilities actually do become inadequate, and the teaching program is placed in jeopardy unless the administration finds a third station. This is the type of arrangement that, if not corrected, will lead to the eventual failure of the program.

The third station needed for this situation may be provided either by the construction of an auxiliary gymnasium or by another folding door (Figures 9–10 and 9–12). The auxiliary gymnasium is preferable and relatively inexpensive, since a low ceiling (14 feet) is satisfactory and the smaller size (40 feet × 70 feet) is considerably less than the standard gymnasium designed for basketball and spectators. Auxiliary stations are readily adaptable for handicapped students.

Administrators should be careful to avoid mistakes of the past in their recommendations. One of these is the traditional multiple-purpose room that is used in many places. This type of room, found in many elementary schools, is used for band, chorus, auditorium, drama, exhibits, parent-teacher meetings, physical education, and sometimes even as a lunchroom. An arrangement such as this is impractical and may well lead to a complete breakdown of *all* programs; moreover, it is frequently a source of friction between departments. Subjects that require intermittent meetings may use the room to advantage, but required subjects that meet daily, such as physical education, always suffer. A resolution by the City and County Supervisors and Directors of the American Alliance of Health, Physical Education and Recreation stated:

Whenever possible and feasible, multiple-purpose rooms in elementary schools should be replaced or supplemented by separate gymnasiums; and if new facilities are being planned, they should include a separate gymnasium appropriately designed and equipped for the age level served.[10]

A more practical arrangement for planning the elementary facility would be to provide three areas: (1) a "cafetorium," (combination lunchroom-auditorium); (2) a multi-purpose room to be used for subjects that meet intermittently, such as music and drama groups; and (3) a physical education room to be used for physical education instruction on a daily scheduled basis. Figures 9–5 and 9–6 portray excellent examples of thoughtful planning for physical education in the elementary school.

If physical education is to meet its objectives, there must be sufficient stations to meet the needs of the students without interference from or conflict with other subjects in the curriculum.

Some administrators may question how a small school in a community with a low economic base can provide an adequate number of teaching stations. There are few small schools that do not have a standard basketball court. This area can be designed for an enrollment of 480 students through the addition of a folding partition. If a school with an enrollment of 960 students can secure two rooms for health instruction, it will have an excellent teaching arrangement for both physical education and health education. The inclusion of health education in the program has an important bearing on construction costs.

The information and recommendations given the architect should include the policy pertaining to health instruction. If health instruction is combined with physical education, then health rooms should be included in planning the teaching stations. It is obvious that the inclusion of health instruction as a teaching subject reduces the cost of construction, since a health teaching station is much less expensive than a physical education station.

Health Education Stations. Many cities and districts include health education instruction in their physical education programs. This necessitates the inclusion of health education stations in the initial planning. Health education classrooms or stations are similar to academic classrooms, but must be planned on a larger scale in order to accommodate the larger classes in health education. An adequately designed health instruction station should allot about 35 square feet of space per student. Essential items to be included in the room are exhibit space, storage space, and electrical outlets. If the teaching content involves laboratory time, running water and hand-washing facilities should be provided.

The Swimming Pool. Designing the swimming pool requires great technical skill. In addition to the architect, the services of a specialist in swimming pool design are usually desirable. Before submitting plans to the architect, administrators must decide what type of pool is needed and the purpose for which it is to be used. The three items discussed in the following paragraphs are the major factors to be considered in planning the pool.

1. *Type of pool.* It is generally agreed that the indoor pool is more practical and may be utilized to a greater degree than the outdoor pool, since it is not affected by weather conditions. If the pool is used jointly for physical education and interschool competition, it must be planned for competition as well as for instruction. Pools may be designed in several ways: (1) with the instructional, competitive, and diving areas in the same unit (the all-purpose pool); (2) with the instructional area located in a separate unit; ((3) with the diving area in a separate unit; and (4) with the diving, swimming, and instructional areas all planned separately. The most practical pool for the secondary school is the all-purpose pool.

2. *Location of the pool.* The location of the pool is of major importance, largely because of the cost factor. The pool can be constructed as a separate unit

away from the school; as a separate unit attached to the school as a part of the physical education facility and using the same service facilities; or it can be constructed on the top or in the basement of the building, with separate service facilities. The most practical design is to have the pool planned in conjunction with the physical education plant, especially if cost is an important factor. This arrangement reduces the cost considerably, since joint use is made of the locker rooms, showers, toilets, and other service facilities.

3. *Size of pool.* The size of the pool is determined by its functions. Instructional pools are usually smaller than the all-purpose pools used for competitions. Age and grade factors also affect pool size. The following dimensions are suggested for pools built for instruction and competition:[11]

Multiple-purpose pool
   width—45′
   length—75′ × 1″
   depth—3.5′–7′ (without diving board)
   depth—3.5′–12′ (with diving board)

   lanes—7′ wide, with 12″ lines down the center and on the bottom of each lane. Each lane should end with a "T" of 30″ × 12″ five feet from the end of the pool.

   ceiling—16′–18′

Other considerations include (1) hand grips flush with the end of the pool, in the center of each lane for backstroke starts; (2) turn targets 30 inches square painted into the end wall in the center of each lane; (3) floor or wall fixtures for pennant lines 15′ from each end of each lane for visibility of backstroke swimmers; (4) water-polo markings; (5) recessed receptacles for water-polo goals on ends of pool or overhead installations that can be raised or lowered.[11]

Smaller pools may be used for elementary instruction, but the dimensions shown above are more desirable when the planning includes community use.

Specific guides for planning. A checklist for planning will be of valuable assistance to the architect. Such a list may be found in the publication by the Athletic Institute:"Checklist for Facility Planners; Planning Facilities for Athletics, Physical Education and Recreation," shown in Figure 9–9.

Refer to the Resource Manual for specific guides in planning for the handicapped.

Guidelines for Administering the Service Areas

The importance of service areas was pointed out in the discussion of the general plan on page 236. Even the most carefully planned teaching area can be ineffective without the proper planning and administration of service areas.

Planning for these areas is not merely a matter of determining the number of shower heads or the size of storage lockers; many more details are involved. Moreover, innovations develop daily in these areas and it is extremely difficult to keep recommendations in line with current developments. However, the following guidelines relating to each service area will assist the administrator in planning.

Dressing Rooms. Dressing rooms should be easily accessible from outside areas and from inside physical education stations. Entrances to dressing rooms should be arranged so that the flow of traffic does not cross the main gymnasium and the traffic corridors. Storage lockers appropriate to the plant design and function should be provided. There are two types of locker arrangements that are generally used for storage of clothes: (1) the separate storage and dressing room, and (2) the combined storage and dressing room.

Separate storage and dressing rooms. The separate storage and dressing room plan places all storage lockers in a separate room. Students enter this room, take their uniforms and locks from their box lockers, and enter the dressing lockers. At the end of the period the procedure is reversed, with students locking their uniforms in the box lockers. There must be enough dressing lockers in this room to accommodate the largest class. This plan is recommended in situations in which outside groups use the dressing facilities. The storage box lockers must be securely locked to prevent outside groups from opening them. Various sizes of box lockers and dressing lockers may be incorporated in this arrangement. However, for practical purposes, the 12″

Figure 9–14. Separate storage and dressing rooms. Box lockers may be seen in the storage room in the background.

× 12″ box locker and 5′ × 12″ × 12″ dressing lockers are recommended. It is also recommended for maintenance purposes that the lockers be placed on concrete bases. The lockers should have slanting tops, as shown in Figure 9–14.

Combined storage and dressing rooms. The combined storage and dressing room provides enough dressing lockers to accommodate the largest class and a sufficient number of storage lockers to accommodate all students scheduled for physical education. This plan involves the use of a box locker–storage locker unit. Specifications usually consist of one 5′ × 12″ × 12″ dressing locker with six-cubic-foot storage lockers attached. Figure 9–15 illustrates this arrangement. See resource manual for space requirements and variations of this plan.

Shower Rooms. Although there are several types of showers, such as gang showers, individually controlled showers, and walk-around showers, the walk-around type of shower is highly recommended. Walk-around showers cost less because less space is required and water consumption is controlled. More time for instruction is provided, since an entire class may walk through the showers in a few minutes. A final advantage of walk-around showers is the low incidence of

behavior problems, since students cannot loiter in the showers.

Walk-around showers are placed in a stagger pattern on both sides of the corridor at the recommended height (Figure 9–16). The water temperature and flow are controlled by the teacher, who operates a valve in the physical education office. As students walk through the

Figure 9–15. Combined storage and dressing lockers.

| AGE GROUP | GRADES | MIRROR HEIGHT | | SHOWER HEIGHT | | SHOWER VALVE HEIGHT |
		VERTICAL LENGTH	TO BOTTOM OF MIRROR	GIRLS	BOYS	
Elementary	2 thru 6	30"	32"	50"	55"	36"
Junior High	7 thru 9	30"	40"	54"	60"	40"
Senior High	10 thru 12	30"	44"	56"	66"	45"
Adults		30"	48"	60"	72"	48"

Notes: 1. Mirror mounting heights apply only to mirrors of size listed. Smaller mirrors are not recommended.
2. Shower heights are for heads 8" from wall. Height should be adjusted if closer to wall.
3. Girls' shower heights are shoulder high.
4. Shower heights are from floor to face of shower head (not rough-in dimension).

Figure 9–16. Recommended heights of shower heads and mirrors. (Courtesy of The Athletic Institute. From *Planning Facilities for Athletics, Physical Education, and Recreation.* Chicago: The Athletic Institute, 1966, p. 151.)

corridor, water is sprayed on them from both sides. The walk-around plan usually includes several individually operated showers for intramural use.

Shower rooms should be constructed adjacent to dressing rooms and swimming pools.

Drying area. A drying area should be located between the shower room and the dressing area. Provisions should be made to hang towels while students are showering. This may be accomplished through the installation of bars or cables. Grab bars should be included in the drying area and mini-rails installed on which students may place their feet while drying.

Towel room. A towel room with a check-out window properly placed at the end of the shower corridor is essential. The room should be large enough to store towels and allow freedom of movement for the person issuing towels.

Showers for girls should be planned differently from showers for boys. Modesty and other considerations make it advisable to have as many private, individual showers and booths as possible. In addition, some walk-around showers should be installed. Figure 9–17 shows shower and locker arrangement for girls.

Athletic Areas. It is recommended that a separate athletic area be provided. This area should include dressing rooms and lockers to accommodate the peak number of athletes; it should also provide adequate shower facilities, drying rooms with pipe racks, temperature- and air-circulation controls, a towel-storage room, a physiotherapy room, and a repair room.

Storage Space. One important factor, usually overlooked in planning, is provision for storage space. Administrators should inform architects of the types of equipment and supplies that will be used in the program. Considerable space is necessary to store mats, table tennis tables, hurdles, and other large pieces of equipment, and for storing and securing supplies such as tennis rackets, golf clubs, balls, and other expensive items. In planning storage rooms, accessibility, security, adaptability, and adequacy should be carefully considered.

OUTDOOR FACILITIES

Outdoor facilities should be designed for school-community use just as indoor facilities are. The type of instructional program conducted by the school and the needs of the community will determine the areas that should be involved in outdoor design. Because of varying programs, weather conditions, and school-community emphasis, it is extremely difficult to describe all of the possibilities that are available for outdoor facilities. The objective of this section is to present certain basic aspects of planning facilities for outdoor programs, including the site plan, surfaces, multiple-use areas, standards for outdoor facilities, and innovative designs for facilities.

Site Plans

The development of site plans for outdoor facilities is extremely important, since weather conditions, subsurface conditions, and drainage are factors that affect cost and functional use of the areas. Plans should reveal the following information on the site to be used:

1. Results of a topographical survey of the grounds on which the areas are to be located.

2. Location and size of the areas.
3. Types of construction of the areas.
4. School-community use of the areas.
5. Approximate cost of each area expressed in dollars per square foot.

The amount of play area for elementary and secondary schools is usually determined by state regulations, but the types of activities involved in the instructional program must also be taken into account. When the area is used partly for instruction and partly for interschool athletics, planning should include the basic requirements of both programs. All play areas should be located some distance from the classrooms, streets, parking lots, and loading zones.

For elementary schools, the area designed for the lower grades should be fenced in and located in a protected area. Various types of permanent equipment, such as climbing apparatus, should be installed in this area. The upper grades should be allotted sufficient space to include concrete multiple-use areas, play fields, and a track area at

Figure 9–17. The arrangement of a girls' shower room. The foreground shows the dressing room, with a section of individual showers in the background.

least 100 yards in length and wide enough for six lanes.

In the secondary schools, the play areas are used jointly by the physical education classes and the athletic teams. This joint use necessitates the allocation of sufficient space for football, track, baseball, softball, tennis, golf, and other sports.

Surfaces

The type of surface used for outdoor play areas varies with the activity. The appropriate types of surfacing for various activities are briefly discussed in the following paragraphs.

Concrete Surfaces. A concrete surface is highly recommended for tennis, badminton, and volleyball courts; roller skating; ice hockey rinks; bowling alleys; table tennis; and outdoor swimming pools. Concrete is relatively inexpensive, impervious to climatic conditions, durable, and easily marked. It is widely used for multiple-use areas and, because it requires so little maintenance, is preferred by many administrators. Concrete may be colored to cut down the glare of the sun.

Asphalt. Asphalt surfacing has many of the qualities needed for a year-round versatile surface for playgrounds. It is durable, low in maintenance cost, can be easily marked, drains easily, and has no-glare qualities that make it desirable for many sports. In some sections of the country, however, unless the ground is properly treated before constructing the area, grass will grow through the asphalt.

Synthetic Surfaces. Several sports —football, softball, hockey, baseball, lacrosse, and soccer—require some type of turf surface. Turf surfaces are safer and in some rebound games, such as tennis, are desirable for the more skillful players.

Recent developments in synthetic turf have revolutionized the surfacing of some game areas and will have important implications in playground construction for the future. Synthetic turf has many advantages over natural grass.

When this type of ground covering is used, play areas have greater daily use and may be utilized year round, since the disintegration of grass in heavily used areas and the problems created by mud are eliminated. Artificial turf areas are free of allergy producing agents and provide better traction for running, punting, and other movements.

Administrators should carefully study the advantages and disadvantages of synthetic turf before recommending adoption of it for playing areas. The most important consideration is the safety factor. Synthetic turf is extremely expensive, but if it provides safer playing conditions, it should be used.

An important study of playing surfaces was made by Steven T. Bramwell *et al.* The study involved 26 high schools playing 228 games in the Seattle area. One brand of synthetic turf was used. The study reported the "injury rates for games played on the synthetic surface were significantly higher than for those played on grass."[12] However, since only one brand of synthetic surface was used, the authors feel that because of the differences in the various brands, generalizations concerning all brands should await epidemiologic investigations.

Experimentation with such synthetics as rubber, cork, and sponge is rapidly producing surfacing that may eventually replace traditional surfaces for some activities. Synthetic materials have been successfully used for running tracks and for approaches for high jumping, pole vaulting and long jumping.

Multiple-Use Areas

The most practical, economical areas for outdoor use are multiple-use areas. Constructed from either concrete or asphalt, multiple-use areas provide for several play areas on one surface. They can be used year round for instruction and competition in basketball, volleyball, tennis, and other activities in which hard surfaces are required. Figure 9–18 shows one of the many uses of a multiple-use area for elementary schools.

Figure 9–18. The multiple-use area is a practical teaching station for elementary physical education. (Courtesy of Norfolk Public Schools, Norfolk, Virginia.)

Recommended Dimensions and Plans for Game Areas

Although standard dimensions are not necessary for physical education instruc-tion, it is important for after-school com-petition and community use to conform to recommended dimensions for game areas. These dimensions are included in the Resource Manual.

REFERENCES

1. William G. Wagner: *Shelter for Physical Education.* College Station, Texas: A & M College, 1961, p. 22.
2. *Ibid.,* p. 47.
3. "Inexpensive Schoolyard Fairway Enables Students to Tee Off on Golf Balls." *Physical Education Newsletter,* September 1, 1965.
3a. Federal Register, Part II. Washington, D.C.: Department of Health, Education and Welfare, June, 1975, p. 24141.
4. "Focus on Facilities." *JOHPER,* April, 1962, p. 42.
5. *Ibid.,* p. 43.
6. *Ibid.,* p. 46.
7. *Ibid.,* p. 46.
8. *Ibid.,* p. 37.
9. "The Physical Education Building." A brochure published by the Public Schools of Brookline, Massachusetts.
10. *Administering City and County School Programs:* Report of a National Conference. Washington, D. C.: AAHPER, 1961, p. 64.
11. "Planning Facilities for Athletics, Physical Education, and Recreation." AAHPER and The Athletic Institute, 1974, p. 188.
12. Steven T. Bramwell *et al.:* "High School Football Injuries: A Pilot Comparison of Playing Surfaces." *Medicine and Science in Sports,* Fall, 1972, p. 166.

SUGGESTED READINGS

Approaches to Problems of Public School Administration in Health, Physical Education and Recreation. Washington, D.C.: AAHPER, 1968.
Castaldi, Basil: *Creative Planning in Educational Facilities.* Chicago: Rand McNally & Co., 1969
Gabrielsen, M. Alexander: *Swimming Pools: A Guide to their Planning, Design, and Operation.* Fort Lauderdale, Fla.: Hoffman Publications, 1969.
Planning Facilities for Athletics, Physical Education and Recreation. Chicago: The Athletic Institute, 1966.

CHAPTER TEN

Administration of the Equipment and Supplies Budget

Although the board of education and the superintendent are responsible for all phases of the school budget, other individuals play an important role in its preparation. Planning the budget is too important to be left to chance. A functional budget should be developed by administrators and teachers working cooperatively.

There are several plans for developing budgets in physical education, the most common being (1) the separate physical education budget and (2) the athletic budget from which physical education receives part of the income. The material in this chapter is based on the separate physical education budget, since the national trend is in this direction. The athletic budget will be discussed in Chapter 13.

THE SEPARATE PHYSICAL EDUCATION BUDGET

In recent years the trend has been away from preparing the physical education and athletic budget jointly. Studies show that in the outstanding school districts of the country 80 per cent of the physical education budgets are prepared separately from the athletic budget.[1] However, in some school systems, the budget in physical education still depends upon the income from gate receipts and other sources of income from the athletic program. This practice places physical education in a disadvantageous position and is not recommended. The instructional program in physical education is important to the health and fitness of all boys and girls, and the program should not be dependent upon fluctuating income from interschool athletic contests. Physical education is the only subject in the school curriculum faced with this problem, and steps should be taken to correct it. However small the allocation for physical education may be, it should come from the same source as the other subjects in the curriculum.

Budget planning in physical education is an integral part of the total school budget, and the procedures for the two are almost parallel. In order to plan wisely and efficiently, physical education administrators and teachers should understand the procedures of budgeting. They should also know in what respects the physical education budget relates to the total budget. More importantly, the administrator should be keenly aware of the fact that his budgetary recommendations establish the parameters within which the physical education program can meet the health needs of all the students in the system. Once budgetary limitations are set, all efforts to carry out objectives must conform to them, at least for the fiscal year for which the budget is approved.

Budget planning not only insures the procurement of items needed for the program, but also assists in improving instruction. A survey of the physical education program reveals present and future needs for facilities, equipment, supplies, and personnel. The survey also reveals the sometimes staggering costs of these items. In order to justify expenditures, aims and objectives are re-

viewed and plans are made showing to what extent the instructional program is meeting these aims and objectives. It is at this point that the quality and effectiveness of instruction are scrutinized. When instruction is good and the outcomes of the program are evident, it is relatively easy to justify and gain approval for additional expenditures. Poor teaching is difficult to sell.

PRINCIPLES OF BUDGETING

Planning for the purchasing of equipment and supplies in physical education involves certain principles of budgeting that should be followed in order for expenditures to be made in an organized and efficient manner. Teachers may plan their instructional program with confidence when they are assured of receiving equipment and supplies in an orderly fashion. The following budgeting principles apply to both single schools and entire systems.

1. Whether the budget is planned for six months, for a year, or for a longer period, it should be prepared several months in advance of the fiscal year for which it is to be presented for approval.
2. Although the superintendent and school board are ultimately responsible for the budget, teachers, principals, and directors who are responsible for the instructional program should be involved in the planning. These instructional leaders should also be involved with any deletions, adjustments, or changes that may be necessary.
3. Budget requests should be ample, but they should be based on the actual needs of the particular school or department. Budget padding is not a sound practice and is difficult to defend.
4. When the budget has been approved, expenditures should be made in accordance with the allocation. Overdrawn budgets cause friction because they incur accounting problems. Embarrassing situations may be avoided by strict adherence to budgetary allocations.
5. Administration of the budget should be handled in an orderly manner. Requisitions and purchase orders should be thoughtfully prepared and should be accurate and descriptive.

STEPS IN BUDGET PLANNING

There are several steps in budget planning: (1) determining the needs of the program; (2) making the inventory; (3) preparing the budget based on needs; (4) presenting the budget; (5) administering the budget; and (6) evaluating the budget.

Determining the Needs of the Program

The purpose of the budget is to assist in providing adequate resources to meet the needs of the program. Needs are determined by the aims and objectives of instruction; they may vary from school to school. In determining needs, two factors should be considered: (1) the curriculum and (2) the nature of the teaching process.

The Curriculum. The type of curriculum determines the financial resources that will be needed to conduct the program. Once the activities that will compose the curriculum have been determined, ample equipment and supplies must be supplied to provide quality instruction for each activity. The budget must take into account the philosophy of the program, the activities for girls, activities for boys, coeducational activities, activities for the handicapped, communication materials such as stationery

and mimeograph paper, and the number of teachers necessary for implementing the program.

After the curriculum has been established, the items needed and how much they will cost should be noted in the budget proposal. Department heads and teachers should help to determine what items they will need to conduct their classes. These needs will vary, since the content for the various grades will be different. For example, the requirements of a 9th-grade teacher who is responsible for golf instruction are different from those of an 8th-grade teacher who teaches tennis. A checklist of the items included in the instructional program is helpful in planning budget requests.

The Nature of the Teaching Process. Probably one of the reasons that physical education does not always occupy a respected place in budget allocations is the nature of the teaching process. The methods and procedures used in teaching demand an important role in establishing accountability and also in determining the equipment and supplies needed for instruction. An instructional program that is based on planned teaching requires considerably more instructional items than a supervised play or recreational program. For instance, using balls to teach perceptual-motor skills effectively to a class of 30 students necessitates providing each student with a ball (see Figure 10-1), whereas the recreational or supervised play approach in an activity such as volleyball would involve only one or two balls, depending on the number of games in progress. The later procedure violates the philosophy of physical education, since individualized instruction for all students is the underlying objective of the instructional program. After the needs of the program are determined, an inventory is the next step in planning the budget.

Making the Inventory

The basic instrument used in collecting and assembling information for determining the rules of the program is the inventory. Careful scrutiny of current and past inventories provides an over-

Figure 10-1. Providing sufficient equipment for each student facilitates individualized instruction. (Courtesy of Norfolk Public Schools.)

view of needed equipment and supplies. The inventory should not only include the items on hand but it should also provide space for equipment and supplies requested for the budget year. A sample inventory sheet is shown in Figure 10–2. Other material may be found in the resource manual.

Preparation of the Budget

After the needs of the program have been determined, the budget should be prepared to reflect these needs. There are several ways to obtain the information needed for preparing the budget. The principal, with or without the help of teachers, may decide what the needs are. The information he provides is used by the administrative staff in the superintendent's office to formulate the working budget. Another method is to prepare the budget in the superintendent's office without assistance from the principal, teachers, or the director. A more democratic—and more effective—method is to delegate the responsibility for making the budget to the director of physical education, who in turn would seek assistance from principals, department heads, and teachers. As a group working cooperatively, these people would collect and assemble information for the budget.

It seems advisable at this point to discuss *cost analysis*—the manner in which allocations are made. In some systems allocations for physical education are included in the total school budget. A fixed amount of money per student is allocated to cover all instructional areas, including physical education. Sometimes this plan is broken down into allocations for each instructional area. For example, allocations for instructional supplies might be: art, $1.00 per student; physical education, $1.25 per student; music, $1.50 per student; and so on. In this plan, allocations for equipment are made by subject areas and are placed in the general equipment account.

Another plan, less commonly used, allocates a stipulated amount of money based on daily attendance. In a few places the superintendent and the board of education determine allocations without consulting the principal, teachers, or directors. There are also instances in which the physical education program depends on income from athletic events.

After information has been collected and assembled and allocation procedures studied, the sources of equipment and supplies should be determined. The cost estimate, quality, order number, make, and other specifications of each item should be indicated. Catalogs from the various manufacturers, distributors, and vendors should be studied. Some systems require that two bids be submitted for each item before entering the cost in the budget.

Presenting the Budget

Many factors are involved in presenting the budget for adoption by the appropriate governing body. Presentations may have to be made at several levels before the budget may be legally adopted. It may have to be presented from teacher to principal or director, from director to superintendent, and from superintendent to school board. Eventually, of course, the budget must be approved by the school board. This approval is usually preceded by one or two public hearings, which allow the public to react to the proposed budget. Public hearings provide a unique opportunity for educators to explain the purposes of the programs to the public, and therefore have tremendous implications for school-community relations.

The purpose of this section is to emphasize the role of physical education personnel in the presentation of the budget. If at any stage before final adoption the budget must be cut, the physical education leader should be available to speak in the interest of the department and to justify the need for the items included in the physical education budget.

Administering the Budget

After the budget has been approved, administrators and department heads are

Form No._____
Code No._____

PERPETUAL INVENTORY FORM

Organization _____

Item Description   Tennis shoes, low-cut, white _____

Vendors   1_____   4_____
          2_____   5_____
          3_____   6_____

Critical Balance (4): 40   Usage Rate (5): [ ]

DATE	REFERENCE (1)	REQUISITIONED HOW (2)	QUAN.	QUAN. REC'D.	DISBURSED HOW (3)	QUAN.	BALANCE	UNIT COST	TOTAL COST
1-1-60							40		
1-5-60	Vendor (1)	P.O. 1693	25 pr.					$3.00	$75.00
1-20-60				25 pr.			65		
1-25-60					I	20	45		

(1) Vendor Code
_____
_____
_____
_____

(2) Code
PO—Purchase Order
PC—Petty Cash
D—Donation
T—Transferred
O—Other

(3) Code
C—Consumed
I—Issued for Use
T—Transferred
D—Discarded
L—Lost or Broken
LO—Loaned Out

(4) Critical Balance
(order when
balance reaches
quantity shown)

(5) Usage Rate
(quantity used
per year or
activity)

Figure 10–2. *A,* The perpetual inventory form. *B,* The periodic inventory of equipment and supplies. From *Equipment and Supplies for Athletics, Physical Education and Recreation.* Chicago, The Athletic Institute, 1966, pp. 67 and 68.)

notified concerning the various allocations for supplies and equipment. The budget now becomes the purchasing guideline for each department of the school.

It is important that purchases be made according to the policies established by the school administration. There are two types of organizational plans for purchasing: centralized and decentralized. In the centralized plan, all purchases are made from a central purchasing office; this plan is most commonly used because it is the most economical and effective. Items needed for all schools are purchased through bids and are stored in a central warehouse. Requisitions are made to the appropriate administrator, and, if approved, deliveries are made from the warehouse.

In the decentralized plan, each school purchases its own supplies and equipment and is responsible for paying the bills and handling the accounts necessary for the school. Some obvious disadvantages to this plan are the absence of the economic advantages of quantity buying and the lack of quality control. The greatest advantage of the decentralized plan is that it is more responsive to unexpected needs, since purchases can be made without a great deal of red tape.

The authors recommend the centralized system for the following reasons: (1) it employs the use of highly qualified people for purchasing; (2) it allows for the purchase of materials in quantity, which provides for economies of scale; (3) in large systems, the centralized plan is more amenable to compu-

EQUIPMENT AND SUPPLIES

PERIODIC INVENTORY OF EQUIPMENT AND SUPPLIES

Form No._____

Activity _____

Program _____

Organization _____

Page No._____

Date of Inventory _____

Item Description	Unit: Each Pair Dozen Gross	Usage Rate: per Yr. per Activity	Location	Previous Inventory	Purchased Since Last Inventory	Total to Be Accounted for	Usable New	Usable Used	Needs Repair	Not Accounted for	Estimated Needs Quantity Required	Estimated Needs Unit Cost	Estimated Needs Total Cost
Softball, Rubber, 12"	each			50	10	60	10	49	0	1	20	$.50	$10.00
Volleyball Stds., Alum.	pair			4	2	6	2	3	1	0	0	0	0

Signature _____

Date _____

Figure 10–2. Continued

B

terized equipment, which permits a more efficient operation. Moreover, the problem of unexpected needs can be solved by establishing in advance a policy through which such needs can be met. Although occasions may arise when supplies will be needed that have not been ordered, thorough planning will help to keep such occasions to a minimum.

There are several procedures involved in providing supplies and equipment for the school after the budget has been approved and allocations have been made. The following steps illustrate the manner in which items needed for the instructional class are procured in systems using the centralized buying plan.

Requisition. The teachers and the department head list the items needed for the department on a requisition form (Figure 10–3), which must be signed by the appropriate school authority, usually the principal.

Purchase Order. The requisition is usually sent to the office of the director of physical education for approval; if it is approved, a purchase order (Figure 10–4) is issued by the purchasing agent and copies are sent to the vendor, to the

school, and to the director of physical education.

The procedure for purchasing is a complicated one and requires rapport between the purchasing agent and the director of physical education. The purchasing agent has the delegated authority to write purchase orders and place bids for large orders. However, he needs the assistance of the director and the teacher in determining specifications for the materials used in the program. The quality of the merchandise, changing designs, and innovative materials are just some of the specifications with which physical educators must be familiar. These and other appropriate specifications should be included in the purchase order.

The buyer or purchasing agent should develop a checklist to be referred to when placing orders. The following list offers important guides to efficient purchasing:

1. The companies from which purchases are made should have a reputation for fairness and honesty and should be in sound financial condition.

2. The vendors should be able to process

Purchase Requisition No. 2652
Board of Education • 470 Sioux Street • West Minneapolis 31, Minnesota

DEPARTMENT: DATE OF REQUEST:
LOCATION: DATE WANTED:
PERSON:

REASON:

APPROVALS:

QUANTITY	DESCRIPTION	SUGGESTED PURCHASE SOURCE

PURCHASING DEPARTMENT INFORMATION
Ordered from: Purchase Order Number:
Date Ordered:
Date Received:

Figure 10–3. Purchase requisition form for ordering supplies.

Purchase Order No. 9449

From: Board of Education • 470 Sioux Street • West Minneapolis 31, Minnesota

TO:

DATE:

PLEASE SHIP AND BILL US FOR THE GOODS LISTED BELOW. IF FOR ANY REASON YOU CANNOT DELIVER WITHIN 30 DAYS, LET US KNOW AT ONCE. PLEASE REFER TO OUR PURCHASE ORDER NUMBER (ABOVE) IN ALL COMMUNI-CATIONS.

SHIP VIA:

QUANTITY	DESCRIPTION	YOUR CAT. NO.	UNIT PRICE	AMOUNT

NOTE: YOUR BILL TO US SHOULD INDICATE ALL YOUR USUAL DISCOUNTS.
PAYMENT WILL BE MADE UPON RECEIPT OF BILL WITH GOODS. ....Purchasing Agent

Figure 10–4. Purchase order for shipment of supplies.

purchase orders quickly and should be willing to make adjustments and exchanges readily.

3. Vendors should have a wealth of information about equipment and supplies and should be readily available to supply needed information and consultive services.

4. Early buying is efficient buying, and should be the general practice established by the purchasing agent.

5. Purchasing from open stock is desirable, since replacements may be facilitated and the cost is usually less.

6. Materials should be standardized with regard to color, type, and style, since items may be bought in greater quantity and therefore at a lower price when they are standardized.

7. Quality purchasing is the best policy. Quality items insure greater safety, durability, and better performance.

8. The buyer should always take advantage of normal discounts, but he should be wary of unusually large discounts, since quality may be sacrificed.

9. The buyer should be concerned with obtaining the best value for the money expended.

10. The buyer needs assistance from his colleagues and should seek it, so long as there is no conflict with legal purchasing procedures.

11. The purchasing agent should be made familiar with the objectives and content of the physical education program, so that he will not only purchase items that cost less, but will also be able to assist the department in realizing its objectives.

12. The buyer should discourage all gifts and favors that may influence his buying or obligate him in any way to the vendor.

13. The buyer should be careful not to show partiality to a particular vendor. He should develop fair and ethical trade procedures with the various suppliers and he should be unbiased in making all decisions relative to quality and other specifications.

Receiving Report. When the vendor delivers the items shown on the purchase order, a receiving report is signed and sent to the central office. The receiving report should not be signed until the shipment is checked with the items and specifications listed on the purchase order and found to be accurate.

After the budget has been in operation for several months, irregularities and weaknesses may appear. It is the responsibility of all individuals who assisted in planning the budget to study these problems and make recommendations to the proper officials to provide a more serviceable instrument. This is done through a formal evaluation of the budget, which is the final step in budget planning.

EVALUATION OF THE BUDGET

The evaluation of the budget is necessary to determine whether or not it is meeting educational needs and resulting in improved instruction. Several methods may be used in evaluating the effectiveness of budget construction and administration. These procedures depend to a great extent on who is making the appraisal. The method of evaluation by a business manager will be quite different from that of a classroom teacher. The business manager would be concerned with balancing his budgeted receipts and expenditures with the actual receipts and expenditures. A budget that has been planned and administered properly would reflect this balance in the annual report. This method of appraising the budget has merit for educators because it encourages them to become more accurate in their planning. However, because it is impossible to foresee all conditions that may arise during a fiscal year, discrepancies between estimated and actual expenditures may justifiably occur.

The teacher uses different criteria in evaluating the budget. His basic concerns are instruction and the procurement of sufficient materials to facilitate his efforts. The teacher's position is far removed from that of the business manager, who reports to the superintendent and the school board. The teacher reports to the principal and the supervisor, and is evaluated on instructional competence. He rarely has more than a vague knowledge of budget techniques; his evaluation of the budget is based on promptness of delivery, adequacy of items needed, and quality of materials.

Sometimes, because of legal requirements, expenditures must be limited to the available income and budgetary allowances cannot be exceeded. Under these circumstances programs must be either curtailed or stopped completely. In order to compensate for this, budget planners sometimes allow plenty of leeway between estimated expenditures and estimated income, so that the budget will balance at the end of the fiscal year. In other words, they pad the budget. Such a procedure defeats the whole purpose of budgeting, which is to provide for accuracy and efficiency in the procurement of supplies and equipment.

Appraisal forms have been developed to determine the strengths and weaknesses of budgets. These forms are more valid when prepared locally, since no standardized form can meet all the existing conditions in several communities.

BUDGETARY CONTROL

Budgetary control is essential to administering the supplies and equipment budget in order to achieve educational objectives. Plans and procedures must be devised to govern the procurement and distribution of equipment and supplies, the evaluation of the quality of items purchased, the maintenance and repairs of equipment, and other functions involved in the successful operation of the budget.

Good records are essential to the successful performance of the functions listed earlier. Three things are involved in successful record keeping and control: (1) an adequate inventory, recording the equipment and supplies that are on hand and those that are on order; (2) records showing the distribution of materials, repair and maintenance costs, and the disposal of unfit materials; and (3) an appraisal of the procedures and methods used to plan the budget. It is essential to have guidelines for the development of policies and procedures for budgetary control; these should be based on principles that have been found to be practical and effective.

Principles of Control

Principles of control are necessary to assist administrators in developing the policies, procedures, records, and methods to be used in the administration of supplies and equipment. The following principles may be used as guidelines in planning the management of supplies and equipment.

1. There should be a direct relationship between the management of equipment and supplies and the objectives of the instructional program. This relationship should be reflected in the control system.
2. The superintendent should have the ultimate responsibility for the control of all equipment and supplies.
3. Budgetary control should be part of the organization and administration of the school program. In physical education, control policies should be an integral part of the total organizational pattern.
4. Policies should be made to determine action in case of theft, fire, loss, misappropriation, or destruction of materials.
5. Record keeping is essential for control and should be developed uniformly for the entire system.
6. Persons to whom equipment and supplies are issued should be held responsible for the care of these materials.
7. Inventories should be kept to insure an accounting of all materials at all times.
8. The administrator may delegate the responsibility for conducting the inventory, but he should approve the final copy.
9. A practical labeling plan should be developed to assist in identifying all equipment and supplies.
10. Records and plans should be developed for the distribution of all equipment and supplies.
11. Policies should be made to govern the disposition of supplies and equipment that are no longer valuable to the program.[2]

Record Forms. A control system requires record forms in order to maintain effective control of equipment and supplies. In preparing these forms, various guidelines should be employed to ensure that certain questions are answered: (1) Is the system effective? (2) Do teachers receive materials at the right time? (3) Is the procedure for supplying materials simple? (4) Does the administration of the system have control over the supply process? (5) Is the supply system organized to operate without excessive supervision and administrative involvement? Sample record forms are shown in the resource manual.

THE SYSTEMS APPROACH TO BUDGETING

The six steps described in the foregoing paragraphs represent the traditional budget-making process. All of these steps are interrelated and none is completed in isolation. To coordinate the various steps, a systems approach to budgeting has emerged over the past few years.

Theoretically, budgeting has always been the means by which educational objectives were implemented. But the taxpayer's demand for accountability in recent years has caused educators to use the budget as one element of a process through which the public can compare actual output with expectations. This has led to a systems approach to educational decision making. One systems approach involves four components: planning, programming, budgeting, and evaluating. Commonly referred to as PPBES (originally PPBS), this process has been called an "educational resources management system" by the Association of School Business Officials.[3]

PPBES was first used by the government in the early sixties as a means of achieving cost effectiveness in various departments. By the late sixties, articles about the application of program budgeting to the educational process began to appear in the professional journals. As demands for accountability increased, school systems began using PPBES as a tool for assisting administrators in determining alternative uses for scarce resources—money, talent, and time.

Many definitions of PPBES have been published. Hartley defines it this way:

Program budgeting relates the output-oriented programs, or activities, of an organization to specific resources that are then stated in terms of budget dollars.

Both programs and resources are projected for at least several years into the future. Emphasis is upon outputs, cost effectiveness methods, rational planning techniques, long-range objectives, and analytical tools for decision making. Probably the most important single task that must be accomplished in moving to this kind of planning and budgeting is the development of a program structure.[4]

To the administrator of physical education, this means that the program must be broadly planned and then translated into performance goals which provide for measurement. For example, activities will be selected and performance expectations of students will be stated. Next follows programming—the setting up of alternative means by which goals may be achieved. After programming, the budgeting component will assign financing to activities, based on priorities established by the administrator and his planning team. Planning and budgeting are often projected over a period of years; high-priority items should be achieved first and others as resources allow. The budgeting component attempts to match program requirements with available resources. The departmental budget document often is subjected to review and approval by top administration, the school board, and the public.

The final component, evaluating, provides a means of determining how effectively the available resources have been put to use to achieve the program objectives. Figure 10–5 shows the relationship of the four components of PPBES.

Strict application of PPBES utilizes the computer and the mathematical anal-

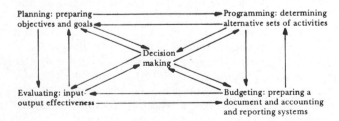

Planning: preparing objectives and goals → Programming: determining alternative sets of activities

Decision making

Evaluating: input-output effectiveness → Budgeting: preparing a document and accounting and reporting systems

Figure 10–5. The major components of PPBES. (From Browder, L. H., Jr., W. A. Atkins, Jr., and E. Kaya: *Developing An Educationally Accountable Program.* Berkeley, Calif.: McCutchan Publishing Corp., 1973, p. 203.)

ysis of operations research in the decision process and may not be formally adopted by a school division or department. However, the philosophy of the systems approach inherent in PPBES has implications for budgeting that the administrator of physical education should not ignore.

DISTRIBUTING EQUIPMENT AND SUPPLIES WITHIN THE SCHOOL

The plan used for storing and distributing equipment and supplies within the school is an important factor in determining the quantity of materials necessary for conducting the program. In the secondary schools, equipment and supplies are usually ordered in sufficient quantity to meet the instructional needs and are stored in a central location. These materials are issued to the individual teachers as needed.

In the elementary school the situation is somewhat different. If the program is conducted by specialists who do all of the teaching in stations designed for physical education, the materials may be stored centrally and issued in the same way as in the secondary schools. In situations in which the classroom teacher is responsible for the program, materials may also be stored centrally and issued as needed. However, some classroom-teacher programs arrange for each classroom to be supplied with sufficient materials. This plan is more expensive, but it provides for a superior instructional program. If each classroom is sufficiently equipped, then an outline such as the one shown in Figure 10–6 of materials needed for a school with 16 classrooms can be used. If each room is not separately equipped, a sufficient quantity of these materials would be stored centrally to meet the needs of the largest number of classes that meet each period either in a gymnasium or on the playground.

INNOVATIVE EQUIPMENT

Sometimes the amount of money allocated for the physical education program is not sufficient to meet instructional needs. This situation may present a real hardship unless other means are available to procure the necessary equipment items. Improvising is one way of solving the problem. Though not the best way to procure supplies and equipment, improvising at least provides some means of meeting an objective that otherwise might have to be abandoned. Moreover, some improvised equipment is innovative and has in some cases been so successful that it has replaced older, more expensive equipment. A little imagination and effort will do wonders when motivation is great and budgetary allocations are limited. Figure 10–7 lists several items of equipment that may be inexpensively constructed locally.

MAINTENANCE AND CARE OF EQUIPMENT AND SUPPLIES

Equipping a physical education department is expensive, and the maintenance and care of equipment and supplies to insure prolonged use should be emphasized. In addition to the cost of supplies and equipment, the element of safety necessitates periodic checks of equipment, with continued emphasis on maintenance to provide maximum safety for all students. Students are required to participate in physical education, and administrators are legally responsible for maintaining safe and adequate equipment at all times.

Care of Supplies

Physical education programs require many more supplies than are needed for interschool athletic programs. Administrators should insist that a reasonable effort be made by teachers to care for the supplies used in class. Common sense is the most valuable asset in caring for physical education supplies. In order to assist teachers, some helpful suggestions concerning the maintenance of supplies are offered.

Care of Balls Various types of balls are used in both the elementary and

			SUPPLIES								EQUIPMENT		
Room	Grade	8½" Balls	Jump + Ropes Short	Long	Soccer balls	Rhythmic Records Albums*	Basket- balls	Soft- balls	Soft- ball Bats	Foot- balls	Mats 5' X 10'	Record Players	Apparatus
1	1	6	6	4	X	2	X	X	X	X	80' -	1	One
2	1	6	6	4	X	2	X	X	X	X	100' of	1	Set (6 Pieces)
3	1	6	6	4	X	2	X	X	X	X	Mat Sur-	1	of
4	2	6	6	4	2	2	X	X	X	X	face are	1	Equipment
5	2	6	6	4	2	2	X	X	X	X	Provided	1	Is Standard
6	3	4	6	4	2	2	X	X	X	X	and May	1	for
7	3	4	6	4	2	2	X	X	X	X	Be Used	1	Each
8	3	4	6	4	2	2	X	X	X	X	Jointly	1	School
9	4	2	6	4	2	2	X	X	X	X	By All	1	
10	4	2	6	4	2	2	X	X	X	X	Classes	1	
11	4	2	6	4	2	2	X	X	X	X	When	1	
12	5	2	6	4	2	2	2	2	2	X	Appro-	1	
13	5	2	6	4	2	2	2	2	2	X	priately	1	
14	5	2	6	4	2	2	2	2	2	X	Scheduled	1	
15	6	2	6	4	2	2	2	2	2	2		1	
16	6	2	6	4	2	2	2	2	2	2		1	
TOTAL													

+ One hank (100') of #10 sash cord cut to appropriate length with taped ends should be minimal.

* A selection of appropriate record albums should be available for use by teachers in the same and adjacent grade levels. This should promote a review of previously learned movements by teachers and students as a basis for rhythmics on their present grade level.

** Not less than six pieces of climbing apparatus for joint class use for each school is standard.

Figure 10–6. Materials needed to enable 16 classrooms to conduct programs independently. (Courtesy of Norfolk Public Schools.)

secondary programs. Rubber and plastic balls are available for basketball and soccer. In many lead-up games, the 8½-inch ball is used. These balls are susceptible to punctures and should be used in areas free from glass, nails, and wire fences with protrusions at the top. Rubber balls should be kept clean at all times by washing them with soap and water. Many plastic and rubber balls may be salvaged by procuring kits to repair punctures and replacing old valves with new ones when leaks are discovered.

Leather balls should be kept clean by using a damp cloth. These balls should not be overinflated, since excessive inflation places a strain on the stitches.

Needles used for inflating balls should be dipped in glycerine before insertion.

Wooden Items. Items made from wood, such as golf clubs, softball bats, tennis racquets, hockey sticks, and bows, may last several years if moderate care is exercised. These itmes should be stored in a dry, cool room. Wooden supplies that cannot be repaired should be discarded.

Nets. Tennis, volleyball, and badminton nets, unless given proper care, may become expensive items in the budget. All nets should be cleaned and stored in a cool, dry room. Moisture causes nets to rot. Nets that are used outside should be creosoted. When storing nets, it is advisable to hang them unrolled rather than rolled or piled together.

Tennis nets that are used by both the community and the school undergo severe treatment, and repairs may be

ITEM	PROCURED FROM	USED FOR
Bowling Pins	Local Alleys	Indoor Bowling
Jumping Standards	School Shop	High Jumping Pole Vaulting
Table Tennis Tables	School Shop (4'x8' Plywood Tops) (5'x9' Plywood Tops)	Table Tennis
Jump Ropes	Buy Bulk Rope - Chop in Desired Lengths - Masking Tape Ends	Rope Skipping
Bowling Backstops	School Shop	Indoor Bowling
Bowling Runners	Indoor-Outdoor Carpeting Cut in Desired Length and Width	Indoor Bowling
Golf Putting	Indoor-Outdoor Carpeting Cut in Desired Length and Width	Indoor Putting
Relay Batons	Old Broom Handles Cut to Size Old Lawn Hose Cut to Size	Relay Races
Starting Blocks	School Shop	Track
Table Tennis Nets	Scrap Canvas Cut to Size - Local Awning Dealers	Table Tennis
Hurdles	Local Shop	Track
Pull-up Bars	Local Machine Shop	Pull-up Tests
Portable Pull-up Bar	Local Shop	Demonstrations
Equipment Boxes	Local Shop	Taking Equipment on the Field
Record Player Cabinets	Local Shop	Protecting Record Player
Fence Tennis Nets	Recreation Department Other Local Sources	Tennis Courts

Figure 10-7. Examples of innovative equipment that may be constructed locally.

costly. Even the rugged wire nets that are installed permanently have not proved to be satisfactory. Students sit on them and they gradually deteriorate. A net made of wire fencing similar to the permanently installed recreation net may be a solution to this problem. The basic difference is ¾-inch pipe that is stretched across the top. These nets have proved to be practical and satisfactory for both physical education and recreational use.

Racquets. For instructional purposes, the metal racquet with metal frame and wire strings is superior. It is inexpensive and with proper care will last for years. These racquets are impervious to most climatic conditions and restringing is unnecessary. Steel racquets should be stored in a dry room to prevent rust.

Care of Equipment

The care of equipment in physical education requires more attention than the care of supplies. Items such as mats,

record players, and film projectors are not only costly but are also subject to extremely rough treatment. Suggestions for the care of these items are offered along with recommendations for the most practical type for use in the physical education class.

Mats. The most practical mat for use in physical education is a felt mat with a duck cover. There should be a plastic cover for the side that is used. The plastic cover may be easily cleaned with soap and water. The same side of the mat should always be placed next to the floor. The canvas side should be cleaned each week with a vacuum cleaner to insure a sanitary surface at all times.

Recently foam rubber mats have become popular because of the ease with which they may be handled. These mats come in all sizes and the sections may be zipped together to form larger areas for participation. The smaller sections may be easily stored in small areas.

Record Players. Record players are delicate instruments and should be carefully handled and stored. Figure 10–8

Figure 10–8. Locally constructed cabinets designed to protect valuable equipment are both practical and functional. The photographs above show how a cabinet may be used to store a record player and also how it may be used in the class.

shows a record cabinet that has been found satisfactory for the protection of record players. The cabinet is constructed on rollers and may be trans- ported from the storage room to the gymnasium. While the record is being played, the top can be closed to prevent balls or other objects from falling on it.

REFERENCES

1. Edward F. Voltmer and Arthur A. Esslinger: *The Organization and Administration of Physical Education*, 4th ed. New York: Appleton-Century-Crofts, 1967, p. 391.
2. *Equipment and Supplies for Athletics, Physical Education and Recreation.* Chicago: The Athletic Institute, 1960, p. 65.
3. Charles W. Foster (ed): *Educational Resources Management Systems.* Chicago: Association of School Business Officials, 1972.
4. Harry Hartley: *Educational Planning—Programming—Budgeting: A Systems Approach.* Englewood Cliffs, N. J.: Prentice-Hall, Inc., 1968, p. 76.

SUGGESTED READINGS

Anderson, Lester W., and Lauren A. Van Dyke: *Secondary School Administration,* 2nd ed. Boston: Houghton Mifflin Co., 1972.
Equipment and Supplies for Athletics, Physical Education and Recreation. Chicago: The Athletic Institute, 1960.
Forsythe, Charles E., and Irvin A. Keller: *Administration of High School Athletics.* Englewood Cliffs, N. J.: Prentice-Hall, Inc., 1972.
How to Budget, Select and Order Athletic Equipment. Chicago: Merchandise Mart Athletic Goods Manufacturers Association, 1962.

III
ADMINISTRATION OF CONTINUING AND RELATED PROGRAMS

CHAPTER ELEVEN

Planning School Health Programs

Current literature on the critical health problems of youth indicates that the need for health programs in the nation's schools is becoming increasingly more important. The three major problems are nutrition, drugs (including alcohol), and venereal disease. Following these in close order are promiscuity (which leads to illegitimacy and abortions), smoking, diseases of the circulatory system, cancer, degenerative diseases, and accidents. The current apathy toward health education should be replaced with a strong plan of action for emphasizing the need for good health programs in the schools.

Although health and physical education are administered separately in many teacher education institutions, this is not the predominant pattern in the schools of America. Most schools in the United States administer health education and physical education together, under one administrative head. The advantages and disadvantages of the combined program and the need for teachers and adminis-

273

trators to understand why this situation exists will be discussed in this chapter.

The total school health program involves, to some degree, the services of every person in the school. In some instances the service may be indirect, such as the custodian's efforts, which are concerned with keeping the building clean. The principal, on the other hand, makes a direct contribution by virtue of supervising the health and safety of everyone in the school.

The responsibility for total health in the modern era of technology is too complex to be delegated to any one person or group. Rapidly changing environmental and other living conditions, continued scientific discoveries in medicine and science, and the explorations of outer space are a few of the facets of modern living that affect the health of all people. If health education is to keep pace with these changes, progressive steps must be initiated to provide all people with factual information and services necessary for the maintenance of optimal good health. This requires a coordinated effort by the home, the school, and the community. Figure 11–1 illustrates an arrangement for organizing groups concerned with the total school health program.

The school health program plays an enormous role in setting the tone of the nation's health for years to come, and thus planning the program presents an important challenge for all concerned. The magnitude of this challenge necessitates the establishment of specific procedures for conducting the planning. The first step should be the preparation of an organizational outline showing the divisions of the total health program and the groups and functions that make up each division. Such an organizational plan is shown on the following pages.

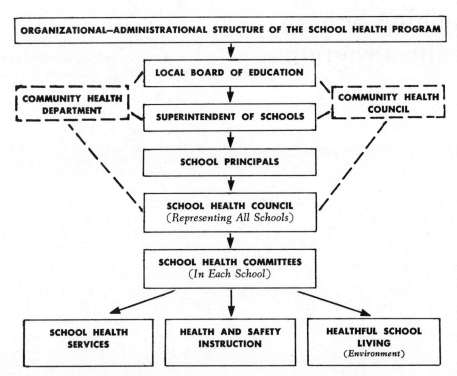

Figure 11–1. Organizational-administrational structure of the school health program. *Note:* The solid lines denote direct authority and the dotted lines indicate indirect authority. (From Smolensky and Bonvechio: *Principles of School Health.* Boston: D. C. Heath & Co., 1966.)

ORGANIZATION OF THE SCHOOL HEALTH PROGRAM

It is generally accepted that the total school health program involves three large divisions: (1) health education, (2) health services, and (3) a healthful school environment. Each of these divisions, with the groups and functions involved, is shown in an outline developed by the Department of Health, Education and Welfare.

The outline shows that parents are basically responsible for the health of their children and that many community groups, along with the schools and the public health department, also have significant responsibilities. Finally, it is strongly recommended that all groups concerned recognize fundamental objectives and share appropriate responsibilities in improving local health programs.

Included in the Department's report are discussions of various areas of concern in health education, such as (1) the students' health instruction, (2) the school staff, (3) parental and community involvement.

In the school environment section of the outline are questions pertaining to (1) the emotional climate of the school, (2) the health aspects of administrative policies and practices, (3) the maintenance of buildings and grounds, (4) prevention of accidents, and (5) food services.

The outline also includes a detailed section on various problems in health services, such as (1) identification of health needs and resources, (2) appropriate selection and use of services and personnel, (3) coordination of programs and services, (4) provision for adequate health facilities, equipment, and supplies, (5) communicable disease control, (6) health appraisal and follow-up activities, (7) management of emergency illness and injury, (8) handicapped children, and (9) maintenance of health of school personnel.[1]

As can be seen from the previous discussion, school health programs involve so many people and departments that, in order to provide direction and supervision for the program, specific areas of responsibility must be determined. The efforts of the various individuals and groups involved in administering school health programs must be coordinated to insure smooth operation of the programs.

STATE CONTROL

The administration of the total health program is usually the joint responsibility of the state board of education and the department of health. The board of education is responsible for health education and works closely with the department of health, which is responsible for health services. This arrangement is consistent with the belief that each department is a specialist in its own area. The health of children and youth can best be served when the expertise of both departments is available. Under this plan, the responsibility for the certification of teachers, the planning of workshops, the development of curriculum guides, the allocation of funds, and policy making belongs to the board of education.

LOCAL CONTROL

The evolution of school health programs has resulted in three types of administrative control: (1) health department, (2) board of education, and (3) joint responsibility of the board of education and health department. Each type of control has its advantages. Control by the health department is probably the least desirable of the three, since the control of health instruction should be delegated to those individuals who are qualified and certified to teach—the health teachers. Administrative control of health programs by the board of education is the most prevalent in the nation's schools. The criticism of this plan is the secondary role assigned to health services, an important aspect of the health program. Joint control by the board of education and the department of health has several advantages:

1. Health instruction and health services have equal status.

2. Health department personnel may serve as consultants in the instructional program.

3. Joint responsibility provides greater access to community resources.

4. Duplication of facilities, personnel, and effort may be avoided.

5. Valuable advice may be available from medical authorities in the development of curriculum content.

6. Health instruction may be administered by educators.

7. The health department has supervision of such areas as sanitation and examinations, which are important for the health of children and adults.

Although many people are involved with planning and organizing school health programs, establishing administrative responsibility for these programs is essential if the program is to be effective.

A report by the National Education Association and the American Medical Association disclosed that administration of the school health program should be the responsibility of the local school board and the superintendent of schools.[2] Through these administrative levels, responsibilities are delegated to others in the system who are more directly involved in the health program. Responsibilities for the various levels of involvement are presented in the following paragraphs.

The Board of Education

The local school board has the legal responsibility for administering all health programs in the schools. It is primarily a policy-making body with broad powers granted by the state. The responsibilities of the local school board include the approval of written policies to improve and give direction to the all-school programs, the appropriation of funds for the operation of the school system, the selection of the superintendent of schools, and the development of good school-community relations. The board of education, although usually elected, may be appointed by the city council, by county commissioners, or by the city manager. The

board of education works closely with the superintendent, who is its chief executive officer.

The Community Health Council

The community health council is a desirable facet of the total health program. It provides a medium for bringing together teachers, parents, and medical groups to assist with the operation of the school health program. The establishment of a community health council not only serves as an instrument for interpreting the school health program but can also be of real help in initiating new and sensitive programs, such as family life education. The following are suggested criteria for the organization and operation of such a council:

1. The purposes, objectives, and policies of the council should be stated clearly and reviewed periodically.

2. The council should include representation from the school administration (superintendent or his administrative representative); parents; the school staff; the health department; medical, dental, and nursing societies; and community agencies with programs related to personal and community health. The organization should remain flexible.

3. Each group should be given an opportunity to select its own representatives. Officers should be elected by the council for a specified term.

4. The council should meet regularly with a prepared agenda.

5. Each group should be permitted to present any health problems of school children for council consideration. Particular attention should be given to problems requiring joint action by the schools and other community agencies and to those that involve participation by two or more professional groups.

6. Use should be made of subcommittees, but these should relate in function to the council as a whole.

7. Although long-term projects are necessary and appropriate, projects which can be completed successfully in a short period of time should not be neglected.

8. Publicity should be given throughout the community to the council's progress and accomplishments.

9. Emphasis should be placed on solving

pertinent problems such as developing written emergency procedures, rather than on organization or on routine procedures.

10. All members of the council should be involved in planning, recommending, and evaluating programs.[3]

The Superintendent

Not only is the superintendent the executive officer of the school board but he is also the educational leader of the school system. Since his responsibilities are so complex and demand so much time, he must delegate many of them to selected individuals who will assist with the operation of the school system. Although he may delegate many duties in the area of school health, he is responsible for:

1. Administering and coordinating the three divisions of the total school health program: health education, health services, and school environment.
2. Cooperating with the state board of education in maintaining established guidelines, both legal and suggested.
3. Developing written guides and policies for the school health program.
4. Preparing the budget and including in it appropriate funds for personnel, equipment, supplies, teaching stations, and other items necessary for implementing the program in school health.
5. Cooperating with the local health department in whatever responsibilities they may have regarding the school health program.
6. Providing for continuous evaluation of the total school health program.
7. Developing a dynamic school-community relations program for acquainting the public with the purposes of school health.
8. Maintaining programs for teacher growth through in-service programs and workshops.

The Health Coordinator

Some cities and districts delegate a qualified individual from the superintendent's office to be responsible for coordinating the total health program.

His duties include (1) supervising health education, health services, and the school environment; (2) maximizing the use of available community resources such as the health department, voluntary agencies, and civic clubs; (3) evaluating the total program; (4) assisting in the development of health education curriculum materials.

The Director or Supervisor

In many places one person is selected from the central office to supervise health education. His duties may also involve the supervision of physical education, but not health services and school environment. The director or supervisor is a specialist in health instruction. He coordinates the city-wide program and is responsible for improving instruction and providing expert supervision in health education. He is responsible for (1) developing city-wide curriculum guidebooks; (2) assisting the evaluation of teachers; (3) assisting in the selection of teachers; (4) developing a balanced program of instruction; (5) apprising teachers of current trends and instructional aids in health education; and (6) assisting teachers in determining student needs and interests.

SCHOOL LEVEL

Many people are responsible for implementing the health program on the school level. However, the success of the program depends on the principal, the health council, the teacher, and certain other individuals discussed in the following paragraphs.

Coordinated effort is, of course, important for the total health program. But the total effort can be effective only when the particular duties of each person responsible for health education have been enumerated.

The Principal

With the exception of the superintendent, the principal probably has more responsibility in the area of school health than anyone else. He supervises construction of the schedule, cooperates in employing teachers, promotes in-service programs, emphasizes and de-emphasizes subjects in the curriculum, prepares budget requests, and serves as the chief supervisor of all subjects. To a large degree, his efforts set the tone for the total health program in his school.

The School Health Council

The school health council, if properly organized and operated, may serve as an invaluable aid to the individual school program. The council should be composed of representatives from each department in the school that has a contribution to make toward the health of the students and the school personnel. One of the important functions of the council is to coordinate the various health services and health environment functions in order to prevent overlapping in health education. Other functions of the council are to discover any health problems that may exist in the school and to make recommendations to correct these problems, to assist in the development of curriculum guides, to make recommendations for improving the health of school personnel, to assist in developing plans for the prevention of accidents in the school and on the playground, and to serve as a coordinating agency for the total school health program, including health services.

The Classroom Teacher

The teacher is the most important person in the school health program. Combining health knowledge with interest, he assists students with their health problems by relating their needs and interests to current scientific facts. Without the dedicated and purposeful efforts of the teacher, the health program cannot be effective. The good classroom teacher:

1. Maintains constant interest in the problems of his students and assists them in solving these problems through teaching and counseling.

2. Keeps abreast of current developments in health and constantly reviews scientific materials for new discoveries and approaches in health education.
3. Provides initiative in developing sound instructional programs in the school and throughout the city.
4. Works with curriculum-planning groups.
5. Works cooperatively with other individuals, such as the doctor, nurse, counselor, custodian, and parents, to improve the health of students.
6. Establishes communication with community agencies and seeks their assistance in conducting the health instruction program.
7. Practices emergency health care and first aid.
8. Promotes public relations through available media.
9. Maintains quality instruction in his classes, particularly on the elementary level.
10. Makes observations of student health, recommends follow-up and referrals, and provides for programs for the handicapped.
11. Maintains personal good health, both physical and emotional.

In addition to the general responsibilities of the teacher, more specific assignments are included at the various growth and development levels of the child. In the elementary school, all teachers have responsibilities in screening tests, making daily observations of students' health status, providing follow-up services, and planning health education programs.

At the secondary level, the responsibility is diminished, since teachers spend so little time with students. However, they should be constantly observant of changing behavior patterns of students and should be available for guidance in the health problems of adolescents. One of the more pressing areas is the drug scene that exists throughout the schools of America. All teachers have a significant role in detecting drug users and taking recommended steps for alleviating the problem.

Other Individuals with Responsibilities

There are other individuals in auxiliary services of the school who render valuable contributions to the total health program. Social workers, guidance counselors, psychologists, specialists in speech and hearing, dieticians, lunchroom managers, nurses, and physicians are but a few of the many people who make daily and sometimes unnoticed contributions to the total health of children. Their duties are specifically outlined for the position they fill, but all of them have the responsibility of cooperating with school health personnel.

In addition to the importance of efficient administration, organizational procedures are also basic for effective implementation of the total school health program. The organization of the three divisions — health education, health services, and healthful school environment — will be discussed in the remainder of the chapter.

ORGANIZATION OF HEALTH EDUCATION

The Need for Health Education

Health has been a basic objective of education for over 50 years. As early as 1918 the Commission on the Reorganization of Secondary Education published the Seven Cardinal Principles of Education. Health was listed first. The Commission stated that:

The secondary school should, therefore, provide health instruction, inculcate health habits, organize an effective program of physical activities, regard health needs in planning work and play, and cooperate with home and community in safeguarding and promoting health interests.[4]

These principles served as guidelines in secondary education for many years. However, problems developing during World War II necessitated a re-evaluation of the purposes of education, and in 1944 a study was made by the Educational Policies Commission of the National Education Association. Health was again recognized as an important objective, and the Commission stated that "All youth need to develop and maintain good health and physical fitness."[5]

The most comprehensive study of secondary education since the Cardinal Principles of 1918 was made in 1973 by the National Commission on the Reform of Secondary Education. The report, *The Reform of Secondary Education,* will probably replace the Seven Cardinal Principles as the blueprint of secondary education for the 21st century. It states that "health is the goal of both Commissions, but while the earlier one stressed physical fitness, today's Commission is concerned with a student's mental and emotional needs and adjustment to the unprecedented acceleration of change."[6]

When the health problems of the young people of our nation are studied, the importance of health education cannot be minimized. The damage that has been done to the health of children by drugs, venereal disease, and poor nutrition has long since passed epidemic levels.

The need for health instruction has been clearly revealed by the startling findings of the School Health Education Study. The study represents 1101 elementary schools involving 529,656 students, and 359 secondary schools with an enrollment of 311,176 students. The report was developed around four concerns: (1) health education practices in the public schools, (2) instructional programs, (3) health behavior of students in the public schools, and (4) teaching and scheduling practices.

Prevailing health education practices were determined by questionnaires sent to school administrators. The data revealed the status of instruction among the districts in such items as content and variation of area emphasis, health topics, and teaching and scheduling practices.

Teachers and administrators listed many problems which they face in conducting effective programs in health instruction. These problems include:

1. Failure of the home to encourage practice of health habits learned in school.
2. Ineffectiveness of instructional methods.
3. Parental and community resistance to certain health topics.
4. Insufficient time in the school day for health instruction.

5. Lack of coordination of the health education program throughout the school grades.

6. Inadequate professional preparation of staff.

7. Disinterest on the part of some teachers assigned to health teaching.

8. Failure of parents to follow up on needed and recommended health services for children.

9. Indifference toward, and hence lack of support for, health education on the part of some teachers, parents, administrators, health officers, and other members of the community.

10. Neglect of the health education course when combined with physical education.

11. Inadequate facilities and instructional materials.

12. Student indifference to health education.

13. Lack of specialized supervisory and consultative services.

An appalling lack of health knowledge and attitudes was revealed when the results of the study were compiled. The findings of the study were based on results in four major categories: (1) differences on scores between sexes and among district groups, (2) strengths and weaknesses on health content areas, (3) subtest scores of 9th-grade students, and (4) health misconceptions of students. The misconceptions are the most startling part of the study, since they underscore the necessity for careful planning and implementation of health education in the nation's schools.

The seriousness of the teaching and scheduling problems is reflected in the results of the study, which are summarized in the statement that "there certainly are a majority of situations where health instruction is virtually nonexistent, or where prevailing practices can be legitimately challenged."[7]

Another study showing the inadequacy of existing health education programs was conducted in the Grand Rapids-Kent County School District, Michigan. The study showed inadequacies in (1) acceptance of health as an area of instruction, (2) health books and guides, (3) staff development programs in health education, (4) health rooms, and (5) supervision.[8]

Some of the factors that have contrib-uted to the apathy for health instruction are (1) disinterested teachers, (2) failure of administrators to recognize the need for health education, (3) inadequate college preparatory courses, and (4) disinterested students.

Defining Health Education

A large number of organizations and health education leaders have defined health education. Probably the most comprehensive definition was developed by the Joint Committee on Health Education Terminology in 1972. The committee defined health education as a process with intellectual, psychological, and social dimensions relating to activities which increase the abilities of people to make informed decisions affecting their personal, family, and community well-being. This process, based on scientific principles, facilitates learning and behavioral change in both health personnel and consumers, including children and youth.[9]

The Aim of Health Education

The aim of health education is to provide children with health knowledge that will conserve and improve their present health, and to assist them in developing attitudes and practices that will increase their potential for health in the years ahead. Figure 11-2 describes the aims of the sophisticated approach to optimal health of the New York State health education program.

Organizing the Curriculum in Health Education

A careful selection of content for health education is extremely important. Random selection of health topics based on the whims of the teacher is likely to be a waste of time. Topics taught in health education should be selected through the use of valid criteria that are scientifically sound and that reflect the needs and interests of students.

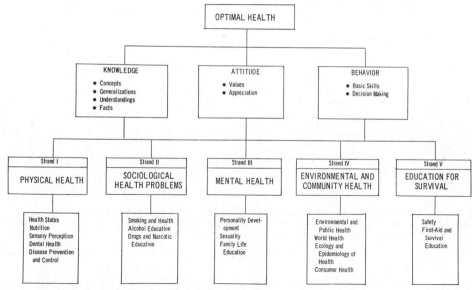

Figure 11–2. Content and basic aims of the New York State Health Education Program. (From Sinacore: New York State Program in Health Sciences, reprinted from the Bulletin of the National Association of Secondary School Principals, March, 1968.)

Several procedures have been used to select the topics to be taught in health education. In many places, committees are appointed to compile material gathered from guides and textbooks. The teachers may also rely on current texts in health education. Sometimes specialists in medicine, psychology, or sociology are asked to suggest topics that they consider important. More than any other subject in the curriculum, health education should be based on the interests and needs of students and on the conditions existing in the community. The following studies illustrate efforts that have been made to develop content based on the interests and needs of students.

The South Carolina Study. In 1971 a statewide evaluation of health education was made in South Carolina. Thirty-one schools were involved and information was obtained through questionnaires and personal interviews. Finding the resources used for curriculum development was an important part of the study. It is interesting to note that the needs and interests of students as a resource tool ranked second, as shown in Figure 11–4. Another part of the study was concerned with determining the

content areas. Figure 11–5 presents, in order of priority, the areas in grades K–12 in which 50 per cent or more of the respondents placed minor or major emphasis.

One unique feature of the study was the emphasis placed on determining

Figure 11–3. Health instruction should have top priority in the schools of America. (Courtesy of Norfolk Public Schools, Norfolk, Virginia.)

	GRADES	
	K-8 (%)	9-12 (%)
State Curriculum Guides	7	8
Local Curriculum Guides	3	6
Individual Teacher Decisions	19	27
Textbooks	35	17
Needs and Interests of Students	28	20
Student-Teacher Planning	4	11
Pretest of Students	0	8
Local Community Influence	4	2

Figure 11-4. Resources used in health education curriculum development. (From Newman, Ian M., and Cyrus Mayshark: "Health Education Planning and Community Perceptions of Local Health Problems." *Journal of School Health,* September, 1973, p. 459.)

community health problems. Figure 11-6 lists the rank order of the health problems of the community as perceived by the citizens. As Figures 11-4 and 11-5 are studied, it becomes obvious that the needs and interests revealed by the school respondents do not coincide with the community health problems perceived by the citizens.

Several questions may be raised as the areas of concern listed by the commu-

nity are compared with the subjects actually taught. Do young people know enough to determine what they need? Since the school respondents did not reflect the community needs in their curriculum, how did they determine areas of instruction? For example, the community felt that heart disease was a major health problem, yet the school people did not even recognize it. Illegitimacy, a major social problem throughout the na-

Content Area	Grades									
	K-3	4	5	6	7	8	9	10	11	12
Accidents	X	X	X	X	-	0	0	0	0	0
Alcohol	-	-	0	0	X	X	0	0	0	0
Communicable Disease	0	0	0	0	0	0	0	0	0	0
Community Health	-	-	0	0	0	0	-	-	-	-
Consumer Health	-	-	-	-	-	-	-	-	0	0
Dental Health	X	X	0	0	0	0	0	0	0	0
Drugs and Narcotics	-	-	0	0	X	X	X	X	X	X
Environmental Health	-	0	0	0	0	X	0	0	0	0
Exercise and Relaxation	X	X	X	X	X	X	0	0	0	0
Family Life Education	-	0	-	0	0	0	0	0	X	X
Nutrition	X	X	X	X	X	X	X	X	X	X
Personal Health	0	0	0	0	X	X	X	0	X	X
Venereal Disease	-	-	-	-	X	-	0	0	0	X
Vision and Hearing	X	X	X	0	X	0	0	0	0	0

X: Fifty percent or more of the respondents indicated that this subject matter area received major instructional emphasis.

0: Fifty percent or more of the respondents indicated that this subject matter area received moderate emphasis.

-: Less than fifty percent of the respondents indicated neither major nor moderate emphasis for these subject matter areas.

Figure 11-5. Curriculum priorities in Grades K-12. (From Newman, Ian M., and Cyrus Mayshark: "Health Education Planning and Community Perceptions of Local Health Problems." *Journal of School Health,* September, 1973, p. 459.)

PROBLEM	
Heart Disease	3.63
Illegitimacy	3.51
Venereal Diseases	3.40
Drug Abuse	3.38
Cancer	3.37
Accidents	3.31
Alcoholism	3.25
Unemployment	3.10
Nutrition	3.07
Urban Renewal	3.03
Water Pollution	3.02
Social Welfare for Elderly	2.98
Consumer Protection	2.88
Availability of Health Services	2.78
Air Pollution	2.67
Infant Mortality	2.56

*The rating scale ranged from five (extremely severe problems) to one (no problem).

Figure 11–6. Rank order of significant community health problems as perceived by local citizens. From Newman, Ian M., and Cyrus Mayshark: "Health Education Planning and Cummunity Perceptions of Local Health Problems." *Journal of School Health,* September, 1973, p. 460.)

tion, did not seem to concern the schools.

The conclusion drawn by the committee was that, as taught in South Carolina, health education is far removed from community needs and students are not learning health facts at a desirable level.[10]

The study substantiates the feeling of many people that school people and students alone should not determine the health education content. It also points to the need for more interaction between the schools and the community and the need for community health councils to assist educators in matching student interests with community needs.

West Virginia Study. Because of the inadequacy of health education, the West Virginia State Department conducted an inventory of student health interests during January, 1970. The inventory was the first step in the development of a curriculum in health education for the state. Five county systems were selected on the basis of socio-economic variables. Four groups of people (counselors, nurses, sophomore and senior students, and parents) were selected within each county to participate in the study. Students completed a Health Education Inventory consisting of 125 health statements in which each student indicated whether he had no interest, low interest, medium interest, or high interest in the area. Parents completed a Health Needs Inventory. Their reaction to the health needs of their children was requested on the same areas. Figure 11–7 shows the health interests of students and the health needs that parents, nurses, and counselors feel are important for students. Some conclusions that were drawn from the study are:

1. There was a clear and significant difference between the health interests of boys and those of girls.
2. The responses of parents concerning health needs were generally similar in all five counties.
3. The responses by school counselors and nurses gave somewhat different results.
4. The study showed that there are health areas in health education which have a high interest for students as well as a high priority among parents, counselors, and nurses.
5. There was a significant difference between the health interests of students and the needs parents, counselors and nurses felt should have priority.[11]

R. O.	Variables	HEALTH INTERESTS		R. O.	Variables	HEALTH NEEDS
		Boys	Girls			Parents, Counselors, Nurses
1	Family Health	29.1	32.5	1	Drugs & Narcotics	34.4
2	Mental Health	28.3	31.8	2	Mental Health	32.5
3	Personal Grooming	27.8	31.5	3	Family Health	32.0
4	Drugs & Narcotics	27.9	3.14	4	Safety Education	31.4
5	Com. & Prev. Dis.	28.3	30.5	5	Alcohol	30.2
6	Safety Education	28.3	30.3	6	Weight Control	29.8
7	Weight Control	27.7	30.6	7	Com. & Prev. Dis.	29.8
8	S. & F. Human Body	27.9	29.8	8	Smoking	29.7
9	Consumer Health	27.4	29.4	9	Consumer Helath	28.8
10	Alcohol	27.2	28.9	10	Community Health	28.8
11	Community Health	27.1	28,4	11	Personal Grooming	28.7
12	Dental Health	27.2	28.3	12	S. & F. Human Body	28.6
13	Nutrition	27.1	28.2	'13	Nutrition	27.9
14	Smoking	26.9	27.7	14	Dental Health	27.4
	Group Means	27.7	29.9		Group Means	30.0
	Number in Group	1507	1656		Number in Group	1584

a/ numbers assessed to responses in Inventories
10.0 = no interest
20.0 = low interest
30.0 = medium interest
40.0 = high interest

Figure 11–7. Rank order and means for health interests and needs of West Virginia High School students. (From Ransdell, Les C.: "An Analysis of the Health Interests and Needs of West Virginia High School Students." *Journal of School Health,* October, 1972, p. 478.)

Other Sources for Selecting Content. In addition to the selection of activities based on needs and interests, other sources for the selection of content are available. These sources usually consist of specialists and committees who, through study and research, develop guides that are helpful in the organization of the curriculum and health education. Such a curriculum may be found in Figure 11–8, which shows the areas of instruction for grades K–12. These areas are planned sequentially.

Once areas of instruction have been determined, administrative action has to be taken regarding the inclusion of health education in the total school program. A careful evaluation of the approaches available for presenting health education is essential for effective administration.

HEALTH EDUCATION IN THE ORGANIZATIONAL FRAMEWORK

Just as administrators have experimented with organizational practices in academic subjects, they have also tried to find better plans for including health education in the organizational framework. Several approaches generally used for placing health education in the curriculum are (1) integration, (2) correlation, and (3) the separate course, or block schedule. Figure 11–9 provides one overview of these approaches.

Integration

Integration is the process of fusing the entire health content with other subjects or broad areas of learning. In this plan,

Suggested Topics	Grade Emphasis			
	K-3	4-6	Junior High	Senior High
Personal Cleanliness and Appearance	X	X	Omit	Omit
Physical Activity, Sleep, Rest and Relaxation	X	X	X	Omit
Nutrition and Growth	X	X	X	Omit
Dental Health	X	X	X	Omit
Body Structure and Operation (including the senses and skin)	X	X	X	Omit
Prevention and Control of Disease	X	X	X	Omit
Safety and First Aid	X	X	X	Omit
Mental Health	X	X	X	X
Sex and Family Living Education	X	X	X	X
Environmental and Community Health	X	X	X	X
Alcohol, Drugs and Tobacco	Omit	X	X	X
Consumer Health	Omit	X	X	X
World Health	Omit	Omit	Omit	X
Health Careers	Omit	Omit	X	X

Figure 11–8. Suggested areas of instruction by grades in health education. (From Willgoose, Carl E. "Saving the Curriculum in Health Education." *Journal of School Health,* March, 1973, p. 191.)

health education loses its identity and depends upon its incidental appearance in other broad areas of instruction. This approach is most prevalent in the elementary school program.

The weakness of this plan is that either health instruction may be excluded completely or, if it is included, many important topics and problems may be omitted in favor of other material more germane to the subject into which the health areas have been integrated. However, there are some everyday health problems of young children that may be successfully integrated in daily instruction by having the teacher constantly remind children of the values of cleanliness, the various procedures necessary for disease control, the many factors of safety around the school, and the importance of eating proper foods. Recent research has disclosed that integration on the secondary level is an unsatisfactory approach for health instruction.

Correlation

Correlation is an approach that attempts to associate health areas with other subjects by utilizing the natural relationships that exist between the two

areas without destroying the identity of either. This approach provides for instruction time in science, social studies, and other subjects for health areas that are related to these subjects. Although this approach offers a better opportunity for health instruction than integration, it has not proved to be successful. The School Health Education Study showed that a separate health course in health education was preferable to either integration or correlation in secondary schools.

The Separate Health Course

Direct instruction through a separate health course has been thought by many to be the most desirable approach for presenting health instruction. The School Health Education Study focuses attention specifically on the need for this approach.[12] The separate health course with direct instruction has many advantages in both elementary and secondary schools. When health education is given a definite place in the school curriculum, all students are assured of instruction in all areas of health education. The program maintains dignity and respectability, since credit for successful com-

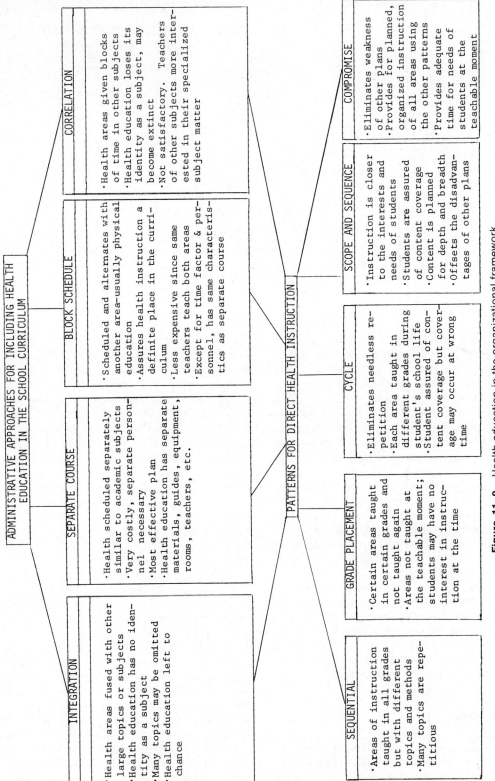

ADMINISTRATIVE APPROACHES FOR INCLUDING HEALTH EDUCATION IN THE SCHOOL CURRICULUM

INTEGRATION
·Health areas fused with other large topics or subjects
·Health education has no identity as a subject
·Many topics may be omitted
·Health education left to chance

SEPARATE COURSE
·Health scheduled separately similar to academic subjects
·Very costly, separate personnel necessary
·Most effective plan
·Health education has separate materials, guides, equipment, rooms, teachers, etc.

BLOCK SCHEDULE
·Scheduled and alternates with another area—usually physical education
·Assures health instruction a definite place in the curriculum
·Less expensive since same teachers teach both areas
·Except for time factor & personnel, has same characteristics as separate course

CORRELATION
·Health areas given blocks of time in other subjects
·Health education loses its identity as a subject, may become extinct
·Not satisfactory. Teachers of other subjects more interested in their specialized subject matter

PATTERNS FOR DIRECT HEALTH INSTRUCTION

SEQUENTIAL
·Areas of instruction taught in all grades but with different topics and methods
·Many topics are repetitious

GRADE PLACEMENT
·Certain areas taught in certain grades and not taught again
·Areas not taught at the teachable moment; students may have no interest in instruction at the time

CYCLE
·Eliminates needless repetition
·Each area taught in different grades during student's school life
·Student assured of content coverage but coverage may occur at wrong time

SCOPE AND SEQUENCE
·Instruction is closer to the interests and needs of students
·Students are assured of content coverage
·Content is planned for depth and breadth
·Offsets the disadvantages of other plans

COMPROMISE
·Eliminates weakness of other plans
·Provides for planned, organized instruction of all areas using the other patterns
·Provides adequate time for needs of students at the teachable moment

Figure 11–9. Health education in the organizational framework.

pletion may be acquired toward graduation, and guides and texts devoted exclusively to the subject may be used. The success of the program does not depend on permissiveness, as in the integrated approach, nor on the cursory manner of presentation offered by the correlation plan. When teachers of health education are provided with classrooms, teaching guides, and other aids, they will be inclined to have as much interest and satisfaction resulting from their efforts as other classroom teachers do.

The separate course involves daily scheduling of health education. The most desirable arrangement is to schedule health education each year from grades K to 12. Compromise arrangements have been made to schedule health education for one semester or year in the junior high school and one semester or year in the senior high school. The basic disadvantage of the arrangement is the intermittent manner in which health teaching is offered. Health instruction is a continuous need throughout one's whole life. Who is sufficiently knowledgeable to say that health instruction can be concentrated in one year and cease after that? What happens in the years prior to or after the one year of instruction? The rapid advances of scientific technology and the findings in health research necessitate the inclusion of health instruction in the curriculum every day throughout the school years and into the post-school years.

While the separate health course is shown to be the most effective approach for including health education in the total curriculum, the organizational difficulties encountered are sometimes overwhelming. This is true in both the elementary and secondary school programs. There are usually only six or seven periods in the school day. Most of these periods are usually reserved on the secondary level for subjects that are required for college entrance, such as English, mathematics, science, and languages. In many schools physical education is required. These requirements present scheduling problems that prevent the inclusion of other areas of in-

struction in the curriculum as separate courses. Competition with other subjects for time in the school program presents difficulties for health education—it must either compromise or be excluded entirely. The compromise provides several alternatives. Health instruction may be either integrated, correlated, or offered as a part of a block program; the last is the most prevalent approach for scheduling health education.

The Block Approach

The block approach assures health education a place in the program by scheduling it with physical education. In this plan, health education alternates with physical education; this alternating arrangement is prevalent throughout the country. The School Health Education Study showed:

In all three districts, two-thirds or more of the health classes in grades 7, 8, and 9, and 90 per cent or more in 10, 11, and 12, in all districts were taught by the teacher with a combined major in health and physical education, or with specialization in physical education only.[13]

Although some educators voice criticisms of this combination, the fact remains that the majority of programs in the country are organized this way and will probably remain so for many years.

The secondary curriculum today has expanded to such an extent that it is becoming increasingly difficult to allot time for both required and elective subjects. Problems of scheduling and providing time for the existing areas are extremely difficult, and administrators are looking for plans to assist them in their efforts.

The combination of health education and physical education, broadly interpreted, is a form of block scheduling, and provides for direct instruction in both areas. Block-time scheduling for various subjects is not unusual, particularly in the junior high school. In many instances, areas that are similar in content and that were formerly taught as separate subjects have been combined into a single nucleus of instruction. One teacher is usually assigned to teach during the entire block of time.

There is much in the literature to support block scheduling of health education and physical education. Bossing and Cramer offer several reasons for advocating the block program:

1. The young students in each grade are assured specially prepared men teachers for boys and women teachers for girls in physical fitness, recreation, and health science—persons who are knowledgeable about the basic physiological and hygienic facts which are so often of special concern to the early adolescent and can be transmitted *without difficult scheduling problems.* When health teaching is scheduled separately, too often the instruction is only incidentally presented in a short homeroom period.

2. Since health instruction is given in regular classrooms two days per week, or in an equivalent block-of-time class, more *teaching space* is available for physical fitness in gymnasiums, auxiliary playrooms, and swimming pools. Thus, costly building space for teaching physical fitness and recreation becomes less of a problem.

3. By combining health and physical fitness instruction into one regular class period, the maximum enrollment of fifty students in physical fitness classes is automatically reduced to *thirty* or *thirty-five,* which correlates with maximum per-class enrollments of other subject areas. This reduction in class size markedly improves the quality of instruction and guidance.

4. With the *same* teachers for health and safety education and physical fitness, including recreation, the teachers are better able to accurately perceive their students' assets, needs, and liabilities. They can thus devise activities suited to the maturity and physical capacities of each student, and give teaching and learning a closer and more meaningful association.

5. Mills reported that virtually all separate health teachers also taught other courses. Since health and physical fitness are more interdependent than other curriculum areas and combined scheduling is more convenient, it is obvious why they are integrated in many junior high schools.

6. Collaboration between parent and teacher is often facilitated when boys relate to a man teacher and girls to a woman teacher in a combined health and physical fitness unity. This is important in the area of sex education. The combined structure also lends itself to easy shifting to coeducational classes for special instruction in folk dancing, square dancing, and social dancing, and is useful for the presentation of school programs and award assemblies.[14]

The chief criticism of the plan is that many teachers of physical education are not interested in or qualified to teach health education. The fact remains, however, that in many sections of the country physical education teachers teach health education as well, and it is the responsibility of the teacher-training institutions to prepare them for this task. Mayshark and Foster showed that of the 500 colleges preparing teachers in physical education in the United States, probably 75 properly prepare them in both areas. The authors discussed a study, presented before the research council of the American School Health Association, that showed that 90 per cent of the direct health instruction in the schools of Indiana was conducted by teachers with majors in both fields. The study also showed that the personal qualities and competencies of the teachers were satisfactory, and, with greater administrative support, a more effective program of instruction would be attained.[15]

It is generally agreed that the best plan for including health instruction in the curriculum is to organize it on a daily separate basis. However, this arrangement has been recommended for many years, and its adoption in the foreseeable future seems unlikely. In the meantime, it is important to examine plans to incorporate health instruction in physical education instruction.

The block program, which combines the two areas into a nucleus of instruction, provides for direct health education. The block arrangement itself is largely an administrative device. The actual instruction in health education within the block is direct, since it is conducted in a classroom and all the materials and tools necessary for direct instruction are available. The health instruction is not correlated or integrated with any other subject. The compromise feature of the plan necessitates the sharing of time with physical education, which is justifiable on the basis of the health objective of the total program. The following plans are generally used for combining physical education and health education.

The Three-Two Plan. The three-two plan allocates two periods to physical education and two periods to health education each week. The fifth period may be scheduled for coeducation or some other form of physical education activity. The plan may also operate on an alternating basis, with physical education scheduled one day and health education the other. The disadvantage of the three-two plan is the erratic way in which health education and physical education would be studied. There is rarely sufficient time to complete a unit of instruction in either area. Figure 11–10 describes the variations of the three-two plan.

The Three-Three Plan. In the three-three plan, three solid weeks are allotted to health education and three weeks to physical education. Although there may be sufficient time for instruction in both areas, physical education generally suffers, since instruction in some seasonal activities may be missed entirely.

The Six-Six Plan. The six-six plan provides for six continuous weeks of health instruction and six continuous weeks of physical education instruction. This plan has the same weakness as the preceding plan. The more continuous time allotted each area, the more seasonal activities missed in physical education.

The Nine-Nine Plan. This plan is similar to the six-six plan. Nine continuous weeks of instruction are allocated to health education and the same for physical education.

The Semester or Yearly Plan. In the semester or yearly plan, physical education instruction and health education alternate on a semester or yearly basis. The advantages for health instruction are obvious, but also obvious is the fact that students miss many months of time from physical education instruction. Another disadvantage of this plan is that large spans of time elapse between the health instruction blocks. It was pointed out earlier that health instruction should be a daily procedure. When weeks or even months elapse without instruction, the health needs of children cannot be met.

The Alternate-Week Plan. The alternate-week plan provides for instruction in both health education and physical education on alternate weeks. This plan evolved after experimentation with other plans of combining health education and physical education in a single block of instructional time. The experimentation included the other plans described above and proved rather conclusively that these plans were unsatisfactory for effective instruction.

There is not sufficient time in the six- or seven-period day to schedule all of the traditional subjects and at the same time include other desirable areas. The alternate-week plan allows teachers and administrators to incorporate both sound instructional content and effective procedures that otherwise would be limited or excluded altogether because of time limitations. Even though administrators may attempt to include such areas as driver education, mental health, family living, physical education, and health education in this schedule, many proponents of these subjects insist on a full period daily for each. Realizing the futility of these demands the administrator includes the areas he thinks important,

Figure 11–10. Variations of the three-two plan for combining health education with physical education.

DAY	PLAN ONE	PLAN TWO
Monday	Physical Education	Physical Education
Tuesday	Physical Education	Health Education
Wednesday	Health Education	Physical Education
Thursday	Health Education	Health Education
Friday	Physical Education (co-education)	Physical Education

to the exclusion of others. Combining all of these areas into an alternate-week arrangement makes it administratively feasible to include desirable content recommended by both educators and lay groups. Figure 11–11 provides an overview of the alternate-week plan, showing the content of both health education and physical education; it also shows the advantages of the plan and the set-up of the intramural laboratory.

In the alternate-week plan, physical education and health education are each allowed one solid week of instruction. These two programs alternate between the activity stations and the health classrooms. While the boys are participating in physical education, the girls are in the health classrooms, and vice versa. Although the two programs are grouped together for administrative expediency in a one-period-daily block of time, they are taught as separate programs with direct instruction in each and with the same teacher.

A visit to schools where each of the two programs has been instituted would reveal certain details of instruction. Since the programs are conducted in clearly defined but separate stations, the fact that they are combined is not noticeable. In health education, the classrooms are equipped with texts, guides, wall charts, audio-visual aids, and other teaching materials. The atmosphere in the classrooms is conducive to good health instruction. In the same manner, instruction is the objective of the physical education program; here adequate teaching stations, equipment, and all the aids necessary for conducting a program geared to the space-age objectives can be found. The alternate-week plan assures both programs a place of dignity and prestige in the curriculum, without infringing upon the time allotted to traditional subjects. The alternate-week plan is required from grades 7 through 10, with full academic credit being granted in the 8th, 9th, and 10th grades. No subjects receive credit in the 7th grade, which is an exploratory program. In the 11th and 12th grades, the program is elective, with full academic credit.

The alternate-week plan provides for a basic curriculum in health education and physical education, with intramurals as a necessary adjunct of the total program. Nowhere in the curriculum is there a more natural interaction of learning than that taking place in the activity program and health education. In no way is the need for instruction in personal hygiene, disease control, safety, and nutrition brought out more clearly than in the teaching of sports skills and attitudes, with health and fitness as the objectives. The alternate-week plan provides an appropriate vehicle to capitalize on this natural interaction.[16]

The alternate-week plan is probably the most satisfactory one because it (1) assures health education a place in the curriculum, (2) provides time for continuous instruction, (3) facilitates administration, and (4) lowers the cost of the program.

Patterns for Including Direct Health Education in the Curriculum

Health education, whether scheduled as a separate course or as a block, may be organized in several different patterns. The most common are the sequential, cycle, grade-placement, scope-and-sequence, and compromise patterns. (See Figure 11–9.)

The Sequential Pattern. The sequential pattern provides for all areas to be taught in all grades in a continuous manner that relates to the current needs and interests of students. Although presented in all grades, the instruction in each area should be approached in a different manner, depending on the growth needs, interests, and experiences of students from one grade to another. The major weakness of the plan is that it is difficult to prevent needless repetition. Students become bored with the same instruction year after year, and motivation decreases sharply.

The Cycle Pattern. The cycle pattern (Figure 11–12) eliminates to some degree the unnecessary duplication and overlapping that exist in the sequential pattern. In this plan, selected areas are

HEALTH INSTRUCTION
(alternates weekly with activity)

ACTIVITY INSTRUCTION
(alternates weekly with health instruction)

Grade Placement of Areas

	7	8	9	10	11	12
Fall Semester	Tobacco; Safety in physical education activities; Personal problems; Problems	Nutrition; Personal hygiene; Personal problems; Problems	Disease control; Venereal disease; Problems	Mental hygiene; Practice driving; Problems	Physiology of exercise; Problems	Public health services; Community health; Problems
Spring Semester	Safety in the home; Bicycle safety; Pedestrian safety; Firearm safety; Problems	First aid and disaster safety; Water safety; Drug abuse; Problems	Driver education class instruction; Problems	Alcohol; Narcotics; Stimulants; Tobacco; Drugs; Fads; False advertising; Practice driving; Problems	Physiology of exercise; Family living; Problems	Home nursing (girls); Health problems (boys); Problems

INTERACTION →

Definition

"A relation between more or less independent entities in which reciprocal influences of one upon the other are possible" —Carter Good (Ed.): **Dictionary of Education.** New York: McGraw-Hill Book Company, 1959, p. 294.

Boys alternate weekly with the girls in the health rooms and activity areas.

Advantages

1. Eliminates double expenditure for supplies and equipment.
2. Allows full week on a given area or topic.
3. Eliminates complications in the joint use of gymnasium, playgrounds, courts, etc., by boys and girls.
4. Provides more facilities for the activity program.

INTERACTION →

INTRAMURAL LABORATORY

Extension of instruction program allows for pupil participation in skills taught in class.

During and at the end of each semester at least one full week is set aside for immediate pupil problems in all areas.

Emphasis on Teaching Skills

Boys	Girls	Orientation in Junior High School	Pupil Choice in Senior High School
Golf; Bowling; Tennis; Wrestling; Table tennis; Softball; Basketball; Exercises; Proficiency tests; Touch football; Track; Tumbling; Horseshoes	Bowling; Tennis; Golf; Table tennis; Basketball; Hockey; Volleyball; Softball; Proficiency tests; Exercises; Rhythmics; Horseshoes; Body mechanics	Emphasis on motivation. Pupils participate in variety of activities. Pupils find out what activities they are suited for anatomically, physiologically and psychologically.	Pupils select activity they are suited for anatomically and psychologically. Pupils aim to perfect performance. Cuts across grade levels. Places expert teacher in activity. Minimizes discipline problems. Minimizes excuses from program. Better staff utilization through team teaching.
Texts used for instruction			
Emphasis on teaching skills			
Actual play after school			

INTERACTION →

Pupils participate after school in skills learned in instruction period.

Figure 11-11. The alternate-week plan provides a setting for effective instruction in health education. (Courtesy of Norfolk Public Schools, Norfolk, Virginia.)

Area	Cycle I Grades 1 2 3	Cycle II Grades 4 5 6	Cycle III Grades 7 8 9	Cycle IV Grades 10 11 12
I. Personal health				
A. Personal hygiene	x	x	x	x
B. Nutrition	x	x	x	x
C. Wholesome activity and rest	x	x	x	x
D. Choice and use of health services and health practices	x	x	x	x
II. Community health				
A. Prevention and control of disease	x	x	x	x
B. Community health services and agencies	x	x	x	x
III. Mental health				
A. Personality and character development	x	x	x	x
B. Alcohol, narcotics, and tobacco	x	x	x	x
C. Individual adjustment to society	x	x	x	x
D. Family living	x	x	x	x
IV. Safe living				
A. Home	x	x	x	x
B. School	x	x	x	x
C. Community	x	x	x	x

Figure 11–12. The cycle plan for health instruction. (From Mayshark, Cyrus, and Roy A. Foster: *Health Education in Secondary Schools,* 3rd ed. St. Louis: C. V. Mosby Co., 1974, p. 112.)

placed in the various grades. For example, personal hygiene may be taught in the 1st, 4th, 7th, and 10th grades. Although it prevents repetition, the cycle plan has several disadvantages. Health problems may appear in the grade in which the area is not taught. This means that, as with the sequential pattern, although problems of personal hygiene may be acute in all grades, instruction is provided only in the 1st, 4th, 7th, and 10th grades. Other weaknesses exist, such as overemphasis of one area to the detriment of another and the exclusion of important areas from the curriculum entirely.

However, many places use the cycle pattern successfully, through careful planning and flexible arrangement of instructional areas.

Scope-and-Sequence Pattern. A curriculum in health education that has far-reaching implications for improving instruction and exploring health areas in depth is described by Hoyman and illustrated in Figure 11–13. The scope-and-sequence framework, as it is called, has enough flexibility to ensure a spiral learning progression with both depth and breadth.

The Grade-Placement Pattern. In the grade-placement pattern, specific areas are taught in certain grades and not taught again. The weakness of this plan is that some of the subject areas may be taught at a time when students have little interest or need for them. In an earlier discussion it was noted that needs and interests are important in arranging curriculum content by grades and that unless there is considerable interest in an area, there will be little retention of knowledge.

The Compromise Pattern. The compromise pattern retains the strong features and eliminates the weaknesses of the other patterns. It arranges some areas on the grade-placement basis, some in cycles, and some sequentially. In addition, a block of time is allotted periodically for discussion of problems in any health area.

The compromise pattern allows the students' interests always to be in focus while assuring a planned, organized presentation of the content of each area. In arranging the placement of certain areas, age determines the grade level for instruction. For example, in teaching practice driving, the bulk of instruction should be given near the age at which the law allows students to drive. Up-to-date research reports should suggest the grade level in which instruction concerning alcohol, drugs, venereal disease, and the use of tobacco should be given.

PROFESSIONAL QUALIFICATIONS OF THE HEALTH EDUCATION TEACHER

The qualifications of the health education teacher are extremely important because of the tremendous amount of health knowledge available and the sophistication of the students enrolled in the health classes. Today's health problems are so serious that health instruction can no longer exist as simply a class in hygiene. The tragedies resulting from the rising incidence of venereal disease, drug abuse, and alcoholism indicate the need for qualified teachers who have a broad knowledge of these areas if health education is to meet the needs of the students enrolled in our schools today. A good health education teacher in today's changing society should be certified as follows:

A. The health teacher should meet the general education requirements for *all* teachers.

B. The preparation of the health teacher should include courses in the biological sciences (such as human biology, anatomy, physiology, and bacteriology), the physical sciences (especially chemistry), and the behavioral sciences (such as psychology, sociology, and cultural anthropology).

C. Minimum professional preparation

MAJOR HEALTH INSTRUCTION AREAS	PRIMARY GRADES				INTERMEDIATE GRADES			JUNIOR HIGH GRADES			SENIOR HIGH GRADES		
	K	1	2	3	4	5	6	7	8	9	10	11	12
Human Ecology and Health, Disease, Longevity	X	X	X	X	X		X		X				X
Human Growth, Development, Maturation, Aging	X	X	X	X	X		X		X				X
Healthful Living and Physical Fitness	X	X	X	X	X		X		X				X
Nutrition and Personal Fitness	X	X	X	X	X		X		X				X
Alcohol, Tobacco, & Narcotics	X	X	X	X	X		X		X				X
Prevention and Control of Disease	X	X	X	X		X			X			X	
Community and Environmental Health	X	X	X	X		X			X			X	
Consumer Health Education	X	X	X	X		X			X			X	
Rise of Modern Scientific Medicine	X	X	X	X		X			X			X	
Safety Education	X	X	X	X	X		X	X		X	X		X
First Aid and Home Nursing	X	X	X	X		X			X		X		X
Personality Development and Mental Health	X	X	X	X		X		X			X		X
Family–Life and Sex Education	X	X	X	X		X		X			X		X
Current Health Events and Problems	X	X	X	X	X	X	X	X	X	X	X	X	X

Figure 11–13. The scope-and-sequence pattern: A schematic health science spiral curriculum for grades K to 12. In grades K to 3 the X's denote topics. In grades 4 to 12, the X's denote units, or major parts of combined units. *Note:* Separate health courses may be scheduled at the junior and senior high school levels as a part of the health science spiral curriculum where this method of scheduling is preferred. (From Hoyman, Howard S.: "An Ecologic View of Health and Health Education." *Journal of School Health,* March, 1965, p. 118.)

requirements for certification in health education should include appropriate study in the following specific areas:

1. The school health program, including the areas of healthful school environment, health services, and health instruction.
2. Mental, emotional, and social health; alcohol, drugs, and tobacco.
3. Dental health; vision; hearing.
4. Emergency care, including first aid.
5. Safety education, including occupational, home, and recreational safety; man-made and natural disasters.
6. Community health, including such aspects of environmental health as air pollution, water pollution, and radiation; fluoridation; agencies promoting community health; official, voluntary, and professional health agencies and organizations.
7. Nutrition in respect to health education, including knowledge of basic food nutrients, wise selection and use of foods; obesity and weight control; food faddism, food fallacies, and controversial food topics.
8. Disease prevention and control, including the communicable and the degenerative diseases, and chronic health disorders.
9. Family life education, including human sexuality, and the psychosocial and cultural factors promoting successful marriage and family relations.
10. Consumer health, including intelligent selection of health products and health services, consumer protection agencies, health misconceptions and superstitions, health insurance plans, and health careers.
11. Study in methods and materials for health instruction.
12. Student teaching in health education.[17]

GUIDELINES FOR EFFECTIVE TEACHING

Administrators should have definite guides to assist them in scheduling health education, evaluating teachers, providing in-service education, appraising teacher qualifications, and handling other factors essential to health education. Johns developed the following set of guidelines, which he describes as essential ingredients in the teaching process. Administrators and teachers could use these guidelines very profitably to improve instruction.

1. The teacher is the key to effective health teaching.
2. The health teacher must have adequate time allotted, in keeping with other academic areas, if health teaching is to be effective.
3. The teacher must have a modern "point of view" of health education to make health teaching effective.
4. The teacher must know and utilize the health resources of both the school and community if health teaching is to be effective.
5. Careful planning by the health teacher is necessary for effective teaching.
6. The health teacher must thoroughly know his students in order to make health teaching effective.
7. The health teacher must formulate objectives in relation to the behavioral changes desired; health knowledge, health attitudes, and health practices.
8. The health teacher must select and organize health content so it has meaning for the students—now, today.
9. Teaching methods, procedures, and techniques used by the teacher must be functional if health teaching is to be effective.
10. The teaching materials that the health teacher selects and uses must be scientifically accurate and up-to-date, to ensure effective teaching.
11. Evaluation is an essential part of health teaching, as it provides evidence of the effectiveness of health teaching.
12. A healthful and wholesome environment contributes to teaching effectiveness.[18]

SCHOOL-COMMUNITY RELATIONS IN HEALTH EDUCATION

School-community relations in education are discussed generally in Chapter 4. In addition to the usual media that may be used for public relations, there are unique procedures that may be used to interpret the health education program to the public. One of the best media for communicating with the public is the Health Education Fair, which brings together a large number of voluntary health organizations, students, and administrators in one large project that has a tremendous impact on the community (Figure 11–14).

EVALUATION OF HEALTH EDUCATION PROGRAMS

Because it is an everchanging discipline, health education requires continuous evaluation. Local checklists are desirable if developed by qualified personnel. A comprehensive evaluation should measure the effectiveness of (a) the organization of the program; (b) the teaching in health knowledge, health attitudes, and health practices; and (c) available facilities.

A suggested evaluation form is shown in Figure 11–15. Evaluation of health knowledge follows the pattern prevalent in academic areas. Recently, evaluation in the cognitive domain by developing performance on behavioral objectives has become standard procedure in many places. The reader is referred to Chapter 8 for the discussion of evaluative techniques, which are applicable to health education.

Unless attitudes and practices change, the mere acquisition of knowledge is useless. The affective domain has received little attention in education; most of the emphasis has been on the cognitive aspects of teaching. However, failure to recognize the affective domain in teaching is to ignore a most important instrument in evaluation. For example, if a student learns about drugs but the knowledge does not change his attitude toward using drugs, has not the time imparting this knowledge been wasted? It is extremely difficult to evaluate health attitudes. Observation of the student's behavior is one way of evaluating attitudes and practices. Changes in health habits, such as watching one's weight, getting enough rest, and exercising for fitness, are examples of attitudinal responses to instruction. Visits to the phy-

Figure 11–14. Projects constructed by students and exhibited in the Health Education Fair provide an excellent medium for school-community relations. (Courtesy of Norfolk Public Schools, Norfolk, Virginia.)

sician for periodic check-ups indicate the effectiveness of the instructional program.

HEALTH EDUCATION FOR THE FUTURE

Several significant trends prevail in health education that may serve as a forecast of the program for the future. The findings of many study and research groups, such as those discussed earlier in the chapter, have focused public attention on the crucial health problems of the American people.

The health program of the future may see educational leaders with sufficient time in the school schedule for adequate instruction. This forward step means that no longer would health education be correlated or integrated with other subjects; it would be a separate course with direct instruction, as in other disciplines. The program would be scheduled daily, with comparable credit granted for satisfactory completion of the allocated blocks of time.

The next few years will see emphasis

I. ORGANIZATION

Checklist

1. Health instruction is provided through separate courses that constitute a planned, sequential program of study.   na 1 2 3 4
2. Elective health education courses are also provided.   na 1 2 3 4
3. Students of comparable grade and developmental levels are scheduled for the same classes.   na 1 2 3 4
4. Wherever appropriate, health education classes are coeducational.   na 1 2 3 4
5. The size of classes permits flexibility in organizing for teaching.   na 1 2 3 4
6. Health education is coordinated with related subject areas.   na 1 2 3 4

7. Time is provided for staff members to develop instructional materials.   na 1 2 3 4
8. Coordination of health education is the responsibility of one individual.   na 1 2 3 4
9. Teachers from the various grade levels plan together to develop a sequential program in health education.   na 1 2 3 4
10. Teachers of the same grade level plan together to develop the health education program at that level.   na 1 2 3 4
11.   na 1 2 3 4

Supplementary Data (Fill in the following table for all courses in health education.)

| | | | | | | Per Week | |
Title of Course	Grade	Enroll-ment	Number of Sections	Required or Elective	Range of Class Size	Number of Periods	Total Minutes

Evaluations

a) *How adequate is the provision for health instruction?*   na 1 2 3 4
b) *Do the time allotments for health education adequately meet the need for health instruction?*   na 1 2 3 4
c) *To what extent are opportunities provided for students to elect additional courses in the area of health education?*   na 1 2 3 4

Comments

A

Figure 11–15, *A* and *B*. Evaluating the health instruction program. (From the National Study of Secondary School Evaluation, Evaluative Criteria, 4th ed. Washington, D.C., 1974, p. 132.)

placed on curriculum planning and implementation of health recommendations made by medical authorities, community research, and the findings of the public health services. Guides will be developed with a strong focus on the needs and interests of children. The emphasis on instruction will not only be at the secondary level but will also include the elementary grades. The elementary curriculum will include such areas as drug education, sex education, smoking education, and nutrition.

A closer school-community relationship will result from the need for expertise from each group. The combined efforts of public health specialists and the teaching corps will be a forward step in meeting the health demands of the future.

As in all areas of instruction, closer ties between the colleges and schools are on the horizon. These two institutions have too long been operating on the periphery of health education. This is unfortunate, since both groups are

II. NATURE OF OFFERINGS

Checklist

The curriculum consists of a variety of content areas which enable the student to:

1. Develop individual responsibility for personal and community health.　　na 1 2 3 4
2. Recognize the influence of values on health behavior.　　na 1 2 3 4
3. Critically appraise and select health services.　　na 1 2 3 4
4. Critically evaluate health information.　　na 1 2 3 4
5. Understand his role in personal relationships (sex education and family life).　　na 1 2 3 4
6. Identify and cope with potential hazards in the environment.　　na 1 2 3 4
7. Recognize the importance of preventive rather than remedial action.　　na 1 2 3 4
8. Understand the growth and development of the human body and their relationship to health.　　na 1 2 3 4
9. Understand human needs and motivation, including sexuality.　　na 1 2 3 4

10. Understand the role and contributions of private, public, and professional organizations in solving health problems of the nation and of individuals.　　na 1 2 3 4
11. Understand factors influencing mental and emotional health.　　na 1 2 3 4
12. Select the foods necessary for the building, regulation, and repair of body tissues.　　na 1 2 3 4
13. Understand the causes and prevention of the major communicable and noncommunicable diseases.　　na 1 2 3 4
14. Understand the hazards as well as the therapeutic benefits, if any, in the use of alcohol, tobacco, and drugs.　　na 1 2 3 4

15.　　na 1 2 3 4

Evaluations

a) *How adequate are the offerings to develop in the student an understanding and appreciation of health?*　　na 1 2 3 4

b) *How adequate are the offerings to develop in the student a responsibility for maintaining and improving health?*　　na 1 2 3 4

Comments

III. PHYSICAL FACILITIES

Checklist

1. Instructional space provides for a wide variety of class activities　　na 1 2 3 4
2. Space is provided for storage of instructional materials.　　na 1 2 3 4
3. Display space is available for student projects and other instructional materials.　　na 1 2 3 4
4. A variety of instructional equipment is available.　　na 1 2 3 4

5. Library facilities are available to students and teachers.　　na 1 2 3 4
6. A private area is available for teacher-student conferences.　　na 1 2 3 4
7. Teachers' work space is available with provision also for collections of reference and resource materials.　　na 1 2 3 4

8.　　na 1 2 3 4

Evaluations

a) *How adequate are physicial facilities for a variety of health education activities?*　　na 1 2 3 4

B **Comments**

Figure 11–15B

needed to provide in-depth instruction for the youth of the country.

Tomorrow's instruction must be quality oriented. Taxpayers and administrators are taking a closer look at education. There is a focus on accountability in all areas of instruction, and programs that do not measure up to established standards will be eliminated from the curriculum. As education stands at the threshold of innovation and experimentation, the health of America's youth is still a basic objective. Effective health education is imperative not only for individual happiness and well-being, but for the future of the nation.

Authoritative groups such as the American Medical Association, the American Dental Association, the National Education Association, the American Public Health Association, and the President's Commission on National Goals have expressed the need for and have strongly supported programs of health education in schools and colleges. The place of the schools in providing health education is pointed out by the Society of State Directors for Health, Physical Education, and Recreation:

The ultimate goal of the Comprehensive School Health Program is to help every young person to achieve his full potential through becoming responsible for his own personal health decisions and practices, through working with others to maintain an ecological balance helpful to man and the environment, and through becoming a discriminating consumer of health information, health services, and health products.[19]

Probably one of the most important statements portraying the importance of health education was made by the American Medical Association. The association advised:

That the American Medical Association reaffirm its longstanding and fundamental belief that health education should be an integral and basic part of school and college curriculums and that state and local medical societies be encouraged to work with the appropriate health and education officials and agencies in their communities to achieve this end.[20]

HEALTH SERVICES

Definition

Health services may be defined as that part of the school health program provided by physicians, nurses, dentists, health educators, other allied health personnel, social workers, teachers, and others to appraise, protect, and promote the health of students and school personnel. Such procedures are designed to (a) appraise the health status of students and school personnel; (b) counsel stu-

dents, teachers, parents, and others for the purpose of helping students obtain health care and for arranging school programs in keeping with their needs; (c) help prevent and control the spread of communicable disease; (d) provide emergency care for injury or sudden illness; (e) promote and provide optimum sanitary conditions and safe facilities; (f) protect and promote the health of school personnel; and (g) provide concurrent learning opportunities which are conducive to the maintenance and promotion of individual and community health.[21]

Responsibility

The responsibility for school health services varies from community to community. One prevalent plan places the responsibility with the local school board and the superintendent. In some places, the local public health department is assigned the responsibility. A more recent plan organizes health services as a joint responsibility of both the local school board and the health department. Whichever plan is used, strong leadership and sufficiently qualified personnel are essential for an effective program.

The individuals responsible for health services also vary throughout the country. Personnel involved with this function should plan their work in conjunction with local policy and with the personnel of the departments of health education and school environment. The duties of the more generally recognized specialists concerned with school health services will be discussed in the following paragraphs.

The School Physician. The school physician usually has the responsibility of examining students and, if necessary, excusing them from certain types of classwork, such as physical education, when health problems are involved. In a number of school systems, the family physician and dentist provide for the periodic examination, and the school physician uses their examinations for school purposes. A discussion of granting excuses from classwork in physical education was presented in Chapter 9.

The School Nurse. The school nurse, whether assigned to one school permanently or to several schools periodically, plays an invaluable role in the school health service program. Her work is both clinical and educational. She may assist with the examination of school children and also render valuable services to the health education teachers.

The Dental Hygienist. The dental hygienist may be a full-time or part-time employee. Her services are varied; she may give x-rays and fluoride treatments, discover abnormalities in the mouth, and serve as a dental consultant for health education, among other duties.

The Dentist. Large school systems usually employ full-time dentists. The dentist's functions in the school health service program are both educational and medical. His examinations may be used as the basis for follow-up treatment, and he may serve as consultant for health education. He provides a valuable service to students and teachers.

Scope and Organization of School Health Services

The scope of school health services varies from state to state. Usually the program consists of the following components: health appraisal, follow-up and interpretation, and related services, such as emergency treatment of sickness and injury and disease prevention and control. Figure 11–16 shows how one school system organizes the health services program and illustrates the scope of the various organizational divisions.

School Health Appraisal

School health appraisal may be defined as:

The process of determining the total health status of a student through such means as parent, teacher, and nurse observations; screening tests; physical fitness tests; study of information concerning the student's past health experience; and medical and dental examinations. This concept recognizes that medical examinations include mental and emotional evaluation and that dental examinations are important in appraising student health. Such examinations, however, need to be supplemented by the other procedures mentioned.[22]

This relatively modern term provides new directions for the total health services program. Unlike the traditional health examination, which was concerned primarily with detection, school health appraisal requires the coordinated efforts of many people and involves many procedures, such as the health history of the student, screening tests, physical growth, psychological tests, health examination, and cumulative health record.

Health History. The health history of students is a most valuable procedure in the health-appraisal program. Questionnaires may be sent to parents for determining the health status of students with regard to accidents, operations, susceptibility to colds, history of rheumatic fever, diabetes, and emotional problems. The health inventory is an important instrument, since it reveals health information that would not be available otherwise. Observations or examinations may not reveal that the child has asthma, infrequent seizures, or that he had rheumatic fever the year before.

Health Observations. The daily health observation of students by all school personnel is a very important phase of the health-appraisal program. The daily association of students with teachers, counselors, physicians, nurses, and others may disclose many physical and emotional variations. These symptoms are of inestimable value in assessing the health of students. Of all the individuals who observe the behavior of school children, the teacher is in the most favorable position to discover symptoms that may not be revealed in any other situation. An outline of symptoms should be available to assist the teacher in his daily observations, so that he can detect variations that should be brought to the attention of the physician.

Screening Tests. Screening tests are used to identify students who need fur-

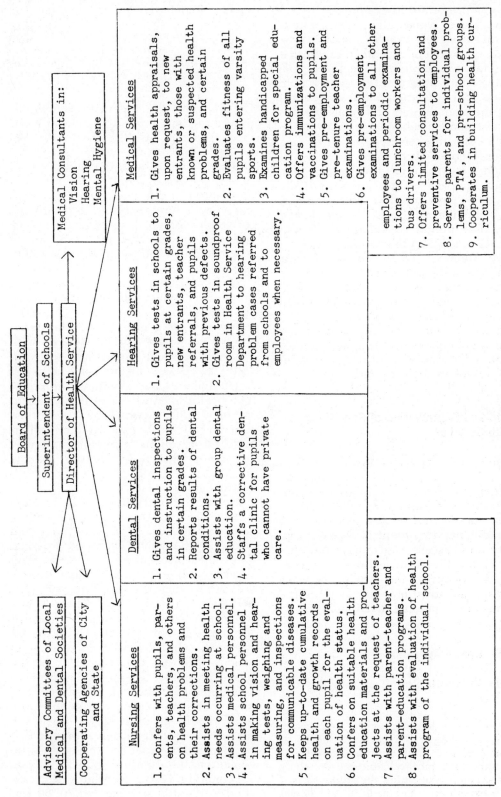

Figure 11–16. Organization of a health service department. (Courtesy of Denver Public Schools, Denver, Colorado.)

ther examination by a physician. These tests should be given at regular intervals, and all results should be accurately recorded. Screening tests for acuity of vision and hearing, tuberculosis, growth, dental defects, and emotional behavior usually make up the screening program. Confused views about growth patterns necessitate a brief discussion here on height and weight and weight interpretation.

Physical Growth. Physical growth is usually determined by measuring height and weight. This procedure should be done several times each year. Either the results may be recorded on the cumulative record card or each student may be provided a separate card showing the results. Data from the growth cards may be used in the health instruction program to motivate student interest in establishing correct eating habits, recognizing the importance of exercise and rest, and developing other health practices necessary for normal growth and development.

Psychological Tests. Psychological tests disclose additional information that is helpful in providing a picture of the total health of children. These tests not only provide information regarding the intelligence of children, but they may also disclose hidden and deep-rooted symptoms of emotional maladjustment, low reading levels, and other factors involved in poor performance in school. The psychologist is the key person in this division of appraisal; but the principal, counselor, classroom teacher, nurse, teaching specialists, and other school personnel may also provide invaluable data.

In addition to the important data accumulated as a result of the classroom teacher's continuous observation, the physical education teacher may find information that may be helpful in discovering hidden emotional factors involved in health appraisal. In the daily physical activity of children, dormant urges are brought to the surface. The wise physical education teacher is able to provide guidance at the teachable moment by taking advantage of the information provided by these behavioral

tests. Continuous observation and counseling by the teacher, using these behavioral patterns as guides for action, develop not only the student's character but his inhibition and adjustment abilities as well. The teacher should not attempt to assume the role of psychologist, however, because the diagnosis and treatment of mental and emotional illnesses are medical functions. The teacher must know when the child is in need of clinical services and refer him to the proper person for help. Nevertheless, the teacher's guidance function is an important one.

The physical education teacher probably does more day-by-day counseling than any other member of the school faculty. Because of his close daily association with students in an informal atmosphere which is closely attuned to normal activity, the physical education teacher becomes the student's friend. Through this friendship and guidance he assists students in adjusting to the group and to the school, in finding outlets for biological needs for activity and self-expression, in developing self-confidence, and in finding release from pent-up emotions. Data discovered while assisting students with problems in these areas provide information that physicians and other personnel need for the total health appraisal of students.

Health Examination. Health examinations of schoolchildren are usually required by law. These examinations are made periodically by a physician and should be given several times during the school life of each student. A recommended procedure is to examine students when they enter the 1st grade and to follow this with a second examination in the intermediate grades, a third at the start of junior high school, and a final one before the student leaves school.

The family physician should assist with the examination. Not only is he able to provide a more thorough examination but he is also in a position to encourage a better student-teacher-parent-nurse relationship. This relationship is essential in providing an adequate examination and remedial measures.

The periodic medical examination may

be an educational experience and it should be closely associated with health instruction in the classroom before and after the examination. Parents can make an effective contribution to the examination if they accompany the child and acquaint the physician with special data that otherwise would be unavailable. The resource manual shows a sample letter to parents that may be used to announce health examinations.

The Cumulative Health Record. The cumulative health record should include the health history of the child, results of the medical examination, and the data gathered by the nurse, teacher, counselor, psychologist, and other personnel in the school. The value of the cumulative health record cannot be overemphasized.

The Health Follow-Up

The follow-up and counseling of students is the second most important procedure in the health-service program. A thorough health appraisal is of little value unless the information revealed is used constructively to correct defects and establish sound counseling procedures. A carefully planned follow-up and counseling program involving the physician, principal, teacher, nurse, guidance counselor, and others should be initiated. The follow-up program should be designed around such procedures as (1) a more detailed medical examination, (2) treatment, correction, or constant medical supervision where necessary, (3) altered or improved home care, and (4) mental health studies.[23]

Related Health Services

A comprehensive health-service program includes special services for handicapped children, disease control programs, emergency care and first aid procedures, accident insurance, and facilities for maintaining the health of school personnel.

HEALTHFUL SCHOOL ENVIRONMENT

Healthful school environment has been defined as "the promotion, maintenance, and utilization of safe and wholesome surroundings, organization, day-by-day experiences and planned learning procedures to influence favorably emotional, physical and social health."[24] The school environment affects not only the health of students but also their scholastic performance. Since students spend approximately one-fourth of their lives in school, it is extremely important that those components of the school environment that affect the health and fitness of students, such as healthful school plant, organization of the school day, and maintenance of the school plant, be carefully evaluated.

Healthful School Plant

It is the responsibility of the admininstrator to provide a school plant that meets all standards of health that will contribute to the mental, physical, and emotional well-being of all students. Buildings should be constructed not only in accordance with local and state building standards but also as examples of architectural beauty and symmetry. For many students the school is a kind of home, in which play and study are sources of lasting joy and happiness.

A qualified representative of the administration should work with the architect in planning the school facility. Chapter 9 describes this cooperative arrangement. The healthful school plant should consist of adequate classrooms designed for effective instruction and equipped with chalkboards, adjustable chairs, storage space, proper illumination, acoustically treated walls, and floors constructed of materials most suitable for the grade levels involved.

Although local and state building codes usually establish standards for school construction, the administrator is responsible for establishing adequate water supply and plumbing facilities. He is also responsible for seeing that there are sufficient toilet facilities, locker rooms, and showers, and that the swimming pool is sanitary. He takes into consideration the importance of sound procedures in cafeteria service and student transportation. The checklist in Chapter 9 shows the essentials involved in a healthful school plant.

Organization of the School Day

The organization of the school day has a direct effect on the health and well-being of students, particularly their emotional health. The pressures that confront students in their day-by-day routines produce symptoms and behavioral patterns that are reflected in the classroom and on the playground. The administration is responsible for adjusting the school curriculum to meet individual differences, and it should recognize the importance of scheduling, length of the school day, testing, teaching loads, extra-class activities, homework, and safety procedures in the organization of the school program.

Maintenance of the School Plant

Adequate maintenance of the school plant is an investment not only in the health and safety of students but also in the economy of operating the school. A well informed custodial staff is able to anticipate and locate many environmental problems that may be detrimental and hazardous to the health and safety of students. Problems may arise from the following conditions:

1. Inadequate heating, which involves faulty piping, thermostatic control, and improper fueling.
2. Improper wiring, overloaded circuits, and faulty connections.
3. Lack of sufficient safety precautions, resulting in faulty stairways, improper glass in doors, and other conditions that may cause accidents.
4. Improper cleaning of rooms, offices, and hallways.

5. Inadequate storage and refrigeration of foods.

Responsibility

There are many individuals responsible for a healthful school environment. A major responsibility of all school personnel is to contribute to the development of a healthful environment for schoolchildren and for all personnel in the school. As the responsibility flows from the superintendent down to the principal, teacher, student, and custodian, probably the one person who has the greatest influence in providing a healthful environment in the school is the custodian. Although all school personnel, including students, contribute to a healthful school environment, the custodian is usually the person who is directly responsible. He supervises care of the floors, windows, chalk boards and erasers, and lavatories, and is responsible for effecting general repairs throughout the building. The custodian is also responsible for periodic inspection of the heating plant and temperature controls, lighting controls, storage of equipment and supplies, and for providing adequate follow-up to correct any adverse conditions he may find.

Other factors which contribute to a healthful school environment include safety in the building and on the playground, the emotional climate of the school, and the administrative practices of the school.

EVALUATION OF SCHOOL HEALTH PROGRAMS

Evaluation of the school health program is essential. Every school needs a carefully organized instrument for measuring the quality of programs in light of established objectives. In view of this, a checklist is suggested for evaluating each of the three facets of the school health program—health services, health education, and school environment. Such a checklist is available from the California State Department of Education.

REFERENCES

1. U. S. Department of Health, Education, and Welfare: *School Health Program—An Outline for School and Community Public Health Service.* Publication No. 834. Washington, D.C.: U. S. Government Printing Office, 1961, pp. 1–4.
2. National Committee on School Health Policies: *Suggested School Health Policies,* 4th ed. Chicago: The American Medical Association, 1966, p. 1.
3. *Ibid.,* pp. xi–xii.
4. Commission on the Reorganization of Secondary Education: *Cardinal Principles of Secondary Education.* Bulletin No. 35. Washington, D.C.: U.S. Government Printing Office, 1918.
5. Educational Policies Commission of the National Education Association: *Education for All American Youth.* Washington, D.C.: The Association, 1944.
6. B. Frank Brown (Chairman): *The Reform of Secondary Education.* New York: McGraw-Hill Book Co., 1973, p. 35.
7. Elena M. Sliepcevich (Director): *School Health Education Study.* Washington, D.C.: School Health Education Study, 1964, pp. 5–12.
8. Daniel Reardon and Scott Scobell: "School Health Inventory Survey." *Journal of School Health,* October, 1965, p. 383.
9. Report of the Joint Committee on Health Education Terminology. *Journal of School Health,* January, 1974, p. 34.
10. Ian M. Newman and Cyrus Mayshark: "Health Education Planning and Community Perceptions of Local Health Problems." *Journal of School Health,* September, 1973, p. 462.
11. Les C. Ramsdell: "An Analysis of Health Interests and Needs of West Virginia High School Students—A Report." *Journal of School Health,* October, 1972, p. 477.
12. Sliepcevich, *op. cit.,* p. 22.
13. *Ibid.,* p. 10.
14. Nelson L. Bossing and Roscoe V. Cramer: *The Junior High School.* Boston: Houghton Mifflin Co., 1965, pp. 217–218.
15. Cyrus Mayshark and Roy A. Foster: *Health Education in Secondary Schools,* 3rd ed. St. Louis: C. V. Mosby Co.,1972, p. 83.
16. *Building Healthier Youth—A Guidebook in Health, Physical, and Safety Education for Secondary Schools.* Norfolk, Va.: Norfolk Public Schools, 1976.
17. "Teacher Preparation in Health Education." A Report of the National Conference Steering Committee, *JOHPER,* February, 1969, p. 32.
18. Edward B. Johns: "Effective Health Teaching." *Journal of School Health,* March, 1964, pp. 123–128.
19. A Statement of Basic Beliefs, Kensington, Md.: The Society of State Directors of Health, Physical Education and Recreation, 1972, p. 2.
20. American Medical Association, Meeting of the House of Delegates, Miami Beach, Florida, June, 1960, p. 196.
21. Report of the 1972–1973 Joint Committee on Health Education Terminology, *Journal of School Health,* January, 1974, p. 36.
22. Donald A. Dukelow (ed.): *Health Appraisal of School Children,* 4th ed. Joint Committee on Health Problems in Education of the NEA and the AMA, 1969, p.2.
23. Alma Nemir and Warren E. Schaller: *The School Health Program,* 4th ed. Philadelphia: W. B. Saunders Co., 1975, p. 285.
24. Report of the 1972–1973 Joint Committee on Health Education Terminology, *op. cit.,* p. 35.

SUGGESTED READINGS

Mayshark, Cyrus, and Ray A. Foster: *Health Education in Secondary Schools,* 3rd ed. St. Louis: C. V. Mosby Co., 1972.
Nemir, Alma, and Warren E. Schaller: *The School Health Program,* 4th ed. Philadelphia: W. B. Saunders Co., 1965.
Smolensky, Jack, and L. Richard Bonvechio: *Principles of School Health.* Boston: D. C. Heath & Co., 1966.
Willgoose, Carl E.: *Health Education in the Elementary School,* 4th ed. Philadelphia: W. B. Saunders Co., 1974.

CHAPTER TWELVE

Intramural Programs

INTRAMURALS AND CHANGING LIFE STYLES

The intramural phase of the total physical education program has had several titles over the years. The term intramural is derived from two Latin words — *intra*, meaning within, and *mural*, meaning wall. The combination of these two words, *intramural*, has been used to define competitive programs and activities played within the confines of one institution or school.

Some authors and administrators have used the term "intramural sports" and others have defined the programs as "intramural activities." In the opinion of many, the term *intramural laboratory* is a more truly definitive title. However, since most of the content of the program involves sports, the term *intramural sports* will be used here to define this phase of the school program.

Ever since intramural activities first appeared in the schools of America, the program has had secondary status. To a

305

large extent, the emphasis on interscholastic athletics served as a deterrent to
intramural growth. The huge allocations
of financial aid to support interscholastic
competition, the urgent need for facilities for varsity practice, and the emphasis on spectators and gate receipts de-
tracted from the support of a faltering
intramural program.

Recent developments in the student
attitudes toward spectator sports and the
emphasis on fitness promise the dawn of
a new era in intramural competition.
Students no longer have the desire for
spectator programs they once had. They
are leaning more toward the philosophy
of activity for all rather than for just the
gifted few. Numerous articles on reports
on physical fitness and health are motivating many people to seek ways to exercise. The popularity of health salons
illustrates this trend. However, if people
had been provided with instruction in
lifetime sports with adequate intramural
competition to improve skills in these
sports, there would be little need for
frequenting these places to improve
their health.

The increase in the amount of leisure
time for the working classes has been so
phenomenal that millions of people actually are finding time on their hands. In
1972 the Secretary of Labor, J. D. Hodg-
son, stated that with the reduction of the
work week, combined with added vacation time and more paid holidays, the
American worker has netted approximately 800 hours of free time annually.[1]
The increase in leisure hours provides
the opportunity for millions of Americans to seek the golf course, the bowling
alley, the ski course, and other places for
individual participation in those activities they enjoy. However, while large
numbers of people *are* utilizing recreational hours effectively, there are still
many who are unable to do so for the
simple reason that they do not know
how.

Actually, this increasing amount of leisure time has created one of the acute
social problems of the last half of the
20th century. How to spend this time
wisely is a question that confronts educators and all individuals concerned

with the welfare of the individual and
the country. Staley stated:

At a recent conference of leading political
and social scientists, it was generally agreed
that the outstanding fact about leisure in the
United States today is that it is growing much
faster than our capacity to use it wisely.[2]

There is considerable evidence pointing
to the need for more vigorous physical
activity not only for organic development
but also for the development of emotional stability. The tensions of everyday living, the frustrations of today's
socio-economic conditions, and the un-
certainties of the future are producing an
increase of grave proportions in emotional problems.

The importance of having well-
organized and carefully planned intramural programs as deterrents to delinquency and other types of emotional instability is well recognized. In all such
programs, the basic ingredient necessary
for deterring emotional instability is continuous, vigorous muscular activity. The
individual who is vigorously active is
usually emotionally stable.

Before the individual's recreational
participation must come his education in
skill and movement. The skills and
movements that are first learned in the
physical education class are practiced
and developed in the intramural program. Experiences and attitudes developed in the intramural program are pro-
totypes of behavior in later life. If these
experiences are constructive, they will
lead to leisure-time pursuits that will
produce an individual better able to
achieve self-realization and satisfying
human relationships.

Education in America's schools is designed to provide all children with the
opportunity to receive adequate instruction in those areas necessary for adaptability to living in a democratic culture.
Since an increasingly important phase of
living in American society is leisure
time, the importance of education for
leisure is becoming more and more evident.

Recent developments point to the
need for greater emphasis on physical

activity during the leisure hours. It was pointed out earlier that there is insufficient time for activity in the regular class period and that provisions must be made for vigorous activity beyond school hours. A national interest in the gravity of the problem has developed, and several organizations are making intensive efforts to acquaint the public with the need for health and fitness and the worthwhile use of leisure time. The President's Council for Physical Fitness and Sports and the National Intramural Sports Council are two such groups. They are providing leadership in promoting and developing programs designed to educate the masses on the need for organizing their leisure-time activity around exercise programs that contribute to health.

INTRAMURAL OBJECTIVES

In addition to the general purpose of physical education, which extends to the intramural phase, there are seven specific objectives of intramurals:

To Supplement the Required Program

It is generally believed that the required physical education class does not provide sufficient time for students to participate in the vigorous daily activity needed for their normal growth and development. The class period, no matter how efficiently it is organized, can provide only 30 to 40 minutes of time for exercise. This is about two or three hours less than the amount of activity required if students are to have the necessary time for normal growth and development. The intramural laboratory provides this time for students to practice more fully the skills learned in class.

To Motivate Students in After-School Participation

The problem of motivating students always confronts the teacher or administrator. The teaching of skills, although basic, is not enough. In addition to acquiring skills, students must be motivated to carry these skills beyond the school day. When the intramural laboratory is planned and organized properly, students will be encouraged to continue the practice of skills beyond the school day, thus maintaining and increasing their interest in the activity.

To Provide Activities for All Students

If the objectives of varsity athletics are both educational and necessary for the gifted, then a comparable program is needed for the thousands of students who are unable to be a part of the varsity program. There can be only five members of the varsity basketball team, but there are thousands of students who can dribble, pass, and shoot effectively. These students who, either by choice or because of inability, are not on the team should have the opportunity to participate in the activities of their choice.

To Provide Supervision for After-School Play

Although too much adult involvement may hamper student programs, there should be an adult to assist with the organization, administration, and supervision of the intramural laboratory. The intramural laboratory is administered by a member of the regular physical education staff who understands the relationship between the instructional class and the laboratory, and is therefore able to organize and administer the laboratory program to meet the established objectives. He can also provide the right amount of supervision to insure a safe environment and, at the same time, allow the degree of freedom that will engender joyful participation.

To Provide Sufficient Facilities and Equipment for All Students to Participate

It is the responsibility of the school administration to provide adequate space, equipment, facilities, and officials for the intramural laboratory. Budgetary considerations must be given to these aspects of the program in order that participating students may have an adequate environment for participation and that desirable goals may be achieved.

To Provide for Individual Differences

There are many students who become disinterested with the school program because of either reading difficulties or apathy toward the traditional curriculum. Well-planned intramural activities may provide the medium for retaining these students and wise counseling may rekindle their interest in other programs.

To Develop Skills in Lifetime Sports and Activities

As an extension of classroom instruction, intramural programs may provide the opportunity for many hours of practice, which is so important for developing individual skills. Such sports as golf and tennis require students to practice many hours in order to attain the skill performance level necessary to enjoy the activity. Time for this is simply not available in the physical education class.

ADMINISTRATIVE RESPONSIBILITIES

The effectiveness of the intramural program depends upon the basic organization and administration of the program. The first and most important step in administering the program is the assignment of personnel and their duties. Figure 12–1 suggests an organizational arrangement through which an intramural program may be conducted. The major responsibilities of the administrators involved in conducting the program are discussed in the following paragraphs.

The School Board and Superintendent

The school board is responsible for determining policy in all programs conducted by the schools within a system. This responsibility includes the instructional programs and all extracurricular activities. The superintendent is the legal executive for administrative policies of the board.

The Director of Physical Education

The director of physical education for the city is responsible for coordination of the programs in all schools of the system. He is also responsible for conducting intramural workshops and scheduling periodical meetings of those individuals who are assigned to directing the program in the schools.

The Principal

The principal is responsible for all programs conducted in the school. Although much of the administrative detail is delegated, the principal remains the administrative officer of the instructional and extracurricular programs.

The School Intramural Director

The importance of who is assigned the responsibility for conducting and supervising the program cannot be overemphasized. The position or title of the person involved varies throughout the country. Edward Bork, supervisor of elementary physical education in Austin, Minnesota, in an effort to determine the extent of intramurals in the state of Minnesota, sent questionnaires to 29 districts. Of 23 respondents, 16 districts had intramural programs. Thirteen of the districts reported the following supervisory arrangements:

1. One district—Elementary physical education specialist.

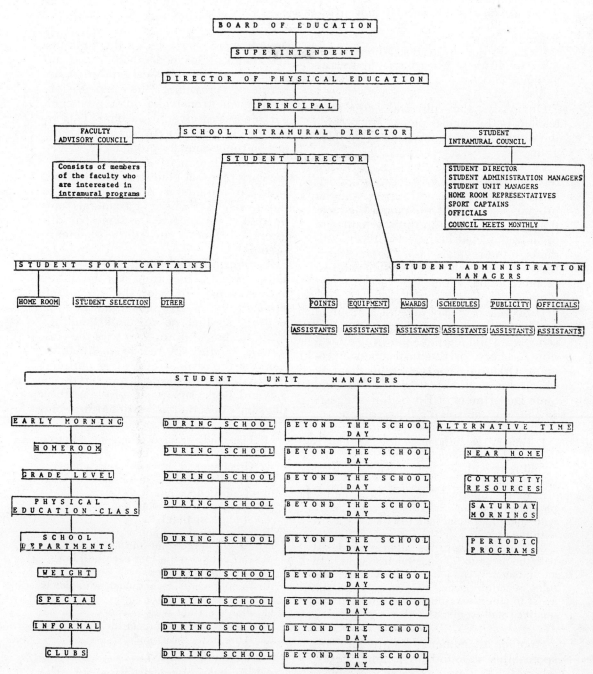

Figure 12-1. Organization of the intramural program.

2. Two districts—Intramural director.
3. Two districts—Physical education consultant.
4. One district—Elementary director.
5. Three districts—Elementary principals.
6. One district—Coordinator of after-school programs.
7. One district—Recreational director.
8. Two districts—Elementary physical education supervisor.[3]

Obviously the physical education teacher is the logical person for providing direction and supervision of the program.

On all levels, a physical education teacher should be given the responsibility for conducting and supervising the program. Not only is the physical education teacher trained in the mechanics of organization, but he meets with the students in the regular class program and is therefore more able to motivate interest in intramurals, which have a carry-over element.

However, this may present a problem in the elementary school, since many schools do not employ physical education teachers for the instructional program. Orlando Savastano, consultant in physical education for the Rhode Island State Department of Education, suggests several ways of solving this problem:

1. Employ an intramural director who is responsible for conducting the program. He would work with and train teachers to assist with the program.
2. In the high schools, the head of the physical education department could work with and train qualified teachers to assist with the program.
3. Students should be allowed to assist with the program. Those students could form an intramural council which would make rules, schedule games, rule on protests, and assist in other ways under the direction of a qualified staff member.[4]

Another assignment of intramural responsibility is found in Abilene, Texas, where W. D. Lawson, director of physical education, reports that 23 elementary schools participate in after-school programs. Each school has an intramural director who receives extra remuneration for this responsibility.

In each of the five junior high schools, physical education teachers are responsible for the program. In each of the high schools, an intramural director conducts the program before and after school.[5]

In Norfolk, Virginia, intramural sports programs are conducted in the 15 junior and senior high schools, with a man and woman from the physical education department providing the supervision. Each teacher receives a differential comparable to that given to coaches. This arrangement provides 30 intramural directors in the secondary program.

In the elementary schools, the elementary physical education teachers are assigned intramural responsibilities in those schools where intramurals are needed. They receive the same pay differential found in the secondary schools.[6]

Responsibilities of the Intramural Director. It is important that the duties and responsibilities of the intramural director be clearly communicated in writing, so that no misunderstandings arise. Responsibilities vary with the conditions existing in the local situation. Some of the responsibilities, as outlined by localities, are shown in a survey by Edward Bork, supervisor of elementary physical education in Austin, Minnesota:

1. Plan and organize programs of activities.
2. Organize and supervise tournaments.
3. Coordinate the intramural program with physical education.
4. Standardize rules and regulations.
5. Set up schedules.
6. Supervise personnel.
7. Secure referees for tournaments.
8. Employ personnel for each building.
9. Plan demonstrations.
10. Keep records (schedules, attendance, seasonal activities, etc.).
11. Plan meetings with teachers.
12. Prepare and administer the budget.
13. Work in the program.[7]

Additional responsibilities of the director would include determining the purpose, aim, objectives, and policies of the program; promoting an intensive public relations program; developing and implementing an awards and point system; and making periodic reports to the director of health and physical education for the system.

Faculty Advisory Council

Some schools plan intramural programs around the faculty advisory council. The council may serve as a strong instrument for promoting intramural programs if it is organized properly. However, because of the demand on teachers' time, it may be difficult to find teachers who are able to effectively assist with intramural programs.

The use of volunteers to assist with officiating and with organizing transportation for extramural and other periodic functions is highly recommended. However, the arrangements for using these people should be made in advance, to avoid conflicting commitments.

Student Intramural Council

A student intramural council is desirable for conducting an effective program in intramurals. The council should consist of representatives from the various segments of the student body.

D. T. Carter, intramural director of E. E. Smith High School, Fayetteville, North Carolina, reports that a student council is responsible for the organization and administration of all intramural activities. The council is composed of five girls and five boys who are seniors in physical education. The committee is responsible for such procedures as eligibility of participants, making rules, keeping records, selecting committees, hearing forfeits and protests, and checking insurance.[8]

Student Director

The director of the school program should select from a list of senior candidates one student to serve as the student director. This student should have had experience with the program and should be familiar with recording results, procuring officials, working with managers, issuing supplies and equip-

ment, handling publicity, arranging for awards, and scheduling.

Student Unit Managers

Each sport or activity should have a manager responsible for the effective conduct of that sport. The manager should work with the team captain and assist him in procuring officials and providing equipment for the sport. The manager's duties include posting game results, securing the names of players from the captains, having all entry sheets filled out on time, notifying teams concerning the time, place, and date of each game, and apprising all players of the eligibility rules.

Student Administrative Managers

Student administrative managers are responsible for the many aspects of conducting the total programs, such as keeping points for participation, procuring and issuing equipment to the unit managers, determining who shall receive awards, preparing schedules, publicizing the program, and securing officials.

Student Sport Captains

Each team or sport should select a captain who is responsible for representing the team or sport and assisting with all the details involved in conducting the program. The duties of team captains include having their teams appear on time for all contests, filing protests, leading their teams in maintaining proper behavior during contests, and keeping an accurate record of the line-up and presenting it to the proper official. The captain also assumes the responsibility for all equipment before and after the contest.

Officials

Capable officials are necessary for the successful operation of an intramural program. In some instances, students may be trained to officiate in an extremely satisfactory manner. Members of the varsity teams have been used successfully in officiating. DeNike found, in his survey of 105 schools, that most schools use student officials.[9] John Phillips, director of intramurals at Cooper High School, Abilene, Texas, describes a very effective plan in which the use of students has solved the officiating problem in Abilene. There, officiating students receive intensive instruction each day from textbooks, rule books, and manuals. Before officiating, the student must pass an extensive examination. Those students in grades 10 to 12 who wish to become officials register for the last period in physical education, in which they learn the techniques of officiating.[10]

In some places, intensive effort has been made to train girls for leadership roles in intramurals. Marion Kneer of East Peoria Community School, East Peoria, Illinois, not only uses student leaders in intramurals but also uses them in class activities. Girls are encouraged to organize intramural programs, conduct tournaments, and arrange workshops in sports. According to Miss Kneer, "The keystone for success of an intramural and extramural program is the manner in which the adult leadership provides opportunities for student leadership to grow." She offers some suggestions for those teachers who wish to organize intramural clubs:

1. Don't try to solve all problems yourself. Let student leaders learn to cope with difficult situations. You will find them stricter and wiser in their dealings with classmates. Furthermore, the decisions will be accepted more readily.

2. Insist on officers fulfilling their responsibilities. Help students to develop policies which will aid them in replacing irresponsible officers and representatives.

3. Avoid big group business meetings. They usually become boring and are difficult to control.

4. Have leaders—with your help—evaluate progress regularly and help them take concrete steps to improve the program.

5. Help club leaders devise some means of contacting the membership or student body when necessary. A newsletter or bulletin board listing scheduled activities and other items of interest should prove helpful.

6. Work with student leaders in planning recognition awards. Use good judgment in their selection. Be sure they stand for something worthwhile.

7. Open intramurals and extramurals to all students—not just club members. Provide bonuses for membership, such as awards, the opportunity to participate in administrative decisions, social events.[11]

POLICIES GOVERNING INTRAMURAL PROGRAMS

Definite policy statments to cover all situations that may arise in the course of the program should be developed and approved by the local board of education. These policies should include the following principles:

1. Intramural programs should be designed to provide the opportunity for *all* students to participate and should include both team and individual sports.

2. Experienced and capable personnel should be employed to administer the program.

3. Sufficient equipment and supplies should be provided for the program.

4. The time frame for conducting intramural competition should be after school. However, because of such conflicts as varsity practice, space, busing schedules, and facilities, it may be necessary to schedule activities before school, during the day, or on Saturdays.

5. All intramural competition should be scheduled outside of the instructional program. Class time is designed for instruction and should be used for this purpose.

6. Intramural participation should be an extension of the instructional program and should include a comprehensive coeducational program.

7. Intramural competition should be confined to individual school programs. If the competition extends to other schools, then it assumes all of the characteristics of the interscholastic program, which limits student participation to a small, highly skilled group. An exception is the extramural program discussed later in this chapter.

8. It is not advisable to charge admission for intramurals. Supplies and equipment should be procured from the physical education department. Charging admission for intramurals is counter to the philosophy of "ac-

tivities for all," which is the basic aim of the program.

9. Students should provide the school with a parental permission form, properly signed, before participating in intramural programs. The form should include a state-

ment releasing the school from responsibility for claims should the child be injured. Many schools carry blanket insurance, which includes intramural contests. The premiums may be paid by the school, the school board, or the participant. Figure 12–2 is an example

```
                PARENTAL  PERMISSION  FORM

                    INTRAMURAL PARTICIPATION


Dear Patron:

     The intramural sports program designed for elementary students begins Monday,
September  15, 1966.  The program will be held before and after school.  The objec-
tives of the program are (1) to serve as an extension of the instructional program
and (2) provide the time for vigorous activity so essential for normal growth and
development.

     The program shall be under the supervision of the physical education teacher at
all times.  All participants should secure the school accident insurance, which may
be procured for a nominal fee.

     The schedule of activities includes the following:

     Fall:  Lead-up games, volleyball, kickball, basketball, fitness tests

     Winter:  Bowling, tumbling, basketball, group games, fitness tests

     Spring:  Softball, kickball, track, fitness tests, lead-up games


_____                    _____
      School                             Physical Education Teacher, Room Teacher
                                         or Principal

-------------------------------Detach and Return--------------------------------

     I do hereby grant permission for my child to participate in the intramural
program, conducted by the school.  This permission includes contests away from
school as well as those held at the school.  I also release the teachers and the
administration from any responsibility or liability for personal injury that may
occur to my child while participating in the program.


_____                          _____
      Date                                      Parent or Guardian


                                                _____
                                                Address


                                                _____
                                                Telephone


                                                _____
                                                Emergency Telephone
```

Figure 12–2. Parental permission form for intramural participation.

of a parental permission form. The form interprets the program, discusses the schedule, and includes a release of liability.

10. All students who participate in intramural contests should have satisfactorily passed a physical examination. The periodic examination conducted by the school should suffice.

POLICIES GOVERNING STUDENT PARTICIPATION

Rules for student participation are extremely important for an effective program; they should be carefully written, and posted conspicuously. The proper consideration of these rules may prevent needless arguments and serious misunderstandings. The following areas illustrate the elements of participation that need consideration when planning the intramural program.

Student Eligibility

All boys and girls enrolled in school are automatically eligible for all intramural privileges, unless they fail to comply with the other eligibility rules, such as the following.

Scholastic Requirements. No scholastic requirements are necessary, unless a student is so far behind the average of his class that his spare time is needed for study.

Varsity and Other Organized Competition. Any student who is or has been a member of a varsity or junior varsity team, and has participated in one or more scheduled games or practice games during the current season, shall be ineligible to compete in that particular intramural sport. The same regulation applies to students who bowl on civic league bowling teams or swim on any organized teams. This rule should be strictly enforced. Special programs should be planned for these students.

Sportsmanship. A player may be ruled ineligible to compete in future contests because of unsportsmanlike conduct, refusal to abide by the decision of an official, or use of improper language.

Best Interest of School. Students may be ruled ineligible to compete by the director for infractions of any rule of the program or for any conduct not in the best interest of the school.

Forfeits

Forfeits are unnecessary if programs are planned properly and if a positive approach is used to show team and players the importance of assuming the responsibility of following the schedule. However, forfeits may occur, and arrangements should be made to consider them. Some rules that should be applied to forfeits are:

1. When teams or individuals fail to appear at the scheduled time, the intramural director may forfeit the contest to the team or individual that reported.
2. A policy should be established for teams that forfeit more than one time in the same tournament. Usually, they are prohibited from further play.
3. Forfeited contests should not be rescheduled, and a forfeit should be recorded as a loss.
4. Teams reporting without a full quota of players may forfeit or play at their discretion.

Protests

Provisions should be made for protests, and a committee or board should be appointed to rule on them. Protests should be allowed only in situations in which players are ineligible or when there is misinterpretation of established rules. An official's judgment or decision is not protestable, but failure of an official to apply correct rulings to a particular situation may be protested. Local administrators should develop procedures applicable to their own particular program. The following policies are recommended:

1. Any protest that involves the judgment of an official will not be allowed.
2. Protests concerning eligibility may be made at any time.
3. Protests other than those concerning eli-

gibility must be made on the field and presented in writing to the intramural coordinator on the day of the game.

4. Individual contestants, team captains, and the officials in charge shall be permitted to present their versions of the case before a decision is made. The decision shall consist of a majority vote of the intramural council or governing body.

5. Games in which a protest is sustained shall be replayed from the beginning of the nearest preceding segment of the contest; i.e., in basketball, from the beginning of the quarter in which the protest arose or occurred.[12]

Postponements

Conflicts within the school, weather conditions, and administrative arrangements may necessitate the postponement of a contest. In such cases, the contest should be held as soon as possible after the postponement.

ORGANIZATION OF THE INTRAMURAL PROGRAM

Classification of Intramural Activities

Originally, most intramural activity was centered around organized leagues and consisted of tournaments planned around the various units found in the college or school. This plan for competition, even though it has desirable features, has failed to meet the interests of all individuals. There are many students who are not interested in being a member of a planned program, or who lack the ability. The highly organized intramural league program is similar to the varsity program, which is designed for the gifted few, thereby restricting participation to a very small number.

The ultimate goal for the intramural laboratory is to provide the opportunity for all students to participate in the activity of their choice. In order to design a program of this nature, the physical educator should know that there are two distinct types of intramural programs: the planned program and the informal pro-

gram. The two types may be used singly or in combination, depending upon the needs of the group involved.

The Planned Program. This phase consists of highly organized leagues designed to meet the needs and interests of those students who excel in motor skills. There is a thin line between the ability of these students and the ability of those who make up the varsity teams. The planned program does provide participation for those highly skillful students who are dropped from the varsity program. However, when the entire student body is considered, it is obvious that the planned program is not entirely satisfactory. In order to meet the needs of the large number of students who are not qualified for this program, another type of program is necessary.

The Informal Program. It was stated earlier that many students are neither interested in nor qualified for formal, highly organized intramural participation. For these students, informal participation is the answer. They may check out basketballs, tennis balls and racquets, or golf equipment, and plan among themselves how they wish to participate. This informal approach lessens the pressure for winning and provides the amount of vigorous activity needed to meet individual needs.

Grouping for Participation

Grouping students for participation is an important phase of planning the intramural laboratory. The organizational structure of most schools is such that several already existing units are available for arranging leagues and tournaments. Some of these units are discussed to show the physical educator that sound grouping is necessary in order to initiate an intramural program.

Homeroom. The homeroom is the most natural and practical unit for developing intramural programs. It is already highly organized and should be the logical unit for developing competitive programs.

Grade Level. The grade level in the school is a popular unit for organizing tournaments and leagues. This plan is used successfully when there are insufficient homerooms available to form a league. Teams formed from each grade level play one another within the grade level.

The Instructional Class. Although the physical education class should not be used for intramural activity, representative students from these classes may form teams to participate. The grade level prevails, making it possible for a class to have several teams that play groups from other classes of the same grade level.

School Department Teams. The various departments of the school, such as vocational, science, mathematics, and social studies, may be used for units of competition. In this plan, each department organizes a team to compete with teams from other departments.

There are other units for organizing the intramural laboratory that have been used effectively. Units such as those to be discussed next are not structural parts of the school, but are units that may be developed by the teacher or director.

Weight Classes. Weight classes are natural units for sports such as wrestling, tug-o-war, and hand wrestling.

Special Groups. The one-day tournament is extremely successful for sports in which the degree of the students' skill is not great. A day is set aside, and all students who report are placed on teams. A straight elimination tournament is held, and the winner is declared. These tournaments should be held following the conclusion of the instructional unit in a particular sport.

The students at Thornton Fractional High School, South Lansing, Illinois, participate in several one-shot types of events. Included in these events is the dual sport night, consisting of tournaments in volleyball and water polo. Individual all-around athletic championships are also held in 10 events: (1) fungo batting for distance, (2) baseball throw for distance, (3) forward pass for distance, (4) punt for distance, (5) 50-yard free style swim, (6) 12-pound shot, (7) 100-yard dash, (8) basketball set shooting, (9) hop-skip-jump, (10) 20-foot rope climb.

Points are awarded for each event and the participant with the most points is the winner.[13]

Informal Selection. Students may democratically form teams and elect a captain. The team lists are turned in to the intramural director or teacher, who uses them for organizing the tournament or league.

Intramural Clubs. Intramural clubs planned by students have been popular on the college level for a number of years. Recently, this unit of competition has also gained favor on the secondary school level. Club competition is found throughout the state of Texas, with tournaments conducted in such sports as rodeo, swimming, and track and field. The clubs are an outgrowth of the school curriculum, and skills are taught in the physical education class.[14]

The groupings just described are the ones most commonly used for intramurals. There are, however, other units that may be desirable in some cases. The director or teacher may wish to experiment with groupings by age, height, weight, the draw system, strength tests, the California exponent plan, age and height, grade, I.Q., the gang, and various combinations of these.

Scheduling Time for Intramurals

Experimenting with various time schedules is important in planning the intramural program. Students, particularly those in the secondary schools, have so many time conflicts that a varied time schedule is mandatory if the needs and interests of all students are to be met. For instance, many students work after school, precluding their participation in the after-school program. For these students, a morning schedule would be appropriate. Some of the time schedules presented in the following paragraphs may help to resolve problems of conflict with other activities.

Beyond School Hours. Over the years, the majority of intramural programs have been planned for the after-school hours. Although this is the ideal time, transportation problems, after-school jobs, school activities, and other conflicts necessitate the inclusion of other time schedules in the planning.

Early Morning. Programs developed for the early morning hours may prove successful for many students. William Michelli, a teacher at West Junior High School, Tiffin, Ohio, conducts an early morning intramural program in basketball, volleyball, and indoor play football. Coeducational volleyball is scheduled on a homeroom basis.[15]

During the School Day. There are many times during the school day that may be used for scheduling intramural programs. Many schools have a club period that may be used for this purpose. In some places the recess period has been arranged to include intramural participation. Merle E. Bradford, a teacher at the J. V. Beach School, Portland, Oregon, conducts such a program. He explains that the general purpose of the noon hour is to provide an organized and supervised period for recreational games and activities. The organization of the program depends upon the time, space, and facilities available. The program is designed to include activities for students in the lower and upper grades. Within these grades, outdoor and indoor programs are planned.[16]

A challenging program consisting of 20 activities is conducted at East High School, Cheyenne, Wyoming, and is held during the noon hour. Competition was originally held during the early morning hours, but owing to schedule changes it was placed during the school day. Rod Phillips, the director, feels that the program has been successful because of the following five elements: (1) intramural bulletin board, (2) individual patches for winners in each event, (3) a total points chart, (4) trophies, and (5) newspaper publicity.[17]

An elementary recess program designed to reinforce the skills taught in class and to motivate interest in physical education has been developed in Setauket, New York. The plan was devised by William Foley, physical education teacher at Nassakeag School, with the major emphasis on participation. The program is flexible both in content and student selection of activities and in or-

ganization. A well-rounded program of activities is available for all 5th and 6th grade students. A comprehensive point system is used and records of the participation are kept by each student. Awards are made in the assembly at the end of each year. The program has grown, with more students participating in all activities. Approximately 80 per cent of all 5th and 6th graders are involved in the program.[18]

Some intramural directors use a combination of time schedules. One director who has successfully combined several time schedules is Ray Welsh of East Orange High School, East Orange, New Jersey. His program functions before, during, and after school. The morning program consists of 50-minute recreational periods each morning from 7:30 to 8:30, and a daily afternoon intramural period from 3:00 to 4:45. He reports that 75 per cent of the boys participate in these morning and afternoon programs. During the school day, each boy has three 45-minute physical education periods per week. Mr. Welsh states, "We believe in giving our students an opportunity to use in competitive and recreational situations all the skills they learn in class."[19]

Alternative Intramurals. Alternative programs in physical education were discussed in Chapter 5. These programs allow students alternatives in instructional content through the utilization of community resources away from the school. Because of the lack of adequate school facilities, many schools are conducting alternative intramural programs away from the school. In some instances the alternative programs are conducted in the school, but on a different time schedule. A few alternative types of programs are:

1. *Near the home.* An objective of intramurals stated earlier is to motivate students to prolong their skill practice beyond the class period. Many students have several hours of free time spent near their homes that may be used for intramurals. Activities in which students compete in small groups and keep their own results are appropriate; one-goal basketball, foul shooting, and pull-ups belong to this group. The results are reported to the

physical education teacher and awards may be given to students who attain prescribed standards.

2. *Community resources.* To provide this participation, community resources are easily available. One of the most popular activities is bowling, yet few schools provide instruction and intramural opportunity in this sport. However, there are some exceptions. Girls in Kiowa Junior and Senior High School, Kiowa, Kansas, use local bowling alleys for five weeks of instructional-intramural bowling. The first week is used for teaching bowling skills and the remaining four weeks are devoted to intramural bowling.[20] The 16 junior and senior high schools in Kansas City, Missouri, utilize local bowling alleys for conducting intramural bowling for boys and girls. The program is sponsored by the Kansas City schools and the Bowling Proprietors Association. Twenty bowling establishments are involved and buses are provided for schools that are too far for students to walk to.[21]

3. *Saturday mornings.* Saturday mornings are an ideal time for highly organized intramural competition. Students are out of school, and many have no constructive activity to occupy their time. Well-planned programs may very well lower the incidence of deviant behavior during these hours. Clark County School District, Las Vegas, Nevada, promotes an outstanding Saturday-morning program. The program includes such activities as table tennis, badminton, archery, volleyball, Frisbee, bicycling, billiards, horseshoes, and spin casting. The Special Sports Committee recommends rules and regulations for the activities.[22]

Periodic Programs. An increasing number of schools and systems schedule periodic tournaments, demonstrations, and field days as an integral part of the intramural program. A typical example of this type of program is the annual Septathlon conducted in the Birmingham, Michigan, Public Schools. The event includes the tug-o-war, high jump, broad jump, softball throw, triple jump, 50-yard dash, and 500-yard shuttle relay with five boys and five girls on each team. The program is designed for 5th- and 6th-grade boys and girls, and Carl A. Pendracki feels that "It is extremely important to give older elementary school boys and girls the opportunity to engage in a varied extensive and regular intramural program."[23]

Another illustration of periodic intramural programs is the Olympic Game contest held at Thornton Fractional High School, South Lansing, Illinois. The components of the 10-item event are (1) one accurate tennis serve, (2) one free throw, (3) a four-foot golf putt, (4) a successful baseball pitch from mound into a garbage can at home plate, (5) a run around the bases, (6) a football extra point kick, (7) a soccer ball kick into the goal, (8) a rope climb to a steel beam, (9) a high jump of three feet six inches, and (10) a swim of two lengths of the pool.[24]

Planning for Competition

After the type of intramural program has been determined and the units for organization and time schedules selected, there remains the choice of a plan for organizing the competition. Several plans have been universally accepted for organizing the competing units.

The most popular plan is the *tournament,* which is used not only for organizing the competition but also for determining winners. The six types of tournaments most often used for determining winners are the single elimination, the double elimination, the consolation elimination, the round-robin tournament or league, the challenge, and meets.

Single-Elimination Tournament. The single elimination is used when time is limited and it is agreed by the parties concerned that a winner should be declared quickly. In the single-elimination tournament, the participants' names are placed in brackets, as shown in Figure 12–3.

When the number of participants exists in powers of two (2, 4, 8, 16, 32), there is no problem (see Figure 12–3, which shows eight players). However, when the number of players does not exist in powers of two, the first round must include "byes." The number of byes is determined by subtracting the number of players from the next power of two. For example, if there are 12 players or teams, the nearest highest power of two is 16. When 12 is subtracted from 16, the result is 4 byes in

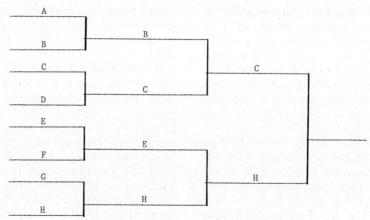

Figure 12–3. Single elimination tournament.

the first round. In the situation illustrated in Figure 12–4, players A, F, G, and L do not participate in the first round. In the single-elimination tournament, the teams or players should be equally placed or seeded throughout the tournament, according to their known ability. This prevents the better players from being eliminated early. In Figure 12–4, the byes are seeded players.

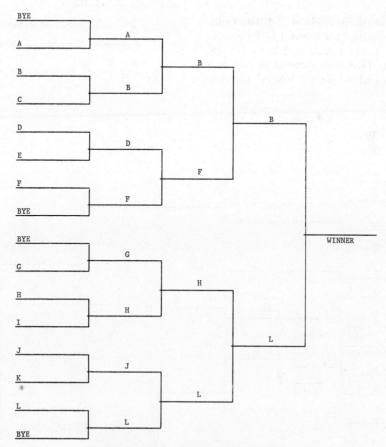

Figure 12–4. Elimination with byes.

Double-Elimination Tournament. In the double-elimination tournament, a player's single defeat does not end his participation, since each player must lose twice before being eliminated from the tournament. The losers in all rounds continue to play in a losers' tournament. The losers from the championship bracket drop down and play the winners in the losers' bracket, as shown in Figure 12–5. If H defeats D, then H is the tournament winner. However, if D defeats H, then they must play again, since this is the first time H has lost.

Another type of double-elimination tournament is shown in Figure 12–6. The winning teams advance to the right and the losing teams advance to the left. The arrows show the placement of the losing teams in the losers' brackets. The winner on the left must play the winner on the right. E must defeat A twice, since E has already lost one game. If A wins the first game, he is declared the champion.

Consolation-Elimination Tournament. In the consolation tournament, the losers of the first round begin to play a losers' tournament. This tournament is not particularly popular, since losers playing losers does not appeal to most participants. As shown in Figure 12–7, winners advance to the right and losers to the left.

Round-Robin Tournament or League. The round robin is a popular and universally accepted organization for tournament or league play. The reason for this popularity is that the procedure is designed primarily for team play, and each team plays every other team at least once. The round robin, being more intricate than the other plans, requires considerable organization. The first step in planning for the round robin is to determine the number of games to be played. The following formula may be helpful.

$$\frac{N(N-1)}{2} = \text{Number of games to be played}$$

N is the number of entries

$$\frac{(\text{Number of teams}) \times (\text{Number of teams} - 1)}{2}$$
$$= \text{Number of games to be played}$$

Example: Number of teams is 6

$$\frac{6 \times 5}{2} = 15 \text{ games to be played}$$

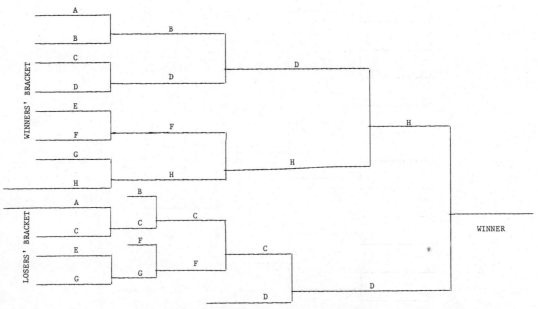

Figure 12–5. Double elimination tournament.

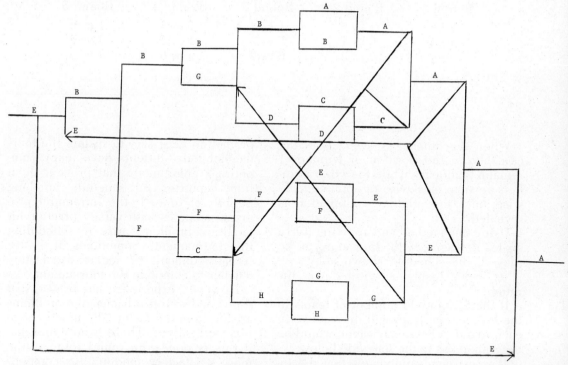

Figure 12–6. Double elimination tournament.

If more than six teams are involved, it is recommended, because of the time element, that another league be formed. When the number of teams has been determined, the next step is to arrange the schedule. The simplest way of doing this is to arrange all teams in two columns as shown:

$$\begin{array}{c}\longleftarrow \\ 1-6 \\ \downarrow\ 2-5\ \uparrow \quad \text{Even number}\\ 3-4 \\ \longrightarrow \end{array}$$

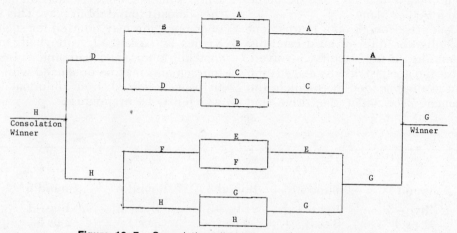

Figure 12–7. Consolation-elimination tournament (8 teams).

Round 1	Round 2	Round 3	Round 4	Round 5
1 vs 6	1 vs 5	1 vs 4	1 vs 3	1 vs 2
2 vs 5	6 vs 4	5 vs 3	4 vs 2	3 vs 6
3 vs 4	2 vs 3	6 vs 2	5 vs 6	4 vs 5

When the number is even, as in the case above, the position of Number 1 remains stationary while the other numbers revolve clockwise or counterclockwise until the original combination is revealed.

Using this method and applying it to a six-team league with 15 games to be played, the schedule shown above results, with teams substituted for the numbers.

If there is an odd number of teams in the league, one team will draw a bye in each round. A five-team league would be determined as in the schedule below.

It is extremely important that the intramural director always have available sufficient mimeographed materials to expedite the organization of the tournament. These materials should include entry forms such as the one shown in Figure 12–8. In addition, league forms should be available for 4-, 5-, 6-, 7-, and 8-team leagues. Figure 12–9 illustrates such a form.

Sometimes it is desirable to conduct a round-robin tournament in conjunction with an elimination style of play-off. Figure 12–10 illustrates this arrangement for four 5-team leagues. See resource manual for other plans.

To conduct a round-robin tournament successfully, the director must carefully consider the many factors involved. Probably the greatest disadvantage is the amount of time needed to complete the tournament. Too often the drive and promotion necessary to sustain the tournament fail. Students have many competing commitments that prevent them from reporting on schedule for long periods of time. If the intramural program competes with varsity practice for facilities, problems arise in scheduling the tournament. Sometimes it is extremely difficult to secure satisfactory officials to complete the tournament.

However, experience has proved that if planned well in advance, the problems arising from the factors discussed above may be resolved. There is no doubt that if this is done, the round robin is the most satisfactory medium for competition. Each team plays each other team at least once or twice. If a double round-robin tournament is held, league standings may be posted. Continuous play is assumed, and the teams may be ranked according to their success in competition.

To insure successful competition, it may be necessary to include some variation of the round-robin type of tournament. One type that deserves mention is the Lombard tournament, which is an instant type of tournament that is desirable when sufficient time is unavailable for the standard round robin play. This type of competition may be used for such activities as basketball, volleyball, touch football, tennis, and badminton. Instant tournaments may be organized with participants selected from informal play which may be in progress.

Round 1	Round 2	Round 3	Round 4	Round 5
Bye–5	Bye–4	Bye–3	Bye–2	Bye–1
1 vs 4	5 vs 3	4 vs 2	3 vs 1	2 vs 5
2 vs 3	1 vs 2	5 vs 1	4 vs 5	3 vs 4

```
                    INTRAMURAL ENTRY BLANK

_____                                    _____
     Date                                                Sex

_____    _____    _____    _____
    Sport              Homeroom           Captain            School


PLAYERS                                    PLAYERS
_____    _____
_____    _____
_____    _____
_____    _____
_____    _____
_____    _____
_____    _____

                                        _____
                                            Homeroom Manager

                                        _____
                                            Homeroom Teacher
```

Figure 12–8. Intramural entry blank.

A Lombard tournament provides for shorter game periods, with the playing time determined by dividing the actual game time by the number of teams playing. For example, if the game time for basketball is 60 minutes and six teams constitute the league, then the game time for the Lombard tournament is 10 minutes. Each team then plays each other team a 10-minute game.

Challenge Tournaments. The challenge tournament is a self-directed, self-organized type of competition. The participants attempt to advance in the hierarchy of competition by challenging and defeating their opponents on a higher level or position. Although there is a deadline for completing the tournament, the contest usually requires a much longer time frame than the round robin type. Arranging the challenge tournament requires creativity and imaginativeness by the director and emphasizes the importance of participant cooperation.

Students desiring to participate in a challenge tournament list their names and telephone numbers with the director and also place them on a tag, which is attached to some type of board such as a

League
_____

ROUNDS	TEAM plays TEAM	PLACE	DATE	TIME	WINNER
1	1 vs 6				
	2 vs 5				
	3 vs 4				
2	1 vs 5				
	6 vs 4				
	2 vs 3				
3	1 vs 4				
	5 vs 3				
	6 vs 2				
4	1 vs 3				
	4 vs 2				
	5 vs 6				
5	1 vs 2				
	3 vs 6				
	4 vs 5				

TEAMS AND CAPTAINS
_____

Team	Captain	Team	Captain
1		4	
2		5	
3		6	

Figure 12–9. A form for a six-team league.

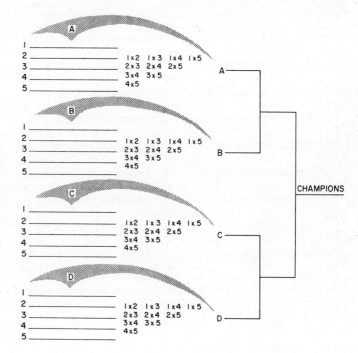

Figure 12–10. A round-robin tournament with a single-elimination play-off. (From Means, Louis: *Intramurals, Their Organization and Administration*, 2nd ed. Englewood Cliffs, N.J.: Prentice-Hall, Inc., 1973, p. 225.)

peg board. The position occupied by the contestants may be determined by ability, by drawing from a lot, or by the time of entry or ranking in a previous tournament.

After the names are posted, participants challenge each other and competition begins. If a challenger defeats a player on a higher position, they change places, but if the defender wins, the positions remain the same. At the expiration date for the tournament, the player in the highest position on the board is the winner.

Challenge tournaments are not suitable for team sports, but are designed for such activities as tennis, handball, and other activities in which the participants may elect the time and conditions of play. These tournaments are an important adjunct to the intramural program. For those students who have neither the time nor the desire to compete in the school round-robin tournaments, the challenge tournament provides the opportunity for exercise, recreation, and pleasurable competition.

Competition in the challenge tournament should be governed by basic rules and regulations, including the following:

1. All challenges must be honored and played within a specified time frame.
2. Participants may challenge anyone in the tournament unless guidelines are devised to limit challenges to two or three positions above.
3. When a participant loses, he must accept another challenge below him before challenging the player who defeated him or attempting to move up.
4. New players may participate in the tournament by challenging a player in the lowest position on the board.

There are several types of challenge tournaments that have evolved from experimentation with the various arrangements for conducting tournaments. The most popular are the ladder, the pyramid, and the funnel.

The *ladder tournament* derives its name from the design, which resembles the rungs of a ladder. The ladder tournament is easy to administer, and when completed, provides a rank order for the participants' ability. This type of tournament can accommodate such a few con-

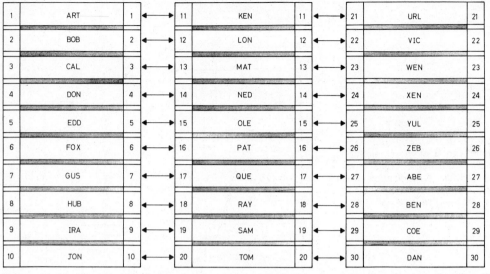

1	ART	1	↔	11	KEN	11	↔	21	URL	21
2	BOB	2	↔	12	LON	12	↔	22	VIC	22
3	CAL	3	↔	13	MAT	13	↔	23	WEN	23
4	DON	4	↔	14	NED	14	↔	24	XEN	24
5	EDD	5	↔	15	OLE	15	↔	25	YUL	25
6	FOX	6	↔	16	PAT	16	↔	26	ZEB	26
7	GUS	7	↔	17	QUE	17	↔	27	ABE	27
8	HUB	8	↔	18	RAY	18	↔	28	BEN	28
9	IRA	9	↔	19	SAM	19	↔	29	COE	29
10	JON	10	↔	20	TOM	20	↔	30	DAN	30

STRUCTURING TOURNAMENTS

Figure 12–11. Combination ladder tournaments, permitting horizontal and vertical challenging. (From Mueller, Pat: *Intramurals: Programming and Administration,* 4th ed. New York: The Ronald Press Co., 1971, p. 161.)

testants, they may be arranged in combination to provide additional entries. Figure 12–11 shows how ladders may be arranged side by side in order to provide horizontal and vertical competition. This arrangement may be used for 10, 20, or 30 players.

The *pyramid tournament* is a popular form of competition and may be used to accommodate more entries than the ladder type. Contestants are usually required to defeat an entry on their own row before challenging someone above. This creates more opportunities for play and prevents anyone from being in last place. (See Figure 12–13.)

A variation of the pyramid tournament is the *crown tournament,* in which three pyramids are arranged in ascending order. When the contestant reaches the top of the lower pyramids, he may challenge horizontally. If he wins, he moves to a position at the bottom of the pyramid on the higher level. The contestant who advances to the highest position in the upper-level pyramid and maintains his position is the winner. (See Figure 12–14.)

The *funnel tournament* combines the pyramid and ladder to form a design resembling a funnel. In this type of tournament, the players sift downward to the bottom of the funnel. A great number of entries are possible when the funnel tournament is used, and by adding more rungs in the ladder section, even more

Figure 12–12. Intramural activities are extremely important as an extension of the elementary physical education instructional program.

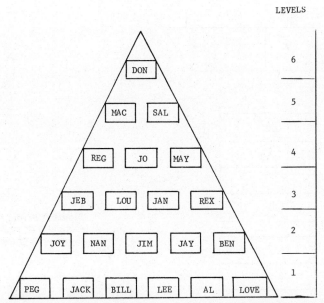

Figure 12–13. Coeducational pyramid tournament. 21 players. Any player in level 1 may challenge any player in level 2. Any player in level 2 may challenge any player in level 3. Any player in level 3 may challenge any player in level 4. Any player in level 4 may challenge any player in level 5. Either Mac or Sal may challenge Don.

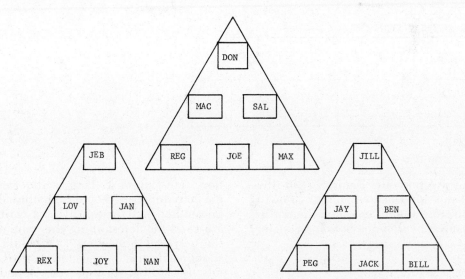

Figure 12–14. Coeducational crown tournament—18 players.

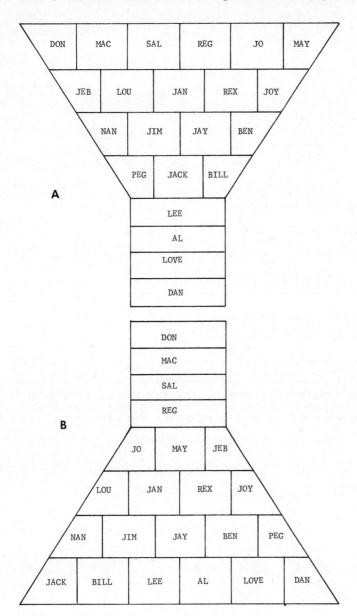

Figure 12–15. *A,* The funnel tournament—22 entries. *B,* The inverted funnel—22 entries.

entries are possible. Figure 12–15 illustrates this type of tournament, showing the inverted tunnel in which the participants advance from the bottom to the top.

Program of Activities

One basic objective of the intramural program is that the program shall be an extension of physical education instruc- tion. This premise largely determines the activities that should be included for intramural participation. Just as criteria are used for determining the content of the physical education curriculum, so should activities be selected for intramurals. In addition to those developed for physical education activities, other criteria should be established.

The comprehensive program conducted in the public schools of Portland, Oregon, outlines the criteria for selecting activities: (1) facilities, equipment, and supplies, (2) time allotment, (3) number of students, (4) interest, (5) seasonal sports, (6) variety, (7) ability levels, (8) coordination with physical education, (9) co-recreation.[25]

The Elementary Program. Students in the elementary school should not participate in the same activities that are included in the secondary schools. One of the criticisms of the elementary intramural program in many places is that it duplicates the secondary school content. When the elementary physical education curriculum is scientifically devised, the elementary intramural program is sound, since intramurals should be an extension of the physical education program. The following paragraphs describe some of the elementary programs conducted in various sections of the country. The reader should appraise them in light of (1) the criteria suggested for selecting instructional activities, discussed in Chapter 6; (2) intramurals as an extension of the instructional program; and (3) the criteria listed in the preceding paragraph.

A survey by Edward Bork involving 16 school districts and 186 elementary schools in Minnesota discloses that the following activities were used:[26]

Fall
Soccer
Touch football
Tetherball
Swimming
Field hockey
Kickball
Spring
Hiking
Bicycling
Track
Swimming
Golf
Winter
Basketball
Volleyball
Wrestling
Gymnastics
Dodgeball
Indian hockey
Four square
Box hockey
Tumbling
Rhythms
Ice hockey

Bowling
Paddleball

An elementary program which represents thoughtful planning is conducted in the Birmingham, Michigan, Public Schools. In addition to such activities as track and field, tumbling, soccer, and basketball, the program includes an athletic achievement program. All 5th- and 6th- graders have the opportunity for recognition if they pass 12 of the 14 tests which constitute the program. Not included in the items is the swimming test. All students who can swim 50 yards without stopping may substitute this performance for any of the 14 tests. Figure 12-16 outlines the program and includes the events and standards for boys and girls.

The Secondary Program. Since intramural programs are more prevalent in secondary schools than in the elementary schools, it is not too difficult to find samples of quality programs. The problem on the secondary level is deciding what activities should *not* be included. It is extremely important to use established criteria in developing intramurals for secondary schools. If the program is conducted on the philosophy that it should be an extension of physical education instruction, then the selection of activities should be relatively easy. In addition to the criteria mentioned earlier, the safety factor should play an important role in developing content for secondary participation.

The girls' physical education department in the Houston, Texas, Independent School District balances team and individual sports in both instruction and intramurals. The intramural offerings include volleyball, basketball, softball, badminton, tennis, archery, swimming, track and field, table tennis, paddle badminton, and soccer. During the school year 1968–69, 27,000 girls registered for intramurals.[27]

Evanston Township High, Evanston, Illinois, enrolled 2000 girls in the intramural program during the year 1968–69. The program is administered by girls and is conducted every day from 3:30 P.M. to 5:00 P.M. One feature of the pro-

BOYS		GIRLS	
EVENT	STANDARD	EVENT	STANDARD
1. 50 yard dash	8.0 sec.	1. 50 yard dash	8.1 sec.
2. 600 yard run-walk	2:22 sec.	2. 600 yard run-walk	2:24 sec.
3. High jump	3'6"	3. High jump	3'5"
4. Standing broad jump	5'5"	4. Standing broad jump	5'4"
5. Pull-ups	6	5. Flexed arm hang	20 sec.
6. Push-ups	25	6. Push-ups (modified)	30
7. Squat thrust (60 sec.)	23	7. Squat thrust (60 sec.)	23
8. Sit-ups	100	8. Sit-ups	75
9. Shuttle run	11.0 sec.	9. Shuttle run	11.2 sec.
10. Basketball free throw	5-10	10. Basketball free throw	5-10
11. Softball throw or	122 ft.	11. Softball throw or	88 ft.
Football pass	25 yds.	Soccer pass	15 yards
12. Football punt	25 yds.	12. Soccer punt	20 yards
13. Shoulder kip	land on ft.	13. Shoulder kip	land on feet
14. Walk on hands or motionless handstand	10 ft. 20 sec.	14. Walk on hands or motionless handstand	10 ft. 15 sec.
15. Scholarship	2.0 average	15. Scholarship	2.0 average

Figure 12–16. Elementary intramural athletic achievement program used in Birmingham, Michigan, Public Schools. (From "Planning Intramurals for Fifth and Sixth Graders." *Physical Education Newsletter,* January 15, 1970.)

gram which deserves attention is the general organization of the student body. The school is divided into four semiautonomous schools, with each school forming an organizational unit. An elaborate point system is used which is based on participation, playing on winning teams, and winning individual events. Annual awards banquets are scheduled which motivate interest in the program. The following activities are included in the program:[28]

The program for intramural activities and sports at Rockville High School, Rockville, Connecticut, owes its success to the Girls' Athletic Activities Club (GAAC). The club sponsors all intramural activities and is an outgrowth of the physical education program. Fifteen different activities are offered each year, with participation restricted to no more than two seasonal activities. Certain participating groups in folk dance, modern dance, and tumbling provide demon-

Fall Activities (September 15–October 24)
Tennis   Swimming   Track and Field

Winter Activities (November 3–March 20)
Gymnastics Volleyball   Archery Roller skating Basketball Fencing
Badminton   Table Tennis Exercise and Conditioning Activities

Spring Activities (March 24–April 22)
Tennis   Swimming   Softball   Track and Field   Badminton

Activity	Girls	Boys	Coed
Aerial Tennis	X		X
Basketball	X	X	X
Bowling	X		X
Field Hockey	X		X
Flag Football	X		X
Soccer		X	
Softball			X
Tug-o-War	X	X	X
Volleyball	X	X	X
Archery	X	X	
Badminton	X		
Century Club (jog 100 miles)	X	X	
Cycle Century Club	X	X	
Miniature Golf	X	X	
One-on-One Basketball	X	X	
Ping Pong	X	X	X
Tennis	X		X
Track	X		

strations for PTA organizations and clinics. Activities included in the intramural program are bowling, basketball, volleyball, softball, golf, archery, badminton, tennis, track, modern dance, tumbling, and folk dance.[29]

An interesting early morning intramural program is conducted at Christiansburg High School, Christiansburg, Virginia. All activities are held each morning from 8:00 to 8:45, with the exception of individual sports and bowling, which are held after school. The activities are evenly balanced in team and individual sports. Officials are selected from the student body and receive no remuneration. The program of activities is as shown in the schedule above.[30]

Procedures in Developing the Program

Sometimes the director of the program, although he may have the necessary knowledge of organization and administration, is unable to make a start, usually because of lack of communication. In order to reach students and acquaint them with the objectives and activities involved, several procedures may be followed.

Promotional Program. To contact students and acquaint them with the dates, time schedule, activities, and other essentials of the program, a practical direct line of communication must be found. The best plan is to make all announcements in the physical education classes. Entry forms may be distributed. The forms, when properly filled out, may be returned to the director (see Figure 12–17).

In conjunction with this procedure, announcements may be made on the public address systems and through other media, such as the bulletin board, auditorium announcements, and the school paper. These procedures must be repeated many times until the program is under way. All student leaders should be involved in assisting with the promotional program.

The handbook is highly recommended as a means of stimulating interest in intramurals and interpreting the program to students, teachers, parents, and administrators. The handbook published by the Cincinnati Public Schools is an excellent guide for secondary programs.[31] A general outline of the book and the cover are shown in Figure 12–18.

ELEMENTARY VOLLEYBALL DEMONSTRATION

ENTRY BLANK

SCHOOL

GRADE

BOYS   GIRLS

Age should be shown in years as of October 22, 1968

LAST NAME FIRST	AGE	LAST NAME FIRST	AGE
1.		1.	
2.		2.	
3.		3.	
4.		4.	
5.		5.	
6.		6.	
7.		7.	
8.		8.	
9.		9.	
10.		10.	
11.		11.	
12.		12.	

Teacher _____   Teacher _____

Room No._____   Room No. _____

This is to certify that the participants listed above are winning members of the team from our school and are the age shown by the name as of tournament date.

_____   _____
            Principal   Physical Education Teacher

Figure 12–17. Entry blank for elementary volleyball demonstration.

The intramural handbook developed by the Birmingham, Michigan, Public Schools is an example of a cooperative effort by teachers to improve the program. The handbook serves as a guide for the organization and administration of intramurals within the city and includes the following sections:[32]

Intramural policies
Duties of the sponsor
Supplemental pay
Length of seasons
Opportunities for boys and girls
Sports days
Intramural in-service meetings
Evaluating and reporting procedures
Sportsmanship goals
Methods of choosing teams
Communications with parents
Permission to play rules
Operational procedures
Setting up tournaments
Record keeping
Special events

Posting Schedules. It is important that attractive and detailed schedules be posted. The student director and leaders should be familiar with the schedules and should assist in this procedure by working with the captains and managers.

Motivation. Motivation is the key to success in all aspects of education. This is particularly true in programs which extend beyond the school day. When successful intramural programs are examined, a high degree of motivation is apparent. Poorly planned programs that ignore the interests of students are sure to fail.

A successful intramural program involves many factors. Coeducational activities in volleyball, tennis, and softball are sure to stimulate interest. Plans to include one-day tournaments should be considered. Mixed doubles in tennis, table tennis, and badminton motivate students to remain after school for competition.

When programs are carefully organized and student leaders are involved, many of the mechanics of developing interest become relatively simple. The results of all contests should be widely publicized through the use of such media as bulletin boards, newspapers, special notices, and announcements to all classes through the intercommunication system. Comprehensive point and awards systems should be developed to recognize handicapped students as well

INTRAMURAL HANDBOOK
PROGRAM for BOYS
in SECONDARY SCHOOLS

FITNESS—FOR—ALL

CINCINNATI   PUBLIC   SCHOOLS

I. Introduction

    A. Philosophy and Objectives

II. Statement of Policy

    A. General Policies
    B. Eligibility for Participation
    C. Intramural Leadership
    D. The Standard Program
    E. A Broad and Varied Program

III. Organization and Leadership

    A. Plan of Organization
    B. The Intramural Council
    C. Faculty Leadership
    D. The Role of Pupil Leadership
    E. Duties of Pupil Leaders

IV. Planning the Program

    A. Publicity and Promotion
    B. Use of Facilities
    C. Adopting Specific Activities
    D. Awards
    E. Equipment and Supplies
    F. The Sports Calendar
    G. Suggested Point System

V. Conducting the Program

    A. Classification for Competition
    B. Health and Safety of Students
    C. Officiating
    D. Protests and Forfeits
    E. Record Keeping and Reports

VI. Methods of Organizing for Competition

    A. The Round Robin Tournament
    B. Single Elimination Tournament
    C. Seeding
    D. Consolation Elimination Tournament
    E. Double Elimination Tournament
    F. Combination Plan
    G. Challenge Tournaments   (31)

Figure 12–18. The Intramural Handbook. (Courtesy of Howard Grimes, Cincinnati Public Schools, Cincinnati, Ohio.)

as those who excel physically. Student leaders may offer invaluable assistance with the implementation of these procedures.

An extramural program, when coordinated with the school program, usually serves as a motivating influence. Extramurals should be the capstone of the intramural program. The dates for these programs should be announced early, thus providing teams and individuals with a definite goal.

Faculty participation in intramural games has proved successful. When teachers are placed on the various teams, the camaraderie is such that a high interest level is maintained.

Developing a balanced program of team and individual sports is essential for creating general interest in intramurals. In addition to the usual activities for male and female students, elaborate coeducational programs should be developed.

Innovative programs are the answer to stimulating and maintaining interest in the intramural program. These programs are developed when teachers and students cooperatively plan for intramural competition. The basic consideration is to plan beyond the traditional tournaments and leagues. Participation in such activities as bicycle racing, roller skating, surfing, mountain climbing, and skiing offer additional opportunity for many students. Telephonic intramurals may be extremely effective and interesting when lack of transportation precludes extramural programs. The results of events such as foul shooting, track and field, and swimming are compared by telephone either at the central office or in the individual schools.

An interesting example of innovative planning is the elementary intramural program at the Fort Bragg Dependents School, Fayetteville, North Carolina. Most of the activities are coeducational. All are chosen by the students on an interest basis. The club organizational plan is used rather than classrooms. The program consists of (1) modified track and field events (grades 3–6); (2) carnival day (grades 1–6), which capitalizes on holidays such as Halloween and includes such activities as beanbag toss games, rope climb, tetherball, and relays; (3) mile run (grades 4–6), in which students run a mile once a week at their own pace; (4) volleyball club (grades 5–6); (5) soccer club (grades 4–6); (6) flag football club (grades 4–6); (7) folk dance club (grades 4–6); and (8) gymnastics leaders club (grades 4–6).[33]

Cumulative Records. Keeping cumulative records is essential for an effective program in intramurals. The student director should be responsible for this procedure. These records may be kept on a 4″ × 6″ card and filed alphabetically (see Figure 12–19.)

Point System and Awards

Awards for intramurals have long been controversial. There are many educators who feel that the intrinsic values of play, the fun derived, and the competition should suffice. On the other hand, the majority of intramural leaders are adamant in their belief that awards are necessary. They point out that we live in a competitive society in which awards are given for scholastic achievement, graduation from school, professional endeavor, and so on.

If awards are given, it is recommended that everyone have the opportunity for recognition and that the awards remain simple. Usually awards consist of medals, monograms, trophies, plaques, and certificates. The certificate is a desirable award because it is inexpensive, attractive, and has tremendous public-relations potential. (See Figure 12–27.)

Point Awards. A point system must be devised in order to regulate the granting of other awards, such as monograms or trophies.

The Cincinnati public school system uses the following point system, which may serve as a guide for planning the secondary program. The plan is flexible and may be modified to meet local needs.

10 points for each entry
2 points for each win
1 point for each loss
0 points for a forfeit; or, if desired, deduction for each forfeit

10 points for each team championship

6 points for second place team championship

3 points for third place team championship

6 points for each individual championship

4 points for second place individual championship

3 points for third place individual championship

3 points per game for officiating

10 points for homeroom representatives

2 points for each meeting attended by homeroom representative[34]

This point system may serve as a basis for awarding certificates, trophies, plaques, banners, medals, ribbons, pins, and monograms for individual and team accomplishments. The following factors

G.R.A. POINT RECORD

NAME _____ PH. _____ MEMBERSHIP SOPH. JR. SR.

INTRAMURALS	10	11	12	EXTRAMURALS	10	11	12	AWARDS		
AERIAL DARTS				CHEERLEADING				SMALL 'W'		
ARCHERY				BEG. CHEERLEADING				BIG 'W'		
BADMINTON				FIRST AID				PIN		
BASKETBALL				FITNESS SWIM				CHARM		
B.B. FREE THROW				PHYSICAL FITNESS CLASS				TOTAL POINTS		
BOWLING				REFEREE				SOPH.		
GOLF				SPORTS MANAGER				JR.		
HOCKEY				STUNTS & TUMBLING				SR.		
SOFTBALL				SYNC. SWIMMING						
SHUFFLEBOARD				TENNIS				HEALTH		
SWIMMING				JR. LIFESAVING				DR.		
TABLE TENNIS				SR. LIFESAVING				DEN.		
VOLLEYBALL				TRACK				EYE		
TOTAL										

A

G.R.A. ACTIVITIES	10	11	12							
PICNIC				GRAND GALA				PLAYDAYS		
CHILI WITH POP				GEN. CHAIRMAN				JR. HIGH		
CHRISTMAS PARTY				AUD.				SPORTS DAYS		
EVENT WITH MOM				CLEAN UP				OTHERS		
FLOAT				CORSAGE						
WORK PROJECT				COURTESY				AWARDS BANQUET		
				DECORATION				MISCELLANEOUS		
				KING & COURT						
				POSTERS						
BANQUET SERVING				PROGRAM						
				REFRESHMENTS						
				TICKETS						

C-563 - C.H.S. Press

B

Figure 12–19. Cumulative record card for intramural and extramural sports. (From "Girls' Recreation Association," West High School, Barkersville, California, 1965.)

should be considered when planning the awards system:

1. Points and awards should be allotted for participation in addition to the system described above. This is in compliance with the purpose of intramurals, which is to recognize individual effort. A separate award, such as a certificate, may be used for those students who participate but do not win.

2. If the point system is used for system-wide programs, points should not be transferred from elementary to junior high school or from junior high school to senior high school. The excessive bookkeeping involved makes the transferral of points from one level to another prohibitive.

3. The number of points necessary for receiving the various awards should be determined and publicized. Points may be carried over from one year to the next, but not from one school level to another.

All point systems should be simple and functional. Highly sophisticated systems such as those used on the college level are not appropriate for elementary and secondary schools. The system should be flexible enough to provide changes to meet individual needs and situations without affecting the total program. When points systems are developed, the motivation of students should receive careful consideration. If student interest is not maintained and broadened, the program may suffer and become extinct owing to lack of participation. All activities should be weighed and points allotted accordingly.

Monograms. Monograms are universally awarded for winning a particular activity and for accumulating a number of points. Monograms are expensive, but if felt or chenille is bought in large quantities, the school homemaking department may make them as a class project.

Certificates. Certificates are the most practical and inexpensive awards, and are used in many school and city programs. They are especially effective as awards for participation, regardless of whether a contestant wins or not.

Other awards, such as cups, plaques, pins, trophies, banners, medals, and ribbons, are universally used for individual and team competition.

Coeducational Intramurals

It has long been recognized by psychologists and sociologists that it is educationally sound for boys and girls to play together in wholesome, vigorous activity. Many activities in the physical education curriculum meet all criteria and are suitable for joint participation by both boys and girls. These activities, when organized and supervised properly, make a tremendous contribution to the objectives of education. Such sports as tennis, golf, swimming, bowling, volleyball, and rhythms are illustrative of activities that boys and girls may play together successfully.

The recent action by the Department of Health, Education and Welfare under Title IX places intramurals in the same category as other school programs in which segregation by sex is no longer allowed.

Figure 12–20. Coeducational activities stimulate interest and enthusiasm for intramural participation. (Courtesy of Clark County School District, Las Vegas, Nevada.)

Planning Coeducational Activities

Coeducational intramural activities must be planned differently from those segregated by sex. The fact that boys and girls are placed in the same play area creates an entirely different climate for competition. Previous to their intramural participation, most of the participants have been playing and competing with members of the same sex. The need for adjusting and adapting codes of conduct, behavior, and attitudes to the new patterns necessitates a thorough study of the factors involved in the selection, organization, and administration of the activities in the coeducational program.

Selection of Activities. Traditionally, during the first three years of elementary education, boys and girls have participated and played together in all aspects of the physical education program, including intramurals and recreation. From the 4th grade through high school, the separation of sexes in physical education is usually practiced. This organizational pattern exists because leaders in physical education feel that because of anatomical, physiological, safety, and social factors, the sexes should be separated.

However, there is an increasing amount of evidence to suggest that if the best interests of boys and girls are to be served, they should be allowed to participate in some coeducational activities. An overview of the growth and development characteristics of boys and girls during puberty reveals marked anatomical and physiological differences. Although the basic instructional program may be segregated by sex, some sports, such as tennis and golf, may be planned as coeducational activities. The following guidelines may be of help in the selection of activities for the program.

ELEMENTARY SCHOOL. Most activities usually found in the elementary curriculum (grades K–6) are educationally sound and satisfactory for inclusion in a coeducational program. An acceptable plan is to list a group of activities that are scientifically appropriate and allow students to select from these the activities in which they wish to participate. Interest is a basic criterion for selection when the activities are educationally and medically sound.

JUNIOR HIGH SCHOOL. It was stated earlier that puberty marks the change in growth patterns of boys and girls. Activities suitable for girls during the earlier years are no longer desirable for junior high programs. Interest should continue to be the basic criterion, but the activities offered should be more carefully screened. There are some schools, for example, in which boys and girls play touch football together. Such programs usually end in disaster, with serious injuries inflicted upon the girl participants. The following are some activities that are desirable and suitable for inclusion in a coeducational program with emphasis on team activity:

Individual Sports
        (Moderate emphasis)
  Tennis
  Golf
  Bowling
  Swimming
  Rhythms

Team Sports
        (Strong emphasis)
  Volleyball
  Softball

SENIOR HIGH SCHOOL. The selection of activities for the senior high school coeducational program is very difficult. Because of the many competing interests, both in and out of school, it is important to provide activities that will arouse a high degree of interest among students. If interests have not already been developed, there is not sufficient time to offer new programs and teach new skills.

An outline of activities that are more generally interesting and desirable for the senior high school follows; note that the emphasis has changed to individual sports:

  Tennis—strong emphasis
  Golf—strong emphasis
  Bowling—strong emphasis
  Swimming—strong emphasis
  Volleyball—emphasis
  Softball—emphasis

Organizing the Program. The process of organizing the program for coeducational intramurals is similar to that outlined under organization of the intramural program (p. 309). Tournaments should be arranged, but the formal type of organization is by far the more desirable for senior high school boys and girls.

Administrative Guidelines. In conjunction with the regulations for administering the traditional intramural program, the conduct of coeducational events involves certain special principles that should be followed. Consideration of these principles and a supervisory structure insuring their implementation is vitally important for a successful coeducational program. Some guidelines that have been found effective are:

1. Coeducational programs should be an integral part of the total intramural organization and should operate under the same general policies.
2. The element of safety should play an important role in the selection of activities for intramural competition. Potentially dangerous activities such as football, karate, and wrestling should be excluded from the program.
3. Rules for coeducational activities should be modified to meet the anatomical differences of the female participant.
4. Students should be involved in planning the program, and selection of the activities should be based on their interests.
5. Intensive supervision is extremely important for the success of coeducational programs. Teachers of both sexes should be present at all contests to insure acceptable behavior.

EXTRAMURAL PROGRAMS

It is no secret that the interschool program is designed for the physically gifted student. It is also generally known that the interschool athletic program involves a very small group of individuals chosen from the many candidates desiring to be members of the interschool teams.

There is a thin line separating the quality of the performance of individuals on the team representing the school and that of the large number of students who are not on the interschool team. Indeed, there have been many instances of students who were dropped from the varsity squad who were superior to those finally selected to represent the school.

This large number of individuals whose potential is greater than the performance level offered in the traditional intramural program and who are not on the school team should have the opportunity to participate with students of comparable caliber from other schools. An extramural program provides such an opportunity.

Another need for extramural competition arises from the criticisms of those opposed to having interschool athletics in the junior high school. These critics say that the formation of leagues, the percentage procedures involving wins and losses, and the overemphasis on winning that usually follows are educationally and medically unsound for junior high school students. The city-wide prgrams involving limited and controlled competition may be the answer to the problem of competition on the junior high school level.

The extramural program may also be designed for students who are not necessarily highly skilled. These programs may be demonstrations in which representatives from several schools meet to compete or to demonstrate the skills involved in the physical education program.

Because of the factors discussed in the preceding paragraphs, extramural programs have emerged as an integral part of the total physical education offering.

These programs differ from the regular intramural program in that they are designed to serve the above-average or near-gifted students. With the addition of the following objectives, the same philosophy guides the program.

Objectives of Extramural Programs

The objectives of the extramural program reflect both its difference from and its similarity to the regular intramural program. The extramural program of intramurals should:

1. Provide opportunity for those gifted students whose performance level is below that of individuals on the varsity programs, so that they may participate with students of similar ability in other schools.
2. Serve as a culmination of the intramural program in the various schools.
3. Motivate students to exercise and compete beyond the school day.

Regulations for Extramural Programs

The larger the school system, the more urgent the need for strong rules governing the extramural program. Careful consideration of these rules of operation in the initial planning will undoubtedly prevent misunderstandings. The following general regulations are essential for the conduct of all extramural programs:

1. Participants in extramural programs should be winners of the individual school program. The teams of individuals who win the school events are the only ones eligible to participate in the extramural program.
2. Since extramurals are designed to attract large numbers of students, competition should be developed from a large base of individual school participation. An example would be to hold extramural tournaments in several grade levels.
3. All extramural participants should be examined by a physician and should carry accident insurance.
4. Eligibility rules developed for school intramurals (p. 314) should apply to extramural competition.
5. Entries for extramurals should be approved by the school principal and director and sent to the coordinator of the city-wide program one week prior to the event.
6. The junior high schools should participate separately from the senior high schools.
7. All results should be compiled and recorded; copies should be made and sent to the schools for posting.
8. All students who, during the current year, are members of a varsity or junior varsity team, or a community league, or any organized group, should be ineligible for competing in the extramural programs.

Types of Extramural Programs

There are numerous types of city-wide events that may be conducted. A study of some of the programs that have developed across the country, described in the following paragraphs, shows that demonstrations, tournaments, and meets are the most popular vehicles for the city-wide program.

City-Wide Demonstrations. In addition to the traditional intramural program of tournaments and informal participation, demonstrations should be included as an integral part of the total intramural program. Demonstrations serve not only as a culminating aspect of the physical education program but also as an excellent medium for public relations. Demonstrations constitute the bulk of city-wide programs reported over the country, and vary depending on the local conditions. Some demonstrations do not involve competition, but consist of groups of students merely demonstrating various aspects of the program. On the other hand, other demonstrations involve a combination of competition and groups demonstrating aspects of the physical education program.

There are certain guidelines or basic principles that should be applied to the planning and they should include the following:

1. All demonstrations should be planned well ahead of the official dateline for presentation, and a checklist of specific items involved in organizing the demonstration should be available.
2. The demonstrations should be designed to include a large segment of the student body, including the gifted and the handicapped as well as the average student. This may be accomplished by providing a large variety of classifications, groupings, and activities.
3. The demonstration should reflect the various activities taught in the instructional program. However, class time should not be used for rehearsing or practicing the event unless it is an integral part of the instructional program.
4. To insure a successful demonstration, it should be organized and conducted in a professional, effective manner. Both specta-

tors and participants will benefit when events are performed on schedule without needless waste of time.

5. Several media should be used to promote the demonstration, such as television, newspaper, printed programs, and bulletin boards.

6. Special guests should be invited to participate in the demonstration. Board members and administrators may have a part in the opening phase. Lay people may assist with officiating and scoring. Parent-teacher groups should assist in promotion.

7. Coeducational activities should be an integral part of the demonstration. Such sports as volleyball, tennis, bowling, golf, and swimming are natural activities for coeducational participation.

8. A public address system should be used; it should be checked well ahead of the starting time.

9. Appropriate awards should be made for participants and winners.

10. The demonstration should be carefully planned. If it is a yearly event, mistakes made should be recorded and corrected the following year.

11. Numbers which involve music should be included.

12. A checklist should be devised showing the equipment, supplies, procedures, and all details involved in conducting the program.

13. A number of rhythmic activities should be included.

14. It is desirable to have a theme for the demonstration.

15. Programs should be printed if possible. Mimeographed programs may be used, but they are not as attractive as the printed programs. Administrators and outstanding citizens should be involved in the demonstration and their names should appear on the program.

16. The content of the demonstration should reflect the local philosophy of physical education.

17. All schools in a district or city should be involved in the demonstration

Interesting demonstrations typifying the extension of the physical education instruction are held throughout the nation. Some examples of such demonstrations are described here to show their scope and variety.

An effective type of demonstration, particularly adaptable to the elementary school, is the parental visitation, which takes place during the school day.

Parents are apprised of the exact time at which their children are assigned to physical education. Special demonstrations are planned each period, involving the various activities taught. Brief opening procedures include welcoming remarks by the principal and comments by the teacher. If there are eight 30-minute classes of 30 students each, approximately 250 parents can visit the school in a day.

Fort Atkinson, Wisconsin. A demonstration involving 750 girls and boys in grades 7 to 12, and viewed by 2000 spectators, was held in Fort Atkinson under the direction of Herb Ostrand. The aim of the demonstration was to emphasize physical fitness and the ideals of liberty. An Olympic torch, lit by the Governor and carried 37 miles by members of the cross-country team, provided a dramatic opening for the participants. Activities included volleyball, basketball, soccer, football, wrestling, tumbling, apparatus, and physical fitness tests.[35]

Special Sports Program. Clark County School District, Las Vegas, Nevada, operates a special sports program which serves as an intermediary step between the intramural program and the interschool athletic program. The program coincides with the purpose of extramurals, which is to provide competition for the gifted who have not reached the level of performance required for varsity competition or for participation in activities not offered in the interschool program.

The program includes competition in badminton, table tennis, archery, chess, billiards, coed volleyball, skiing, golf, bicycling, gymkhanas, and swimming. Each school sends one boy and one girl from each grade level (7–12) to compete in the county-wide competition. The special sports program operates on the schedule shown on the opposite page.[36]

City-Wide Tournaments. The tournament is an important vehicle for the city-wide programs. For students who have won individual school events to be able to compete with other schools in a one-day tournament is a desirable extension of the program; moreover, it is educationally sound. These city-wide tourna-

1974--1975 SCHOOL YEAR

Event	Host	Date

October, 1974

Sr. High Swim Meet	Basic	October 5
Jr. & Sr. High Archery Tournament	Western	October 19

November, 1974

Jr. & Sr. High Coed Volleyball Tournament	Volley	November 9

December, 1974

Jr. & Sr. High Chess Tournament	Cashman	December 7

January, 1975

Jr. High Ski Meet	Fremont	To be announced
Sr. High Ski Meet	Rancho	To be announced

January, 1975

Jr. & Sr. High Billiards Tournament	Knudson	January 11

February, 1975

Jr. & Sr. High Badminton Tournament	Hyde Park	February 8

March, 1975

Jr. & Sr. High Table Tennis Tournament	J. D. Smith	March 1

April, 1975

Jr. & Sr. High Bicycling Tournament	Chaparral	April 19

May, 1975

Jr. High Golf Tournament	Orr	May 1

Additional Events

Gymkhana (4 dates)	Eldorado	To be announced

ments, in addition to providing the opportunity for winners of the individual schools to compete with each other, also serve as a culmination of the year's program.

One city has conducted a city-wide volleyball tournament for 17 consecutive years. The tournament features the 6th- and 7th-grade boys and girls in all of the city's 55 elementary schools. The schools are placed in three geographical divisions, with each division operating separately. Figure 12–21 outlines the rules and regulations governing the tournament. The event serves as a culmination of the year's instruction in volleyball, and is a powerful motivating medium for encouraging boys and girls to extend their class instruction beyond the school day.

Extramural Meets. There are several types of meets frequently used for determining city-wide winners. An innovative meet that is still undergoing experimentation at present is the telephonic contest, in which the results are telephoned to the central office from the individual schools. An outstanding city-wide program of this type is held in Fort Wayne, Indiana, conducted by Clarence A. Biedenweg. The program is held each year for 5th- and 6th-grade boys and girls. The purpose of the event is to allow students to compare their skill performances with those of other schools. The contest is an outgrowth of the instructional program in which the best performances in each grade are submitted by telephone to the central offices. The 38 schools are divided into four divisions on the basis of enrollment, and a division winner is declared for each activity, based on total points. All students whose scores are submitted are awarded ribbons or certificates. On the divisional level the first five winners in each event are awarded ribbons. The various events used in the telephonic contests are:[37]

Softball
 Overhand throw for accuracy
 Underhand throw for accuracy
 Underhand pitch for accuracy
 Overhand throw for distance
 Basic running for time
 Overhand catching and throwing relay

Football
 Pass for distance
 Punt for distance
 Placement kick for distance
 Pass for accuracy
 Team-passing relay
Track and Field Meet
 60-yard dash (5th-grade boys and girls)
 75-yard dash (6th-grade boys and girls)
 600-yard walk and run
 Standing broad jump
 Running high jump
 Shuttle relay race
Basketball
 Free throw
 Lay-up shooting for speed and accuracy
 Chest pass for speed and accuracy
 Jump and reach for height
 Team dribbling relay

George Calkins, coordinator of elementary physical education, Livonia Public Schools, Livonia, Michigan, reports an annual event known as Elementary Physical Education Days. Fifth- and 6th-grade boys and girls from 31 schools participate in 13 events. An attractive brochure is used to promote the program. The schedule of events is included in the handbook. Figure 12–22 describes the schedule of events included in the brochure.

The traditional track and field meet is universally well regarded. A program designed for intermediate grade students that deserves recognition is held yearly in the Laramie County School District, Cheyenne, Wyoming. All boys and girls of the district's 23 elementary schools are involved in events such as the 75-yard dash, 50-yard hurdle over, 600-yard run-walk, running long jump, running high jump, softball throw, 200-yard shuttle relay, 220-yard pursuit relay, and coeducational potato race relay. The district is divided into four divisions, with the winner of each division competing in the city-wide meet.

In order to facilitate the scheduling of events and compile the 50 events in two or three hours, the meet is divided into three categories—track, field, and relay events. The students from each grade compete in one of the three categories simultaneously. After the three grades have competed in the events of each category, which is called a go-around, they

NORFOLK CITY PUBLIC SCHOOLS
ELEMENTARY VOLLEYBALL TOURNAMENT AND LEAD-UP EVENTS
RULES AND REGULATIONS - 1976

REGULATIONS:

Who Participates:	Winning 6th grade homeroom team (Boys & Girls)
Court Dimensions:	25' X 48'
Height of Net:	7' (Boys & Girls)
Number of Players on Team:	9 (Boys & Girls)
Substitution:	3 per team

POINTS PER GAME:

School Meets: Two of three games, 15 points each, or rounds may be
                    played on time limit basis as shown under city meet.

Divisional Meets: Ten minutes time limit -- two five (5) minute halves with
                    a one (1) minute break between halves. Four (4) minute
                    break between rounds.

DATES FOR MEETS:

School Meets: October 14 - October 18, 1974
Divisional Meets: Assigned school in your division, October 22-24, 1974
                    Alternate date - same day of the following week.

AWARDS:

School Meets: A certificate will be awarded to each member of the school
                    championship teams.
                    Ribbons will be awarded to divisional first, second and
                    third place winners.

RULES:

1. All members of a team must be members of the same homeroom with only one
   exception: When a homeroom does not have an adequate number of members to
   field a nine (9) member team, they may select members from another class
   of the same grade or lower grade level providing these selected players have
   not been chosen as a member for that classroom's team in school competition.
2. Each contestant must wear identification tag pinned to front of participant's
   shirt showing school and grade number. The tags will be furnished by the
   Physical Education Department.
3. The team winning the flip of the coin will serve at the beginning of the
   game. Teams will change side of court at half time. Team losing coin flip
   will begin serve the second half.
4. Girls are allowed an assist on the serve and may set up the ball for themselves.
5. Side out will be called in event of let balls.
6. Rotation: All teams will rotate as shown in school demonstrations: Volleyball, page 62, Elementary Basic Curriculum Guide.
7. Time-Outs: In school meets where two out of three games are played, a time-
   out may be allowed after either team has scored eight points or when an injury occurs for substitution. In the area meets, all rounds will start and
   end simultaneously. Substitutions may be made between halves and round.
8. Officials: Physical education and classroom teachers will serve as officials
   in school and division meets.
9. In the event of a tie score at the end of a game in a division meet, a three
   minute extension of play will decide the winner of the game.
10. Regulation volleyball rules will apply in all other instances.
11. Age Requirements: A. Sixth grade - participants must have not reached their
    thirteenth birthday by October 22, 1976. B. Overage Team Tournament: If a
    school has a sufficient number of participants in grade six who are too old
    to meet age requirement for grade level tournament, they may enter an over-
    age team. All schools entering an overage team must notify the Physical
    Education Office prior to Wednesday, October 2, 1976, in order that court
    assignment may be completed.

Figure 12–21. Guidelines for extramural volleyball tournament. (Courtesy of Norfolk Public Schools, Norfolk, Virginia.)

THE INTRAMURAL LABORATORY

LIVONIA PUBLIC SCHOOLS
Division of Instruction
Livonia, Michigan

PHYSICAL EDUCATION DAY SCHEDULE OF EVENTS

EVENTS	PARTICIPANTS (per classroom)				NUMBER OF TRIALS	AWARDS		EQUIPMENT NEEDED
	GIRLS		BOYS			Individual 1st, 2nd, 3rd	Team 1st only	
	5th	6th	5th	6th				
GROUP A								
Running Broad Jump	2	2	2	2	2	X	X	Take-off Board and Jumping Pit - Measuring Tape or Board
Standing Broad Jump	4	4	4	4	2	X	X	Take-off Line Measured Area
Softball Throw for Distance	2	2	2	2	2	X	X	Throwing Line and 12" Softball - Measured Area
600-Yard Run-Walk	4	4	4	4	1	X	1st,2nd & 3rd Teams	Measured course Starting Line
Softball Throw for Accuracy	2	2	2	2	4	X	X	Canvas Target 12" (Girls - 30') Softball throwing Line (Boys - 50')
Pull-Ups for Boys			3	3	1	X	X	Outside parallel bars
Pull-Ups for Girls (FLEXED ARM HANG)	3	3						
GROUP B								
50-Yard Dash	4	4	4	4	1	X		Starting and Finish Line - Measured course
Shuttle Relay	4	4	4	4	1		1st,2nd & 3rd Teams	Batons, Starting Line and Measured course
Running High Jump	2	2	2	2	2	X		High-Jump Standards Pit and Bamboo Pole
Tug-of-War	6	6	6	6	2 out of 3 pulls Elimination Series		1st,2nd & 3rd Teams	Rope and Measured Area
Rope Climb	2	2	2	2	2	X	X	Rope and Tambourine
SEPARATE EVENT Volleyball (A school with more than one 6th gr. class may enter 1 or 2 teams.)	All team members from one class (12), the team may have a combination of:				(A point is scored every time the ball is served)		1st & 2nd	Net, Volleyball,& Court - 30' x 20'
	4 girls		8 boys					
	Team members from more than one class, team must be composed of:				15-point Game Elimination Series			
	6 girls		6 boys					

Figure 12–22. Schedule of events for Physical Education Day. (Courtesy of Livonia Public Schools, Livonia, Michigan.)

rotate to the second and then the third go-around. The activities in each division meet and city-wide meet are arranged in go-arounds as follows:

First go-around
 Fourth grade – Track
 Fifth grade – Field
 Sixth grade – Relay
Second go-around
 Fourth grade – Relay
 Fifth grade – Track
 Sixth grade – Field
Third go-around
 Fourth grade – Field
 Fifth grade – Relay
 Sixth grade – Track

With this plan in operation, no student may compete in more than one event in each of the categories.

Planning for and conducting an event of this type requires the cooperation of many people. Working together and utilizing available facilities are basic to the success of the program. Figure 12–23 describes how the area is marked for the meet.

An elementary city-wide track and

field meet for boys and girls is conducted yearly in the public schools of Eugene, Oregon. All 5th- and 6th-grade students receive instruction in the events, and the meet is truly an extension of the physical education class. Members of the secondary track teams perform all of the officiating. Special certificates of accomplishment are awarded for first-, second-, and third-place winners.[38]

Organization of Extramurals

The organization of city-wide programs requires a tremendous amount of ability and effort on the part of the planners. The more schools involved, the more intricate are the details and problems that arise. Probably the reason that so many cities do not develop more programs of this kind is the enormous challenge they present. Inadequate planning usually results in unsatisfactory programs that defeat the purposes. The need for careful planning cannot be overemphasized; obviously such planning is time-consuming. When several thousand children are brought to a central location for the first time to compete in a variety of activities, the results can be chaotic, hazardous, and generally deplorable unless each detail has been carefully thought out well in advance.

Probably the best way of explaining the intricacies involved in conducting city-wide events is to outline, step by step, the procedures of a particular program. On the next few pages an annual demonstration involving 2000 students and 54 elementary schools is described. The demonstration is unique for the following reasons:

1. It has initial involvement of 30,000 students in grades 4 to 7. This will be described later.
2. The demonstration is sponsored by a local civic club, which assists with interpreting the program to the public.
3. It is held on Saturday mornings, providing ample time for participation.
4. Parents are encouraged to bring their children. They are usually able to do this, since many do not have to work on Saturdays.
5. Students compete against a score, and rarely know who their competitors are.

The demonstration consists of two distinct phases: (1) the school phase, and (2) the Leisure Time Fitness Day.

The School Phase. All boys and girls

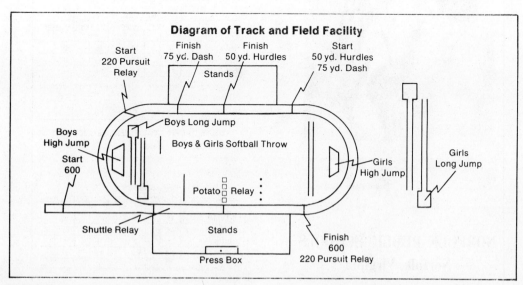

Figure 12–23. An example of a well-planned arrangement for conducting an elementary track and field meet. (From "Intermediate Grade Students Compete in City-Wide Track and Field Meet." *Physical Education Newsletter*, March 1, 1973.)

in grades 4 to 7 are involved in the school phase of the intramural program. They practice the events that constitute the program, working in groups of three. After equaling or surpassing the norms, each participant signs the entry blank and, after obtaining his parents' signatures, returns it to the physical education teacher, who then presents him with a Leisure Time Fitness button. This button allows the student to enter the Leisure Time Fitness Day program, which includes all the students from the 57 elementary schools who have earned their leisure time buttons. (See Figure 12–24.)

Leisure Time Fitness Day. All students who have earned their leisure time buttons in the various schools are eligible to participate in the Leisure Time Fitness Day activities, after submitting a signed parental permission form. (See Figure 12–2.) The eight steps to successful planning of the Fitness Day are enumerated below. The title and general information of the event are shown on the printed program, which is sent to all individuals involved with the planning-participants, parents, principals, teachers, administrators, and civic groups.

HEALTH - SAFETY
AND
PHYSICAL EDUCATION

HANDBOOK

for

PUPILS and PARENTS

On the broad and firm foundation of health alone can the loftiest and most enduring structures of the intellect be reared.

Horace Mann (1845)

NORFOLK PUBLIC SCHOOLS
Norfolk, Virginia

LEISURE TIME FITNESS PROGRAM
INSTRUCTIONS

All boys and girls in the 4, 5, 6 and 7 grades are allowed to participate. However, they must comply with the following requirements:

1. TIME—All tests must be taken after school.
2. ORGANIZATION—All pupils will work in groups of three. They will help each other administer the tests and sign the cards when completed.
3. SCORING—Each pupil must equal or excel the averages in all tests to qualify for the fitness button.
4. AWARD—When all tests are completed and the card is properly signed, give it to your physical education teacher. He will present your physical fitness button.
5. PHYSICAL FITNESS DAY—All pupils who win buttons will be given an official entry and score sheet, and will be eligible to participate in the City-Wide Physical Fitness Day in May.

LEISURE TIME PHYSICAL FITNESS TESTS FOR **GIRLS**

Name................ School................ Grade................
Address................ Teacher................
P. E. Teacher................

EVENTS	GRADES			
	AV. SCORE 4	AV. SCORE 5	AV. SCORE 6	AV. SCORE 7
Sit-Up (30 Sec.)	16	17	18	19
Hop, Step, Jump	12'3"	13'0"	14'0"	15'
Dash (40 Yds.)	7.6	7.2	7.0	6.7

The above tests were scored in my presence and are valid
Parent's Signature ....
Witness................ Witness................

LEISURE TIME PHYSICAL FITNESS TESTS FOR **BOYS**

Name................ School................ Grade................
Address................ Teacher................
P. E. Teacher................

EVENTS	GRADES			
	AV. SCORE 4	AV. SCORE 5	AV. SCORE 6	AV. SCORE 7
Sit-Up (30 Sec.)	18	19	20	21
Std. Broad Jump	54"	58"	62"	67"
Pull-Up	2	3	4	5
Dash (50 Yds.)	8.4	8.3	7.8	7.7

The above tests were scored in my presence and are valid
Parent's Signature ....
Witness................ Witness................

Figure 12–24. The school phase of the Leisure Time Fitness Program.

I. General Items
   A. Separate areas for boys and girls and for each event.
   B. All areas roped off with line-up lanes if possible.
   C. Scoreboards (portable blackboards) out front for running score of leading participants.
   D. Use red or blue pencils for scoring.
   E. Members of Northside Norfolk Rotary Club score at head tables.
   F. Explain procedure for reporting results by name (printed), school, grade, score
   G. Count score sheets turned in by students to obtain total number participating.

II. Head Tables - Rope off to keep participants away
   A. Loudspeaker unit with record player on one table.
   B. Eight tables, 16 chairs needed for officials.
   C. Certificate and trophies to be given out during meet.
   D. Four portable blackboards with erasers and chalk.
   E. Flag - pledge of allegiance.
   F. National Anthem Record.

III. Materials for Marking Field
   A. String, nails, lime marker and lime, tape measures.
   B. For running-off events:
      1. Sit-up, (boys and girls)-one stopwatch, 40 pencils, 1 mat cover each, 40 clipboards.
      2. Dash, (Boys and girls)-15 stopwatches (one per lane), pistol and blanks, 30 pencils, nail to eject cartridges, 30 clipboards.
      3. Pull-up (boys only)-10 pencils. 10 clipboards.
      4. Standing Broad Jump - 20 pencils, 8 tape measures, 18 yardsticks, large staples to hold tapes down, 16 clipboards.
      5. Hop-Step-Jump-Eight tapes, staples, 18 yardsticks, 20 pencils, 16 clipboards.
   C. Signs:
      1. Two signs for each event-boys on red poster board, girls on white poster board.
         a. One for line-up of officials.
         b. One for designation of events.
      2. Large poster boards-boys on red poster boards, girls on white poster board.

IV.

Officials line up here

Girls

| H.S.J. | Sit-Up | Dash |

Boys

| Broad Jump | Sit-Up | Dash | Pull-Up |

   3. Grade level signs for tables for boys and girls to turn in score sheets.

Officials Needed by Events

Events	Sex	Line-Up Official	
S. Broad Jump	B	10	16 to measure and score
Pull-Ups	B	10	12 to count and score
Sit-Ups	B	10	20 to hold feet, count and score
Dash	B	10	15 to time and score, thereafter to start races
Dash	G	10	15 to time and score, thereafter to start races
Hop, Step, Jump	G	10	16 to measure and score
Sit-Ups	G	10	20 to hold feet, count, and score

Figure 12-25. A checklist is helpful in planning demonstrations.

1. **Announcing the Program.** The first step is making the official announcement of the program. This step is very important. The announcement should be made several months in advance of the demonstrations.

2. **The Checklist.** A checklist that has been kept over the years provides the necessary information for the initial planning of the demonstration. The list provides the administrator with a detailed procedure to follow based on the experience of previous years and incorporating new procedures to take care of any organizational changes or new school policies. (See Figure 12–25.)

3. **Selection of Student Officials.** The officials are selected from the junior high school where the demonstration is to be held. The teachers in the school cooperate in the task of securing the officials. Several times, prior to the demonstration, the officials are briefed about their duties and responsibilities.

4. **Teacher Assignments.** Each event is supervised by a teacher responsible for assisting the student officials in the performance of their duties.

5. **Diagram of the Field.** If the majority of students participating in the demonstration have never been to the site prior to the day on which it is held, it is desirable to have a layout of the field, displaying where the activities are to be held. All persons, including the participants and officials, should have one of these diagrams.

6. **Official Score Sheets.** All students who have earned their leisure time buttons must procure an official score sheet from the teacher who issued them their buttons. The teacher signs this blank to insure its validity. These blanks, each bearing a teacher's s gnature, are presented to the official at each event before participation. (See Figure 12–26.)

7. **Winner's Sheet.** The winners of the demonstration are determined on a point basis. Cumulative scores are kept by members of the sponsoring club and are announced at the conclusion of the demonstration.

8. **Awards.** All participants are given certificates, as illustrated in Figure 12–27. The first-place winners of each event in all grade levels are awarded trophies. Note that the event is sponsored by the Rotary Club.

PARENTAL APPROVAL, MEDICAL EXAMINATION, AND LIABILITY

It is important that all students participating in extramural programs have parental permission before competing. (See Figure 12–2 for a suggested form.) A medical examination should be mandatory for participating in extramural contests. Usually the examination conducted periodically by the school is sufficient.

Some schools provide blanket insurance coverage for extracurricular activities, including extramurals. Since transportation is essential for these programs, sponsors of extramurals should be apprised of the legal aspects of transporting students away from school. When commercial or school vehicles are used, they should carry insurance for this purpose. Group insurance is available for this; the premiums may be paid by the participants, the school, or the board of education.

INTERPRETING THE INTRAMURAL-EXTRAMURAL PROGRAM

To a large extent, the success of the city-wide intramural program depends on how well it is regarded by the community. The administrator must use every means available to him to enhance the school-community relationship. The procedures for promoting interest in all phases of the intramural laboratory are the same as those suggested for the physical education program, as described in Chapter 3. The nature of both the individual school program and the city-wide phase is such that developing good public relations is relatively easy. The intramural laboratory is basically a public relations medium used to interpret to the community the philosophy and activities of the physical education program. Indeed, intramurals have been described as windows through which the public may observe the physical education offering.

There are many groups and individuals who should be acquainted with the program and who may be invited to observe the events. Prominent representatives of various civic groups, members of parent-teacher organizations, school administrators, and school board members are examples of individuals

LEISURE TIME FITNESS DAY

BIRTH DATE_____

HEALTH, PHYSICAL EDUCATION AND SAFETY DEPARTMENT
NORFOLK CITY PUBLIC SCHOOLS

9 YEAR OLD
G I R L S

Official Score Card

Print
Name _____
First   Middle   Last   School   Physical Education Teacher

SIT-UP (Knees Flexed - Number in 30 Seconds)

Score	16	17	18	19	20	21	22	23	24	25	26	27	28	29	30	Total Points
Points	1	2	3	4	5	6	7	8	9	10	11	12	13	14	15	

STANDING BROAD JUMP (Inches)

Score	54"	55"	56"	57"	58"	59"	60"	61"	62"	63"	64"	65"	66"	67"	68"	Total Points
Points	1	2	3	4	5	6	7	8	9	10	11	12	13	14	15	

AGILITY RUN (101 Yds. - Seconds and Tenths)

Score	29.4	29.3 29.2	29.1 29.0	28.9 28.6	28.5 28.0	27.9 27.6	27.5 27.3	27.2 27.0	26.9 26.6	26.5 26.3	26.2 26.0	25.9 25.6	25.5 25.3	25.2 25.1	25.0	Total Points
Points	1	2	3	4	5	6	7	8	9	10	11	12	13	14	15	

50 YARD DASH (Seconds and Tenths)

Score	8.8	8.7	8.6	8.5	8.4	8.3	8.2	8.1	8.0	7.9	7.8	7.7	7.6	7.5	7.4	Total Points
Points	1	2	3	4	5	6	7	8	9	10	11	12	13	14	15	

IMPORTANT INSTRUCTIONS

1. Your physical fitness button should be worn to participate.
2. Do not make any marks on this card except your name, school, teacher and birth date.
3. Go to event with least number of participants--take test and have official enter score and initial.
4. When all tests have been completed, take score card to official table. Receive participation certificate.
5. Officials--circle the block in which score and points were attained, initial and enter score in total points column.
6. Trophies will be awarded to age level winners at end of meet.

TOTAL SCORE ☐

LEISURE TIME FITNESS DAY

BIRTH DATE_____

HEALTH, PHYSICAL EDUCATION AND SAFETY DEPARTMENT
NORFOLK CITY PUBLIC SCHOOLS

9 YEAR OLD
B O Y S

Official Score Card

Print
Name _____
First   Middle   Last   School   Physical Education Teacher

PULL-UP (Number)

Score	3	4	5	6	7	8	9	10	11	12	13	14	15	16	17	Total Points
Points	1	2	3	4	5	6	7	8	9	10	11	12	13	14	15	

SIT-UP (Knees Flexed - Number in 30 Seconds)

Score	18	19	20	21	22	23	24	25	26	27	28	29	30	31	32	Total Points
Points	1	2	3	4	5	6	7	8	9	10	11	12	13	14	15	

STANDING BROAD JUMP (Inches)

Score	57"	58"	59"	60"	61"	62"	63"	64" 65"	66"	67"	68"	69"	70"	71"	72"	Total Points
Points	1	2	3	4	5	6	7	8	9	10	11	12	13	14	15	

AGILITY RUN (101 Yds. - Seconds and Tenths)

Score	28.6	28.5 28.4	28.3 28.0	27.9 27.6	27.5 27.3	27.2 27.0	26.9 26.6	26.5 26.3	26.2 26.0	25.9 25.6	25.5 25.3	25.2 25.0	24.9 24.6	24.5 24.1	24.0	Total Points
Points	1	2	3	4	5	6	7	8	9	10	11	12	13	14	15	

50 YARD DASH (Seconds and Tenths)

Score	8.5	8.4	8.3	8.2	8.1	8.0	7.9	7.8	7.7	7.6	7.5	7.4	7.3	7.2	7.1	Total Points
Points	1	2	3	4	5	6	7	8	9	10	11	12	13	14	15	

IMPORTANT INSTRUCTIONS

1. Your physical fitness button should be worn to participate.
2. Do not make any marks on this card except your name, school, teacher and birth date.
3. Go to event with least number of participants--take test and have official enter score and initial.
4. When all tests have been completed, take score card to official table. Receive participation certificate.
5. Officials--circle the block in which score and points were attained, initial and enter score in total points column.
6. Trophies will be awarded to age level winners at end of meet.

TOTAL SCORE ☐

Figure 12-26. Official score sheets for 9-year-old girls and boys.

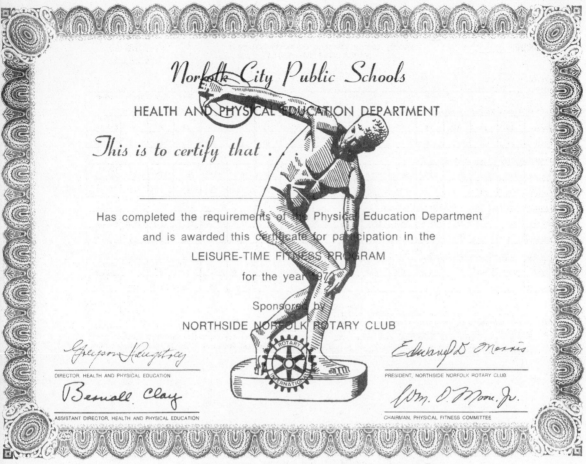

Norfolk City Public Schools

HEALTH AND PHYSICAL EDUCATION DEPARTMENT

This is to certify that . . .

_____

Has completed the requirements of the Physical Education Department
and is awarded this certificate for participation in the
LEISURE-TIME FITNESS PROGRAM
for the year 197
Sponsored by
NORTHSIDE NORFOLK ROTARY CLUB

DIRECTOR, HEALTH AND PHYSICAL EDUCATION

ASSISTANT DIRECTOR, HEALTH AND PHYSICAL EDUCATION

PRESIDENT, NORTHSIDE NORFOLK ROTARY CLUB

CHAIRMAN, PHYSICAL FITNESS COMMITTEE

Figure 12–27. Award certificate for Fitness Day.

who should attend the programs. In addition to the public relations media described in Chapter 3, there are others that have proved helpful in promoting city-wide contests.

Sponsors. Many civic groups and clubs are interested in sponsoring youth activities. Some of them have youth and health committees that are responsible for assisting with and supporting youth programs. Usually these groups will not only furnish adult help in sponsoring programs but also donate trophies and other awards for the events which they sponsor. (See Figure 12–27.)

Programs. All intramural events should be properly announced well in advance of the actual date. The printed program is by far the best medium for announcing all intramural events, particularly the city-wide contests. Printed programs are not only effective in presenting general information, such as dates, time, and place, but may also include valuable information concerning philosophy, objectives, and descriptions of the events; all of these are important tools for acquainting the public with the program. People who play a role in the power structure of the city, such as the school superintendent and board members, should be given a place on the program. These prominent people have many demands on their time and sometimes attend only if they have a definite part in the event.

Awards for City-Wide Intramurals

Planners of city-wide intramural programs are confronted with the same problems in granting awards that apply to individual school events. These programs become expensive as the number of participants and events increases. For example, to award trophies for the individual winners of a volleyball tournament would be costly. If, when the tournament is planned, provisions are made for broadening the base for competition, all 7th-, 8th-, and 9th-grade winners for both boys and girls will be represented. This would mean that the 36 winners (18 boys and 18 girls) would be eligible to receive a trophy. The cost of trophies varies. Assuming that one costing two dollars was selected, the cost for the individual awards would be $72. This, in addition to the cost of providing team awards for winners in all grades, would mean that approximately $100 would be spent in awards for the volleyball tournament. This cost, in addition to the expense of other city-wide programs, could easily result in an expenditure of $1000 or more yearly for awards, a prohibitive figure for most systems. As mentioned earlier, in the award system for individual school programs, the certificate is highly recommended for individual awards.

Certificates printed in large numbers cost about 10 cents each. The team winners may be awarded trophies in addition to the certificates that are given to all individuals who serve on the winning team.

In addition to this awards arrangement, it is suggested that the possibility of securing sponsors for these events be considered. Not only will sponsors gladly furnish awards, but school-community relations benefit greatly as a result of cooperating with these groups. Figure 12–27 is an example of how one civic club assists in promoting an activity.

Periodic Reports

In large school systems involving many schools, reports on student participation are desirable. It is impossible for the director or supervisor to visit each school in the system often enough to know the extent of participation or the response of students to the programs in the various schools. It is important to have an overview for presentation to the superintendent and the school board. Cedar Rapids Community School District, Cedar Rapids, Iowa, uses reports to serve this function. Figure 12–28 illustrates how this city secures participation reports.

FINANCING THE INTRAMURAL LABORATORY

Intramural programs should be financed in the same way as other phases of the school program are. With the exception of remuneration for the teacher responsible for conducting the program, the cost is relatively small. The same equipment used for the physical education program may be used, since the intramural laboratory is an extension of the required program. The awards are relatively inexpensive, and sponsors may be found to finance them.

There are two ways in which teachers may be compensated for time spent supervising the program: (1) by allowing them released time, and (2) by compensating them for their assignment in the same way that coaches are paid. At this point it is appropriate to justify the need for the intramural program by comparing it with the interschool athletic program.

The interschool athletic program has been accepted as educationally desirable for the gifted few. The same health and social values that are derived from the interschool program will be derived from the intramural program, which involves all members of the student body.

In order to justify the intramural program, it is necessary to show that the program not only can provide the same opportunities but in many instances is more educationally sound for large numbers of students than the interschool program is for a few. An effective intramural program provides ample justification for the inference that the good derived by the few from interscholastics will also be derived by the masses of

INTRAMURAL PARTICIPATION REPORT - ELEMENTARY

To: All Elementary School Intramural Instructors:

In order to have a uniform annual report on activities which can be made into a complete report for the Superintendent of Schools, will you please fill out the form below. The report is to cover the entire school year. All reports must be completed and forwarded before the last week of the school year. Send one copy to the Physical Welfare Office. A duplicate report should be left with your Principal.

_____School_____Teacher_____Date Forwarded

LIST ACTIVITIES	NO. OF TEAMS	NO. OF PUPILS PARTICIPATING	SEASON OF YEAR	AVERAGE NO. OF GAMES PER PUPIL	TYPE OF TOURNA-MENT (1)	TIME OF DAY (2)	GRADE LEVEL OF PARTICIPANTS
BOYS:							
GIRLS:							
CO-RECREATION:							

(1) Round Robin - elimination, ladder, etc.   (2) Hour of day when play was conducted
What was the total number of games, contests, matches, and meets you had during the year with other schools?_____

Figure 12–28. Intramural participation report for elementary schools. (Courtesy of Cedar Rapids Community School District, Cedar Rapids, Iowa.)

students through intramural participation.

COMPARING THE INTRAMURAL PROGRAM AND INTERSCHOOL ATHLETICS

It is generally agreed by leaders in physical education that interschool athletics should subscribe to the same objectives advanced for education and physical education.

Several groups have prepared and published objectives for physical education. For the purpose of this comparison, the list of objectives developed by the American Alliance for Health, Physical Education and Recreation and the Society of State Directors of Health, Physical Education and Recreation will be used. These objectives, published in 1950, were selected because of their specificity. In conjunction with these objectives, several secondary objectives gen-

erally advanced by coaches and administrators are also listed. (See Figure 12–29.)

EVALUATION OF INTRAMURAL-EXTRAMURAL PROGRAMS

Any program in a school or system should be evaluated according to definite guidelines for evaluation. These guidelines may be included in a checklist (Figure 12–30). The intramural programs should be appraised just as the physical education and the academic programs are.

One guide for the evaluation of the intramural program is the number of individuals involved. The purpose of the intramural laboratory is to serve as an extension of the instructional program. This means that a great percentage of students (at least 50 per cent) should participate in some part of the beyond-school intramural program.

OBJECTIVES	INTERSCHOOL ATHLETICS	INTRAMURAL SPORTS
Develop and maintain maximum physical efficiency.	Rates high during the competitive years, for the gifted few. However, in team sports activity usually ends when school years are over.	Rates high throughout life since the program is designed for the masses and the level of physical efficiency is geared to individual needs.
Develop useful skills.	Rates high for the particular sport. Rates low if there is not a varied participation.	Rates high since a varied program is always available.
Conduct himself in socially acceptable ways.	Could rate high or low. Pressure on winning sometimes brings about anti-social behavior.	Rates high since winning is not as important.
Enjoy wholesome recreation.	Too often athletes have limited experience in a variety of activities. Team sport participants usually have little experience in individual sports.	Rates high since intramurals are geared to recreation and life time sports.
SECONDARY OBJECTIVES		
Physical Fitness	Rates high.	Rates high.
Sportsmanship	Rates high and low.	Rates high.
Health and Fitness	Rates high for a few.	Rates high.
Spectator Appeal	Rates high. Necessary for financial survival.	Rates low. Not necessary.

Figure 12–29. Comparison of the objectives of the intramural program and those of interschool athletics.

AN INTRAMURAL CHECKLIST

Before the Season

	YES	NO
1. Do I have adequate facilities?		
2. Do I have adequate supplies and equipment?		
3. Have I a good storage system?		
4. Are all items marked and identified?		
5. Have I planned for adequate safety supervision?		
6. Have I scheduled a variety of seasonal sports?		
7. Have I informed my administrator as to what we plan to do?		
8. Have I involved as many faculty members as possible?		
9. Have I informed and involved the PTA whenever practical?		
10. Have I advertised the program by daily bulletins, PE class announcements, signs, posters, and newspaper releases?		
11. Have I checked all community agencies to reduce conflicts in scheduling?		
12. Have I planned seasonal activities that are neither too long nor too short?		
13. Am I really enthusiastic about the program?		
14. Do I have a standings bulletin board in a prominent place?		
15. Have I posted clear-cut rules governing all activities for all to see and do I insist that everyone understand and follow the rules?		
16. Have I posted a schedule of all proposed intramural activities?		
17. Do I have well-trained student officials?		
18. Do I have good captains who know their jobs?		
19. Do the captains and team members know the rules of the league and the sports they're playing?		

Seasonal Organization and Operation

	YES	NO
1. Have I organized teams using a system that will work in our school?		
2. Have I planned so that all who want to participate may participate?		
3. Have I included activities for all grades and abilities?		

Figure 12–30. A checklist for evaluating the intramural program. (Adopted from "An Intramural Evaluation Checklist," *Physical Education Newsletter,* March 1, 1966.)

	YES	NO

4. Have I made being on a team attractive for all?

5. Do I have an effective means of checking attendance?

6. Do all teams know who, when, and where they play?

7. Have I developed a system to control absenteeism?

8. Do I have a plan to reorganize leagues if teams drop out?

9. Do I have a method of publicizing games (photography and journalism clubs)?

After the Season

1. Do I have a good awards program?

2. Have I based my awards on attendance and participation as well as ability?

3. Do I have team awards and trophies?

4. Do I have an all-star vs. league champion game at the end of each season in each sport?

5. Do I have an awards day (father-son night, letter day)?

6. Have I kept up-to-date records?

7. Do I have sports clinics in all activities?

8. Have I evaluated the program to improve it?

9. Have I written thank-you notes to all who have helped during the season?

Figure 12–30. *Continued.*

SUPERVISION OF THE INTRA-MURAL-EXTRAMURAL PROGRAM

Programs of intramural activities which are conducted in the individual schools require constant supervision.

Intramurals improve through intensive observation, just as physical education programs do. When school intramural programs are directed by teachers within the physical education department, the principal, supervisor of physical education, and the school department head have supervisory responsibility. Such factors as organization of the program based on intramural philosophy; establishing guidelines regarding activities, grouping, time frames, and units of competition; student leadership; and finances are included in the supervisory function.

When school intramurals extend into the extramural category, coordination and supervision from the central office becomes necessary. The organization of city-wide programs and tournaments requires a tremendous amount of planning, which should take into account such factors as location of the contests, transportation, certification, officials, dates, and finances.

Those responsible for supervision should have an in-depth knowledge of the program. The use of a checklist is always helpful. A functional checklist serves as a guideline not only for the supervisor but also for the intramural director.

REFERENCES

1. "Leisure and the American Worker." *JOHPER*, March, 1972, p. 38.
2. Edwin J. Staley: "Critical Issues in Recreation and Outdoor Education." *JOHPER*, June, 1964, p. 17.
3. Edward J Bork: "Intramural Programs in Sixteen Minnesota School Districts." Mimeographed Report, 1969.
4. "Solutions to Common Problems in Intramural Sports." *Physical Education Newsletter*, January 1, 1969.
5. W. D. Lawson, Director of Physical Education, Abilene, Texas. Personal communication.
6. *Building Healthier Youth.* Norfolk Public Schools, Norfolk, Virginia, 1975.
7. Bork, *op. cit.*
8. D. T. Carter: "A Student Steering Committee Runs the Varied Intramural Program in Fayetteville." *JOHPER*, March, 1974, p. 40.
9. Howard R. Denike: "How Good is Your Intramural Sports Program?" *The Physical Educator*, October, 1965, p. 117.
10. "Student Officials Handle High School Intramurals and Interscholastics." *Physical Education Newsletter*, September 15, 1965.
11. "Training Leaders for Girls' Physical Education and Intramurals." *Physical Education Newsletter*, November 15, 1965.
12. Cincinnati Public Schools, Intramural Program for Boys in Secondary Schools. Materials sent by request.
13. "Intramural Ideas to Try." *Physical Education Newsletter*, April 15, 1971.
14. "High School Sports Clubs." *Physical Education Newsletter*, November 1, 1968.
15. "A Small Gym, Lack of Outdoor Facilities Need Not Stop You From Conducting Intramurals." *Physical Education Newsletter*, May 15, 1969.
16. *Noon Hour Activities forElementary Schools.* Portland Public Schools, Portland, Oregon.
17. Rod Phillips: "Emphasis on Promotion Effectively Sells the Full Intramural Program at the Cheyenne, Wyoming, High School." *JOHPER*, March, 1974, p. 44.
18. "The Daily Recess Period—A Stimulant for Fifth and Sixth Grade Intramurals." *Physical Education Newsletter*, September 1, 1967.
19. "Games, Sports, Tumbling, Gymnastics: Before, During, and After School." *Physical Education Newsletter*, April 1, 1965.
20. "Using Community Facilities to Establish a Class and Intramural Bowling Program." *Physical Education Newsletter*, January 1, 1967.
21. *Ibid.*
22. Tom Birch: "The Saturday Approach Provides Special Sports for Clark County Students in Nevada." *JOHPER*, March, 1974, p. 46.
23. "Planning Intramurals for Fifth and Sixth Graders." *Physical Education Newsletter*, January 15, 1970.
24. "Intramural Ideas to Try." *Physical Education Newsletter*, April 15, 1971.
25. *A Guide for Planning an After School Intramural Program in the Elementary Schools.* Portland Public Schools, Portland, Oregon.
26. Bork, *op. cit.*
27. "Plan Balanced Team and Individual Sports in High School Intramurals for Girls." *Physical Education Newsletter*, August 15, 1970.
28. "Intramurals, Interscholastics Highlight Girls' Activities." *Physical Education Newsletter*, December 1, 1970.
29. Clare Albom: "The Girls' Athletic Club Promotes Intramurals and Provides for Responsible Student Participation in Activities." *JOHPER*, March, 1974, p. 48.
30. Pamela Gunsten: "Intramurals—The Christiansburg Way." *JOHPER*, March, 1974, p. 51.
31. Howard Grimes: *Intramural Handbook, Program for Boys in Secondary Schools.* Cincinnati Public Schools, Cincinnati, Ohio.
32. "Providing Intramurals for All." Perspective, *Physical Education Newsletter*, February, 1971.
33. Joe Lukaszewski: "Elementary Program Allows all Children to Express and Enjoy Themselves Through Sports and Play." *JOHPER*, March, 1974, p. 47.

34. Grimes, *op. cit.*
35. "Demonstration Ideas That Score." *Physical Education Newsletter,* April 1, 1970.
36. Clark County School District, Las Vegas, Nevada. Mimeographed materials sent on request.
37. "Telephonic Contests for Fifth and Sixth Graders Stimulate Improvement in Sports Skills." *Physical Education Newsletter,* March 15, 1968.
38. "Fifth and Sixth Graders Compete in City-Wide Track and Field Events." *Physical Education Newsletter,* April 1, 1968.

SUGGESTED READINGS

Means, Louis E.: *Intramurals,* 2nd ed. Englewood Cliffs, N.J.: Prentice-Hall, Inc., 1973.
Mueller, Pat: *Intramurals: Programming and Administration,* 4th ed. New York: The Ronald Press Co., 1971.
Rokosz, Francis M.: *Structured Intramurals.* Philadelphia: W. B. Saunders Co., 1975.
Werner, George I.: *After-School Games and Sports.* Washington, D.C.: AAHPER, 1968.

Courtesy of S. H. Ringo, *The Virginian Pilot*, Norfolk, Virginia

THE PLACE OF INTERSCHOOL
ATHLETICS IN EDUCATION

ADMINISTRATIVE RESPONSIBILITIES IN
INTERSCHOOL ATHLETICS

CRUCIAL ISSUES OF INTERSCHOOL
ATHLETICS

ADMINISTRATIVE CONCERNS IN
INTERSCHOOL ATHLETICS

ADMINISTRATIVE POLICY FOR
INTERSCHOOL ATHLETICS

SUPERVISION OF THE INTERSCHOOL
ATHLETIC PROGRAM

CHAPTER THIRTEEN

Interschool Athletics

THE PLACE OF INTERSCHOOL ATHLETICS IN EDUCATION

A study of the evolution of interschool sports reveals that for many years they had no place in the school program. They developed outside of the school, without control, and the bitter rivalry that resulted produced such practices as proselyting, unsportsmanlike conduct, and commercialism. This situation existed largely because the formal educational philosophy of the period did not encompass an interschool sports program; it emerged, therefore, without sanction, administration, or direction.

Paradoxically, educators accepted interschool athletics as a part of the educational program largely because of the unethical practices that existed. As the years passed and the interschool program gained popularity despite the unscrupulous activities permeating it, enlightened leaders saw the educational values that could accrue in a controlled program of athletic competition between schools. The control and direction exercised by educational institutions redeemed and protected the educational values of the program, and interschool athletics gradually became recognized as an integral part of the educational scene.

Acceptance of interschool athletics as a part of the educational pattern has been substantiated by leaders in athletics, education, and physical education. Paul Briggs, Superintendent of Schools, Cleveland, Ohio, has this to say about the results of a survey of athletics in five secondary schools:

Athletics are not only keeping students in school, but are providing them with future education opportunities. I have seen so many success stories come out of the athletic plant that I have become perhaps the strongest advocate of any of the city superintendents in the United States on behalf of effective programs.[1]

The Division of Men's Athletics of the American Alliance for Health, Physical Education and Recreation (now the National Association for Sport and Physical Education) emphasized the place of interschool athletics in education when the program is organized and conducted in accordance with the following basic principles:

1. Interscholastic and intercollegiate athletic programs should be regarded as integral parts of the total educational program and should be so conducted that they are worthy of such regard.

2. Interscholastic and intercollegiate athletic programs should supplement rather than serve as substitutes for basic physical education programs, physical recreation programs, and intramural athletic programs.

3. Interscholastic and intercollegiate athletic programs should be subject to the same administrative control as the total education program.

4. Interscholastic and intercollegiate athletic programs should be conducted by men with adequate training in physical education.

5. Interscholastic and intercollegiate athletic programs should be so conducted that the physical welfare and safety of the participants are protected and fostered.

6. Interscholastic and intercollegiate athletic programs should be conducted in accordance with the letter and the spirit of the rules and regulations of appropriate conference, state, and national athletic associations.[2]

Too often lay people confuse the program of interschool athletics with programs in physical education. This is a logical mistake, however, since both programs usually include many of the same activities and the interschool program receives intensive publicity through the newspapers and television.

Although they are related and are sometimes administered by the same individual, the programs are quite different. The comparison on the following page shows some major differences.

How, then, can the interschool program be defined?

Definition

The interschool athletic program may be defined as a contest between selected individuals or teams representing two or more schools organized and controlled by school authorities. It is extremely important for teachers and administrators to be able to delineate the two programs. Many problems which arise in administering the programs could be eliminated if the programs were interpreted properly to all administrators and lay groups.

Objectives

The objectives of the interschool athletic program should coincide with the general objectives of education. In addition to the general aims, there should be specific objectives important in serving as guidelines in conducting the program. They are:

1. To provide the opportunity for students who are naturally gifted to develop a high level of performance and physiological fitness commensurate with their natural endowments.

2. To learn a higher level of skills under the direction of expert coaches.

3. To learn teamwork and cooperation with other individuals of comparable ability.

4. To meet individuals from other communities and broaden the social horizon through association with these individuals.

CHARACTERISTICS OF PHYSICAL EDUCATION AND ATHLETICS

Physical Education	Athletics
Designed for all pupils	Designed for the gifted few
Normal	
Handicapped	
Gifted	
Concerned with individual differences	Concerned with the best performance
Usually required	Voluntary participation
Part of the school curriculum	Extracurricular activity
Not concerned with spectators	Deeply concerned with spectators
Concerned primarily with teaching skills rather than competition	Deeply concerned with competition
Program conducted at the school for large numbers	Many games held away from the school
	Numbers restricted

5. To develop lifetime friendships through participating in programs that test courage, strength, performance, and ability to cooperate.

6. To respect the athletic prowess of other individuals.

7. To learn how to lose gracefully and how to win modestly.

Values Derived from Interschool Athletics

The values derived from interschool athletics are vitally important in the present culture of our country. The efforts to exist today no longer demand the power, strength, and fitness so necessary for survival in the early years of our nation. A once-rugged way of life has become an increasingly sedentary one, beset with many influences that may have deleterious long-run effects on the nation. History shows that a nation's educational system must be sensitive to such influences and offset them if the nation is to survive. A basic objective of education today is survival, though not in the same interpretation of the word which prevailed when the nation was young. Will our nation be able to survive the deadly and disintegrating inroads that are being made into the health and fitness of our youth? The increasing incidence of drug addiction, venereal disease, and promiscuity is an indication of a greater ensuing weakness—the deterioration of character—that will emerge to-

morrow. The rugged, competitive factors involved in interschool athletics serve as strong countermeasures to offset some of the disintegrating forces so prevalent today.

The Division of Men's Athletics in a platform statement justified its belief that participation in athletics should be included in the educational experiences of students. This participation is important, the statement pointed out:

Because athletics are of historical and social significance in our national culture...

Because athletics provide a primary means through which may be developed and maintained the physical vigor and stamina required to defend successfully our concept of freedom, and to realize fully our potential as Americans...

Because athletics provide a primary means through which may be developed the habits, attitudes, and ideals requisite to ethical competition and effective cooperation in a free society...

Because athletics provide a primary means through which may be utilized in a healthful and wholesome fashion the leisure of our citizens and youth...

Because athletics have a powerful appeal for young people during their formative years and can be utilized to further the harmonious development of youth...[3]

Interschool athletics provide for the physically gifted students the same opportunity for expression that accelerated programs provide for the academically gifted. The history of interschool athletics reveals that these programs initially were student initiated. Students who were interested in furthering their physical prowess beyond school hours organized teams and challenged similar groups from other schools. School officials were forced to assume control of these programs in order to provide direction and supervision for them. It would appear that without school sponsorship the programs would exist anyway for these gifted students.

Standards in Interschool Athletics

The nature of interschool athletics necessitates the establishing of standards to assist administrators in conducting and evaluating the program. Unlike other areas in the school program, interschool athletics are concerned with competition, contests away from school, gate receipts, spectators, community pressure, and other factors that create administrative problems. Probably the most comprehensive set of guidelines for conducting an interschool program was made in 1951 by a joint committee of the National Federation of High School Athletic Associations, the National Association of Secondary School Principals, and the AAHPER. These standards appear in the *JOHPER*.[4]

The state of California has been a leader in all phases of education, including interschool athletics. A committee of school superintendents developed a set of standards that deserves attention. These standards are presented for study by those administrators interested in establishing sound guidelines for the interschool program:

1. All interscholastic championship games, insofar as possible, should be limited to local leagues.
2. There should be a revision of the organization of local leagues, considering size of schools, and limiting the number of schools in the league so as to reduce the number of games.

3. With the exception of San Diego, Bakersfield, Eureka, and possibly a few other places, long distance travel by athletic teams, involving staying overnight, should be eliminated.
4. American football should not be played in grades below the tenth.
5. Spring and summer football practice by all schools should be eliminated.
6. The use of the terms "major" and "minor" sports should be eliminated and the proper emphasis placed on all sports according to their educational values to those who participate.
7. More emphasis should be placed upon the sports that follow through into after-school years, such as volleyball, handball, golf, tennis, and swimming.
8. Athletic awards of intrinsic value should be eliminated, and school letters should be substituted for all students who meet the minimum requirements in mental, social, and physical efficiency.
9. The reduction to an absolute minimum of ticket selling within the school for athletic contests should be effected.
10. Emphasis on interscholastic athletics should be decreased and emphasis on intramural athletics increased.
11. Students should be required to pass a physical examination by a licensed physician before they are permitted to participate in any athletic competition.
12. The use of unpaid adult and student officials in all games, with the exception of league games in football, basketball, and baseball, should prevail. For these games adult officials should be appointed by the school authorities, and the officiating done, insofar as possible, by school people. The compensation for officials should be standardized by the local leagues.
13. The superintendents and city and county supervisors of physical education should have a definite responsibility, together with the high school principals, in determining interscholastic relationships.
14. The high school principals of the state, in cooperation with the superintendents and city and county supervisors of physical education, should use the foundation laid by the California Interscholastic Federation in developing a larger group of local leagues and in increasing the personnel of the governing body.
15. The Chief of the Division of Health and Physical Education in California should be a member of the governing body which determines all interscholastic relationships.[5]

ADMINISTRATIVE RESPONSIBILITIES IN INTERSCHOOL ATHLETICS

Interschool athletics are organized in somewhat the same manner as the intercollegiate program. The program is controlled by three organizations: the local organization, the state association, and the national association. Interschool programs become so involved with a multiplicity of problems that without the help and control of these organizations the program would probably retrogress to the level of competition that existed in the early years.

Local Control

Local control of interschool athletics is the responsibility of many individuals and several groups of people. The size of the school or system determines the number of people involved with the administration of the program. The responsibilities of these individuals and groups will now be discussed.

The Superintendent. The superintendent is the chief executive officer for the school system. He has the final responsibility for approving policies governing the program and interpreting these policies to the board of education, to his staff, and to the public. Although responsibility for many of the procedures included in the operation of the program may be delegated to others, the superintendent is the person who makes the final decisions. Some of the areas in which the superintendent should assume leadership in establishing policies are:

Determining the place of interschool athletics in the educational pattern. The place of interschool athletics in the educational pattern has already been established. The program is an integral part of the educational framework and the superintendent is responsible to see that it functions as such. Because it is a part of the educational pattern, the question arises relative to its relationship with the physical education program. The prevailing pattern on the secondary level is to administer the interschool athletic program as part of the physical education program. However, there is strong opinion in some places that the interschool program is an extraclass activity and should be administered as such. The superintendent should study the advantages and disadvantages of both plans and establish a written policy regarding the matter.

Establishing responsibilities of other school officials. The responsibilities of other school officials involved in the program should be clearly defined. The superintendent should assume leadership in establishing these responsibilities and have written policies governing them.

Evaluating the program. The superintendent should devise plans for constantly evaluating the program. Problems of player attitudes, spectator behavior, educational objectives, coaching procedures and behavior, and cost of the program are but a few of the areas that should be evaluated periodically.

Maintaining leadership in community relations. The superintendent is responsible for maintaining leadership in community relations. Although individual schools share this responsibility, the superintendent must study the relationship of interschool athletics with outside groups, such as the "boosters' club," the "quarterback club," and other organizations that may develop into pressure groups. He should discuss the program with the board of education, civic groups, parent-teacher groups, and individuals interested in the program. The need for this leadership is greater in small systems than in large cities. People living in large urban areas have varied interests, and for them the concern over the wins and losses of the team is not as intense. Without this leadership by the superintendent in community relations, the schools may lose control of the program.

Establishing policy for use of facilities. The superintendent should establish written policies regarding the use of facilities. Usually facilities in the school must be shared by the instructional program, the intramural program, and the interschool athletic program. Unless a written policy is available stating the time and manner in which these groups should share the use of the facility, friction and bitterness may result.

Financing the program. The superintendent should survey existing methods of financing the program and provide a written statement regarding the plan under which the program will function. A definite decision and policy should be made, stating whether the program will be financed by the board of education or from gate receipts.

Establishing policy for athletic injuries. A written policy should be available concerning the medical cost of athletic injuries. The superintendent should determine whether the school or the board of education should be responsible through insurance or other means for the cost of these injuries.

Establishing policy for girls' interschool programs. The arguments for and against girls' interschool programs should be carefully weighed by the superintendent and a policy developed concerning this issue.

Establishing policy for junior high school programs. The superintendent, after studying the pros and cons of the place of the junior high school in the interschool program, should develop a clear-cut policy relative to the role of the junior high school in interschool competition.

Reporting to the board. The superintendent is responsible for informing the board of education about all matters concerning interschool programs and for securing board approval for all policies and procedures.

Planning cooperatively. Planning cooperatively is recognized as the best procedure for effective administration of interschool programs. The superintendent should provide leadership in this process by utilizing the experience and knowledge of the principal, the director of physical education, and other qualified individuals to assist him in formulating policies in the organization and administration of interschool athletics.

The City-Wide Athletic Council. The athletic council is the body that advises and assists the administration with the many facets of interschool athletics. Because the interschool program involves so many people and procedures, the council is needed to keep the program in its proper educational perspective. City-wide athletic councils are prevalent in large cities such as Detroit, Michigan; Chicago, Illinois; Philadelphia, Pennsylvania; and Los Angeles, California. These cities have enough schools so that outside competition is unnecessary. The councils should be composed of the director of physical education, the high school principals, the directors of athletics from the individual schools, and several coaches. These individuals are usually appointed by the superintendent. Among the functions of the councils are determination of policies regarding contests, scheduling, eligibility, and awards, and the approval of the sports included in the program.

In Akron, Ohio, an athletic advisory committee consisting of representatives from the student body, parents, businessmen, medical profession, coaches, physical education teachers, administrators, parent-teacher leaders, police department, the press, and the school board meets periodically to discuss and resolve problems in interschool athletics. The committee is presently concerned with girls' athletics, spectator sportsmanship, competitive sports, and construction, including swimming pools.[6]

The athletic program in the Parma Public Schools, Parma, Ohio, is managed by an athletic council. The council exercises control over the program through continuous evaluation and the development of sound policies for regulating the various aspects of interschool competition. Regulations to prevent unreasonable competition and harmful practices are strongly enforced. The council assists with the preparation of the budget and determination of the use of facilities, and defines the duties and responsibilities of both junior and senior high school staffs and their relationship to each other. The council endeavors to:

—Provide a well-planned and well-balanced program of interscholastic athletics for as many secondary school students as possible, consistent with available facilities, personnel, and financial support; to operate and manage these athletic activities in harmony with the basic policy of the Parma Board of Education and the Ohio High School Athletic Association.
—Promote cooperative thinking and unification of interest and effort among the coaches of the respective Parma secondary schools. Develop and maintain the highest type of sportsmanship: to develop proper attitudes toward winning and losing; to encourage and develop respect for fellow athletes whether they be teammates or members of opposing teams.
—Develop the desire for perfection among athletes in terms of team play, fair play, sportsmanship, and character development; to encourage competition, not only for the tangible rewards but also for the intrinsic values that make athletic competition valuable and worthwhile.
—Promote competitive activity as part of the total educational program and be concerned with the total development of the student.

The Parma Athletic Council continuously evaluates the program, controls and regulates athletics by developing policies consistent with sound educational aims and objectives, and promotes and develops policies and procedures to protect participants from unreasonable competition and from harmful practices or activities. The Council also acts in an advisory capacity in preparing the budget, helps in determining the scope of the total program, prepares a long-range program for the development and extension of facilities for each sport, unifies coaching objectives with regard to the total program, and determines the relationship that should exist between high school and junior high school coaching staffs.[7]

The Principal. The principal shares with the superintendent some of the general responsibilities of administering the interschool program. However, cooperating with the athletic council and with his staff, the principal is concerned with more detailed problems and procedures. Some of the principal's responsibilities are:

Delegating responsibility. The principal must delegate responsibility to other members of his staff. The interschool athletic program is but one of the many phases of the school program for which the principal is responsible. The selection of capable individuals to assume some of the responsibility for conducting the program is the first step in effective administration.

Determining eligible players. The principal, although the details may be delegated, is responsible for the eligibility of all participants. The eligibility of players is determined by local and state policies and regulations and covers such factors as the amateur rule, age, attendance, enrollment, dates, residence, participation on non-school teams, medical examination, scholastic requirements, awards, undue influence, and parents' consent.

Supervising the program. Since he is responsible for the conduct of players at all times, the principal should supervise practice sessions and attend as many games as possible. He is responsible to the superintendent for the conduct of the program and unless he sees the players in practice and in the actual game situation, he will be unable to make an informed evaluation of the program.

Controlling student behavior. The principal is responsible for the behavior of the students during interschool contests. He should discuss the importance of good sportsmanship with the student body and the faculty. Efforts should be made to have the principles of good citizenship permeate the classroom instruction, student councils, and all school clubs and organizations that may affect the behavior of students away from school. Attending as many games as possible has high priority in the principal's efforts to control behavior during interschool contests.

Defining responsibility. The principal has the important task of defining the responsibility of other individuals regarding game officials, finances, schedules, maintenance of playing facilities, spectator control, and other factors involved in conducting the program.

Enforcing policy on use of facilities. The principal is responsible for enforcing the policy on use of facilities. Since the facilities are usually used jointly for intramurals, interschool athletics, and physical education, definite plans should be developed to prevent friction and misunderstanding.

Understanding the program. The principal should thoroughly understand the program. He should be familiar with the philosophy and objectives of interschool athletics. He should constantly strive for the educational approach in conducting the program. There is a greater goal in interschool athletics than winning games and emphasizing gate receipts. Programs that place winning and making money above the educational values will eventually fail. Collegiate preparation for administrators should include information regarding the standards and policies that constitute good interschool athletic administration.

Selecting the coaches. The principal is responsible for the selection of coaches, subject to the approval of the superintendent and the board of education. The coach is the most important person in the interschool program. Many of the problems that have existed in the program have developed because of the employment of unqualified individuals. The coach has more contact with participants than any other person. A qualified coach, because of his daily contact with students, can not only provide technical knowledge of sports, but can also help the students develop patterns of socially acceptable behavior. His opportunities for this guidance are unequaled by any other member of the faculty. The coach who has a passion for coaching, who has the virtues of good character and integrity, and who is endowed with the health and fitness of youth can prevent many of the bad practices that occur in the interschool program. The most important responsibility of the principal in the selection of a coach is to choose a teacher who possesses the qualities of a good teacher. In his evaluation of coaches, the principal should look for the following qualities suggested by the Educational Policies Commission:

1. They recognize that coaching is teaching.
2. They make their work an integral part of the school program, giving special attention to its educational contribution.
3. They insist on the enforcement of all rules of athletic eligibility and seek no favors for athletes.
4. They are fair and unprejudiced in relationships with students.
5. They pay careful attention to the physical condition of players at all times.
6. They see to it that only competent games officials are selected and then support their decisions.
7. They teach students to use only legitimate and ethical means in trying to win.
8. They counteract rumors of questionable practices by opponents.
9. They seek to prevent gambling, obscene language, and other offenses against honesty and decency.
10. They set good examples for boys to follow.
11. They help student athletes to understand that they are neither more nor less important than their fellow students.[8]

The School Athletic Council. School athletic councils are highly desirable for effective athletic administration. These councils operate in somewhat the same manner as city-wide councils. Their membership should include the principal, students, faculty members, athletic directors and coaches. Organizational procedures for these councils including their duties and responsibilities are shown in Figure 13–1 and discussed in the following paragraphs.

The New Britain Public School system, New Britain, Connecticut, operates its secondary school athletic program by utilizing the services of the athletic council. Figure 13–2 illustrates the organization of the New Britain council.

The Athletic Director. The athletic director is responsible to the principal for administering the details of the interschool athletic program. The effectiveness of the program to a large extent depends on the manner in which he

| | SIZE OF SCHOOL | | |
	Large N-217	Medium N-195	Small N-179
The Duties of the Committee Are:			
Policy Making	93	57	24
Advisory Only	46	40	33
Veto Power over Actions of the Committee			
Exercised by:			
Principal	57	29	26
Board of Education	41	23	7
Superintendent	24	15	15
Athletic Director	1	2	3
The More Common Duties of the Committee Are:			
General Policies	32	22	10
Approve Budget and Finances	36	13	8
Approve Schedules	24	14	11
Approve Awards	26	12	10
Approve Purchase of Equipment	9	7	5
Approve Admission Prices	8	3	5
Determine Eligibility	4	4	2
Publicity	2	3	2
Advise and Help Raise Funds	1	2	4
Plan Rallies	2	3	1
Ticket Sales	0	4	1

Figure 13–1. Duties of the Athletic Council. (From Harry Bennett Adams: "A Report on Current Practices in the Administration of Interscholastic Athletics in 591 Selected Secondary Schools of the United States." Unpublished master's thesis, University of North Carolina, p. 80. In Voltmer, Edward F., and Arthur A. Esslinger: *The Organization and Administration of Physical Education,* 4th ed. New York: Appleton-Century-Crofts, Inc., 1967, p. 279.)

discharges his duties. Some of the duties of the athletic director are:

Scheduling contests. Scheduling contests is a cooperative function between the coach and director and is subject to the approval of the athletic council and principal. When developing the schedule, the director should take into consideration conference regulations, policies of the local school or system, conflict with other school programs, and the recommended limit of the number of games to be played.

Contracting officials. Contracting officials is one of the more important responsibilities of the director. The better officials should be contracted early and the names of those selected should be submitted to visiting teams. A list of certified officials is provided by athletic associations and stipulates that officials from this list should be used. All officials should be required to pass examinations on the rules and officiating procedures and techniques.

Establishing travel procedures. The athletic director arranges travel procedures and is responsible for providing the necessary safety measures to assure parents and others that every effort has been made to ensure a safe trip for the players. Players should be apprised of the safety rules of traveling and the importance of following these rules when traveling away from home. It is standard practice that the team should stay together when traveling. The director should take into consideration other procedures, such as securing parental approval for the trip; notifying parents of the hotel where players will be registered; attending to finances, game details, eligibility of players, game contracts, equipment used by players, time of departure and arrival; and handling other details involved with transporting contestants away from home. Figure 13–3 describes one type of letter that may be used for securing parental permission.

Supervising coaches. Although the principal is responsible for the supervision of coaches, he may delegate this responsibility to the athletic director. Too often coaches are selected on their own prowess in athletic competition and not on their knowledge of training, kinesiology, physiology, and other areas necessary for effective coaching. The coach is basically a teacher, and he should possess those qualities essential for good teaching. In addition, he should be a master of techniques and the art of working with players and developing a rapport that places emphasis on character, good sportsmanship, and health.

Supervising practice sessions. As an administrator, the director of athletics should be responsible for supervising the practice sessions to determine if proper training procedures are used to ensure the safety of participants regarding adequate equipment. He should be watchful for contraindicated exercises, such as the deep knee bend and other movements that have been found to be

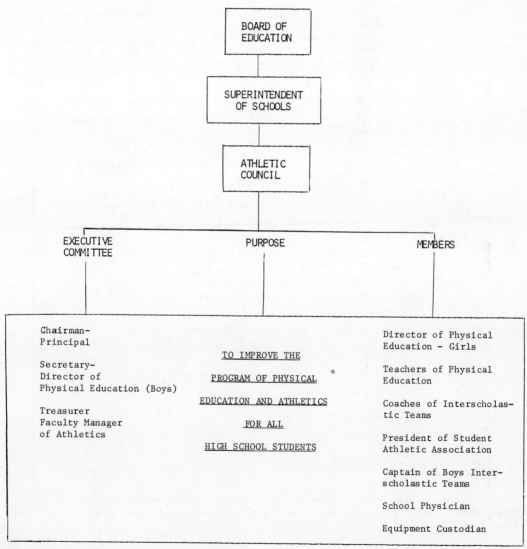

Figure 13–2. Organization of the athletic council. (Courtesy of New Britain Public Schools, New Britain, Connecticut.)

```
                                        January 16, 19--

Mr. Louis C. Jorndt, Director
Bureau of Health, Physical Education
Safety, & Driver Education

Dear Mr. Jorndt:

    _____ requests permission to sign a contract for
     (Name of High School)
the _____ team to play on _____
     (Type of Contest and Team Classification)            (Day and
____ at _____ in the _____    against
Date)  (Town or City)       (Name of School's Gym or Field)
_____ which is a member of its State High School
(Name of Out-of Town School)
Association.

    Mr._____ will accompany and be responsible for
         (Name or Names of Coaches)
the _____ players.  The group of _____
    (Number of Players)                            (Number of Players & Coaches)
will travel by _____ a
               (Name of Approved Bd. of Ed. Company Transporting)
fully insured company.

    The team will leave Chicago _____, and will arrive back
                                (Time and Date)
in Chicago at _____.  Disposition of players after arriving in
              (Time and Date)
Chicago will be in proximity of their homes.

    The _____ players will be housed in the _____
        (Number of Players)                                   (hotel or
_____ with faculty supervision.
 motel)
    There (will) (will not) be non-playing members in attendance.  These
students will travel by _____ to and from the
                        (Bus Co. or other Transportation)
game and will be supervised by faculty members.


         [      ]   on the buses       [      ]   at the game

             (CHECK SQUARES WHICH APPLY)
    An accurate accounting of all finances will be kept and be on file
for future audit.  Parental permission will be required for each boy.

Approved:                          Sincerely yours,



_____
Area Associate Superintendent      _____
                                   (Signature of Principal)



_____
District Superintendent



_____
Director, Bureau of Health,
Physical Education, Safety,
  and Driver Education
```

Figure 13–3. Parental approval for out-of-town contests. (Courtesy of Chicago Public Schools, Chicago, Illinois.)

injurious to various segments of the body. He should be familiar with the various local and state regulations and be ever watchful for violations of these regulations.

Maintaining eligibility lists. Eligibility lists of participants are required by most state associations. These lists are approved by the principal and exchanged with competing teams, and a copy is sent to the state association. Figure 13–4 illustrates a form used by a large city school system for listing eligible players. Eligibility regulations vary from state to state. These regulations usually include the age of the participant, time of enrollment, limit on seasons of play, parental approval, scholarship semesters of attendance, physical examination, transfer, undue influence, awards limit, and amateurism.

Preparing contracts. Contracts signed by the representatives from competing schools are essential for effective operation of the interschool program. Verbal agreements are not sufficient. The use of contracts may prevent distrust, bitterness, and misunderstandings that may undermine the program. The contract requires the signature of the principal, who may request the signature of the director of athletics.

Preparing for contests. The preparation for home contests requires a multiplicity of detailed procedures. The difficulty arises from the time and effort needed to prepare for them. To forget one of the many items necessary for the contest may result in confusion and embarrassment. A checklist may prove an invaluable aid in preparing for the event. Such a checklist is shown:

Before-Game Preparation
  Contracts
  Eligibility records
  Physical examinations
  Parent's permission
  Athlete's permission to participate
  Athletic officials
  Equipment
  Field or court
  Publicity
  Courtesies to the visiting school
  Reserve games
  Tickets
  Contest programs
  Concessions
  Ushers
  Police protection and parking
  Reserved areas
  Cheerleaders
  Scoreboards
  Condition of stadium, bleachers, or gymnasium
  Bands and half-time arrangements
  Decorations
  Public-address system
  Physician at contests
  Scorers, timers, judges

Game Responsibilities
  Supplies and equipment
  Tickets
  Ushers
  Contest programs
  Officials' quarters
  Visiting-team quarters and courtesies
  Flag raising
  Intermission program
  Players' benches
  Physician
  Bands
  Contracts
  Contract guarantees and payments
  Eligibility lists
  Scoreboard arrangements
  Guards for dressing rooms
  Extra clothing for substitutes
  Concessions
  Cheerleaders
  Police
  Public address system
  Rest rooms
  Guarding extra equipment

After-Game Responsibilities
  Payment of officials
  Payment of visiting school
  Storage of equipment
  Contest receipts
  General financial statement
  Concessions report
  Record of officials
  Participation records
  Filing of contest data[9]

Certifying medical services. Yearly medical examinations of all athletes should be made in *each sport before uniforms are issued.* Many serious injuries occurring during practice may have been prevented if the director of athletics or the coach had known the results of a medical examination by a qualified physician. Conditions such as rupture or a

(H.P.E. 103)
102

OFFICIAL ELIGIBILITY CERTIFICATE

Chicago Public High Schools Athletic Association

CHICAGO PUBLIC SCHOOLS
Division of Health
and Physical Education

This Is to Certify that the following are eligible to represent the...High School,

in the Athletic Contest of...

Played with...at... ....................A.M.
(Park or Gymnasium)   P.M.

On the.....................................day of... Class...
(Junior or Senior)

FACULTY REPRESENTATIVE....................................... PRINCIPAL...
(Signature)   (Signature)

COACH... BOARD OF CONTROL MEMBER...
(Signature)   (Signature)

| NAMES OF CONTESTANTS | | | UNIFORM NUMBER | | BIRTH DATE | IS NOW IN | |
LAST NAME	FIRST	INITIAL	HOME	AWAY	MO. DAY YR.	SEM. NO.	SEASON NO.
1.							
2.							
3.							
4.							
5.							
6.							
7.							
8.							
9.							
10.							
11.							
12.							
13.							
14.							
15.							
16.							
17.							
18.							
19.							
20.							

Figure 13–4. Eligibility list for interschool athletics. (Courtesy of Chicago Public Schools, Chicago, Illinois.)

heart abnormality may lead to results just as serious in a practice session as in the actual game. The director of athletics is responsible for certifying that the participants have had an examination by the family or school physician before the issuance of uniforms. This procedure protects not only the participant but the administrator and coach as well. Some cities and states combine the medical examination with parental approval. Figure 13–13 shows one type of form used by a city for recording the medical examination, parental permission, and other pertinent information.

In addition to the physical examination, the director is responsible for arranging medical consultations and insuring that there is a physician present at all games. Medical services for athletes will be discussed later in this chapter.

Preparation of the budget. The athletic director is usually given the authority by the athletic council or principal to prepare the budget. The appropriation of money to finance the athletic program presents a serious problem in many schools. Those programs that finance interschool athletics from sources other than tax money are usually handicapped because of insufficient funds. This means that the purchasing of equipment and supplies must be done in a systematic and businesslike manner. It is extremely important that a definite policy be established regarding the quality of materials, the character of the vendor, and the source of funds. Preparation of the athletic budget is basically the same as outlined in Chapter 10, except that the source of income for financing the athletic program necessitates additional planning. Many schools rely on sources other than tax funds to finance the program, and these sources have to appear in the budget.

The issue of sources of income is highly controversial. Gate receipts for many years have been the chief source of raising funds. This is a satisfactory procedure when the school has a winning team, but experience has shown that school administrators cannot depend on gate receipts alone to finance the program. The sale of season tickets

for athletic contests and general student tickets are standard sources of income in many schools. When general student tickets are sold, in addition to athletic contests, such activities as subscription to the school paper, admission to parties, and admission to plays and concerts are included.

Many schools resort to raising funds through school carnivals, beauty queen contests, sponsors, selling candy and Christmas trees, concessions, dances, and the like. Many sources of raising funds are of questionable nature, which is why boards of education are gradually assuming control of the interschool program.

Preparing the athletic budget should be a joint effort of the athletic director, the coaches, and the principal. Definite guidelines such as the following should be developed.

1. The inventory forms should be your guide in estimating new equipment needs for the next year.

2. An accurate record should be kept of all financial transactions involving athletics. This should be done by individual sports and should include such things as new equipment costs, transportation, medical expenses, insurance, publicity, officials, scouting, laundry and dry cleaning, awards, guarantees, repairs, and so on. This information, if properly kept, will be the basis for making the following year's budgetary estimates.

3. An accurate record should be kept of all athletic receipts. This should include gate receipts, donations, advertising revenue, and so on. This information will help you determine (a) the estimated availability of funds for next year's budget, and (b) what portion of the budget must be financed from the school's general fund (if such funds are available).

4. All budgetary estimates should be as accurate as possible.

5. The budget should not be "padded." There may be reasons for cutting the budget, but "padding" should never be one of them.

6. Some provisions should be made in the budget for unforeseen expenses and emergencies.

7. The coach and athletic director should thoroughly familiarize themselves with the cost of new equipment. If adequate estimates for new equipment are to be made, you must have concrete knowledge of the prices of

new equipment and school purchasing procedures. Your athletic equipment dealers and school purchasing manager can help you on these matters.

8. The athletic budget should be drafted by the athletic director or, in small schools, by the head coach.

9. Before the budget is submitted to the chief school administrator, it should be thoroughly discussed with the entire coaching staff, the school principal, and the school business manager.

10. Purchases of athletic equipment should be made as soon as possible after the

budget has been approved and funds are made available.[10]

The final budget should include receipts and expenditures. Expenditures should be itemized by sports. Figure 13–5 shows a typical budget. Other examples are shown in the resource manual.

In addition to preparing the budget, the athletic director should be familiar with the selection and care of equipment and supplies, and the best dates for purchasing these materials. He should refer

Balance	49.09	Disbursements	1977.29
Receipts	2493.90	Balance	565.70
Subtotal	2542.99	Total Outstanding Bills	525.00

	Budget	Spent This Month	Spent to Date	Balance
Varsity Football	3,984.25		4,025.05	-130.80
Jr. Varsity Football	330.00		505.90	-175.90
Freshman Football	232.00		182.75	49.25
Junior High Football	203.00		83.25	119.75
5th & 6th Grade Football	67.00		45.00	22.00
Varsity Basketball	3,061.25	208.70	3,201.27	-140.02
Jr. Varsity Basketball	407.50	28.00	296.00	111.50
Freshman Basketball	358.40		417.22	- 58.82
Junior High Basketball	178.00	75.00	200.00	- 22.00
Grade Basketball	75.00			75.00
Girls' Gymnastics	775.00	338.00	519.56	255.44
Cheerleaders	180.00	11.34	143.09	36.91
Wrestling	1,160.40	99.50	1,352.65	-192.25
Skiing	186.00		240.76	- 54.76
Golf	255.00	254.26	311.99	- 56.99
Tennis	385.50	505.12	569.75	-184.25
Track	850.55	398.17	686.27	164.28
Administration	910.00	59.20	971.91	- 61.91

Figure 13–5. A sample budget showing the summary of receipts and disbursements, from Iron Mountain High School, Iron Mountain, Michigan. (From Forsythe, Charles E., and Irvin A. Keller: *Administration of High School Athletics*, 5th ed. (Englewood Cliffs, N.J.: Prentice-Hall, Inc., 1972, p. 238.)

```
Physical Education                                              Baltimore City
Division of                                                    Public School


                    INTERSCHOLASTIC ATHLETIC ACCIDENT REPORT

                                    Procedure

        Immediately after an injury occurs, this form shall be filled out in triplicate. Upon receipt of
    the bill from the physician or dentist, two copies, with the bill attached, shall be forwarded to the
    office of the Director of Physical Education.


        ALL CLAIMS FOR PAYMENT MUST BE MADE WITHIN SIXTY DAYS FROM THE
    DATE OF THE ACCIDENT.


    Name (Print)                                               School No.
                        LAST          FIRST       INITIAL

    Address

    Type of Accident

    Place of Accident                                  Date          Time

    Activity in which accident occurred

    Attending Physician or Dentist

                        ⎧  Site of Accident

    Place of Treatment: ⎨  Physician's Office

                        ⎩  Name of Hospital

    Amount Claimed           Scheduled Benefit        Amount Paid

        Submitted By:                             Date
                            SIGNATURE
```

Figure 13–6. Interscholastic athletic accident report. (Courtesy of Baltimore City Public Schools, Baltimore, Maryland.)

to *How to Budget, Select and Order Athletic Equipment* for a detailed description of these areas. (See the References at the end of the chapter for the address.)

Reporting accidents. The director of athletics is responsible for developing a policy for the reporting of all accidents and injuries. Each accident should be reported in writing and copies sent to the proper authorities as designated by the athletic council. Figure 13–6 illustrates one type of accident report.

Evaluation of the athletic director. The duties of athletic directors are of such vital importance that periodic evaluation should be made of the manner in which they are carried out. Probably the best vehicle for appraising the administrator of the athletic program is a self-evaluation checklist. Self-evaluation, while the results may be biased in favor of the scorer, has the distinct advantage of apprising him of the areas of concern in the administration of the program.

A checklist outlining the criteria of a successful athletic administration is shown in Figure 13–7. The checklist includes a rating card for athletic direc-

INTERSCHOOL ATHLETICS

Criteria and Division	Performance in this area is given:		
	Great Attention	Moderate Attention	Little Attention
FINANCIAL SOUNDNESS			
1. He operates on a sound financial basis.			
2. There is an equitable balance in the budget for all sports.			
ORGANIZATION OF THE DEPARTMENT			
3. He handles the business of the department in an efficient and prompt manner.			
4. All members of the department handle their work assignments efficiently.			
5. He operates effectively without undue waste of time or materials.			
6. He develops close co-operation between all members of his staff.			
7. Policies and procedures are written out and are made clear to both players and staff members.			
8. He co-operates with other departments of the institution, and he maintains good relations with the administration.			
9. He is fair and firmly in control of his staff and he never fails to recognize organizational channels.			
10. He is easily available to anyone with an interest in the athletic program.			
WELL-BEING OF THE STAFF			
11. He has developed a high degree of esprit de corps among all members of his department.			
12. He selects a staff who believe in high standards of competitive athletics.			
13. He develops a staff of men with high professional standards and education.			
14. He is loyal to his staff and gets facts before making a move.			
WELL-BEING OF THE STUDENTS			
15. The health protection of athletes is rated high.			
16. He insists that athletes strive to keep up with their class.			
17. The best possible education for the boy is the most important criterion.			
18. He produces a program that appeals to a large number of participants.			
19. He considers the after-graduation success of former athletes a measure of success of the athletic department.			
20. He prefers that athletes carry on a career program of study.			
21. He has understanding of and co-operates with general student body interests.			
22. Students assigned to work in the department give reasonable service for money earned.			
PROFESSIONAL STATUS OF THE STAFF			
23. His operations are in harmony with the spirit and rule of amateur athletic codes established by the NCAA.			
24. He is able to justify the athletic program as an important phase of education.			
25. The director is an educator. His status in the institution is high.			
26. He works with the faculty and keeps them informed.			
PUBLIC RELATIONS			
27. There is an efficient program of public relations.			
28. He maintains friendly press and radio relations.			
29. He conducts athletics in an efficient, crowd-pleasing manner.			
30. He insists that squad members are institutional representatives at all times and that they conduct themselves accordingly.			
31. The activities of the department are well received by the faculty and the community.			
32. The over-all win and loss record of all competitive teams under his administration is high.			
CARE OF PROPERTY AND EQUIPMENT			
33. Teams are well equipped, neat and clean.			
34. The equipment of the department is cared for in an excellent manner and according to sound procedures.			
35. The buildings and grounds under the supervision of the director are kept in excellent condition.			

Figure 13–7. A self-evaluation checklist for athletic directors. (From Kelliher, M. S.: "Successful Athletic Administration," *JOHPER,* November, 1957, p. 30.)

tors to use in evaluating the administration of the program. The card consists of 35 criteria that fall into seven divisions.

Student Managers. Student managers are necessary for efficient administration of the interschool program. Not only are they indispensable to the coach in the daily operation of his program, but they also serve as public relations agents while associating with the students and faculty. Student managers may be either elected or appointed; their duties are delegated by the coach. Some of the duties of student managers are outlined in the *Guidebook for Athletics*, New Britain Public Schools, New Britain, Connecticut. The outline follows:

Equipment Duties. The student manager should:

1. Assist the coach in a pre-season inventory. Coach orders needed equipment through the faculty manager, subject to the approval of director.

2. Keep equipment clean and in working order.

3. Issue out and check in equipment accurately and in a businesslike manner, in the presence of a coach. Use equipment form cards issued by faculty manager.

4. Compile a checklist of equipment needed for practice and games and refer to it constantly as a guide.

5. Be alert to safeguard all equipment during practice and games.

6. Check all equipment at the end of the season for breakage or needed repairs.

7. Have all equipment cleaned and supervise the packing of it at the season's conclusion.

8. Assist head coach in checking inventory of all football equipment at the end of the season and submit final report to director and faculty manager.

9. Keep a close check on all equipment issued, see that there is no pilfering by members of the squad. Report any such incident to the coach. Don't issue equipment without approval.

10. See that members of the squad keep equipment clean and that shoes are oiled.

11. Check to be sure football shoes are worn only at the field.

12. Check with school physician and see that first-aid kit is well supplied. Report needs to coach in writing.

13. Turn in worn out, discarded equipment to faculty manager.

14. Make sure that boys who quit team

return all equipment. Report any irregularity to coach and faculty manager.

Practice Session Duties. The student manager should:

1. Record daily the attendance of team candidates and members and hand it to coaches at end of the day's practice session.

2. Check the weight of team members before and after practice.

3. Have stretcher and water buckets on field.

4. Guard and watch all equipment at practice session.

Game Duties. The student manager should:

1. Greet all visiting teams and officials in a courteous manner and assist them in any way possible.

2. Oversee the arrangement of team comfort.

3. Designate an assistant to the visiting team and officials.

4. Designate assistants to safeguard equipment around the field.

5. Provide good drinking water for both teams.

6. Designate an assistant manager to tend to the football equipment during and after the game.

Locker Room Duties. The student manager should:

1. Compile a list of the names and squad numbers, addresses, class schedules, telephone numbers, etc.

2. Save all newspaper clippings to form a complete record of the season, and post on bulletin board.

3. Divide the work of the assistants and try to avoid overloading any one individual.

4. At the close of the season, suggest to the incoming manager, the athletic director, and coaches any possible improvements.

5. Have assistants sweep and dust locker room, equipment room and coaches' room on Monday, Wednesday, and Friday.

6. Keep all football equipment together but separated so that an inventory can be made at any time the coaches desire.

7. See that all rooms are locked and locker room entrance door is locked, after everyone has left.

8. Assist coach in keeping bulletin board up-to-date with notices, schedules, and other matters pertaining to the track team.

9. Manager should report to locker room at 2:05 P.M. and leave no later than 6:00 P.M. on practice days. Report to coach before leaving, only after all boys have left locker room.

10. Have each member of squad sign for towel for showers. Towels must be returned

by squad member and names checked off. (Managers are not to go around picking up towels for players.)

11. Secure keys for locker room from coach and return to him when request is made.

Final Reports at Close of Season. The student manager should:

1. Submit in writing all suggestions for the improvement of any phase of the program.

2. Add any changes to his report that arise from his experience.

3. Make sure to receive a final approval of all responsibilities (equipment, keys, condition of room, bulletin board, etc.) as having been completed satisfactorily from coach, faculty manager, and director.[11]

The Coach. Although the coach is basically responsible for coaching the team, he has other responsibilities which are quite different from those of the teacher, but are just as important. The coach is responsible to the administrator, the parent, and the public. Many cities and districts have developed instruments for evaluating teachers, but procedures for appraising coaches are rare.

An evaluative instrument designed to improve the quality of coaching was developed by the Beaverton School District, Beaverton, Oregon. It involves five classifications: (1) administration, (2) skills, (3) relationships, (4) performance, and (5) self-improvement. See Figure 13–8 for a detailed outline of the instrument.

Although coaches are appraised by both administration and the public, too often the players' evaluation of the coach is ignored. Successful coaches usually have excellent rapport with the members of their team. What players expect from coaches is summarized by an athlete who states that he expects coaches to have:

1. *An inspiring personality.* Their conduct sets a personal example for players on and off the field.

2. Loyalty. A coach cannot expect much of his players if he himself is not loyal to his team.

3. *Technical knowledge.* The coach and the athletic director both should be professional people with a sound educational background. Both should have an excellent background of training in athletics, health, and physical education.

4. *Leadership.* All athletes look to their coach for leadership.

5. *Knowledge of their team members.* The coach and athletic director should be especially concerned with the athlete's (1) physical well-being, (2) character development, and (3) academic guidance.

6. *Self-discipline.* The coach and athletic director should exercise the same self-discipline they expect of the players. They should emphasize that the primary purpose of attending school is to acquire an education.

7. *Fitness.* The coach and athletic director should keep themselves mentally, morally, and physically fit.[12]

The Trainer. For a number of years athletic trainers have been recognized as invaluable members of the athletic staffs of colleges and universities. However, only recently have high schools begun to employ individuals for this position. A recent article reports that of the 25,000 high schools in this country, of which 60 per cent participate in interschool football, only approximately 100 schools employ full-time trainers.[13]

The National Athletic Trainers Association has long recognized that the athletic trainer is an integral part of the athletic program. Supported by such organizations as the American Medical Association, the NATA is dedicated to three goals for assuring employers of adequate preparation of athletic trainers:

1. Seek the development of specific athletic training curricula which would meet the approval of the NATA.

2. Carry out certification of the NATA membership through a standardized testing procedure which requires a certified athletic trainer to meet minimal competencies.

3. Convince high school administrators and boards of education of the need for qualified teacher-athletic trainers at the secondary level. Actively recruit high school and college students for the athletic training curriculum.[14]

State Athletic Control

All states have associations for athletic control. However, the names of these as-

**DEPARTMENT OF ATHLETICS
SCHOOL DISTRICT NO. 48**
Beaverton, Oregon

CODE: O—Outstanding
      S—Satisfactory
      NI—Needs Improvement
      US—Unsatisfactory
      NA—Nonapplicable

COACH_____

ASSIGNMENT_____

EVALUATOR_____

DATE_____

Each coach is to be evaluated only on criteria applicable to his assignment.

A. ADMINISTRATION   Circle One

1. Care of equipment   O S NI US NA
   (issue, inventory, cleaning, etc.)
   Comments: _____
         (This line is repeated for each item.)

2. Organization of Staff   O S NI US NA

3. Organization of practices   O S NI US NA

4. Communication with coaches   O S NI US NA

5. Adherence to district and school philosophy   O S NI US NA
   and policies (eligibility reports, inventories,
   budgets, rosters, insurance forms, and
   follow-up, scores reported)

6. Public Relations   O S NI US NA

7. Supervision   O S NI US NA

B. SKILLS

1. Knowledge and presentation of fundamentals   O S NI US NA

2. Conditioning   O S NI US NA

3. Game preparation   O S NI US NA

4. Prevention and care of injuries   O S NI US NA
   (follow-up with parents)

C. RELATIONSHIPS

1. Enthusiasm
   a. for working with students   O S NI US NA
   b. for working with staff   O S NI US NA
      (support of other programs)
   c. for working with academic staff   O S NI US NA
      (other nonsport activities)
   d. for the sport itself   O S NI US NA

2. Discipline
   a. firm but fair   O S NI US NA
   b. consistent   O S NI US NA

3. Communication with players
   a. individual   O S NI US NA
   b. as a team   O S NI US NA

D. PERFORMANCE

1. Appearance and execution of team   O S NI US NA
   on the field or floor
2. Attitude of the team   O S NI US NA
3. Conduct of coach during game   O S NI US NA

E. SELF-IMPROVEMENT

1. Attends in-district meetings and clinics   O S NI US NA
2. Attends out-of-district clinics   O S NI US NA
   and statewide coaching meetings
3. Keeps updated by reading   O S NI US NA
   current literature
4. Aspirations made evident   O S NI US NA
   by statement of goals

_____   _____
   Coach   Evaluator

STEPS TO COACH'S EVALUATION

1. (To be completed prior to the start of
   coaching assignment.)

   Statement of personal goals and/or program
   goals as they relate to your coaching
   assignment.

   _____
   _____
   _____
   _____
   _____

2. To be completed at the conclusion of your
   coaching assignment, a self-evaluation
   on applicable criteria and statement
   relative to completion of goals statement.

   _____
   _____
   _____
   _____

3. Review by building athletic coordinator
   with coach (district athletic coordinator
   will review all evaluations before
   forwarding to principal.)

   _____
   _____
   _____
   _____

4. Signed by _____
                Coach

   _____
                Evaluator

Further comments: _____
   _____
   _____
   _____
   _____

5. To be placed in working papers of principal
   and forwarded to personnel office with
   yearly teaching evaluation.

Figure 13–8. An evaluation instrument for coaches. Courtesy of Beaverton School District, Beaverton, Oregon.)

sociations vary from state to state. In some sections of the country activities associations have been formed that exercise control of music, academic, and dramatic, as well as athletic contests. In a number of states the principals' associations exercise control over the athletic programs.

The purposes of state associations are stated in the constitutions of the various state organizations. The general objectives of the associations are to regulate and control interschool competition, contribute to the educational growth of high school students, improve the quality of amateur competition, protect the interests of member schools, and promote a more wholesome attitude toward all interschool competition. The following excerpt from the Handbook of the Virginia High School League is typical of the purposes of state associations:

The object of the Virginia High School League shall be to foster among the public high schools of Virginia a broad program of supervised competitions and desirable school activities as an aid in the total education of pupils.[15]

State associations are of three types: (1) voluntary organizations, (2) state department of education-affiliated, and (3) controlled through an institution of higher learning. The voluntary associations are the most numerous and all of them have effective regulations for the control of interschool programs. Some of the states that have voluntary associations are Washington, Kansas, Florida, and Pennsylvania. Associations affiliated with state departments of education place legal control of the interschool program with the state. This plan has been in effect in the state of Michigan since 1924. In 1938 the New York Board of regents made athletics in New York a definite part of the physical education program. The state associations in South Carolina, Virginia, and Texas are affiliated with the state universities in these states and are examples of highly organized associations with administrative control exercised by the state university.

Functions of State Associations. State associations have many functions and re-

sponsibilities in administering the state-wide program. Some of the functions that are generally recognized are:

1. Determining eligibility of contestants
2. Establishing regulations for conducting contests
3. Interpreting rules for playing
4. Developing insurance plans
5. Handling registration and classification of officials
6. Conducting tournaments and meets
7. Establishing athletic standards
8. Providing judicial service
9. Providing service
10. Sponsoring workshops and clinics.

The National Federation of State High School Associations

The National Federation of State High School Associations is composed of state athletic associations and exercises national control and direction over high school athletics. This association grew out of the efforts of educators to maintain state and local control of athletic programs and to keep these programs within the boundaries of the state. At the time of its formation, many outside groups were interested in school athletics not as educational programs but as a medium for commercialism. The National Federation attempts to advise and guide member associations and to protect their interests in interstate affairs. The objectives of the National Federation are clearly stated in its constitution:

The object of this Federation shall be to protect and supervise the interstate athletic interests of the high schools belonging to the state associations, to assist in those activities of the state associations which can best be operated on a nationwide scale, to sponsor meetings, publications and activities which will permit each state association to profit by the experience of all other member associations, and to coordinate the work so that wasted effort and unnecessary duplication will be avoided.[16]

Services of the National Federation. Founded in 1920, the National Federation is a service organization which presently influences the policies of

22,000 high schools. The most recent responsibility undertaken by the Federation is that of writing rules for girls' interscholastic programs. The services which the Federation provides include (1) adapting sports to the high school program; (2) coordinating nationwide experimentation on testing in an effort to improve sports; (3) authorizing experimentation in rules variations to assist in maintaining a meaningful code of rules; (4) promoting and supporting a rules publication and training program; (5) sustaining a rule-writing program which provides high schools with a voice in developing rules; (6) publishing official rules in basketball, baseball, gymnastics, and soccer; (7) authorizing the national alliance track and field rules and records book; (8) disseminating through the National Federation press service articles and materials to high school administrators and coaches; and (9) promoting research in athletics, particularly in safety. Because of national concern regarding protective equipment in sports, the National Federation, in conjunction with the Athletic Goods Manufacturers Association, the American College Health Association, the National Athletic Trainers Association, the National Collegiate Athletic Association, and the National Junior College Athletic Association, created the National Operating Committee for Safety in Athletic Equipment (NOCSAE). The committee authorized Wayne University to experiment with protective equipment, and is planning other research in an effort to establish standards to assist manufacturers in producing the safest equipment possible for players. NOCSAE established the following objectives:

1. To promote, conduct, and foster research; to study and analyze the collection of data and statistics relating to athletic equipment, with a view of encouraging the establishment of standards in the manufacture and use thereof for the benefit of amateur athletics.
2. To disseminate information and promote, conduct, and foster other activities designed to increase knowledge and understanding of the safety, comfort, utility, and legal aspects of athletic equipment.

3. To provide a forum in which individuals and organizations may consult and cooperate in considering problems relating to athletic equipment.
4. To do all of the foregoing exclusively for charitable, educational, and scientific purposes.[17]

Cardinal Athletic Principles. The cardinal principles were developed by a joint committee of the National Federation and the American Association (Alliance) for Health, Physical Education and Recreation. These principles were designed to produce maximum effectiveness of the interschool athletic program. The committee maintained that an effective program is composed of a blending of restrictions and freedom; mental growth and development; and liberties and restraints. Although these principles were established in 1948, they have withstood the ravages of time and are even more important today than they were the year they were adopted. These principles stipulate that to insure effectiveness the interschool program will:

1. Be closely coordinated with the general instructional program and properly articulated with other departments of the school.
2. Be such that the number of students accommodated and the educational aims achieved justify the use of tax funds for its support and also justify use of other sources of income, provided the time and attention which is given to the collection of such funds is not such as to interfere with the efficiency of the athletic program or of any other department of the school.
3. Be based on the spirit of nonprofessionalism so that participation is regarded as a privilege to be won by training and proficiency and to be valued highly enough to eliminate any need for excessive use of adulatory demonstrations or of expensive prizes or awards.
4. Confine the school athletic activity to events which are sponsored and supervised by the proper school authorities, so that exploitation or improper use of prestige built up by school teams or members of such teams may be avoided.
5. Be planned so as to result in opportunity for many individuals to explore a wide variety of sports and in reasonable season limits for each sport.

6. Be controlled so as to avoid the elements of professionalism and commercialism which tend to grow up in connection with widely publicized "bowl" contests, barnstorming trips and interstate or intersectional contests which require excessive travel expense or loss of school time or which are bracketed with educational travel claims in an attempt to justify privileges for a few at the expense of decreased opportunity for many.

7. Be kept free from the type of contests which involve a gathering of so-called "allstars" from different schools to participate in contests which may be used as a gathering place for representatives of certain colleges or professional organizations who are interested in soliciting athletic talent.

8. Include training in conduct and game ethics to reach all nonparticipating students and community followers of the school teams, in order to insure a proper understanding and appreciation of the sports skills and of the need for adherence to principles of fair play.

9. Encourage a balanced program of intramural activity in grades below the ninth, to make it unnecessary to sponsor contests of a championship nature in these grades.

10. Engender respect for the local, state and national rules and policies under which the school program is conducted.[18]

Examples of the Recommendations of the National Federation. The influence of the National Federation on state and local athletic programs has been so great that some examples of its accomplishments should be reviewed. Over the years this organization has achieved many of the goals established during its formative period. Progress made by the National Association has been astounding, and the need for assistance from this body in the future cannot be minimized. As competition develops on a large scale and spectator interest increases, more problems will develop. The National Federation is of sufficient strength and size to exercise the same or even more effective control in the future as it has in the past. Some of the recommendations of the Federation that may help to establish confidence in its strength for the future are:

1. Development of standards for member schools

2. Development of greater uniformity in minimum eligibility requirements

3. Elimination of national championships

4. Sanction of interstate meets and tournaments

5. Scheduling of interstate contests

6. Writing of playing rules

7. Cost reduction and approval of athletic equipment

8. Approval of records

9. Establishment of national policies concerning:
   a. solicitation of high school athletes by colleges
   b. agreement between professional baseball and the National Federation
   c. bowls, charity, and all-star games
   d. national championships (not allowed)
   e. nonschool promotions
   f. major-minor league rules

10. Adoption of the 10 cardinal athletic principles

11. Opposition to national promotions involving high school athletics[19]

National Council of Secondary School Athletic Directors

The National Council of Secondary School Athletic Directors was organized by the AAHPER in 1969, as a result of the need for a national body to assist in the administration and improvement of interschool competition. The council is administered by an executive committee consisting of a chairperson-elect, the past chairperson, and three representatives at large. Ex-officio members include representatives from the National Association of Secondary School Principals, the National Federation of State High School Associations, the American Association of School Administrators, and the vice-president of the AAHPER, who are responsible for administering and coordinating interschool athletic programs.

The Council, in its effort to strengthen the role of secondary school athletic directors in their efforts to attain educational objectives, has the following clearly defined goals:

1. To improve the educational aspects of interscholastic athletics and their articulation in the total educational program.

2. To foster high standards of professional proficiency and ethics.

3. To improve understanding of athletics throughout the nation.

4. To establish closer working relationships with related professional groups.

5. To promote greater unity, good will, and fellowship among all members.

6. To provide for an exchange of ideas.

7. To assist and cooperate with existing state athletic directors' organizations.

8. To make available to members special resource materials through publication, conferences, and consultant services.[20]

CRUCIAL ISSUES OF INTERSCHOOL ATHLETICS

The Educational Policies Commission in 1954 in its prestigious publication *School Athletics* conducted a thorough study of crucial issues confronting administrators of interschool athletic programs. It is amazing to find that these false values and bad practices, so prevalent then, are still facing us today. It seems appropriate that these concerns, so evident in athletics over the years, be mentioned at this time.

False Values

Among the false values that appear today on the interschool scene are (1) overemphasis on winning; (2) glorification of star athletes; (3) disparaging of nonathletes; and (4) presenting school games as public spectacles.

Bad Athletic Practices

There are many athletic practices existing today that are bad for young people, bad for the schools, and bad for the community. Some practices which should cause concern are (1) overemphasis on varsity athletic teams; (2) distortions in the educational program, such as lowering standards to meet eligibility requirements; (3) putting coaches under pressure to produce winning teams at all costs; (4) financial difficulties resulting

in the raising of money becoming the basic aim of the program; (5) recruiting by colleges; (6) involving younger children in high pressure competition; (7) neglecting female athletes; and (8) distorting school organization. The entire outline of false values and bad practices is found in *School Athletics*.[21]

It should be noted that the Commission also highly praised the many good values and practices that do exist in our schools today, while reiterating that the bad values and practices serve as a disintegrating influence and, unless resolved, will eventually undermine the entire interschool program.

The crucial issues just discussed have created many problems for administrators. These problems and the ethics involved in them are discussed in the following paragraphs.

ADMINISTRATIVE CONCERNS IN INTERSCHOOL ATHLETICS

Because of the tremendous growth of the interschool athletic program, the intense emphasis on competition, the trend toward spectator appeal, and the influence of the public on the program, administrative concerns in interschool athletics have developed. Some of these concerns are recruitment, scouting, overemphasis, community pressure, financing the interschool athletic program, certification of and additional remuneration for coaches, accident benefit plans, spectator control, legal responsibility of schools, and awards.

Recruitment

Some of the practices exercised by colleges in recruiting high school athletes are far from desirable. There are many instances in which the athletes are pampered and promised certain inducements to enroll in a particular college. Financial assistance has been approved and admission requirements have been waived. Recruitment practices in many instances have been so unethical that some states have established rules to discourage unethical practices to induce athletes to enter a particular college.

The situation has become so serious that the violations include payments to high school stars, tampering with grades, forging transcripts, finding substitutes to take students' exams, promising jobs to students' parents, and even buying the students automobiles. All of these practices violate the recruiting code of rules of the National Collegiate Athletic Association.[22]

The National Federation of State High School Associations for many years has recognized the problems created by solicitation pressures placed on high school athletics by college recruiters. The National Federation, in cooperation with the National Collegiate Athletic Association, developed a Recruiting Code of Good Conduct. which serves as a guideline for recruiting. However, even with the use of this code abuses did occur, and the National Federation in 1969 suggested a revision of the code to include the following:

(a) To reasonably limit the number of visits members of athletic staffs may make to prospective student athletes.

(b) To limit the number of expense-paid trips a prospective student athlete may make to a given campus.

(c) To limit the total number of expense-paid trips a student athlete may make to all campuses.

(d) To cause representatives of athletic staffs to arrange with the individual principal any visitations to a high school.

(e) To secure, through the principal, a profile of the prospective student athlete's high school academic record.

(f) To encourage colleges to refrain from overly publicizing interest in a boy who has not completed his high school education.

(g) To refrain from contacting a prospective student athlete immediately before or during an interscholastic contest.[23]

Scouting

Although colleges initiated scouting of opponents' teams in action, high school coaches in recent years have developed this technique extensively. Scouting opponents when they play other teams may be acceptable, but resorting to unethical practices cannot be condoned. The American Football Coaches Association issued the following statement regarding scouting:

It shall be considered unethical under any circumstances to scout any team, by any means whatsoever, except in regularly scheduled games. Any attempt to scout practice sessions shall be considered unethical. The head football coach of each institution shall be responsible for all scouting. This shall include the use of moving pictures.[24]

Overemphasis

Overemphasis on the interschool athletic program develops problems which adversely affect the student body, the administration, and the players themselves. Overemphasis in many places restricts the use of facilities to varsity practice and games, a practice which prevents conducting a broad intramural program for the entire student body. The pressure may become so great that sometimes teachers must lower standards in order that players remain on the eligibility list. Physical education instruction may be replaced by using this time for athletes to practice. The players are affected because they assume false and unethical values of interschool athletics, which in turn distorts their perspective in adjusting to actual life situations in later years.

These practices should not be condoned by administrators. Eventually, when overemphasis replaces the proper educational perspective for athletics, the program deteriorates and loses public support. When this happens, the survival of interschool athletics is placed in jeopardy as a phase of the educational effort.

Community Pressure

The program of interschool athletics is a spectator program and is designed to involve as many spectators as possible. Spectators are loyal to their teams and exert individual and group effort to assist in producing a winning team. Such groups as booster clubs, quarterback clubs, and touchdown clubs have been known to exert extreme pressure for a winning team. Parents may become involved with groups that are concerned with winning regardless of consequences. Promotional programs sponsored by clinic clubs or other community groups, in their efforts to produce successful spectacles, may undermine the objectives of interschool athletics.

It is the responsibility of the superintendent and the board of education to establish policies that will prevent lay groups from dominating the athletic program. Trends in the direction in which promotional groups are gaining control of the school program may be anticipated, and the necessary steps to curtail these attempts should be taken. Strong action on the part of the principal, the director of athletics, and the coach in most instances is sufficient to prevent these situations from developing. This does not mean that the school should attempt to exclude community help. All interschool programs need the assistance of the community. It does mean, however, that small pressure groups should not be allowed to gain control of any phase of the school educational program. These groups are not representing the community but are usually operating from selfish motives with private endorsement.

Financing the Interschool Athletic Program

Financing the interschool athletic program is an administrative problem that becomes increasingly critical each year. As costs for other school programs increase, the cost of supporting the athletic program also increases.

Financing the program in interschool athletics is usually accomplished through three methods: (1) the school supports the program entirely through gate receipts, fund raising programs, and student fees; (2) the school partially supports the program, with the board of ed-

ucation assuming some of the cost; and (3) the board of education assumes the entire cost of the program. Of the three plans, the third is by far the best. It is the opinion of many people that if all interschool athletic programs were financed by the board of education, many of the problems that arise in interschool athletics would diminish. Irrespective of the difficulties involved in providing tax funds for the support of the program, efforts should be made to secure such funds for this purpose. Some of the advantages of supporting the program through tax funds are:

1. The high school athletic program has ceased to be a commerical enterprise, dependent on gate receipts. Outside pressures for postseason, charity, all-star, and "curtain raiser" games have been eliminated.
2. More adequate health and safety protection is accomplished by having fewer games and contests, avoiding play during inclement weather, providing safe equipment and safe transportation, and valuing the health of the participant above the winning of the game.
3. Most football games are now played on week-end afternoons, with resulting decrease in such problems as vandalism and rowdyism.
4. All schools within a system are assured of equal quality of equipment and supplies. Through central purchasing savings can be had.
5. Some of the hidden costs of public high schools, athletic fees, are reduced for the student.[25]

Certification of Coaches

Coaching a team involves so much more than sports expertise that certification of coaches seems to be a necessary step if quality coaching is to be expected. Universally, the single criterion for selecting coaches is the fact that the individual played on the college team. It is felt by many that a minor in physical education is the minimum acceptable requirement for coaching. However, one out of four head coaches does not meet this standard. Although knowledge of the sport is essential, many other factors are involved.

Unless the coach has knowledge of

some of the areas included in the physical education curriculum, neither he nor the team can be expected to meet educational objectives. Many of the injuries that occur in interschool contests could be prevented if coaches were familiar with human anatomy and kinesiology.

The American Alliance for Health, Physical Education, and Recreation, through the division of men's athletics, appointed a committee to study this problem. The committee concluded that the best way to alleviate the problem of unqualified coaches was to establish certification standards for students majoring in academic subjects who desired to coach. The committee felt that the standards should include minimum essentials that every coach should have. The courses, with the major aspects of each course, are outlined here.

Additional Remuneration for Coaches

The emphasis on interschool athletics and the importance of securing teachers who are qualified for both teaching and coaching necessitates additional remuneration for coaches. Coaches spend an enormous amount of time beyond the normal teaching day coaching the team, accompanying the team on trips during weekends, and attending clinics. They spend several nights each week with the team when games are played. They should receive compensation for this additional time and effort. Moreover, many teachers must supplement their regular teaching salaries through outside employment. Since coaching involves that time which might otherwise be used for this purpose, these teachers may be

Courses	Semester Hours
Medical Aspects of Athletic Coaching	3
I. Medical aspects	
II. Protective equipment and facilities	
III. Training	
IV. Injuries	
V. Medical and safety problems	
VI. In-service training — care of the athlete	
VII. Medical research related to athletics	
Principles and Problems of Coaching	3
I. Personal relationships	
II. Organization	
III. Important considerations	
Theory and Techniques of Coaching	6
I. Educational implications of the sport	
II. Fundamentals detailed	
III. Technical information	
IV. Scouting	
V. Conditioning for a specific sport	
VI. Organization and management	
VII. Practice sessions	
VIII. Safety aspects of a particular sport	
IX. Rules and regulations	
X. Evaluation	
Kinesiological Foundations in Coaching	2
I. Anatomical factors	
II. Mechanics of movement	
Physiological Foundations of Coaching	2
I. Physiological factors	
II. Exercise physiology factors[26]	

handicapped financially unless arrangements are made for extra pay.

There are several ways in which consideration is given for extra services for coaching. In some places, teachers are allowed free periods. Another plan is to allow teachers free periods in addition to extra pay. The plan most generally used is to provide extra remuneration for such services, in addition to the regular salary. This plan usually takes into consideration the number of extra hours involved plus other factors that are involved in coaching.

A salary schedule based on a formula was developed by Thurston, which includes such factors as length of school day, time spent in each sport each day, time spent per year, and the length of the normal school year. The first step in the formula is to develop an index to serve as a basis for the schedule shown at the bottom of the page.

In addition to the basic index, "additive indices" should be determined. These indices consider factors other than clock hours that should be involved in the extra pay schedule. For example, the basketball coach with the basic index of .125 might receive "additive indexes" of .03 for pressure, .005 for responsibility, .01 for travel, and .005 for liability. His total index would be .125 + .03 + .005 + .01 + .005 or .175. Assuming that he has a base salary of $11,000 his differential for coaching would be determined by multiplying $11,000 by .175, or $1925.[27]

The coaching staff of Watertown High School, Watertown, New York, developed an instrument to provide coaches with extra pay for their services. The plan was constructed around several indices, which included (1) hours involved, (2) number of students involved, (3) experience necessary, (4) spectator and public pressure, (5) equipment and faculty responsibility, (6) indoor and outdoor coaching environment, and (7) travel.

The coaches felt that they should be paid a percentage of their salary for coaching and that the percentage system would:

1. Recognize after-school physical education activities as educational functions.
2. Give credit for educational training and experience.
3. Provide for an annual pay raise related to the credit given for training and experience in the teaching schedule.
4. Provide a built-in automatic adjustment of the extra pay scale to accommodate changes made in the district-wide teacher salary schedule.
5. Encourage and tend to hold high caliber personnel in the field of interscholastic coaching.[28]

The differentials resulting from the application of indices to each sport are shown in Figure 13–9.

$$\frac{\text{Amount of Time Spent in Activity Per Day}}{\text{Amount of Time in Normal School Day}} \times \frac{\text{Amount of Time Spent in the Activity During the Year}}{\text{Length of Normal School Year (either months, weeks, or days)}} = \text{Index}$$

For the first example, the high school varsity basketball coach, the formula works as follows:

$$\frac{\text{2-hr. Practice of Playing Time Per Day}}{\text{8-hr. Normal Day}} \times \frac{\text{5-month Long Season}}{\text{10-month School Year}} = \text{Index}$$

$$\text{Or} \qquad \frac{2}{8} \times \frac{5}{10} \qquad = .125$$

```
                        COACHING DIFFERENTIALS

1.09      Head Coaches of Varsity Basketball, Football, Wrestling
1.08      Varsity Swimming
1.07      Varsity Gymnastics
1.06      Head Coaches of Varsity Baseball, Lacrosse, Soccer & Track
1.06      Varsity Asst. in Football, Head J. V. Football, J. V. Wrestling,
          J. V. Basketball
1.05      Varsity Cross-country
1.045     J. V. Baseball, J. V. Lacrosse, Asst. Varsity Track, Asst. J. V.
          Football
1.04      9th grade Basketball, 7th & 8th grade basketball, Varsity Tennis,
          Jr. High Track, 9th gr. football
1.035     Varsity Golf, Jr. High Cross-country, Jr. High Soccer, 9th grade
          Football Asst.

1.  The above indices would be applied to the individual's own step on
    the salary schedule, relative to his years of coaching experience,
    not his years of teaching experience,

2.  We strongly recommend a minimum of $300 for any full-time interscholastic
    coaching assignment; (in case of a beginning teacher receiving 1.035 and
    it might not bring him to the $300 level.)

3.  We also request the Randle committee to evaluate and place a fair remunera-
    tion on the five days of football practice (before Sept. 1st).

4.  We suggest the following remuneration for all intramurals:

            $5.00/hr. - 1st yr.
             5.50/hr. - 2nd yr.
             6.00/hr. - 3rd yr. and thereafter

    Maximums:  to be set by the Director of Physical Education and the
    Board of Education.
```

Figure 13–9. Coaching differentials for various sports, based on indices. (From Watertown High School, Watertown, New York.)

Accident Benefit Plans

Wisconsin was the first state to establish an accident benefit plan for interschool athletics. The data on injuries compiled by this state and also by New York provide valuable material for study. Recommendations for the improvement of equipment and changes in rules resulted from the study, which in turn made sports participation safer.

For a number of years many states developed accident benefit plans for the protection of players. These plans and the statistics involved in implementing the plans illustrate the important role state associations have played in the evaluation of interschool athletics.

In recent years commercial insurance companies have become interested in athletic insurance. These companies have followed to a large degree the plans developed by the state associations. The plans offered by the commercial companies have broadened the coverage to include all activities, which in turn involve more pupils.

Spectator Control

The administration of interschool contests in some places involves problems of spectator control that may be serious and difficult to handle. Crowd enthusiasm and disapproval sometimes result in mob action and riots in which the personal safety of spectators is threatened. Interschool athletics are a part of the total educational pattern, and it is the responsibility of school officials to administer them in accordance with the objectives of education.

There is concern because of the behavior of spectators that the future and continuance of interschool programs may be seriously threatened. The problem is a national one. Many schools have discontinued all of their night contests and are scheduling games in the afternoon. There are two alternatives in alleviating the problem: establish measures for controlling the behavior of spectators or discontinue the program.

A survey of the 22 members of the Connecticut Association of the Administration of Health and Physical Education revealed the seriousness of the problem. The results of the survey show that:

1. Spectator or control problems are increasing and at a faster rate in the larger cities.

2. All school districts take the greatest precautions in football and basketball. Hockey, where played, rates high.

3. Most school districts hire teachers to supervise at athletic events, and most have increased this coverage in the past three years.

4. All school districts use police protection at football and basketball games. Half have found it necessary to increase this protection in the past three years. Large cities find it necessary to cover more sports than suburban cities.

5. All school districts rely heavily on sports assemblies and pep rallies to stress sportsmanship.

6. There has been an increase of both major and minor incidents in the past three years.

7. Two large city school districts have experienced problems during the playing of the national anthem. Seven felt the incidents at the Mexican Olympics would have an unfavorable reaction, and 14 indicated the action of the Olympic Committee would have a favorable reaction on our problems.

8. Sportsmanship assemblies, uniformed police protection, examples of coaches and faculty supervision were listed most often as "successful techniques."[29]

Many cities have studied the problem and have adopted effective procedures for controlling crowds and ensuring a safe environment for the thousands of spectators not involved with disorder.

Hilton Murphy, Director of Athletics and Community Service, Toledo, Ohio, Public Schools, feels that behavior problems occurring at interschool contests are caused by a small group of juvenile delinquents and school dropouts. He recommends advance planning, ample resources, and quiet decisive action by the groups concerned as the answer to preventing small groups from disrupting the entire interschool program.[30]

A study of 70 athletic directors selected from different sections of the country showed that the practices and procedures listed below are used at present in crowd control. The percentages indicate the number using the procedure.

Limitation of spectator attendance at games—13%
Afternoon League schedules—24%
Restriction of gate ticket sales—7%
Utilization of school personnel for control purposes
    Faculty supervision—51%
    Faculty paid extra—25%
    Paid civilian security guards—11%
    No school personnel used—5%
Utilization of local police department for control purposes
    Regular police—76%
    Off-duty police—19%
Development of student sportsmanship programs in all schools—89%
    (assemblies and awards were the two techniques most often mentioned)
Utilizing student cheerleaders and pep squads—87%
Evaluating attitudes of coaches, players, and spectators following game performance—50%
Evaluating quality of officiating
    By coaches—61%
    By athletic commission—15%
Establishing programs of human relations within and between schools—65%
Reviewing facilities for athletic events for maximum safety and security—82%
Establishing a local athletic advisory committee to review and recommend policies for athletic events—59%.[31]

The Chicago Public School System, which has the second largest interscholastic program for boys in the world, has approached the problem of spectator control realistically. Under the direction of Louis C. Jorndt, Director, Division of Health, Physical Education, and staff, the combined efforts of the schools, the police, and city transportation authorities are utilized to provide measures for controlling crowds attending the afternoon contests. Meetings of representatives from the schools involved are scheduled two weeks before the competitive season begins. Problems of scheduling, home teams, spectators, faculty supervision, and entertainment are discussed at these meetings. Each Wednesday prior to the games scheduled on Thursday, Friday, and Saturday afternoons, a meeting is held that brings together police, juvenile officers, Chicago Transit Authority, and human relations representatives. At this meeting, past games are discussed and future contests are evaluated according to possible tension, rivalry, and anticipated crowds. The various agencies are assigned to supervise the games, based on the evaluation. For example, more police, faculty supervision, and all available help from every source would be sent to the game with the largest anticipated attendance and rivalry.

A written policy for controlling crowds has been developed; this policy includes recommendations designed to ensure the welfare and security of all persons attending interschool contests. The functions and responsibilities of all coaches, students, and faculty are outlined in the brochure; provisions are also included for arrangements with the stadium management, police, and transit authorities. This policy has proved to be effective and, because it illustrates so well the importance of pre-planning, the sections that include recommendations for the various groups are presented in the Resource Manual. The groups involved are coaches, students, faculty, stadium managers, police, and the transit authority.[32]

A checklist is used by Chicago schools in conjunction with the crowd-control recommendations. This checklist is made in duplicate; the principal keeps one copy and the other is sent to the superintendent one day prior to the contest. A copy of the checklist is shown in Figure 13–10.

Legal Responsibility of Schools. In all athletic contests, the schools have definite legal responsibilities for the safety of spectators as well as participants. If there is an injury to a spectator as the result of an accident, any employer of the school district may be liable for negligence. It seems that after the spectator has purchased a ticket and has been seated, he has definite legal status within the framework of the actions and responsibilities of the sponsoring agency. Precedents set in court cases have established that the school district is ultimately responsible for conducting and supervising the event, and is under a legal duty to provide for the safety of the spectators through provision for all foreseeable circumstances. This duty encompasses control of the crowd and individuals, and failure to carry out that duty adequately may render the agency and/or individuals liable for injuries resulting from that failure, if negligence is involved.[33]

Awards for Interschool Competition

Granting extrinsic awards for athletic competition is a universal practice. Providing awards for interschool competition follows the same pattern that permeates most endeavors throughout life. Academic performance is rewarded with a mark. Excellence in academic achievement is recognized on the college level by the coveted Phi Beta Kappa key. Everyone expects monetary remuneration for teaching, or for practicing law or medicine. Architects and engineers are often awarded for their services, and all governmental agencies operate on awards programs. Some people feel that intrinsic satisfaction is sufficient reward for athletic competition, and there is a great deal of merit in this belief. However, in our culture, where the majority of people believe in rewards for a job well done, it is difficult to deny an individual

(Make out in duplicate - Retain one copy; send other to District Superintendent)

Game: Football _____ vs _____

Field _____ Time _____ Date _____

ESTIMATE OF TENSION (Check one) HEAVY _____ MEDIUM_____ LIGHT _____
Check each item below indicating attention given; remarks, if any.

STUDENT INFORMATION AND EDUCATION

_____ Sportsmanship Assembly _____
_____ Transportation Information _____
_____ Field Seating Arrangements _____
_____ Field Dispersal Plan _____

FACULTY PERSONNEL

_____ Faculty Representative in Charge _____
_____ Explanation of duties; Station Assignment: (Field, Building, Bleachers)
_____ Pre Game _____
_____ During Game _____
_____ After Game _____

STADIUM AND FIELD MANAGEMENT

_____ Faculty Representative in Charge _____
_____ Seating Arrangements _____
_____ First Aid Station _____
_____ Comfort Stations _____
_____ Locker Rooms _____
_____ Ticket Sellers _____
_____ Ticket Takers _____
_____ Gate Men _____
_____ Pass Gate _____
_____ Barricades and Signs _____

POLICE DEPARTMENT SERVICE
        Request for a Detail via Director's Office
        (DE 2-7800 - Ext. 365)

_____ Local Field Control Plan Discussed with Police _____
_____ Dispersal Plans Discussed with Police _____
_____ Name of Police Officer in Charge at Game _____

CHICAGO TRANSIT AUTHORITY SERVICE

        Request to Local District Superintendent
_____ for additional Transportation Service _____
_____ Transfer Points Discussed _____
_____ Loading Point Plans Discussed _____

_____ Date _____
Signature of Person Completing Check List
_____
                            High School

Figure 13-10. A checklist of arrangements and preparations for spectator control. (Courtesy of Chicago Public Schools, Chicago, Illinois.)

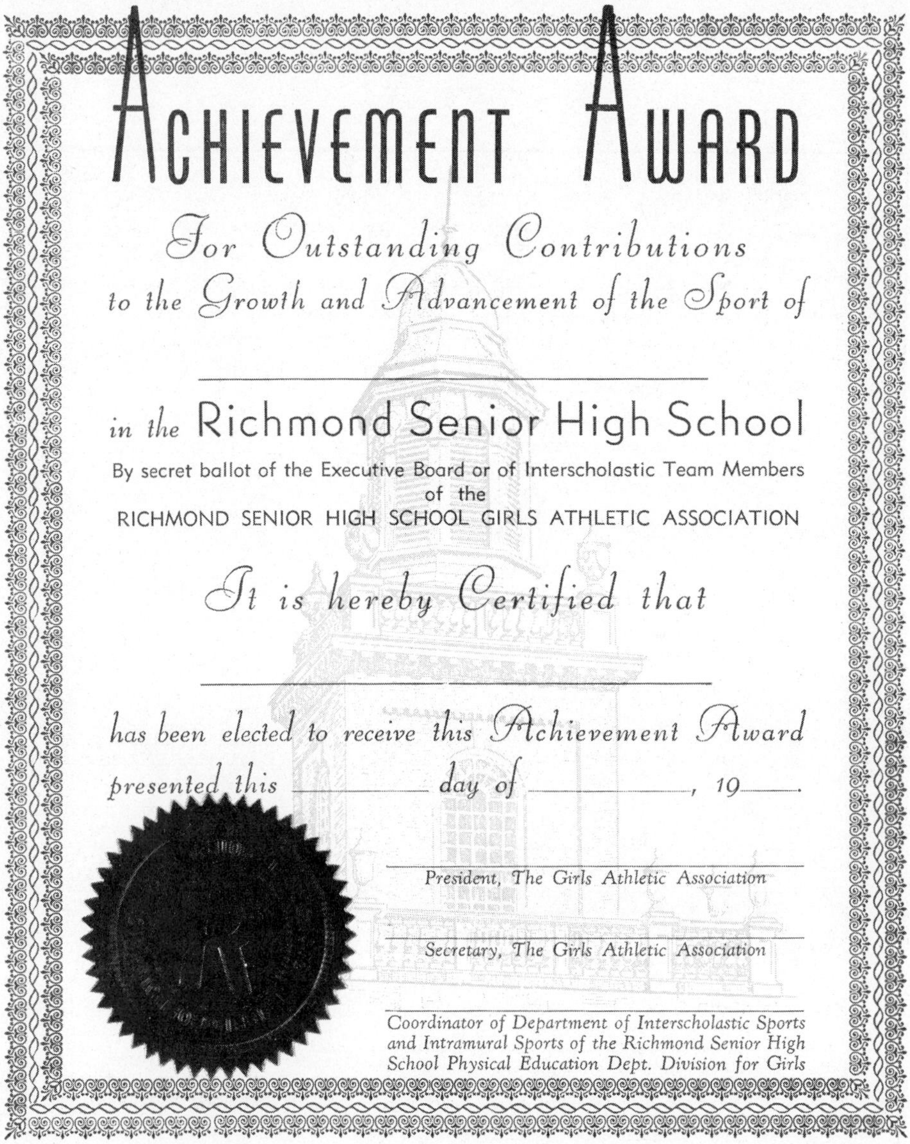

ACHIEVEMENT AWARD

For Outstanding Contributions
to the Growth and Advancement of the Sport of

____

in the Richmond Senior High School

By secret ballot of the Executive Board or of Interscholastic Team Members
of the
RICHMOND SENIOR HIGH SCHOOL GIRLS ATHLETIC ASSOCIATION

It is hereby Certified that

____

has been elected to receive this Achievement Award
presented this ________ *day of* ____________, *19*____.

____
President, The Girls Athletic Association

____
Secretary, The Girls Athletic Association

____
Coordinator of Department of Interscholastic Sports
and Intramural Sports of the Richmond Senior High
School Physical Education Dept. Division for Girls

Figure 13–11. An athletic award that is both appropriate and inexpensive. (Courtesy of Richmond Senior High School, Richmond, Indiana.)

this recognition. Probably the answer is to provide modest awards with emphasis on intrinsic values. Inexpensive monograms and certificates seem to be the most generally accepted type of award for athletic competition. Figure 13–11 shows an inexpensive certificate for outstanding achievement in athletics. Although this is a special award, it is the type of inexpensive recognition that may be used for athetic accomplishments.

The monogram or school letter is the standard award for most athletic competition. Although some schools distinguish between major and minor sports, the majority award the same letter for all sports.

Usually individual schools develop their own requirements for granting letters based on the recommendation of the coach and the athletic council. The St. Louis Public Schools use the following requirements in awarding letters for nine sports.

Basic Requirements

1. All eligibility requirements of the Missouri State High School Activities Association and of the St. Louis Public High School League must be met for a boy to be considered eligible for consideration for an athletic letter.

2. The boy, to be considered for an athletic letter, must have displayed good sportsmanship in competition and have been regular in attendance at practice and at games.

3. The coach shall recommend the boys to be considered for athletic letters at the end of each sport season.

4. This list of recommendations by the coach shall be submitted to the principals, and each boy so recommended must be approved by the principal.

5. A letter and a certificate shall be awarded to each boy the first time he qualifies in each separate sport. Thereafter, he shall be awarded a certificate only in lieu of a duplicate letter for the sport.

Specific Requirements

1. *Football.* Participation in at least one-third of the quarters played by the team in the total schedule.

2. *Basketball.* Participation in at least one-third of the quarters played by the team in the total schedule, or participation in State Tournament.

3. *Baseball.* Participation in at least one-fourth of the innings or one-third of the games played by the team in the total schedule, or participation in State Final. *Exception:* Pitchers may be recommended for letters without an established requirement of participation. No more than two base coaches may be recommended for letters without an established requirement of participation.

4. *Track.* Score an average of two points for the dual meets in the total schedule of the team or qualify in the District or League Meet.

5. *Swimming.* Score an average of two points for the dual meets in the total schedule of the team or qualify in the State Meet.

6. *Tennis.* Participation in at least one-half of the matches played by the team in the total schedule.

7. *Cross Country.* Participation in at least one-half of the meets run by the team in the total schedule and finishing among the first seven men of his school in one-half the meets.

8. *Soccer.* Participation in at least one-half of the halves played by the team in the total schedule.

9. *Wrestling.* (a) A boy will score points in each match according to the rules—2 for draw, 3 for decision, 5 for pin; (b) if no points are scored, one point per match will be awarded for participation; (c) a letter will be awarded for averaging one point per match in the total schedule of the team, or for scoring two or more points in District Meet.

10. *Service Letter.* May be awarded to a boy who has been faithful in practice and participation for at least two years and has completed the sport season during his senior year without having reached the required standards, either because of injury or lack of skill.

11. *Manager's Letter.* May be awarded for a minimum of one season of service as team manager and such letters shall be limited to not more than two per year.[34]

The giving of a manager's letter is being done by an increasing number of schools. These students perform a service for both the athletes and the school. Recognition of these services certainly is appropriate.

ADMINISTRATIVE POLICY FOR INTERSCHOOL ATHLETICS

There are several facets of the interschool program that necessitate the establishing of a written policy by the board of education. The most important of these are (1) interschool athletics in the junior high school, (2) interschool athletics for elementary school children, (3) interschool athletics for girls, and (4) medical services.

Interschool Athletics in the Junior High School

Although interschool athletics have been accepted as a part of the educational pattern on the senior high school level, a similar program for the junior high school is still a controversial issue. It is interesting to note that through the years national organizations and leaders in education and medicine have prepared statements in opposition to junior high school programs, and a few years later other committees and individuals supported such programs. The issue is a critical one, since the health and fitness of thousands of children are involved. Both sides of the controversy are discussed in the following paragraphs.

Groups Opposing the Program. In 1954 the Educational Policies Commission, consisting of representatives from the National Education Association and the American Association of School Administrators, in their publication *School Athletics,* included the following statement opposing programs of interschool athletics in the junior high school:

No junior high school should have a "school team" that competes with school teams of other junior high schools in organized leagues or tournaments. Varsity-type interscholastics of junior high school boys and girls should not be permitted.[35]

In 1951 the American Association of School Administrators issued a statement regarding interschool athletics in the junior high schools:

Interscholastic athletics are not recommended for junior high school boys. At these levels most boys are prepubescent, growing rapidly and insufficiently developed to withstand the physical and emotional strain of interscholastic competition. Their needs can be met best by a varied program of intramural activities. In a similar way it is recommended that girls' programs be limited to intramurals, sports days and club programs.[36]

Individuals Opposing the Program. The opinions of scientists and physicians are extremely important in studying interschool athletics in the junior high school. Krogman represents the feeling of many individuals opposing the program. He states:

As a human biologist I hold it basically unsound to impose upon the rapidly growing organism excessive physical demands. The catch here is, of course, the definition of the word "excessive." In a sense the definition must refer to the skills, aptitude, and potential of the individual; this means a demand-evaluation based on the child's own growth progress. In a larger sense, however, this means that the entire circum-pubertal period, roughly 11–14 in girls, 12–15 in boys, is one in which maximum protection must be given

to the growing child, for balance between energy-intake and energy-use (in function and in growth dynamics) is finely drawn—there is too often no reservoir of excess energy upon which to draw. By "protection" I mean that the child in such a growth surge should not be required to lavish energy upon various kinds and degrees of athletic performance.

I should like to point out that I am not in the least condemning. I am admonishing. I am certain that Physical Education as a discipline will implement growth thinking into any and all programs of athletic skills, be they merely curricular (as gym classes) or competitive (as intramural or interschool). My thinking applies mostly to the latter, and especially to the vigorously aggressive contact sports. (There is no profit it seems to me, in risking traumata—either morphological or physiological—at a time when the child (especially the boy) is depositing all his energy in the bank of growth. It will yield him a high rate of interest in normal, health progress toward maturity. Why, then, endanger the yield by a too-great withdrawal from the energy account?[37]

Medical opinion is available in opposition to programs of interschool competition in the junior high school. Dukelow expresses his opinion in the following statement:

Most pupils in the elementary and junior high schools, and a few in the first year or two of high school are not physically and emotionally stabilized. In the presence of such emotional stresses as victory and defeat or failure to "make the team," they may develop all sorts of compensations. At this age, too, there are discrepancies in body proportion; muscles and ligaments are not adjusted to new responsibilities produced by longer bones; and injury to growth areas of bones is possible.[38]

Reichert, a physician of renown, reports the results of a study of junior high boys in Cleveland, Ohio, who participated in interschool athletics:

An extensive study...showed that a group engaged in highly competitive interschool athletics did not gain as much in height, weight, and lung capacity as did a comparable group of boys in the same school who were participating in a program of physical education and intramural athletics.[39]

Those Favoring the Program.
Proponents who favor the inclusion of interschool athletics in the junior high school are just as positive in their stand. Alley summarizes the arguments of those who advocate interschool programs in the junior high school. He states:

1. Preadolescent and adolescent boys are growing, developing organisms; and injuries do occur in programs of athletics for this age group. However, there is no evidence that boys are injured more frequently or more seriously in well-organized and well-conducted programs of athletics in junior high schools than in such programs in senior high schools.

2. Admittedly, boys of junior high school age vary widely in respect to height, weight, and physiological maturity. However, studies have shown rather conclusively that the boys who succeed in athletics are boys who, in terms of height, weight, and (or) physiological maturity, are advanced for their ages. These boys will comprise the interscholastic team in any given school and, to some degree, will be protected from injury because of their advanced physiological maturity.

3. The view that the normal heart may be injured by excessive exercise is not shared by a number of medical authorities who hold that the inability of the body to meet the demands of the exercise will cause the person to diminish or cease the exercise before the normal heart is placed in jeopardy because of excessive strain.

4. The evidence purported to indicate that participation in interscholastic athletics interferes with the normal growth pattern of junior high school boys is sparse and inconclusive. The deviation from normal that is reflected in the growth patterns of junior high school athletes is probably due to the fact that these boys are, in respect to growth and maturity, advanced for their ages.

5. Rather than adversely affecting emotional and social development, participation in competition of the nature usually provided in junior high school programs of athletics fosters emotional control and desirable social development. Youngsters who participate in athletics programs gain confidence in themselves and obtain added recognition from their peers.

6. The failure of the teacher-coach or other school personnel to provide adequate physical education and intramural programs is an administrative problem, the solution to which is dependent upon the personnel and the facilities that are available in each school and upon the administrative policies concerning the manner in which the time of the school personnel is spent. The removal of interscholastic athletics from the school scene would not necessarily result in improved physical education and intramural programs.[40]

A later study of the issue was made by a joint committee sponsored by the American Association for Health, Physical Education, and Recreation; the National Association of Secondary School Principals; and the National Federation of State High School Athletic Associations. This report evaluated the arguments offered for both sides of the issue and reaffirmed the belief that participation in these programs provides wholesome recreation and contributes to the development of (1) strength, endurance, and organic vigor, (2) proficiency in physical skills; and (3) the ability to compete ethically and to cooperate effectively.[41]

The report recommended that the required program in physical education, the intramural program, and the physical recreation program should have priority in all junior high schools. If these programs are adequate, the report recommends an interschool athletic program organized with the following principles serving as guidelines:

1. The interscholastic athletic program for boys in the junior high school should make definite contributions toward the accomplishment of the educational objectives of the school.

2. The interscholastic athletics program for boys in the junior high school should supplement—rather than serve as a substitute for—an adequate program of required physical education, intramurals, and physical recreation for all students.

3. The interscholastic athletics program for boys in the junior high school should, under the administration and the supervision of the appropriate school officials, be conducted by men with adequate professional preparation in physical education.

4. The interscholastic athletics program for boys in the junior high school should be so conducted that the physical welfare of the participants is protected and fostered.[42]

The recommendations of the committee were made with reservations. For example, the report stated, "The committee recognizes that in most junior high schools the benefits that may be derived from participation in competitive athletics can be realized as readily through intramural athletics as through interscholastic athletics."[43]

Administrators should weigh the arguments carefully before initiating interschool athletic programs in the junior high school. Medical opinion and study should play a prominent role in making the decision.

One argument used by the proponents of these programs is that boys will participate in these programs whether the school sponsors them or not. This is not a sound argument. School administrators are highly trained and knowledgeable regarding the growth and development of children. They should take the lead in providing scientifically sound programs and not be influenced by pressure groups. There are many programs functioning in the community that are not acceptable in the school curriculum. In some places groups sponsor boxing and tackle football for small children. Should the same rationale—that the school should sponsor these activities—be applied here?

In addition to the arguments pro and con regarding the issue of including interschool activities in the junior high school, the following factors are involved:

1. The costs would be prohibitive. The program would have to be financed through gate receipts. This in turn places pressure on the coaches to produce winning teams, which in turn results in overemphasis for a few gifted pupils.

2. The program would conflict with the intramural program in the use of facilities. Intramurals involving thousands of pupils would have to be abandoned for a small number of varsity players.

3. Increased emphasis on intramurals with city-wide tournaments growing out of intramurals would be a more suitable program for the boys and girls in the junior high schools.

4. All the objectives advanced for interschool athletics may be attained through a well-organized intramural program. Moreover, the intramural program is designed to meet the needs of many pupils.

We, the authors, are deeply concerned with this issue. The concern increases as the recommendations of the various groups are studied and conflicting opinions are in evidence. The issue is a grave one. If there is even a remote possibility that injuries such as those described by some physicians may occur, these programs should be abolished and individuals who continue to sponsor them should be condemned. The authors would like to recommend that a committee to study the problem and make recommendations be formed, composed of representatives from all interested groups. Physicians who have had experience in working with young children and who have a knowledge of the growth and development of children should be among the members. Representatives from the following organizations should be included on the committee:

American Medical Association
National Education Association
American Association of School Administrators
American Association for Health, Physical Education, and Recreation
Society of State Directors of Health, Physical Education and Recreation
National Council of State Consultants in Elementary Education
Department of Elementary Principals
Division of Men's Athletics of the American Association of Health, Physical Education and Recreation

Interschool Athletics for Elementary School Children

Interschool athletics for elementary school children is not as controversial as the junior high school program. Although some schools sponsor these programs, the practice is not universal. Educators are opposed to these programs for elementary school children not only because of medical opinion that opposes them, but for educational and social reasons as well.

Until further research and study are available, the recommendations of the joint committee report of the American Association for Health, Physical Education, and Recreation; the Society of State Directors of Health, Physical Education, and Recreation; the National Council of State Consultants in Elementary Education; and the Department of Elementary School Principals may serve as guidelines to follow. The committee recommended:

Instruction in Physical Education for All

The best interests of all children are served when school and community give priority — in professional personnel, space and facilities, equipment and supplies, time and money — to a broad program of instruction in physical education, based upon individual and group needs, for all boys and girls.

Voluntary Informal Recreation and Intramurals

Next in importance is a broad and varied program of voluntary informal recreation for children of all ages, and an interesting extensive program of intramural activities for boys and girls in upper elementary grades and above. "Intramural activities" means individual, dual, and team sports with competition limited to contests between teams within the individual school (or neighborhood recreation center).

Play Days, Sports Days, Informal Games

Activities such as play days and sports days and occasional invitational games, which involve children of two or more schools and which have high social values, are to be encouraged. The emphasis should be upon social participation with the competitive aspect subordinated. Play days involve teams or groups made up of children from several schools, all intermixed. Sports days include activities in which the playing units are composed of members of the same school. A few invitational contests in certain sports between schools (or natural neighborhood groups) on an informal basis might be carried on — but only as a supplement to good instruction in physical education, recreational opportunities for all children within the school and additional informal recreational opportunities during out-of-school hours.

Activities should be appropriate to the level of maturity, skills and interests of the participants. Tackle football for children below the ninth-grade age and boxing for children and youth of all ages are definitely disapproved.

No Interschool Competition of a Varsity Pattern

Interschool competition of a varsity pattern and similarly organized competition under auspices of other community agencies are definitely disapproved for children below the ninth grade.[44]

Interschool Athletics for Girls

Widespread emphasis on competition for girls and women, particularly in the Olympic Games, has focused attention on interschool athletic programs for girls. In the past there has been considerable controversy relative to the desirability of these programs. Many statements have been advanced by those opposing the participation of girls in interschool programs. The proponents of interschool competition for girls are just as positive in their stand and offer strong arguments supporting their views.

The opponents of these programs argue that girls should not participate in highly organized competition for medical reasons. They claim that this type of competition might have a deleterious effect on the sexual organs and that the emotional nature of women is not compatible with the pressure of interschool competition.

Those who advocate interschool programs for girls argue that girls have the same rights as boys to participate in interschool competition. They feel that programs should be offered for those girls gifted in skill performance to have the opportunity of furthering this potential just as boys do.

Since there is no evidence, medical or otherwise, to show that girls will be adversely affected by interschool competition, the question is raised: Why the opposition to the program? Probably the answer lies not so much in the program itself as in the fears of how it may be conducted. Administrators familiar with the undesirable practices that have occurred in the program for boys are reluctant to promote programs for girls that may present the same problems.

The National Association for Girls and Women in Sport (NAGWS). The National Association for Girls and Women in Sport, a division of the American Alliance for Health, Physical Education and Recreation, has provided leadership in determining policy for interschool athletics for girls for many years. The organization, formerly The Division for Girls' and Women's Sports, has been aware of the consequences that may result from interschool programs for girls and shares the same fears that administrators have expressed. The purpose of NAGWS is to foster the development of sports programs for the enrichment of the life of the participants. In its efforts to serve the needs of all persons concerned with sports programs for girls and women, NAGWS stated the following beliefs:

1. Sports are an integral part of the culture in which we live.
2. Sports programs are a part of the total educational experience of the participant when conducted in educational institutions.
3. Opportunities for instruction and participation in sports appropriate to her skill level should be included in the experience of every girl.
4. Sports skills and sports participation are valuable social and recreational tools which may be used to enrich the lives of women in our society.
5. Competition and cooperation may be demonstrated in all sports programs, although the type and intensity of the competition and cooperation will vary with the degree or level of skill of the participants.
6. An understanding of the relationship between competition and cooperation and the utilization of both within the accepted framework of our society is one of the desirable outcomes of sports participation.
7. Physical activity is important in the maintenance of the general health of the participant.
8. Participation in sports contributes to the development of self-confidence and to the establishment of desirable interpersonal relationships.[45]

Among the many functions of NAGWS, the most important are (1) formulating and publicizing guiding principles and standards for the administrator, leader, official, and player; (2) publishing and interpreting rules governing sports for girls and women; (3) providing the means for training, evaluating, and rating officials; (4) disseminating information on the conduct of girls' and women's sports; (5) stimulating, evaluating, and disseminating research in the field of girls' and women's sports; (6) cooperating with allied groups interested in girls' and women's sports, in order to formulate policies and rules that affect the conduct of women's sports; and (7) providing opportunities for the development of leadership among girls and women for the conduct of their sports programs.[46]

Realizing the increased interest in interschool programs for girls, the NAGWS approved a statement of policy for girls' competition for both the senior and junior high schools. On both levels they specify that the interschool program is one form of competition that may exist and that it should complement the intramural and instructional program.

In junior high school, it is desirable that intramural programs of competitive activities be closely integrated with the basic physical education program. Appropriate competition at this ´level should be composed of intramural and informal extramural events consistent with social needs and recreational interests. A well-organized and well-conducted sports program should take into account the various skill levels and thus meet the needs of the more highly skilled.

In senior high school, a program of intramural-extramural participation should be arranged to augment a sound and inclusive instructional program in physical education. It should be recognized that an interscholastic program will require professional leadership, time and funds in addition to those provided for the intramural programs. Facilities should be such that the intramural and instructional programs need not be eliminated or seriously curtailed if an interscholastic program is offered.

Specifically, the following standards should prevail:

1. The medical status of the player is ascertained by a physician and the health of the

players is carefully supervised.

2. Activities for girls and women are planned to meet their needs, and not for the personal glorification of coaches and/or sponsoring organizations.

3. The salary retention and promotion of an instructor are not dependent upon the outcome of the games.

4. Qualified women, teach, coach, and officiate wherever and whenever possible, and in all cases the professional background and experience of the leader meet established standards.

5. Rules approved by the DGWS are used.

6. Schedules do not exceed the ability and endurance relative to the maturity and physiological conditioning of the participants. Standards for specific sports are defined by the DGWS and appear in sports guides published by the American Association for Health, Physical Education and Recreation, 1201 16th St., N. W., Washington, D. C.

7. Sports activities for girls and women are scheduled independently from boys' and men's sports. Exceptions will occur when the activities and/or time and facilities are appropriate for both.

8. Girls and women may participate in appropriate corecreational activities or teams. Girls and women may not participate as members of boys' and men's teams.

9. The program, including health insurance for players, is financed by budgeted school or organization funds rather than entirely by admission charges.

10. Provision is made by the school or organization for safe transportation by bonded carriers, with chaperones who are responsible to the sponsoring group.

11. Where deemed necessary, standards for a specific sport may be defined by the respective sport committee of the DGWS.[47]

NAGWS further explores the interschool athletic program for girls by delineating the guidelines for both the junior and senior high school programs. On the junior high school level, the importance of exploration in a wide variety of team and individual sports is recommended. The National Association strongly recommends competition through a limited number of sports days at the end of the intramural season. The guidelines for such a program on the junior and senior high school levels are set down in *Philosophy and Standards for Girls' and Women's Sports*, published by the DGWS.[48, 49]

NAGWS has had a tremendous influence on sports and competition for both girls and women. The research on the subject which the organization has sponsored provides scientific guidelines for female competition. However, with the tremendous interest and demand for girls' athletics on the secondary level, many women leaders felt the need for a specific emphasis on direction for secondary girls' programs.

In August 1971 at Estes Park, Colorado, the first National Conference on Girls' Sports Programs for Secondary Schools was held. The primary purpose of the conference was to examine the present status and future direction of girls' sports in grades 7 through 12. In addition the delegates discussed such areas as the scope of sports, financing, ethics and values, high school athletic leagues, officiating, scheduling, public relations, and social change. The conference adopted eight resolutions, which are shown in Figure 13–12.

In April 1974 NAGWS released a position paper which provided the most recent beliefs of the Division of Girls' and Women's Sports. They are:

1. The Division for Girls' and Women's Sports believes girls and women should have athletic programs equal to but separate from those provided for boys and men. The several court cases which have sought to give girls the right to play on boys' teams should not be viewed as presenting a solution for the future of sports for girls and women. There are a few girls who can qualify with boys for positions on a team. If there is only one team, the majority of girls who wish to have the opportunity to compete will not be served at all. If girls are permitted to play on boys' teams, it is logical to postulate that in cases where girls have teams that are unavailable to boys, the boys could request to play on the girls' teams. This would mean, in many cases, that there would be more boys than girls on the girls' team, making a second varsity team dominated by male membership.

2. DGWS recognizes that separate sports programs for girls, while on the increase, can rarely be equated with boys' teams in terms of funding, staffing, and use of facilities. This is partly due to the long held societal prejudice that participation by girls in organized athletics is unladylike and, in fact, harmful to the physical and social development of the

RESOLUTIONS ADOPTED AT THE DGWS NATIONAL CONFERENCE
ON GIRLS SPORTS PROGRAMS FOR SECONDARY SCHOOLS
August 20-25, 1971, Estes Park, Colorado

RESOLUTION I

WHEREAS the participants of the DGWS National Conference on Girls Sports Programs for Secondary Schools have gathered to examine the current status and explore future directions for secondary school sports programs for girls throughout the United States, and have recognized the scope of existing programs and policies, therefore
BE IT RESOLVED that all participants attending this conference will return to their areas of responsibility and make every effort:

(1) To discover and publicize existing policies regulating instructional, intramural, extramural, and interscholastic girls sports programs.
(2) To enlist support of colleagues and other appropriate persons to plan, organize, and implement sports programs which will meet the needs of all students, based on educationally sound standards and philosophy.
(3) To seek ways of securing responsible leadership roles in agencies governing secondary school athletics.

RESOLUTION II

WHEREAS the participants of the DGWS National Conference on Girls Sports Programs for Secondary Schools that believe education is for all, and that the sports program contributes to the educational process, and
WHEREAS it is the responsibility of the local school board to provide an equitable sports program for all girls and boys, therefore
BE IT RESOLVED that the local school board be urged to:

(1) Provide sports programs that include instructional, intramural, extramural, and interscholastic experiences.
(2) Provide an equitable budget to finance all aspects of the sports programs.
(3) Ensure that the use of facilities is based on the needs of all students.
(4) Employ personnel who are educationally qualified and knowledgeable about students and their respective sports programs.
(5) Compensate all personnel on an equitable basis.

RESOLUTION III

WHEREAS the state high school athletic or activities association is the regulatory body for secondary school programs, therefore
BE IT RESOLVED that the DGWS Executive Council:

(1) Encourage professional preparation institutions to include within their curriculums instruction in the history,

role, and structure of high school athletic or activities associations.
(2) Define the role of DGWS in relation to state high school athletic or activities associations.
(3) Encourage the Officiating Services Area to cooperate with each state high school athletic or activities association in recruiting, training, and listing officials.

RESOLUTION IV

WHEREAS the needs of girls sports programs on the secondary school level are such that they deserve concentrated attention and service from the DGWS, therefore
BE IT RESOLVED that the DGWS Executive Council incorporate within its structure a permanent body to concern itself with the specific needs of girls secondary school sports programs.

RESOLUTION V

WHEREAS attention has been directed to the need for additional coaches and officials qualified to implement girls sports programs, therefore
BE IT RESOLVED that the DGWS Executive Council encourage teacher preparation institutions to include in their curriculums

(1) In-depth experience in the areas of officiating and coaching girls interscholastic sports programs.
(2) Instruction in the history, structure, and role of the DGWS in the development of sports programs for secondary school girls.

RESOLUTION VI

WHEREAS personnel currently assigned responsibility for the conduct of girls sports programs need opportunities to improve their skills in order to keep pace with the expansion of competitive sports programs for girls, therefore
BE IT RESOLVED that the DGWS, in conjunction with appropriate professional organizations, sponsor regional institutes on coaching in specified sports as determined by the needs of prospective participants.

RESOLUTION VII

WHEREAS the DGWS is to be commended for providing this opportunity to examine the current status and explore future directions of secondary school sports programs for girls, therefore
BE IT RESOLVED that the DGWS continue to provide for the concerns and interests of the leaders of secondary school girls sports programs in future conferences.

Figure 13–12. Resolutions of the DGWS. (From Barron, Alice A.: "Report of the First DGWS National Conference on Girls' Programs for Secondary Schools." Washington, D.C.: *JOHPER,* November-December, 1971, p. 16.)

female. Research does not support the claim that girls are physiologically or socially harmed by participation in sports, and the current approach of society toward the role of girls and women repudiates such outdated ideas and practices.

3. DGWS believes that sports programs in high schools and colleges should be an outgrowth of the physical education program and should provide a variety of opportunities for participation and appropriate competition for all students (both male and female). Funds, facilities, equipment, and staff should be made available for girls' and women's programs on the basis of parity with boys' and men's programs.

4. The Division further believes it is essential that women physical educators, coaches, and athletic directors be involved in the planning, development, and administration of girls' and women's sports programs and be included on boards and councils which develop policies for girls' athletics.

5. In addition, DGWS believes that those responsible for the administration of sports programs for girls and women should be concerned with training adequate numbers of women officials and with developing minimum certification standards for coaches of girls' and women's teams.

6. Finally, the Division feels that there must be a united effort if female students are

to be given the opportunity for high-level performance, achievement, and competition within the framework of girls' and women's varsity sports.[50]

The guidelines on sports and competition for women contained in the preceding paragraphs have been most useful for administrators who have developed programs for girls. However, with the advent of Title IX, the program of competitive sports for women is viewed in an entirely different perspective. Title IX states that:

a. *General.* No person shall, on the basis of sex, be excluded from participation in, be denied the benefits of, be treated differently from another person or otherwise be discriminated against in any interscholastic, intercollegiate, club or intramural athletics offered by recipient, and no recipient shall provide any such athletics separately on such basis.

b. *Separate teams.* Notwithstanding the requirements of paragraph (a) of this section, a recipient may operate or sponsor separate teams for members of each sex where selection for such teams is based upon competitive skill or the activity involved is a contact sport. However, where a recipient operates or sponsors a team in a particular sport for members of one sex but operates or sponsors no such team for members of the other sex, and athletic opportunities for members of that sex have previously been limited, members of the excluded sex must be allowed to try-out for the team offered unless the sport involved is a contact sport. For the purposes of this part, contact sports include boxing, wrestling, rugby, ice hockey, football, basketball, and other sports, the purpose or major activity of which involves bodily contact.

c. *Equal opportunity.* A recipient which operates or sponsors interscholastic, intercollegiate, club or intramural athletics shall provide equal athletic opportunity for members of both sexes. In determining whether equal opportunities are available the Director will consider, among other factors:

   i. Whether the selection of sports and levels of competition effectively accommodate the interests and abilities of members of both sexes;

   ii. The provision of equipment and supplies;

   iii. Scheduling of games and practice time;

   iv. Travel and per diem allowance;

   v. Opportunity to receive coaching and academic tutoring;

   vi. Assignment and compensation of coaches and tutors;

   vii. Provision of locker rooms, practice and competitive facilities;

   viii. Provision of medical and training facilities and services;

   ix. Provision of housing and dining facilities and services;

   x. Publicity.[51]

This trend in women's competition is an outgrowth of expressions by leading women professionals and the insistence of equal rights of women in interschool and intercollegiate athletic competition. This is as it should be. Girls and women should have the same opportunity to develop to the fullest their athletic potential. However, the view which is outlined in Title IX, if it remains in its present form, surely is not the answer. Merely to allow girls and women to participate on men's teams is to create the false assumption that equal rights have been provided. Few women ever attain the strength and speed of most men, and to compete with men for team membership would be disadvantageous for girls and women. Some girls may compete satisfactorily with boys during the early years, but this is not true after puberty. Irrespective of what some outstanding professional athletes, who are usually unknowledgeable in the fields of anatomy or physiology, may say, women *are* different from men, both anatomically and physiologically. This was pointed out in Chapter 6. Although the purpose of Title IX was to prohibit sex discrimination in education, the wording is such that interpretation is vague, and to implement the mandate as it stands could produce serious consequences.

The NAGWS has long felt that girls and women should have athletic programs equal to but entirely separate from those of men. The Division takes the view that if only one team exists and women are allowed to play on the team, the program does not meet their needs. This situation provides them the opportunity to compete with men, but does not assure them equal athletic participation.

The courts have reviewed several cases of discriminatory practices in athletics for girls and women, and when integration in previously all-male teams has been sought, the court has ruled in favor in some cases and against in others. However, in all cases where separate but equal teams for boys and girls were under consideration, the courts ruled that separate but equal teams should be provided, with legal provisions prohibiting play on a sex integrated basis. In the majority of cases in which the courts ruled to allow girls access to previously all-male teams, the courts suggested the need for separate but equal teams.[52]

Providing Medical Services

The school has a definite responsibility for providing medical services for all athletes. These services are essential for the safety and welfare of the players and to insure effective performance on the field. They should include (1) physical examinations, (2) medical consultation, and (3) medical supervision during the game.

Physical Examination. Most states require annual physical examinations of athletes before participation in a game. Sometimes these examinations are given a day or so prior to the first game, in order to comply with the requirement. Such hurriedly arranged plans are unsatisfactory, because they are likely to be given in a cursory manner with little thought given to the health of the players.

As stated earlier, examinations should be given *prior to the first practice in each sport.* Many aspirants report to practice without an examination. This is unwise, since practice sessions can be more demanding than the actual game situation. It is also important to examine candidates before practice in each sport, since many complications may develop during the time lapse between seasons.

The cost of physical examinations may be defrayed by the school, or the player may be required to assume this responsibility. Usually the family physician performs this service. In some cases involving indigent students, the public health department provides the examination. Whichever plan is followed, the objective should be to require the candidate to obtain the best medical examination available. Figure 13–13 shows a typical form which may be used for the examination.

Medical Consultation. The examination of players is only one of the medical services the school is obligated to provide in the conduct of interschool athletics. In addition to the physical examination, continuous consultation with physicians is extremely important. These consultations should include all of the factors essential for improving and maintaining the optimum health of the player. The major factors are conditioning, diet, proper protective equipment, consultation relative to the player's health history, and follow-up resulting from the physical examination.

Medical Supervision During the Game. Team physicians should be present at all games in such sports as football, hockey, basketball, and wrestling. Physicians should be present during scrimmage and on call at all times. Players who have emotional problems should be under the supervision of the team physician. After an injury the team physician should work closely with the coaching staff. His recommendation as to when, or if, an injured player should resume competition should be final.

SUPERVISION OF THE INTERSCHOOL ATHLETIC PROGRAM

A written policy should be established by the school superintendent and approved by the board defining responsibility for the supervision of interschool athletics. This supervision should be administered on the city-wide level from the superintendent's office and also on the school level. Usually the principal is responsible for supervising the program on the school level. However, the principal rarely has the time to observe the day-by-day operation of the program. Because of this, the coach and director of athletics must be assigned the responsibility for assuring parents and the administration that the safety and welfare of the players are basic objectives of the program. In addition to the safety of athletes, the false values and abuses that occur in the program should be under constant observation.

Probably the reason that current literature reports such startling criticisms of the interschool program is that the program is not properly and adequately supervised. The August 1972 issue of the *American School Board Journal* included articles entitled "Are Competitive Sports Wasting Money and Ruining Kids?," "Don't Let the Sports Tail Wag the Dog," and "Are High School Sports Teaching Brutality?" The existing conditions that these titles imply are not helping the interschool program, particularly in these days of austere budgets and accountability. One article stated that "Incidents of spectator violence and brutal player-coach behavior have grown to such proportions in some places that school boards have barred all non-student spectators from sports events." Such conditions do not help those schools who do conduct sound programs of interschool competition.[53]

The first person in the hierarchy of responsible supervision of the athletic program is the coach. He is the only one who is in daily contact with the player and the various segments of the program. His basic supervisory responsibilities are (1) supervision of player behavior, (2) supervision of player health, (3) supervision of the athletic playing conditions, and (4) supervision of playing areas.

The coach is responsible for developing player attitude and instilling sportsmanship in the daily routine on the practice field, in the locker room, and in the school. By setting positive examples of sportsmanship and emotional inhibition, the coach can go a long way toward improving the behavior of his players.

The health of each athlete is of great concern to the coach. Not only is good health essential for effective performance but the coach is responsible to the parent and to the player himself for health guidance. Included in these responsibilities are diet; conditioning; intensity of practice; length of practice sessions; protective equipment; first aid; prevention of foot cramps, heat exhaustion, and heat stroke; and proper classification of players to prevent overmatching. Unfortunately, too many coaches are not qualified to supervise these areas, and adverse conditions are the result.

Providing a healthful environment is essentially a responsibility of the coach. He should refuse to permit practice when adequate sanitary conditions do not exist. Sufficient towels, soap, clean uniforms, clean equipment, clean showers and toilets are among the items the coach supervises in the daily performance of his job. The coach is also responsible for providing health education regarding how infection may be spread by using other players' combs, towels, drinking cups, socks, supports, and clothing.

All playing areas should be examined each day to insure safe playing conditions. The field, jumping pits, tracks, and other areas should be free of glass or other objects that may injure the player. Locker rooms should have mats to prevent slipping and lockers should be arranged to prevent accidents. Supervision of the locker and shower room are essential to prevent accidents, which often result from deviant behavior in these areas.

An evaluative instrument that may be used in the supervision of coaches is shown in Figure 13–8. In addition to adequate professional preparation, a good coach usually exhibits the following characteristics:

1. A vigorous, forceful, and inspiring personality.
2. Concern for personal appearance and good taste in personal grooming.
3. The kind of observation and analysis of sports which enables one to size up the important points quickly in a sports situation and propose remedial action.
4. Emotional stability and self-control, with power to concentrate when highly emotional conditions prevail.
5. The substantial character which makes

VIRGINIA HIGH SCHOOL LEAGUE

FORM 2

P. O. Box 3697, Charlottesville, Virginia 22903

Athletic Participation / Parental Consent / Physician's Certificate Form

(Separate form required for each school year. File in the Office of the Principal.)

PART I—ATHLETIC PARTICIPATION

(To be filled in and signed by the student)

Name: ....School Year: ....
     (Last)   (First)   (Middle Initial)

Home address: ....Home address of parents: ....

City: ....City: ....

Date of birth: ....Place of birth: ....

This is my .... semester in .... High School, and my .... semester since entering the ninth grade of high school or prep school, or since first enrolling in a school year after passing four eighth-grade subjects (whichever occurred first). Last semester I attended .... School and passed .... subjects, and I taking .... credit subjects this semester. I have read the condensed individual eligibility rules of the Virginia High School League that appear below and believe I am eligible to represent my present high school in athletics. If accepted as a team member, I agree to make every effort to keep up my school work and to abide by the rules and regulations of the school authorities and of the Virginia High School League.

Date: ....Signed: ....
                                                     (Student)

INDIVIDUAL ELIGIBILITY RULES

Attention, Athlete! To be eligible to represent your school in any interscholastic athletic contest you—

——must be a regular bona fide student in good standing of the school you represent.

——must have been promoted to the ninth grade or must have passed four eighth-grade subjects in a school year preceding the present one (eighth-grade students who do not qualify for varsity participation under the foregoing provision are eligible for junior-varsity competition).

——must have enrolled not later than the tenth day of the current semester.

——must have passed at least four credit subjects the previous semester and must be currently taking no less than four credit subjects.

——must not have reached your nineteenth birthday on or before the first of March which precedes the current school year (and after July 1, 1975, you must not have reached your nineteenth birthday on or before the first of October of the current school year).

——must have been in residence at your present high school, or at a junior high school from which your high school receives its students, during the last full semester

    ——unless you are transferring from a public or private school with a corresponding move on the part of your parents into the area served by your present school.

    ——unless you are entering the ninth grade for the first time or you are enrolling in the current school year after passing four eighth-grade subjects in a previous school year.

    ——unless your former school was discontinued or consolidated and you were required to transfer to your present school.

    ——unless you are legally adopted, are a foreign exchange student, are under the guidance of an orphanage or the State Department of Welfare and Institutions, or are required to change residence by court order.

——must not, after entering the ninth grade for the first time or after first enrolling in a school year after passing four eighth-grade subjects, have been enrolled in or been eligible for enrollment in high school more than eight consecutive semesters, nor have represented a high school or prep school in a varsity sport more than four years.

——must be an amateur as defined by the Virginia High School League:"An amateur athlete is one who engages in athletics for the educational, physical, mental and social benefits he derives therefrom, and to whom athletics are nothing more more than an avocation."

——must have submitted to your principal before becoming a member of any school athletic team an Athletic Participation/Parental Consent/Physician's Certificate Form, completely filled in and properly signed, attesting that you have been examined and found to be physically fit for athletic competition and that your parents consent to your participation.

——must not have transferred from one school to another for athletic purposes as a result of undue influence or persuasion by any person or group of people.

——must not have received in recognition of your ability as a high school athlete any award not presented or approved by your school or the League.

——must not, while a member of a school's team in any sport, become a member of any other organized team or participate in an unsanctioned meet or tournament in the same sport during the school sport season.

——must not have participated in any all-star contest between teams whose players are selected from more than one high school.

Eligibility to participate in interscholastic athletics is a privilege you earn by meeting not only the above-listed minimum standards, but also all other standards set by your League, district, and school. If you have any question regarding your eligibility or are in doubt about the effect an activity might have on your eligibility, check with your principal or athletic director; they are aware of the various interpretations and exceptions provided under League rules. Meeting the intent and spirit of League standards will prevent your team, school, and community from being penalized.

PART II—PARENTAL CONSENT

(To be filled in and signed by the parent or guardian)
(See Part I)

In accordance with the rules of the Virginia High School League, I give my consent and approval to the participation of the student named above for the sports NOT MARKED OUT BELOW:

BASEBALL	FOOTBALL	SOFTBALL	TRACK
BASKETBALL	GOLF	SPEEDBALL	VOLLEYBALL
CROSS COUNTRY	GYMNASTICS	SWIMMING	WRESTLING
FIELD HOCKEY	SOCCER	TENNIS	OTHERS——

I understand that participation may include, when necessary, early dismissal from classes and travel to participate in interscholastic athletic contests. I will not hold the school authorities responsible in case of accident or injury as a result of this participation. *Please check appropriate space:* He/She has student accident insurance available through the school ( ); has football insurance coverage available through the school ( ); is insured to our satisfaction ( ).

I also give my consent and approval for the above named student to receive a physical examination, as required in Part IV, Physician's Certificate, of this form, by ....M.D., or by a qualified, registered physician as recommended by the named student's school administration.

Date: ....Signed: ....
                                     (over)   (Parent or Guardian)

A

Figure 13–13. *A,* Parental consent form for athletic participation. *B,* Physician's medical examination form. (From Virginia High School League, Charlottesville, Virginia.)

PART III—STUDENT'S MEDICAL HISTORY
(To be completed by parents or family physician)

Name of student .... Age ....

Address .... Tel. No. ....

1. Has had injuries requiring medical attention	Yes	No
2. Has had illness lasting more than a week	Yes	No
3. Is under a physician's care now	Yes	No
4. Takes medication now	Yes	No
5. Wears glasses	Yes	No
contact lenses	Yes	No
6. Has had a surgical operation	Yes	No
7. Has been in hospital (except for tonsillectomy)	Yes	No
8. Do you know of any reason why this individual should not participate in all sports?	Yes	No

Please explain any "Yes" answers to above questions:

....

....

9. Has had complete poliomyelitis immunization by oral vaccine (Sabin) or inoculations (Salk)   Yes   No

10. Has had primary series of tetanus toxoid (DPT or DT) and a booster within the last 10 years   Yes   No

Date: .... Signed: ....

(Parent or Physician)

PART IV—PHYSICIAN'S CERTIFICATE
(To be filled in and signed by the examining physician)
(Separate examination and certificate required for each school year, July 1 through the ensuing June 30)

(Cooperatively prepared by the National Federation of State High School Associations and the Committee on Medical Aspects of Sports of the American Medical Association.)

(Please Print)   Name of Student   City and School

Grade .... Age .... Height .... Weight .... Blood Pressure ....

Significant Past Illness or Injury ....

Eyes .... R 20/ ; L 20/ ; Ears .... Hearing R /15; L /15

Respiratory ....

Cardiovascular ....

Liver .... Spleen .... Hernia ....

Musculoskeletal .... Skin ....

Neurological .... Genitalia ....

Laboratory: Urinalysis .... Other: ....

Comments ....

Completed Immunizations: Polio .... Tetanus ....

                                Date   Date

Other ....

I certify that I have on this date examined this student and find him/her physically able to compete in the supervised activities NOT CROSSED OUT BELOW.

BASEBALL	FOOTBALL	SOFTBALL	TRACK
BASKETBALL	GOLF	SPEEDBALL	VOLLEYBALL
CROSS COUNTRY	GYMNASTICS	SWIMMING	*WRESTLING
FIELD HOCKEY	SOCCER	TENNIS	OTHERS——

*Weight loss permitted to make lower weight class: Yes .... No .... If "Yes," may lose .... pounds.

Date of Examination: .... Signed: ...., M.D.

                                             (Examining Physician)

Physician's Address .... Telephone ....

GSS—23—R—5741689

B

Figure 13–13. *Continued*

one a worthy associate and personal example for his players, both on and off the playing field.

6. Love of sport and of players with enthusiasm for sport.

7. Ability to plan and organize for steady progress toward efficient sports achievement.[54]

The director of athletics is responsible for supervising the entire program. This responsibility includes evaluation of the coaches, handling school-community relations, providing interpretation of the program, and overseeing the general administration of the program. At this level of supervision, so many problems can occur that, unless they are resolved properly, adverse conditions are sure to arise. The importance of selecting a capable, knowledgeable, and efficient director of athletics cannot be overestimated. Supervision and evaluation operate hand in hand, and this necessitates accurate instruments of evaluation. Figure 13–7 shows such an instrument and includes the various components of effective athletic directorship.

Since the principal is the head of the entire school program of instruction and extracurricular activities, he is responsible for supervision of the interschool athletic program. Where you find a competent principal you will find a well-administered program, properly supervised and effectively organized. The principal should use the *Standards in Athletics for Boys in the Secondary Schools*[4] as a guide for evaluating the school program.

The following checklist, developed by the Committee on the Medical Aspects of Sports of the American Medical Association and the National Federation of State High School Associations, supports the view that intensive supervision is essential in athletics:

Proper conditioning helps to prevent injuries by hardening the body and increasing resistance to fatigue.

1. Are prospective players given directions and activities for pre-season conditioning?

2. Is there a minimum of three weeks' practice before the first game or contest?

3. Is each player required to warm up thoroughly prior to participation?

4. Are substitutions made without hesitation when players evidence disability?

Careful coaching leads to skilled performance, which lowers the incidence of injuries.

1. Is emphasis given to safety in teaching techniques and elements of play?

2. Are injuries carefully analyzed to determine causes and to suggest preventive programs?

3. Are tactics discouraged that may increase the hazards and thus the incidence of injuries?

4. Are practice periods carefully planned and of reasonable duration?

Good officiating promotes enjoyment of the game as well as protection of players.

1. Are players as well as coaches thoroughly schooled in the rules of the game?

2. Are rules and regulations strictly enforced in practice periods as well as in games?

3. Are officials employed who are qualified both emotionally and technically for their responsibility?

Right equipment and facilities serve a unique purpose in protection of players.

1. Is the best protective equipment provided for contact sports?

2. Is careful attention given to proper fitting and adjustment of equipment?

3. Is equipment properly maintained, and worn and outmoded items discarded?

4. Are proper areas for play provided and carefully maintained?

Adequate medical care is a necessity in the prevention and control of athletic injuries.

1. Is there a thorough pre-season health history and medical examination?

2. Is a physician present at contests and readily available during practice sessions?

3. Does the physician make the decision as to whether an athlete should return to play following injury during games?

4. Is authority from a physician required before an athlete can return to practice after being out of play because of disabling injury?

5. Is the care given athletes by coach or trainer limited to first aid and medically prescribed services?[55]

REFERENCES

1. "An Inner City Superintendent Supports Physical Education." *Physical Education Newsletter*, June, 1971.
2. *Athletics in Education*. Washington, D.C.: AAHPER, 1963.
3. *Ibid.*
4. Joint Committee Report: "Standards in Athletics for Boys in Secondary Schools." *JOHPER*, September, 1951, p. 17.
5. John M. Cooper and Clinton Strong: *The Physical Education Curriculum*, 8th ed. Columbia, Mo.: Lucas Brothers, Publishers, 1973, p. 87.
6. "Establishing an Athletic Advisory Committee Helps to Improve Physical Education and Athletics." *Physical Education Newsletter,* March 1, 1970.
7. "The School Athletic Director's Role as a Professional Administrator." *Physical Education Newsletter,* February 15, 1973.
8. Educational Policies Commission: *School Athletics*. Washington, D.C.: NEA, 1954, p. 61.
9. Charles E. Forsythe and Irvin A. Keller: *Administration of High School Athletics*, 5th ed. Englewood Cliffs, N.J.: Prentice-Hall, Inc., 1972, p. 174.
10. *How to Budget, Select and Order Athletic Equipment*. Chicago: Athletic Goods Manufacturers Association, 1962, p. 10.
11. Charles T. Avedisian (ed.): *Guidebook for Athletics*. New Britain, Conn.: New Britain Public Schools, pp. 46–50.
12. John R. Midgett: "What a Student Expects of His Coach." In *Secondary School Athletic Administration: A New Look*. Washington, D.C.: AAHPER, 1969, p. 111.
13. Walter C. Schwank and Sayers J. Miller: "New Dimensions for the Athletic Training Profession." *JOHPER*, September, 1971, p. 41.
14. *Ibid.*, p. 43.
15. *Virginia High School League Handbook*. Charlottesville, Va.: Virginia High School League, 1969, p. 16.
16. *National Federation of State High School Associations: Official Handbook*. Elgin, Ill.: The Association, 1973, p. 8.
17. *Ibid.*, p. 18.
18. "Cardinal Athletic Principles. " In *National Federation of State High School Associations: Official Handbook*. Elgin, Ill.: The Association, 1973, p. 22.
19. Forsythe and Keller, *op. cit.*, p. 17.
20. "National Council of Secondary School Athletic Directors." *JOHPER*, April, 1969, p. 48.
21. Educational Policies Commission, *op. cit.*, pp. 6–10.
22. "Sports Recruiting: A College Crisis." *Readers Digest*, July, 1974, p. 107.
23. *National Federation of State High School Associates: Official Handbook*, *op. cit.*, p. 46.
24. Dudley Degroot: "Code of Ethics of the American Football Coaches Association." *JOHPER*, February, 1953, p. 51.
25. Educational Policies Commission, *op. cit.*, p. 66.
26. Arthur A. Esslinger: "A Proposed Plan for Certification of High School Coaches." In *Certification of High School Coaches*. Washington, D.C.: AAHPER, October, 1968, p. 42.
27. James Thurston: "A Formula for Extra Duty." *JOHPER*, April, 1968, p. 31.
28. Extra Pay for Extra Service. Watertown High School, Watertown, New York. From materials sent on request.
29. Robert M. Pate: "Crowd Control." *JOHPER*, April, 1969, p. 30.
30. Hilton Murphy: "Crowd Control." *JOHPER*, April 1969, p. 28.
31. George J. Kozak: "Crowd Control." *JOHPER*, April, 1969, p. 29.
32. Louis C. Jorndt: "A Reference Paper on Big City Approach to Crowd Control for Interscholastic Competition." In *Approaches to Problems of Public School Administration in Health, Physical Education, and Recreation*. Washington, D.C.: AAHPER, 1969, p. 101.
33. Howard C. Leibee: "The Law and the Spectator." In *Crowd Control for High School Athletics*. Washington, D.C.: AAHPER, 1970, pp. 35–36.
34. St. Louis Public High School League: *Boys' Handbook for Physical Education and Athletics*, 1969–70, pp. 27–28. From Forsythe and Keller, *op. cit.*, p. 222.
35. Educational Policies Commission, *op. cit.*, p. 36.
36. *Health in Schools*. Twentieth Yearbook of the American Association of School Administrators. Washington, D.C.: National Education Association, 1951, p. 197.
37. Wilton Krogman: "Factors of Physical Growth of Children as They May Apply to Physical Education." In *Proceedings: 1954 National Convention of the AAHPER*, p. 63. (From Edward F. Voltmer and Arthur A. Esslinger: *The Organization and Administration of Physical Education*. New York: Appleton-Century-Crofts, 1967, p. 315.
38. Donald Dukelow: "A Doctor Looks at Exercise and Fitness." *JOHPER*, September, 1957, p. 26.
39. John Reichert: "A Pediatrician's View of Competitive Sports Before the Teens." *Today's Health*, October, 1957, p. 29.

40. Louis Alley: "Interscholastic Athletics for Junior High School Boys." In *Current Administrative Problems*. Washington, D.C.: AAHPER, 1960, pp. 97–98.
41. *Standards for Junior High School Athletics*. Washington, D.C.: AAHPER, 1963, p.14.
42. *Ibid.*, p. 14.
43. *Ibid.*, p. 16.
44. Joint Committee Report: *Desirable Athletic Competition for Children*. Washington, D.C.: AAHPER, 1953, p. 3.
45. Division for Girls' and Women's Sports: *Philosophy and Standards for Girls' and Women's Sports*. Washington, D.C.: AAHPER, 1973, pp. 5–6.
46. *Ibid.*, p. 6.
47. Division for Girls' and Women's Sports: *Philosophy and Standards for Girls' and Women's Sports*. Washington, D.C.: AAHPER, 1973, p. 34.
48. *Ibid.*, p. 39.
49. *Ibid.*, p. 43.
50. "Sports Programs for Girls and Women," a position paper of the DGWS. Washington, D.C.: *JOHPER*, April, 1974, p. 12.
51. Federal Register (Part II), Department of Health, Education and Welfare, Washington, D.C., June 4, 1975, p. 24142.
52. Dorothy McNight and Joan Hult: "Girls' and Women's Sports," *JOHPER* (June, 1974), p. 46.
53. Jack Razor: "Control the Fans; They can Brutalize Your High School Sports Program," *The American School Board Journal* (August, 1972), p. 24.
54. *Coaches' Handbook*. Washington, D.C.: AAHPER, 1960, p. 3.
55. Charles C. Wilson (ed.): *School Health Services*. Chicago: AMA, 1964, p. 276.

SUGGESTED READINGS

Forsythe, Charles E., and Irvina Keller: *Administration of High School Athletics*, 5th ed. Englewood Cliffs, N.J.: Prentice-Hall, Inc., 1972.
George, J. F., and Lehman, H. A.: *School Athletic Administration*. New York: Harper & Row, 1966.
Grieve, A. W.: *Directing High School Athletics*. Englewood Cliffs, N.J.: Prentice-Hall, Inc., 1963.
Hixson, C. G.: *The Administration of Interscholastic Athletics*. New York: J. Lowell Pratt & Co., 1967.

CHAPTER FOURTEEN

Physical Education for the Exceptional Child

Education is the inalienable right of every individual, irrespective of his or her anatomical, psychological, or physiological structure. Physical education has been defined as education through the physical. This definition emphasizes the wholeness of the individual as opposed to the older philosophy that the body consists of two separate entities, mental and physical. It also means the inclusion of all individuals in the instructional program; the fact that some students deviate from an established pattern defined as "normal" should not exclude these students from the program.

The special education program differs from the regular program in modification only. It is a program designed to meet the individual differences of students. No two students are the same anatomically, physiologically, or psychologically; the students who comprise any class vary structurally and functionally. It is the individual who deviates to a marked degree who needs special attention.

407

Providing equal educational opportunity for handicapped children became law in 1970 under the Education of the Handicapped Act. The signing of this law ushered in a new era for education. Before this act became law, many handicapped children received inadequate attention.

ADMINISTRATIVE PRINCIPLES IN ADAPTED PHYSICAL EDUCATION

Administrators, teachers, and specialists who plan to develop programs for exceptional children should be aware of the many factors involved in planning programs for them. Because of their deviation from average children, exceptional children require teachers with special training, skills, and abilities.

For many years, physicians and physical education leaders were concerned with providing programs for the exceptional child. As an outgrowth of their concern, a committee on adapted physical education was formed by the AAHPER. This committee developed a set of principles for adapted physical education which were approved by the joint committee of the American Medical Association and the National Education Association. This statement of principles was prepared for schools and colleges rather than for special schools for the handicapped. The *definition* of adapted physical education appears in principle number one. The principles are as follows:

1. *There is need for common understanding regarding the nature of adapted physical education.* Adapted physical education is a diversified program of developmental activities, games, sports, and rhythms suited to the interests, capacities, and limitations of students with disabilities who may not safely or successfully engage in unrestricted participation in the vigorous activities of the general physical education program.

2. *There is need for adapted physical education in schools and colleges.* According to the best estimates, there are in the United States about 4 million children of school age with physical handicaps. Only 11 per cent of this group requiring special educational services are receiving such services through special schools and classes. The vast majority of exceptional children are attending regular schools.

The major disabling conditions, each affecting thousands of children, are cerebral palsy, poliomyelitis, epilepsy, tuberculosis, traumatic injuries, neurological problems, and heart disease. Further evidence indicates that on the college level there is a significant percentage of students requiring special consideration for either temporary or permanent disabilities.

3. *Adapted physical education has much to offer the individual who faces the combined problem of seeking an education and living most effectively with a handicap.* Through adapted physical education the individual can (a) be observed and referred when the need for medical or other services is suspected; (b) be guided in avoidance of situations which would aggravate the condition or subject him to unnecessary risks or injury; (c) improve neuromuscular skills, general strength, and endurance following convalescence from acute illness or injury; (d) be provided with opportunities for improved psychological adjustment and social development.

4. *The direct and related services essential for the proper conduct of adapted physical education should be available to our schools.* These services should include (a) adequate and periodic health examinations; (b) classification for physical education based on the health examination and other pertinent tests and observations; (c) guidance of individuals needing special considerations with respect to physical activity, general health practices, recreational pursuits, vocational planning, psychological adjustment, and social development; (d) arrangement of appropriate adapted physical education programs; (e) evaluation and recording of progress through observations, appropriate measurements, and consultations; (f) integrated relationships with other school personnel, medical and auxiliary services, and with the family to assure continuous guidance and supervisory services; (g) cumulative records for each individual, which should be transferred from school to school.

5. *It is essential that adequate medical guidance be available for teachers of adapted physical education.* The possibility of serious pathology requires that programs of adapted physical education should not be attempted without the diagnosis, written recommendation, and supervision of a physician. The planned program of activities must be predicated upon medical findings and ac-

complished by competent teachers working with medical supervision and guidance. There should be an effective referral service involving physicians, physical educators, and parents, aimed at proper safeguards and maximum student benefits. School administrators alert to the special needs of handicapped children should make every effort to provide adequate staff and facilities necessary for a program of adapted physical education.

6. *Teachers of adapted education have a great responsibility as well as an unusual opportunity.* Physical educators engaged in teaching adapted physical education should (a) have adequate professional education to implement the recommendations provided by medical personnel; (b) be motivated by the highest ideals with respect to the importance of total student development and satisfactory human relationships; (c) develop the ability to establish rapport with students who may exhibit social maladjustment as a result of disability; (d) be aware of a student's attitude toward his disability; (e) be objective in relationships with students; (f) be prepared to give the time and effort necessary to help a student overcome a difficulty; (g) consider as strictly confidential information related to personal problems of the student; (h) stress similarities rather than deviations, and abilities instead of disabilities.

7. *Adapted physical education is necessary at all school levels.* The student with a disability faces the dual problem of overcoming a handicap and acquiring an education which will enable him to take his place in society as a respected citizen. Failure to assist a student with his problems may retard the growth and development process.

Offering adapted physical education in the elementary grades and continuing through the secondary school and college will assist the individual to improve function and make adequate psychological and social adjustments. It will be a factor in his attaining maximum growth and development within the limits of the disability. It will minimize attitudes of defeat and fears of insecurity. It will help him face the future with confidence.[1]

ADMINISTRATIVE PROCEDURES

Usually administrators follow certain prescribed steps in developing programs for exceptional children. Each step should be carefully planned and implemented. The ultimate success of adapted programs is based on the initial groundwork. These steps include (1) appointing advisory committees, (2) establishing objectives, (3) surveying the school or community to determine the number of exceptional children, and (4) scheduling students for participation.

Advisory Committees

Advisory committees are most helpful in planning the adapted program in physical education. Not only may they serve as a liaison between the schools and the community, but they also provide expert professional help in developing the program. Two types of committees are prevalent: the system type and the school-community type. The system-wide type usually consists of a physician, administrators, a nurse, a counselor, the supervisor of adaptive physical education, representatives from the parent-teacher organization, a classroom teacher, a physical education teacher, and others who have strong dedication to promoting programs for the exceptional child. The individual school program should involve the same personnel suggested in the formation of the system-wide committee, with the inclusion of a counselor and a student. The school committee has the basic responsibility for implementing the program at the school level, and serves in an advisory capacity to the principal, teachers, and others who are responsible for the program.

Establishing Objectives

In addition to the guiding principles outlined in earlier paragraphs, definite objectives should be developed to provide direction for the program and to be used as evaluative criteria. The following objectives may serve such a purpose and assist the student in gaining maximum benefits from the program:

1. To help students correct conditions that can be improved.
2. To help students protect themselves and

any physical conditions that would be aggravated through certain physical activities.

3. To provide students with an opportunity to learn and to participate in a number of appropriate recreational leisure-time sports and activities.

4. To improve physical fitness through the maximal development of organic and neuro-muscular systems.

5. To help each student to develop a knowledge and an appreciation of his physical and mental limitations.

6. To help students make social adjustments and to develop a feeling of self-worth and value.

7. To aid each student to develop knowledge and appreciation relative to good body mechanics.

8. To help students understand and appreciate a variety of sports that they can enjoy as a nonparticipant or a spectator.[2]

Survey of the School or System

Surveys are essential in the preliminary stages of planning. Inventories should be made in each school to determine the number of exceptional children registered. This may be accomplished through searching the health evaluation records. Figure 14–1 shows a form that may be used for this purpose. Observations in the physical education classes, the interests and needs of children, and the results of psychomotor skills tests may also be used for locating exceptional children.

The survey should also include the number and qualifications of teachers, types of facilities available, type of equipment that may be used, attitudes of principals and other administrators, and means of transportation for those attending special centers.

Scheduling Exceptional Children

Scheduling exceptional children properly is a difficult task for administrators. Lack of sufficient information, inadequate facilities, a poorly planned curriculum, and unqualified teachers are some of the obstacles that prevent effective scheduling of these children.

Too frequently, exceptional students are excused from all activity and allowed to spend the time in a study hall or a similar place. Exceptional children need the experiences offered in a well-planned program of physical education, and to excuse them without a strong reason is a serious mistake. There is medical opinion to support this premise, as shown in the following statement by the American Medical Association:

Waiving a student's privilege of participation in physical education is a serious decision for a physician, one that can profoundly influence the student's physical growth and emotional development. Physical education's important role in building healthy personalities as well as healthy bodies needs to be more widely understood. Unnecessary restrictions of physical activity can hamper personal development and interfere with group acceptance of a student.[3]

Strong interaction between the administrator and the physician is essential for effective placement of exceptional children in physical education. The communication between the physician and the school assists the physician in appraising the total offerings and making decisions regarding the assignment of the student in physical education. Where a varied program of activities exists, permanent excuses in physical education are unnecessary, and knowledge of the program assists the physician in prescribing the right activity. The medical profession again comments on physical education and the exceptional child:

Offering a variety of activities attracts and involves all students, including the temporarily or permanently handicapped. These students may be in greater need of activity programs than other students. Too often, handicapped students are excused and relegated to the roles of nonparticipants, spectators, or scorekeepers.

Exercise not only enhances rehabilitation of atrophied or unused muscles, but provides opportunity for maintaining optimum organic fitness, acquiring functional skills, and developing greater self-confidence. Limited or modified activities beneficial to the handicapped are almost always available. These

DENVER PUBLIC SCHOOLS
Health Service Department

HEALTH EVALUATION OF PUPILS FOR PLACEMENT IN SPECIAL EDUCATION PROGRAMS

Name of child_____ Date_____
Birthday of child_____ School attended (if any)_____
Address_____ Phone_____
Parent, guardian, or other informant_____
Reason for examination:_____

		Date Last Seen
Name of clinics, hospitals, or doctors serving child	Clinic_____	_____
	Private M.D._____	_____
	Specialist_____	_____

PAST AND FAMILY HISTORY: (Parent present ☐ or if not, nurse obtains data from home)
Birth: (type, weight, trauma, etc.)_____ Convulsions_____
Mother's health during this pregnancy_____
Health, age, sex of siblings_____
Child stat up_____ Talked_____ Walked_____ Child's difficulty first noted_____
Diseases_____ Accidents_____
Operations: T&A_____ Others_____

PHYSICAL EXAMINATION: Height_____ Weight_____
Vision test (current) Rt._____ Lt._____ Comments_____
Hearing test (current) Rt._____ Lt._____ Comments_____
Check below (o) if essentially negative or (x) if abnormal and describe on back of sheet.

Mouth_____ Glands_____ Heart_____ Genitalia_____ Skin_____ Coordination_____
Teeth_____ Eyes_____ Abdomen_____ Hernia_____ Gait_____ Skel. deform._____
Tonsils_____ Ears_____ Extremities_____ Nutrition_____ Allergies_____ Toilet habits_____

IMPRESSION OF CHILD AND MEDICAL RECOMMENDATIONS FOR EDUCATIONAL PROGRAM:
1. General physical condition is_____
2. Health practices seem to be_____
3. Family attitudes apparently are_____
_____
_____

4. Specific health problems include: Vision ☐ Hearing ☐ Motor Incoordination ☐ Hyperactivity ☐
Convulsive Disorder ☐ (on medication ☐ no medication ☐) Frequency of Episodes_____
Date of last episode, etc._____
Other:_____
_____
_____

5. Recommendations:
Further attention to_____
Placement in limited P.E. ☐ Regular P.E. ☐ Swimming ☐
Other:_____

_____   _____
Date of Evaluation   Signature of Physician

FORM 808 DSP 8-64-5M B-621-54560

Figure 14–1. Health evaluation of students for placement in special education programs. (Courtesy of Health Service Department, Denver Public Schools, Denver, Colorado, 1964, p. 71.)

are most likely to be of benefit when assigned by the physical educator and family physician working together.[4]

When varied programs exist, it is advisable to schedule exceptional children with the regular physical education class. This is effective, since these students change classes with their peer groups, and separate schedules are unnecessary. Modifications and provision for special programs may be made within the regular class schedule. It was pointed out earlier that for the majority of exceptional children, the regular instructional program may be adapted to meet their needs. In addition to a varied curriculum, careful attention should be given to ability grouping and the modification of activities.

The physician, in making his decision for assigning the exceptional child to physical education, is usually guided by a classification of activities which will permit student participation to a maximum potential. It is this type of placement that allows the student to attain the greatest values from the program. The generally accepted groupings are based on functional testing, physical skills, interests, attitudes and concerns, and previous physical education experience. The most important criterion used in grouping students is the medical examination. The following categories were derived from the results of such examinations:

1. *Unrestricted activity.* Full participation in physical education and athletic activities.
2. *Moderate restriction.* Participation in designated physical education and athletic activities.
3. *Severe restriction.* Participation in only a limited number of events at a low level of activity.
4. *Reconstructive or rehabilitative activity.* Participation in a prescribed program of corrective exercises or adapted sports.

The objectives of these classifications are to (1) safeguard the health of participants, (2) group students for effective learning, (3) equalize competitive conditions, and (4) facilitate progress and achievement.[5]

Categories 2, 3, and 4 cover activities for youths who are convalescing from illness and need a gradual return to activity; students in whom certain muscle groups need strengthening; the handicapped, who will benefit from physical activity; and those with postural deviations or other conditions medically determined as subject to improvement through prescribed activities. A program of reconstructive physical education is possible only when medical supervision and the services of a corrective or physical therapist are available.[6]

An instrument that has been successfully used to facilitate communication between the school and the physician is the physician's report. Prepared forms should be available which include, among other items, the classification of activities. Such a form is shown in Figure 14–2.

DETERMINING THE CATEGORIES FOR ADAPTIVE PROGRAMS

All exceptional children may be grouped into one of three categories: (1) the mentally exceptional, (2) the physically handicapped, and (3) the emotionally disturbed. Children in any of these groups need a particular type of activity and specialized guidance, depending on the degree of disability.

Mental Deviates

Deviation from mental normality may be in two directions—retardation or giftedness. These are the opposite ends of the continuum on which the normalcy of the masses is plotted.

The Gifted Child. The gifted child is blessed with a superior physical endowment; a high level of neuromuscular coordination enables him to move with grace and to develop skills rapidly, and he is usually highly motivated. The interschool athletic program and the intramural laboratory usually provide the necessary media for students who are gifted.

The Mentally Retarded. Children in this category have limited development

STATE OF CALIFORNIA

REFERRAL FORM

PHYSICIAN'S RECOMMENDATION FOR PHYSICAL EDUCATION AND
OTHER PHYSICAL ACTIVITIES

Dear Physician:

All pupils enrolled in the public schools participate in physical education
activities which are designed to meet the growth and developmental needs of boys
and girls. In addition many pupils participate in other types of physical activity
such as intramural programs, interschool athletics, band, drill team. To identify
specific needs of each pupil, the physician, parents, and school personnel must
work cooperatively. Will you please provide us with the information listed below
so that we can provide appropriate activities for:_____

(Pupil's name)

FINDINGS AND RECOMMENDATIONS TO THE SCHOOL

I have examined_____and find the following handicaps,

(Pupil's Name)

if any:_____

_____

I recommend the following: (check appropriate item or items)

_____ 1. No restriction on any type of activity.

_____ 2. Participation in all activities (intramural and other activities
          in addition to physical education) with the exception of inter-
          school athletics.

_____ 3. No restriction on activities in physical education.

      4. Adaptions in physical education to fit individual needs:

          ____a. Little running or jumping

          ____b. No running or jumping

          ____c. No activities involving body contact

          ____d. Exercises designed for rehabilitation

          ____e. Strenuous conditioning exercises

      5. Other adaptions: (specify)_____

          _____

I recommend the adaptation for: ____2 weeks, ____1 month, ____3 months, ____6 months

Date_____   Signature_____

                                       Address:_____

Please mail this form to: (Name and address of school should be given here)

Form approved in compliance with Education Code section 11906, Superintendent of
Public Instruction, State of California 10/25/62.

Figure 14–2. Physician's report on referral for physical education. (From Willgoose, C. E.: *The Curriculum in Physical Education,* 2nd ed. Englewood Cliffs, N.J.: Prentice-Hall, Inc., 1974, p. 290.)

of the brain, which prevents them from learning, using their resources, and adjusting to life as normal children do. The condition, which is permanent, ranges from slight impairment to complete disability. Mentally retarded children fall into three groups: the educable, the trainable, and the totally dependent.

EDUCABLE. Educable children progress academically at a much slower rate than normal children. They usually adjust socially, but may develop antisocial behavior when they learn of their relatively inferior performance levels. They may be awkward in some skill techniques, but they may also develop at a remarkable rate when taught properly. Stein reports:

Recent trends in research show that the lack of intellectual ability resulting from arrested mental development need not affect the levels of physical fitness and motor development of the retarded. Two studies have shown that the mentally retarded respond and progress as much as normal boys and girls when given specialized training or instruction in a systematic and progressive physical education program.[7]

TRAINABLE. Children in the trainable category learn much more slowly than those in the educable group. Their skill performance level is low, and simple repetitive movements constitute the major portion of their movement program. These students will need guidance, care, and support throughout their lives. However, research shows that these children show remarkable improvement in strength and endurance when participating in programs emphasizing organic fitness.[8]

TOTALLY DEPENDENT. Students in the totally dependent group will need help and support all their lives. They will learn very little, and their skill performance will remain very low.

Wheeler and Hooley list the characteristics of the trainable and totally dependent groups as distinguished from those of normal children:

1. They seem younger socially.
2. They do not move well. They seem awkward and show little of the sequential movement of confident people. Posture and body mechanics are both poor.
3. Many are obese.
4. Many have little energy.
5. Some move constantly, but with little purpose.
6. They do not seem able to concentrate, follow directions, or even learn through their senses as well as children who speak well, see well, and generally seem aware of the environment.
7. The retention span is short, and they must relearn what the normal child remembers easily.
8. They take part in group activity, but often seem to work for individual participation and success rather than for the success of the team.[9]

One of the basic needs of children in this group is the coordination which grows out of skill development. Other needs are programs of physical fitness and leisure-time activities. Teachers need guidelines in working with these children, particularly in the area of motor skills. Figure 14–3 illustrates an arrangement of fundamental skills ranging from minimum to maximum development.[10]

The Physically Handicapped

Individuals in the physically handicapped group are usually children who have orthopedic, visual, hearing, speech, respiratory, cardiac, or menstrual problems; or who suffer from diabetes, anemia, hernia, overweight, skin diseases, epilepsy, or nutritional deficiencies.

This is such a broad category that lack of space prevents an adequate discussion of each group. The reader is referred to the texts listed at the end of the chapter for this information.

The Emotionally Disturbed

Emotionally disturbed children usually suffer from problems ranging from the extreme afflictions of emotional

Skill	Minimum achievements	Maximum achievements
A. Walking	Ability to walk with good coordination. Will rarely trip or fall.	Ability to stride, like an adult. Can step forward, backward, and sidewise.
B. Running	Ability to run with assurance. Can turn and stop without falling.	Ability to race fluidly and gracefully. Will pace self when running.
C. Climbing stairs	Ability to ascend and descend with alternate steps and without support.	Ability to walk or run up or down stairs with objects in arms. Can climb ladders and trees.
D. Skipping	Ability to attempt to skip. Will skip "one-legged" in an awkward and clumsy manner.	Ability to break into a skipping motion from a walking or running start.
E. Marching	Ability to walk rhythmically when accompanied by a definite rhythm and beat.	Ability to march gracefully in intricate patterns and to intricate directions.
F. Dancing	Ability to imitate simple bodily movements when music is played.	Ability to enter into group or social dancing with evident satisfaction.
G. Throwing	Ability to throw a ball with one hand with overhead motion but slightly off balance.	Ability to throw a ball at different rate of speed with good judgment of distance.
H. Catching	Ability to catch a ball by convulsively closing in of arms. Arms will be held at sides and raised stiffly.	Ability to catch a ball most of the time from a set or running position. Will hold hands in front of body with elbows bent in a preparatory set.

Figure 14–3. Minimum and maximum achievements of the trainable mentally retarded child. (From Arnheim, D. D., *et al.: Principles and Methods of Adapted Physical Education,* 2nd ed. St. Louis: The C. V. Mosby Co., 1973, p. 261.)

instability, such as schizophrenia and paranoia, to delinquency. Many of them must be institutionalized for life. Some of them, usually the delinquent, receive treatment and return to school. In addition, there is a borderline group that remains in school but needs guidance or psychiatric treatment.

A prerequisite of success in teaching emotionally disturbed children is early detection. Children are more adaptable and receive greater benefits from physical education if their emotional problems are discovered early, before they have developed strong, hostile attitudes toward school, parents, and their peers. Early detection by the teacher is easier when he is aware of a sequence of be-

havior patterns that is observable. This sequence usually precedes a severe disturbance. The following symptoms are typical:

1. Trivial, everyday disturbances that teachers cannot study in detail, such as giggling or lack of concentration. Action can be met with counteraction to eliminate this form of disturbance.

2. Repetitious behavior that must be interpreted as a sign of deeper underlying tension.

3. Repetitious behavior accompanied by a serious single disturbance—a tantrum or breaking into tears.

4. A succession of different disturbances—talking when roll is taken, poking the person standing next to him, staring into space, etc., on different days. This type of be-

havior is indicative of deep-seated tension and requires the services of a psychologist or a psychiatrist.[10]

INSTRUCTIONAL GUIDELINES

Assigning exceptional students for instruction requires careful review of the classifications and categorical groups discussed earlier. The majority of these students should be assigned to the regular physical education class. Only in extreme cases should they be taught separately. When scheduled for separate classes, they should be reassigned to the regular class as improvement justifies the change.

When the physical education program is varied and students are grouped by ability, exceptional children automatically find their place. With individualized instruction and careful guidance they may progress satisfactorily in the regular class. In some instances, in addition to ability grouping, activities should be modified to allow for variations in disabilities.

Joan Nelson and Gail A. Harris, in a study of educable handicapped children in the schools of Michigan, found that these children participate in most of the activities of normal children. However, they offer the following as modified teaching procedures necessary for an effective program:

1. Progress slowly, offering familiar activities first. Use repetition, because these students need reinforcement of learning.

2. Introduce new activities during the early part of class, before the class gets tired.

3. Be kind, firm, and patient, using a positive approach.

4. Be clear in directions, without talking down to the class. Use concrete examples.

5. Attempt to keep each child active.

6. Demonstrate and take part in the activities.

7. Offer activities which could be useful at recess time, after school hours, and later on in life.

8. Remember the characteristics of the children, and consider individual abilities and attention spans.

9. Let children compete with themselves. Some simple tests and measurement devices provide an incentive.

10. Give the children goals in which they can have some measure of success, and use praise as often as possible.

11. Allow them to have some choice of activities, and allow them to suggest activities.

12. Include rhythmical activities, such as simple folk and square dancing.

13. Aid the children in developing skills such as running, jumping, and ball handling.

14. Correlate good health habits with physical education.

15. Keep records of physical fitness.

16. Aim for progression in social and physical skills.[11]

Figure 14-4. When regular classes are grouped by ability, exceptional children may be appropriately assigned according to their level of performance.

INSTRUCTIONAL PROCEDURES INVOLVING STUDENT ASSISTANCE

When exceptional children are assigned to the regular physical education class, several teaching procedures are indicated. Team teaching may become an important aid in providing the necessary supervision and instruction for these students. For example, when a regular grade level of students is assigned to a physical education period, several teachers will be present. If tumbling is the instructional area for the particular period, the class may be divided into three ability groups: beginners, intermediate, and advanced. Teachers are assigned to each of the three groups according to their qualifications. The teacher who is the most interested and best qualified teaches the group to which the exceptional students are assigned, depending upon the extent of disability. The students progress to higher groups as their performance improves.

If only one teacher is available, the class may be organized in the same manner, except that student leaders assist with the instruction. Pilot programs which have used students to assist in teaching exceptional children have produced outstanding results.[12] Student leaders provide the enthusiasm, ability, dedication, and peer leadership that seem to be particularly adaptable to individualized instruction for exceptional children.

Peer instruction has proved to be of inestimable value in academic instruction, but has not been universally developed in physical education. With the increased enrollment of exceptional children in the schools, using students to assist the classroom teacher, the physical education teacher, and the special education teacher may be the answer to personnel problems.

The advantages of using students for teaching responsibilities are many, particularly when working with exceptional children. Exceptional children relate to their peers in a positive manner that is difficult to explain. They respond in a manner which sometimes borders on adulation. Children who are handicapped develop a close attachment to other students, probably because these students have the patience and understanding so necessary in the world of exceptional children. Senior high school students, when given the proper instruction in skills, can do an exceptional teaching job. Many students involved in assisting with adapted programs are members of varsity teams and with this background may relate to the younger children in such a manner that effective instruction is assured. Many secondary school students have great leadership ability, and this potential is manifested when they are allowed to assist with the instruction of exceptional children. Finally, all students need an opportunity for self-expression. Those students who are selected to work with exceptional children have the opportunity to express themselves through guiding and helping the exceptional child. The chapter opening photograph illustrates how well children respond to being taught by other students.

EVALUATION OF PROGRAMS FOR EXCEPTIONAL CHILDREN

Programs for exceptional children should be carefully evaluated. The first requirement for these programs is that the total physical education offering be consistent with the philosophy outlined in this chapter. The physical education program should include varied activities based on the growth needs of children and on procedures for grouping students by ability. In addition, arrangements should be made for providing modifications of a sufficient number of activities to meet the needs of those exceptional children enrolled in the class.

Finally, attention should be given to appraising the total physical education program by evaluating the factors involved in conducting programs for the exceptional child. A form that includes the necessary ingredients for evaluating adaptive programs is shown in Figure 14–5.

I. ORGANIZATION

Checklist

1. Policies and procedures for establishing and operating special education programs are clearly defined and make provision for all handicapped students. . na 1 2 3 4
2. Special education teachers have a major role in establishing procedures for the identification, evaluation, placement, and transfer of the handicapped. na 1 2 3 4
3. The special education program(s) operates under the leadership of a trained special education administrator. . na 1 2 3 4
4. Supervisory services are provided for special education teachers and program. na 1 2 3 4
5. The special education education program is an integral part of the instructional program. na 1 2 3 4
6. The staff is offered the same considerations as other staff members. na 1 2 3 4
7. Opportunities for staff professional development, curriculum development, and in-service training are provided. na 1 2 3 4
8. Budgets for special education programs are formulated as part of the school budget. na 1 2 3 4
9. Appropriate teacher-student ratios are in effect and meet state standards. na 1 2 3 4
10. Teachers are members of an interdisciplinary team that participates in decisions regarding placement, curriculum, evaluation, and instruction. na 1 2 3 4
11. Before a student is transferred to or placed in a special education program, both parents and student receive a complete orientation to the program. na 1 2 3 4

12. Students are provided special supportive services as needed. na 1 2 3 4
13. A systematic plan is in effect for evaluating the quality of special education services. na 1 2 3 4
14. Clerical personnel are available. na 1 2 3 4
15. The school maintains an approved and continuing screening and referral procedure. na 1 2 3 4
16. The school cooperates with professional and lay groups to coordinate activities concerned with the referral of handicapped children and youth. na 1 2 3 4
17. Referrals are made to other agencies to secure diagnostic information. na 1 2 3 4
18. Professional records, including cumulative records, psychological findings, case histories, and medical reports, are available and used by appropriate personnel. na 1 2 3 4
19. Handicapped children in organized programs are re-evaluated at intervals to verify their continued eligibility. na 1 2 3 4
20. Teachers from the various grade levels plan together to develop a sequential program in special education. na 1 2 3 4
21. Teachers of the same grade level plan together to develop the special education program at that level. na 1 2 3 4
22. na 1 2 3 4

Evaluations

a) How effective are the policies pertaining to special education programs? na 1 2 3 4
b) How effective is the administrative leadership? na 1 2 3 4
c) How adequate is the financial support for special education programs and services? na 1 2 3 4
d) To what extent is the special education program an essential component of this school's program? na 1 2 3 4
e) How accurate and complete is identification and assessment of the handicapped? na 1 2 3 4
f) To what extent are referrals made to proper services? na 1 2 3 4
g) How adequate is the follow-up after clinical referrals? na 1 2 3 4
h) How adequate are the supportive services? na 1 2 3 4

Comments

A

Figure 14–5. *A* and *B,* Evaluation of the adapted program. (From National Study of Secondary School Evaluation: *Evaluative Criteria,* 4th ed. Washington, D.C., 1969, p. 235.)

II. NATURE OF OFFERINGS

Checklist

1. The curriculum is designed to meet the needs of handicapped children and youth.   na 1 2 3 4
2. Students have an opportunity to develop specific talents and abilities as well as to strengthen areas of weakness.   na 1 2 3 4
3. Handicapped students are assigned to regular classes in those cases where such placement is appropriate.   na 1 2 3 4
4. Special students are involved in the regular program *only* as their progress determines this to be desirable.   na 1 2 3 4
5. The school has special services to take care of assessment and referral needs (check if available):   na 1 2 3 4
   ____Audiologist.
   ____Educational diagnostician.

____General medical practitioner.
____Neurologist.
____Occupational therapist.
____Ophthalmologist.
____Orthopedic surgeon.
____Otologist.
____Pediatrician.
____Physical therapist.
____Psychiatrist.
____School psychologist.
____Social worker.
____Speech therapist.
____Other _____

6.   na 1 2 3 4

Supplementary Data

1. If the program titles listed below do not describe the programs offered, make appropriate changes. Include only offerings that are a regular part of the school program.

PROGRAMS, BY NATURE OF HANDICAP	ENROLLMENT OF STUDENTS, BY NATURE OF INSTRUCTION				FULL-TIME EQUIVALENCY OF TEACHERS IN EACH PROGRAM	NUMBER OF HANDICAPPED STUDENTS IN REGULAR PROGRAM CLASSES
	In Self-Contained Classroom	Resource Teachers	Itinerant Teachers	Total		
1. Hearing impaired						
2. Vision impaired						
3. Speech handicaps						
4. Orthopedic handicaps						
5. Other health impairments						
6. Retarded, educable						
7. Retarded, trainable						
8. Slow learners						
9. Socially/emotionally maladjusted						
10. Learning disabilities						
11. Multiple handicaps						
12. Hospital- or home-bound						
13.						
14.						

B

Figure 14–5. *Continued.*

REFERENCES

1. Committee on Adapted Physical Education: "Guiding Principles for Adapted Physical Education." *JOHPER*, April, 1952, p. 15.
2. Daniel D. Arnheim, *et al.*: Principles and Methods of Adapted Physical Education, 2nd ed. St. Louis: C. V. Mosby Co., 1973, p. 65.
3. Committee on Exercise and Physical Fitness: *"Classification of Students for Physical Education.* Chicago: AMA, 1967, p. 265.
4. "Need for Varied Activities in Physical Education Programs." *JOHPER*, June, 1965, p. 6.
5. Committee on Exercise and Physical Fitness, *op. cit.*
6. *Ibid.*
7. Julian Stein: "The Potential of Physical Activity for the Mentally Retarded Child." *JOHPER*, April, 1966, p. 25.
8. *Ibid*, p. 26.
9. Ruth H. Wheeler and Agnes M. Hooley: *Physical Education for the Handicapped.* Philadelphia: Lea & Febiger, 1969, p. 290.
10. Arnheim, *op. cit.*, p. 272.
11. Joan Nelson and Gail A. Harris: "Teaching Suggestions." *JOHPER*, April, 1966, p. 27.
12. Vicki Arrand: "PELT – Physical Education Leadership Training." *JOHPER*, October, 1973, p. 50.

SUGGESTED READINGS

Arnheim, Daniel D., David Auxter and Walter C. Crowe: *Principles and Methods of Adapted Physical Education*, 2nd ed. St. Louis: C. V. Mosby Co., 1973.
Hirst, Cynthia C., and Elaine Michales: *Developmental Activities for Children in Special Education.* Springfield, Ill. Charles C Thomas, 1972.
Logan, Gene A.: *Adapted Physical Education.* Dubuque, Iowa: Wm. C. Brown Co., 1972.
Vodola, Thomas M.: *Individualized Physical Education Program for the Handicapped Child.* Englewood Cliffs, N. J.: Prentice-Hall, Inc., 1973.

Courtesy of University of Wyoming, Laramie, Wyoming

CHAPTER FIFTEEN

Recreation and Outdoor Education

AN OVERVIEW OF RECREATION

Definition of Recreation

Play and recreation have been synonymous with life since time immemorial. Play during childhood is essential for normal growth and development. It is nature's way of providing sufficient activity during the formative years.

Although the terms play and recreation are often used to refer to the same thing, there is an important distinction between them. Play, particularly during childhood, occurs at any time, whereas recreation, which includes play, usually occurs after the day's work is completed, during vacation, or after the school day. Recreation has been defined as "Experience or activity carried on within leisure, voluntarily chosen and providing pleasure or a sense of well-being."[1]

Need for Recreation

The need for recreation has been shown by leaders in psychology, sociology, medicine, and education for many years. Every generation has realized the need for some form of recreation. The rapid rise of industrialization, the trend toward more leisure time, the affluence enjoyed by a large part of the population, and the conditions existing in the inner cities are making disintegrating inroads into our culture. Evidence that these conditions have reached a critical stage is seen in the high incidence of dropouts in the schools, the increase in crime and delinquency, the grave problem of drug abuse and alcoholism among young people, the widespread unrest on the college campuses and in the streets, and the increasing problem of mental illness. The picture painted by these conditions is not a pretty one. Although recreation cannot solve all of these problems, there is evidence that many of these problems could be alleviated by well-planned and properly administered programs in recreation. A discussion of this premise is in order at this time.

Crime and Delinquency. It seems logical to assume that if a small fraction of the money, time, and effort placed on rehabilitation and law enforcement were spent on prevention, crime and delinquency would not be the problem it now is. Hetherington stated many years ago that "play gone wrong is the source of most of the bad habits known to childhood and youth."[2] Children will have their play whether we like it or not. If play is not guided along socially acceptable channels, it may be directed toward unacceptable behavior. It is the responsibility of adults to provide the type of recreation that meets the needs of boys and girls.

It is during the play life of children that the most effective guidance programs take place. The rugged, rough-and-tumble aspects of play bring out the innate character traits of children. The teacher is able to see these moods, attitudes, and actions that reflect character, and, through counsel, he may guide the children into socially acceptable behavior. The desire for play is so strong and so fundamental to life that growing children may be guided through play to accept codes of behavior willingly. Be-

cause of this, teachers are able to assist children in developing strong standards of behavior necessary for a life of health and happiness.

An outgrowth of misguided play is the disorder on the streets and campuses. Although cities and colleges have playgrounds and playfields, the question is raised: How are they used? No longer are traditional programs and facilities adequate for providing millions of people with a way of using leisure time wisely. Programs must be developed that not only serve as a medium for releasing tension but also are designed to develop creativity.

Delinquency, crime, rioting, and other antisocial acts may be the results of frustration and boredom; but in most instances, they are the results of emotional instability. The only way, other than by heredity, to have a strong stable nervous system is through vigorous exercise during the formative years. Layman states, "The fact that play is spontaneous self-expression and involves joyful and exuberant emotions renders it a 'must' for adequate emotional health."[3]

The importance of physical education programs cannot be overestimated. However, physical education is concerned with instruction, and the bulk of exercise occurs in the recreation program of children. Skills of play are learned in the physical education class and applied in those afterschool programs in which there is sufficient time to practice them. Morehouse and Miller, in describing the value of exercise through play, state:

If the exercise is pleasant in itself, as in games, part of the benefit derives from the relief of tensions and of the monotony of daily activity. There are psychological benefits of a similar nature to be gained from types of exercise which are not themselves pleasurable, but they are more likely to result from the emotional relaxation resulting from physical fatigue and to require greater effort for the same return.[4]

A survey of the opinions of 24 psychiatrists showed that they believed moderate exercise would relieve tension. The respondents gave the highest priorities to walking, swimming, bowling, golf, tennis, square dancing, social dancing, folk dancing, creative dancing, calisthenics, bag-punching, basketball, fishing, boating, gardening, and relaxing exercises. It is interesting to note the dominance of individual sports rather than spectator sports in the survey. All of the activities shown are easily adapted to recreational programs and could be available for all age groups.[5]

School Dropouts. The increasing incidence of school dropouts presents a perplexing problem for educators. Approximately one-fourth of the students entering the ninth grade do not graduate. The causes of the problem are known and considerable effort is being made by local, state, and national agencies to combat the situation. Douglass states that:

The dropout problem is largely a curriculum problem as far as schools are concerned, but it extends beyond the confines of formal education, and part of the solution will come from extensive social and economic realignments.[6]

Among the reasons pupils drop out of school is lack of interest. This is probably a result of their inability to meet prescribed standards in the academic curriculum. In too many schools the experiences and materials do not seem to be in harmony with the concerns of the potential dropout.[7]

A new look at the curriculum is indicated, with emphasis on adjusting the curriculum to the needs of students rather than forcing the student to meet the demands of an inflexible program of studies. Emphasis on providing physical education in all grades that would lead to recreational pursuits beyond the school day would provide holding power for the potential dropout. As Conant so effectively stated:

If I had to choose one department in any high school that can do most to reduce dropouts, to hold the youngster emotionally to the institution, it would be physical education.[8]

Too often, after skills are learned in the physical education class, no provi-

sion is made to provide the opportunity for practice beyond the school day. Situations like this need to be remedied. To deny students the opportunity to become involved in purposeful recreational pursuits beyond the school day is to encourage them to participate in socially unacceptable activities.

ADMINISTRATION OF RECREATIONAL PROGRAMS

There are several plans generally used throughout the country for administering recreational programs. Irrespective of which plan is used, a great amount of cooperation must exist among the various agencies and the public. Four widely used plans are (1) the park board plan, (2) the recreation commission plan, (3) the school board plan, and (4) the joint school board–park board plan.

The Park Board Plan

The park board plan for administering recreation is widely employed by both

Figure 15–1. Play is nature's way of providing sufficient exercise for normal growth and development. (Courtesy of New Zealand Schools.)

large and small cities. There are sound arguments for the park board plan; yet many people are opposed to the plan.

Arguments Against the Plan. The arguments against the plan include the following:

1. Under this plan, recreation would be of secondary consideration; the major emphasis would be on zoos, gardens, construction, and landscaping.
2. Park leaders are primarily concerned with and trained for developing parks, landscaping, and engineering; and the leadership would be in this direction. Recreation would suffer because of lack of interest.
3. Recreation would suffer from lack of adequate appropriations, since budget cuts would be in favor of the parks program.
4. Recreation needs indoor facilities and these may not be available. If they are constructed, the duplication of already existing facilities is costly and impractical.

Arguments for the Plan. Proponents of the park plan are just as strong in giving their reasons for it. They argue that:

1. Since land is already owned by the park board, it is relatively easy to convert some of it into playgrounds.
2. They already employ a staff of experienced people who are available for maintenance, landscaping, and constructing facilities.
3. The park budget is sufficiently large to provide for recreation.
4. The board already controls playgrounds, swimming pools, beaches, camping areas, and other facilities that may easily be made available for recreation.

The Recreation Commission Plan

The recreation commission plan is found in many large cities. Under this plan a board is formed, consisting of individuals interested in recreation. The members are either elected or appointed by the mayor. The board organizes recreation programs around municipal facilities owned by the city, such as schools, parks, and the waterfront; it may also use private facilities that may be loaned to or rented by the city. The school system usually has representatives on the commission to serve as a liaison between the two agencies.

The School Board Plan

Many cities provide recreation under the school board plan, an arrangement which is usually made possible by state legislation. There are arguments for and against this plan, as outlined in the following paragraphs.

Arguments for the Plan. Some of the arguments for the plan are:

1. Schools, particularly elementary schools, are close to the children and already serve as a center for many activities.
2. Schools already have the facilities for physical education, art, music, and other instructional areas that may easily be used for recreation.
3. Schools have physical education programs in the curriculum designed for teaching skills. Recreation may be an extension of the physical education program in which pupils may practice the skills learned in class.
4. Highly qualified teachers are already in the schools. They may be employed to conduct the recreation program beyond school hours. This prevents duplication of personnel effort.

Arguments Against the Plan. There are arguments against the plan, and those opposing it offer the following reasons for their opposition:

1. The school is still primarily interested in children. Recreation planning should include programs for adults as well. If the school board plan is used, the main interest would be in programs for children of school age.
2. The recreation program would suffer from lack of appropriations, since the educational leaders are primarily interested in education.
3. The school board would not be interested in or have access to parks and other municipal areas. This would prevent the establishment of a broad program in recreation.
4. Teachers are not professionally qualified to conduct or supervise recreational programs. Their background has been in teaching children, and if required to work with adults, they would not perform satisfactorily.

5. Physical education teachers are not interested in or qualified to conduct activities other than those in the physical education curriculum. If recreation is placed in the physical education department, it would suffer from lack of experienced leadership.

School Recreation Programs. Recreation programs conducted by the local boards of education are rapidly assuming leadership in recreation throughout the country. Enabling laws have been passed by California, Michigan, Pennsylvania, and other states, making provisions for local school boards to sponsor recreation programs. There are many reasons for this arrangement, but the overriding argument for school-sponsored programs is that wasteful and costly duplication of facilities is prevented. In addition to this justification, there are other considerations that apply to school-sponsored recreation. They are:

1. Schools are charged with the responsibility to develop lifelong interests, attitudes, and skills in physical education, art, outdoor education, music, literature, and dramatics.
2. Leisure is growing with the end nowhere in sight.
3. The school is where the bulk of the tax dollar is usually expended and where the facilities are invariably suited for community-wide use for all ages.
4. The school's facilities are usually unused from 3:30 or 4:00 to 10:00 or 11:00 at night, the time when the community has the greatest needs for recreational service.
5. Many of the activities taught by the school are similar to many of the activities included in the recreational program.
6. The swimming pool, gymnasium, shop, home economics room, music room, athletic field, library, school camp, and classrooms are splendidly suited for recreational pursuits for all age groups.
7. Much of what the school normally includes in its music, industrial arts, art, home economics, dramatics, and physical education programs is closely related to preparation for leisure-time activities in current and later years.
8. The extracurricular program in the average school closely embodies the choice-exercising features of recreation.
9. The school is responsible for the provision of areas where the various recreational activities taught during the school day can be practiced, interests deepened, and skills perfected.
10. The opportunities to develop lifelong interests and leisure-time pursuits during the formative years are indeed a responsibility that the school, among the other community agencies, cannot afford to overlook.[9]

Planning School Programs. Planning school recreation programs is a task that requires considerable time and effort. The same procedures involved in planning the school curriculum are essential in developing a program in school recreation. Three aspects of planning that should receive serious consideration are: (1) objectives, (2) needs and interests of pupils, and (3) developing the program.

Objectives should be developed that state the recreational needs of the present. Objectives of yesterday are not applicable to the future. The objectives might be developed from the following concepts:

The program should be based on restudy of the interests and needs of children. Too often adults are prone to superimpose adult programs on children. These programs are not accepted by children and may result in a communications gap between the children and the recreation leader. A better understanding of the play interests of children may be of immense value to adults in their efforts to plan recreational programs for boys and girls.

The recreational program should be an outgrowth of well-planned physical education programs. Physical education is primarily concerned with instruction in skills of sports and related activities. The recreational program should be an outgrowth of this instruction. Recreation should be heavy with physical activity geared to the physical education instruction, in addition to art, crafts, and nature study. If tennis and golf are taught in the school, for example, then recreational planning should provide for participation in these skills beyond the school day.

There is a tendency to plan recreation programs for the gifted only. This phase of recreation, while important, should not dominate the program. This narrow type of program rules out participation by the masses. For example, the average basketball league consists of eight teams or a total of 40 pupils. This plan of organization precludes the masses who would enjoy recreational basketball. An alternative would be an informal type of program planned in conjunction with league play. This does not rule out the league organization, but it does provide activity for individuals who are not among the 40 selected. Another aspect of recreational planning is the need for more activities and programs for girls. There are many places where emphasis is placed on the boys' program with little attention given to the needs of girls. Finally, programs for senior citizens and pre-school children should be developed in order for these groups to have the opportunity of benefiting from wise use of leisure time.

In a school-centered recreation program, the responsibility of the principal cannot be overestimated. There are many organizational and administrative problems involved in planning school recreation programs. The use of facilities, the program, and coordinating the various activities that constitute the recreation program are a few of the problems confronting principals in conducting school recreation.

The following guidelines have been developed to point out the areas of the principal's responsibility:

1. Whenever possible, select or recommend teachers for school recreation responsibilities and inspire them to relate their playground experiences to the classroom instruction.
2. Recruit for recreation.
3. Assume creative and positive community leadership with regard to use of school plant and its facilities for both school and nonschool recreation.
4. Leagalize, formalize, and publicize conditions of use.
5. Realize that school recreation is worth the cost. Mountains of materials, testimonials, and textbooks attest to this, although statistically there is no definite proof. The values lie in less objective results: school and community well-being, prevention of delinquency, a rise in the fitness level, high cultural standards. But what about costs?
6. Seek the revenue where it may best be found.[10]

Joint School Board–Park Board Plan

Joint effort by the school board and the park board seems to be the most logical and effective method for administering recreational programs. With both groups operating under the same objectives, better utilization of facilities and personnel is assured.

It is difficult to justify the construction of separate facilities for recreation when most school buildings are closed evenings and during the summer. A survey in 1971 revealed that of the 25,000 gymnasiums in over 17,000 school districts in the United States, most of these facilities are used during the school hours and remain idle evenings and summers.[11] Joint planning by both the school board and the park board should utilize these facilities and extend the instructional program to leisure-time participation.

Not only are the facilities available, but personnel for recreation may be found in the physical education and other staffs of the schools. By appropriately increasing the salaries of these teachers, adequate and qualified personnel may be provided to conduct various types of recreational activities. It is unjustifiable to employ full-time recreational leaders who work in the evening and do busy work during the day in an attempt to qualify for full-time employment.

There are many examples of joint usage of facilities and staff for education and recreation. The community school concept pioneered by the C. S. Mott Foundation in Flint, Michigan, is a vivid illustration.

In Tulsa, Oklahoma, the school board, park and recreation board, and the city government combined their resources and efforts to produce a positive approach for providing recreational programs for their citizenry. The creation of the Community School Coordinating Committee in 1972 marked the beginning of an expanded recreational program which included in its membership representatives from the Tulsa Public Schools, Board of Education, City of Tulsa Park and Recreation Board, and the

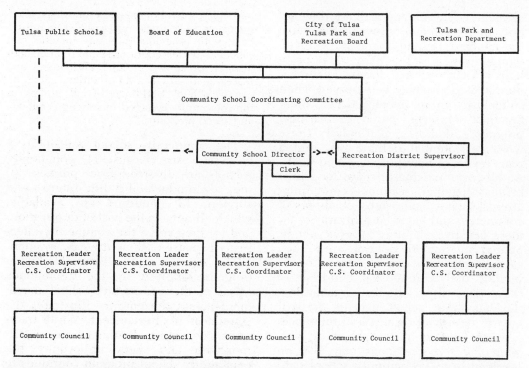

Figure 15-2. Tulsa model for community planning. (From Nance, Everette E., and Donna Pond: "Community Education: Broad Based Comprehensive Community Planning, the Tulsa Model." *JOHPER*, April, 1974, p. 23.)

Tulsa Park and Recreation Department. Figure 15-2 illustrates the administration arrangement of the program.

The authors of this text would be remiss in their efforts if they failed to mention the recreational program of the Milwaukee Public Schools. Milwaukee was the first city in America to benefit from a state law allowing cities to levy taxes for community use of schools. The "city of the lighted schoolhouse," as Milwaukee is known in recreational circles, has grown from a lighted playground program in 1912 to a diversified program of fantastic proportions. Today, as the program approaches its 65th anniversary, the city is using 128 of its 158 school buildings for recreational and adult programs. In addition to buildings, there are 125 play areas and field houses and other facilities spread throughout the city. The program also assists 110 industries in the development of industrial recreation. The entire program is directed by an assistant superintendent and has expanded to include in its recreational centers over 200 activities which include (1) creative interests—arts, crafts, drama, music; (2) contemporary interests—family living, home and household, investment planning, foreign languages, driver education; (3) personal health—figure analysis, physical fitness, indoor sports; (4) recreational skills—golf, gun safety, mountaineering, watercraft safety; and (5) sports and athletic contests—friendly competition, mixed activity. In addition, programs for the elderly and adaptive recreation for over 1000 handicapped children are conducted.[12]

The Community School Concept. A prerequisite for reading this section of the chapter should be a review of the community school concept discussed in Chapter 5.

One of the first steps in developing the community school is to keep the schools open on a 24-hour basis. The schools belong to all of the people and may be used for all age groups. When schools are kept open on a round-the-clock basis, the programs that follow not only strengthen family ties but also raise the standards of living through the development of new skills. Many social problems—drugs, venereal disease, malnutrition, and so on—may be resolved when community groups meet and face them together. Through varied recreational programs, teenagers, particularly those who are potential delinquents, find a place to learn new purposes and goals. An all-encompassing program for adults brings together various community groups, such as civic clubs, chambers of commerce, and health organizations, for more effective planning for civic needs. School programs in delicate areas such as sex education can be expanded to include both parents and children. In these days of racial misunderstanding, the community school may be the real answer to mutual respect and tolerance. The growing need for providing programs for senior citizens may also be resolved in the community school concept. Cities such as Flint, Michigan; Milwaukee, Wisconsin; and Tulsa, Oklahoma, have discovered many ways to fill the creative and recreational needs of older people.

Spiraling costs demand a new look at the financial aspects of recreational and educational programs. Programs involving duplication of effort, facilities, and personnel must be eliminated. When the planning for education and recreation is made a joint effort of school officials, community groups, and citizens, the community school becomes an instrument for revitalizing the total educational and recreational effort. True community education is:

—a philosophy that pervades all segments of educational planning;
—a school which serves as a catalytic agent by providing leadership to mobilize community resources to solve identified community problems;
—based on the premise that education must be relevant to people's needs and that people affected by educational programs should be involved in decisions about these programs;
—the marshalling of all forces in the community to bring about change, with the school extending itself to all people;

—keeping school doors open mornings, afternoons, and evenings, up to twelve months a year, with programs that may include preschool activities, continuing and remedial education for adults, cultural enrichment and recreational activities for all citizens, and the use of school buildings by all groups in the community engaged in solving economic and social problems.[13]

The community school concept is a successful one because (1) community schools are divorced from politics; (2) they are products of public interest and support; (3) facilities are available, which eliminates the cost of duplication; and (4) they serve the community effectively because of their strategic location.

The success of the Flint, Michigan, program followed by the tremendous surge of the community school movement across the country illustrates the soundness of the concept. While traditional education flounders in experimentation and shaky philosophy, the community school program continues to grow.

The Flint, Michigan, program mobilizes the human and institutional resources of the community in such a manner that (1) senseless and costly duplication is avoided; (2) people of all classes and creeds are given the necessary encouragement and opportunity to help themselves to a better life; and (3) local institutions, schools, governments, and businesses become genuinely responsive to human wants and needs.[14]

Developing Recreational Programs. The foregoing guidelines for planning recreational programs necessitate providing increased and varied facilities. One gymnasium, a playground, and one tennis court may have been adequate 25 years ago, but current and future planning demands many gymnasiums, playgrounds, and courts. One of the reasons leisure-time programs have been restricted is the lack of adequate facilities. It is at this point that the school-community concept should be considered.

The majority of school buildings throughout the country are closed at the end of the school day, during holidays, and throughout the summer. This is particularly true of elementary schools. It is difficult to believe that the taxpayer has allowed this situation to exist. Billions of dollars are invested in buildings that are used six hours daily and nine months of the year.

Planning for expanded programs designed for the future must include finding ways to meet the needs of millions of individuals seeking participation. There are several ways of providing for this increased participation:

Joint Use of School Facilities. For years some school systems have developed programs around the school-community concept. Classrooms, gymnasiums, playgrounds, and other areas have been used by the community before school, after school, and through the summer. Flint, Michigan, is one of the best illustrations of the manner in which programs of this type may be developed. Gary, Indiana, utilizes school facilities to develop the school-community concept, as does Baltimore County, Maryland.

Extension of School Programs. Although separate community programs using school facilities are desirable, extension of the school programs is necessary.

A child's education does not end at three o'clock or on June 15th. It is outside of the school influence that antisocial attitudes and practices may be developed. The influence of the school should be extended beyond the usual school day or term. Florida operates an outstanding extended-school program. It is planned around the Florida Summer Enrichment Program and has been in operation since 1953.

Many school systems provide intramural programs that extend the physical education programs beyond the school day and term. Some illustrations are Abilene, Texas; Omaha, Nebraska; Los Angeles, California; Sherwood, New York; Austin, Texas; La Crosse, Wisconsin; Portland, Oregon; Skokie, Illinois; Pontiac, Michigan; Weymouth, Massachusetts; Battle Creek, Michigan; and Cincinnati, Ohio.

Emphasis on Positive Values of Mutual Use. As outside groups take over school facilities, many problems arise. Whether school officials like it or not, ex-tended-day programs by community groups are here to stay. Some of the problems that arise are the misuse of equipment and facilities, conflict of objectives that may affect the instructional time, and disruption of classes. Many problems grow out of mutual use of facilities; however, the positive values that accrue from these programs overshadow the problems that arise from mutual use.

Planning Cooperatively for School-Community Programs. Probably the real cause of most of the problems that exist in school-community programs is the lack of cooperative planning. Leaders, directors of both physical education and recreation, school boards, administrators, and sponsoring agencies should be involved in the establishment of policies for the use of facilities.

The President's Council on Youth Fitness recommended a community committee for organizing recreation programs. Figure 15-3 shows the various organizations represented in the committee. The objectives of the committee are:

1. To develop and carry out a community-wide plan, emphasizing physical fitness, which involves all organizations and agencies having recreation interests.
2. To provide opportunities for and encourage daily participation in vigorous physical activities by all age groups, in all programs, wherever feasible and appropriate; to encourage individual citizens to employ the self-discipline necessary to fulfill their own commitments to regular exercise.
3. To provide year-round opportunities for development of physical fitness through fitness centers and sports clubs.
4. To make the widest possible use of available leadership and facilities, working, where necessary, for enactment of state enabling legislation and local ordinances which authorize use of public property or funds for recreation.[15]

The Council suggested various responsibilities of the committee:

1. Determine physical fitness needs as they relate to recreation for all age groups.
2. Determine what each organization is doing to meet physical fitness needs of the people it serves.
3. Determine the scope and effectiveness

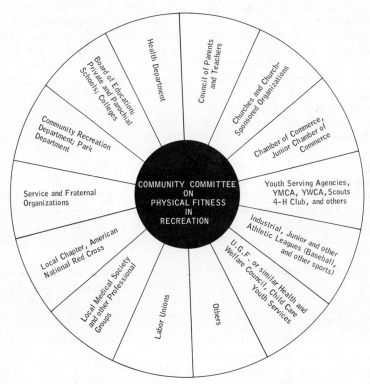

Figure 15–3. A community committee for organizing recreation programs. (Redrawn from *Physical Fitness Elements in Recreation*, President's Council for Youth Fitness, 1962.)

of the existing programs for improving physical fitness of all community members.

4. Identify voids where organizations are not meeting the physical fitness needs of various segments of the population.

5. Determine whether existing organizations can meet these fitness needs or if new programs should be established. Take appropriate steps to provide the necessary programs and services.

6. Identify undesirable overlapping of physical fitness programs and other duplication of effort; work out the desired adjustments.

7. Recommend means for strengthening existing physical fitness programs.

8. Secure maximum utilization of all facilities in the community, including evening, weekend, and summer use.

9. Work out a plan for the most efficient use of professional and volunteer personnel in carrying out the total community physical fitness program.

10. Initiate action for planning and financing new physical fitness facilities.

11. Develop a comprehensive plan for public interpretation of the need for physical fitness.[16]

PUBLIC RELATIONS

The public relations program should be planned to reach the many "publics" involved in the power structure of a community. There is no one public. Opinions vary within each public. A comprehensive program in public relations should be designed to influence the thinking of administrators, teachers, pupils, civic groups, parent-teacher groups, religious groups, volunteer medical groups, business, and industry. Many of these groups will be involved in the school-community programs through actual participation in the activities available in these programs. These and other concepts relating to the necessity for a public relations program are presented in Chapter 4.

THE OUTDOOR EDUCATION MOVEMENT

The history of American culture reveals that our civilization had its inception in the great outdoors. The early col-

onies were founded in locations bounded by rivers, streams, and forests. As towns grew into cities, pioneer movements surged across the prairies of the Midwest and finally settled on the coast of the Pacific Ocean. The great cities developing on the coasts, with their factories and vast industries, provided very little of the outdoor living characteristic of the first hundred years of American life.

A back-to-nature movement, reflecting man's rebellion against the crowded, smog-filled city, has reached immense proportions in the last 25 years. The magnitude of this movement is difficult to describe. The increased sales of camping equipment, trailers, and all types and sizes of boats are indications of the surge away from city life toward the freedom and leisure of the great outdoors. Millions of people are spending weekends and vacations at the seashore, at the lakes, and in the great parks that are scattered across the country.

An important overview of outdoor education, which includes an evaluation of and projections for the future, was made by the National Conference on Outdoor Education sponsored by the Outdoor Education Project of the American Alliance for Health, Physical Education, and Recreation. The recommendations of the conferees should affect programs in outdoor education for years to come, since so many leaders in education, recreation, conservation, and industry participated in the conference. The most important conclusions resulting from their deliberations are summarized:

1. The need for education in and for the outdoors is greater than ever before.

2. Outdoor education, as a means of curriculum enrichment and good program development, should be stressed in schools and colleges and in conservation, recreation, and other agency programs.

3. All agencies and organizations concerned with education and with the management of outdoor resources and facilities should work together in making experiences in the outdoors a reality for more children, youth and adults.

4. The American Association for Health, Physical Education, and Recreation should give strong leadership to outdoor education with special attention to the implications of

the outdoor Recreation Resources Review Commission report.[17]

A later conference developed guidelines for the future that should serve as priorities for action by the Project. These guidelines showed the need for:

1. More workshops and clinics in and near large population centers for school and community recreation leaders.
2. The activation of state leadership in outdoor education through committees and workshops.
3. The acceleration of efforts in teacher and leadership preparation through college- and university-sponsored courses and workshops.
4. Continued work with schools and colleges based on the promising developments now underway.
5. Cooperation with the Bureau of Outdoor Recreation and other federal and state agencies and organizations concerned with outdoor education.[18]

Many schools and districts throughout the country have developed outdoor education programs. These programs are forms of alternative education and are usually extensions of the physical education program. An example of such a program is the outdoor development in the Rochester High School, Rochester, Vermont. The program began in the mid 1960's and includes these activities: hiking (fall and spring), snowshoe hiking (winter), hunter safety (fall and spring), archery (fall and spring), skiing (winter), first aid and medical self-help (spring), swimming (fall and spring), canoeing (fall and spring), skating (winter), gymnasium activity (winter), and horseback riding (fall and spring).

In addition to the activities just listed, the curriculum provides instruction in bowling, golf, camping, tennis, sailing, mountaineering, modern dance, square dancing, bicycling, track, baseball, touch football, soccer, rappelling, and canoe building. Additional time may be allotted for activities requiring large blocks of time. One of the outstanding phases of the program is the overnight expedition, which includes hikes, bike rides, canoe trips, and horseback riding.[19]

Outdoor education programs for elementary students are also conducted in Frederick County Schools, Maryland; San Diego City Schools, San Diego, California; Heath Junior High School, Gruly, Colorado; and Berkin School, Hamburg, Wisconsin. The programs include camping activities, field trips, recreation, ecology, hikes, and similar activities.[20]

One phase of the outdoor education movement is camping. Seeking an environment far removed from the crowded life of the city, individuals, groups, and families are finding a new experience in camping. An overview of camping in this country reveals that several types of camps are in existence at present.

Types of Camps

The camp movement has been so great that many types of camps have developed through the years. The various types of camps fall into two categories: the informal camp and the organized camp. The informal camp involves the many individuals, groups, or families who include camping as a part of their vacation program. The thousands of camp trailers seen on the highways and in trailer camps are part of this informal camping movement.

The organized camp program consists of those types of camps that have definite sponsorship by individuals or agencies. These camps vary in operation, depending on the purpose and objectives defined by the sponsoring groups. Some of these camps conduct programs on a daily basis; others operate for weekends, one- or two-week periods, or for an entire summer. The following types of camps belong to the organized-camping category.

Youth Hostels. The youth hostel movement began in Europe and was introduced in the United States during the early 1930's. The purpose of the movement is to provide overnight accommodations for those who travel and wish inexpensive facilities with a camp atmosphere. Minimal facilities are provided and cooking areas are available for the campers, who bring their own utensils.

The hostel accommodations are developed along predetermined travel routes and maps are available showing locations of the hostels. Membership by the camper in American Youth Hostels, Inc., is required in order for him to use the facilities.

Public Camps. Public camps are operated by municipal governments and are supported by tax money from local, state, or federal funds. The camps may be operated in conjunction with the existing playgrounds or they may be conducted on an organized basis as separate entities.

Private Camps. Private camps have been operated by individuals and groups for many years. These camps serve a purpose for families who wish their children to derive the benefits of camping experiences.

Community-Organization Camps. Community-organization camps are conducted and supported by community agencies, such as the Boy Scouts, Girl Scouts, YMCA, YWCA, Boys' Clubs, and other similar groups. Such camps have been an established part of the parent organizations for many years and serve as a means of furthering their objectives within a camp environment.

School Camps. School camps are operated by schools to serve as a continuation of the school instructional program in a camp setting. These camps have developed from a rather modest beginning centered around field trips and one-day excursions to a broader concept involving the development of full-time camping programs.

Since school camps are integral parts of the instructional program of the school and because many of the activities are related to physical and health education, in many instances the responsibility for administering the program is placed in the physical education department. The remainder of the chapter will therefore be devoted to the organization and administration of the school camp.

ORGANIZATION AND ADMINISTRATION OF THE SCHOOL CAMP

Purpose of the School Camp

The purpose of the school camp is to further the instructional program of the school in an outdoor setting; it serves to enrich educational experiences and motivate interest in the acquisition of knowledge and skills. The inflexible routine that exists in so many schools deters rather than promotes pupils' progress toward the objectives of the educational program. Placing boys and girls in an environment close to nature and free from the frustrations that exist in school life enhances the learning process and contributes to the mental, physical, social and emotional development of children. This premise represents a revival of Rousseau's theory that the young of all species learn best in an environment provided by nature. Associating the camp with the school provides purposeful direction and control and represents a modern refinement of Rousseau's theory.

Objectives of the School Camp

The objectives of the school camp should be consistent with the objectives of education. Pupils embarking on a camping program should not just be taken outdoors for a recreational or play program. These programs should be planned around a purpose or goal. Some specific objectives that may serve as guides in planning and evaluating the camp program are contained in the following statements. Camping experiences should help:

1. To serve as an extension of the school instructional program in a more natural environment.
2. To improve personal attitudes, establish new goals, and develop, through special counseling, better ways of spending leisure time.
3. To develop a sense of responsibility and cooperation through participation in the camp routine.

4. To develop wholesome and sound health habits and attitudes through health education, nutritional practices, and first aid.

5. To develop and improve personal self-image and physical potential.

6. To develop and broaden the cultural potential of boys and girls through actual participation in music, drama, and art.

Administrative Responsibilities for Operating the Camp

A properly planned camp utilizes the services of various people, and the administrative responsibilities for operating the camp should be outlined in writing. The selection of personnel for conducting the camp requires careful consideration of the character, personality, and educational background of the applicant. The close association of campers with camp leaders involves a type of decision making and action unlike any other phase of a child's education. Counselors and others responsible for programming and supervision of campers should always be conscious of the need for safety measures in all phases of camp life. The need for continuous guidance of campers is so important in camping that a background in this area should be a major criterion in the selection of personnel. The responsibilities and duties of individuals who are operating the camp are discussed below. Although the administrative organization of the camp varies depending upon local policy, the positions described below are usually found among camping personnel.

The Camp Director. The camp director is the chief administrator of the camp and should excel as an organizer and leader. The success of the camp's operation depends largely on the director's ability to organize, plan, delegate authority, and work with adults as well as children. The director should understand people and be sympathetic yet firm in carrying out the policies of the camp.

The director has many duties to per-

form in the operation of the camp. Some of the more important ones are:

PREPARATION OF THE BUDGET. The preparation of the budget is a responsibility that requires thought and time. The director should seek the aid of his staff in compiling the items necessary for operating the various programs. Materials needed for programs in art, music, crafts, sports, photography, and other areas should be carefully studied before preparing the final budget. An inventory of items on hand should be the first step in the over-all planning of budgetary needs.

SUPERVISION OF THE PROGRAM. The director must exercise general supervision over the entire program. Since he is responsible to the board of education for the operation and management of the camp, he must be aware of the many personnel and program problems that exist in the camp's operation. Supervision with authority is as basic to quality education in camping as it is in school.

COORDINATING DUTIES. The director is responsible for coordinating the entire program. Each phase of camp life must have its place in the total program. Coordinating the various programs is essential for smooth, effective administration.

SELECTION OF PERSONNEL. The camp director, with the assistance of others, is responsible for the selection of the people who work with him. A careful appraisal of the qualifications of the applicants for the various positions is of extreme importance. Knowing the requirements for each job is, of course, an essential corollary.

PUBLIC RELATIONS. The camp director has an important role in public relations and in interpreting the purpose and objectives of the program to the many publics. He should use all available media, including the newspaper and television, for focusing attention on the camp program.

OTHER DUTIES. Other duties of the director include conducting orientation, holding staff meetings, planning the program, arranging transportation, keeping records, planning meals, planning field trips, and reporting the results of the year's program to the board of education.

The Program Director. The larger camps usually employ an assistant director responsible for planning and conducting the program of activities. Some of his specific duties are to:

1. Develop the program of activities.
2. Conduct in-service and training programs for camp personnel.
3. Supervise activity personnel.
4. Maintain morale among the personnel.
5. Assist in maintaining safety standards in the conduct of all activities.

Counselors. Counselors are the backbone of the camp program. They have the closest association with campers and have guidance responsibilities that make camping a home away from home. The counselor must be endowed with certain basic qualities that are essential to the successful fulfillment of his responsibilities. These qualities are identified in a self-evaluation chart shown in Figure 15–4. The chart lists items in three categories: (1) health, (2) acceptability to others, and (3) emotional maturity. Each item is arranged so that it may be checked in five evaluative levels: (1) poor, (2) below average, (3) average, (4) above average, and (5) superior.

Duties of counselors may include the following:

1. Meeting campers when they arrive; supervising the unloading of equipment; assigning the cabins; touring the facilities.
2. Developing friendly relationships with campers through learning their names, discovering innate potentialities, and assisting them in adjusting to camp life.
3. Orienting campers to the various phases of camp life and to the activities involved.
4. Planning and teaching effectively.
5. Staying with the group at all times to insure safety and continuous instruction.
6. Reporting all accidents immediately.
7. Providing daily health education through direct instruction and incidental teaching. This instruction should give cleanliness a high priority.
8. Supervising and assisting campers in developing proper table manners, in assuming responsibilities for serving, and in performing duties involved in before- and after-meal chores.
9. Encouraging and directing creative effort when discovered.
10. Providing adequate equipment and supplies for each activity.
11. Assisting in coordinating the total program.

Counselors are specialists in teaching and supervising the daily camping program. They are with the campers throughout the day and in some camps may also be assigned to remain with the group in the cabin for the night.

Junior Counselors. Junior counselors are necessary to assist with the over-all operation of the camping program. Their chief responsibility should be to stay with their cabin group at night and to assist the senior counselor with the various responsibilities that occur during the day. Duties of the junior counselor may include:

1. Supervising the campers in the performance of their chores, which may include sweeping the floors, emptying wastebaskets, making beds, hanging clothes, arranging toilet articles properly, keeping areas around cabins clean and sanitary, and following the rules for toilet and shower cleanliness and sanitation.
2. Being responsible for the safety of campers at all times.
3. Being familiar with the rules and regulations of the camp and enforcing them at all times.
4. Knowing the whereabouts of each camper at all times.
5. Reporting all irregularities to the senior counselor or director.

The Caretaker. Year-round camps usually include a caretaker who performs duties similar to the school custodian. The caretaker is responsible to the director for maintaining a safe and sanitary environment in the building and on the grounds, for serving as a watchman on the premises, and for maintaining the buildings and grounds in satisfactory condition for the effective operation of

Health	Poor 1	Below Average 2	Average 3	Above Average 4	Superior 5
1. Stamina enough to last through a strenuous day					
2. Well-balanced meals eaten regularly					
3. Regular sleep in sufficient quantity					
4. Smoking, not at all or moderately and in an appropriate place					
5. No intoxicating liquors (can't be tolerated at camp)					
6. Sufficient vigorous exercise each day					

Acceptability to Others	Poor 1	Below Average 2	Average 3	Above Average 4	Superior 5
7. Pleasing and neat appearance					
8. Cleanliness of person and clothing					
9. Graciousness and mannerliness					
10. Tact (speak truthfully, but without unnecessarily offending or hurting others)					
11. Cooperativeness (even when carrying out the plans of others)					
12. Cheerfulness (no sulking or moodiness)					
13. Sense of humor (even when the joke's on you)					
14. Good English (no excess slang or profanity)					
15. Warmth (a friendly personality that attracts others to you)					
16. Poise (even in emergencies or embarrassing situations)					
17. Appreciation of the beautiful in deed, music, nature and literature					
18. Sincere liking for children (even unattractive and "naughty" ones)					
19. Enjoyment of hard work (even when it means getting yourself and your clothing dirty)					
20. Skills and knowledge of outdoor living (in rain, as well as sunshine)					
21. Adaptability (can happily change plans to fit in with others or the weather)					
22. Can "take" as well as "give" orders					
23. Love of fun (can see possibilities for enjoyment in almost any situation)					
24. Interested in many things					
25. Specialization (ability to "do" at least one camp activity well)					
26. Initiative (ability to start without outside prodding or suggestion)					
27. Promptness at all appointments and in performing all tasks					
28. Dependability (do *what* you say you will *when* you say you will)					
29. Industry (want to be constantly up and doing)					
30. Persistence (finish what you start with dispatch and thoroughness)					
31. Curiosity (want to know about many things just for the sake of knowing)					
32. Neatness (keep own living quarters neat and clean)					

Figure 15–4. A self-evaluation checklist for camp counselors. (From Mitchell, A. Viola, *et al.: Camp Counseling,* 4th ed. Philadelphia: W. B. Saunders Co., 1970, p. 59.)

EMOTIONAL MATURITY	Poor	Below Average	Average	Above Average	Superior
	1	2	3	4	5
1. Can you accept criticism without undue anger or hurt, acting upon it if justified, disregarding it if not?					
2. Are you tolerant of others and willing to overlook their faults?					
3. Do you feel genuinely happy at the success of others and sincerely congratulate them?					
4. Do you refrain from listening to and repeating undue gossip about others?					
5. Do you converse about other things and persons? Test it by checking your conversation to see how frequently you use "I."					
6. Are you altruistic, often putting the welfare and happiness of others above your own?					
7. Do you refrain from emotional outbursts of anger, tears, etc.?					
8. Do you face disagreeable duties promptly and without trying to escape by playing sick or making excuses?					
9. Can you stay away from home a month or more without undue homesickness?					
10. Can you weigh facts and make decisions promptly, then abide by your decisions?					
11. Are you willing to postpone things you want to do now in favor of greater benefits or pleasure later?					
12. Are you usually on good terms with your family and associates?					
13. When things go wrong, can you objectively determine the cause and remedy it without alibiing for yourself and blaming it on other people or things?					
14. When disagreeing with another, can you discuss it calmly and usually work out a mutually satisfactory agreement without hard feelings?					
15. Can you enter into informal social events of many types wholeheartedly?					
16. Do you really enjoy doing little things for others, even though you know they will likely go unknown and unappreciated?					
17. Do you dress neatly and modestly without tendency to gaudiness or overdress?					
18. Can you dismiss past sins and mistakes that can't be remedied now without dwelling on them?					
19. Can you make decisions regarding others objectively, disregarding your personal dislike or resentment of them?					
20. As a leader, do you work democratically without dictating or forcing your will on others?					
21. Are you loyal to your friends, minimizing or not mentioning their faults to others?					
22. Are you free from "touchiness," so that others do not have to handle you with kid gloves?					
23. Do you act according to your honest convictions regardless of what others may think or say about it?					
24. Do you have a kindly feeling toward most people, a deep affection for some, and no unhealthy attachments to any?					
25. Do you feel that you usually get about what you deserve? Are you free from a feeling that others "have it in for" you?					

Figure 15–4. *Continued.*

the camp program. Specific responsibilities of the caretaker are to:

1. Check security of facilities daily or seasonally according to need.
2. Be responsible for maintenance, cleanliness, and sanitation of the camp buildings and grounds.
3. Inform the director about specific problems and needs as they arise.
4. Maintain an adequate supply of janitorial materials and equipment and supervise economical use of these supplies.
5. Make repairs to buildings as needed and approved by director.
6. Make necessary trips related to camp as outlined by the director.
7. Be on duty, as assigned by the director, when camp is being used by designated community groups.
8. Maintain an inventory of equipment and supplies.
9. Request necessary repairs by written requisition to the maintenance department.
10. Report by phone and written report to the director, maintenance department, or camp supervisor damage to or loss of property.
11. Maintain usual working hours of 40 hours per week (7-hour work day, 5 days per week, and 5-hour work day, 1 day per week).
12. Check maintenance of equipment daily or seasonally as needed.
13. Remain on the premises except when absence is approved in advance by the director.
14. Cooperate with and be respectful in language and bearing toward administrative officials, camp staff personnel, campers, and visitors.
15. Request mosquito-control services as needed.

The Camp Physician. The camp physician has a very important role in the administration of the camp program. The physician should be either in residence or available on immediate call. It is the responsibility of the board of education and the camp director to provide the camp with medical assistance.

The Camp Nurse. The camp nurse should be in residence for long-term camp programs. Her responsibilities include first-aid instruction and practice and assisting with the health education

program. Specific duties of the nurse may be to:

1. Supervise the health and sanitation program and make daily inspection of rooms, cabins, and other facilities.
2. Direct the activity of the infirmary.
3. Administer first aid or guide its administration.
4. Assist the doctor when his services are used.
5. Be aware of the health status of the campers and advise the administrative staff of unusual conditions, such as physical handicaps, allergies, etc., and follow up on conditions of these children.
6. Make arrangements with a local doctor for emergency calls.
7. Inform the camp director when parents need to be notified.
8. Assist in the preparation of lesson plans in health instruction.
9. Instruct in health and safety education.
10. Keep accurate records on health and first-aid treatment of campers.
11. Maintain inventory of supplies and keep the director informed of needed items.

The Dietitian. The dietitian has the responsibility for planning meals, supervising the cooks and kitchen help, and maintaining an attractive and clean environment within the kitchen and dining hall.

Auxiliary Personnel. Camps of longer duration include in the administrative planning auxiliary personnel, such as librarians, hostesses, and other personnel necessary for the effective operation of the program.

Types of School Camps

Several types of school camps exist in the country at the present time. The type of camp that is operated by the school depends on local philosophy, facilities, and financial appropriations for the program. The more prominent types are briefly discussed.

The Day Camp. Day-camp programs are planned around activities that can be provided during the day. Pupils are transported to the camp site, where they participate in the extended school program, and return home in the afternoon. Although the usual school instructional program is maintained, the emphasis is on outdoor education.

A comprehensive day-camp program operated by the Norfolk Public Schools emphasizes instruction. Through the assistance of the Elementary and Secondary Education Act, Title I, disadvantaged children have their classroom instruction extended to the camp environment. The 30-acre camp, which is owned by the Norfolk School Board, consists of three swimming pools (one enclosed for year-round instruction), an eight-cabin dormitory, recreation hall, dining room–kitchen complex, caretaker's home, arts and crafts building, nature study building, music cabin, outdoor amphitheater for drama, reading room clinic, and 10 sleeping cabins. The outdoor facilities include two multiple-use concrete areas, two outdoor bowling alleys, a softball-football field, a nature trail, and waterfront facilities for boating, fishing, and crabbing.

Students are transported daily to the camp by bus after parents have signed permission slips (see Figure 15–5). The camp program includes instruction in art, music, drama, physical education, health education, reading, nature study, boating, fishing, and photography.

The Weekend Camp. Some school-camp programs are developed around weekend trips to the camp site. These programs simulate the summer camping program as much as possible. The advantage of the weekend plan over the day camp is the overnight experience. An experiment in weekend camping was made with disadvantaged children in the Norfolk, Virginia, public schools. The program was designed to assist and guide those children from the city schools to develop proper study habits and learning experiences in an outdoor camp atmosphere. Eighty students were given permission by their parents to spend two consecutive weekends at Camp Young, which is owned by the Norfolk School Board. The program was financed through the Elementary and Secondary Education Act. The students

were transported to the camp by bus on Friday afternoon and returned home on Sunday afternoon. Letters were sent to the parents of each child requesting permission for him to attend camp (see Figure 15–5). The camp program usually consists of experiences in art, music, drama, sports education counseling, and health education.

Weekend camp programs, when properly organized, may serve as incentives for study, for developing creativity, and for establishing better attitudes toward school.

An evaluation of the program reveals that students show a tremendous amount of interest in all aspects of the camp program and that their attitudes toward school are improved. The relaxed atmosphere of the camp, the association with adults who take time to listen to their problems, and the participation in activities of their choice provide many of the children with a new outlook on life.

The Summer Camp. The summer camp more nearly meets the objectives of school camping. Boys and girls are able to spend sufficient time to really experience the thrill of participating in the many activities provided by the outdoor summer program. The period of time spent by the students in the summer camp varies with local policy. Many school systems plan programs around a one- or two-week interval, arranged according to grade level.

The day-camp program for disadvantaged children, described earlier, continues during the summer and is designed for elementary students. The camp operates on a weekly basis, with a different group being transported to the camp each week. See Figure 15–6 for an overview of the camp activities.

Administrative Problems

Operating a school camp presents administrative problems that should be discussed during the early stages of planning. The more important problems that are pertinent in all school camp programs are briefly considered here.

Legal Authority. Before a school

HEALTH, PHYSICAL EDUCATION AND SAFETY DEPARTMENT
NORFOLK CITY PUBLIC SCHOOLS
CAMP E. W. YOUNG
Parental Consent for Attending Day Camp

Dear Parents:

The Administration of the Norfolk City Public Schools is conducting for the fourth consecutive year a day camping program at Camp E. W. Young. This program is sponsored by the Office of Special Projects and administered by the Health, Physical Education and Safety Department

The purpose of this program is to extend the regular school instructional program into a more natural environment, which will enhance the growth and development of our students in this complex society in which we live today. The daily program includes instruction in arts and crafts, music, drama, nature study, reading, health education, physical education, and swimming.

Transportation

The camp will provide transportation for students to and from camp daily without cost. A classroom tacher will accompany the students to and from the camp on the bus.

Food Service

Lunch and a snack will be prepared and served at camp free to students. A snack will be served before students depart camp. This service is under the supervision of the camp dietician.

Participation Dates

The participation days for your child will be the week of _____
                                                                Date
through _____.
                Date

Student Camp Supply List

Items checked below are things your child will need to bring to camp daily.

_____ 1 Notebook   _____ Raincoat, hat and boots

_____ Text book   _____ Bathing Suit

_____ Pencil(s)   _____ Bathing Cap (Girls)

_____ Tennis Shoes   _____ Gym Bag

PLEASE RETURN PERMISSION SLIP BELOW TOMORROW

PARENTAL PERMISSION SLIP

School _____

I hereby give permission for my child:

Name _____ Grade _____ Age _____

Address _____ Phone No. _____

to participate in the Day Camping Program beginning Monday,
_____ through_____ and to receive whatever medical,
        Date   Date
surgical or nursing services that may be necessary at the camp by any professional persons selected by the camp counselors, director or nurse.

Check: ( )
_____ My child is taking medication

_____ I do not wish my child to take swimming.   _____

_____ I do not wish my child to go to camp.   Signature(s) of Parents/Guardians

Figure 15-5. Parental consent for attending day camp.

Figure 15–6. Various camp activities at Camp E. W. Young. (Courtesy of Norfolk Public Schools, Norfolk, Virginia.)

camp may operate, local boards of education must determine if they have the legal authority to expend tax money for camp programs. Several states, such as New York and Michigan, have laws that make provisions for camping in the school program.

Health Inspection. Camps must be planned so as to comply with the health inspection standards outlined by the state. These standards include such items as adequate toilet facilities, proper washing facilities for dishes and cooking utensils, adequate food storage and refrigeration, and standards for treating water in swimming pools to prevent infection and spread of disease.

Health of Campers. All campers should be examined prior to admission to camp. The periodic examination given in school should suffice. However, it is important that these examinations be reviewed before allowing pupils to register at the camp.

Financing the Camp. Cities that finance camping as a part of the instructional program are very fortunate. Many cities are not able to procure adequate funds for camping from tax money and must find other means to finance the program. Some of the plans used to finance the program other than using tax funds include camp fees, donations, and contributions by parents. However, until camping becomes an integral part of the school budget and money is appropriated each year for this program, camping will not achieve the goals for which it has such a rich potential.

Selecting the Activities. In addition to the usual camp activities shown in the preceding pages, the activities of a school-operated camp should follow the curriculum of the school. The basic differences between the activities of the school and the camp are the teaching procedures and the more natural environment found in camp life.

REFERENCES

1. Richard G. Kraus and Joseph E. Curtis: *Creative Administration in Recreation and Parks.* St. Louis: C. V. Mosby Co., 1973, p. 3.
2. Clark Hetherington: *School Program in Physical Education.* Yonkers on Hudson, N.Y.: World Book Co., 1922, p. 87.
3. Emma McCloy Layman: *Mental Health Through Physical Education and Recreation.* Minneapolis: Burgess Publishing Co., 1955, p. 352.
4. Laurence E. Morehouse and Augustus T. Miller: *Physiology of Exercise,* 6th ed. St. Louis: C. V. Mosby Co., 1971, p. 300.
5. Oliver Byrd: "A Survey of Beliefs and Practices of Psychiatrists on the Relief of Tension by Moderate Exercise." *Journal of School Health,* November, 1963, p. 427.
6. Harl R. Douglass: *The High School Curriculum,* 3rd ed. New York: Dodd, Mead & Co., 1965, p. 24.
7. Albert I. Oliver: *Curriculum Improvement.* New York: Dodd, Mead & Co., 1965, p. 24.
8. James Conant: "What They Said." *JOHPER,* March, 1963, p. 41.
9. H. Dan Corbin: "School-Sponsored Recreation." *JOHPER,* February, 1962, p. 23.
10. Ted Gordan: "School Recreation Personnel, Facilities, and Financing." *Current Administrative Problems* (Washington, D.C.: AAHPER), 1960, pp. 151–153.
11. Patrick J. Bird: "Community Education: The Potential of Physical Education." *JOHPER,* April, 1974, p. 21.
12. George T. Wilson: "Milwaukee—City of the Lighted School House." *JOHPER,* January, 1973, p. 65.
13. "Getting Community Education in Orbit." Leaflet published by the National Community School Education Association, Flint, Michigan.
14. Peter L. Clancy: "The Flint Community School Concept." Community Education Center, Charlottesville, Virginia.
15. *Physical Fitness Elements in Recreation.* President's Council on Youth Fitness, October, 1962, pp. 4–5.
16. *Ibid.*
17. *National Conference on Outdoor Education,* A Professional Report. *JOHPER,* November, 1962, p. 29.
18. Julian W. Smith: *After Eight Years,* Report of the Outdoor Education Project. *JOHPER,* March, 1973, p. 37.

19. "An Innovative Outdoor Education and Physical Education Program." *Physical Education Newsletter,* February 15, 1974.
20. "Better Outdoor Education Programs." *Physical Education Newsletter:* Perspective, September, 1970.

SUGGESTED READINGS

Kraus, Richard G., and Joseph Curtis: *Creative Administration in Recreation and Parks.* St. Louis: C. V. Mosby Co., 1973.
Lynn, Rodney S., and Phyllis M. Ford: *Camp Administration.* New York: The Ronald Press Co., 1971.

IV
THE ORGANIZATION AND ADMINISTRATION OF PHYSICAL EDUCATION IN COLLEGES AND UNIVERSITIES

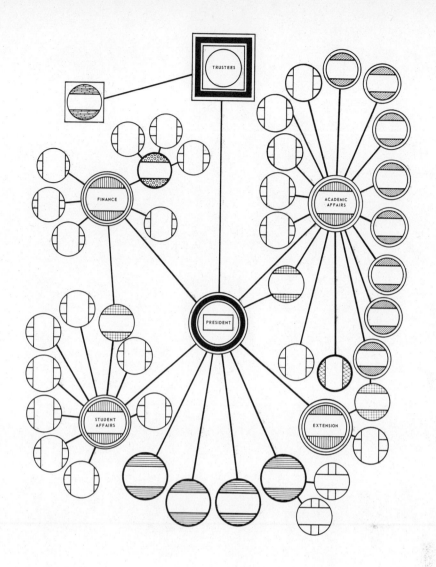

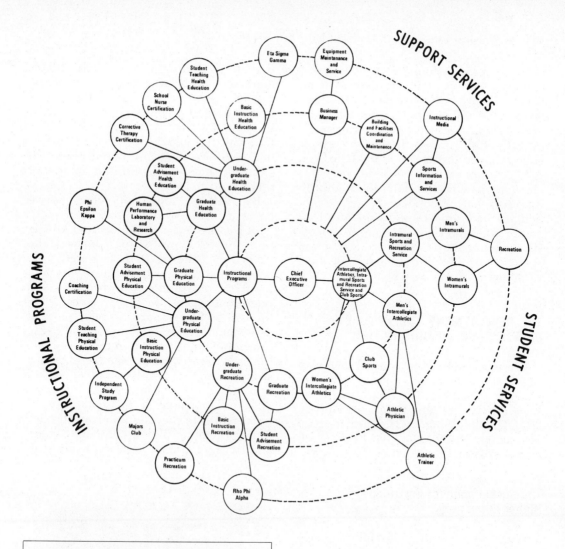

CHAPTER SIXTEEN

Academic Administration and Higher Education

In attempting to set forth administrative policies and procedures for physical education within the structure of higher education, we must first obtain an understanding of the structure and nature of the total administration of the college or university. All too often, serious administrative errors are found to be the direct result of faulty administrative decision making at the department or college level. The problem is that decisions are made which are not in keeping with the overall administrative framework established for the institution as a whole.

As has been observed in previous chapters, it would be folly to attempt to establish and recommend one set of policies and procedures to be used no matter what the circumstance. By necessity, administrative form and function change with the requirements of each situation.

THE DEVELOPMENT AND NATURE OF ACADEMIC ADMINISTRATION

It was noted in the historical review of physical education, presented in Chapter 1, that physical education in the United States began at Harvard University. The founding of Harvard in 1636 also marked the beginning of the development of American higher education.

The Development of American Higher Education

With the founding of Harvard, academic administration in the United States was created. During those early years in our history, education was dominated by Protestant sectarian beliefs and practices. With the passing of time and the changes in society, religious influence gradually decreased and privately endowed institutions, such as Princeton and Yale, were opened. Leyden University in Italy, established in 1575, was one of the first universities to adopt a system of administrative control by an external board. The University of Edinburgh also adopted this plan. Since Yale and Princeton used Scotland as a model for their organization, they incorporated the principle of external control as well. This adoption, then, set the precedent for the future organization of higher education in the United States. The curriculum of the early colleges was largely centered on the classics, al-

though beginning in the early 1800's more emphasis was placed upon the sciences, mathematics, and other disciplines. Usefulness was not an important standard for the early classical curriculum, but it gradually became an important criterion for many people both inside and outside institutions of higher education.

By 1910 the "university idea," as we know it in the United States today, was well established, and all forms of education for all types of people was the American pattern. It is generally accepted that the great growth in size and numbers of American institutions has been made possible in part because in the United States there has been more of an economic margin to be devoted to the development of education than has been the case in many other countries. A great strength in the development of higher education in this country has been the close relationship of the colleges and universities to the aspirations of the majority of people. With few exceptions, institutions of higher education are cor-

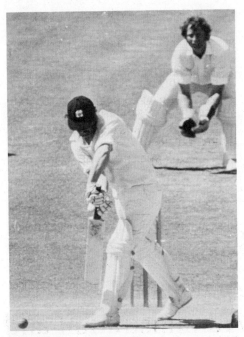

Figure 16-1. "Cricket was a popular sport in the early classical curriculum." (Courtesy of the Dunedin [New Zealand] Evening Star.)

porate bodies. If a majority of the members of a governing board are popularly elected or are appointed by the legislature, the governor, or some other public body or official, then the governing board is considered to be a public corporation.[1]

The development of the American pattern of higher education, although financially costly, has been phenomenal in both magnitude and accomplishment. With some 2000 institutions of higher learning in the United States, employing approximately 1,000,000 individuals, academia does indeed contribute significantly to the economic base of the country. In 1970 there were more than 7,000,000 students enrolled in American colleges and universities. Many of them, at that time, were demonstrating for more involvement in shaping their own worlds.

The development of institutions of higher learning in both Canada and the United Kingdom has somewhat paralleled the growth of colleges and universities in the United States. One of the most crucial questions dominating British academics and administrators deals with the purposes of a contemporary university. As British universities near the end of their 1972–1977 quinquennium, it is evident that they are still expanding, but their rate of growth has been slowed, as have enrollments and programs in the United States. Many countries are concerned with defining the purposes of contemporary higher education and with fulfilling the new aspirations for social relevance of both students and employers.

In the late sixties and early seventies it became evident that American universities were in financial difficulty. The years of booming enrollments and unlimited spending had vanished, and in their place state-supported universities experienced operating deficits and curtailments of some academic building and maintenance programs. The early seventies saw institutions borrowing heavily and spending private endowment funds in order to maintain their operations. As student enrollments stabilized, academic institutions had to follow a "hold the line" budget. Reports on the financing of higher education reveal that a combination of increased tuition and sophisticated management methods may represent the only way that financially pressed colleges and universities can survive. Suggestions have been made that institutions consider "variable tuition rates" for different programs, depending on the cost of providing such programs. Institutions may also have to adopt a more hard-nosed business approach in order to survive financially.

Some Canadian universities are considering the adoption of a 10½-month university year in place of their present 7½-month academic calendar. This proposal is designed to increase productivity, which a recent Canadian Economic Council report says has been declining in Canadian universities in recent years.

University Government — Organization for Purpose

So far there has been little systematic theory or precise empirical study of the administrative process in colleges and universities. "Administration is, of course, complex human behavior and difficult to analyze in any context. Universities are devoted to the tasks of discovering and disseminating knowledge. Much more understanding of how our institutions of higher education are organized and administered is needed before we can adequately judge how they should be organized to cope with the problems of great growth facing our educational community."[2]

Although the preceding quotation came from a publication which is over 10 years old, it still has relevance today, even though the growth problems facing the educational community have somewhat diminished.

Colleges and universities have the characteristics of bureaucratic organizations. They are, or should be, organized to provide experiences from which certain knowledge and skills are gained that are required in later life. The purposes of the university are the discovery, dissemination, advancement, and transmission of knowledge. Rosencrance states that the general aims of a college are to (1) serve society, (2) perpetuate itself, and (3) serve the individual. The specific aims of any college or university may be revealed by a close examination of the academic curricula offered by the colleges and departments that make up the institution.[3]

Curricular offerings for most colleges and universities are usually presented in areas of broad-field courses and courses for specialization. Subject matter areas in the *humanities* are designed to introduce the student to possible areas for future growth. The *social sciences* have as their objective the basic understanding of the fundamental ideas upon which our society has been built in order to give meaning to the rights and well-being of others. The objectives of the so-called *pure science* areas are to acquaint the student with the types of problems that may possibly be solved through the use of scientific techniques and the development of a basic understanding of all the scientific disciplines. "A good college program should enable graduates to do difficult things well and should make them eternally curious about life—its opportunities, challenges, and meanings."[4]

Institutional Administration. The overall objectives of a company, school, or college are the responsibility of top management—the president, the board of directors, the chairman of the board, and members of executive committees. It is also true that in any organization there must be a *cohesive and disciplinary* force that helps maintain membership, facilitates group interaction, and directs the members of the unit in the pursuit of some goal.[5] Executive members of organizations must at times make decisions of such major importance that they must be made without complete regard for the views of subordinates.

The legal framework of higher education within which administrators work in the United States is quite different from the pattern in most other countries. "The typical continental university is an arm of government, with a Minister of Education or similar functionary serving as the actual operating head of the national university system and professors having a status not totally unlike that of civil servants."[6] In the United Kingdom, the government has relatively little to say about the running of institutions of higher learning. A typical British university is run by its professors, with a rotating presiding officer who is more of a ceremonial figurehead than an administrator.

In 1972, 72 years after it received its Royal Charter, one of Britain's major universities, the University of Birmingham, was placed under independent scrutiny by an academic review body headed by a former leader of the Liberal Party. This review of a prestigious British university amounts to an in-depth evaluation of the contemporary British university in the context of changes in both its inner government and its external role in the community at large. In the early 1960's it was suggested that higher education in Britain should transmit a common culture and common standards of citizenship. Specific ramifications which are being studied at the present time have evolved from basic beliefs that include the following:

1. A university cannot stand aside from the moral issues and problems of society.
2. A university cannot pursue a line or policy, either by action or apathy—such as preventing the publication of research—which conflicts with its primary duty to higher learning.
3. A university, in its long-term contribution to the community, should be involved in philosophical, religious, and political issues, and should provide a source of leadership for social and political change.
4. Acceptance of such a stance as basic to a university in the modern world requires that its concern should be made clear, not for the establishment of some new orthodoxy, but rather for the persistent enlightened exploration of problems for the common good.[7]

In both the United States and Canada, there is great concern over the role of universities in contemporary societies. A marked difference is, however, found in the governance of academic institutions in these two countries, in that universities and colleges in the United States usually operate under the unique supervision of a lay governing board.

It is to this lay board that institutions are responsible. The rights and privileges of presidents, faculty, and students are determined by the governing board. Among the duties and responsibilities of the governing board are:

1. The determination and establishment of the fundamental policies of the institution.
2. The selection and appointment of the president, and the delegation to him of powers commensurate with his responsibilities.
3. The preservation of capital assets and the financial integrity of the institution.
4. The functions of a board of review for the actions of the administrative officers.
5. The appointment of members of the faculty.[8]

The typical American college or university, therefore, begins with an authoritarian chain of command from the trustees through the president to the campus. This lay board of governors, then, has the over-all responsibility for maintaining the integrity of the institution under its governance.

If an institution is well organized, clear definitions of function and authority will be evident and "like" functions at every organizational level will be placed under the supervision of a single administrator. There are four principal areas of administration in an institution of higher education. They are:

1. Academic administration.
2. Student personnel service administration.
3. Business administration.
4. Public relations and extension services administration.

Because this discussion is primarily about academic administration, only a brief review of this administrative area will be provided.

The second organizational pattern, which is not necessarily new but has been adopted by several schools in recent years, is the divisional plan whereby all subjects are grouped under broad categories, such as the humanities, the social sciences, and the natural sciences. Supporters of this administrative plan believe that it favors greater coordination of curriculum content among departments, eliminates the duplication of courses, and assists students to solve problems that cut across departmental lines. It would appear that such an organization of offerings would be more beneficial in small institutions or institutions of a liberal or general college nature.

In either of the above administrative patterns, instruction and research are the primary concerns of both the president and vice-president (or dean) for academic affairs. The history of American higher education supports the contention that institutions of higher learning make significant progress only under the leadership of an outstanding president. There is no doubt that the present role of the university president has become much more difficult and demanding than ever before. In an attempt to clarify the role of the chief executive officer and to specify basic principles for his administration, the American Association of State Colleges and Universities prepared a statement of the basic rights and responsibilities of college and university presidents. The following is a brief overview of this statement:

BASIC PRINCIPLES

1. A college or university exists to serve the general society which created it and which supports it; such an institution does not belong to a particular group of persons within the society or within that institution.

2. A college or university serves many constituencies—faculty, staff, students, alumni, and parents of students.

3. Legally defined, a college or university does not consist of any one or combination of these constituencies. In the eyes of the law, a college or university is its governing board, most commonly known as the board of trustees.

4. The major functions of a public college or university are teaching, learning, scholarship, research, and appropriate public service, as determined ultimately by the board of trustees. These functions cannot be illegally interfered with or eliminated except at the risk of destroying the institution.

THE ROLE OF THE PRESIDENT

The president serves as chief executive officer of the college or university. In this capacity, he reports and recommends directly to the board of trustees. Although the president listens to the voices of all constituent groups, it must be recognized that he functions primarily as the administrative arm of the board and that all legal governing authority resides with the board.

The selection of the president is the board of trustees' most important decision. Having once made that selection, the board must insure that the president is vested with all the authority necessary to carry out the duties and responsibilities for which he is held accountable. As chief executive officer, the president is responsible for recommending broad policies for consideration by the board and implementing these policies once they have been approved by the board. Major areas of presidential responsibility include:

1. The direction of current and long-range planning related to institutional goals, academic programs and teaching approaches, research, public service, enrollment projections, and physical plant development.

2. The development and maintenance of an appropriate administrative organization and policy-making structure for the most efficient and effective utilization of institutional resources.

3. The development and maintenance of a personnel system concerned with the recruitment, selection, assignment, supervision, evaluation, and promotion and tenure of all personnel employed by the institution.

4. The preparation and presentation of the financial budget and the allocation and supervision of all appropriations and other funds that finance any activities under the jurisdiction of the college.

5. The development and maintenance of the facilities and equipment necessary for the support of the university's functions.

THE VICE-PRESIDENT FOR ACADEMIC AFFAIRS

The general duties and responsibilities of a vice-president for academic affairs and his role in the university administrative structure involve the following:

1. The direction of the academic activities of the university.

2. Serving as chief advisor to the president in matters pertaining to policies of the institution.

3. The formulation of policies and the presentation of them to the faculty or the president for consideration.

4. Directing the attention of the faculty to changing educational thought and practice, with particular reference to present academic trends in higher education.

5. The transmission to the president of academic budget recommendations.

6. The supervision of curricula, courses, and methods of instruction.

7. The supervision of academic programs and the academic welfare of students.

8. The overall administration of the academic disciplinary problems of the institution.

9. Serving as a member of the administrative council.

10. The nomination of faculty members for tenure and promotion in cooperation with academic departments and committees.

By the middle of the 19th century, as more specialization in academic areas became necessary, college faculties began to subdivide into departments, which were administered by a department *head* or *chairman*. The primary responsibility of a department chairperson is that of leadership, and his or her major duty is that of making recommendations. Such recommendations include proposals for course offerings, time schedules, academic curricula at both the undergraduate and graduate levels, employment of faculty and staff, the nature and use of departmental facilities, and policies for faculty retainment, salary, and promotion.

RIGHTS AND RESPONSIBILITIES OF FACULTY AND STUDENTS

If one were to ask a university or college professor, "What are your primary rights and responsibilities as a member of an academic faculty?" the majority of academics would probably reply, "To exercise and cherish academic freedom." This right and responsibility includes the diffusion of knowledge through teaching, the augmentation of knowledge through investigation (research) and publication, and the attainment and application of expertise to the problems of a particular discipline and to society as a whole. These, briefly stated, are the primary reasons for the existence of a college faculty.

It is of vital importance to note that most faculties are primarily employed by academic institutions to convey knowledge, usually by teaching. Accordingly, one must assume that students attend (by free choice) an institution of higher education *to learn, because they believe that the vast majority of the faculty of their chosen institution have acquired knowledge which they themselves must acquire because they deem this knowledge or training to be of vital importance for their future.* This premise must not be overlooked by any administration. Many educators believe that without some *administrative discipline* there can be no effective education at any level.

The turbulence and dissension experienced by higher education in the United States during the sixties and early seventies has been tempered by an influx of new students who are concerned with the problems of society yet are anxious to return to the search for a worthwhile and meaningful education. Now, in the middle seventies, the academic pendulum has swung a full course. The dogmatic, authoritarian, administrative dictatorships of the early 20th century had, in the late 1960's, given way to administrations in which power and discipline were abandoned for student rule. The 1970's witnessed a return to sensibility, with students, faculty, and administrators working together. This return to cooperative university government saw the demise of several radical student organizations, including the 42-year-old Canadian Union of Students, which was disbanded as a result of its own radical politics.

Outbursts of student violence during the 1960's, bolstered by several sweeping court decisions, forced the nation's schools and colleges to recognize that youth is no barrier to possessing and exercising rights. Institutions have undergone and are undergoing a change of both faculty and student attitudes regarding the rights and responsibilities of professors and students. The American Civil Liberties Union (ACLU) has done much to provide factual information and to support the constitutional rights of students. A 1971 White House Educational Task Force on Youth declared that America's democratic system is rooted in the belief that all citizens who are affected by the system should have a voice in deciding how the system is to be run. This concept of a representative democracy has not been universally accepted in our nation's educational institutions. The task force went on to state that students must be thought of as *participants* in, and not merely recipients of, the educational process. Several recommendations of the early seventies urged that students have a voice in the policy and governance of their educational system and that all educational institutions adopt codes of student

454 / **Physical Education in Colleges and Universities**

rights, responsibilities, and conduct. Student codes should define the legal and social relationships of the institution to the student and of the student to the institution in such areas as speech, demonstrations, dress, housing, and class attendance. "In order for any aspect of society to maintain itself as a functioning community, a framework must be provided within which its several members may operate. Historically, on many university and college campuses, such frameworks have remained unwritten or ambiguous."[10]

Statements of student conduct, rights, and responsibilities usually include the state or local laws under which an institution must function, so that both students and faculty may be aware of the governing policies of the college or university. These laws are usually then augmented to include resolutions pertaining to rights and responsibilities by the board of trustees or the governing body of the institution. In addition, principles of student life are presented, noting that the freedom of individuals is never absolute but is subject to reasonable restrictions. Statements of student responsibilities and a code for the operation of the institution are usually intended to set forth general principles of rights and responsibilities in relation to the institution. Such principles serve as *guidelines* for all members of the university community to follow in the conduct of matters pertaining to student and faculty life. Both student and faculty codes are usually formulated by select committees made up of students, faculty, and the administration.

In the discussion and formulation of the rights and responsibilities of faculty and students, an administrator in today's academic climate must believe in and support the need for an "administrative discipline" which will make it possible for teachers to teach and students to study, and which will prevent external and internal power factions from interfering with academic organization and administration. In turn, an administrator *must* be provided with the necessary support from his superiors as well as the power and authority to cope successfully

with the problems of his organization. If these conditions are not met, it is doubtful that higher education as we know it in America today will survive in the 21st century.

ACADEMIC ADMINISTRATION AND THE CURRICULUM

Student and faculty interests and their demands for more participation in the policy-making decisions of institutions have led to important curriculum changes. These changes have been labeled everything from "innovation" to "faddism." They have contained, among other things, pass-fail grading systems, academic calendar changes, and student-directed academic programs.

For the most part these changes were not necessarily new—many had been attempted or were already in operation in other institutions. What is extremely interesting is the fact that these changes or innovations did not reflect any change in the basic philosophy, objectives, or assumptions of the institutions involved.

Perhaps the most influential factor in program and curriculum change during the 1970's has been the monetary cutbacks experienced by state colleges and universities. In many instances, programs and curricula were reduced or completely curtailed by university administrators because of insufficient funding. In one or two instances, it was reported that large universities had placed academic departments or divisions in "receivership," which is fairly common in business and industry but is almost unheard of in higher education.

Educational Philosophies, Goals, and the College Curriculum

Educational administrators at any level in the educational spectrum should be familiar with the various educational philosophies (rationalism, progressivism, and so on) upon which college and university curricula are founded. The administrator must then attempt to determine the expressed philosophy of his institution as a whole and of the chief administrators who provide the overall administrative leadership. Administrative decision making (regarding curriculum) should then be based upon the attainment of goals in keeping with these expressed philosophical beliefs.

The American university has sometimes been compared to a "firehouse on the corner" that responds to any and all requests for assistance. For a long time, thanks to faithful and generous public support, this appeared to be a role which most universities accepted. In recent years, however, many educational, social, and economic circumstances have arisen which have made it necessary for many institutions to reassess their goals. During the 1960's there were new demands, especially from students, for colleges to assume new roles and serve new interests. During the early 1970's a widespread financial crisis made it imperative for colleges to specify the objectives to which limited resources could be directed. With approximately 2600 institutions of higher education in the United States, the development of institutional goals as a conceptual tool took on new meaning, as goals are extremely useful in deliberating, determining, and evaluating policy and practice in educational organizations. The broad purposes of teaching, research, and public service are by necessity provided in numerous ways, as only some 300 of the 2600 institutions grant doctorate degrees, while some 350 colleges and universities are controlled by the Roman Catholic Church and some 450 colleges are affiliated with one or another of the Protestant denominations. In attempting to meet the needs of many diverse institutions, the institutional research program for higher education of the Educational Testing Service developed an *institutional goals inventory*. The IGI was developed as a tool to help college communities delineate goals and establish priorities.[11] The IGI, by assisting the development of clear conceptions of institutional goals, assists colleges and universities in putting the goals to work. Institutional goals are used as follows: (1) as fundamentals of policy, (2) as general decision guides, (3) in planning, (4) in management information systems, and (5) in institutional evaluation. Descriptions of the 20 goal areas in the institutional goals inventory are included in the manual.

Curriculum Criticisms and Trends

Criticisms of the curriculum by both students and faculty are often laid at the feet of the administrator. These criticisms appear to be common for all disciplines and revolve around (1) unstated objectives, (2) overlap, repetition, and boredom, and (3) stereotyped approaches to instruction. Students have also complained that there is a lack of "intellectual stimulation," especially during the freshman year. It is of interest to note that faculty interests, publicity, institutional prestige, opportunism, and experience in responding to pressures or to availability of financial resources are more potent determiners of specific change than is deliberation based on educational goals, social needs, and the abilities and aspirations of students.

Much has been accomplished and more remains to be undertaken in alleviating criticism of the curriculum. The participation of competent and mature students on departmental and institutional curriculum committees has greatly helped to eliminate unstated objectives and the offering of outmoded courses. Student evaluation of faculty has also contributed to the improvement of instruction.

Undergraduate curriculum trends have definitely moved toward more individualized learning experiences, and students and faculty alike have been openly critical of courses that are mandatory for entire student populations. It is envisioned that within the next few years very few, if any, institutional requirements will remain. A modern university curriculum must be functionally viewed by the student. Higher education is far too costly and time-consuming to embrace curricular offerings that are illogically conceived and poorly taught.

PHYSICAL EDUCATION AND HIGHER EDUCATION

The purpose of this chapter is to present a brief introduction to selected general concepts of the administration of higher education. Now that these concepts have been discussed, it is important to review the general nature and scope of professional physical education and how this discipline takes its place in the overall college or university structure.

Administrative Organization

The history of physical education in America reveals that the many and varied aspects of this discipline had a closely connected association with interscholastic and intercollegiate athletics. As athletic programs grew in magnitude and in importance to the general public, professional programs of study housed under athletic administrations began to suffer. For this reason many of the larger institutions desirous of promoting nationally prominent athletic programs changed their administrative organization in order to provide an administratively independent department, school, or college of physical education or of health, physical education, and recreation.

The specifics of such administrative organization will be discussed in a later chapter; however, it is important to note here that, as is perhaps true of all changes, this separation of physical education from intercollegiate athletics created new administrative problems. *There is no doubt, however, that the positive aspects of this separation greatly outweigh the problems that have arisen.* In smaller institutions, which do not appear to be seeking national prominence by means of big-time athletics, physical education and intercollegiate athletic programs are offered under a common administration in a department of physical education or of physical education and athletics. The administrative organization of health, phys-

ical education, and recreation and park administration in large institutions varies considerably, then, from that of the so-called "smaller" schools. As course offerings expand, it is common to find the creation of separate departments for each of the disciplines of health education, physical education, and recreation-park administration.

Academic and Service Programs

Academic programs offered by the larger universities in physical education and associated fields are numerous. Usual offerings for most departments of health, physical education, and recreation include courses dealing with the academic areas stated in the title of the department. Not all departments, however, offer major areas of concentration or supporting fields of study in health education, physical education, and professional recreation even though their title suggests otherwise. State colleges and smaller private colleges will usually offer selected major programs of study at the undergraduate level and a limited graduate program toward a master's degree. The professional autonomy being sought by health educators and professional recreation leaders is long overdue, and in small and large institutions alike the desire for autonomous departments in these disciplines is evident.

There is no doubt that the breadth and scope of an administrative unit containing physical education and associated areas make it one of the largest and most complex administrative units in higher education. It is quite common to find the administrator of such a division responsible for physical education activity programs, intramurals, professional physical education for both men and women, recreational use of numerous outdoor and indoor facilities, and in some cases the over-all administration of professional programs of study in recreation and park administration. This wide diversification of academic offerings and service programs has created many administrative and organizational problems.

Financing Programs

Institutions of higher learning are basically financed by the (1) allocation of state funds, (2) appropriation of federal funds, (3) student fees, and (4) private gifts and contributions. The generation of monies to finance higher education programs is one of the most critical issues of our time. Many colleges and universities are feeling the financial squeeze because state legislatures cannot meet the budgetary requests of institutions faced with increases in operational expenses that far exceed available monies. The end results of such situations are bare "hold-the-line" budgets that do not permit expanded academic and service programs and reveal increased pressure for the procurement of federal grants and research funds.

This financial climate, then, is the one under which college and university administrators are forced to operate in many of our institutions. The ramifications of insufficient institutional funding are perhaps more severely felt by administrative divisions of physical education than by other academic divisions. Physical education departments, divisions, schools, and colleges must generate funds primarily by legislative-university appropriation. It is generally true that when monies are in short supply, non-academic or service offerings of the institution are cut back or curtailed. This makes it extremely difficult for the administrator in charge of intramural sports programs, recreational activity programs, and physical education activity programs to provide funds for ever-increasing student and faculty demands. Limited budgets have thus promoted the "art of grantsmanship" in order to attempt to obtain federal funding for various academic and research programs. It is all too evident that such monies are in short supply for pertinent areas that are a vital part of professional physical education. For this reason accusations have been made that some researchers are promoting research that has little if any relationship to the profession in order to perpetuate and expand research facilities by means of federal funds.

State Appropriations Per Capita

	Per Capita Appropriation	Rank		Per Capita Appropriation	Rank
Alabama	$ 44.20	37	Montana	$ 52.04	22
Alaska	107.04	1	Nebraska	55.35	19
Arizona	70.85	3	Nevada	51.87	23
Arkansas	39.97	45	New Hampshire	22.75	50
California	65.33	8	New Jersey	39.50	46
Colorado	66.97	6	New Mexico	54.71	21
Connecticut	43.80	38	New York	64.04	12
Delaware	64.93	9	North Carolina	62.85	14
Florida	50.96	25	North Dakota	49.81	28
Georgia	48.63	33	Ohio	35.95	48
Hawaii	69.35	4	Oklahoma	39.12	47
Idaho	62.88	13	Oregon	57.32	16
Illinois	55.03	20	Pennsylvania*	41.00	44
Indiana	46.36	35	Rhode Island	50.20	27
Iowa	51.76	24	South Carolina	64.86	10
Kansas	55.73	18	South Dakota	47.24	34
Kentucky	50.52	26	Tennessee	41.13	43
Louisiana	49.29	32	Texas	42.26	41
Maine	43.65	39	Utah	64.57	11
Maryland	44.38	36	Vermont	42.81	40
Massachusetts*	34.44	49	Virginia	49.38	30
Michigan	57.61	15	Washington	66.84	7
Minnesota	49.33	31	West Virginia	49.71	29
Mississippi	56.25	17	Wisconsin*	71.69	2
Missouri	41.24	42	Wyoming	67.70	5
			Total U.S.	51.86	

* Estimated appropriation

Figure 16–2. Estimates of the 1974 state populations were used to calculate the per-capita appropriations for higher education for 1974–1975. (Courtesy of *The Chronicle of Higher Education.*)

The administrative specifics of budgetary organization, requests, and expenditures are presented in a later chapter. It is, however, deemed necessary to point out here that program offerings of *quality* are mandatory if an administrator expects to be able to generate funds in today's academic climate. Budgetary requests must be well organized and presented for sound, functional programs of high quality and of definite and unquestionable value to the institution.

With total expenditures for higher education in the United States approaching some 25 billion dollars, the recommendations on who should pay for higher education are being viewed with deep concern. Student payments for tuition and other fees approximate some 21 per cent of the total cost of financing colleges and universities. State and local governments contribute an additional 30 per cent, and the federal government provides 28 per cent. Gifts and endowment earnings account for some 10 per cent, with auxiliary enterprises and other activities contributing an additional 11 per cent. With costs rising at an unpredictable rate, and with equipment and material in relatively short supply, institutions are carefully scrutinizing cost analyses for academic offerings. In 1973, a report of the Carnegie Commission of Higher Education stated that the taxpayers' share of monetary outlays in higher education should be increased modestly over the next several years as student-aid funds expand to assist students from low-income families. This report also recommended that states with regressive tax structures develop more progressive tax systems in the interests of greater equity and adequacy in the financing of education. It was also concluded that the balance of public support for higher education must shift over the coming decade if the goal of universal access is to be achieved, and that federal funds should partially relieve the states of added financial burdens. The Commission also recommended that federal support of higher education gradually expand so that by the 1980's about one-half of the cost of higher education will be borne by the federal government. Private colleges and universities must carefully study their educational costs per student and consider restructuring their tuition charges, making tuition relatively low for lower-division students and somewhat higher for upper-division students.

Colleges and schools of education that increased their output of graduates during the last 25 years to overcome a reported teacher shortage are today facing a teacher surplus. As a result of this surplus, which began in the early seventies, some institutions curbed their enrollments through selective admissions, while many others relied on attempting to counsel students out of the field by warning them of the relatively poor job prospects. The National Education Association estimates that some 240,000 new teachers each year compete for only 116,000 positions. The NEA also reports that this oversupply could grow to as much as 730,000 teachers by 1977 if nothing is done to create more jobs or to limit access to the profession. This problem of a shrinking demand and an expanding supply is especially critical in the field of professional physical education. However, some school personnel experts predict that the low point in enrollment will be reached by 1975 and that after 1985 enrollments will grow rapidly. By 1990, if teaching programs continue to be curtailed, a severe shortage of teachers may exist.

For decades, institutions of higher learning have been justifying their operational budgets to state legislative bodies on the basis of increased student enrollments. It is extremely difficult to re-educate legislators to the "quality, not quantity" concept after they have been "instructed" in the other direction for so long. Physical education organizations have also played the "numbers game" for many years and are now faced with a severe curtailment of programs because of decreasing enrollments. It is indeed unfortunate that some departments and schools continue to actively recruit students no matter what their interests or qualifications in order to attempt to justify the preservation of large physical plants and faculties. Some educators believe that they do not have the moral right to restrict entry into the profession, even when positions are scarce. In many instances, the decision to limit enrollments has been prompted not only by the teacher surplus but also by the money squeeze in higher education that has left schools of education without the faculty to handle additional students.

REFERENCES

1. Thomas E. Blackwell: *College and University Administration.* New York: The Center for Applied Research in Education, Inc., 1966, p. 5.
2. Robert H. Kroepsch: *The Study of Academic Administration.* Boulder, Colorado: Western Interstate Commission for Higher Education, 1963.
3. F. C. Rosencrance: *The American College and Its Teachers.* New York: The MacMillan Co., 1962, p. 91.
4. *Ibid.,* p. 104.

5. Carroll L. Shartle: *Executive Performance and Leadership.* Englewood Cliffs, N. J.: Prentice-Hall, Inc., 1956, pp. 117–118.
6. Buell G. Gallagher: "Who Runs the Institution?" In *The Rights and Responsibilities of Faculty and Students.* Boulder, Colorado: Western Interstate Commission for Higher Education, October, 1965.
7. Brian MacArthur: "Who Should Govern Universities?" *The Chronicle of Higher Education,* October 16, 1972.
8. Blackwell, *op. cit.,* p. 8.
9. Bernard F. Engel: "So You Want To Be Department Chairman?" *The Chronicle of Higher Education,* May 6, 1974.
10. William D. Carlson, President, The University of Wyoming: *Student Conduct, Rights and Responsibilities.* January, 1973.
11. Institutional Research Program for Higher Education: *Institutional Goals Inventory.* Princeton, N.J.: Educational Testing Service, 1973.
12. Paul L. Dressel and Frances H. DeLisle: "Undergraduate Curriculum Trends." Michigan State Office of Institutional Research, American Council on Education, 1969.

SUGGESTED READINGS

Browder, Lesley H., *et al.: Developing an Educationally Accountable Program.* Berkeley, Calif.: McCutchan Publishing Corp., 1973.
Frank, Roland G.: "Community Education—A Role for Higher Education." *JOHPER,* April, 1974, p. 26.
Popham, W. James, and Eva L. Baker: *Establishing Instructional Goals.* Englewood Cliffs, N.J.: Prentice-Hall, Inc., 1970.
Redfern, George B.: "Evaluating Administrator Productivity." *School Administrator,* AASA, April, 1974, p. 18.
The Chronicle of Higher Education (selected issues).
"Thinking About Outcome—Oriented Planning in Higher Education: An Introduction." Boulder Colorado: National Center for Higher Education Management Systems, WICHE, Vol. 2, No. 1, 1972.

THE TWO—YEAR
COLLEGE—ORGANIZATION FOR
PURPOSE

PHYSICAL EDUCATION AND
INTRAMURALS

COMMUNITY COLLEGE ATHLETICS

CHAPTER SEVENTEEN

Physical Education and the Community College

Perhaps the educational institution most neglected by authors concerned with the administration of physical education programs has been the American two-year college. The available data on the recent growth of two-year colleges in the United States reveal an astonishing development. In the period from 1921 to 1922, for example, there were approximately 16,000 students enrolled in some 207 community colleges in this country. By 1968 this figure had climbed to 1,954,116 students enrolled in 993 colleges, with a total of 11,215 administrative employees.

By late 1974 public community colleges were no longer growing at the phenomenal rates of the 1960's. Like their senior "partners," community colleges began to redefine their mission and to look for new kinds of students in an effort to maintain the momentum they had enjoyed during their boom. In the mid seventies only five or six new colleges were opened each year in comparison to as many as 50 per year in the 1960's. Those educators with a sincere interest in community college development urge the re-emphasis of goals stressing a wide range of community services.

During the fall semester of 1974 approximately 3,400,000 students were enrolled in some 1000 public community colleges throughout the United States, according to the American Association of Junior Colleges. By the fall semester of 1977 these enrollments were expected to increase to slightly over 4,000,000 for some 1200 institutions.

In spite of these data, very little pertinent information is available regarding physical education and athletic programs at the community college level. No doubt much of this neglect is due to the many similarities that exist between the physical education activities and intramural offerings of four-year institutions and those of the two-year colleges. The physical education administrator in the two-year institution must, however, remember that if the college does believe that its *raison d'être* is (a) terminal education, (b) transfer education, and (c) community service, physical education programs must meet these objectives.

THE TWO–YEAR COLLEGE—ORGANIZATION FOR PURPOSE

In the introductory paragraphs of this chapter the terms "junior college" and "community college" were used almost interchangeably. The distinctions between these terms are perhaps best defined by Hillway:

Junior college may be regarded as the generic term to identify an institution of higher learning which offers two years of education beyond the high school. Community college is the name applied to an institution which is primarily concerned with providing educational services on the collegiate level to a particular community. The community college draws a student body almost exclusively from among the graduates of the local high schools, while the typical junior colleges may draw from a wide area. The community college most frequently is under public control and is a part of the local school system, whereas the junior college not primarily interested in community service may be privately or church controlled.[1]

In recent years the term *community college* has come to be widely used as a designation for most junior colleges. Junior colleges as such originated in the United States as extensions of high schools or academies and as transformations of some church-related colleges

from four-year to two-year institutions. Some two-year colleges were also developed to provide post-high school education for rural areas; other colleges were created by philanthropic groups.

Community colleges are usually designed to achieve educational goals, organizational goals, goals related to four-year institutions, and goals related to the community. These goals were expressed as early as 1924.[2] In 1947 a President's Commission on Higher Education proposed reduced emphasis upon the preparatory or transfer function and more upon the terminal function, for two-year "community-serving" institutions. This commission stated the primary functions of the two-year college to be: (1) training for the semi-professions, or those occupations requiring no more than two years of college; (2) general education for students who will complete their formal education at the end of the 14th grade; (3) adult education in the late-afternoon and evening classes; and (4) some provision for those young people who will transfer after two years to colleges offering more advanced degrees. Many educators knowledgeable about present-day two-year colleges agree that programs now tend to promote curricula in the first two years that will be sufficient for transfer to a four-year institution. The unique service of two-year institutions will be lost if this apparent trend continues. It is essential to remember, however, that not all these institutions are alike and a fairly unanimous agreement appears to exist among educators that a junior college or community college should provide whatever educational services are needed for a particular student body in a particular community.

Most community colleges are created by voters in order to meet the needs for post-high school education and training in a particular city or county. Colleges are dedicated to assisting the individual in preparing for a career, life in the community, and leisure time, by providing continuing educational experiences. In order to meet these needs, courses are offered in the areas of academic, vocational-technical, and community services education. Academic programs prepare students for transfer to four-year institutions, while vocational-technical programs provide up to two years of experience and education, with the aim of preparing students to gainfully enter the world of work. Community services education may consist of work leading to the equivalent of a high school diploma or may provide general information and cultural opportunities. An expressed goal of many community colleges is to make the college an educational institution for all people.

Financial Support

Privately controlled two-year institutions of both independent and denominational structure derive their main financial support from student fees, private gifts, and income from endowments. These institutions usually do not receive public financing. Public two-year colleges, on the other hand, do receive public appropriations, with such funds coming from varying sources in each state. Chief sources of income are (1) student tuition, (2) state appropriations, (3) federal appropriations, (4) property taxes, (city, county, district, etc.), and (5) limited funds from private gifts and institutional earnings. It is of interest to note that state governments are providing more and more of the monies necessary to operate public two-year colleges.

"The community college, largely dependent upon local tax support in the past, now looks toward the state for the major share of its financial means. What the state is willing to pay for is expected to have a lot to do with the kinds of services offered by the institutions. And there are numerous examples of financial support patterns that impede rather than encourage movement toward the generally perceived goals of the community college."[3] Some educators predict that within 10 years the community college is going to be primarily a community service institution and yet, in several states, state funds have not been available for that function. In many

states, in order to determine suitable means for financial support of community and junior colleges, the state must first determine the functional role of these institutions within their total state educational system.

Administrative Organization

There are two main types of administrative organization for two-year publicly supported colleges—local control and state control. Such public institutions are usually the outgrowth of the upward extension of secondary schools. Locally controlled colleges are usually administered by boards of education or trustees elected on a county, district, local, or municipal level. Colleges controlled by the state are administered in most cases by elected or appointed state boards of education. Local public colleges are primarily supported out of the general budget for the school district in which they are located, with state-controlled colleges usually financed by state appropriations. California, which is considered to have an advanced two-year college system, employs three types of public junior college districts: (1) the local school district, coterminous with the high school district; (2) the union district, embracing two or more contiguous high school districts; and (3) the county, including all county territory not already in a high school district.[4]

"Good governance, whatever its style or participatory dimensions, is that which moves the college to better service for students and community. It lays the base, through broad policy formations, for the right things to happen. Administration then arranges the action in accordance with purpose."[5] The two-year college trustee is a relatively new concept in the history of governing boards for academic institutions in the United States. Approximately one-half of the two-year college governing boards have come into existence within the last 20 years. Over half of publicly controlled community and junior colleges have their own local governing boards, which usually have between seven and nine members, with a majority of the trustees being elected by popular district elections. In the 1970's more and more of the important administrative decisions concerning the development of community colleges were being made by individuals who were not necessarily directly involved in institutional operations. The creation of state-level boards of control caused a shift in the community college power structure and resulted in the new position of State Director of community college education.

The internal administrative structure for the majority of junior colleges and community colleges generally follows that found in colleges and universities. A basic principle for community college administration is that such institutions should be component parts of the public education system of the state and be integrated with this system.

Student-Centered Curricula

The curriculum for two-year colleges developed as the colleges themselves

developed, from many different sources with many different features and varied offerings. The availability of a wide variety of curricular offerings is said to be one of the distinguishing features of the two-year college movement. Another distinguishing feature has been the belief that American community colleges are the only educational institution that can truly be considered an American social invention. The adoption of a philosophy of equal educational opportunity for all and the promotion of open admissions created colleges which were *not* an offshoot of the classical higher education pattern in the United States.

A basic two-year college curriculum provides courses in the areas of general education, pre-professional or preparatory education, and vocational education. General education is considered to be the nonspecialized portion of the student's program, although it is very difficult to separate general education from pre-professional requisites in many instances. Specific undergraduate professional offerings related to transfer programs are considered as pre-professional

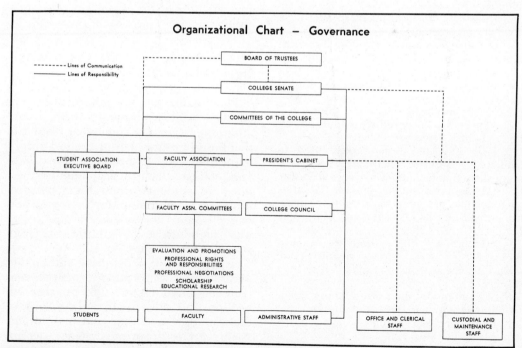

Figure 17–1. The organizational chart of a community college. Note that several distinct groups contribute to the governance system. (Courtesy of Daniel P. Simon, AACJC.)

curricula, whereas vocational programs are offered for students who desire skills and understandings necessary for full-time employment after leaving the two-year college. It is generally considered that community college programs that are geared toward transfer to four-year institutions attract students who are in the upper half of their high school graduating classes in academic aptitude. Career programs are, of course, open and available to any student who wishes to pursue immediate occupational enrichment. Open admission policies are prevalent in many community and junior colleges, and an increased amount of administrative time is now devoted to the inclusion of relevant work-related education. An increasing attempt is also being made to shape the curriculum to the students rather than shaping the students to the curriculum.

Several years ago, at the 50th anniversary convention of the American Association of Junior Colleges, it was emphasized that community colleges should be:

1. Available to all in the community who need service.
2. Responsive to local needs in offering a diversity of programs, many of which need not lead to degrees or to any formal certification.
3. Truly comprehensive, by catering to a variety of student needs, from vocational training programs through programs providing transfer credits to four-year institutions.
4. Especially concerned with adult education and mid-career refresher programs.
5. Fully involved in and committed to community service, including the willingness to operate "outreach" programs away from the campus and to provide facilities such as day care centers to assure that education is made available to everyone who wants it.
6. Supportive of curricular experimentation, encouraging new definitions of what a course is or who is qualified to be a teacher.
7. Willing to find their own identity rather than relying on standards and definitions that are "traditional" and "accepted."[6]

Accountability, or the "management of change," has come to community colleges just as it has to the majority of four-year degree granting institutions. For the community college, accountability means its obligation to answer to its constituency for carrying out delegated responsibilities; in other words, the obligation of members of the college to produce an account-for-results column, in terms of the objective or assignments which have been delegated.[7]

Physical Education and Intramurals

In addition to promoting the idea that universal higher education is the right of any person who can profit from it, community colleges were also founded on the basic ideal that they exist to serve the society which supports them. As stated previously, community colleges should be flexible institutions, and their campuses should reflect the college's willingness for innovation and experimentation. Where, then, do physical education intramural and intercollegiate athletic programs find their place within such an organization as it attempts to answer the call for educational accountability?

Organization and Administration

The organization and administration of two-year college physical education and athletic programs is somewhat similar to that found in the small or limited enrollment four-year institution. Many two-year colleges have in fact opened their doors to students when their physical education department (for both men and women) consisted of only a single faculty member and a borrowed high school gymnasium.

As their enrollments grew and faculty and facilities were added, the two-year college tended to pattern its physical education and athletic organization after that found in most four-year institutions. A director or department head was appointed to provide the administrative leadership for physical education (usually for both men and women), intramurals, and athletics. In large two-year colleges, subadministrative positions were established as the "span of control" grew larger, and administrative authority and responsibility were delegated to heads or coordinators of men's physical education, women's physical education, and intramural activities. In institutions where a large athletic program had developed, a director of athletics was also appointed.

As in the four-year college, the departmental or divisional administrator in the two-year college is responsible to either an academic dean or the college president. In large two-year institutions, the chief administrator for intercollegiate athletics may be directly responsible to the college president or to one of his vice-presidents. Community colleges tend to pattern their physical education and athletic organization after the structures found in four-year institutions, but in so doing, many colleges tend to lose sight of their basic aims and objectives in meeting the needs of the local community.

It is very unfortunate that most two-year institutions emphasize their intercollegiate athletic programs rather than their intramural programs for men and women. As was stated earlier, the major objectives of most two-year colleges are terminal education, transfer education, and community service. With these objectives in mind, one of the first programs which the college should offer is a quality intramural program. The program should be varied enough so as to meet the activity and skill needs of the entire student population. When feasible, the programs should be coeducational and should reflect a harmonious and close cooperative relationship between men's and women's departments. Indoor and outdoor facilities should reflect the administrative objective of providing worthwhile physical activity for *all* students. If intramural programs of quality are going to materialize in two-year colleges, boards of trustees, presidents, and physical education administrators must provide the necessary leadership.

Basic Instruction Programs

Most community college physical education programs have been patterned after the programs used in four-year institutions. Typical of many such programs are course offerings in the areas of developmental activities, recreational activities, aquatic activities, and, in some instances, introductory courses in "human movement." The two-year college may or may not have a required basic instruction or "service" program. Students who are pursuing programs of study for possible transfer to four-year institutions elect the necessary courses or credits of physical activity in order to meet the requirements of the college to which they wish to transfer.

The curriculum of physical education activities should be formulated to meet the physical and recreational needs of the students for the rest of their lives. That is not to say that *all* course offerings must meet this need, but a vast majority of the two-year programs should be so designed. As students master the skills taught in activity courses, they may wish to participate in intramural programs to improve their proficiency and to compete against their peers. Physical education activity programs should not merely give "lip service" to the development of improved health habits, better physical well-being, and valuable recreational skills, but should actually provide measurable results. Each physical education faculty member should be held accountable for his or her contribution to the overall objectives of the program. In the "management-by-objectives" process, specific objectives may be applied to any area, field, subject, discipline, body of knowledge, or desired teaching outcome.

As the community college formulates its taxonomy of objectives, physical education departments must scrutinize their formal and informal offerings in order to determine how they contribute to:

a. *Policy objectives:* derived from the mission of the college and expressed as goals.

b. *Program objectives:* statements describing predicted measurable accomplishments of a program director and/or department of the college.

1. departmental objectives
2. unit or team objectives
3. personal development

c. *Learner objectives:* measurable predictions of what a learner will be able to do or produce in order to demonstrate his knowledge, skills, preferences, or beliefs resulting from an instructional experience.

1. curricular objectives
2. instructional objectives
3. task objectives

Many physical education and intramural programs in community colleges across the country are committed to total educational accountability. They provide excellent curricula that include individualized programs, extended off-campus programs, and lifetime sports activities that are offered either within the community college or in cooperation with the community at large, in order to provide activities which meet the needs and interests of students of all ages and from all walks of life.

Two-Year Professional Programs

Two-year colleges are faced with the ever-increasing responsibility for the professional preparation of prospective physical educators. Freshmen and sophomores seeking an undergraduate specialization in physical education must be provided with a sound professional beginning if they are to achieve academic success in four-year institutions. Colleges offering the first two years of such specialization must adhere to accepted national standards, as presented by the American Alliance for Health, Physical Education and Recreation.

Some two-year colleges have been most anxious to foster the development of a professional physical education curriculum, in order to insure academic eligibility for varsity athletes. If the administrative leaders of the physical education and athletics program support and promote this type of philosophy, they should be replaced. If replacement is not possible, then professional physical education should be provided with a separate administrative unit.

It is of vital importance that two-year colleges offering freshman-sophomore professional preparation do not attempt to offer highly specialized courses if they do not have the necessary facilities and a well-qualified faculty. Curricula for the first two years of professional preparation and the need for the coordination of transfer programs with four-year colleges and universities will be presented in later chapters dealing with the total undergraduate program of studies.

Faculty

In order to develop and promote an outstanding organization, a college or university administrator must recruit a competent and industrious faculty and staff. In order to obtain a faculty of high quality, an administrator must be able to provide: (a) superior physical facilities; (b) above-average salaries and fringe benefits; (c) a healthful community climate and atmosphere in which to live; and, perhaps most important, (d) an academic atmosphere in which innovation and creativity are welcomed.

In several ways faculty salaries are directly related to projected goals and state and local support. The AAJC reports that the two-year college movement is not confined to public colleges but is reflected in projected enrollments in independent colleges as well. In a College and University Personnel Association research report for 1974–1975, the *mean* salary reported for community college directors of athletics and physical education was $16,791. This mean was compiled using data gathered from 138 individuals. The highest salary reported was in the $28,500 to $28,999 bracket, with the lowest salary reported being under $5000.

As is true for any institution, the two-year college should employ only individuals who are professionally prepared in the subject matter to which they are assigned. It is unfortunate that many colleges continue to employ persons who are not qualified in the curricular areas which they are to teach.

A two-year college faculty member

need not be expected to have completed the doctorate unless such expertise is required for instruction in selected scientific areas. It is, however, beneficial if the departmental or divisional administrator holds an earned doctorate *in physical education,* as this individual must be knowledgeable of the total scope and quality of undergraduate professional and "service" offerings. A "fifth year" of professional training or a master's degree should be a *minimum* requirement for all faculty teaching in professional programs. Selected course work (in physical education) beyond the master's should be encouraged in order to provide individual competencies, which should in turn strengthen instruction.

Nature and Use of Facilities

The design and use of physical education and athletic facilities for a two-year college are (as in other comparisons) very similar to those of the four-year college or university. Planning, modern design concepts, and details regarding the specifics of indoor and outdoor areas are found in a later chapter dealing solely with facilities. It is pertinent at this point, however, to discuss the nature and use of such facilities as they may differ for the two-year college.

The "total campus" of a two-year college should reflect the *comprehensiveness, uniqueness, and purposes* of the college. "It must be a place which enhances the programs of the college and a place where those programs can be readily carried on by the students, faculty, and staff."[8] Physical education-athletic facilities are no different, nor should they be considered different, from other campus facilities and they should be planned and constructed to reflect the comprehensiveness, uniqueness, and purpose of a given institution. It is strongly recommended that both indoor and outdoor facilities be initially designed and constructed to meet the needs and objectives of a quality physical education activity program, intramurals, and freshman-sophomore professional programs (if desired) *for both men and women.* Many, if not all, activity facilities should be designed for coeducational use, as now demanded by federal law if the institution receives federal support funds. The expenditure of state and local funds for duplication of facilities for men and women should not be permitted. An effective "physical environment" will depend directly upon the correct initial organization of space—space for the maximal development of coeducational activities with *limited* allocations for "separated" classes, mass team games, and intercollegiate athletics. The physical plant for all institutions in today's quickly changing educational world must possess the qualities of *expansibility, convertibility,* and *versatility,* but nowhere is this more important than for the two-year college.

When possible, both indoor and outdoor community facilities should be obtained for use when they are not being used to capacity by the local public. Many colleges have been able to construct outstanding indoor areas for specific activities if they have not become "overextended" by attempting to build minimal facilities for many different programs. Once again the administrator must keep in mind the basic objectives of his college and do his utmost to provide a campus that supports these purposes in form and function.

Coordination with Four-Year Institutions

The so-called preparatory or transfer segment of the two-year college curriculum should come under thorough and constant evaluation. The administrator of physical education has the responsibility of providing both physical activity programs and beginning professional courses that will meet the requirements of the four-year colleges in regard to course content, prerequisites, and credit-hour values. Many colleges and universities differ in this regard and "the curriculum-planner for the community college, as a consequence of this lack of uniformity, must become an academic

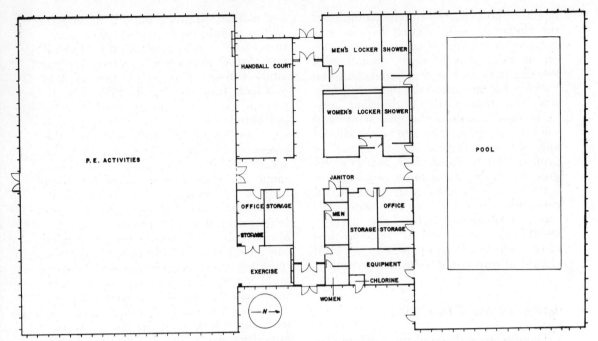

Figure 17–2. An inexpensive and realistic community college physical education building plan. (Courtesy of Laramie County Community College, Cheyenne, Wyoming.)

juggler, keeping as many 'balls' in the air as there are colleges to which the students will transfer."[9]

A close working relationship between the two-year college and four-year institutions in the immediate locale is of vital importance if students are to transfer with a minimum of difficulty. The departmental or divisional administrator of physical education should obtain complete information for activity course content (and credit) as well as those specifics which are pertinent for professional programs. This information should be provided for all advisors involved in the transfer curriculum and students should be made aware of transfer problems that may arise. Information dealing with the physical education activity requirements of four-year institutions should be used both to establish two-year college activity programs and to assist students with the proper selection of such courses. Professional activity-methodology courses and theory courses should be patterned as closely as possible to aca-demically sound courses of well-established institutions offering baccalaureate degrees. It is an excellent procedure to promote "curriculum conferences" between two- and four-year institutions in order to facilitate the transfer process.

In attempting to coordinate two-year college programs with four-year institutions, the administrator should be aware of the characteristics of the transfer student. Studies conducted in the past have shown that approximately 75 per cent of community college students who go on to four-year degree granting institutions do not achieve their bachelor's degrees until their fourth year *after transfer.* Many students also experience a decline in their level of academic achievement, as measured by college grades, and some community college transfer students transfer to institutions whose academic standards they cannot meet. In many states, the present organizational machinery for a smooth articulation between two- and four-year degree granting institutions is inadequate to solve

the types of problems which both the students and the institutions will face.

COMMUNITY COLLEGE ATHLETICS

The most glamorous and exciting, and at the same time the most potentially dangerous, area of student extracurricular participation is the junior college athletic program. The National Junior College Athletic Association was formed on May 14, 1938, largely as a result of athletic meetings held in Fresno, California, in 1937. Since the inception of this organization and the resultant promotion of junior college athletics, two-year colleges have rapidly adopted the athletic pattern of four-year colleges and universities. A very informative early study dealing with junior college athletics was undertaken, the results of which were published by Swenson in 1952. Swenson reported the following:

1. There was little uniformity among the institutions as to what they were attempting to achieve educationally and otherwise through their athletic programs.
2. Most often the objectives stressed were individual achievement in team play and sportsmanship, mental and social development, organic or physical growth, and recreational skill.
3. In very few instances did institutions use athletics to promote the welfare of the student group as a whole, of the faculty, of the academic program, or of the community.
4. The accomplishment of worthwhile objectives in intercollegiate athletic programs was partially prevented by:
   a. Questionable practices in obtaining athletes.
   b. Lack of adequate finances.
   c. Lack of proper facilities.
   d. Inadequate leadership.
   e. Lack of equitable competition within a reasonable distance.
   f. Poor attitudes and habits of athletes.
   g. Incompatible philosophies and standards of schools and the public.[10]

In some areas significant steps have been taken to improve programs since Swenson's report was published. However, pressures to expand schedules and to win have increased, and programs have flourished in spite of the few voices raised to question the value of overemphasized activities. Few, if any, doubts have been raised regarding the value of athletic programs for both men and women, *so long as such programs are kept within reasonable bounds and attempt to meet some institutional objectives.* Many athletic administrators and coaches still emphatically insist that the athletic program in the two-year college *should* be "educational" in nature. Unfortunately, in many institutions educational objectives are ruthlessly subordinated to the main goal—to win. If junior college athletics are indeed contributing to the educational goals of the institution, the athletic program should be *controlled by the college faculty and not by the college administration.*

In an attempt to insure that two-year college physical education-athletic programs do indeed meet (or attempt to meet) the educational and service objectives of the institution, the chairperson of such administrative divisions must be an individual whose personal and educational philosophies are such that he will insure a well-balanced, total program. After service and professional curricula have been developed and a well-balanced intramural program has been initiated, intercollegiate athletics should be introduced on a reasonable and sensible basis *if student interest and demand are present.* If such is not the case, however, athletic programs should not be permitted simply to provide "coaching reputations" and a two-year "athletic farm system" for four-year colleges and universities.

In 1974 community colleges receiving federal financial support, and even those which did not, found themselves facing additional problems as a result of the passage of federal legislation prohibiting discriminatory practices in athletics based on an individual's sex. This important legislation provided the necessary impetus for community colleges to begin the active recruitment of female athletes.

REFERENCES

1. Tyrus Hillway: *The American Two-Year College*. New York: Harper & Brothers, 1958, p. 8.
2. Leonard V. Koos: *The Junior College*. Minneapolis: Research Publications of the University of Minnesota Education Series, No. 5, 1924.
3. Edmund J. Gleazer, Jr.: "AACJC Approach." *Community and Junior College Journal*, December-January, 1973, p. 6.
4. James A. Starrak and Raymond M. Hughes: *The Community College in the United States*. Ames, Iowa: The Iowa State College Press, 1954, p. 33.
5. William G. Shannon: "AACJI Approach, Thoughts on Good Governance." *Community and Junior College Journal*, October, 1973, p. 6.
6. William H. Jones: "Minority Groups Press Demands for Changes in Junior Colleges." *The Chronicle of Higher Education*, March 16, 1970, p. 2.
7. John E. Roueche *et al.: The Management of Change. Accountability and the Community College*. Washington, D.C.: The American Association of Community and Junior Colleges, 1972, p. 23.
8. Thomas E. O'Connell: *Community Colleges—A President's View.* Urbana, Ill.: University of Illinois Press, 1968, p. 95.
9. James W. Reynolds: *The Junior College*. New York: The Center for Applied Research in Education, Inc., 1965, p. 33.
10. Reed K. Swenson: "Status of JUCO Athletic Programs." *NJCAA Bulletin*, June, 1952.

SUGGESTED READINGS

"Athletics and Social Crisis." *JOHPER*, April, 1972, pp. 39–50.

Freischlag, Jerry: "Competency-Based Instruction." *JOHPER*, January, 1974, p. 29.

Hodges, Patrick B.: "Status and Structure of Physical Education in Public Two-Year Colleges of the Midwest." *JOHPER*, June, 1974, p. 13.

Johnson, William P. and Richard P. Kleva: "The Community Dimension of College Physical Education." *JOHPER*, April, 1973, p. 40.

Junior College Journal (selected readings).

"Leisure Today: Community Education." *JOHPER*, April, 1974, pp. 33–62.

CHAPTER EIGHTEEN

College and University Programs

The organization, supervision, and administration of college and university physical education programs is a difficult and very complicated task. The administration of such an organization is usually so diverse that few (if any) other academic administrators are faced with so many varied responsibilities. Many physical education deans, directors, and department heads must not only provide the overall professional leadership for several semiautonomous academic disciplines but also accept the administrative responsibility for one or more "service" subdivisions providing student-faculty recreation and intramural participation. These duties are further complicated by the additional responsibility for a vast array of indoor and outdoor facilities, totaling thousands or millions of dollars of financial expenditure for construction and maintenance.

When the magnitude of such administrative responsibility is realized, the question is quickly asked, "Where are administrators for such organizations obtained and what is their experience and training for such responsible positions?"

471

Unfortunately this question is not easily answered. There are several avenues for advancement (if administration is indeed an advancement) that may place an individual in an administrative position. In some instances, unfortunately, the Peter Principle is followed, which states, "In a hierarchy every employee tends to rise to his level of incompetence."[1] In other cases, young neophytes are employed for difficult situations in which "fools walk in where experienced administrators fear to tread." Fortunately, these two illustrations are not always the rule. Large universities are frequently fortunate in that they have in the past been able to attract seasoned administrators of quality by offering high salaries, above-average fringe benefits, prestigious positions, and a healthy administrative atmosphere.

Decreasing or stabilizing student enrollments together with budgetary limitations have caused several major changes in academic administration. The nation's 2000-odd institutions became concerned with the promotion of quality rather than quantity in supporting academic programs. The capital outlay for institutions of higher education began to stabilize in the late 1960's and actually showed a slight decline during the early 1970's (see Table 19–1). Such funding limitations have made it increasingly difficult for departments and colleges of physical education to attract outstanding administrators from other institutions. Many institutions are experiencing a "no-growth reality" of their tenured and administrative faculty. Because there is decreasing opportunity for the academic advancement of young faculty within departments, there is very little "new growth" created by new additions. The stimulation provided by academic growth is thus limited, as are opportunities to recruit administrators from outside the institution. In some instances, positions of leadership are announced and advertised throughout the country when the institutions do not in fact have the available resources to employ an individual "from the outside." Such "witch hunts" are deemed to be unethical but are caused by state and university regulations demanding that new positions be advertised.

In spite of hold-the-line budgeting, administrative salaries continue to show two-year gains of approximately 10 per cent. The largest average salary increases among college and university administrators generally occur in two areas, both of them dominated by women — nursing and home economics. Presidential salaries in 1975 ranged from some $10,000 to $75,000, with deans or directors of education receiving an average total compensation of approximately $30,000 per year. The average nationwide yearly salary for a director of intercollegiate athletics was reported in 1974 to be $18,742, with a range from less than $10,000 to more than $45,000 per year.

Physical education and athletic administrators who only recently were avidly recruiting new faculty members and coaches are now experiencing the unpleasant task of attempting to decide whom to terminate on their faculties and having to employ probationary faculty with the understanding that they probably will not be recommended for tenure. The financial problems of the seventies have created many additional administrative problems for department heads and deans and made their work far more difficult than it had been in the past, even counting the problems of student unrest experienced in the sixties. These and other problems have made it increasingly difficult for departments and colleges to obtain competent and well-qualified individuals who wish to pursue academic administration.

Few, if any, formalized programs are in existence that provide the necessary experience and training for physical education administrators. It is hoped that the materials presented in this chapter will assist both present and future administrators in their quest for outstanding professional leadership.

THE ORGANIZATION AND ADMINISTRATION OF PHYSICAL EDUCATION IN HIGHER EDUCATION

Organization should exist only in terms of *purpose,* and administration

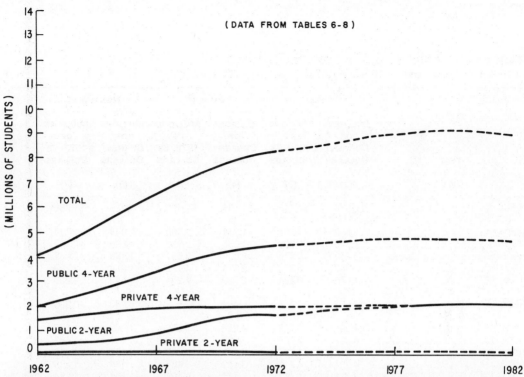

Figure 18–1. Total degree-credit enrollment in institutions of higher education, by control and type of institution: United States, 1962 to 1982. (Courtesy of the U.S. Department of Health, Education and Welfare, 1974.)

should exist only to provide group *guidance, leadership,* and *control* of efforts toward some valuable common goal. Thus the organization and identification of college and university physical education is complex and varied, because different academic hierarchies may view our purposes in different lights.

Several studies have been conducted dealing with the different organizational and administrative structures for departments, schools, and colleges of physical education. In a national study conducted by Hall and Jantzen at the University of Southern California in 1968, it was found that there were some 27 different official titles being used at that time to identify a physical education administrative unit.[2] The most prevalent organizational title was found to be that of a Department of Physical Education or Department of Health, Physical Education and Recreation. Approximately 17 per cent of the institutions responding to this survey reported that they were

housed administratively in a division of health, physical education, and recreation or a department of physical education and athletics. In a study conducted by McKinney in 1966, it was found that 23 colleges and universities were identified at that time by the administrative nomenclature of college or school of physical education.[3]

A more recent survey of the organizational structure of college programs in health, physical education, and recreation was conducted by Mehn in 1970.[4] A questionnaire was used in this study in an attempt to determine the organizational structure for 147 colleges and universities offering a major degree in one or more of the programs of health, physical education, and recreation. The survey was limited to institutions with an enrollment of over 6500 students. A total of 96 institutions replied to the questionnaire, and of this total, 68 stated that their basic administrative structure for health, physical education, and recrea-

TABLE 18–1. CAPITAL OUTLAY OF INSTITUTIONS OF HIGHER EDUCATION: UNITED STATES, 1962–63 TO 1982–83

YEAR	TOTAL		PUBLIC		NONPUBLIC	
	MILLIONS OF CURRENT DOLLARS	MILLIONS OF 1972–73 DOLLARS	MILLIONS OF CURRENT DOLLARS	MILLIONS OF 1972–73 DOLLARS	MILLIONS OF CURRENT DOLLARS	MILLIONS OF 1972–73 DOLLARS
(1)	(2)	(3)	(4)	(5)	(6)	(7)
1962–63[1]	$2,534	$4,748	$1,596	$2,990	$938	$1,758
1963–64	2,466	4,497	1,518	2,768	948	1,729
1964–65[1]	2,825	5,023	1,595	2,836	1,230	2,187
1965–66	3,253	5,575	2,064	3,537	1,189	2,038
1966–67	3,943	6,394	2,573	4,172	1,370	2,222
1967–68	4,175	6,424	2,732	4,204	1,443	2,220
1963–64 to 1967–68	16,662	27,913	10,482	17,517	6,180	10,396
1968–69	4,297	6,118	3,218	4,575	1,079	1,543
1969–70	4,332	5,759	3,066	4,076	1,266	1,683
1970–71	4,344	5,255	3,147	3,807	1,197	1,448
1971–72[2]	4,333	4,719	3,153	3,434	1,180	1,285
1972–73[2]	4,771	4,771	3,487	3,487	1,284	1,284
1968–69 to 1972–73	22,077	26,622	16,071	19,379	6,006	7,243
Projected[3]						
1973–74	5,206	4,842	3,822	3,555	1,384	1,287
1974–75	5,660	4,921	4,168	3,624	1,492	1,297
1975–76		5,024		3,714		1,310
1976–77		5,131		3,803		1,328
1977–78		5,226		3,882		1,344
1973–74 to 1977–78		25,144		18,578		6,566
1978–79		5,299		3,942		1,357
1979–80		5,329		3,972		1,357
1980–81		5,334		3,983		1,351
1981–82		5,324		3,980		1,344
1982–83		5,266		3,944		1,322
1978–79 to 1982–83		26,552		19,821		6,731

[1]Interpolation based on reported value of plant at close of previous year and the beginning of following year.

[2]Estimated.

[3]The projection of capital outlay is based on observation of the relationship of total capital outlay per full-time-equivalent (FTE) enrollment during the base period. This observation supports a theory that capital outlay can be expected to level off during periods of little or no increase or decrease in FTE enrollment. The projection is based on projected FTE enrollment and capital outlay per-FTE enrollment, 1971–72.

NOTE.—Data are for 50 States and the District of Columbia for all years.

SOURCES: Capital outlay data from U.S. Department of Health, Education, and Welfare, Office of Education, publication: *Financial Statistics of Institutions of Higher Education*, 1961–62 through 1968–69; and unpublished data for 1969–70 and 1970–71.

TABLE 18–2. ESTIMATED FULL-TIME-EQUIVALENT ENROLLMENT
IN ALL INSTITUTIONS OF HIGHER EDUCATION, BY DEGREE-CREDIT
STATUS AND INSTITUTIONAL CONTROL: UNITED STATES,
FALL 1962 TO 1982[1]

[RESIDENT AND EXTENSION OPENING FALL ENROLLMENT—IN THOUSANDS]

Year (Fall) (1)	All Students			Students Taking Work Creditable Toward a Bachelor's or Higher Degree			Students in Occupational or General Studies Programs Not Chiefly Creditable Toward a Bachelor's Degree		
	Total (2)	Public (3)	Private (4)	Total (5)	Public (6)	Private (7)	Total (8)	Public (9)	Private (10)
1962	3,455	2,145	1,310	3,322	2,041	1,281	133	104	29
1963	3,696	2,351	1,345	3,539	2,225	1,314	157	126	31
1964	4,115	2,671	1,444	3,924	2,504	1,421	191	167	24
1965	4,671	3,094	1,577	4,443	2,895	1,548	228	199	29
1966	5,070	3,398	1,672	4,792	3,154	1,637	278	243	35
1967	5,480	3,761	1,719	5,168	3,482	1,686	312	279	33
1968	5,954	4,228	1,726	5,594	3,899	1,695	360	329	31
1969	6,319	4,564	1,755	5,997	4,268	1,729	322	296	26
1970	7,721	4,937	1,783	6,299	4,539	1,761	421	399	22
1971	7,003	5,218	1,785	6,482	4,727	1,755	522	491	30
1972	7,083	5,300	1,783	6,511	4,757	1,754	572	543	29
Projected[1]									
1973	7,191	5,403	1,788	6,581	4,820	1,761	610	583	27
1974	7,310	5,508	1,802	6,663	4,888	1,775	647	620	27
1975	7,465	5,645	1,820	6,771	4,978	1,793	694	667	27
1976	7,624	5,780	1,844	6,891	5,074	1,817	733	706	27
1977	7,766	5,899	1,867	7,001	5,161	1,840	765	738	27
1978	7,876	5,991	1,885	7,075	5,217	1,858	801	774	27
1979	7,922	6,037	1,885	7,092	5,234	1,858	830	803	27
1980	7,930	6,054	1,876	7,081	5,232	1,849	849	822	27
1981	7,916	6,049	1,867	7,040	5,200	1,840	876	849	27
1982	7,830	5,994	1,836	6,940	5,130	1,810	890	864	26

[1]The estimations, 1962 to 1972, and the projections of the full-time equivalent of part-time enrollment are based on the assumption that the 1964 percentages of part-time enrollment equivalent to full-time enrollment (33 per cent for degree-credit students and 28 per cent for non-degree-credit students) have remained constant, 1962 to 1982.
For further methodological details, see appendix A, table A-1.

NOTE.—Data are for 50 States and the District of Columbia for all years. Because of rounding, detail may not add to totals.

SOURCES: Enrollment data and estimates are based on U.S. Department of Health, Education, and Welfare, Office of Education, publications: (1) *Opening (Fall) Enrollment in Higher Education,* annually, 1962 through 1968, 1971, and 1972, (2) *Fall Enrollment in Higher Education, Supplementary Information,* 1969 and 1970, (3) unpublished data from *Resident and Extension Enrollment in Institutions of Higher Education,* fall 1966 and 1967, (4) *Resident and Extension Enrollment in Institutions of Higher Education, First Term 1961,* and (5) Sample survey of full-time-equivalent enrollments and credit hours, fall 1964 (unpublished).

tion was at the departmental level. Six universities reported that they were housed in a College; nine reported Division status; and 13 indicated that their administrative structure was that of a School. Of the institutions who reported departmental status, 48 replied that health, physical education, and recreation programs should be grouped as a school or unit separate from other disciplines and operated as an autonomous academic body. This attempt to establish separate departments under the organizational framework of a school or college of physical education has been prevalent for many years. School or college status has been achieved by several institutions each year for the past 15 or 20 years, and there appears to be a continuous attempt to achieve this academic structure by many of the larger departments or divisions across the country.

Hall and Jantzen also provide interesting information regarding the title of the chief administrator for each of the above organizations, as indicated below:[5]

The Department

The basic organizational unit, referred to as a "department," was briefly discussed earlier, in the chapter dealing with academic administration. Department organization is usually considered the backbone of institutional organization, and as such provides the basic structure in which common curricula are housed. In order to provide an academic organization that is administratively sound, *a department should be composed only of homogeneous offerings and should exist only if the administrator or department chairperson can main-* *tain a reasonable span of control.* If varied programs come into existence which propose (a) uncommon objectives and (b) a body of knowledge that is heterogeneous, additional and separate administrative units should be formed. A delegation of responsibility and authority should also be initiated when a leader cannot function efficiently within a reasonable span of administrative control. Several guidelines must, however, assist with the determination of the feasibility for the creation of new administrative units. A general principle which is considered to be organizationally sound is that no departmental structure should be created with fewer than four full-time faculty members and an established curriculum oriented to a specific body of knowledge. Once again administrative procedures must remain flexible and there may well be exceptions to this general rule. Many university presidents and boards of trustees are reluctant to initiate additional administrative structures, since much criticism has been given to the large institutional bureaucracy already in existence. For this reason many so-called "departments" may in actuality be operated as a college, school, or division. This subterfuge provides only additional administrative difficulties and in many instances makes it unnecessarily difficult (if not impossible) to employ outstanding faculty and generate much-needed funds and facilities.

Generally speaking, the title used to describe a department will (or should) illustrate administrative responsibilities. Thus the title Department of Health, Physical Education and Recreation suggests that the department encompasses the disciplines of health education, physical education (for both men

NUMBER OF SCHOOLS	PER CENT	TITLE
112	54.1	Chairman
37	17.9	Head
27	13.0	Director
9	4.3	Chairman and Director of Athletics
2	1.0	Director of Physical Education and Athletics
1	.5	Executive Head

and women), and professional recreation. In some instances, departments will organizationally house many areas under a single heading, which does not provide for administrative clarity.

The primary duties and responsibilities of a department head or chairperson are:

1. The determination and request of departmental operating funds.
2. The allocation of department funds to the various professional and service areas within the department.
3. The recommendation for faculty and staff employment, advancement in rank, tenure, salaries, and teaching or work schedule.
4. The determination of departmental course offerings at the undergraduate and graduate levels.
5. The coordination of the entire department in attempting to meet the professional and service objectives of the department, the college, and the institution.

The theoretical distinction between a department "head" and a department "chairperson" is usually one of degree of authority. In the truest sense, a department chairperson is a chairperson for the departmental faculty, whereas a department head does not necessarily have to concur with the wishes of "the majority."

The School

The administrative organization of a "School of . . ." appears to be as different in structure and administrative flow as are the purposes and objectives of the institutions in which they are found.

The most commonly accepted purpose for the organization and creation of a school of health, physical education, and recreation is to offer professional and service programs in these closely related disciplines. One must assume, however, that the premise is correct and that these three disciplines are indeed closely related and that it is for the betterment of all that they should be housed under one administrative roof. The *need, justification,* and *rationale* for this separate organization have been explicitly presented in

a proposal by the University of Georgia for a school of health, physical education, and recreation:

The Need — All three areas of University function (in HPER); education, service and research can and should receive equal import while emanating from one specific focal point within the university structure. The vast expansion in the program responsibilities of the College of Education requires diligent and conscious attention to those matters that are *primarily* in the 'domain' of education and restricts the effort that can be devoted to programs of a 'peripheral' nature. . . . In order to achieve maximum articulation of the programs of health, physical education and recreation with the administration of the University, it is apparent that it would be mutually advantageous to separate the program from the College of Education and to locate it in a School of Health, Physical Education and Recreation.

Justification — Health, Physical Education and Recreation are professional disciplines requiring a body of knowledge that is germane only to these fields.

Rationale — A separate School of Health, Physical Education and Recreation will open the way to self-government and self-determination. The separate school will afford freedom of administrative operation in matters pertaining to philosophy, curriculum, budget, faculty and facilities. All of these, to be sure, are governed by the policy structure administered by the University. . . . A separate School of Health, Physical Education and Recreation will provide better identification and status and permit the development of greater 'esprit de corps' amongst faculty members and student body.

Organizationally such administrative structures are either located with a college, such as a college of education, or are established as entities of their own. In the latter case, the director or dean of the school reports directly to the pres-

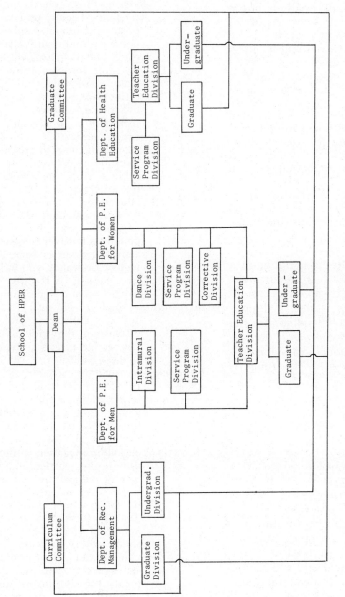

Figure 18-2. Organization of a school of health, physical education, and recreation in a large university. (Courtesy of the University of Oregon.)

All graduate programs must be conducted under the policies of the University Graduate Council and the School of Health, Physical Education and Recreation Graduate Committee. All undergraduate profession curricular matters are referred to the Minor Faculty through the school Curriculum Committee.

ident, vice-president, or an academic dean. When a school is created within a college, the director of the school is administratively responsible to the dean of the college. Departments or divisions are then housed within the School when they are considered necessary and administratively feasible. A fairly common pattern found in state colleges is the "divisional" plan, in which a division of physical education is located within a college, such as a college of education.

The distinction between a division and a school depends upon the autonomy provided by the administration of the college or the institution. Divisions are frequently established within an institution to organize non-academic administrative structures, such as a division of intercollegiate athletics. The athletic director is the administrative head of such divisions and usually reports directly to a vice-president or to the president and the board of trustees.

The most important benefit derived from the organization of a school is the autonomy of the organization to establish and control (within reasonable limits) curriculum, philosophy, budget, faculty, and facilities. *If such autonomy is not granted, the entire purpose for the organization of such an administrative unit is lost.*

The College

As was previously stated, the distinction between a school and a college is dependent upon institutional structuring and the authority, responsibility and autonomy provided by the university administration. Colleges have the autonomy to award degrees and in some instances this autonomy is also given to schools. It is also true that colleges per se are usually found in large institutions or universities composed of many colleges. The term university refers to an educational institution of the highest level, typically with one or more undergraduate schools or colleges.

In a typical college, the dean of the college deals directly with the president or a vice-president of the institution. Administratively this is the most efficient and beneficial organizational structure for combining the academic units of health education, physical education for both men and women, and recreation and park administration. *This statement is based on the premise that it is desirable to house these disciplines together because they desire maximum articulation among one another and have some commonality of curricula and purpose.* The dean of such a college has a direct "administrative flow" to the president's office and thus eliminates the intermediary usually found in a school, where the director of the school must present his requests to a college dean. It is, of course, beneficial to eliminate as many intermediaries as possible between departmental structures and the highest administrative office of the institution.

The duties and responsibilities of the dean of the college are similar in nature to those of the department head with the exception that this administrator is responsible for the leadership of several academic and service departments. *It is the expressed duty of the dean to provide a professional and financial climate which enables maximal advancement and growth for each of the administrative divisions under his direction.* This charge is founded upon the necessity for an unbiased and impartial philosophy on behalf of the individual holding this office. It is also true that a philosophy of "equal advancement" of all administrative units simultaneously (one for all and all for one) may prove to be disastrous for divisional initiative and creativity.

Present Administrative Trends and Future Planning

Several studies conducted within the past five to ten years tend to indicate that there exists an administrative trend toward the continued creation of schools and colleges of physical education and closely aligned disciplines. In many instances, new administrative units are apparently created by necessity, because of the great diversification of curricular and service offerings.

Increased size is one of the most com-

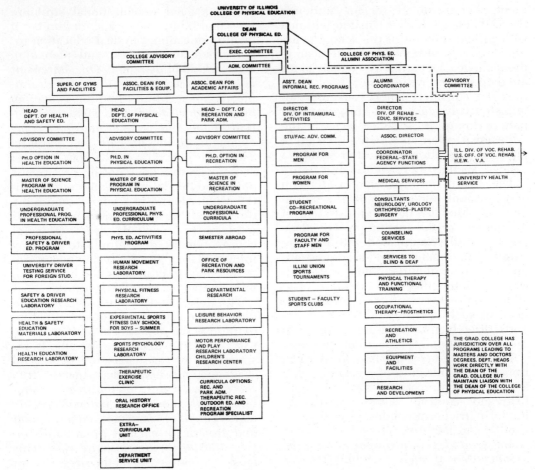

Figure 18–3. The organizational chart of one of the largest colleges of physical education in the United States. (Courtesy of the University of Illinois, 1972.)

mon pleas presented by physical education administrators in their quest for an autonomous administrative unit. Certainly size is a factor, but perhaps the most important justification is the organizational and administrative grouping of the body of knowledge dealing with the total academic area of Human Movement. There appears to be a serious transition around the world for academicians in the areas of physical education, movement education, and the basic human movement sciences to use the term Human Movement as an all-encompassing organizational umbrella. *Physical education is considered to be that phase or part of human movement which is spe-cifically oriented toward the preparation of teachers.* Scientific areas of research such as kinesiology or biomechanics, recreology, perceptual motor learning and, in some instances, physical therapy and orthopedics are considered to be administrative departments or areas within the total framework of human movement. It is argued that, because of their diversity, these specific bodies of knowledge cannot logically be assigned to the humanities, the fine arts, the sciences, or education. Those supporting and promoting colleges of physical education and human movement believe that the discipline is distinct unto itself. Physical education logically should be housed administratively in such a college, since the content and general nature of courses taught in this area are frequently very different from other offerings in the college of education or the college of arts and sciences.

Administratively these are the *chief functional reasons* for having separate administrative units. *This structure provides the most effective and efficient organization for the administrator to carry out the duties and responsibilities with which he is charged.* The creation of such administrative structures does not necessarily *have* to depend upon *size* as a sole prerequisite.

The "structural future" for physical education, health education, and recreation and park administration depends to a large degree upon the quality and nature of the administrative leadership for these entities. If one takes an overall look at the national academic organizations for our profession it quickly becomes apparent that many (if not most) of the institutions known nationally and internationally for superior programs are organized in such a manner in order to provide administrative autonomy. If such autonomy is necessary for excellence and strong professional growth, then administrators should strive for separate organizational structures. This statement also implies that the areas of health education and recreation and park administration might be better housed in other schools or colleges or in organizational units by themselves. The administrative leadership in these areas must make this decision and make their recommendations accordingly.

In discussing future administrative planning, it must be noted that higher education decision makers have gone to great lengths to find out what programs cost as they ponder the many problems concerned with "outcome-oriented planning." "What is needed is a reorientation in thinking toward an emphasis on outcomes. Outcome-oriented planning in higher education simply means utilizing outcomes, results, and benefits as a primary basis for determining the directions for higher education. It means

picking a destination and then determining the best way to get there."[6] An excellent example of a large "traditional" college of physical education is the University of Illinois at Urbana-Champaign, Illinois.

The curriculum for physical education teachers at Urbana-Champaign began in the college of education in 1919, and in 1932 this program became the school of physical education, containing separate departments for health and safety education, physical education, recreation and park administration, rehabilitation-educational services, and intramural activities. This college is an autonomous unit, granting its own degrees, and it also operates many interdisciplinary programs with other colleges on the Urbana-Champaign campus. The college's programs are designed to prepare professionals who, through school and agency programs, will help Illinois residents to realize their maximum physical-social development. The accomplishment of this goal in this, the most automated and frustrating period of man's history, will be crucial to our society's survival in the years immediately ahead.

In contrast to the traditional pattern of organization, new patterns are being created in both the United States and Canada. One of the newer, more innovative approaches is found at the University of Waterloo in Waterloo, Ontario, Canada. This university began with the school of physical and health education in 1966. This school later developed into the school of physical education and recreation, and in 1972 the Faculty of Human Kinetics and Leisure Studies was officially formed, which is presently composed of three departments: *kinesiology* and *recreation* (which administer the academic and research programs); and *athletics*, which conducts programs at the intercollegiate, intramural, and service levels. The organizational structure of the faculty at the University of Waterloo focuses on the belief that the major emphasis of the faculty should be physical activity per se, regardless of its form or the place in which it occurred. Thus the study of human

Figure 18–4. The new Physical Education and Activities Center at the University of Illinois, Urbana-Champaign.

movement and those factors which affect and effect such movement are the basic concern of this organizational and administrative structure.

McIntyre cites several examples from business and industry relating that outmoded, nonproductive organizational structures which do not reflect the needs and desires of the people working within them are the main cause for failure in an organization.[7] This author does not believe that the line-and-staff structure of health, physical education, recreation, and athletics is suitable for modern administration. He recommends instead a circular organizational chart which provides for an outward flow in all directions of formal authority. This tends to minimize centralization and may also tend to alleviate faculty members' anxieties and doubts about themselves, since it stresses program function, coordination, and simplicity.

Long-range planning for the organization and administration of physical education must include clearly defined administrative structuring. If present institutional funding difficulties are indicative of inadequate funding in the future, it is clearly recognizable that every academic organization will be forced to adapt to minimal organization structures and to the maintenance and promotion of superior programs of proven worth.

The Use of Computerized Techniques in Organization and Administration

Many administrators are aware that computers are now being widely used in colleges and universities, but a great number of those who are "aware" quickly admit that they know very little about computers and systems analysis.

"The basic administrative uses of computers are either transactional or managerial."[8] Many institutions have automated computer systems for accounting, budgets, student registration, cumulative records, grade reporting, and scheduling. In fact, there are very few major colleges and universities today that do not support a fairly sophisticated computer facility. The existence of such a center does not necessarily lead to its functional use by the faculty or administration. Such facilities must be used to advantage, and administrators who do not investigate the potential of computerized systems for physical education are neglecting opportunities that may provide a valuable tool for allocating resources with optimum efficiency.

Systems planning centers can be invaluable guides to deans and directors of physical education and athletic programs. The objective of management systems is to provide for coordination of all the elements in a system. "Resource requirements prediction models" are being developed by the National Center for Higher Education Management Systems as a tool for analyzing present costs and projecting future costs under various alternative situations. Computerized systems programs can develop standard ways to calculate cost per student, as is being demanded today by both state and federal governments.

Rushall states that computers have greatly increased the scope and detail of data analysis in physical education and the facility for multivariate experiments:

Research projects which ten years ago were a Ph.D. dissertation scope, today are laboratory exercises. No longer should an individual receive a degree for persistence in collecting data or performing a particularly laborious mathematical analysis. Rather the merits for research design, innovation, and the comprehensive investigation of a topic should be some of the more important criteria considered for the granting of degrees.[9]

Administrative Systems. The functions of an automated administrative computer system may be grouped under three headings: transactions; control; and planning.[10] *"Transactional purposes"* facilitate repetitive functions, such as the processing of applications, registration, recording and reporting grades, and preparing student records. *"Control purposes"* assist with the administration of the system in operational functions, such as program evaluations, supervision of personnel, and maintenance of facilities. *"Planning purposes"* involve automated administrative systems for forecasting, simulating, and modeling. Such a system will provide great dividends for the improvement of program design, as well as new and better ways of problem solving. With the assistance of computer programing, an administrator may be able to *predict* and study the effects of various administrative decisions and policies *before* a decision is reached.

Computerized Master Schedule Construction. Very little intensive use of systems analysis techniques is in evidence for physical education programs.

The faculty of physical education at the University of Alberta in Edmonton, Canada, has in the past used computerized scheduling for physical education. Overall major advantages to such programing have been found to be: (1) faster means of preparing and updating a master schedule; (2) timesaving, especially for the student (refers to student class scheduling); (3) physical facilities can be used more effectively; (4) needs of students can be satisfied more easily; (5) fast overview of existing logistical situation; (6) better allocation of manpower; and (7) speed, time, and accuracy.

The utility of computer-based systems for scheduling universities is well established; however, without a well-planned set of institutional policies, efficient and accurate data collection procedures, and well-organized files and useful available outputs, a scheduling procedure is doomed.[11]

Computers and Tests and Measurements. Some studies conducted in the late 1960's showed that computers were not being used extensively by most physical educators. Recently, use of computers has increased, and new programs are assisting teachers in scheduling classes, assigning students, and doing mathematical analyses. Computer programs are available for calculating percentile scores, printing profile records, making performance comparisons, and performing many other tasks; the possibilities are limited only by the imagination of the user. Many physical educators have used computers to stimulate measurement and evaluation classes, and for practical measurement and evaluation processes. Generally such classes do not have as their major purpose the teaching of programing as such; rather, the aim is to teach the utilization of the computer for its calculating speed and accuracy. Programs of this nature have been conducted at many institutions, among them the School of Physical and Health Education at the University of Windsor, Windsor, Ontario, Canada, and the Department of Physical Education at West Chester State College, West Chester, Pennsylvania.

BUDGET AND FINANCE

Although the growth rate of college and university enrollments is slowing, costs continue to spiral upward with inflation, and estimates are that the total expenditure for higher education in the United States increases by over 1.5 billion dollars per year. Federal funding alone in the middle seventies was in excess of two billion dollars per year for support programs in the Department of Health, Education and Welfare.

Basic problems concerning the financial role of state and federal governments in the funding of higher education are in evidence throughout the world. State governments are pouring more and more money into state universities and also into financial aid programs to assist students in paying the costs of higher education.

General Funding

"In the final analysis *finance* is concerned with: (1) obtaining money, and (2) spending it. In a narrow sense the *budget* is a statement of estimated receipts and expenditures; in a broader sense it anticipates the needs of the department prior to the time of expenditure and insures the necessary economies."[12]

A successful administrator is one who is able to generate the necessary funds with which to meet the demands of his organization.

Without operating funds, it is, of course, impossible to operate any organization and, within reasonable limits, the greater the financial resources available to the administrator, the greater the scope and quality of programs he can organize. The various administrative aspects of budget and finance, then, are of the utmost importance to an organization, and the many duties associated with budgetary procedures should be considered as the single most important responsibility of department head, director, or dean. One can see the validity of this statement by noting that the majority of well-organized faculties, departments, schools, and colleges of physical education in the United States and Canada report *annual* operating budgets ranging from $500,000 to over $2,000,000. These amounts usually exclude capital expenditures and reveal that by far the largest allocations are for faculty and staff salaries. Such financial expenditures are indeed large, and every effort must be made to insure that efficient financial management is practiced in order to obtain the maximum benefit from available revenue.

Despite the great importance of this phase of their duties, few directors are prepared for the efficient financial administration of the physical education department when they first undertake it. The great majority of administrators learn by the trial-and-error method. Experience may be the best teacher; but it is an expensive teacher, particularly where finance is concerned. . . . The professional physical education programs should make some provision to prepare physical educators for the financial responsibilities that they will encounter in their positions.[13]

The budgetary preparation and detail required for an academic organizational unit in physical education and its related disciplines does not usually deal with the wide variability encountered in intercollegiate athletic budgetary procedures. In some instances, however, organizational units for physical education, health education, recreation and park administration, and intramural sports have budgets and finance reports just as complicated and varied as any found in intercollegiate athletics. The active participation of the federal government in the allocation of federal funds for the construction of facilities and the conducting of research has further complicated budgetary procedures.

State and Federal Support. As has been discussed previously, the *principal* financial support for public institutions is by means of local or state taxation, or both. The percentage of state support for institutions of higher learning is naturally increasing in the attempt to meet rapidly rising costs. Many university presidents are experiencing "financial frustration" in their attempts to generate sufficient funds to enable their institutions to meet the many academic demands of present-day higher education. For this reason increased emphasis has been placed on every organization in the university to become actively involved with seeking and obtaining federal support. In academic departments in which federal support programs are more readily available, many programs have flourished and have even been able to develop new and innovative approaches to research and teaching. The criticism is often heard that such programs are not stable, since federal funds may be curtailed, depending upon the whims of Congress, leaving programs and faculty without financial support. It is envisioned, however, that federal support of higher education will, through necessity, increase in the foreseeable future, because state support in many states simply cannot keep pace with increased costs.

State financing of a public institution is determined by the financial resources of the state and by the willingness of the people to support education. The president of a university will begin his budgetary request by first determining the needs of his institution. This is accomplished in cooperation with a board of regents or trustees and other administrative officers of the university. Deans and department heads are consulted and asked to submit their financial needs for a fiscal year or for a biennium, depending on how often the state legislative body meets. Such requests are reviewed by the administration and the governing board and are then presented to the legislature. These requests are usually made in light of the financial realities of what the state may be able or expected to provide. Any academic administrator must attempt to determine the "financial climate" of his institution and state in order to present a feasible budgetary request in keeping with the wherewithal of available finances. Nothing is more frustrating and detrimental to the administrator's organization than repeated attempts to generate monies of a magnitude simply not possible or permissible in the eyes of the administra-

tion. Department heads, in particular, must become knowledgeable of the budgetary and financial intricacies of their college and institution so that they may be effective in this aspect of their administrative duties.

Federal support programs for the areas of Health Education, Physical Education, and Recreation-Park Administration have not been of the first magnitude as far as institutions of higher learning have been concerned. Thus many administrators have permitted faculty research to become almost completely divorced from the primary objective of their organization in order to generate federal funds. Nothing could be more detrimental to the furthering of the professional goals of physical education than to permit this to occur.

Budget Preparation and Request

Departments, divisions, schools, and colleges of physical education must be permitted to formulate and control (within reasonable limits) their own autonomous budgets. Because financial support is the key factor in all organization, this is an absolute necessity for the development and maintenance of quality programs. Departmental physical education budgets *should not* be combined with those for other departments in a given college or with an intercollegiate athletic budget. This is also true for departments housed within a college of physical education, since it is deemed of the utmost importance that departmental administrators be permitted to formulate the financial needs for their administrative unit and present such requirements as a separate entity of the over-all budgetary requests of the college and the institution. All too often such is not the case and, inevitably, departmental budgets suffer.

Administrators at any academic level should strive to eliminate as many intermediaries as possible between themselves and the individual or governing body that actually allocates funds. This procedure is simply a common-sense approach to budget and finance, since no one can better present the financial needs of an organization than the immediate administrator of that organization. Caution must be observed, however, because one of the most direct methods of becoming involved in administrative disloyalty is to by-pass established organizational channels in the request for funds. Determinations must be made and priorities established in such requests, and resultant administrative action thus becomes the greatest single responsibility of the leaders of the institution. It is essential that the administrators who make such decisions know the nature and scope of the organization for which they must make such determinations. Budget requests for physical education, intramurals, and basic instruction programs are many times not wholly understood or deemed of significant importance by deans of colleges who believe the prime objectives of their college lie in other areas. It is of interest to note again here that institutions which have developed national and international reputations for excellence in physical education, health education, and recreation-park administration, have apparently done so because they have been administratively housed together in a college or school and have thus been funded by budgets submitted directly to the highest administrators of their institutions. Such budgets are presented by an administrator who fully comprehends their varied needs. This is true for small as well as large colleges and universities.

Organizational units with large student enrollments at both the undergraduate and graduate levels have in the past supported their financial requests by the "numbers game," as did many other units within the college or university. Declining enrollments and accountability programs have now placed such organizational units in financial difficulty. Every attempt should be made by physical education administrators to justify programs based on *quality curricula and student needs*—not on the basis of attempting to generate numbers or a top-heavy bureaucratic structure.

All institutions must have an "expen-

diture code" under which they classify expenditures in accordance with established standards. These codes will, of course, vary from institution to institution, but for the most part an administrative breakdown of expenditures may be classified under headings such as the following:

Personal Services—All salary and wage compensation for officers and employees.
Salaries: set by law (statutory and controlled)
classified (permanent positions)
other (temporary)
Contractual Services—Expenditures for services rendered to the institution; includes purchase of materials, repairs, and maintenance to real property.
Supplies—Commodities purchased for consumption or inventory in correct usage and considered expendable (may be considered as several years' life expectancy and less than $50 cost for each or per set).
Equipment—Money outlay for nonconsumable items acquired with a net cost of over $50; freight and installation charges should be considered part of original costs.
Fixed Charges—Continuing costs for rental of real estate or equipment. Contracts in which no contracted personal service is rendered on a predictable basis.
Grants and Aid Payments—Includes payment to local governments, private organizations, and individuals of grants and benefits of state aid distribution. Distribution of federal aid and grant monies earmarked for specific purposes and programs.
Capital Expenditures—For land, land improvements, building purchases, construction, additions, and major remodeling.
Non-operating Expenditures—Fiscal transactions and expenditures, the costs of which are not usually ultimately borne by or chargeable to the state spending or distributing department.

Each of these major budgetary headings, as well as each subheading, is assigned an institutional budget number for classification. In small departmental organizations it is not considered administratively sound to fragment the overall budget allocation into small segments for each aspect of the department's total operation. *Budget allocations should be directly dependent upon a just and unbiased determination of need and not on the overemphasis of any given area.* If such an approach to budget and finance can be successful it will provide a great deal of the financial flexibility required to meet the unexpected needs of any single unit within the total organization. In large administrative units it is considered wise to formulate and operate within specific budgetary requests for each sub-organization within the parent structure.

FACULTY AND STAFF

One of the most difficult and time-consuming responsibilities of an academic administrator is the successful recruitment and maintenance of an outstanding faculty and staff. "A competent staff with a sound educational philosophy, working with virile and dynamic leadership, is an element in the school administrative process for which there is no satisfactory substitute."[14]

For the purpose of clarification, the term "faculty" is used in these chapters to designate full- or part-time professors who are professionally prepared physical education teachers. The term "staff" is used to designate clerical, equipment, facility, and custodial positions.

Selection and Retention of Faculty

The recruitment and employment of faculty are generally quite standardized techniques, involving the determination of the professional capabilities required by the nature of the available position and the "selling" of the institution to the prospective professor. Creating faculty interest in the college or university is not deemed to be a difficult task with the present oversupply and diminishing demand for academicians. The ability *to maintain an outstanding* faculty is quite another matter. Post-employment relationships (both personal and professional) between the administrator and colleagues who are in a subordinate role are steeped with all the subtleties involved with leadership, communication, morale, and conflict. Such relationships are further complicated in present-day administrative structures by the necessity of scientifically evaluating university teaching as well as the "no-growth reality" of tenured faculty, which was mentioned previously. The limited growth reality of present faculty and the lack of future advancement for young professors is one of the most serious administrative problems facing departments. From 1945 to 1970 it is estimated that there was a 700 per cent increase in the number of individuals holding doctorate degrees in the United States. It is further estimated that between 1970 and 1980 there will be an additional 45,000 doctorates vying for academic appointments. In spite of these many problems, a study conducted in 1973 reported that department heads considered informal contact with faculty as one of their most enjoyable activities. The least satisfying role of departmental administrators was their responsibility as an evaluator of faculty effort. The same study reported that the vast majority of department heads desired more autonomy, more resources, and more administrative assistance.[15]

Such factors as orientation to people and subsequent internal peace are vital to efficient administration. Internal harmony depends to a large extent on *morale.* Morale is a most subtle concept to isolate and is said to be a state of mind as reflected in attitude. Motivation and morale go hand in hand in the development of *esprit de corps.* The development of realistic incentives contributes a great deal to motivation and to the improvement of faculty morale. Above-average salary scales, appropriate facilities and equipment, reasonable fringe benefits, administrative support, and a sincere feeling of being an integral part of the organization are all factors contributing to both motivation and morale.

Howard and Masonbrink believe that the most important considerations for the development and maintenance of faculty morale are:

1. The explicit definition of responsibilities.
2. The accordance of individual respect to each individual faculty member.
3. The provision of administrative leader-

ship for both individual and departmental professional growth.

4. The assurance of faculty participation in the determination of organizational and administrative policy.

5. The provision of ready communication.

6. The provision of desirable working conditions.

7. The provision of reward for merit.[16]

The attitudes or feelings that an administrator must obtain in order to create a progressive and worthwhile organization are *industry, loyalty, enthusiasm,* and *pride.* It is hypothesized that as the distance between the "top" and the "bottom" grows greater in any organization, the problems of individual and group morale become more severe. It is not only the morale of the rank and file that may suffer; it is also true that the more remote an administrative officer is (or feels) from the point at which his recommendations are acted on, the less secure he is likely to feel in his administrative role. Extreme care must be taken in faculty relationships to insure that a span of control is established that will permit both the delegation of power and authority and the maintenance of personal communication.

There are, therefore, four basic objectives that an administrator should accomplish with respect to his subordinates:

1. To motivate them to do their work promptly, capably, and economically.

2. To hold them.

3. To draw from among them the best personnel for assignment to positions of greater responsibility.

4. To assure their being effective missionaries for the department or company.[17]

The Selection Process. There are naturally many different techniques and varied approaches to the selection of a college or university faculty. It is recognized that what may be a successful approach for one institution may prove to be very ineffective for another. It is safe to assume that all institutions are desirous of obtaining individuals of professional quality and expertise who will contribute to the excellence of their given academic discipline.

The nature and scope of a departmental or institutional selection process in most instances depends upon the position to be filled. Junior-level appointments at the rank of instructor or assistant professor do not usually receive the "in-depth" investigation required of appointments made at higher ranks or for administrative positions. This is not to imply that junior-level appointments are not important, for this is certainly not the case. At the higher ranks recommendations for tenure usually have to be made before a second- or third-year appointment is made. In some instances, full professors are awarded immediate tenure. Unlike European universities, institutions in the United States do not make administrative appointments for life. Tenure may be granted to an administrator in his or her area of teaching competency, but the administrative appointment may be revoked whenever such action is deemed necessary or appropriate by the institution.

Although higher than average salaries are important in attracting prospective employees, qualified individuals are also seeking a healthful living environment for themselves and their families, as well as new and modern facilities, better than average fringe benefits, and an administratively progressive academic climate in which to work. As vacancies occur or new positions are created they are announced either through academic placement agencies or by very select professional contacts. Many administrators prefer to personally solicit professional recommendations from well-known colleagues in various parts of the country. By so doing, the administrator is usually assured that only well-qualified individuals will be asked to submit applications and he will therefore not be deluged by applications. The use of select professional contacts in soliciting recommendations is quickly disappearing, however, because institutions must now conform to established laws guaranteeing that they are Equal Opportunity and Affirmative Action Employers.

Specific selection criteria vary considerably from one institution to another, but among those deemed most important are:

1. A professionally sound undergraduate and graduate education in the academic area for which the applicant is being considered.
2. Demonstrated successful experience.
3. Expertise in the subject matter area required of the position.
4. Sufficient personal health to adequately meet the demands of the position.
5. Superior mental and emotional qualities.
6. Outstanding professional recommendations from the candidate's peers and superiors.

Recommendations are only as valid as the reputation and sincerity of the individuals who provide them. That is why it is a sound selection procedure to require a personal interview. Some institutions ask that the interview take place at the candidate's place of residence, so that he may be observed in both family and professional associations and so that those individuals who provided recommendations for the applicant may be interviewed. It is an administrative "truism" that *a thorough investigation and evaluation of a prospective faculty member during the selection process will greatly alleviate future administrative problems dealing with promotion and retention.* A candidate should be explicitly informed of the basic philosophies and objectives of the department and institution so that he, in turn, may relate his own personal beliefs in this regard. Such frank and open discussions during an interview will help to eliminate unfortunate misunderstandings which might completely disrupt departmental harmony and cohesiveness at some time in the future.

It is indeed unfortunate that outstanding candidates of true *professional quality* are still quite difficult to obtain in spite of a "buyers'" market place. This apparent scarcity has, in fact, promoted the necessity in some institutions of rampant inbreeding or the literal "selling" of the institution to an outside candidate, often at the expense of completely ignoring sound professional requirements in order to fill a vacancy.

Evaluation and Retention. If a thorough investigation and evaluation is undertaken during the time of faculty recruitment, the evaluation and retention process is made much easier for the administrator. Faculty are, of course, further evaluated during periods of allocation and reallocation of resources, at promotion time, and in planning sessions. They are judged every day on the basis of their work and the success or failure of their decisions. It has been evident for many years that the procedures, criteria, and influences on which evaluation is based are less than clear. In many instances the evaluations provided by departmental administrators are not efficiency ratings but are rather compatibility ratings which reflect the degree to which the faculty member relates with his colleagues and with his administrator. There are both official and unofficial bases of evaluation, and unofficial criteria, such as consensus with superiors and personal compatibility, are of great importance.

The Center for Research and Development in Higher Education at the University of California at Berkeley has published a report dealing with the results of a study which was undertaken on "evaluating university teaching."[18] The principal results of this study indicated that students characterized their *best* teachers in terms of the following: (1) analytic-synthetic approach; (2) organizational clarity; (3) instructor-group interaction; (4) instructor–individual student interaction; and finally (5) dynamism-enthusiasm. An analysis of the items characterizing *best teachers as perceived by colleagues* also produced five scales: (1) research activity and recognition; (2) intellectual breadth; (3) participation in the academic community; (4) relations with students; and (5) concern for teaching. There was excellent agreement among students and faculty about the effectiveness of given teachers. Although this study dealt primarily with students' evaluations of teachers, it also showed that different types of teaching appropriate to different settings could be assessed and that a variety of types of effective teaching could be identified. Since one of the major objectives of evaluating university teaching is to provide feedback to the instructor for self-improvement, a more constructive approach, such as that presented by Popham,[19] might be more appropriate. This approach presents six self-instruction programs designed to be completed individually by the instructor. As a self-instructional approach, the evaluation of instruction is designed to deal with various aspects of evaluation and to provide a set of tangible competencies that can be employed by teachers or other educational personnel as they evaluate instruction. In this approach, required evaluation of teaching is not directed "from above."

A professionally "healthy" academic department must promote and foster some divergence of thought by its faculty or the discipline will tend to stagnate in its own self-esteem and well-being. On the other hand, one may cite several instances in which faculties were recruited who expressed such divergence of philosophy that entire departmental structures collapsed. This, then, is the difficult challenge facing the administrator; *he must evaluate fairly and objectively on the basis of several criteria, two of which are (a) teaching and research competence; and (b) personal compatibility with superiors, peers, and students.* If this approach is not taken, departmental morale will be severely damaged.

Staff members, to be most effective, must see the goals and purposes of the institution and the department as worthy of their best efforts; feel that in working toward these goals they are also achieving a high degree of self-realization; and recognize meaningful relationships between their own efforts and achievements and the accomplishment of the purposes of the department and the institution. . . . It is also important that each individual view his work as challenging and sometimes even difficult. If it does not call for strenuous effort and creative thinking, it becomes monotonous and meaningless. A sense of personal worth and importance is maintained only when all the capabilities, ingenuities, and resources of the individual are called upon. When this occurs and when the efforts of staff members are perceived as contributing in a significant way to the education of the students and eventually the betterment of society, the relationships will be seen as supportive.[20]

Evaluations, although always a concern, become an especially personal and direct concern to faculty members being considered for continued employment or tenure, promotion in rank, and salary increments. Specific criteria commonly considered during such an evaluation may be grouped into general areas such as (a) instruction and/or administration; (b) research and experimentation; (c) service to the institution, community, and state; and (d) general criteria, which may include such aspects as service and participation in professional organizations. Each individual department, school, or college will then formulate specific criteria for each of these general areas. Educational evaluation in any form is a difficult task indeed, and the evaluation of academic faculty is considered to be one of the most (if not *the* most) difficult of all. For many years educators have been in the difficult position of attempting to determine a valid and reliable method for evaluating "quality instruction," as well as attempting to determine what constitutes "research." It would certainly seem reasonable for an administrator to expect that a competent and professionally active member of the faculty should receive superior proficiency ratings as a director of learning and also that he should in some manner be productive as a researcher, experimenter, or writer. Many institutions ask (or require) that student evaluations be conducted each semester as one means of attempting to determine the teaching competencies of all nontenured faculty. If correctly administered, this technique is very beneficial, provided the results are considered as just one of several evaluative criteria.

Recommendations concerning reappointment, nonretention, and tenure are usually initiated annually by the department or division chairperson or by the dean of the college when appropriate (i.e., in colleges not departmentalized and, in the case of tenure, when the department or division head does not hold tenure). Such recommendations are contained in a written report evaluating the teaching ability, productive scholarship, and other relevant qualifications and characteristics of the faculty member under consideration. If the recommendation is prepared by a department or division chairperson it is then forwarded to the appropriate dean, who adds his recommendation and forwards all reports to the president of the institution.

The factors involved in faculty retention are in many instances much the same as those deemed important for faculty recruitment. The four most important considerations are: (1) salary and fringe benefits; (2) the nature and use of academic facilities; (3) local community living conditions; and (4) a "healthful" administrative climate. Another realistic consideration involved with faculty retention is the "no new-growth reality" facing many institutions. Junior-level faculty, in many instances, are employed with the clear understanding that at the end of their probationary appointment they will not be granted continuing tenure and will be released. This is necessitated by the present lack of faculty mobility and in certain instances by the reduction of the instructional staff.

Faculty Teaching Assignments and Load

One of the more important factors affecting teacher morale is to insure that each teacher has a teaching assignment in which he is interested and for which he is prepared. Prospective faculty members should be consulted in this regard when they are interviewed and not simply assigned to whatever happens to be available. *One of the most serious administrative mistakes is to assign a new faculty member to teach the exact courses that were assigned to the individual he or she replaced.* Also, new teachers should be assigned to a lighter teaching load during their first semester

of employment in order that they may become quickly settled in their position and learn the many intricacies of a new organization. All faculty should be consulted from time to time in a personal interview regarding any change of interest or new academic preparation they may have which may lead to strengthened teaching skills. Each member of the department should also be informed of his or her teaching assignment for the next semester well in advance. In many departments, when schedules are first available, instructors waste valuable time comparing their teaching loads with those of their colleagues.

Unless there are extenuating circumstances dictating otherwise, physical education departments should be permitted to determine their own teaching-load policies. Because of the variability encountered in both theory and activity courses, and the many other complications such as athletic duties and intramural assignments, the teaching load should be determined by those who know and understand such assignments. FTE (Full-Time Equivalencies) should be determined and approved by the physical education administrator, because activity instruction does not receive favorable weighting when the amount of time spent in class by an instructor is divided by the normal required university load.

An interesting study conducted by Gray revealed that there was a wide variation of physical education faculty load weighting practices in colleges and universities throughout the United States.[21] Of great significance was the finding that less than one-third of the 148 institutions responding had a written faculty load weighting policy. Of those schools that stated that they did have such a written policy, the "credit hour" appeared to be the most common measure of faculty load, and its use was more common in state colleges than in universities. Student credit hours and student contact hours were also used by some institutions in the determination of faculty load.

Many different criteria are used to determine teaching loads, and such determinations depend to some extent on the service and professional objectives of the department and the institution. Among criteria that may be considered are teaching, graduate assignments, advisement of students, university committee assignments, administration, state and national professional leadership, consultant service and extension teaching, intramural assignments, and intercollegiate athletics.

A faculty load weighting policy that appears to have merit as a *reasonable* requirement for a semester organization is one which provides a base of 12 semester hours of theory instruction or not more than 12 contact hours (actual class instruction) per week. This plan utilizes this load as a normal base and does not permit, for example, an assignment of more than three four-semester credit hour courses to constitute a normal load. It also equates the credit hour with the clock hour. Such a plan includes a normal base of nine semester hours or 16 contact hours per week for total physical education activity instruction. From these normal loads reductions are then made for undergraduate and graduate advisement, graduate paper and theses direction, intercollegiate athletics, intramurals, and departmental administration. Although this may appear to some to be a "light" load policy, it provides for and should indeed demand faculty involvement in professional activities of service, research, and publication.

It is strongly recommended that *all* head intercollegiate athletic coaches be assigned to not more than one half of a normal base teaching load *per academic year*. With the continued emphasis and pressures being placed on intercollegiate athletic programs today in our colleges and universities, all head coaches, no matter what their sport, should not be required to teach more than half the time during *any* semester or quarter. Head coaches of football and basketball in large institutions that stress national prominence in these sports should not be required to teach more than one or two courses per year if at all. This recommendation is made in the best interest of both the teacher-coach and the physical education programs they are assigned to instruct.

Staff Employment and Retention

The determination of the quality and nature of staff personnel required to effectively and efficiently operate a college or university department is one of the most important administrative responsibilities a leader will encounter. An outstanding administrator and a superior faculty may well be reduced to mere mediocrity without the able assistance of a clerical, custodial, and supervisory staff that has sincere and professional interest in the organization. The employment and retention of such personnel are just as important to the development and maintenance of an outstanding department as the recruitment and retention of a superior faculty. Dedicated individuals to fill such staff positions are difficult to obtain, and for the most part administrative employment and retention procedures have been greatly neglected. In many instances the determination of competencies and the retention and/or dismissal of such personnel rests in the hands of administrative units completely divorced from the department in which they work. Unionization and civil service requirements have assisted in some respects, but, unfortunately, in other matters such requirements have made it increasingly difficult for administrators to demand and receive a continued high level of competency.

The personal demands and requirements of individuals filling staff positions are much the same as those for faculty. Salary, fringe benefits, working conditions, facilities, and equipment are some of the most important variables that must be taken into consideration. If they are to maintain a high level of morale and proficiency, a staff must be provided with a "work climate" that fosters the development of personal pride both for their work as individuals and in the operation of the organization as a whole. Salary increments should be based on an appropriate cost of living increase each year as well as a merit increment for work well done. "Across the board" salary increases for all, no matter what their level of proficiency or contribution to the organization, do not promote the much needed desire to excel.

Clerical Staff. Organizational offices are the center of all administrative and academic activity in a college or university. Such offices provide the focal point for the total operation of the organization, and without the efficient and dedicated performance of the clerical staff that maintains these units, the organization could not continue to function. Unless the administrative unit is very large, a secretary will usually be required to undertake many office duties at any given time.

One of the greatest assets of any department is a competent and well-qualified secretarial staff to whom routine administrative and organizational matters may be delegated. Individuals to staff such positions should be recruited with great care because their capabilities are of vital importance to the effective operation of the organization. In many instances it is a wise administrative decision not to hire individuals who are seeking short-term employment, but rather to attempt to secure those who are career specialists. It is of great importance for a chief administrator to personally select his own secretary especially if he is new to his position. His predecessor's secretary may remain as a valuable asset to the department in another capacity. The close working relationship required between the administrator and his secretary demands total loyalty as well as mutual appreciation and understanding.

The employment and retention of clerical personnel may be delegated to the chief administrator's secretary or to one of the senior secretaries in the organization. Such delegation of responsibility is administratively sound in that the administrator is not usually knowledgeable in the specific skill requirements deemed necessary for the efficient operation of the department. The division of labor and work schedules should

also be delegated to the individual responsible for such selection and retention. Efficient office management will depend upon the nature and quality of the organization and supervision provided by the staff member charged with this responsibility.

Facilities and Equipment Personnel. In a departmental organization that contains the numerous and varied responsibilities associated with indoor and outdoor facilities for physical activity, supervisory and equipment personnel are of vital importance. An administrator who is not concerned with a well-planned and efficient operation for this aspect of his organization will quickly discover a total breakdown of internal function. Many of the chief administrative problems associated with physical education are directly related to the supervision of facilities and the distribution and maintenance of equipment and supplies.

The employment of competent personnel to staff such positions should be one of the chief responsibilities of the departmental chairperson or of his designated representative. Every effort should be made to employ individuals who are qualified in physical health, experience, and required skill. All too often such positions are considered to be of low priority in regard to financial compensation and required expertise. Because of inadequate salaries and in some instances unpopular working hours, semiretired, retired, or even those in poor health are employed to fill positions that usually demand full dedication as well as a great deal of patience and personal vitality. This is not to imply categorically that semiretired or retired persons are not suitable for selected positions of this nature, but great care should be taken to insure that such personnel do have the requisites demanded of the position. The chief administrator of a department, school, or college may be so removed from the duties and responsibilities of such personnel that he may wish to delegate the responsibility and authority for their supervision to a faculty member who is not so removed. In any case, there should be well-defined avenues of communication as to the exact nature and duties of such positions.

Custodial Personnel. Personnel associated with the maintenance of the physical plant are, for the most part, selected and employed by a college or university office organized and maintained specifically for this purpose. This is especially true in state-supported institutions. The quality of persons staffing custodial positions is perhaps more important in physical education facilities than in any other physical facility in the institution.

Physical activity facilities, including natatoria, locker rooms, and shower areas, *must* be maintained at a higher level of cleanliness than any other area. Custodial personnel must receive constant supervision and direction to insure that high standards for such work are met. The physical education administrator should do his utmost to work cooperatively with the director of custodial personnel and, if possible, assist with the selection and deployment of custodians for all facilities under his jurisdiction. Written reports should be drawn up for the administrative director of institutional facilities, to keep him informed about the maintenance and upkeep of the department's physical plant.

BASIC INSTRUCTION PROGRAMS

Physical education activity programs that provide instruction in various sports skills are the basic underlying foundation of many physical education departments at the college and university level. The nature and scope of such programs have generated considerable professional soul-searching and controversy for many years. Activity courses, required or elective, have been referred to as programs of "service," "basic instruction," or "foundations for skill and health." Physical educators as well as those not associated with the profession have debated the pros and cons of such programs, but the principal issues are: (1) Should physical education activity programs be required in an institution of higher learning? (2) For what level of skill attainment should instruction be

provided? and (3) Should such courses be offered for academic credit?

There is no doubt that in many institutions basic physical education instruction programs have lagged far behind what is considered desirable in light of sound professional philosophies. This breach between what should be and what actually is is primarily due to *inadequate facilities and disinterested faculty.* Many institutions have encountered difficulty in adequately providing faculty and facilities to meet the demands of increased student enrollments in required programs. The results are usually inappropriate course selection by students, overcrowding of classes, and increased faculty loads. In other instances, difficulties occur when departments or colleges are forced to justify a large percentage of their graduate assistants and junior-level faculty by claiming the necessity for instructors in order to meet the demands of a required program. In some institutions, graduate programs in physical education are dependent upon the maintenance of an activity requirement, since many, if not most, students pursuing graduate degrees do so only if attracted by teaching assistantships or junior faculty positions. Full-time faculty, who have been recruited primarily for intercollegiate coaching assignments and are then required to teach part time in activity programs in order to justify a portion of their salary, have also presented serious problems.

Present Programs

Required or elective basic instruction programs in physical education are usually designed to promote an understanding of and appreciation for the cultural, healthful, and recreational values of physical activity. The teaching of physical skills and the attempted development of positive attitudes toward so-called "play activities" are said to be the principal objectives. If these objectives are met, students should complete programs with an increased level of skill attainment in selected sports, and they should also have developed a more positive attitude toward actively participating in these and other physical activities. It is comparatively easy to measure skill improvement, but it is quite difficult to measure attitude.

Some colleges offer separate curriculum divisions for physical education activity programs. These divisions present courses in: (1) introduction or orientation; (2) developmental or physical fitness; (3) aquatics; (4) recreational activities; (5) adapted or modified programs; and, in some instances, (6) varsity athletic activities. Varied procedures are then followed by different institutions as to how the student proceeds to participate in the curriculum. Such procedures depend to a large extent on whether the activity program is required or elective, or perhaps required with individual electives permitted within specified areas. In many instances the elective process is stressed *after* the student has mastered basic skill or fitness requirements.

The scope or variability of activity curricula naturally depends upon the wishes of the department and the availability of faculty, facilities, and financial support. Present programs tend to offer, in addition to the traditional courses that have been the basic foundation of curricula in the past, an increased emphasis on innovative individual and dual sports which truly meet the interests of students. Courses such as mountain climbing and orienteering, skin and scuba diving, sail flying, European team handball, and the traditional favorites of tennis, golf, and bowling are very popular. The decline in student enrollments which many institutions have experienced has assisted in permitting departments to offer courses with a realistic faculty-student instructional ratio. Thus, in many instances, the quality of instruction has improved, as has student interest and learning.

Required vs. Elective Programs

Determination of a "best approach" for a department's responsibility in offering a required or elective program of

Figure 18-5. Basic instruction programs in physical education provide the basic skills necessary for recreational play as well as organized competition. (Courtesy of the Dunedin Evening Star, New Zealand.)

basic instruction must be left in the hands of the chairperson and his or her faculty. Such a decision may, however, be based upon the determination and evaluation of the following: (1) the scope and quality of elementary and secondary school physical education programs from which the student population is drawn; (2) the availability of skilled and competent instructors; (3) the availability of adequate physical facilities; and (4) the availability of adequate financial resources. *The maintenance or establishment of a required program should not be permitted if such activities are deemed to be detrimental in any manner to their established objectives.* For example, if students are found to be completing a compulsory program that in actuality develops negative habits and attitudes toward physical education and physical activity, the program should be immediately revised or discontinued altogether. Many professional educators believe that healthful attitudes must be developed in the primary or secondary grades, since it is much more difficult to change a person's attitudes once he has become a young adult. College and university physical activity programs must be of a superior nature or they may only reinforce poor attitudes developed in earlier years.

Figure 18–6. The "martial arts" are a very popular aspect of college and university basic instruction programs. (Courtesy of Dakota State College.)

It is envisioned that, in the future, courses which are at present required for "total" student populations will be increasingly difficult to support. Physical education departments in various parts of the country are beginning to sense a student-faculty uneasiness with regard to required programs. A recent "position paper" of the Western College Men's

Figure 18–7. One physical education activity course that has attracted a great deal of interest by both men and women is SCUBA diving. (Courtesy of the University of Wyoming.)

Physical Education Society (WCMPES), which dealt with the general purpose of physical education, clarified the role of basic instruction programs in higher education as follows:

The purpose of physical education in the educational setting is to provide progressive planned learning experiences to fulfill human needs so that the individual understands alternate opportunities in, and elects freely a life style of, physical activity that is appropriate to time and place.[22]

The WCMPES further asserts that:

—Physical education contributes to the optimal development of every individual as a member of an ever-changing environment, thus furthering his full participation in day-to-day living.
—Physical education provides the opportunity for individuals to attain movement skills at a level which will bring satisfaction, thus serving as an incentive to promote subsequent participation.[22]

Proficiency Testing. Proficiency testing which has been of concern to physical educators for many years, has now taken on new significance as departments and institutions move to performance-based or competency-based programs.

The College Physical Education Commission of the AAHPER states, "We define the term 'proficiency test' as a test administered to a student upon his request, to determine whether he meets a predetermined standard of performance and knowledge in a specific sport or physical education activity."[23] As acknowledged by these authors, the difficulty with this definition arises over the acceptance and definition of "predetermined standard of performance." Many colleges have used performance tests for years in order to determine the skill or knowledge level of students prior to instruction. The results of such tests have been used for placing students in beginning, intermediate, or advanced skill levels, and as pre-instructional data that assist the instructor in determining a final grade or evaluation. Recently, proficiency testing for physical education activities has been used to determine whether exemption from a required course or courses is valid.

If proficiency testing is to be initiated in a basic instruction program, a great deal of pre-orientation and pre-organization needs to be undertaken by the department or faculty that will be involved. "In-house" policies and procedures must be alleviated regarding the administration of the program, the role of students and faculty, and the levels of proficiency that are expected. "A proficiency testing program which is carefully conceived, thoroughly prepared, and well conducted will result in sound educational experiences and decisions."[24]

In addition to the increased emphasis on providing proficiency testing, departments are also initiating various forms of *diagnostic fitness testing* and *student-choice programs.* If students so desire, they may be placed in diagnostic fitness courses during their first term in school and provided with a rather thorough evaluation of their physical fitness level. Students are then counseled and assisted in selecting courses from the curricula which are of interest and which will assist them to achieve increased fitness levels if they so desire. Institutions that do not have required programs provide a wide variety of individual, dual, and team activities specifically geared to student interests.

Several studies conducted in the late 1960's and early 1970's showed a slight decrease in the number of credit hours required in physical education at the college level since 1955. At present, the curtailment of required programs is *not* a national trend, as departments do not voluntarily recommend the elimination of such university requirements. Institutions of all sizes have shown considerable increases in the number of coeducational offerings, and this trend is expected to continue as governmental agencies demand the elimination of sex discrimination. Of considerable interest in this regard are remarks made by Hodgkinson, who states:

In general, research indicates that collegiate environments change students as a

lens gathers light—simply focusing and sharpening what was there to begin with. . . . If one thinks of the huge battery of student services provided on most campuses to feed them, house them, entertain them, and counsel them, one wonders how long we can justify the expense if they make so little difference in the development patterns of students.[25]

It is common knowledge that the students who most need physical activity are those who do not receive it in a totally elective program. If departmental resources exist to cope with the organization and administration of proficiency tests, this procedure may be considered to waive the participation of superiorly skilled students in required programs. Some institutions have initiated rather creative procedures in this regard by permitting students to substitute individualized leisure-time activities for departmental requirements. *No matter what procedure is followed, however, the primary goal is to have students develop positive mental and emotional attitudes toward present and future physical activity participation.*

Student Evaluation

Educators generally agree that student evaluation is perhaps the most important aspect of any form of formalized instruction. It is also considered the most *difficult* task a teacher faces. Solley makes an excellent statement regarding physical educators' problems with grading:

. . . . physical educators find that grading presents almost insurmountable problems in practice. They begin to disagree about how grading should be accomplished—what should be evaluated—how it should be tested—and how often. They sometimes feel that they are misunderstood and misrepresented because of their grading procedures. Physical education grades are suspect—by students, administrators, colleagues, and parents.[26]

There are perhaps as many different approaches to student evaluation at the college and university level as there are professors teaching courses. One of the more common practices followed in basic instruction programs in physical education is the attempted evaluation of students on such criteria as written knowledge tests, demonstrated skill ability, attitude, interest, and a variety of supporting criteria, such as attendance and dress. Whatever procedure is followed, the administrator should make sure that grading practices are clearly outlined by the department and the instructor and that students are informed as to what these practices are. Although instructors must be permitted academic freedom, there is a great deal of merit in attempting to standardize to some degree the evaluation practices and criteria for all courses offered within a department. Some educators believe that physical education activities must be graded only on achievement, while others believe that grades should be determined and given on the basis of many different criteria. The authors believe that the following guidelines should be followed for activity-oriented courses at the college level:

1. In any activity program the *major* emphasis should be placed on the development of desirable student attitudes toward participation. Any evaluation techniques that distract from this objective should be eliminated.

2. Physical education activities should be deemed unique by their very nature and may well necessitate a unique evaluation procedure that may or may not be in keeping with the established criteria for the total institution.

3. Administrators should not unnecessarily subject activity programs to undue criticism and ridicule by dogmatically demanding academic credit and grades, unless such demands are mirrored by evaluation techniques and procedures that are above reproach.

Several studies have indicated that some physical education departments have not changed their basic grading procedures for many years. The letter grade is the predominant method of grade assignment, and the great majority of institutions do not provide the student with the opportunity to take proficiency tests. This is, of course, due to the addi-

tional expenditure of faculty time and the additional use of facilities required for administering proficiency tests. It is estimated that over 70 per cent of institutions of higher education in the United States still include the grade for a physical education activity in the student's grade-point average and in determining scholastic honors as well.

Several innovative approaches to evaluation and grading are worthy of consideration. Washington State University initiated an "A," "S," and "F" system in 1967 in which the A and the F are used in determining a student's grade-point average, but the S is not. Students at that university have accepted this type of grading favorably. Such a system is better than the simpler "S" or "U" system in that it separates the average student from the highly skilled and thus retains some motivational incentive. It also removes much of the heavy evaluation pressures from faculty members and permits more class time for actual student participation.

Some institutions have changed from a letter grading system to the satisfactory or unsatisfactory approach. In some instances, "student choice" prevails, and a student can *choose* to be graded on either the S – U or A – F scale. A survey of grading systems throughout the country indicates that the greater the frequency of "nontraditional" grades on a student's record, the greater the degree of difficulty the student will have in transferring to another college or gaining admission to graduate or professional schools.[27] Difficulty will also be experienced in obtaining financial aid, employment, and in being accepted for graduate study. It is generally believed that the less traditional the grading system, the more an institution will rely on standardized test results, letters of recommendation, individual grade interpretations, and the reputation of the institution from which the student graduated.

As stated previously, grading in the basic instruction program should not be so stringent that it has an adverse effect on the student's interest and attitude toward physical activity and fitness. In the *professional academic program,* however, evaluation and grading should result in a determination of above-average, average, and below-average academic achievement. Most institutions find traditional grading patterns acceptable, but when undergraduate institutions are compared with graduate schools, it is quickly apparent that only a very small percentage of graduate schools find nontraditional grades acceptable.

Curriculum Development

One of the profession's most frustrating and ineffective approaches in curriculum development has been our unsuccessful attempt to obtain academic respectability by mirroring the programs, instruction, credit and evaluation practices of other academic areas. We as physical educators have become bogged down with attempting to design basic instruction programs that will conform to the "basic tenets of democracy" and that will be all things to all people, while still achieving the "academic respectability" of our peers. *Academic respectability must be earned; it cannot be copied.* Basically it must be earned by the quality and demonstrated expertise of the individuals comprising the profession, but it may also be earned by quality curricular offerings of demonstrated and proven worth.

In many instances ineffective basic instructional activity programs have been caused by patterning college curricula and methodology after the programs used in the elementary and secondary schools. This mere continuation of elementary and secondary school programs in higher education is certainly not in keeping with desirable curriculum standards.

The logic of educational continuum demands increasing excellence in degree and quality of skill. In every division of the college curriculum the student is challenged toward expanding skills, knowledge, and understanding. The physical education requirement for the general student must effectively cope with the same high criteria for its program. Higher education must be precisely

what its name implies. It builds on the foundations that its students present and it requires ever higher standards of achievement.[28]

In some areas of the United States, public school physical education is deemed to be of such low quality that colleges must provide programs based upon a minimal previous acquisition of skill. Unfortunate as it may seem, this is true more often than is realized; when this situation occurs, institutions of higher education are required to provide beginning-level activity curricula. In fact, the physical education profession might well be ineffectively devoting a large percentage of its *academic* resources to the development of *fundamental* skill, knowledge, and understanding. Such resources might better be devoted to the improvement of undergraduate professional curricula designed, in turn, to improve the scope and quality of physical education instruction in the public schools.

In developing a basic instruction curriculum for a university, guiding principles must first be established which take into account departmental, college, and professional objectives. Consideration is usually given to sociological, physiological, and psychological principles as they relate to the student population and to the discipline. It is a wise administrative procedure to delegate the responsibility and authority for the total basic instruction program to one or two faculty members and require that they work cooperatively with other faculty and with the department chairperson or dean. As indicated previously, a recent trend in such curricula has been the increased offering of coeducational courses, which *may* necessitate the delegation of responsibility to both a male and female member of the faculty. These *coordinators* or *directors* may then, in turn, delegate the responsibility for various aspects of the activity curriculum (e.g., aquatics) to selected faculty who are directly involved with the actual instruction and curriculum content. The overall coordinators are, however, charged with the responsibilities of recommending schedules, curriculum changes, and faculty assignments; purchasing needed equipment and supplies; and taking any action deemed necessary to better conduct the total program.

Some of the most worthwhile and innovative curriculum developments of recent years are:

1. The enactment of college pre-admission area credit for high school physical education by which students are permitted to enter college classes only if they have no high school physical education deficiencies.

2. The offering of intermediate and advanced skill courses as regular college curricula, with beginning-level courses deemed as high school deficiencies (as related to item no. 1).

3. The increased offering of coeducational activity classes, to the extent that almost all basic instruction courses are now coeducational.

4. The increased emphasis on individual and dual sport activities.

5. The development of individualized activity programs in which students are permitted to participate by themselves and if necessary during their free time.

6. The use of proficiency or achievement tests in waiving specific requirements.

7. The use of flexible scheduling to meet specialized objectives.

8. The minimization of student "coercion" and the maximization of student self-direction, achievement, and individual choice.

UNDERGRADUATE PROFESSIONAL PREPARATION

Formalized instruction in any discipline is an effort on the part of a faculty to assist or to shape growth. Bruner believes that intellectual growth involves an increasing capacity to say to oneself and others, by means of words or symbols, what one has done or what one will do.[29] He further states that a theory of instruction is a vital component of education in that it sets forth rules concerning the most effective way of achieving knowledge or skills. It also provides a yardstick for criticizing or evaluating any particular way of teaching or learning. Theories of instruction set criteria and

state the conditions for meeting them. Such theories should:

1. Specify the experiences which most effectively implant in the individual a predisposition toward learning — learning in general or a particular type of learning.

2. Specify the ways in which a body of knowledge should be structured so that it can be most readily grasped by the learner.

3. Specify the most effective sequences in which to present the materials to be learned.

4. Specify the nature and placing of rewards and punishments in the process of learning and teaching.[30]

Educators must begin by establishing and setting forth the intellectual substance of what is to be taught; otherwise there can be no sense of what challenges and shapes the curiosity of the learner. "A teacher is supposedly the intermediary between the uneducated student and the educated world. Too often the teacher simply looks like an untouchable example of that far-off world, rather than a safe bridge."[31]

Professional Leadership

The propagation of any academic discipline is naturally directly dependent upon its present and future leaders. The scholarly and intuitive direction of present leaders will to a large degree determine the present education and professional preparation of young educators who will carry on their shoulders the future of the profession. Our nation's very rapid advancement in all forms of technology, which tends to promote a sedentary way of life and an overwhelming expansion of knowledge, makes the present a very crucial time in the history of physical education and human movement. As has been discussed previously, physical *inactivity* is apparently increasing, and more and more pressure for time is being evidenced in our schools and institutions of higher learning as available knowledge quickly outdistances the time available to convey it to students. Administrators and leaders in professional physical education must be aware of present trends and quickly perceive pertinent indicators of what may be expected in the future.

As aptly stated by Zeigler, the "now" physical education leadership must display accountability, relevance, and involvement.[32] The administrative leadership of the profession must (1) sharpen the issues; (2) place them in some order of priority; and (3) tell professional colleagues how the field can once again "get in step."[33] Zeigler flatly states that the "shotgun approach" and the "treadmill approach" of professional preparation have got to go. New program developments at the State University at Tyler, Texas, East Stroudsburg State College, The University of Massachusetts, the University of Waterloo, and many other colleges and universities are making major efforts to offer "now" physical education curricula to keep pace with our rapidly moving society. For example, the proposed program at the new state university at Tyler, Texas, has the following as its basic objectives.

1. To prepare individuals to diagnose, prescribe, implement, and evaluate physical development based on an understanding of and skills in physical structure and functions.
2. To offer professional alternatives in teacher education for elementary, secondary, and all level assignments.
3. To offer professional alternatives for roles in industry, business, and community service.
4. To create a greater intrinsic value of self as a function of personal, community, and family health.
5. To promote and guide student inquiry *by faculty example and involvement* in the pursuit of knowledge and skills.

At East Stroudsburg State College, the School of Health Sciences and Physical Education offers approximately 12 different curriculum options for majors in physical education. The School of Physical Education at the University of Massachusetts has organized its physical education department into areas of Exercise Science, Athletics, Leisure Studies and Services, Sports Studies, and Professional Preparation in Physical Education and Dance. This new organizational structure is designed to promote

curricula and academic endeavor which will be more functional and of a higher degree of interest to students and faculty. Unique in the United States but fairly common in Canada, New Zealand, and the United Kingdom are "faculties" which are organized specifically to pursue the study of the academic discipline of human movement. Such "faculties" are not necessarily concerned with the professional preparation of teachers but are generally organized to pursue the study of an academic discipline. Examples are found in Canada at both Simon Frazier University in British Columbia and at the University of Waterloo in Ontario.

Physical educators in positions of academic leadership should be aware that such adaptations are being considered and in some instances implemented, so that they may evaluate the implications for undergraduate professional preparation in their departments and colleges.

A major trend is the increasingly important role played by the community colleges in transfer education. The effects of having large numbers of students transfer from two-year colleges to senior institutions must be given serious consideration in planning future professional undergraduate curricula. It also appears that there will be an increased separation between the structures and functions assigned to undergraduate education as it relates to graduate education and research. The cause of this separation will be increasing demands from funding agencies for accountability and for greater economic efficiency. *State universities usually report a per capita annual cost of undergraduate education of two to five times that of the junior college.*

Administrators must also use their leadership and authority to see that some measure of quality control is maintained at both undergraduate and graduate levels of instruction. This is a difficult task in light of decreasing student enrollments and increasing pressures to maintain students. Within the past few years, many institutions have experienced a decline in student failure rates as student evaluations of their professors and administrative pressures to maintain student enrollments have contributed to higher grading curves. There is also the temptation to attract students who may not have the necessary prerequisites to pursue a university degree. Colleges and universities must become less concerned with academic prestige and more concerned with becoming centers of effective learning. As expressed by Malchlup, "Higher education is too high for the average intelligence, much too high for the average interest, and vastly too high for the average patience and perseverance of the people, here and anywhere. Attempts to expose from 30 to 50 per cent of the people to higher education are completely useless."[34] Malchlup further states that institutions should not reduce academic requirements and the level of their offerings in the name of social justice and equality of opportunity in order to accommodate more individuals who are not prepared to take higher education. That *quality attracts quality* is once again emphasized. Professional leaders should *demand* that every institution follow a sound program of selective admission and retention as well as quality academic programs. It must be realized, of course, that the "quality" pendulum can very well swing too far in either direction; admission and retention programs must be reasonable in their objectives and requirements.

Schools and colleges should do their utmost to thoroughly review undergraduate and graduate degree requirements, examine the content of courses, and explore new teaching methods and new curricula so that basic instruction programs do not become just a "rehash" of high school physical education. Physical education should seriously consider various interdisciplinary approaches and the initiation of nonteaching degrees. Every effort should be made not to let "growth" subvert quality in the recruiting of students. In the future, administrators may very well experience 10 to 20 per cent across-the-board reductions in operating budgets by boards of control and university administrators. Such reductions would be made arbitrarily, and then organizational units which have experienced such reductions would have to justify their reinstatement.

Professional Curricula

The purpose of physical education in 1980 should be to study the effect of movement on man and the effects of man's movement on society.[35]

Undergraduate professional curricula in many institutions are in the midst of change. Traditional programs, curricula, and service offerings are experiencing what may well prove to be the most significant changes made in the profession in the past several decades. Physical education departments that for years were concerned only with teaching pedagogy are now experiencing new pressures to provide courses and curricula that are not solely concerned with preparing elementary and secondary school teachers. Nonteaching degrees are being created, and special emphasis is being given to courses dealing with recreation and leisure. More undergraduate curricula are being developed to study the "academic discipline" via the basic sciences, and more and more programs are providing students with the option of whether or not to seek teacher's certification. Institutions with large student enrollments still tend to offer curricula that provide a greater degree of specialization in a specific area such as motor learning, exercise physiology, and methods and curriculum. A very large percentage of undergraduates majoring in physical education still desire to become successful coaches. This desire is now a career goal for both men and women, and was brought about for women by an increased emphasis on girls' and women's sports.

In the past, the Professional Preparation Panel of the AAHPER was constantly striving to improve undergraduate and graduate preparation by actively supporting projects dealing with certification among states, the development of elementary certification, the certification of interscholastic coaches, institutional flexibility of certification requirements, the development of specialty areas within the physical education major, and the abolishment of the physical education minor. In 1973, at a Professional Preparation Conference, a special task force dealing with certification was vitally concerned with the following:

1. Performance-based teacher certification.
2. The "approved program" concept in contrast with "individual credential" certification.
3. Certification reciprocity.
4. The role of state and federal departments and government in certification.
5. The role of professional associations in certification.
6. Differentiated staffing in certification:
   a. paraprofessionals
   b. specific certification for inner-city programs or other purposes
7. Specialized certification in such areas as coaching, dance, driver education, health education, and recreation.

It is expected that state boards of education will move toward competency-based certification *as soon as competencies can be adequately defined and measured.* Some states have already agreed that teachers must have a wide range of competencies and that professional preparation (both pre-service and in-service) throughout teaching careers must be developed around such competencies. In the state of Florida, performance-based certification suggests that the evidence used to designate those qualified as teachers should be directly related to teaching performance, rather than assuming that course credit hours or degrees will describe the qualified teacher. The success of the Florida program, and that of such plans in other states, will depend upon how well individuals and institutions develop and implement new techniques for training personnel and evaluating their performance.

Coeducational Curricula

One of the most critically difficult issues in the undergraduate professional preparation of physical educators is the need to develop coeducational curricula. It is incomprehensible that academic administrators responsible for the funding and allocation of institutional resources have for so long permitted the duplication of faculty and facilities that is found in many of our institutions of higher learning. This separation of the sexes was brought to an end when the Federal Department of Health, Education and Welfare released its long-awaited regulations providing for the implementation of Title IX of the 1972 educational amendments. Title IX states that "No person...shall on the basis of sex be excluded from participation in, be denied the benefits of, or be subjected to discrimination under any education program or activity receiving Federal financial assistance."[36] This legislation is similar to Title VI of the Civil Rights Act, which prohibits discrimination on the basis of race in educational programs. This regulation affects nearly all public school systems in the country, as well as the nearly 2500 institutions of post-secondary education that receive federal funds. *Title IX covers three major areas—admissions, treatment of students, and employment.* The regulations that have the greatest importance for physical education and athletics are included in the area of "treatment of students." In the sub-area entitled "athletics," the general provision states that:

No person, on the basis of sex, shall be excluded from participation in, be denied the benefits of, be treated differently from other persons, or otherwise be discriminated against in any physical education or athletic program operated by a recipient, and no recipient shall provide any physical education or athletic program separately on such basis; provided, however, that a recipient may operate or sponsor separate teams for members of each sex where selection for teams is based on competitive skill.

Each recipient that operates or sponsors athletics shall (1) determine, at least annually and using a method to be selected by the recipient which is acceptable to the Director of the Office of Civil Rights (HEW), in what sports members of each sex would desire to compete; (2) where athletic opportunities previously have been limited, the recipient shall make affirmative efforts to inform both men *and* women of the availability of athletic opportunities and provide support and training activities designed to improve and expand the capabilities of those interested in participating in such opportunities. Further provisions on athletics state that when separate teams are operated on the basis of sex, there shall be no discrimination on the basis of sex in the provision of equipment or supplies for each team, or in any other manner. Provisions of this section, however, should not be interpreted to mean that equal aggregate expenditures are required for athletics for members of each sex.

Other provisions of Title IX which specifically affect physical education are in the area of treatment of students with regard to course offerings.

Course offerings or other educational activities shall not be provided separately on the basis of sex; an institution may not require or refuse participation therein by any of its students on such basis, including health, physical education, industrial, business, vocational, technical, home economics, music, and adult education courses.[37]

Performance-Based Teacher Preparation

One of the most controversial issues ever faced by departments and colleges involved in the professional preparation of teachers is that of competency-based and/or performance-based teacher education. Despite much controversy, competency-based approaches are still being demanded as institutions attempt to become "accountable."

There are two extreme approaches to performance-based teacher preparation. One approach is to view teaching as an art, not a science; the other is the "behavioral analysis–systems design" attitude, which reduces the teaching process to a long list of rigidly defined competencies. Many physical educators believe that a physical education teacher should be performance-based rather than competency-based. They feel that successful physical education experiences should be process-oriented and field-centered. Traditional courses in educational psychology, history, philosophy, and teaching methods, capped by a brief stint of student teaching, have in some instances been replaced by a sequential curriculum in which each course combines classroom work with field experience in school and community settings and in progressively more complexed teaching-learning situations. A successful program at Brooklyn College in New York City is based upon the assumption that teachers should be educated to be aware of and play a major role in shaping the changes that seem certain to occur in the field of education.[38] Another basic assumption of this program is that the education of teachers should involve not only the professional institution but also the public schools, community school boards, parents, teachers' unions, and educational industries. Most performance-based teacher preparation programs are designed to place prospective teachers in real classrooms or gymnasia very early in their professional preparation. Some course work is often conducted in a school rather than on a campus, so that faculty members can bring in teachers who are working successfully with particular methods or materials. Clinical experiences, such as student teaching, are usually expanded, and the ability to draw up lists of behavioral objectives or performance criteria in terms of knowledge and attitudes is a skill which students are expected to develop in their course of training.

Non-teaching degrees for physical educators are also becoming more popular, and professional curricula have been specifically developed in several universities to accomplish this end. Such curricula usually follow the traditional physical education pattern but delete clinical experiences that are specifically designed for schools as well as other professional education courses dealing specifically with elementary and secondary education. In their place, appropriate courses are selected (with the assistance of an advisor) which deal specifically with the student's future occupational plans. In this way courses are tailored to meet the needs of students in such areas as athletic training, pre-physical therapy, graduate level research, and sports-oriented positions in health spas, YMCA's and YWCA's.

One of the most serious problems facing the development of professional curricula around the world lies in the apparent dichotomy between the physical education researcher and the teaching practitioner. Some physical educators believe that the type of practitioner being produced by present physical education programs is merely an "overeducated technician," and that present curricula are only providing a thin overlay of science and scientific method so that students can discuss matters only in a superficial (although professionally accepted) manner. For example, Loughborough College in England believes that physical education, sports science, and recreation are cross-disciplinary approaches to the study of man's movement, performance, and behavior in relation to play, physical exercise, sport, and leisure. Because there has been such a tremendous growth of knowledge concerning human performance over the past 30 years, the faculty at Loughborough believes that the term *physical education* has been stretched beyond its logical limits. The scientific components of the study of human movement — including biomechanics, exercise physiology, perceptual-motor learning, and the social-cultural aspects of human movement (in the historical, philosophical, sociological, and comparative studies in sports) — have enormously increased the scope of physical education. Because the subject has matured into the study of man as a whole, as he participates in the total sport phenomena, Loughborough College has renamed its physical education department and restructured it into the three areas of physical education, sport science, and recreation. It will be interesting to see whether the specialized programs now being developed in

New Zealand, Canada, and the United Kingdom will have any effect upon American curricula. There was a general agreement among program administrators in the late 1960's that undergraduate curricula in physical education should prepare a "generalist." Very few institutions have emphasized "competencies" rather than "time" spent in courses. The average number of physical education credit hours required in professional curricula is still approximately 42 semester hours or 63 quarter hours, with the average number of credit hours necessary for graduation being some 128 semester hours or 192 quarter hours.

Program Evaluation

The evaluation of undergraduate professional programs of study requires several different approaches and procedures. Such evaluation may or may not involve accreditation, but it must always be conducted in light of *established standards*. These standards may be self-imposed or they may be established in cooperation with other institutions, national professional organizations, or accreditation agencies. Today, however, the development of standards must include the establishment of instructional goals, the development of an educationally accountable program, and the many requirements of competency-based teacher education. "The physical educator must have an understanding of the meaning and significance of movement, the growth and development of the individual and the application of physical, biological and behavioral sciences to assist individuals in reaching awareness of self and others."[39]

In 1965 the Professional Preparation Panel of the AAHPER introduced a "Self-Evaluation Check List," prepared from materials contained in the 1962 Report of the National Conference on Professional Preparation. This checklist contains the following seven standards: (1) Objectives of Professional Preparation; (2) Organization and Administration; (3) Student Personnel; (4) Faculty; (5) Curriculum; (6) Professional Laboratory Experiences; and (7) Facilities and Instructional Materials.

The 1962 National Conference on Undergraduate Professional Preparation recommended that formulated guidelines be periodically revised. Therefore, in 1972, an additional National Conference was sponsored by the AAHPER, at which revisions were made by each of the eight administrative divisions. The conference's planning committee desired that the conference focus on new ideas, concepts, competencies, and experiences which might have significance in professional preparation programs. It was hoped that the deliberation of the conferees would have immediate implications for professional preparation and a great impact on future programs. "The profession fully recognizes that the endeavor to improve professional preparation programs is not a culminating activity itself but a reaffirmation of our commitment to meet the needs and interests of the people served."[40]

The 1972 Professional Preparation Conference provided program evaluation guides for each of the special interest areas of dance, physical education, recreation education, safety education, and school health education. These guidelines should be consulted as pertinent areas of reference prior to program evaluation. Recommendations made in physical education centered on the basic concept that teacher preparation programs should be performance- or competency-based, with a field-centered approach. The key concerns included:

1. Identification of skills, knowledges, and attitudes to be demonstrated by the students.
2. Identification of experiences designed to accomplish these competencies.
3. Determination of criteria to be accepted as proof of achievement.
4. Constant assessment of the student's rate of progress, based on performance rather than on time or course completion.
5. Attention focused on "exit behavior."

Appraisal and fact finding are basic to the evaluation process and often result in recommendations for change. Total evaluation is not achieved until valid changes are made and, in turn, evaluated in terms of desired results.

All physical educators should become familiar with the results and recommendations of the 1972 Conference. In addition, the results of a 1972 conference on professional preparation of the elementary specialists should be of vital interest to students and educators interested in the field of elementary physical education. This conference was co-sponsored by the AAHPER Elementary School Physical Education Commission of the Physical Education Division and the Task Force on Children's Dance of the Dance Division. The specific purposes of this conference were to:

1. Review beliefs about children and their needs for movement, esthetic, and rhythmical experiences.
2. Develop insights concerning the significance and uniqueness of comprehensive development programs for children.
3. Clarify the role of dance in a comprehensive physical education program.
4. Examine guidelines for professional preparation.
5. Identify recommendations for action by members and by the association.[41]

Accreditation assists with evaluation in that it involves the establishment of certain minimum standards by a professional body or association and the assessment of whether or not these standards are being met. The results of such evaluations are then published. Accreditation for teacher education was initiated in the United States in 1927 when the American Association of Teachers Colleges began to issue membership lists. In 1948 the American Association of Colleges for Teacher Education (AACTE) was organized, which in 1954 transferred its accrediting function to the National Council for Accreditation of Teacher Education (NCATE). In 1960 the national AAHPER approved the recommendation that NCATE be accepted as the accrediting organization for teacher education in health education, physical education, and recreation education. The AAHPER then urged that state departments of education grant teacher certification only to graduates of institutions accredited by NCATE.

Administrators of physical education professional programs must realize that the standards usually presented by national or regional professional agencies or by state departments of education are *minimal* standards, and that every effort must be made to go beyond mediocrity.

Selection and Retention of Students

The striving for excellence and the upholding of standards are to a large extent directly dependent upon a department's or college's authority and responsibility for the initial selection and continued retention of its students.

In many institutions in which physical education is a department within a College of Education or a College of Arts and Sciences, the selection and retention process is performed by a college committee operating under the guidance of standards set for the total college. Representation on such a committee may or may not consist of a faculty member from each department in the college. These committees, like national or regional accreditation associations, usually grant admission or permit retention based on minimal standards. In most instances physical education departments are of sufficient size to form selection and retention committees within their own administrative organization and to base their recommendations upon *both* the overall standards set by their college and those criteria deemed pertinent and vital to maintaining standards and promoting excellence in physical education. In this procedure, the professors who know the students *best* are involved in recommendations for retention. A representative of the total college, appointed by the dean, also sits on the committee, to ensure that general college policies are adhered to. This same procedure is followed for Colleges of Health, Physical Education, and Recreation that contain separate departments for each discipline. The underlying principle of this procedure is that

no attempt should be made at any administrative or organizational level to enforce a standardization of selection and retention policies *that do not permit departments to raise standards beyond the expected minimum.*

Specific policies and procedures then should be developed and enforced within the department of physical education in accordance with departmental objectives, the recommendations of national and regional professional agencies and associations, and certification requirements. It is regrettably true that in many institutions professional programs are experiencing a "high grade syndrome" as a result of increasingly liberal grading policies. Declining student enrollments and the increasing importance given by administrators to student evaluations of their professors have both contributed to a higher grading curve.

GRADUATE STUDY

Since Columbia University offered the first master's degree in physical education in 1901 and the first doctorate (Ph.D.) degree in 1924, graduate study for physical educators has undergone criticism, change, and, for the most part, an unfortunate lack of national consensus as to purpose and direction. This lack of unanimity is not restricted to physical education; it is a serious problem in many other disciplines as well.

In 1971, in the total field of education, some 90,000 master's degrees were awarded for both men and women, and approximately 6400 doctoral degrees were earned.[42] Of these totals, over 4300 master's degrees were awarded in physical education (excluding health education), and some 280 doctoral degrees were granted. Tabulated data for the same year reveal that approximately 25,000 bachelor's degrees were given to both men and women in physical education, by far the largest total for any discipline within the total field of education. In spite of the apparent oversupply of individuals with advanced degrees, the National Board on Graduate Education continues to support "student choice" as the best guide to policy on graduate study in the United States.[43] This board attempts to forecast and determine the manpower needs for doctorates in the various professions. The board does not believe that the United States should as yet become involved in "manpower planning" and "human capital analysis," as is practiced in many socialistic and developing nations. Instead, it feels that students should be provided with factual information on the labor market and institutions, and that the government should examine carefully the need for additional degree programs. New graduate programs that merely duplicate existing programs should not be approved.

The Nature of Graduate Study

Graduate study is usually considered to be any formalized study that is pursued after the successful completion of the first professional or baccalaureate degree. The purpose of graduate study is to discover, disseminate, and preserve knowledge. Doctoral degree programs are primarily concerned with the training of individuals for faculty positions in institutions of higher learning or for positions in business and industry. Such training may involve programs designed primarily for instruction or research or a combination of both. Prior to the initiation of graduate study at Yale in 1861, scholars from the United States pursued advanced degrees in Germany. Graduate programs in Germany maintained a heavy emphasis upon independent study and research; thus, when advanced degrees were introduced in this country, they were primarily patterned after German programs. The introduction of the Doctor of Education degree at Harvard University in 1921 was later followed by the first awarding of these degrees in physical education at Stanford University and the University of Pittsburgh in 1929. Doctor of Education programs were designed with less emphasis upon independent study and research and more provision for subject matter content, designed to improve teaching and educational supervision.

Some physical educators believe that graduate study should be concerned with philosophy, history, principles, and research, rather than with the continuation of skills and techniques. "Graduate education should be designed to develop the ability of students to read widely and rapidly with comprehension; to find and use available source materials in the solution of problems; to produce work of an original nature; to do independent and critical thinking; to find, organize, and evaluate evidence; and to formulate and defend conclusions."[44] Graduate programs have traditionally emphasized a concentrated and specialized form of study centered on investigation and research, and were based upon high standards of excellence. During the past 10 years, however, the nature of graduate study in education has changed considerably with the initiation of fifth-year programs that were brought about primarily because school districts demanded that their teachers attain additional course work beyond the baccalaureate. Since not all teachers were deemed competent to pursue traditional master's degree programs, an additional year of course work that did not lead to a graduate degree was initiated by some institutions. Problems in this approach quickly became evident. Once admitted for such "limited" study, students then wanted to change and complete a graduate program leading to a degree. Some master's degree programs thus became "diluted" and, in many instances, students came to expect that if they had successfully completed their baccalaureate they were "entitled" to a master's degree. This unfortunate situation has led to the concept of offering two types of degree programs at the master's level.

Paralleling this course of action, doctoral programs have for some time followed the concept that there are two approaches to advanced study. The Doctor of Philosophy degree is generally designated as the research oriented program, whereas the Doctor of Education emphasizes professional expertise related to teaching. No differentiation should be made regarding quality but a difference should exist regarding the uses to which such specialized knowledge is put.

Doctoral programs should certainly provide a much more concentrated and specialized form of study and investigation than was evidenced at either the undergraduate or master's levels. There does not appear to be much doubt, however, that master's degree programs in education are becoming (or have become) for the most part an extension of undergraduate preparation.

An outdated view of academic life as a pastoral existence separate from the rest of society, the application of a single standard of excellence to diverse institutions, and an unfounded opinion that America has overdeveloped its system of advanced education have prevented the nation's graduate schools from making significant changes to meet the needs of new types of students seeking graduate study.[45]

Present Programs

Graduate curricula in health education, physical education, and recreation and park administration are now offered by almost all state universities, many state colleges, and some private institutions in the United States and Canada.

Degrees that are commonly awarded include the Master of Arts, Master of Education, Doctor of Education, and Doctor of Philosophy. Two institutions offer a Physical Education Doctorate, and several offer a Director's diploma or the Professional diploma—Specialist in Education, which is a sixth-year program between the master's and the doctorate. The specific nature of graduate study leading to such degrees is quite varied and depends upon the objectives and emphases of individual institutions. Curricula are usually organized into programs of concentrated study and research in each of the three academic disciplines commonly housed in departments, divisions, schools, or colleges of Health, Physical Education, and Recrea-

tion. Administrative units designated as divisions, schools, or colleges in an institution of higher education may or may not be primarily responsible for the awarding of graduate degrees. Departmental structures must, of course, work in cooperation with a college and/or an institutional administrator responsible for graduate study, such as a dean of the graduate school. In some universities, departments work directly with the graduate school dean; in others, they must function through the college in which they are housed. In some instances, schools or colleges of physical education have the autonomy to regulate and award their own graduate degrees.

Present programs have been assisted by the recommendations of two national conferences dealing with graduate study. The first of these conferences was held in 1950 and the latest in 1967.[46, 47] The Pere Marquette conference in 1950 presented the overall objectives of graduate study: (a) the production of better teachers, leaders, administrators, and creative scholars; (b) the stimulation and improvement of the quality of research and its consumption; and (c) the development of specialists who have preparation in particular lines of endeavor beyond the bachelor's degree.

Higher education has already witnessed the development of post-doctoral programs in many disciplines, and such programs are now deemed necessary in several areas of physical education. The so-called "knowledge explosion" and the demand that all public school teachers receive a minimum of five years of formal academic education may well lead to required post-doctoral study.

Organization, Administration, and Evaluation

The determination of the nature and direction of graduate study programs in physical education should be the joint responsibility of (a) the department chairperson, director, or dean, and (b) the institutional director of graduate study. All decisions of this nature should be evaluated carefully by these two administrators and, depending upon the magnitude of the problem, they should seek consultation and recommendations from graduate faculty, institutional graduate committees, and possibly an outside graduate consultant. There are five essential criteria upon which quality graduate curricula are based:

1. The necessary financial support of the institution required to provide *above-average facilities, equipment, supplies, and faculty.*
2. The required number of *competent and well-qualified faculty* who have a high degree of specific expertise, in order to provide the instruction demanded for *all courses* in the desired curriculum.
3. The availability of *well-qualified students.*
4. The *organizational and administrative structure* which will permit internal organization, quality control, and semiautonomous or autonomous budgetary control.
5. The *instructional and research resources* of a complete university, if doctoral programs are to be offered.

At the doctoral level, several requirements in addition to those just cited are demanded. Many doctoral programs, for example, concentrate on some aspect of the basic sciences and the related aspects of medicine, so that a biomedical library is almost a necessity. This is not usually found in institutions that do not have a school of medicine. In order to provide a program of excellence in administration, strong supporting work is required in areas of commerce and business as well as from a department of higher education. Administrators are just as prone as their faculty to actively encourage and lobby for the initiation of advanced degree programs when, in fact, such programs may prove to be substandard and indeed reduce the quality and scope of undergraduate or master's programs.

If graduate programs have been organized and put into operation they should be under the direct administrative supervision of an individual who is knowledgeable about their structure and function. Even in relatively small departments if one or more master's degrees are offered they should be under the supervision of a member of the faculty who has been delegated this responsibility and provided with the necessary authority to see that the graduate program functions efficiently and smoothly. This individual should be responsible for making recommendations pertaining to graduate faculty assignments; teaching loads; purchase of supplies and equipment; admission and retention; course offerings; and the initiation of graduate curricula modification. This person should also represent the department or college in institu-

Figure 18–8. Sophisticated research in biomechanics and motor learning is an important aspect of graduate study in physical education. (Courtesy of Penn State University.)

tional graduate policy making committees as well as in those research committees deemed pertinent.

The Professional Preparation Panel of the AAHPER has prepared a Self-Evaluation Check List for Graduate Programs[48] which includes items from the report of the AAHPER Conference on Graduate Education. This checklist may prove to be of value to administrators who desire to quickly evaluate their programs in each of five areas.

Admission and Retention of Students

If the broad purposes of graduate study in physical education are indeed to extend the boundaries of knowledge through programs of research and to further professional preparation of personnel for positions requiring educational competence and leadership, the profession should have the right to develop and enforce graduate admission and retention policies. Such a requirement is stated as one of several criteria in the self-evaluation checklist published by the AAHPER. This statement reads, "The department exercises control over its graduate enrollment in accordance with its ability to develop and maintain a high quality program.[49] The self-evaluation report goes on to state that admission to graduate study in physical education should be based upon many factors which may include professional preparation, previous experience, intelligence and knowledge, communication skills, personal integrity, and professional interest and diligence. No matter what criteria are established, there should be a written statement of policies concerning the selection and retention or dismissal of students from the graduate program.

Specific criteria found to be in common practice across the country for initial admission to graduate study are the graduate record examinations, undergraduate grade point average (cumulative total for four years, total for last two years, and total physical education for four years), letters of recommendation, and institutional entrance examinations

for colleges of education. The GRE aptitude test (verbal ability and quantitative ability) has in many institutions replaced the Miller Analogies as the single criterion most frequently used for graduate admissions. Some colleges or universities require a minimal GRE *total* aptitude score of 800 for master's admission and 1000 for admission to doctoral programs. Such levels are not considered high, since only 22 per cent of all men score below 400 on verbal ability and 21 per cent score below 400 on quantitative ability. These figures for a doctoral level score of 1000 (500 each area) are 50 per cent and 46 per cent respectively.[50] Undergraduate grade point averages are generally considered to be a good indicator of predicted success at graduate levels. If an extensive selection and admission procedure is carried out it would be reasonable to assume that a greater majority of students who were admitted would successfully graduate. *The single most important element in selection and admission is that careful consideration be given beforehand to the establishment of policies and that once they have been established, they be applied with consistency to all candidates.*

The modernization of graduate curricula and reforms in advanced degree programs are going to affect graduate study in physical education just as they affect other academic areas. Significant attempts are being made to provide (a) a component of discipline-related work outside the university walls; (b) an increase in the number of female and minority students in graduate admissions; (c) the development within graduate schools and programs of statements of goals and functions; (d) the development of alternative standards of evaluation for different types of graduate schools; (e) the equal weighting of faculty teaching and community service with research and publication; and (f) the periodic re-evaluation of subject matter. Several universities have also developed new programs in which a Doctor of Arts Degree is granted, with emphasis upon the academic preparation of college and university teachers.

Research

Bookwalter and Vanderzwaag state, "Research is the unbiased, systematic, and accurate collection, analysis, and interpretation of facts related to a definite problem or hypothesis in order to effect its solution and to generalize thereon."[51] These authors conclude that research extends man's intelligence. The age-old argument over the relative importance of research and how it relates to teaching certainly cannot be solved here. Administratively, the nature of research, its scope and quality, and its many roles in the organization are some of the most pressing and difficult problems in higher education.

The nature and quality of research per se will depend upon the primary objectives and the nature of the graduate or undergraduate programs with which it is associated. Most institutions place little, if any, emphasis upon investigation and research at the undergraduate level. If physical education is to progress as a profession at both the undergraduate and graduate levels, we as physical educators must (1) attain greater accord in our philosophy of physical education; (2) synthesize in a scholarly manner the principles and practices recommended by our better sources; (3) contribute more to the basic and practical research in our field; and (4) if possible, synthesize the isolated particles of research into a science.[52]

Regardless of which graduate emphasis a student decides to pursue, if such direction leads to the awarding of a graduate degree, he should be required to receive, as part of his graduate education, course work dealing with the *fundamental* aspects of research and advanced measurement. Teachers at any level must be able to intelligently interpret test scores as well as pertinent new findings in their discipline if they are to continue to improve professionally. Students pursuing doctoral programs (no matter what their emphasis) should be required to take intermediate or advanced courses in both research methods and statistical analysis. Often students who do not intend to become "research specialists" will state that such a requirement is not appropriate for their future desires, yet they fail to realize that by far the greatest majority of them will become members of graduate faculties in colleges or universities. They will thus become graduate advisors or members of graduate committees, and if they are not at least minimally knowledgeable in research and analysis, the *quality* of graduate studies conducted under their direction will suffer greatly.

Physical education academic administrators should do their utmost to ensure that graduate research is practical and relevant. All too often, research programs are promoted that are not basically related or considered practical in light of the needs and objectives of the profession. The lure of research grants for study in peripheral disciplines is indeed tempting, but graduate study and research programs should not be permitted to "stray" until such time as pertinent basic needs are satisfied. Once again, we must not forget that *academic respectability cannot be copied; it must be earned.*

INTRAMURAL SPORTS PROGRAMS

Intramural sports programs for both men and women continue to play an increasingly important role in the lives of countless thousands of college and university students in the United States and throughout the world. Because of the philosophically sound educational relationship that must exist between physical education and intramural sports, the authors firmly believe that physical educators and physical education administrators must be thoroughly knowledgeable in the areas of intramural supervision, organization, and administration. Means supports this view with the following statement:

Intramurals are a pleasing combination of the elements of physical education and the modern concept of recreation. They form the physical recreation phase of applied physical education. From knowledges and skills learned in the physical education class, to the voluntary utilization of these basic elements in the recreation setting, one realizes the scope and potential of the good program. The rapid surge toward automation, the growing problem of seasonal or prolonged unemployment, and the changed pattern of American living have all conspired to place new importance on recreational sports as an integral and indispensable part of modern living. Thus intramurals as a part of education in preparation for living have taken on deeper meaning.[53]

Intramurals for both men and women should provide activities in which the knowledge and skills learned in physical education activity programs can be utilized by all students. *The organization and administration of such programs, as they pertain to the physical education administrator, are of vital importance.*

Administrative Organization

The administration of intramural sports programs in universities and colleges is usually placed in the hands of a director of intramurals. The director's duties and responsibilities should be clearly defined in relation to the organizational plan within which he is to function. If he is to be the administrator of a college or university program, the director should be professionally trained in some phase of physical education, intramurals, or recreation, and should have earned a master's degree. Mutual planning and cooperation with other members of the physical education or athletic faculty (or both) is a necessity. In small colleges the director may be assigned to a reduced teaching load in physical education in addition to providing the leadership for intramurals. The director should not be required, however, to teach more than one-half of what is considered to be a normal teaching load, and he should be provided with a sufficient number of teaching assistants or other faculty to assist him with his duties. He should also be provided with an intramural office and a full-time secretary.

Most institutions have one of three different types of organizational control for the administration of intramural programs. These traditional approaches have usually revolved around (a) a combined department or administrative unit of intercollegiate athletics, physical education, recreation, and intramural sports; (b) a separate physical education department, school, or college, with an administrative division for intramural sports for men and women; (c) an independent intramural department organized for intramural sports and campus recreation. The success of the administration of intramurals as a part of physical education and separated from intercollegiate athletics depends to a large degree on the availability of facilities. If the physical education–intramural department is provided with sufficient indoor and outdoor facilities, these two programs can make maximal use of such areas 18 hours per day. If only a few activity areas are available,

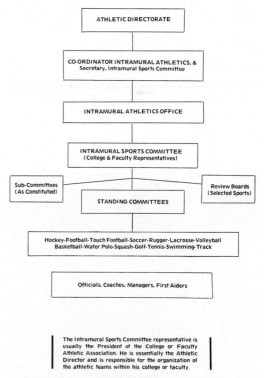

Figure 18–9. An example of the organization of a university intramural program, where the intramural athletic program is responsible to the "Athletic Directorate." (Courtesy of the University of Toronto.)

intercollegiate programs often have to limit their intramural offerings. In smaller colleges in which national prominence in athletics is not demanded at "all costs," combined administrative units appear to function very well. It is also true that in very large universities with outstanding physical facilities for physical education, intramurals, and athletics, a separate school or college plan will function well. Almost all aspects of physical education programs can and do coordinate well with intramural programs for men and women, but there is a definite time scheduling difficulty between many intramural programs and intercollegiate athletics. As the scope of athletic programs for women increases, this conflict of interest will also become a problem for intramurals for women. No matter what type of organization is involved, the nature and quality of intramural programs, like any other offering, is directly dependent upon the compe-

tencies of the various individuals involved.

In 1969, Berg presented three trends that he believed would have considerable impact on intramural sports and on those who administer such programs. These trends were:

1. The suggestion that intramural sports should no longer be structured as a department under the auspices of physical education and recreation or athletics, but should be structured in such a way that the director of intramural sports would answer and be directly responsible to an administrative officer at the vice-presidential level of the institution.

2. The belief that as the popularity of sports clubs expands they should come under the jurisdiction and administration of the intramural sports department.

3. The development and offering of various sports programs for children and youth of surrounding communities who are not students or affiliated in any way with the institution. Such programs would be offered

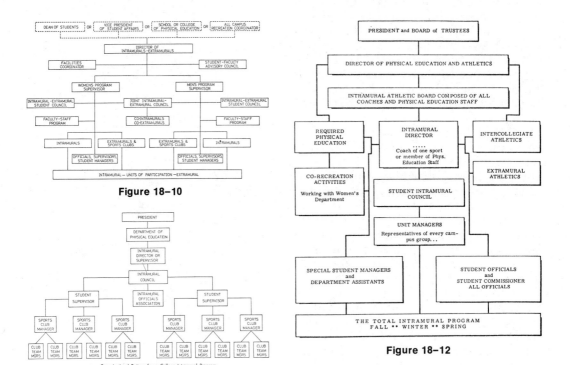

Figure 18–10

Figure 18–11

Figure 18–12

Figures 18–10, 18–11, and 18–12. These figures illustrate three of the most common organizational patterns found in colleges and universities. (From Mueller, Pat: *Intramurals: Programming and Administration.* New York: The Ronald Press Co., 1971.)

during the summer months when the institution's recreational facilities are not in full use by students and faculty.[54]

Physical education administrators and intramural directors should be cognizant of the many ramifications and implications of these possible directions for the future. The administration of sports clubs may well be suitably housed in intramural departments, and certainly there can be no argument about the merit of opening facilities during the summer months; clearly, this trend is long overdue. However, the suggestion that intramural sports should be structured as an entirely different organization from that of physical education raises serious implications. If correctly organized and administered, there should be many advantages to a close working relationship between physical education and intramurals, in keeping with the definition of intramurals presented at the beginning of this discussion. The sharing of faculty, facilities, and equipment—three procedures that require a high degree of coordination—illustrates a most efficient expenditure of state monies. In many instances it is also educationally desirable to coordinate physical education instruction with the intramural sports programs, so that students will have the opportunity to practice their acquired skill during or immediately after they have participated in an instructional program. In situations where intramural programs have been separated from physical education, much coordinated endeavor for the betterment of both programs has been lost.

Intramural programs for women should be administered by an intramural director who is organizationally coordinated with women's physical education. Many of the identical procedures discussed for the men's program should also be followed for the women's program. The increase in coeducational or "social-recreational" activities in college programs is a desirable and valuable part of a complete and modern program. "Co-recreational sports offer just one more valuable method of effecting and approximating the socially, mentally, and phy-

sically adjusted individual who will be better prepared to meet his adult responsibilities."[55] If intramural programs for women are associated with the department, school, or college of physical education, it is desirable to provide an intramural sports department under which both men's and women's programs are administered. Title IX requires that there be no discrimination or separation on the basis of sex. If programs for both men and women are housed together in a division or department of intramural sports, it greatly facilitates the use of supplies, equipment, part-time help, and facilities.

Intramural Finance

There are several different methods of financing intramural sports programs. As with physical education, the most important administrative concerns are facilities, finance, supplies, and equipment. Sources of income or overall funding are usually derived from student activity fees; physical education budgets, general university funds, allocations from intercollegiate athletic gate receipts, entry and forfeit fees, "gate receipts" generated from admission charges, organizational dues, and miscellaneous sources such as contributions and various fund raising activities. In some instances a combination of two or more of these methods is employed. *Irrespective of which of these approaches is followed, intramural programs for both men and women in large departments or colleges should have specifically designated and separate budget allocations.* Such budgets should be under the delegated supervision of intramural directors, and these individuals should be responsible for their preparation and submission.

Outline of Budget Items[56]

I. Personnel
   A. Full and/or Part-time Staff
   B. Student Miscellaneous Employees
      1. Game officials

2. Area supervisors
3. Office clerks and messengers
4. Swimming lifeguards
5. Publicity reporters and photographers
II. Equipment
  A. Sports Equipment
  B. Office Furniture
  C. Office Machines
III. Supplies
  A. Office Supplies
    1. Stencils, marking pens
    2. Stationery, envelopes
    3. Paper supplies
  B. Publicity
    1. Newsletters and posters
    2. Handbooks
    3. Orientation folders
    4. Photographic supplies
  C. Awards
    1. Individual and team trophies
    2. Medals, ribbons, certificates
    3. T-shirts, jackets, blankets
IV. Expenses
  A. Transportation
    1. For extramural participants
    2. For national and regional meetings
  B. Professional Literature and Dues
  C. Insurance Premiums
  D. Telephone and Telegraph
  E. Special Events
  F. Contingency Fund

In most universities the organization of budgets for intramural sports follows the general budgetary patterns for the total institution. Budgetary allocations may therefore be line-itemed or they may be an all-encompassing allocation that is left up to the administrative discretion of the supervisor. Financial expenditures for intramural sports must be conducted in such a manner that all programs can demonstrate a high degree of accountability, to the students and to the institution as a whole. Intramural supervisors and directors should be able to provide a clear and concise outline of their program objectives as well as set policies and procedures for the smooth operation of the various programs. Many intramural programs in the United States grew and are growing rapidly, with very little, if any, planning for the future based on projections of student interest, needs, and enrollments.

Permitting total student funding of in-tramural programs is not considered a financially sound administrative procedure unless such funds are designated as part of the overall institutional student activity fee. Even if funds are generated in this manner, they may still be subject to withdrawal, as has been witnessed in several recent cases of student protests involving student fee requirements to finance intercollegiate athletic programs. The necessity of planning programs based on monies obtained from intramural projects is also not in keeping with the need for a balanced continuous offering. Appropriations from student senates also fluctuate from year to year, depending upon the wishes of elected senators. By far the most appropriate and sound approach is to request that intramural budgets be obtained from appropriated institutional funds. These programs are certainly worthy of institutional support and may be justified in many different ways by the intramural director and the departmental head or dean under whose administration the program is housed.

Sports Clubs

Student sports clubs date back many years in American higher education. Records indicate that both Stanford and Purdue Universities had several different student sports clubs as early as 1905. The current impetus for the creation and support of sports clubs began during the early 1960's, and sports clubs today are increasing dynamically in both scope and numbers. This renewed interest in sports club activities has primarily come about because of the curtailment or limitations being placed on some intercollegiate athletic activities. As intercollegiate athletic funding becomes more difficult, institutions are eliminating selected varsity sports altogether or recommending that they be placed on a sports club basis, funded from student fees, or set up as a regularly budgeted university offering. Such activities as tennis, golf, rugby, and soccer have received considerable student financial support and interest when operated on a "club" basis.

By the late 1960's several studies revealed that there was a great deal of diversification in the administrative policies governing sports clubs. In the majority of instances sports clubs are placed under the administrative jurisdiction of departments of physical education. In other instances they are organized and supervised by athletic departments and various student organizational units, or in an autonomous intramural department. "Early affiliation between sports clubs and a single responsible school unit is most desirable. The department of physical education is the most logical choice for official attachment, as most sports clubs are dependent upon facilities, qualified guidance and instruction, scheduling, provision for officials, eligibility, and other related matters."[57] The director of intramural sports is the most qualified individual to provide the assistance and guidance required for successful club programs. Working cooperatively with the institutional dean of students or with his or her representative, the director of intramural sports can assist club members to promote, finance, conduct, and continue their programs. Like any other student program, sports clubs should establish program objectives and clearly indicate criteria for expansion and growth. Club membership should include established controls over eligibility, liability, and instruction, and all clubs should have a faculty or staff advisor.

INTERCOLLEGIATE ATHLETICS FOR MEN AND WOMEN

Intercollegiate athletic programs for men and women, if conducted in the proper educational perspective and organized and administered with sound professional objectives, are a vital part of a complete physical education curriculum in a small college or university. It has been stated for years that competitive athletics serve as a laboratory for teaching special skills and developing desirable habits and attitudes. This is certainly *possible*, and in fact is the *actual* practice in many institutions. Unfortunately there are perhaps just as many instances in which this statement has become a popular cliché to express the values of athletic programs, whereas in actual practice little, if any, attempt is made to do anything more than develop national championships. If this is indeed the basic goal of intercollegiate programs, it should be clearly stated and programs operated accordingly.

Title IX of the 1972 Education Amendments Act has had the most far-reaching effect on intercollegiate athletic competition of any federal legislation ever enacted. The development of national legislation regarding discrimination on the basis of sex was brought about by increasing concern and documentation of the problems of sex discrimination in educational institutions. As quoted previously, "No person... shall on the basis of sex, be excluded from participation in, be denied the benefits of, or be subjected to discrimination under any education program or activity receiving federal assistance." The general provision applies specifically to athletics when separate teams are operated on the basis of sex. There shall be no sex discrimination in the provision of necessary supplies for each team or in any other manner. Provisions in this section, however, are not interpreted to require equal aggregate expenditures for athletics for members of each sex. Institutions that are recipients of federal monies may *not* provide any physical education or athletic program separately on the basis of sex; they *should* provide support and training activities for members of each sex, with the aim of improving and expanding their capabilities for and interest in such opportunities.

As a result of this legislation and an increased emphasis on intercollegiate athletic competition for women, it is now inappropriate to discuss men's and women's programs separately; therefore the following discussion will cover intercollegiate athletics for *all* students.

Organization and Administration

The Athletic Director's Creed
I believe in the inherent educational values of intercollegiate athletics. As Athletic

Director I accept the responsibility to exert my best efforts to promote and administer this program consistent with the highest aims and objectives of my institution.

If this athletic director's creed were followed sincerely, problems with the organization and administration of intercollegiate athletic programs would be rare. In fairness to those who serve in the capacity of director or chairperson, it must be mentioned that undue public pressures for the success of athletic teams sometimes make adherence to this creed impossible. Such external pressure is often felt throughout the entire institution, and even the highest administrative offices are not immune. For this reason, and to ensure the sound administration of programs, the place and purpose of intercollegiate athletics in relation to the overall educational curriculum should be clearly defined. A report of the Second National Athletic Directors Conference, held in 1962, provides the following objectives:

1. To complement and supplement the goals of general education and those of the local school and college.

2. To place the welfare of the participant above any other consideration.

3. To carry forth the intercollegiate athletic program under the guidance of a strong faculty committee on athletics.

4. To provide qualified professional educators who are specialists in the area of athletics and who meet the same standards of competence as other members of the faculty.

5. To provide continuous medical supervision of all aspects of the intercollegiate athletic program.

6. To provide officiating of such quality that the contest is played under conditions which will insure the educational outcomes implicit in the rules and in the best traditions of the game.

7. To provide a continuous program of school-community relations designed to emphasize the educational, health, social, and recreational values of competitive sports as integral parts of the educational curriculum.

8. To provide facilities and equipment for the program of intercollegiate athletics which conform to all aspects of the official rules of the game and to optimum health and safety standards, and which are sufficient in number

and kind to provide a diversified program of sports activities for all students.

9. To provide academic supervision of all participants of the intercollegiate program.[58]

Intercollegiate athletics, like any other organization within an institution of higher education, may be organized and administered in a variety of ways. Some common patterns are:

1. A combined department of physical education and athletics, usually found in small colleges and universities.

2. A division of physical education and athletics with a divisional director and administrative heads for departments of physical education and athletics.

3. A separate division of intercollegiate athletics not directly associated with physical education.

4. A school or college of physical education and athletics.

In patterns 1 and 2, the overall department head or divisional director is usually an individual who has earned a doctorate and had professional training and experience in both physical education and athletics. A delegation of authority and responsibility is then made to sub-administrators for any area housed within the overall organizational structure. Patterns that combine physical education and athletics into a coordinated administrative unit are usually considered to be the most functional, and provide the best possible arrangement for both programs. Such patterns appear to operate smoothly until internal or external pressures for national athletic prominence or for athletic independence are encountered. When such pressures occur, internal factions can quickly destroy organizational unity and morale. Patterns 1, 2, and 3 imply that the chief administrator is vitally concerned with the promotion and maintenance of *both* sound physical education programs and successful athletic programs. *In any organizational pattern, intercollegiate athletics should not be permitted to function as a detriment to professional physical education.* If physical education curricula are being *"used"* to support athletes and athletic programs, they should become a separate administrative unit under the guidance and leadership of an administrator who follows sound policies and procedures in keeping with professional goals.

Intercollegiate athletic programs in many institutions have become major administrative units because of the increasing complexities of budget and finance, schedules, personnel, and maintenance of facilities. In such instances a separate division of intercollegiate athletics is usually formed.

Since the late 1960's athletic administrators have been troubled with "athletic revolutions" involving protests on issues ranging from the United States military involvement in Cambodia to the length of an athlete's hair and whether or not the growing of a mustache is permissible. Student movements, the black liberation movement, and the growing counter-culture have all had an effect on high school and college athletics during the late 1960's and are still in evidence now in the 1970's. Intercollegiate programs usually reflect the values of the total educational structure within which they are found. In order to exist and survive, intercollegiate athletics must reflect a value orientation that meets with the approval of students, alumni, and university administrators. It is very doubtful that any significant changes in these programs will occur without a major change in the fundamental educational structure within which they operate. "Ethical abuses in the recruiting, subsidy, and handling of college athletes are serious enough to warrant a major national clean-up campaign."[59] This campaign has been called for by the American Council on Education, which believes that severe athletic financial problems are forcing many college and university presidents to pay more attention to intercollegiate athletics. Operating costs continue to rise as income levels off, and rising tuition automatically increases the cost of athletic scholarships. In addition, women are demanding that more be spent on their currently underfinanced programs. The

most significant question asked by the American Council on Education was whether or not colleges and universities should be in the business of providing public entertainment through their football, basketball, hockey, or other teams. In spite of the many problems facing athletic programs throughout the country, there are still many positive aspects of college sports.

In 1973 the National Collegiate Athletic Association released new divisional alignments for its member institutions under an approved reorganization plan. The colleges and universities selected their divisions themselves, and the new alignment determines which national championships a school will play in and lets each division set up its own rules for financial aid for athletes, academic eligibility, and recruiting. All three divisions have separate championships in baseball, basketball, cross country, golf, soccer, swimming, tennis, outdoor track and field, and wrestling. Teams in all three divisions will be eligible for a single championship in fencing, hockey, skiing, indoor track, volleyball, and water polo. This new alignment contains 665 colleges and universities, which are organized into eight geographic districts within the United States.

In 1962 college and university athletic directors attending a national directors conference expressed their belief that all coaches and athletic administrative personnel should take an active role in the academic life of the university. They also said that coaches should make a constructive contribution to the life of the university and that coaches and athletic directors should be given academic rank and tenure if they could qualify for such academically.

In a previous section of this book, the statement was made that *head coaches*, no matter what their sport, should not be required to teach more than one-half of a normal teaching load *at any time*. This recommendation is intended to serve the best interest of both the coaches and the physical education programs to which they are assigned. Certainly, in large universities head coaches and some-

times assistant coaches of the major revenue producing sports should be assigned solely to their coaching duties,
with possibly an occasional teaching assignment in their area of interest and expertise. In programs primarily operated
for men, this would include the coaches
of football and basketball. For those
sports primarily offered for women, it
would include basketball and volleyball
coaches. Coaches should be paid for
such teaching assignments solely
through the Division of Intercollegiate
Athletics, since in this way they may be
paid under the salary schedules established for the Division and reimbursed
for outstanding seasons. Coaches who
are assigned to split appointments between the Division of Intercollegiate
Athletics and the Division of Physical
Education should be paid for their academic assignment on the basis of their
professional education, competencies,
and teaching duties.

Regarding academic rank and tenure,
coaches and athletic personnel should
be given these institutional benefits if
they so qualify. Just as in the selection
and employment of regular faculty, if
care is taken in the selection process to
ensure that basic requisites have been
met, rank and tenure should not become
a problem at a later date. If coaches are
hired who do not hold a master's degree
in physical education and who do not
have an area of teaching competency appropriate to the department, they should
not be granted professional rank and
tenure in physical education. All too
often, physical education departments
are made the dumping ground for old
coaches who are not trained in the profession and who have little expertise or
interest in teaching physical education.

Professional Preparation of
Coaches

There has been a major concern for
many years regarding the improvement
of the professional preparation and qualifications of both high school and college

and university coaches. The desire to
improve the professional preparation of
the high school coach is justifiable, as is
the improvement of coaches who are
employed by smaller colleges and universities where a large part of their assignment is academic in nature. Many
coaches and athletic administrators in
larger universities have received one or
more academic degrees, many in physical education or the general field of educational administration. If coaches are to
be eligible for academic tenure, they
must have received graduate professional preparation which will qualify
them as a faculty member in an academic department or division of the university.

The September 1970 issue of *JOHPER*
contained the following statement
regarding the professional preparation of
the administrator of athletics:

The growth of athletics in schools and
colleges, the expanding public interest, and
the complex cultural aspect of sports have
resulted in athletic administration becoming
a type of administration which is sufficiently
unique to require specialized professional
preparation.[60]

A joint committee on physical education
and athletics recommended that athletic
administrators be qualified professional
educators who are specialists in the area
of athletics and who meet the same standards of competence as other members
of the faculty. Candidates should be able
to do graduate work which meets the institutional requirements for admission to
the graduate school. Competencies to be
mastered in the professional preparation
of administrators of athletics at the graduate level include an awareness and understanding of the following:

1. The role of athletics in education and
our society and the rules, regulations, policies, and procedures of the various governing
bodies.
2. Sound business procedures as related to
athletics administration.
3. Administrative problems as related to
equipment and supplies.
4. Problems related to facilities.
5. Law and legal liability.

6. Factors involved in the conduct of athletic events.

Women in Athletics

Much has been written and discussed recently regarding intercollegiate athletics for women. There seems little doubt that such programs in the United States are just beginning a dramatic and rapid rise to prominence. Readily apparent problems that are and will be associated with women's athletic programs are going to demand a great deal of time and professional leadership on the part of women administrators.

At the first National Conference of College and University Administrators, held in Washington, D.C., in 1967, the functions of a Commission on Intercollegiate Athletics for Women were presented.[61] *Procedures for Intercollegiate Athletic Events,* published by the AAHPER in 1967 and revised in 1968, has been revised again, since several recommended procedures are already considered out of date. Another helpful publication by the Division of Girls' and Women's Sports is *Philosophy and Standards for Girls' and Women's Sports,* published in 1969.

Intercollegiate athletic standards and philosophy as expressed by such organizations as the DGWS have in the past attempted to improve and extend present competition and to expand opportunities for girls and women to compete. At the same time these organizations have desired that the administrative leadership for women's athletic programs remain under the control and guidelines of the DGWS and departments of physical education for women. During the past several years women athletes have achieved a new status in sports, which has resulted in expanded programs, increased emphasis to compete and win, and the establishment of an increasing number of athletic scholarships for women. This equalization of athletic status was brought about primarily by the increased

success of professional women athletes and by the end of sex discrimination in sports.

Organization and Administration of Women's Programs. For many decades in small colleges and universities where men's and women's physical education and intercollegiate athletics were combined in one administrative structure, women physical educators provided a great deal of the professional leadership and scholarly endeavor. It was a well-accepted fact that in many small institutions where male physical educators were employed to both teach and coach, women physical educators provided much of the professional leadership and possessed a sincere dedication toward the professional preparation of competent physical education teachers. Women's *athletics* did not play an important role in women's programs, as professional time and effort was instead spent on educating and training physical *educators.* Athletics for women were under the administrative control of women's physical education, as were sports days and play days.

With the growth and development of high school interscholastic athletic programs for girls, women's physical education departments across the country found themselves facing increased pressure to prepare majors to officiate and coach in addition to teaching physical education. This new emphasis necessitated curriculum changes to provide the necessary courses. Young women also desired to be active participants in intercollegiate competition, in order to establish playing experience which would be beneficial for later coaching assignments. As coaching and officiating courses were established and women's intercollegiate athletics increased in scope and emphasis, women physical educators found themselves faced with many administrative problems and concerns that they had not before experienced.

A sincere effort has been made by women in the profession to "control" women's athletics and keep programs within reasonable administrative and academic boundaries. As programs and emphases have been expanded, however, the control of athletics by physical education departments has become more and more difficult. Young women are attracted to major in women's physical education because of their interest and experience in high school interscholastic programs. More and more women employed as physical education teachers at both the college and high school levels have participated in varsity programs and are interested in initiating such programs in order to coach. As has been experienced in men's programs for years, administrators are finding it more and more difficult to employ young faculty who do not want to be actively involved in athletics.

At present, athletic programs for women are administratively housed as a subdivision of the department of women's physical education or as an administrative and organizational unit within a division of intercollegiate athletics. Many schools have established the new position of Women's Director of Intercollegiate Athletics. This administrator and the intercollegiate athletic program for women should be housed as one component of the overall institutional division of intercollegiate athletics. If both professional physical education and intercollegiate athletic programs are to flourish in the future, it would appear that they should have administrative independence.

Funding of Women's Programs. The Association for Intercollegiate Athletics for Women (AIAW) is composed of an affiliation of colleges and universities for the organization, administration, and improvement of women's intercollegiate athletic programs. The AIAW has been very concerned with the funding of women's programs and has done much to see that women receive adequate funding on an equal basis with programs for men. In the past, funds for women's programs have come from student activity fees and physical education departmental budgets. Student funding is not desirable, however, because of its fluctuation from year to year and its lack of continuity. The new requirements of Title IX have provided more stable budgetary allocations for women's programs through the same operational budgeting that is used for men's athletics. A study conducted by Murphey and Vincent in 1973 revealed that the majority of schools in the AIAW believe that funding from the women's physical education department budget was the best source of revenue for women's intercollegiate programs.[62] Although this type of support was preferred, over 80 per cent of the schools responding anticipated an increase in funds for the future from either a women's athletic department budget or a school budget "line" allocation. This study reported that approximately 95 per cent of the administrative leadership for intercollegiate athletic programs for women was furnished by the women's physical education faculty. In the majority of cases, the only remuneration for coaching received by women faculty was released time or teaching load credit. By 1975 there was a major effort to fund women's intercollegiate programs on an equal basis with men's programs.

Implications for Physical Education

Administrators of both men's and women's physical education programs are becoming acutely aware of the problems which the profession faces as women's and girls' athletic programs at the college and high school levels continue to expand. School programs have been initiated before qualified coaches and officials were trained, and colleges and universities are now faced with the immediate implementation of athletic programs and courses at all levels. Such expansion requires educational leadership to ensure that present instructional and extramural programs are not placed in jeopardy.

Women's athletic programs *should be independent,* or under the overall organizational umbrella of an institutional Division of Intercollegiate Athletics. It seems clear that in most institutions women's athletic programs will eventually achieve their own status, independent of physical education programs.

REFERENCES

1. Laurence F. Peter and Raymond Hull: *The Peter Principle.* New York: William Morrow & Company, Inc., 1969.
2. J. Tillman Hall and Jan Jantzen: "Some Administrative Policies and Practices in 214 College and University Physical Education Departments." University of Southern California, January, 1968.
3. Don McKinney: Unpublished Master's Thesis. Kearney, Nebraska: Nebraska State Teachers College, 1966.
4. Duane B. Mehn: "Survey of the Organizational Structure of College Programs in Health, Physical Education and Recreation." Ogden, Utah: Weber State College, 1970, p. 1.
5. Hall and Jantzen, *op. cit.,* p. 4.
6. "Thinking About Outcome-Oriented Planning in Higher Education." In *An Introduction: Higher Education Management,* Vol. II, No. 1. Boulder, Colorado: Western Interstate Commission for Higher Education, 1972, p. 1.
7. Martin McIntyre: "A Model for the Seventies." *JOHPER,* November-December, 1973, p. 28.
8. John Caffrey and Charles J. Mosmann: *Computers on Campus.* Washington, D.C.: American Council on Education, 1967, p. 6.
9. Brent S. Rushall: "Computers in Physical Education Research." *JOPHER,* September, 1972, p. 37.
10. Caffrey and Mosmann: *op. cit.,* p. 34.
11. Thomas L. Yates: "Non-Computational Aspects of Scheduling Systems." *Data Processing for Education,* Vol. 8, No. 2, April, 1969, p. 5.
12. Jesse F. Williams, Clifford L. Brownell, and Elmon L. Vernier: *The Administration of Health Education and Physical Education.* Philadelphia: W. B. Saunders Company, 6th ed., 1964, p. 48.
13. Edward F. Voltmer and Arthur A. Esslinger: *The Organization and Administration of Physical Education.* New York: Appleton-Century-Crofts, Inc., 1967, pp. 390–391.
14. B. J. Chandler and Paul V. Petty: *Personnel Management in School Administration.* New York: World Book Co., 1955, p. vii.
15. Gerald McLaughlin *et al.:* "Selected Characteristics, Roles, Goals and Satisfactions of Department Chairman in State and Land Grant Universities." Blacksburg, Va.: Virginia Polytechnic Institute and State University, 1973.
16. Glenn W. Howard and Edward Masonbrink: *Administration of Physical Education.* New York: Harper & Row, 1963, pp. 361–391.
17. C. T. Hardwick and B. F. Landuyt: *Administrative Strategy and Decision Making.* Cincinnati, Ohio: South-Western Publishing Co., 1966, p. 163.
18. Milton Hildebrand: *Evaluating University Teaching.* Berkeley, Calif. Center for Research and Development in Higher Education, University of California, 1971.
19. W. James Popham: *Evaluating Instruction.* Englewood Cliffs, N. J. Prentice-Hall, Inc., 1973.
20. Reuben B. Frost: "Promoting and Maintaining Human Effectiveness." In Hall, J. Tillman, *et al.: Administration, Principles, Theory and Practice.* Pacific Palisades, Calif.: Goodyear Publishing Co., 1973, p. 45.
21. Roy R. Gray: "An Investigation of Faculty Load Weighting Procedures Utilized in Physical Education Departments for Men in Selected Colleges and Universities." Unpublished Master's Thesis. Chadron, Nebr.: Chadron State College, 1968.
22. "General Purpose of Physical Education." Position paper of Western College Men's Physical Education Society, Reno, Nevada, 1973.
23. Rosemary McGee and Fred Drews: *Proficiency Testing for Physical Education.* Washington, D.C.: AAHPER, 1974.
24. *Ibid.,* p. 22.
25. Harold L. Hodgkinson: "Does a College's Unique Environment Really Do Anything for Its Students?" *The Chronicle of Higher Education,* May, 1974.
26. William H. Solley: "Grading in Physical Education." *JOHPER,* May, 1967, p. 34.
27. Beverly T. Watkins: "A to F Grading System Heavily Favored by Undergraduate and Graduate Institutions." *The Chronicle of Higher Education,* November 12, 1973.
28. Natalie Shepard: "New Patterns Meet Changing Needs." *JOHPER,* November-December, 1967, p. 28.
29. Jerome S. Bruner: *Toward a Theory of Instruction.* New York: W. W. Norton & Co., 1966, p. 18.
30. *Ibid.,* p. 36.
31. Donald H. Clark: *The Psychology of Education.* New York: The Free Press, 1967, p. 51.
32. Earle F. Ziegler: "Five Stances That Have Got To Go." *JOHPER,* September, 1973, p. 48.
33. *Ibid.,* p. 48.
34. Fritz Malchlup: "Two Views of Higher Education." *Newsletter for Teacher Educators.* Washington, D.C.: American Association of Colleges for Teacher Education, February, 1971, p. 3.
35. "General Purpose of Physical Education," *op. cit.*

36. "Resource Center on Sex Roles in Education." Published by the National Foundation for Improvement of Education, June 26, 1974, p. 4.
37. *Ibid.,* p. 3.
38. Gloria Stashower: "Performance-Based Teacher Training Grows in Brooklyn." *College Management,* April, 1974, p. 21.
39. *Preparing the Elementary Specialist: A Report of the Proceedings of the National Conference on Professional Preparation of the Elementary Specialist.* Washington, D.C.: AAHPER, 1973.
40. *Ibid.,* p. 6.
41. *Professional Preparation in Dance, Physical Education, Recreation Education, Safety Education and School Health Education.* Washington, D.C.: AAHPER, 1974.
42. *The Chronicle of Higher Education,* October 23, 1973.
43. "Student Choice Called Best Guide to Policy on Graduate Study." *The Chronicle of Higher Education,* September 17, 1973.
44. Arthur A. Esslinger: "Professional Preparation: Undergraduate vs. Graduate Study." JOHPER, November, 1966, pp. 63–64.
45. "Outdated View Said to Hinder Graduate Study." *The Chronicle of Higher Education,* December 3, 1973, p. 1.
46. "Graduate Study in Health Education, Physical Education and Recreation." In *Report of the National Conference on Graduate Study in Health Education, Physical Education and Recreation,* January, 1950.
47. "Graduate Education in Health Education, Physical Education, Recreation Education, Safety Education and Dance." Washington, D.C.: Report of a National Conference of the AAHPER, January, 1967.
48. "Self Evaluation Check List for Graduate Programs in Health Education, Physical Education, Recreation Education, Safety Education and Dance." Washington, D.C.: AAHPER, 1969.
49. *Ibid,* p. 7.
50. "GRE Guide to the Use of the Graduate Record Examinations." Educational Testing Service, Princeton, N.J.: 1974–75, p. 11.
51. Karl W. Bookwalter and Harold J. VanderSwaag: *Foundations and Principles of Physical Education.* Philadelphia: W.B. Saunders Co., 1969, p. 360.
52. *Ibid.,* p. 360.
53. Louis E. Means: *Intramurals—Their Organization and Administration.* Englewood Cliffs, N.J.: Prentice-Hall, Inc., 1973, p. 11.
54. Otto Berg: "Future Trends in the Administration of Intramural Sports at the College Level." In *20th Annual Conference Proceedings of the National Intramural Association.* Dubuque, Iowa: Kendall Hunt Publishing Co., 1969, pp. 75–77.
55. Means, *op. cit.,* p. 279.
56. Pat Mueller: *Intramurals: Programming and Administration.* New York: The Ronald Press Co., 1971, p. 59.
57. Means, *op. cit.,* p. 379.
58. "Athletic Administration in Colleges and Universities." Report of the Second National Athletic Directors Conference. *JOHPER,* 1963, p. 18.
59. "Sports: A Clean-up is Called For." *The Chronicle of Higher Education,* July, 1974, p. 13.
60. "Professional Preparation of the Administrator of Athletics." *JOHPER,* September, 1970, p. 22.
61. "Athletic Administration in Colleges and Universities," *op cit.,* p. 18.
62. Elizabeth Murphey and Marilyn Vincent: "Status of Funding of Women's Intercollegiate Athletics." *JOHPER,* October, 1973, p. 15.

SUGGESTED READINGS

Chronicle of Higher Education, The. (Selected readings on Title IX, Athletics, Funding, and other topics related to physical education.)
Hall, et al.: *Administration: Principles, Theory, and Practice.* Pacific Palisades: Goodyear Publishing Co., 1973. (Selected readings.)
Popham, W. James: *Evaluating Instruction.* Englewood Cliffs, N.J.: Prentice-Hall, Inc., 1973.
Professional Preparation in Dance, Physical Education, Recreation Education, Safety Education and School Health Education. Washington, D.C.: AAHPER, 1974.
Singer, R. N., et al.: *Physical Education: An Interdisciplinary Approach.* New York: The Macmillan Co., 1972.
Thinking About Outcome-Oriented Planning in Higher Education. In *An Introduction: Higher Education Management,* Vol. II, No. 1. Boulder, Colorado: Western Interstate Commission for Higher Education, 1972, p. 1.

FACILITIES PLANNING
CONSTRUCTION AND DESIGN
MANAGEMENT AND SUPERVISION OF
FACILITIES

CHAPTER NINETEEN

College and University Facilities

In Chapter 18, "Physical Education and the Community College," it was stated that a two-year college campus should reflect the *comprehensiveness*, *uniqueness*, and *purposes* of the college. This statement is just as true for four-year institutions. College and university decision makers must deal with the difficult problem of analyzing, planning, programing, and managing their indoor and outdoor facilities. Expansibility, convertibility, and versatility continue to be vital factors in planning the physical plant in a rapidly changing educational setting.

In the planning and construction of most new facilities, many problems are increased rather than diminished, since usually the most expedient procedure is to duplicate existing design and construction and, in the process, to duplicate previous problems. Physical education administrators must have a set of clearly described, detailed, illustrative methods and criteria for planning and constructing what is, in many instances, the largest capital outlay for any physical plant in the institution. There should be an honest attempt to provide not only for the immediate and future needs of the department and the institution but also for an interaction between the institution and the surrounding community.

The purpose of this chapter is not to attempt to duplicate facilities guides that are already in existence, but rather to provide basic procedures and principles as well as illustrative materials that may assist the administrator with his responsibilities in the planning, design, and construction of facilities.

FACILITIES PLANNING

Before an administrator or a facilities planning committee can consider either the renovation of existing buildings or the construction of new facilities, *basic objectives and needs must first be stated and understood.* This is a most important preliminary stage in the development of any type of facilities design and construction. These prerequisites must be thoughtfully formulated for the total operation of the organization and must be based upon the desires of the department, school, or college as well as upon the wishes of the administration of the institution. Consideration must be given to present and future goals, enrollment estimates, and economic feasibility. Grandiose desires are all too often not in keeping with the expressed wishes of the institutional administration or with the availability of economic resources.

An excellent illustration of facilities planning for institutions of higher education was one undertaken by the Management Information Systems Program of the Western Interstate Commission for Higher Education. This program is a Space Analysis Manuals project (SAM) that leads to the publication of higher education facilities planning and management manuals. These space analysis manuals are designed to:

1. Measure, analyze, and evaluate the allocation and utilization of building facilities in terms of the program loads and activities of the college or university.

2. Describe alternative processes of assignment, scheduling, and management of building facilities—as resources for the accomplishment of academic and support programs.

3. Illustrate workable methods for the projection and programing of building facilities requirements within the context of the comprehensive program plan for the institution.

The approach outlined on the opposite page and its many variations should serve exceptionally well for the planning and evaluation of physical education, intramural, and athletic facilities.

The planning of activity and professional facilities which contribute to the physical and educational environment of the institution is considered of vital importance. In this regard, Caudill of Rice University presents the following theorems:

1. Whether it is the planning of a new campus or the development of an old one, the effectiveness of achieving the right kind of physical environment will depend upon the subdivision and organization of space.

2. Buildings are important, but not as important as the students, their professors and their programs. *Function, form* and *cost* are inseparable and they must be dealt with simultaneously.

3. Only through a simultaneous consideration of function, form and cost can a really good campus plan, college building, or piece of educational equipment be achieved. (Obviously if we limit our thinking to only function and form, we might have a most thoroughly programmed project and a beautifully conceived design, but if it costs too much to build, time and effort are wasted.)[1]

Caudill goes on to state that the campus and each of its buildings should be planned for flexibility more than for exactitude. A successful educational plant is organic and must grow. If it does not, it must change, since in this fast-moving educational world nothing stands still. Accordingly, any physical plant must possess the qualities of *expansibility, convertibility,* and *versatility.*

If physical education and intramural programs are accepted as educationally sound and vital components of higher education, the principles basic to planning areas and facilities for these programs must then be formulated and stated. The fourth national facilities conference, held in 1967 in cooperation with The Athletic Institute and the AAHPER, drew up the following princi-

---

NEW CONSTRUCTION

Organizational Procedures — New Facility

A. Academic Programs — Planning
Project Building Committee
  Dean
  Faculty
  Finance Office
  Physical Plant
  Campus Planning

B. Site Selection

C. Employment of Architect
Owner-Architect Agreement
A.I.A. Regulations

D. Schematic
Design Development — State Codes O.S.H.A.
  Drawings — Cost Estimates
Construction Drawings (Blueprints)

E. Advertise for Bids (Tenders)
Award Contract
Construction Period
Additional Considerations — Penalty Clauses
                    — Early Completion Award Clause

F. Substantial Completion

G. Final Inspection
Final Payment

H. Warranty Conditions

---

ples based upon the assumptions that physical education and its related disciplines are important educational experiences for all students.

A. Good facilities are essential to a satisfactory program in health and safety education, physical education, recreation, and athletics.

B. All planning should be within the scope of a master plan for the institution.

C. The type, location, and dimensions of areas and facilities planned should be related to existing facilities of all kinds.

D. All planning should conform to state and local regulations and accepted standards.

E. Planning should include provision for the needs of the atypical.

F. All interested and qualified individuals and groups should be given an opportunity to share in the planning.

G. Initial planning should be pointed at the ideal.

H. A professional consultant in planning health and safety education, physical education, recreation and athletic facilities should be retained.

I. Every available source of funds should be investigated.

J. Professionals must be constantly aware of future needs and must continuously investigate the possibility of obtaining new space.

K. Planning functions should be carefully organized.

    1. A professional planning office.
    2. A campus planning committee.
    3. A project planning committee.
    4. Program specialist subcommittees.[2]

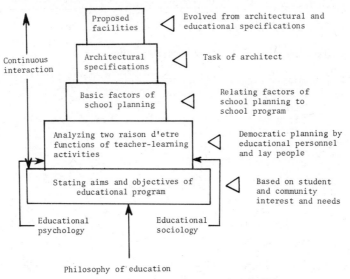

Figure 19–1. Procedure for planning facilities.

Meeting Needs

As has been mentioned, facilities must be designed to meet the needs of the organization and its programs. This may not always be possible, but a sincere attempt should be made to do so. The following questions may be asked in order to determine requirements:

1. How many years of instruction in physical education will be required of all students?
2. Is the instructional physical education program to be broad in scope, with opportunities for the development of interests and skills in a great variety of sports?
3. Are professional curricula in health and safety education, physical education, and recreation to be a part of the program?
4. What responsibility does the college or university take for the physical recreation and physical fitness of its faculty and staff?
5. Will research in health, safety education, recreation and athletics be an aspect of the professional program?
6. What will be the scope of the intercollegiate and extramural athletic programs?
7. What will be the scope of the intramural sports program?
8. What are the environmental factors which will affect the program and facilities for the college or university?[3]

Several other considerations will require attention, depending upon the specific variables that are found at any given institution.

Administrative Considerations

The department head, director, or dean of physical education should be the chairperson of an institutional planning or building committee, which is formed to make recommendations concerning renovation or new construction, if such facilities will be used jointly by physical education, intramurals, and athletics. Often such is not the case, but this recommendation is made on the premise that the administrator who holds this position will be more knowledgeable of the objectives and needs of the *total* organization.

In many instances, several committees will be formed if the building project is large. There may be an institutional committee, comprised of one or more individuals from the department, division, or college, whose proposal is being considered, as well as various representatives from "concerned" aspects of the university. Subcommittees should then be formed, composed of faculty with expertise in specific areas. Depending upon the nature of the proposal and the "professional climate" within the department, it may prove advisable not to have the department head serve on a committee at the departmental level. An elected chairperson or one appointed by the administration may serve in this capacity while the chief administrator represents the department on the over-all university committee. If this approach is used, the administrator is relatively free to act as a mediator if curtailments or cutbacks are required. The building committee chairperson at any level should be provided with a statement of the responsibilities with which the committee is charged. *It is very important that building or facilities planning committees be given direction as to their specific duties.* It is the duty of the department director or dean of physical education to support actively and, in fact, demand that the designing and construction of facilities be undertaken in such a manner that they meet professional objectives and needs.

A departmental administrator who is going to become involved in facilities planning and construction should be familiar with such building details as: assignable square footage desired; basic construction costs per cubic or per square foot; architectural fees (usually a percentage of construction costs based on a sliding scale as project costs increase); cost of new utilities or extension of present utilities cost; expenditure for site clearance, land acquisition, and site improvement; administrative account funds for legal advertising and inspector's fees; contingency funds, or neglected inclusions; and estimated costs for equipment and supplies. These expenditures make up the majority of the total project cost.

CONSTRUCTION AND DESIGN

A successful 31.5 million dollar venture in the Houston Astrodome promoted the feasibility of bringing athletic events indoors. It is now apparent to the general public, students, and faculty that there are alternatives to the institutional expenditure of millions of dollars for facilities in which "few entertained many"

only several times per year. New design and construction concepts are providing facilities for active participation by both the few and the many in year-round, day and night activity areas. Lifetime sports are in demand, and students and faculty desire year-round participation in tennis, badminton, swimming, skating, and many other activities that require a climate-controlled space. Many such physical education–athletic facilities have been constructed in the United States during the past 10 years.

Indoor Facilities

In the past several years many colleges and universities have designed and constructed new indoor physical education, intramural, recreation, and athletic facilities. Large and innovative gymnasia, natatoria, and indoor individual and dual sport areas have been built at such institutions as Harvard University (vinyl-coated nylon air support structure); University of Illinois – Urbana-Champaign (10 million dollar physical education athletic facility); Graceland College – Lamoni, Iowa (steel suspension covered with polyurethane foam); University of Notre Dame (physical education–athletic complex covering 10.5 acres); and the University of Utah (physi-

Figure 19–2. An excellent example of a vinyl-coated nylon cable system is this tennis center at Wheeling, West Virginia. (Courtesy of Birdair Structures, Inc.)

cal education–recreation–athletic complex includes five buildings and an estimated cost of 9.4 million dollars).

Many other outstanding facilities can be found in other institutions both large and small throughout the United States and Canada. The new physical education student center at the University of Ottawa, in Ottawa, Canada, is an outstanding example of combining physical education and recreation areas with an overall student center. Perhaps one of the most innovative new facilities in the United States is the one which was constructed at the University of Northern Iowa (see Chapter introductory photo). This "uni-dome" was constructed at a cost of some 5 million dollars, and the 19,000-seat domed stadium is air-conditioned and heated to provide a constant climate control for a wide range of activities.

Air Structures and Cable Domes

Several air support structures, or air shelter systems, as well as "cabled" envelope systems, have become popular for enclosing athletic and physical education facilities within the past several years. Beginning with "bubbles" at the University of Alaska and Harvard University, this type of construction has spread rapidly for use in enclosing tennis courts, tracks, gymnasia, swimming pools, and indoor multi-purpose arenas.

Basically there are four different types of air shelter and cabled construction. The simplest design in the *noncabled* air shelter. This type of structure is a simple air shelter covered with a *vinyl-nylon cover* and could be constructed for an approximate cost of 3 dollars per square foot in 1974. The approximate life span of this type of air shelter is from 7 to 10 years. A *cable reinforced* air shelter is covered with the same type of vinyl-nylon material and has approximately the same life expectancy. Because of the cable reinforcement, costs are increased to approximately 8 to 10 dollars per square foot; this sum no doubt will continue to increase. *Cabledome* structures

are under a patented trademark and have a top covering of coated *vinyl-glass* which has a life expectancy of 12 to 15 years. New types of Cabledome facilities are now being constructed with a "cabled roof" design, and have life expectancies in excess of 20 years. They consist of new units of *Teflon-glass* which in 1975 cost approximately 6 to 9 dollars a square foot for the floor area that is covered. Annual operation and maintenance costs for such facilities will vary, depending upon how the structure is used. Companies manufacturing these products estimate that the average annual costs for operation and maintenance will be approximately 15 per cent of the total price of the complete system per year.

Cable designed systems and Cabledomes are usually sold and installed as complete packages which include the cabled envelope of vinyl-fiberglass, auxiliary support columns, inflation system blowers, anchorage hardware, and door equipment. Additional options that are available are thermal/acoustical liners, special urethane topcoatings, air conditioning, heating, lighting, offices, locker rooms, rest rooms, and spectator seating.

The lightweight structural envelopes of this nature, which are made from vinyl-coated nylon fabrics, have an approximate total weight of 28 ounces per square yard. The present trend in this type of construction is toward more permanent types of structures rather than ones which can be quickly dismantled and moved. Air shelter components for any type of air shelter equipment include (1) the envelope; (2) the inflation system; (3) the anchorage system; and (4) doors and access equipment. In operation, the envelope does not contain the air entirely, but permits some loss through doors, vents, and anchorages. As a result, a continuous supply of air must be fed into the structure to keep it firmly erect. Capacities of the free-delivery air blowers which are necessary to support this type of structure are from 3300 cfm to 30,100 cfm.

The following types of materials are presently being used for air support and lightweight tension structures.[4]

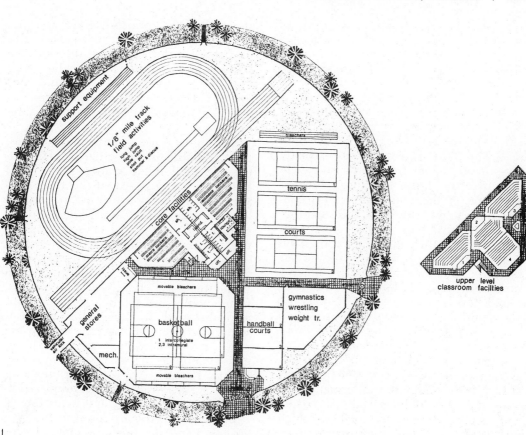

Figure 19-3. Circular Cabledome structures can provide a variety of indoor physical education and athletic activity areas. (Courtesy of Birdair Structures, Inc.)

1. *Clear vinyl film.* Life expectancy 3 to 4 years.

2. *Vinyl-coated nylon, fiberglass, or polyester.* Life expectancy 7 to 10 years, with various materials being used which are coated to a total weight of 23 to 30 ounces per square yard. A fiberglass base material is also used in some instances. Comprises about 85 per cent of the present market.

3. *Neoprene or hypalon-coated nylon, polyester, or glass.* Life expectancy 12 to 15 years. These materials are also used in various weights and require initial and periodic (every 4 to 5 years) painting to assure an extended service life.

4. *Teflon-coated fiberglass.* Life expectancy is predicted to be in excess of 20 years.

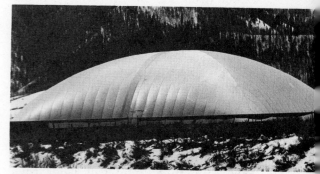

Figure 19-4. Improved construction and design enable cable-reinforced structures to withstand many different kinds of climatic conditions. (Courtesy of Thermo-Flex, Inc.)

Materials have a total weight of some 35 to 45 ounces per square yard and have an extended service life. Costs approximately four to five times more than vinyl-coated nylon or fiberglass.

Other materials which are being used for these types of structures are polyvinyl chloride (PVC) coated nylon fabrics. This type of construction usually uses an 8000-pound test polyester webbing over the entire structure, with the exception of the end seams. PVC construction adds strength and stability to the air structure. It also greatly reduces the tensile load on the fabric itself and creates "convolutions" in the air structure, thus breaking up the reflective surface which, if left flat, produces sound levels that can be distracting. Standards for this type of construction have been developed by Canvas Products Association International.

A unique architectural fabric is in use as the roof system for two new buildings at LaVerne College in California. These roofs are of "fiberglass fabric" coated with a new Dupont formulation which incorporates a *Teflon fluorocarbon resin.* The fabric is woven from fiberglass yarn made by Owens-Corning Fiberglass Corporation. Life expectancy for this material is to be in excess of 20 years. The project entails fabric roofs fastened over steel cables held under tension to shelter a 215-seat theater in one building and physical education areas in another. The fabric, which is treated with fluorocarbon resin, has the advantage of being fire resistant, weather resistant, and so strong that it is able to support from 200 to 1000 pounds per square inch.

Rigid Frame Construction

"Rigid frame" types of construction for physical education, intramural, and athletic facilities are natually very varied in nature and design, as is the combination of air-support and rigid wall panel structures.

One type of structural design that shows promise for the future consists of a combination of an air-support roof structure with pre-cast concrete wall panels. The air-support roof systems are said to allow for increased interior area while costing approximately one-third less than conventional structural systems. This combination also permits a more column-free development of interior space.

Many new types of flexible design are also available in attractive steel buildings of rigid frame construction. Steel buildings are less expensive than conventional types of construction because of their lower labor costs.[5] The main advantage of this type of construction appears to be the elimination of preparing drawings, taking bids, awarding contracts, preparing sites, and construction involving a "step-by-step" process. Components and modular wall systems are fabricated at manufacturing plants while the prime contractor prepares the site. Another advantage to this type of construction is the very short construction time required to complete the facility, as well as the ease of future additions. Interior painting and insulation, if desired, must be considered in the construction costs for this type of facility.

Multi-Purpose Sports Surfaces

During the past several years, multipurpose sports surfaces have come under close scrutiny. The early "rush" by many institutions to install artificial sports surfaces has somewhat diminished along with the initial emphasis to provide identical facilities with other schools in the "conference." Educational administrators as well as physicians are closely evaluating all surfaces with regard to their suitability for human activity and their cost *vs.* longevity.

At present there are very few manufacturers marketing synthetic grasses, although many corporations are very active in the manufacture and distribution of various types of *polyvinyl chloride* and *polyurethane elastomer* floor coverings. These synthetics are widely sold and are used for both indoor and outdoor activities. Horse racing, tennis, basketball, and many other types of activities are now being conducted on a wide variety of artificial surfaces which are not of the grass "family." Most of these surfaces are in their third or fourth "generation" and are installed over either a concrete or bituminous asphalt subsurface. Many can be laid over any type of smooth existing surface, including hardwood floors. In many instances the purchaser may choose whether or not the installation is to be "poured in place" or laid in pre-cast sheets and cemented in place. The advantages of these types of sports surfaces are that they can flex under strain, be easily repaired, are impervious to most types of damage, come in a variety of colors, and in many instances are less expensive than surfaces (such as wood) which would normally be used.[6] Predictions for the future are that "natural" surfaces will no longer be available and that all of our activity surfaces will be of the synthetic nature. Maintenance costs for chlorides and elastomers are usually not as high for outdoor areas such

as running tracks, but they may require just as much maintenance when used for indoor surfaces such as tennis and basketball courts. Most have to be resurfaced with a clear covering every one to five years, depending on traffic. Sanding and coating are much the same as that for wooden surfaces.

Other types of artificial floor coverings which provide excellent playing surfaces for varied activities are those of the *synthetic textile carpet* and *acrylic asphalt* nature. The synthetic textile surfaces provide an indoor surface which is used for tennis, badminton, volleyball, basketball, gymnastics, and similar sports. They can be glued to existing surfaces of asphalt, concrete, or wood, and are cleaned by dry vacuuming. The textile carpet surface does not reflect light and results in better acoustics. Acrylic applications over asphalt provide a uniform texture which can be colored to provide excellent surfaces for activities such as tennis. Manufacturers of these products

Figure 19–5. A modern athletic fieldhouse illustrating an Astro Turf* field and a Tartan† track. (Courtesy of the United States Air Force Academy.)

*Manufactured by the Monsanto Company, St. Louis, Missouri.
†Manufactured by the Minnesota Mining and Manufacturing Company, St. Paul, Minnesota.

state that they provide a medium ball speed and a bounce that is free from skidding.[7]

Lighting

Just as there are many different types of basic construction and a great multitude of artificial floor coverings and sport surfaces, there are many different types of lighting systems for use in indoor and outdoor physical education and athletic facilities. Three of the more prominent lighting systems in use are (1) quartz; (2) multi-vapor or metal halide; and (3) fluorescent. Most of these systems are of aluminum- or zinc-coated steel and are basically maintenance free, with the exception of the replacement of lamps.[8]

Quartz Systems. Quartz lighting systems are one of the most natural types in use today. At least 40 foot-candles of light is usually required on playing surfaces, and lamps are rated at approximately 2000 hours under normal conditions. Initially this system is the most economical to install, but the operation cost to the consumer is higher than that of any other system.

Multi-Vapor Systems. This type of system is usually used to light various playing surfaces which are housed in

"banks" such as tennis courts. Color rendition is not quite as good as with the fluorescent or quartz systems. The advantage of the multi-vapor system is that it requires a very low power consumption. Lamp life on this type of system is approximately 12,000 hours. Various types of metal halide lighting systems have high efficiency, economically reasonable life, and good color-rendering ability and lumen maintenance.

Factors which should be considered in the selection of a lighting system are (1) the type and degree of usage; (2) color of light desired; (3) availability of funds for purchase and maintenance; (4) power consumption; (5) power source; and (6) the facility in which the system is to be used. Some lighting systems have been designed specifically for use in steel buildings or in air-support structures.

MANAGEMENT AND SUPERVISION OF FACILITIES

The department chairperson, director, or dean is the administrator directly responsible for the total operation of the physical plant that has been provided for his organization. This administrator is responsible for these facilities and has the authority to supervise and con-

Figure 19–6. New multi-sports lighting used indoors as a vital part of the renovation of an existing gymnasium and shower area. (Courtesy of the University of Wyoming.)

trol their operation. Physical education areas designed for physical activities of a recreational or intramural nature should be open and available to students and faculty in accordance with their needs. This usually necessitates the availability of some areas 12 to 16 hours per day, seven days per week. Activity facilities are of absolutely no value when they are closed; yet the administrator must realize that the institution cannot leave a facility that cost hundreds of thousands of dollars open and unattended. This factor must be presented to the institutional administration along with the request for funds to provide adequate supervision to meet student-faculty demands as well as the demands of the community at large. In keeping with recommendations presented at the beginning of this chapter, all state-financed facilities should be available for selected public use when they are not being used by the institution. A sincere attempt should be made to provide for interaction between the institution and the surrounding community.

In the operation of indoor and outdoor areas, the administrator should formulate specific policies and procedures to govern use and control of the areas. These requirements should be communicated to every member of the department as well as to all other appropriate or interested individuals. *Priorities for use must be established* and scheduling conducted according to these priorities. Priorities for facilities under the direction and control of a department of physical education may be considered in the following order:

1. Instructional programs. Basic instruction courses, undergraduate professional courses for men and women, and graduate offerings.
2. Intramural sports programs for both men and women.
3. Instructional programs offered by other academic departments or colleges in the university.
4. University-sponsored organizations.
5. Community organizations.

If facilities must be shared with intercollegiate athletics, such programs would receive a priority in keeping with the wishes of the administration.

Supervision and Control

The chief administrator of the physical education organization should, in most instances, delegate the authority and responsibility for the control and supervision of facilities. In large institutions, a single individual or several individuals may be given this responsibility. In small colleges, this task may be assigned to a faculty member, who is then provided with a reduced teaching load. If the total operation and responsibility is not considered to be too large, the director of intramural sports or his assistant may be assigned to control and schedule areas. No matter which pattern is followed, close cooperation and communication between the facilities' coordinator and other members of the organization is a necessity.

The director of facilities must be provided with the necessary authority to conduct his duties effectively. This individual should be administratively responsible for all scheduling and for the supervision of staff personnel employed to assist him. Examples of scheduling forms and organizational procedures are provided in the *Resource Manual* for this text.

Excellent coordination is required among all those using facilities, and schedules should be formulated on a weekly and monthly basis and posted in predetermined locations. Strict scheduling and access control should be maintained in order to insure adequate supervision and appropriate usage of facilities. The controlled use of indoor areas is directly dependent upon the maintenance of supervision over building access. A common belief is that if faculty and staff are worthy of being members of the organization, they are worthy of having access to all facilities. Unfortunately, this is not always the case, and many departments provide faculty and staff with access only to the specific areas in which they work.

REFERENCES

1. William W. Caudill: "Housing the Educational Program: The Physical Plant as Educational Environment." In *Long Range Planning in Higher Education,* Boulder, Colorado: Western Interstate Commission for Higher Education, 1967.
2. *College and University Facilities Guide for Health, Physical Education, Recreation and Athletics."* Washington, D.C.: AAHPER and The Athletic Institute, 1968, p. 4.
3. *Ibid.,* p. 5.
4. Birdair Structures Inc., 2015 Walden Ave., Buffalo, New York, 1973.
5. Stran-Steel Corporation, Houston, Texas, 1974.
6. "Proturf," Professional Products Inc., A Division of Cook Industries Inc., Pittsburg, Kansas.
7. California Products Corporation, Cambridge, Massachusetts.
8. All Sport Lighting Inc., North Miami, Florida.

SUGGESTED READINGS

"Air Structures for School Sports." New York: Educational Facilities Laboratories, Inc.

American Institute of Architects, 1735 New York Avenue, N.W., Washington, D.C. 20006. (Selected readings.)

Bronzon, R. T.: *New Concepts in Planning and Funding Athletic Physical Education and Recreation Facilities.* Phoenix Intermedia, Inc., 1974.

Keller, Roy J.: *Modern Management of Facilities for Physical Education.* Champaign, Ill.: Stipes Publishing Co., 1973.

"Planning Facilities for Athletics, Physical Education and Recreation." Washington, D.C.: AAHPER and The Athletic Institute, 1974.

Selected issues of *The Chronicle of Higher Education* (Innovative Athletic and Recreational Facilities).

INDEX